on, 1817, by Samuel Lovett Waldo (The Metropolitan
s Fund, 1906, 06.197)

JACKSON'S W

Jackson's Way

Andrew Jackson and the People of the Western Waters

————∞∞∞————

John Buchanan

CASTLE BOOKS

This edition published in 2005 by
CASTLE BOOKS ®
A division of Book Sales, Inc.
114 Northfield Avenue
Edison, NJ 08837

This edition published by arrangement with and permission of
John Wiley & Sons, Inc.
111 River Street
Hoboken, New Jersey 07030

This publication is designed to provide accurate and authoritative information in regard to the subject matter provided. It is sold with the understanding that the publisher is not engaged in rendering professional services. If professional advice or other expert assistance is required, the services of a competent professional person should be sought.

Library of Congress Cataloging-in-Publication Data:

Buchanan, John.
Jackson's way : Andrew Jackson and the people of the western waters /
John Buchanan.
p.   cm.
Includes bibliographical references (p.   ) and index.
1.   Jackson, Andrew, 1767-1845. 2. Southwest, Old—History. 3. United States—Territorial expansion. 4. United States—Politics and government—1783-1809. 5. United States—Politics and government—1809-1817. 6. Frontier and pioneer life—Southwest, Old. 7. Pioneers—Southwest, Old—History—19th Century. 8. Indians of North America—Wars—Southwest, Old. 9. Generals—United States—Biography.
10. Presidents—United States—Biography. I. Title.

E382 .B89 2001
976—dc21   00-040818

ISBN-13: 978-0-7858-2060-4
ISBN-10: 0-7858-2060-4

Printed in the United States of America

In memory of my parents,
Charles Walker and Helen Hutchins Buchanan,
and Susi's parents,
Georg and Babette Erhardt

CONTENTS

ILLUSTRATIONS AND MAPS

Preface

The struggle for the great empire that lay between the Appalachian Mountains and the Mississippi River began a century before the American victory in the War of the Revolution and the recognition by Great Britain in 1783 of the United States of America. The contest would continue for another four decades. The prize was all of that territory south of the Ohio River—the modern states of Kentucky, Tennessee, Mississippi, Alabama, and Louisiana. Florida also hung in the balance.

It is a tale once familiar to Americans but little known today. For the near total emphasis in our time on the occupation of the country between the Mississippi River and the Pacific Ocean, with its endless streams of horse Indians and cavalry and cowboys and those blips on historical radar, homicidal gunfighters, has rendered hazy in our national memory that earlier, far greater conflict. Yet in its significance for the future of North America, in savagery and loss of life, plot and counterplot, larger-than-life players, and an outcome that remained for contemporaries unpredictable almost to the end, the struggle for what was once called the Old Southwest was an epic, whereas the filling of the trans-Mississippi West was but an interlude between a fight for empire and the emergence of the United States as a world power in the twentieth century. To put it in military terms, the earlier conflict was a war, the latter a mopping-up operation.

Doubters may point to the Texas Revolution (1835–1836) and the Mexican War (1846–1848) as major exceptions. But the Texans' revolt against Mexico lasted only seven months and had one decisive battle—an eighteen-minute skirmish, really—at San Jacinto, where the Mexican army melted at first contact. In the Mexican War, the big, decisive battles were fought in Mexico.

Historians have traditionally taken liberties with the geography of the Old Southwest, and I shall join them in doing so. The heart of the territory was Tennessee, Alabama, and Mississippi. I shall have little to say about Kentucky, for it has received considerable attention since the magical name of Kaintuck surfaced in colonial literature, and became the topic of innumerable unrecorded discussions in genteel eastern drawing rooms and before rude hearths of long-crumbled frontier cabins.

Tennessee is our destination. And Mississippi and Alabama, Louisiana and the Florida Panhandle, and western Georgia. Under the Peace of Paris of 1783 most of this vast country was ceded to the United States by Great Britain, who had won it from France in the French and Indian War (1754–1763). But Spain had reconquered Florida from Britain during the American Revolution, still held Louisiana, had garrisons at Natchez and St. Louis, and claimed territory northward into Tennessee. And there were Frenchmen who had dreams of regaining the Mississippi Valley and were prepared to act on them.

Most of the Old Southwest, however, was Indian country, the ancestral homes of powerful, unconquered nations who refused to recognize a scrap of paper written in Paris. The Creeks were the most powerful. Their towns ranged from western Georgia to central Alabama. An offshoot of the Creeks, the Seminoles, were well established in Spanish Florida. The numerous Choctaws controlled lower and central Mississippi. Northern Mississippi was the home of a kindred people, the Chickasaws, who also effectively claimed as their hunting grounds the entire western half of Tennessee, from a line roughly parallel with Nashville to the Mississippi River, and the southwestern corner of Kentucky. The Cherokee towns were in the southeastern corner of Tennessee and northwestern Georgia, but they claimed as hunting grounds a vast area stretching north through the Cumberland country of Tennessee and on through Kentucky to the Ohio River. A breakaway element of Cherokees known as the Chickamaugas had settled in the Tennessee River Valley on Chickamauga Creek near the present site of Chattanooga, Tennessee, and eventually spread their Five Lower Towns west along the Tennessee River Valley into the northern Alabama hill country. Other contenders, the Shawnees and allied tribes in Ohio and Indiana, still contested Kentucky with the Americans and hunted and raided southward into southwestern Virginia and Tennessee.

That is why the bloody border fighting, which is one of the defining themes of American history, is often placed where it belongs—front and center—as I try to tell what happened, how it happened, why it happened. For into this country bitterly hostile to their presence came an aggressive, swarming people called by their foes Americans. Among them were many players, a few still famous, others shooting stars. But most were mute and faceless, occasionally revealed by chance and the pens of others. They came first as long hunters who ranged hundreds of miles in advance of the frontier in search of game and came home with wondrous tales of newfound lands, then families and small parties, then as hosts over mountains, along valleys, down rivers, through forests, ignoring treaties and royal governors and presidents, determined to take the land and "hold it in Defiance of every Power." The People of the Western Waters, as the emigrants west of the Appalachians were called, found leaders who wanted what they wanted, and eventually they found the greatest of them all. Gradually, then quite suddenly, Andrew Jackson, one of the most powerful figures in American history, will move to center stage and thereafter dominate our story.

Now to turn to a few technical matters. In this Preface I used the names of modern states, yet none of those states had been created when our story begins, and only one, Georgia, was one of the original thirteen states. To avoid confusion for the modern reader, however, I have used the names of states to make the geography clear. Explanations will appear in their proper places in the text during the course of our story.

Which brings me to the subject of endnotes. Readers for whom notes are annoying distractions from the flow of the narrative may safely ignore them. My general rule on notes is that if information is important enough to include in the book, then it belongs in the text. With rare exceptions— all rules are made to be broken, of course—the notes are bare citations provided for readers who demand such supporting apparatus.

Major John Reid, Jackson's aide during the Creek War and at New Orleans, wrote only the first four chapters of the very important book *The Life of Andrew Jackson* (1817) before his premature death. It was finished by the man who became Reid's coauthor, John Henry Eaton, from Reid's notes and his own and manuscripts gathered by both authors. For simplicity's sake, however, throughout the text I refer only to Major Reid as the author, even for material in those chapters written by Eaton. Although a lieutenant of Tennessee Volunteers when he first joined Jackson, I refer to him throughout as Major Reid, which was his eventual brevet rank in the U.S. Army. I should also mention that subsequent editions of this work, by Eaton, are highly politicized and unreliable; the student's choice should be the 1817 edition or, even better, the University of Alabama Press edition (1974) of the 1817 printing, superbly edited by Frank L. Owsley Jr.

As is my practice, I have left the delightful and imaginative spelling and capitalization of those days as I found them, without the intrusion of the annoying *sic*. Punctuation has also largely been left as written, but in the interests of clarity I have on occasion modernized punctuation, without, I hasten to add, creating ambiguities or changing meanings.

My wife, Susi, has read and reread and listened, always willing to drop what she is doing and come to my aid, whether it be for clarity's sake or to commiserate over my frustrations with, for me, the unfathomable mysteries of computers and printers. Her presence for whatever purpose is cherished, her support indispensable.

Our good friends Charles and Sandy Ellis bear a large share of responsibility for the appearance of this book. I can only hope that I have met their expectations.

My editor, Hana Umlauf Lane, combines mastery of her craft with the blessed gift of editorial restraint, yet on those rare occasions when she intervenes she is invariably right. The pleasure of working with her is beyond my powers of expression. I am also deeply grateful to the production editor, John Simko, for his patience and smooth professionalism, and to the copy editor, James Gullickson, for his accuracy and awesome attention to detail.

How could I ever forget Michele Fuortes, who saved the entire manuscript after I had lost it in the unforgiving bowels of my computer; and Lisa Pilosi, who led me to Michele.

How can I ever repay Robert M. Calhoon of Greensboro, North Carolina, for his friendship and advice? For many things I owe him a debt I can never satisfy. Bob Calhoon took on the daunting task of reading the entire manuscript. I owe him much for whatever merits it has, but he bears no responsibility for errors or my judgments on people and affairs. I am also deeply grateful to Ken Anthony, whom Bob recruited to read certain chapters.

Another good friend, Cherel Bolin Henderson of Knoxville, on numerous occasions graciously broke into her jammed and hectic schedule to share with me her extensive knowledge and well-researched writings on East Tennessee, and was kind enough to read chapter 3. Again, there are debts incurred that are beyond repayment.

John Alden Reid, park ranger and interpreter at Horseshoe Bend National Military Park, was more than generous in sharing his own research and also in giving a careful reading to the chapters on the Creek War. A close student of the war, John Reid saved me from a few embarrassing errors.

Tom Kanon of the Tennessee State Library and Archives, a keen student of the War of 1812, also shared results of his research, read the Creek War and Gulf campaign chapters, and offered insights testifying to his deep knowledge of the subjects.

Wanda Lee Dickey, park ranger, Jean Lafitte National Historical Preserve, and Jack Collier, chief ranger, Cumberland Gap National Historical Park, were generous with time and information.

Allen Haynes of Castilian Springs, Tennessee, read chapters on the establishment of and the struggle over the Cumberland Settlements. He also generously supplied materials as well as knowledge, for which I am most grateful. These chapters were also read by Walter T. Durham of nearby Gallatin, whose fine work *The Great Leap Westward* reveals the value of well-done local and regional history. Naturally, Mr. Durham and all of the readers mentioned above bear no responsibility for my failures.

Mary Parkey, genealogist, of Lee County, Virginia; Margaret M. O'Bryant of the Albermarle County Historical Society, Virginia; and Jennifer McDaid of *Virginia Cavalcade* kindly helped with the Frances Dickenson Scott incident.

Michael M. Bailey of Fort Morgan, Alabama, sent me precisely what I needed on old Fort Bowyer. Dr. Norwood Kerr of the Alabama Department of Archives and History generously provided me with guides to historic sites.

I would like to thank the Tennessee Historical Society for granting permission to quote from John Donelson's *Journal of a Voyage*.

Librarians and archivists are the writer's indispensable support troops, and I begin with the ever-helpful librarians at two of New York City's treasures: the New York Public Library and the New York Society Library. At the latter I must not fail to single out Susan O'Brien, who handled quickly and efficiently interlibrary loans and requests for articles. Carol Briggs, librarian of the Hillsdale Public Library, Hillsdale, New York, once again secured interlibrary loans. Elsewhere my gratitude extends to Julia Rather, marathoner and mother, of the Tennessee State Library and Archives; Debra Blake of the North Carolina Department of Archives and History; Andy Phydras of the Georgia Department of Archives and History; and Jennifer Luna of the Library of Congress.

William Woodson of Lawrenceburg, Tennessee, shared with me a fascinating slice of southern history, and went out of his way to lead me to William McDonald of Florence, Alabama. Colonel McDonald told me how to find Coldwater and gave me helpful information on Muscle Shoals.

Others who have given help and understanding are B. Anthony Guzzi of the Hermitage, Joyce P. Kobasa of the New York State Office of Parks, Recreation and Historic Preservation, and Daisy Njoku of the Smithsonian Institution.

I recall with sorrow yet fond memories the interest and encouragement of my friend Tom Baker of Guilford Courthouse National Military Park, taken from us in his prime.

The enthusiasm, interest, and generous friendship of Luther Wannamaker of St. Matthews, South Carolina, and the hospitality of his wife, Doraine, in a time of adversity are among my most treasured memories.

Finally, and once again, thanks to my brother Pete for accompanying me to Signal Point on a tornado-lashed day so I could look far below upon the waters of the Tennessee, close my eyes, and picture for myself the pilgrims on their way to the promised land. Pete, I'll try to find something equally thrilling next time.

PROLOGUE

Five miles below Charlotte, North Carolina, on a hot day in September 1780, a fourteen-year-old girl named Susan stood behind a window in her home and looked south along the road that led from Camden in South Carolina. It was in the area called the Waxhaws, that broad swath of Back Country between Charlotte and Camden, including much of the present Mecklenburg, Union, and Anson Counties in North Carolina, and Lancaster, Chester, and York Counties in South Carolina. In later years Mrs. Susan Smart was in the habit of telling the following story to her intimate friends.

Every day young Susan stood behind the window and watched the road leading from the south. Her father and brother had been in the American army that General Horatio Gates had led to disaster at Camden against the British under Lord Cornwallis. That had been on the sixteenth of August and now it was September, and the family had no idea of the fate of father and brother. Susan's job upon spotting travelers was to race out to them and ask for news.

Late that hot afternoon a dust trail rose behind a rider coming quickly from the southward. Susan flew out of the house. The rider was a boy, a year younger than Susan, and the most forlorn figure she had ever seen. He was a tall, "gangling fellow," she recalled, legs so long they could almost meet beneath his shaggy "grass pony," as the swamp horses of South Carolina were then called. He was covered with dust and looked too tired to sit his horse. A battered wide-brimmed southern countryman's hat flopped over his narrow face. Susan hailed him and he reined in.

"Where are you from?" she asked.

"From below."

"Where are your going?"

"Above."

"Who are you for?"

"The Congress."

"What are you doing below?"

"Oh, we are popping them still."

Young Susan thought that dubious if this worn-out, ridiculous-looking boy was doing the popping.

"What's your name?"
"Andrew Jackson."[1]

He was born in the Waxhaws on 15 March 1767. His parents, Andrew and Elizabeth Hutchinson Jackson, were poor Scotch Irish immigrants from Northern Ireland. The people we call Scotch Irish, known in the old country as Ulster Scots, were largely descendants of mixed Germanic peoples who over many centuries had moved into and taken over the Scottish Lowlands. Beginning in the early seventeenth century many migrated to Ulster in Northern Ireland, and starting about 1715 the Scotch Irish began a massive migration to America. By 1775, when the War of the Revolution began, some quarter million had arrived. Most of them ended in the Back Country from Pennsylvania south into Georgia.[2]

The boy's parents entered British North America at either Charleston or farther north through one of the Delaware River ports, perhaps Philadelphia, or Newcastle, from where they made their way to the Waxhaws. Historians differ. His father was either an "extremely poor" squatter who "never *owned* in America one acre of land," or owned as he claimed about two hundred acres on Twelve Mile Creek, a tributary of the Catawba River. Depending upon the biographer, Andrew was born just before or just after or "about the time" his father died. The states of South and North Carolina contend for his place of birth, each claiming the honor, although Jackson always maintained that he had been born in South Carolina, and presumably he had that information from his mother. These minor controversies are fitting, for controversy swirled about him throughout his life and beyond the grave to our time.[3]

We do know that after his father's death Andrew's mother took up residence on the South Carolina side of the line as housekeeper in the home of her semi-invalid sister, Jane, and her brother-in-law, James Crawford. There Andrew and his two older brothers, Hugh and Robert, grew up as poor relations with their eight Crawford cousins.

His mother intended him for the Presbyterian ministry, and when he was of age he was sent to a local academy where he was taught, but did not learn much Latin and Greek or anything else outside of reading, writing, and arithmetic. He was never a student, our Andrew Jackson, and "his education," in the words of his twentieth-century biographer, "simply did not take." But education, or lack of it, is not necessarily a measure of intellectual power, and as Andrew Jackson matured and undertook responsibilities that probably amazed those who knew him as a boy, he would reveal an intellect as powerful as his iron will.[4]

That will, for which he became famous, was manifest as a boy. Wrestling among youths was then a very popular sport and Andrew, described by a schoolmate as "remarkably athletic," loved to wrestle. Another schoolmate told James Parton, Jackson's leading nineteenth-century biographer, "I could throw him three times out of four, but he would never *stay throwed*. He was dead game, even then, and never *would* give up." He was an overbearing bully, too, took offense quickly, was "*very* irascible" and generally "difficult to get along with." But one who knew him then said that "of all the boys he had ever known, Andrew Jackson was the only bully who was also not a coward."[5]

His rages of temper became legendary. As a boy, it is said, they could degenerate into such paroxysms that he would slobber. When it occurred, wrote James Parton, "woe to any boy who presumed to jest at this misfortune! Andy was upon him incontinently, and there was either a fight or a drubbing." A modern political scientist seized upon this story and launched into flights of Freudian fancy at a time when psychologists were "poised for a mass flight from Freud." What is important to ask about Jackson's temper on each occasion when it was unleashed is whether it was real or feigned, for there is considerable evidence in his later life from men who were with him often and knew him well that beneath some of the famous rages lay careful calculation. But real or feigned, those who witnessed the temper never forgot it. Boy and man, to challenge him, to cross him, was to risk an explosive, frightening wrath.[6]

In 1775, when Andrew was eight years old, the War of the American Revolution began. For the first four years most of the heavy fighting was in the northern states, but in 1779 the action began to move to the South, and the little Jackson family suffered its first calamity. After the Battle of Stono Ferry near Charleston in June 1779, Andrew's brother Hugh, serving in William Richardson Davie's regiment, died of the "excessive heat of the weather, and the fatigues of the day."[7] The following year, at three o'clock on the afternoon of the twenty-ninth of May, under a blazing Carolina sun, the war struck the Waxhaws with shocking suddenness and ferocity.

On the road between Camden, South Carolina, and Charlotte, a few miles south of the North Carolina line, approximately in the center of the Waxhaws, Lieutenant Colonel Banastre Tarleton's British Legion, made up of northern Tory regulars, attacked and overran 350 Virginia Continentals commanded by Colonel Abraham Buford, ignored their white flag and pleas for quarter, butchered 113, and captured the rest, of whom 150 were wounded, many grievously. The Scotch Irish of the Waxhaws buried Buford's dead soldiers where they died and nursed the wounded at the Waxhaws Presbyterian Church. One of the nurses was Elizabeth Jackson, and it was on this occasion that her surviving sons first witnessed the awful reality of war.[8]

It is reasonable to speculate that Andrew saw here for the first time a man who would became one of his teachers. Major John Stokes was one of the American soldiers brutally mangled at Buford's Massacre. Stokes received twenty-three wounds, including four bayonet thrusts through his body and several severe saber cuts to his head and limbs, one of which "cut off his right hand through the metacarpal bones."[9]

In common with many boys of a time and place torn by the War of the Revolution, thirteen-year-old Andrew Jackson rode with men who made war. He was not a combatant, but he was often so close to the action that danger lurked at every turn. He was given a pistol by William Richardson Davie and joined his band as "a mounted orderly or messenger, for which I was well fitted, being a good rider and knowing all the roads." Davie was brave, elegant, refined, well educated, and a superb small unit combat commander, and by all accounts he became Jackson's beau ideal as an officer. Given Davie's military accomplishments and the dashing figure he cut the story is quite believable.[10]

Andrew was with Davie's command on 6 August 1780 when the South Carolina partisan commander General Thomas Sumter led the Rebels to victory over a large Tory force at Hanging Rock in the Waxhaws. And on one occasion, he recalled many years later, when the British army was advancing through the countryside, Banastre Tarleton's British Legion "passed thro the Waxhaw settlement to the cotauba [Cawtaba Indians] nation passing our dwelling but all were *hid out*. Tarleton passed within a hundred yards of where I & a cousin crawford, had concealed ourselves. I could have shot him." The words *"hid out"* were apt for the inhabitants of the Carolina Back Country during those terrible years in which armies marched and countermarched and mounted partisans of both sides raided, pillaged, and burned. Civilians and irregulars, Rebel and Tory alike, were ready at moment's notice to flee to the woods at the approach of the enemy, for mercy was uncommon in those times and many a man taken by his enemies swung from the nearest tree without benefit of trial.[11]

That is how Andrew, his family, friends, and neighbors spent his thirteenth and fourteenth years. When the British retired after a raid or an advance by their army, "we returned home." Following the debacle of the American army under Horatio Gates at Camden, "on the advance of Cornwallice we again retired & passed Charlott in McLenburge county a few hours before the British entered it [26 September 1780]. When Cornwallace passed on leaving [South] Carolina [22 January 1781] we again returned to our place of Residence. . . ."[12]

Young Andrew now experienced the most terrible time of his young life. Although the main armies had moved into northern North Carolina, partisan warfare soon erupted behind them and "men hunted each other like beasts of prey. . . ." The boy never forgot the horror of one man who apparently went temporarily mad when a friend was murdered and mutilated and in a fury hunted down and murdered twenty Tories before he came to his senses. Nor would he forget his own travail that began on 10 April 1781, when a British force of horse and foot under Major John Coffin "marched with Great precippitation" from Camden to the Waxhaws, "burned the Waxhaw meeting House & next day captured me and my brother."[13]

They were taken in the house of their cousin, Lieutenant Thomas Crawford, and it was there that a famous incident took place. While the house was being ransacked, the British dragoon commander ordered Andrew to clean his boots. The boy refused. The officer raised his saber and slashed at Andrew, who threw up his left hand in an attempt to protect his head. Years later he wrote, "The sword point reached my head, & has left a mark there as durable as the scull, as well as on the fingers." His brother Robert suffered a "deep cut" on the head when he refused a similar command and was immediately attacked by the officer.[14]

The boys were taken with other prisoners to Camden Jail and thrown in with about 250 other prisoners. Jackson told James McLaughlin in 1843 that "my bother, cousin and myself, as Soon as our relationship was known, were separated from each other. No attention whatever was paid to the wounds or to the comfort of the prisoners, and the small pox having broken out among them, for want of proper care, many fell victims to it. I frequently heard them groaning in the agonies of death and no regard was paid to them."[15]

Andrew was in a room on the second floor, from where could be seen the encampment before Camden of the American army under General Nathanael Greene. When the British boarded up the window, Andrew and another prisoner used the razor blade provided to divide their rations and cut a pine knot out of one of the planks, and through this hole they were able to see on 25 April 1781 the Battle of Hobkirk's Hill, in which Greene was defeated by the British garrison under Lord Rawdon.[16]

During their imprisonment both Andrew and his brother Robert caught smallpox, and Robert may also have had that other great wartime killer, dysentery. A few days after the battle an exchange of prisoners took place in which their mother, who had come to Camden, had a hand, and Andrew and Robert were among those released. Elizabeth Jackson procured two horses, and "my brother, on account of weakness caused by a severe bowel complaint and the wound he received on his head, being obliged to be held on the horse, and my mother riding the other, I was compelled to walk the whole way." Mother and sons traveled forty-five miles that day. Andrew was barefoot because the British had taken his shoes. For several hours during the journey they were drenched by a violent rainstorm. The smallpox he had caught in prison now raged within his weakened body and "consequently the next day I was dangerously ill."[17]

Two days later his brother Robert died. Andrew lay seriously ill. His mother buried the older boy and nursed her remaining child well into the summer. In the meantime word came to the Waxhaws of the sufferings of American prisoners on the British prison hulks anchored in Charleston harbor. Some were Waxhaw men, among them Andrew's cousins William and James Crawford, whom Elizabeth Jackson had helped raise. She knew at first hand what conditions prisoners suffered, and as soon as Andrew was out of danger, this brave and generous woman left him in care of her Crawford kin and joined with other women of the Waxhaws who traveled with medicine and clothing to Charleston and boarded the stinking, pestilence-ridden ships to treat their countrymen. During that time she visited a relative, William Barton, who lived two and one-half miles outside of Charleston. But she had brought within her from the hulks a dread disease sometimes called, appropriately, ship's fever. We know it as cholera. Her illness was brief, her death quick, her grave unmarked. Her clothes in a small bundle were sent upcountry to her orphaned son.[18]

The loss of his mother undoubtedly affected fourteen-year-old Andrew Jackson strongly. Perhaps it was traumatic, as some have claimed, but trauma in the sense of a disordered mental state is so overused in our time one has strong reservations about inflicting it on people long dead. And to base an interpretation of Jackson on the death of his mother is fraught with peril.[19] In the absence of testimony from Jackson we simply do not know his reaction to his mother's departure for Charleston and her death. There is no record of his commenting on it, other than to say, this is what happened.

We do know this about him. He was reared in a crude, violent Back Country society. His aggressiveness, his belligerence, the violence so close to the surface were exhibited years before his mother's death. We also know that Andrew Jackson was of a people who had spent centuries of hardscrabble living on the fringes, had arrived through an accident of history at a time and place of unique opportunity, and were determined to make the most of it. He was a son of that people writ large. His aim was their aim, and among a people noted for a fierce, burning drive he became a legend in his own time. In Jackson the virtues and faults of an entire people were magnified.

He hated fiercely, but not the Indian as so often charged. He would fight the Indian relentlessly and, as one with his people, was determined to displace him. But it was the British Jackson hated, and it was a passion carried to the grave. The war had killed his mother and brothers and left him still a boy without immediate family. He had seen friends and neighbors killed and maimed and his boyhood countryside, the garden of the Waxhaws, ravaged by British and Tory legions. He had personally experienced the haughtiness, disdain, and thoughtless cruelty of a British officer. Andrew Jackson grew up in the middle of a war, at one of its most savage moments, and it left its mark on him.

When his mother died, Andrew was still recovering in the home of his uncle, Major Thomas Crawford. Also living in the house was a commissary officer, a Captain Galbraith, who had, according to Andrew, a "very proud and haughty disposition," and "for some reason, I forget now what, he threatened to chastise me. I immediately, answered, 'that I had arrived at an age to know my rights, and although weak and feeble from disease, I had courage to defend them, and if he attempted anything of that kind I would most assuredly Send him to the other world.' "[20]

Galbraith retreated. But tension between the two led to Andrew removing to the home of Mrs. Crawford's uncle, Joseph White. It was a good solution, for young Andrew, bereft forever of mother and brothers, still very ill, needed something worthwhile on which to fix his attention and fill his days. White's son was a saddler, and Andrew loved horses and was an accomplished rider. He spent six months, whenever his health permitted, working in the saddlery.[21]

Andrew was also preoccupied by other interests. Living nearby were several rich and prominent Charleston families who had taken refuge in the Back Country from the British occupation of the city. Andrew got to know the young men of these families and in the summer and autumn of 1782 joined them in drinking, horse racing, and cockfighting, and in general, as James Parton put it, "comported himself in the style usually affected by dissipated young fools of that day." But the boy was thoroughly enjoying himself, and when the British evacuated Charleston in December 1782 and his new friends left for home, Andrew followed on his "fine and valuable" horse and resumed a life "more merry than wise." But he soon spent his meager funds, an inheritance from his grandfather, and found himself in debt to his landlord. In a tavern he chanced upon a crap game. A player offered to wager $200 against Andrew's splendid horse on one throw of the dice. Andrew accepted, threw the dice, and won. The next morning he paid his bill and left Charleston. Years later he said, "My calculation was that, if a loser in the game I would give the landlord my saddle and bridle, as far as they would go toward the payment of his bill, ask a credit for the balance, and walk away from the city; but being successful, I had new spirits infused into me, left the table, and from that moment to the present time I have never thrown dice for a wager."[22]

Jackson did not then become Andrew sobersides. He loved sport, and his passions for horse racing and cockfighting would remain. He continued to like good liquor and later operated his own still and traveled with a carrying case that had room for an ample supply of spirits. He would be well remembered in Salisbury, North Carolina, where he would read for the bar, as a leader of the young blades in town in carousing and high jinks, including that time-honored rural practice that I remember from my youth: sneaking into yards at night and lifting and moving outhouses great distances.

But this and other admittedly wild escapades he engaged in during his youth are signs of exuberance, not dissipation; the sowing of wild oats, not the road to ruin. The Charleston episode and the resolve he showed at age fifteen offer further evidence of that iron willpower for which he became famous.[23]

He returned to the Waxhaws and went to a school in present-day York County, South Carolina, run by Robert McCulloch, for languages and a "desultory course of studies," without, we suspect, much of it taking. But at a time when any educational attainment was rare, it was enough to get him a job as a schoolteacher for a year or two. His sights, however, were set elsewhere. In 1784, the first full year of peace following the War of the Revolution, he left the Waxhaws, never to return. His immediate goal was Salisbury, North Carolina, an important Back Country town forty miles northwest of Charlotte. There he intended to pursue a subject and a profession then and now dear—some think obsessively—to the hearts of ambitious Americans.[24]

Arriving at Salisbury in the winter of 1784, for some reason he pushed on sixty miles westward to Morganton, where he applied to Colonel Waightstill Avery, a famous lawyer said to own the best law library in those parts, to board in his home and read law under him. But Colonel Avery, who lived in a log home, lacked the room, and Jackson turned his horse back toward Salisbury. There another eminent lawyer, Spruce McCay, agreed to accept him. Jackson was then about three months shy of his eighteenth birthday.[25]

He spent almost two years with McCay and his fellow students, including one named John McNairy, who would become a close friend. Once more he was not by any means a good scholar, but he learned enough. And those two years in Salisbury, leading the students in their adventures, attending dancing school, chasing girls, consorting with townspeople, were as much a part of his education as what he read in the law books or absorbed from Spruce McCay. That socializing process was probably more important to him in the long run. Perhaps, as Robert Remini observed, it was in Salisbury that he either learned the social graces that would in later life surprise those who expected a rude backwoodsman or glimpsed enough to build on as he moved forward and upward.[26]

In late 1786 he left McCay's office to finish his education in law with Colonel John Stokes. We described earlier Stokes's travail at Buford's Massacre and the possibility that Jackson had seen the terribly wounded man not long after the action. A silver knob had replaced the hand lost to a saber blow in the Waxhaws. Stokes used it to bang on tables when he wished to emphasize a point. To young Andrew Jackson, that silver knob was another reminder of the war and British massacre.

On 26 September 1787, Jackson was admitted to the North Carolina bar. One month later this young man of "unblemished moral character," as his law license stated, was arrested, along with four other young lawyers, by the sheriff of Rowan County for trespass that caused damage in the amount of 500 pounds. At age twenty, it seems, he had still not quite grown up. But that is all we know of the incident, as neither court documents nor other records reveal the nature or the disposition of the case. Jackson moved north to Guilford County.[27]

For the next year he followed his profession in a circuit that stretched more than one hundred miles, and he was admitted to practice in several North Carolina counties. Clients, however, did not flock to Andrew Jackson, attorney at law. On the contrary, he had time to spare. In Martinsville, in Guilford County, he stayed with two friends, Joseph Henderson and Bennett Searcy, who ran a country store. He helped his friends in the store, and according to tradition was appointed a constable. Gambling occupied some of his time. Horse racing remained a passion. Just another lawyer among many whose prospects appeared not at all bright, without a patron to open the right doors and smooth over the rough spots. Are we surprised, then, that this young man of resolve and fierce ambition, who as a boy "would never *stay throwed*," looked to new horizons, to the lands where the waters ran west?

His opportunity came when John McNairy, his friend and fellow student from Spruce McCay's office, was elected by the legislature to be Superior Court judge for the Western District of North Carolina, a huge district west of the Appalachians that stretched to the Mississippi River and would one day become the state of Tennessee. McNairy needed to appoint a public prosecutor for the district and offered the post to Jackson. It was not a job much sought after, and one unpopular on the frontier, but it offered a steady income, and Jackson could practice privately at the same time. And it was new country, where possibly boundless opportunities existed. He accepted, and in the spring or early summer of 1788 rendezvoused at Morganton with McNairy, Bennett Searcy, who was the newly appointed clerk of the court, and three or four other young lawyers seeking their fortune, a few among the flood of hopefuls headed for the promised land.

Andrew Jackson had by then attained his majority. He was twenty-one years old and fully grown: six feet one in his stocking feet, 140 pounds soaking wet. All skin and bones, it seemed, he never changed, never in a long and action-packed life became fat and soft. His chiseled face defied the efforts of artists to soften the harsh features. Those features were not meant to be soft. They were meant to confront a hostile world he meant to conquer. They framed intense, deep blue eyes that could mesmerize and frighten. They were topped, the skin and bones and chiseled face, by a distinctive mane of thick, sandy hair that in old age turned white but never thinned. When he was old and sick and toothless, he was still quite recognizable as the fierce and unrelenting warrior he had been throughout his life.

Up the steep, narrow trails of the Appalachians Jackson and his companions rode, to the lands where the waters ran west, still fiercely contested by Chickamauga and Chickasaw and Creek and Shawnee, where there was no neat frontier line but settlements here and there in southwestern Virginia and Kentucky and the land that became Tennessee, some barely hanging on, between them vast tracts of wilderness that were veritable no-man's-lands.

The bitter conflict between whites and Indians was of long standing and would continue for decades after Jackson's arrival west of the mountains. It had begun a century earlier, complicated by the clash of imperial nations. Thus we need to step back and examine what came before in order to understand what followed.

Chapter 1

‑‑‑❧‑‑‑

BEGINNINGS

"BE INFORMED THAT I CAME
TO GET ACQUAINTED WITH THE COUNTRY"

In the summer of 1685, 250 riders escorting a pack train left the young town of Charleston in the province of South Carolina and headed up-country. They were led by an experienced and intrepid English frontiersman, Dr. Henry Woodward (c. 1646–c. 1686): physician, adventurer, agent of empire. Woodward and his men had a long way to go, through the watery, fever-ridden Low Country and the featureless pine barrens beyond, into the hills of the Piedmont, described over a century later as enjoying a "free, open air." They forded the Savannah River and kept heading west through the present state of Georgia and forded in succession the Ogeechee, Oconee, Ocmulgee, and Flint Rivers. They had been in Indian country since early in their journey, but they made no attempt to hide their presence. The packhorses had bells on their tack, so the handlers could more easily round them up every morning. To the continual ringing of the bells and cracking of whips and whooping and hollering, the riders pushed on, their destination the great Lower Creek town of Coweta in modern Russell County, Alabama, near the falls of the Chattahoochee River.[1]

The great naturalist William Bartram, traveling the Creek country of south-central Alabama with a pack train in November 1777, left us a vivid picture of a centuries-old scene of pandemonium now out of memory. Bartram thought his old horse "would give up," especially when he discovered what he considered the "mad manner" in which the traders traveled. "They seldom decamp until the sun is high and hot; each one having a whip made of the toughest cow-skin, they start all at once, the horses having ranged themselves in regular Indian file . . . then the chief drives with the crack of his whip, and a whoop or shriek, which rings through the forests and plains . . . which is repeated by all the company, when we start at once, keeping up a brisk and constant trot, which is incessantly urged and continued as long as these miserable creatures are able to move forward. . . . The constant ringing and clattering of the bells, smacking of the whips, whooping and too frequent cursing these miserable quadrupeds, cause an incessant uproar and confusion, inexpressibly disagreeable."[2]

Trade was also Henry Woodward's purpose. English goods for the skins of the whitetail deer that grazed the forests and swamps and savannas of the South in such vast numbers that in 1682 Thomas Ashe wrote, "There is such infinite Herds that the whole Country seems but one continued Park." For well over a century the beaver trade of the North and the Rocky Mountains had lured most historians and writers, attracted by its importance and romance, but in the South the pelts of beaver and other fur-bearing animals were hardly worth mentioning in comparison to the skins of the whitetail deer. For decades deer hides were by far the mainstay of the southern Indian trade and remained significant for most of the colonial period. Forty-five thousand deerskins a year were shipped from Charleston to London between 1699 and 1705, and from 1705 to 1715 the hide trade provided South Carolina's most valuable export. As late as 1747–1748, when the value of beaver pelts exported was 300 pounds, deerskin exports were second only to rice in total value: 252,000 pounds in South Carolina currency. To get a slice of that pie men were willing to risk life and limb, to connive and cajole, to participate in mayhem and massacre.[3]

Although this was a pioneering English effort to establish relations with the Creeks, and solicited by those powerful people, the Creeks were not unaccustomed to dealing with Europeans. Preceding Henry Woodward and his men by a century and a half, Spanish explorers and colonizers had traveled far and wide through the American South, and they had taught the Creeks and other Indians that the white man brought many things with him. He brought death, destruction, and disease, but also guns, and knives and hatchets made of hard metals, and woven cloth dyed with bright colors, and beads and baubles that delighted the eye. Thus they were tempted, and the temptations overcame their shock at the profound changes wrought by the invaders, and tempered their resistance to ways alien to theirs.

Hernando de Soto, conquistador, gave the ancestors of the Creeks and other interior tribes their first experience of Europeans. Brave, brutal, reckless, de Soto had fought under Pizarro in Peru and had profited from the fabulous treasures of the Incas. In May 1539, hoping to establish a colony of his own to rival Mexico and Peru, he began a fruitless quest for gold on the Gulf Coast of Florida that carried him northward through the present states of Georgia and South Carolina, across the Appalachians to the southeastern corner of Tennessee, then southwesterly through Alabama, Mississippi, Arkansas, and a slice of Texas before turning back. It ended in May 1542 when his men lowered his fever-ravaged corpse into the Mississippi. Of his meandering three-year march we can say that he came, he saw, he went, for he was no Caesar. He found no treasure, he built no empires, he left no monuments. He wrought only death and destruction. Behind him, like the ocean erasing the wake of a ship, the great forests and the mist-shrouded mountains and the deep swamps healed and closed and in the fullness of time showed no outward sign of his passing. His primary accomplishment was inadvertent: he softened up the tribes and left them terribly vulnerable to other waves of European and American invaders for the next three centuries.[4]

Spanish steel and Spanish fury were only part of the story. De Soto and other Europeans who preceded and followed him brought with them an invisible weapon far more terrible than Toledo blades wielded by conquistadors. European diseases to which the native peoples had no immunity felled Indians by the tens of thousands. Whole towns were wiped out, tribes decimated, survivors numbed by an experience beyond their ken. The pox was among them, and it would never go away, for this was a tale that would be repeated decade after dreary decade.

There is one more matter to consider before we leave de Soto and his six hundred Spaniards. They had marched and fought their way through thousands of miles of wilderness, surrounded for three years by thousands of brave and skillful warriors. Finally, desperate, their leader dead of fever and only half their number left, the survivors fought their way out and managed to escape. The Spanish adventurers considered their survival a gift from God. What a pity that the Indians lacked a written language, for it would be interesting to know to what they attributed their failure to overwhelm the Spaniards by sheer numbers and destroy them, leaving not a man to tell the tale.

Despite their violent reaction to the Spanish invasion, for the Creeks and their neighbors a dangerous attraction developed that was like a slow-working cancer within their societies. Having seen what wondrous results could come of being armed with guns, the Indians eagerly sought them from other Spaniards who appeared among them. And they would as eagerly seek them from the English, who arrived in South Carolina and founded Charleston in 1670, and from the French, who first established themselves on the Gulf Coast, on Biloxi Bay, in 1699.

It was the Creek desire for guns to protect themselves from the Westo Indians, who had procured theirs from English traders from Virginia, that prompted them to send a delegation to Charleston with an invitation to the English to come among them and trade. Thus was introduced into the very innards of their society a fifth column.[5] Unlike the twentieth-century version, it was not a figment of the imagination. The arrival of the English on the Chattahoochee was a watershed for the Creeks. Never again would things be the same.

The Spanish marched up from Pensacola and temporarily chased out the English. Henry Woodward, exhibiting supreme confidence—some would say arrogance—and a sense of humor, left a letter for the Spanish commander, Lieutenant Antonio Matheos: "I am very sorry that I came with so small a following that I cannot await your arrival. Be informed that I came to get acquainted with the country, its mountains, the seacoast, and Apalache. I trust in God that I shall meet you gentlemen later when I have a large following. September 2, 1685."[6]

"WE ARE FAR FROM ACKNOWLEDGING THAT FLORIDA
BELONGS TO THE KING OF SPAIN"

Other Englishmen fanned out from Charleston to "get acquainted with the country" and trade with the Indians. By the early 1690s British traders were among the Upper Creeks in present-day Alabama, and in 1698 Thomas Welch actually crossed the Mississippi and established a trading post in the Quapaw Indian village at the mouth of the Arkansas River. Spanish and French officials reported the presence of English traders throughout the interior, diverting the Indian trade to Charleston, subverting attachments the Indians might have to the Spanish and French. Next to the giants of Spanish and French exploration—the de Sotos, the Ponce de Leons, the LaSalles— these largely anonymous Englishmen remain unheralded and for the most part forgotten. But they sowed deeper. They were especially successful among the Chickasaws, who lived in present-day northern Mississippi and western Tennessee. It was a relatively small tribe, but it occupied a strategic location on the Mississippi River, and its warriors had a deserved reputation for valor. Almost a century later they would continue to play an important role on the American frontier. The preeminent historian of that period of English expansion stated that the alliance the traders forged with the Chicka- saws "more than any other single factor, was destined to thwart the complete attainment of the French design in the lower Mississippi Valley."[7]

The greatest of those early frontiersmen was a Scot, Thomas Nairne (?–1715). He was South Carolina's first Indian agent, appointed in 1707 to bring order and regularity to an enterprise increasingly known for abuse of the Indians by rough and crooked traders. He did not succeed in this endeavor, and the injustices of the Indian trade would remain to bedevil throughout its long and sordid history British colonial and U.S. officials alike. But Nairne was a very competent man, an acute observer whose *Jour- nals* are a treasure trove for historians and anthropologists, and a visionary who planned for the expulsion of the Spanish and French and the creation of a vast British empire in what became the southeastern United States.[8]

The Spanish were a familiar threat, not just to English ambitions but to the young colony of South Carolina itself. It has been suggested, however, that the French were never more than a nuisance. This may be true. But we must be concerned with what contemporaries thought. In 1699, the year the French built Fort Maurepas on Biloxi Bay, the surveyor general of His Majesty's Customs for North America, Edward Randolph, wrote to the Board of Trade during an official visit to Charleston, "I find the Inhabitants greatly alarmed upon the news that the French continue their resolution to make a settling at Messasipi River, from [whence] they may come over land to the head of the Ashley River without opposition. . . ." Randolph wrote on the eve of the outbreak of the War of Spanish Succession (1701–1714; Queen Anne's War in the colonies), a war everyone knew was coming as soon as the childless Charles II of Spain died, which was anticipated on an almost daily basis and occurred on 1 November 1700.[9]

Governor James Moore of South Carolina also feared a French invasion, warning the assembly in August 1701 that whether "warr or peace we are sure to be always in danger and under the trouble and charge of keeping out guards, even in time of Peace, so long as those French live so near to us. To put you in mind of the French of Canada's neighborhood to the inhabitants of New England is to say enough on the subject."[10]

The key to control of the Gulf Coast, the Mississippi, and the vast hinterland was to get the powerful Indian nations on your side: Yamasees, Cherokees, Creeks, Choctaws, Chickasaws, and, until their destruction by the French (1729–1731), Natchez. Thomas Nairne observed that England's Indian allies were "hardy, active, and good Marksmen, excellent at Ambuscade, and who are brought together with little or no Charge." The security of South Carolina, he wrote, could only be effected by "drawing over to our Side, or destroying, all the *Indians* within 700 miles of *Charlestown.*" By the beginning of Queen Anne's War the English influence was strong among all except the Choctaws, who leaned to the French at Mobile. The Chickasaws made unsafe the passage of French convoys on the Mississippi between Canada and Louisiana. Thomas Nairne considered the "Cherikee nation now Entirely Subject to us are extremely well Scituate to Keep of any Incursions which Either the Illinois or any other french Indians may think of making into Carolina . . . they are now our only defence on the Back parts." This English effort to draw to them as allies as many tribes as possible to oppose the Spanish, the French, and especially the Indian allies of each was not a unique strategy in world history. Undoubtedly without knowing it, Nairne was adapting for British North America the classical imperial Chinese policy of using barbarians to fight barbarians.[11]

The most dramatic English action was taken against the Spanish, and it brings into sharp focus the crucial need of Indian allies in this early period and beyond. It also highlights the English attitude toward Spanish control of Florida, perhaps best expressed in 1730 by the Board of Trade in London: "We are far from acknowledging that Florida belongs to the King of Spain."[12]

By 1686 the English had all but driven the Spanish from Guale (present-day Georgia). The outbreak of Queen Anne's War was all South Carolina needed to launch a massive attack on the land the Spanish called La Florida. Between 1702 and 1706, James Moore of South Carolina, first as governor and later leading a private army sanctioned by the assembly, launched a series of devastating attacks. He was joined by Creeks and Yamasees as well as large numbers of Spanish mission Indians who had begun rejecting Christianity and Spanish hegemony before the interference of the English. The town of St. Augustine was destroyed, although the stone fort of San Marcos and its garrison and refugees survived. But the countryside was devastated by Moore's army of slave hunters, of whom there were fifty Englishmen and a thousand Creek warriors.

But inciting Indians to join in war was one thing, controlling them quite another. The horror of the destruction of the missions as recorded in

Spanish documents rings down over the centuries. Friars were tortured to death. Loyal mission Indians were not exempt from massacre. A Spanish reconnaissance patrol "found many burned bodies and . . . some women pierced by sticks and half roasted, many children impaled on poles, and others killed with arrows, their arms and legs cut off." At the fortified ranch of La Chua, Creek warriors quartered a black ranch hand. Almost all of the mission Indians from the town of Ivitachuco and their chief, the accultur-ated and literate Patricio de Hinachuba, were massacred by Creeks and rene-gade Apalachees within sight of the walls of St. Augustine. Many Spaniards and their Indian allies were skinned alive. Their tormentors "put them in stocks and there cut off the scalps from the heads, and the breasts from the women, and dried them on some long sticks. . . ." After a battle lost by the Spanish, the Indians took hold of one Balthazar Francisco, who "cried out to call on God and to Our Lady . . . spoke with an able tongue to the Indians, as he knew them well as an old soldier, who had been more than fourteen years in garrison in Apalachee; and that he wished it recorded, he heard him say, that he was from the Island of Teneriffe, of the region of Los Silos." The Indians honored Balthazar Francisco by giving him a "crown [of] the beaks of parroquets, deer hair, and wild animal hair, such as are much used in the dances which the pagans have for *tascayas* or *norocos,* names which are given to the courageous Indians"; and then they "cut out his tongue and eyes, cut off his ears, slashed him all over, stuck burning splinters in the wounds, and set fire to him while he was tied at the foot of a cross."[13]

On 16 April 1704 James Moore wrote to the Lords Proprietors in En-gland that he had "killed, and taken as slaves 325 men, and have taken slaves 4,000 women and children."[14]

For Africans were not the only people enslaved in the colonies of the European powers. The Spanish enslaved thousands of Indians in the Caribbean. The French in Louisiana retaliated against the English and their allies by sending captured Chickasaws to the French West Indies for sale as slaves. And the Indians themselves did not emerge from the Indian slave trade with clean hands. English traders encouraged and rewarded Creek and Chickasaw warriors for capturing other Indians, who were transported to Charleston and sent in chains to New England and Barbados. The warriors took to it with enthusiasm. Thomas Nairne reported that "no imployment pleases the Chicasaws so well as slave Catching. A lucky hitt at that besides the Honor procures them a whole Estate at once, one slave brings a Gun, ammunition, horse, hatchet, and a suit of Cloathes, which would not be pro-cured without much tedious toil a hunting." In this respect, the warriors matched the avaricious Charleston traders.[15]

Thomas Nairne was one of the slavers on the Moore expedition. He wrote to the earl of Sunderland in 1708, "The garrison of St. Augustine is by this warr, Reduced to the bare walls their Castle and Indian towns all Consumed Either by us in our Invasion . . . or by our Indian Subjects Since who in the quest of Booty are now obliged to goe down as farr on the point of Florida as the firm land will permit. They have drove the Floridians to the

Islands of the Cape, have brought in and sold many hundreds of them, and dayly now Continue that trade so that in some few years they'le Reduce these Barbarians to a farr less number." If the reader suspects Nairne of exaggerating, consider the fate of the once bold and prosperous Apalachee Indians, whose fierce resistance to de Soto in the winter of 1539–1540 kept the Spanish camp in a state of siege. They numbered about twenty-five thousand in the early 1600s, when Spanish missionaries began efforts to convert them. By the 1680s their numbers had been reduced to an estimated six thousand to ten thousand. The few who were left following the Anglo-Creek fury either took shelter at St. Augustine or went west to the relative safety of the Spanish and French garrison towns of Pensacola and Mobile. When Spain lost Florida to England in 1763, some of the remnants may eventually have ended up in Mexico in Vera Cruz; the rest went to Louisiana. By the 1830s history lost track of them. They disappeared as a people.[16]

From Apalachee to the Keys, from the stone walls of St. Augustine to lonely Pensacola, Creek and Yamasee war parties instigated by Englishmen roamed—killing, torturing, burning, pillaging, enslaving. The terror and devastation visited upon the friars and their Indian charges was unrelenting, and the wounds inflicted on the mission system, carefully built up over a century and a half, were mortal.

THE INDIANS "EFFECT THEM MOST WHO SELL BEST CHEAP"

Excessive pride now overcame the Creeks. Flushed with victory, they stormed Spanish Pensacola in 1707 and burned the town and did the same in October 1708, but on both occasions were unable to take the fort, and thereby revealed a chronic Indian military weakness: their inability stemming from both lack of technique and fighting style to take fortified places held by alert, determined defenders. In May 1709 they went after the French and besieged Mobile, where a "wild sortie by French soldiers repulsed them with loss." In 1711 the South Carolinian Colonel Theophillus Hastings led thirteen hundred Lower Creek warriors against the Choctaws.[17]

The English were also consumed with a pride barely discernible from arrogance, and the ones who felt it most were the Indians, especially their allies the Yamasees and the Creeks. The traders had long abused their clients, and the abuse was financial, mental, and physical: overpricing, cheating on weights and measures, extending credit until Indians were mired in debt from which they could not possibly escape, seizure of Indian property and the repossession of goods, holding relatives of the biggest debtors prisoners, actually beating Indians, and conniving with corrupt *micos,* whose daughters were often traders' wives or mistresses, with presents and favorable conditions of debt. By 1715 Indians owed the traders and merchants an approximate debt of £100,000 sterling ($9.2 million). To make matters worse, the Yamasee, whom South Carolina had enticed up from Florida to settle lands south of Charleston as a buffer against the Spanish, watched as a burgeoning white population began encroaching on the lands they had been given.[18]

Need the list be longer? Did the traders and settlers have any inkling that they were playing with fire?

Which is literally what occurred, on Good Friday, 15 April 1715. Rumors of an Indian conspiracy had filtered down-country. On 14 April Thomas Nairne, William Bray, and Samuel Warner met at the Yamasee town of Pocataligo to offer the Indians redress of grievances. The traders Bray and Warner were on an official mission. They had brought warnings to Charleston and had been sent to Pocataligo to head off a rising. Nairne had learned of the planned uprising independently and had come from his plantation on Saint Helena Island. They slept that night in Pocataligo. On Good Friday morning they were awakened by war cries and seized by warriors painted red and black. William Bray and Samuel Warner were killed immediately. But for Thomas Nairne the Yamasee reserved a special treatment, as befitted an important man who had won honors in war.

He was stripped and tied to a stake, probably with the customary thong that allowed him some freedom of movement. Splinters were stuck into his body and lighted. The Indians would have watched him closely. If he showed signs of fear, or begged for mercy, they would have laughed at him, for that was their way. A fire was built. Not a large fire. That would have ended his travail too quickly. For three days he was roasted "*à petit feu*" (a small fire). On the third day he died.[19]

The Yamasee War came close to destroying South Carolina. Four hundred settlers (6% of the population) were killed. Ninety percent of the traders were killed in the Yamasee and Creek Nations, from South Carolina's Low Country to central Alabama. Charleston's defensive perimeter was reduced to a radius of some thirty-five miles and that was not totally secure. In August 1715 several hundred warriors penetrated the outskirts of Charleston before being repulsed. The degree of danger can be measured by the arming of hundreds of black slaves to fight alongside white militiamen. All of the southeastern tribes had risen except two: the Chickasaws on the Mississippi, who stayed loyal and protected their traders; and the Cherokees, who were thinking over Creek overtures. The Chickasaws were too far away and too few to intervene. The Cherokees, however, were quite a different story. They were on the doorsteps of both Carolinas and they could muster 4,000 warriors. If the Cherokees joined the alliance, what could follow? The evacuation of Charleston?[20]

In the late fall of 1715 Colonels James Moore and George Chicken with 300 militiamen were sent up-country to the lower Cherokee towns as a show of force and to negotiate an alliance. At the same time Creek envoys were in the towns seeking their own alliance, and a large force of Creek warriors were concealed in the forests awaiting the signal for a Cherokee-Creek attack on the English force. The Cherokees took their time and negotiated with both sides. Finally, in January 1716, they made their decision. The Creek envoys were murdered by their hosts and a Cherokee-English force did the attacking and sent the waiting Creek warriors fleeing for their lives.[21]

The Cherokee decision saved South Carolina. Historians have given pride of place to the Indian alliances that led to the Pequot War (1636–1638) and King Philip's War (1675–1676) in New England, and the rising of the northwestern tribes in Pontiac's Rebellion (1763–1765). This is not unusual, given the general neglect of southern history during the colonial and revolutionary periods. But the alliance that led to the Yamasee War was the "greatest Indian alliance in colonial history with the potential to eradicate not just South Carolina but also North Carolina and Virginia." The failure of all of the southern tribes to unite against the invader at this favorable moment is striking, and we should keep it in mind as we arrive at various junctions in our story.[22]

As the English got the upper hand, an Anglican clergyman writing from South Carolina described the situation. "It is certain Many of the Yammonses and Creek Indians were against the war all along; But our Military Men are so bent upon Revenge, and so desirous to enrich themselves by making all the Indians Slaves that fall into their hands, but such as they kill (without making the least distinction between the guilty and the innocent, and without considering the Barbarous usage these poor Savages met from our villainous Traders) that it is in vain to represent to them the Cruelty and injustice of Such a procedure. And therefore all that we can doe is, to lament in Secret those Sins, which have brought this Judgement upon us; for what we Say out of the pulpit, are words of course, and are little minded, nowithstanding the general calamity."[23]

Johnston's final sentence, admitting clerical helplessness in a sea of striving and money grubbing, speaks volumes for the difference between England and its rivals in the great struggle for empire. Spain would cling to Florida for several decades. France took advantage of South Carolina's desperate situation during the Yamasee War. In 1717, at the invitation of the Alabama Indians, a people of the Creek Confederacy, the French built Fort Toulouse as a trading and listening post on the Coosa River in the heart of the Upper Creek country, near where the Coosa joins the Tallapoosa just north of modern Montgomery to form the Alabama. They would remain for almost half a century.[24] Spain, weakened but still to be reckoned with, and France to a greater extent, were continually in the minds of British ministers, colonial officials, merchants, and traders. But we know that even when the contest began a sea change in history promised England the upper hand. Thomas Nairne put his finger on it in 1708 in his *Memorial* to the earl of Sunderland: "May it Please Your Lordship the English trade for Cloath always atracts and maintains the obedience and friendship of the Indians. They Effect them most who sell best cheap."[25]

England had entered the modern world. Spain had not. And when France entered the fray in the South at the end of the seventeenth century, that absolutist monarchy also found itself hobbled by an archaic economic system. Let us not delude ourselves. Spain and France remained strong contenders, served by loyal, sometimes gifted, colonial soldiers and governors, and legions of fearless priests. But this ruthless contest for empire turned not on the salvation of souls but the creation of wealth. In manufacturing, banking, and the ease with which her system produced cheap high-quality goods and extended credit to merchant adventurers, England left her continental rivals in the dust. Added to her superior system of economic organization was the nature of the men behind it and those who served them in the field. They were the English counterparts of the conquistador Hernando de Soto, whether in the counting houses of London and Charleston or plunging alone and ever deeper into the wilderness, dependent always for life itself on the loyalty and good nature of their Indian hosts. Hard, often intrepid men on the make, they differed from de Soto in at least one crucial respect. They were heralds of the modern world.[26]

"THEY COULD NOT LIVE WITHOUT THE ENGLISH"

The upheaval of the war brought a dramatic change in Creek diplomacy. The war and its aftermath taught them that all eggs should not be placed in a single basket. Words written several decades later by a knowledgeable British observer applied to the Creeks: "No people in the World understand and pursue their true National Interest, better than the Indians." Under the wise and skillful leadership of Old Brims of the Lower Creeks, neutrality toward the English, the Spanish, and the French became policy throughout the rest of the colonial period. Among the Upper Creeks, the Alabamas clearly explained their policy to a French officer, Lieutenant François Hazeur, who reported in 1740 that "they had long held as a maxim not to meddle at all in the quarrels that the Europeans had among themselves; that they had profited by it, since by means of this policy they were well received by all and received benefits from all sides." Given the nature of the Creek Confederacy, which we will discuss later in the narrative, neutrality had its detractors and was not always followed, and hot-blooded young warriors were not above going off on their own in quest of scalps and glory. But it was the starting point for policy discussions in council. Finely attuned to their own interests, the Creeks would promise the English this, the Spanish that, the French something else, play one against the other, strive mightily to get the most they could from each. Imperfect and messy, as human affairs are, the neutrality policy nevertheless served the Creeks well.[27]

But the deerskin trade remained, and it continued as a serious problem in relations between the English and the Indians, especially the Creeks and the Cherokees. Both sides were wed to it—the English for profit, the Indians because the English had what they craved and needed, for they had either forgotten or abandoned the old ways. The Indians knew it and admitted it, on more than one occasion with brutal candor. In 1725, Colonel George Chicken, South Carolina's Indian commissioner, reported from the Cherokee town of Tunisee that the "head Warriour . . . got up and made the following Speech to me and the People of the Town. 'That they must now mind and Consider that all their Old men were gone, and that they have been brought up after another Manner than their forefathers and that they must Consider that they could not live without the English.'" Forty-one years later two Creek headmen, Ishenphoaphe and Escochabey, implored Governor James Wright of Georgia not to embargo the trade for the killing of a trader by a Creek warrior: "for we are so used to the white people and their clothing that we should be very poor without them."

White testimony on Indian addiction to trade was given by the British commander in chief in America, General Thomas Gage: "Our Manufactures are as much desired by the Indians, as their Peltry is sought for by us; what was originally deemed a Superfluity or a Luxury to the Natives is now become a Necessary; they are disused to the Bow, and can neither hunt nor make war, without Fire-Arms, Powder, and Lead. The British Provinces only can Supply them with their Necessarys; which they know, and for their own Sakes they would protect the Trade; which they actually do at present."[28]

The separate provinces attempted to control the trade and curb the excesses of the traders, but hundreds of miles of rugged Back Country in an age of primitive communications separated well-meaning provincial officials and "refractory and insolent traders," in the words of South Carolina governor Francis Nicholson. It took many months for transgressions to come to light, many more until judgments were rendered, and, in the absence of adequate enforcement, traders could usually ignore official findings and orders with impunity. In 1723, Governor Nicholson admitted that the attitude of the powerful, well-connected Charleston merchants who controlled the trade and profited most from it was the crucial factor in the problem: "the Various interests of the Persons concerned in the . . . Trade makes it very Difficult to Manage it." In this short but telling admission we glimpse early on the deep-rooted American preference for unfettered private enterprise.[29]

But efforts continued to be made to exert imperial control over the trade. In 1755, a South Carolinian submitted a report and a plan to the Board of Trade in London that shed much light on frontier conditions. Edmund Atkin (1707–1761), himself a successful Charleston merchant in the Indian trade, was tactless, quarrelsome, pompous, arrogant, and inept. And he did not play favorites, angering whites and Indians alike. One incident highlights the personal danger of operating in Indian country, the volatile atmosphere that always lurked beneath the surface when whites and Indians met, and the damage that could be done by offensive deportment or ill-chosen words. It was described by the trader James Adair, on one occasion while in council in the Upper Creek town of Tuckabatchee, which was located in present-day Elmore County, Alabama, northeast of modern Montgomery. Atkin so enraged the Creek warrior Tobacco Eater, "who had always before been very kind to the British traders," that Tobacco Eater "jumped up in a rage, and darted his tomahawk at his head." The blade hit a beam as it came down and struck Atkin only a glancing blow. But blood spurted, and pandemonium ensued. Traders fearing all would be massacred fled in every direction. But several Creeks friendly to the English sprang upon Tobacco Eater and threw him to the ground and bound him. Thus, Adair wrote, was "prevented those dangerous consequences which must otherwise have immediately followed.

Had the aimed blow succeeded, the savages would have immediately put up the war and death whoop, destroyed most of the white people there on the spot, and set off in great bodies, both to the Cherakee country, and against our valuable settlements."[30]

Yet Atkin was intelligent, well educated, and a good observer. And unlike many, if not most, of his fellow merchants, he believed strongly that central control and regulation of the Indian trade was necessary if England was to best France in the momentous war for North America then being waged. His general approach was neither unique nor new to the authorities in London. Various proposals by well-known colonials had been submitted to the Board of Trade during the early 1750s. But his plan, wrote the historian Wilbur Jacobs, "was truly the first comprehensive, well-organized design for Indian management submitted to British authorities."[31]

Atkin divided the colonies into northern and southern departments, with a superintendent of Indian affairs for each. The northern superintendency would be filled by the famous and very able Anglo Irishman Sir William Johnson, whose main responsibility would be the powerful Iroquois Confederacy of central and western New York, among whom he lived, married, and begot children. His baronial home, Johnson Hall, still stands in the Mohawk Valley. Atkin was made superintendent of the Southern Department, in which he served from his appointment in 1756 until his death in October 1761.

A PEOPLE "LAWLESS AND LICENTIOUS"

The new organization, however, was living on borrowed time. Mass migration to America had begun well before Edmund Atkin made his proposal and would continue after his death. It would accelerate a process that had begun with the first landings of English colonists on the Atlantic Coast of North America early in the seventeenth century, in Virginia and Massachusetts. The reader may question my use of the term *mass migration,* for Americans associate its beginning with the flight of the Celtic Irish from the Great Famine of the mid-nineteenth century. But mass migration actually began in the early eighteenth century and steadily rose in volume until the American Revolution temporarily shut off the flow. Unlike the mass movements of the nineteenth and early twentieth centuries, it numbered in hundreds of thousands instead of millions. But in a century of low population levels, especially in North America, the eighteenth-century migrants came in big numbers and took literally the biblical command to be fruitful and multiply. They were mostly Scotch Irish and German Protestants. Among them were smaller groups of Welsh and French Protestants. Thousands of them and their descendants headed for the southern frontier in search of cheap land, joined by English and Scotch Irish settlers pushing out of the southern Piedmont from Maryland to Georgia. In this book the frontier-bound folk are our concern.[32]

The Long Hunters, ca. 1810, by unknown artist (Courtesy of the East Tennessee Historical Society, Knoxville)

They swarmed. From the north, out of Pennsylvania, from the east, out of the Piedmont, down the Great Valley of Virginia, the beautiful and fertile Shenandoah, pressing into the mountain valleys of southwestern Virginia, slipping sideways and descending into the Back Country of the Carolinas and Georgia, a trickle, then a flood of settlers appeared. They sought land and opportunity, and they had something in common with the great movements of peoples of past ages in Asia, Europe, and the Americas: they were not concerned at whose expense they attained their goals. They were for the most part poor but not rabble, contrary to the deep-seated prejudices of their alleged betters, such as General Thomas Gage, who described them as "lawless and Licentious. . . ."[33]

It was these aggressive, pressing people, not traders, who represented the great threat to the Indian owners of the land. Many traders and their pack-horsemen and other employees were crude, greedy, crooked, violent, and sexual predators. Bernard Romans, an eighteenth-century naturalist and cartographer, knew them well and did not mince words in describing them: "monsters in human form, the very scum and outcast of the earth . . . with . . . an inclination for deceit and over reaching. . . ." Their behavior at times drove Indians to violence, as in the Yamasee War and later in Pontiac's Rebellion in the Northwest. But traders and Indians were satisfied with the general state of affairs. The traders had no desire to push the Indians off their land, for they had a solid stake in the status quo. Their living revolved around the white-tailed deer, whose numbers by the time our tale begins were dwindling from heavy hunting and the increasing presence of settlers. Traders had no desire to see hordes of settlers squat on Indian land, kill off the game, and goad the Indians to war. Traders had from the beginning changed the Indian world, but they had not supplanted it and had no wish to do so. Nor did the Indians wish to see the permanent departure of the traders, who supplied their avid desire for European goods. The coming of the settlers, however, and their unceasing flow changed the equation forever.[34]

The French and Indian War (1754–1763) further imperiled the situation of the Indians by driving France from North America. In general the French have never been a nation of migrants, thus they did not represent a threat to Indian occupancy of the land or their way of life. The British, however, not only migrated—they opened the doors to others, especially Germans. Under the terms of the peace treaty England took Canada and all of the lands claimed by France west of the Appalachians to the Mississippi River, and from Spain all of Florida. New Orleans went to Spain. The Indians vigorously objected to the transfer. "We tell you now the French never conquered us neither did they purchase a foot of our Country, nor have they a right to give it to you, we gave them liberty to settle for which they always rewarded us & treated us with great Civility while they had it in their power, but as they are become now your people, if you expect to keep these Posts, we will expect to have proper returns from you."[35]

The British ignored the warning. Yet at the same time they wanted to avoid conflict with the Indians and arrange an orderly administration of new territories. The Royal Proclamation of 1763 was designed to do just that by, among other things, fixing a line that ran from the "heads or sources of any of the rivers which fall into the Atlantic Ocean from the West or northwest. . . ." In the South the line ran along the crest of the Appalachian Mountains. Beyond the line, where the waters ran west, settlers and speculators were forbidden to go. That was Indian country, "reserved to them . . . as their hunting grounds," by the Crown. Private purchases of Indian lands were also forbidden. Only the Crown could accept cessions or purchase land from the Indians. Only the Crown could grant "special leave and license" for "purchases or settlements. . . ." The British government did not regard the line as permanent. But "for the present, and until our further pleasure be known," it was meant to regulate future expansion and to keep Indian relations firmly in control of the government. To British colonists the proclamation was regarded with hostility and disdain. George Washington, then actively engaged in land speculation, described the Proclamation Line of 1763 as a "temporary expedient to quiet the minds of the Indians." Speculators and humbler citizens ignored it. For this was America, where age-old obedience to authority was crumbling, where anything was possible for those who dared, where the king in London was far away, where British soldiers and officials were stretched too thin to consistently enforce royal decrees, where juries of friends and neighbors were quite ready to acquit transgressors against Indians.[36]

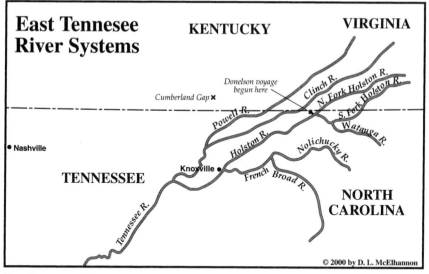

East Tennessee River Systems

"DRAGGING CANOE TOLD THEM IT WAS THE BLOODY GROUND"

At least as early as 1768 a few pioneers from Virginia and North Carolina were pushing into what is today the northeastern corner of the state of Tennessee, beyond the Proclamation Line. Then it was part of North Carolina, which claimed what is now Tennessee all the way to the Mississippi River. Late that year a long hunter, Gilbert Christian, led a hunting party down the valley of the Holston River, which flows from the confluence of its north and south forks in northeastern Tennessee southward to unite with the French Broad River four and one-half miles above modern Knoxville. There the Holston and the French Broad form another river, which will become familiar to us as we follow the fortunes and misfortunes of pioneers and Indians—the Tennessee.[37] The hunters found three families at the Holston's headwaters. Upon their return in February 1769, Christian was astounded to come on several cabins some twenty to thirty miles northeast of modern Kingsport, Tennessee, on lands watered by the Watauga River, a tributary of the Holston. One belonged to William Bean, who had come over the mountains from Pittsylvania County, Virginia. Bean is called Tennessee's first white settler, which may or may not be true. But he was joined by several kinfolk and friends, which prompted a historian of Tennessee, Stanley J. Folmsbee, to write that "his work as a colonizer transcends in importance his alleged priority in time."[38]

The following year a man traveling alone came among them. His name was James Robertson (1742–1814) and he had come from east of the mountains looking for good land for his family and friends. Robertson was born in Brunswick County, Virginia, the eldest son of Scotch Irish parents, John and Mary Gower Robertson. The family moved to Wake County, North Carolina, in James's youth. There James married Charlotte Reeves, with whom he was fruitful and multiplied to the number of eleven children. James and Charlotte Reeves Robertson were strong in body and character. Remember their names.

About 1766 James and Charlotte moved their family west to Orange County, North Carolina, and it was from there that James set out on his solo trek over the mountains. In August 1770, in the valley of the Watauga near modern Elizabethton, Tennessee, Robertson planted corn in an old Indian field before setting out for home, with the intention of returning with his party the following spring. He became lost in the mountains and probably would have died had he not met two hunters who gave him food and directions. The next year Roberton returned to the Watauga with Charlotte, their children, and several other families. James Roberston had become a colonizer, and he was not through with that work.

There were four settlements in the northeastern corner of Tennessee in the early 1770s. Only one, the North Holston Settlements, was outside Indian country. The pioneers in Carter's Valley west of the Holston, on the Watauga, and to the south in the Nolichucky Settlements on the Nolichucky River, a tributary of the Tennessee, were squatters on Cherokee land. Another settler of note was John Sevier (pronounced "severe"), who had come from New Market, Virginia, in the Shenandoah Valley. He eventually settled on the Nolichucky, whence his nickname, Chucky John. Much has been made of Sevier's French Huguenot ancestry, which came from his grandfather, a French Protestant who fled to England to escape religious persecution. In London he married an Englishwoman. In America Sevier's French-English father married Joanna Goad, and on her side Sevier was a fifth-generation American out of English stock. John Sevier (1745–1815) was a partisan chief of uncommon ability and a fierce political antagonist. Remember his name, too.[39]

The British agent for the Cherokees, Alexander Cameron, ordered the Watauga and Nolichucky settlers to abandon the land and leave Indian country. The Nolichucky settlers moved to Watauga, and there the combined groups defied the British government. James Robertson and John Bean visited the Overhill Cherokees at their principal town of Chota, south of Knoxville, and asked to lease the land. The famous Cherokee chief Attakullakulla knew the whites well. In 1730 he and other chiefs had made an official visit to London, where they met the king and became the toast of the town. Felix Walker, who saw Attakullakulla in council three years later, wrote that the name given him by whites, Little Carpenter, was an "allusion, say the Indians, to his deep, artful, and ingenious diplomatic abilities, ably demonstrated in negotiating treaties with white people, and influence in their national councils; like as a white carpenter would make every notch and joint fit in wood, so he could bring all his views to fill and fit their places in the political machinery of his nation. He was the most celebrated and influential Indian among all the tribes then known; considered the Solon of his day. He was said to be about ninety years of age, a very small man, and so lean and light habited, that I scarcely believe he . . . exceeded" ninety pounds. "He was marked with two large scores or scars on each cheek, his ears cut and banded with silver, hanging nearly down on each shoulder, the ancient Indian mode of distinction in some tribes and fashion in others."[40]

Attakullakulla is reported to have said of Robertson's and Bean's request to lease the land, "It is but a little spot of ground you ask, and I am willing that your people should live upon it. I pity the white people. . . ." Whereupon the leader of the Nolichucky settlements, Jacob Brown, hearing of Attakullakulla's generosity, made the same request for the Nolichucky settlers, which was also granted. The foot, a little foot to be sure but still a foot, was in the door.[41]

Finding themselves outside the realm of any organized government, the Wataugans felt the need to create their own, and on 8 May 1772 signed "Written Articles of Association." The document was lost, but the Wataugans described their government as a court empowered to act as both a legislature and a judiciary, with a clerk, a sheriff, and other officials, to prevent the area from becoming a haven for debtors seeking "to defraud their creditors; considering also the necessity of recording Deeds, Wills, and doing other public business. . . ." James Robertson was probably one of the five members of the court. Lord Dunmore, governor of Virginia, was aghast when he learned of the Watauga Association, claiming that the Wataugans had "to all intents and purposes erected themselves into an inconsiderable yet a Separate State . . . it, at least, Sets a dangerous example to the people of America of forming governments distinct from and independent of His Majesty's Authority." Modern students of the affair disagree with Dunmore that the Wataugans meant to create an independent state. Their purpose was almost certainly an emergency measure taken for the simple reason that there was no law west of the Appalachians and they did not wish to live in a lawless state. They duly reported what they had done to royal authorities in North Carolina. Lord Dunmore, however, was certainly right in stating that they had set a "dangerous example." Theirs was a precedent for moving beyond legal boundaries, dealing directly with the Indians, and establishing, if only on a temporary basis, their own system of government without a by-your-leave of colonial authorities. Their "dangerous example" was a clear sign of the loosening of traditional chains of authority, which had been slowly building in American colonies, and of the truly radical nature of the American Revolution.[42]

There matters stood until the early spring of 1775. An uneasy peace had prevailed, punctuated by bursts of violence between whites and Indians. But a development was taking place that had vast repercussions in the Old Southwest. On 6 January 1775 Judge Richard Henderson of North Carolina and several associates formed the Transylvania Company and undertook to do what the proclamation of 1763 expressly forbade: purchase land privately from the Indians without royal "leave or license." Where the Watauga sings over the rocks at Sycamore Shoals, at modern Elizabethton, Tennessee, about 1,200 Indians and 600 whites met in March 1775. James Robertson was there, and a surveyor named John Donelson, who had a daughter named Rachel. It is almost certain that during the conference Judge Henderson, James Robertson, and John Donelson discussed establishing a settlement deep in the western wilderness where the Cumberland River reaches far-thest south before angling north toward the Ohio. For several days Hender-son and others negotiated with Attakullakulla and other Cherokee chiefs. John Vann was the interpreter, but according to a man present "sundry Indian traders . . . were present at the Conferences, and that the Indians seemed to design them as a check upon Vann, in case he should not inter-pret their Talks justly. . . ."[43]

At first the Cherokees offered Henderson the lands north of the Ken-tucky River. Henderson refused. He wanted the lands south of that, the great swath of territory between the Kentucky and Cumberland Rivers. At this point a young Cherokee by the name of Dragging Canoe, a son of Attakullakulla, rose in council and denounced the proceedings, accusing the old chiefs of selling the Cherokee birthright. Their disappearance as a race would be the consequence. But the old chiefs persisted in their design, and on 19 March a private treaty was signed between the Transylvania Company and the Cherokees. That Indian land tenure did not recognize the concept of private property, that the chiefs could not sign away what was claimed in common by all Cherokees, was ignored, as it always was in treaty making between whites and Indians. For $10,000 in trade goods, Henderson had struck a deal for 20 million acres between the Kentucky and Cumberland Rivers.

Young Dragging Canoe, described by an early observer as "a large 6 feet slim Indian, good looking, a Keen Smart Chief," rose in council. He was in a fury at what his father and the other old men had done. A man who was there, Samuel Wilson, watched him and listened to his prophetic words: "the Dragging Canoe told them it was the Bloody Ground, and would be dark, and difficult to settle it."[44]

Sycamore Shoals was one of the most important treaties of the colonial era, but its effect awaited events occurring on the frontier and in far-off places. In Massachusetts a month later, on 19 April 1775, on Lexington Common the shot was fired heard 'round the world. The War of the Amer-ican Revolution had begun.

The Wataugans and the settlers on the Nolichucky took advantage of the gathering at Sycamore Shoals to buy from the Cherokees their leased lands. But by the spring of 1776 the Cherokees had declared for England and demanded that the settlers vacate their lands. They were given forty days to comply. James Robertson and others appealed to North Carolina and Vir-ginia for aid, but neither wanted to get involved in an Indian war while they had the British to deal with. Most of the settlers, however, made of stern stuff, cinched their belts and made ready to fight it out. They were also not

without guile. Their leaders, including James Robertson, had been corre-
sponding with British Indian agent Alexander Cameron and the then deputy
superintendent of Indian affairs in the Southern Department, Henry Stuart,
brother of the superintendent, John Stuart, in an effort to buy time while
they built forts at Sycamore Shoals and elsewhere. Henry Stuart had arrived
in Chota from Mobile on 24 April 1776 with twenty-one packhorses loaded
with five thousand pounds of powder and lead. It was escorted by Cherokee
warriors under Dragging Canoe, who had gone to Mobile seeking just such
a bonanza.[45]

Stuart and Cameron wrote to the Watauga and Nolichucky settlers,
enclosing a demand from the chiefs that they evacuate their lands. The trader
Isaac Thomas, who delivered the letter, later swore that American settlers told
him that a Wataugan, Jesse Bean, had rewritten it to describe a joint British-
Indian plan to attack the frontier and drive the settlers out. The homes of
frontier Tories would be marked in order to spare them. The forgery was
first sent to the Committee of Safety of Fincastle County, Virginia, then widely
circulated, printed in the *Virginia Gazette,* creating a sensation all the way to
Philadelphia and members of the Continental Congress. Rebellious Americans were quite ready to believe anything dastardly of the British, including
collusion in unleashing the horrors of border war. Fincastle County's Committee of Safety now agreed to send help. But before it arrived the Indians
struck. Henry Stuart and Alexander Cameron urged the Cherokees to wait
and act in concert with a British offensive, but they should have known better than to supply Indians with the wherewithal to make war and not expect
them to put it to immediate use.

It seems that for the Cherokees the arrival in Chota of a delegation of
fourteen Shawnees, Delawares, and Mohawks calling for combined action
against the Americans decided the issue. The northerners were painted black,
for war, and carried with them the war belt, nine feet long and six inches
wide, made of purple wampum and covered with vermilion. In council a
Shawnee offered the belt to Dragging Canoe, who took it, then passed it on
to the Raven, who chanted the war song. One by one young warriors eager
for battle against the invader took up the belt.

Virginia, the Carolinas, Georgia: on every border Cherokee warriors
carried the tomahawk, the scalping knife, the faggot, meting out death and
destruction. Our concern, however, is with the small, vulnerable settlements
on the cutting edge of the American frontier—on the Nolichucky, the
Watauga, and the Holston. They got early warning from traders, who had
received it from a famous Cherokee woman, Nancy Ward, a niece of
Attakullakulla.

Three columns totaling 600 to 700 warriors moved north up the Great
Valley of East Tennessee. Dragging Canoe led the center column against
Eaton's Station near Long Island on the Holston, now in the neighborhood
of Kingsport, Tennessee. Old Abram went after Nolichucky and Watauga. To
the west the Raven struck into Carter's Valley, where the settlers were scattered and defenseless. Raven's column devastated the valley as the settlers fled

before the warriors. Cabins and crops were burned, livestock slaughtered, those who failed to get away fast enough killed and scalped. The Raven drove into Virginia as far as Seven Mile Ford on the South Fork of the Holston.

Scouts spotted Dragging Canoe's column making for Eaton's Station. The fighting men numbered about 170 and were commanded by six militia captains: James Thompson, who was senior and at least in nominal overall command, James Shelby, William Buchanan, John Campbell, William Cocke, and Thomas Madison. On the morning of 20 July 1776, it was decided to meet the warriors in the open. "We marched in two divisions," the captains reported, "with flankers on each side and scouts before." The scouts came on 20 warriors. Fire was exchanged. Then "our men rushed on them with such violence that they were obliged to make a precipitate retreat." Fearing that a large party of Indians might be nearby, they decided to return to the fort, but they had gone only about a mile when Dragging Canoe and his main force, "not inferior to ours, attacked us in the rear. Our men sustained the attack with great bravery and intrepidity, immediately forming a line. The Indians endeavoured to surround us, but were prevented by the uncommon fortitude and vigilance of Captain James Shelby, who took possession of an eminence that prevented their design. Our line of battle extended about a quarter of a mile. We killed about thirteen on the spot, whom we found. . . . There were streams of blood every way, and it was generally thought there was never so much execution done in so short a time on the frontiers." It is said that Dragging Canoe himself was shot in the leg and suffered a broken thigh. Thus ended the Battle of Island Flats, a skirmish really, but important nonetheless.[46]

The following day, 21 July, Old Abram's warriors fiercely assaulted Fort Caswell on the Watauga, Colonel John Carter commanding. With him were Captain James Robertson and Lieutenant John Sevier. The latter had evacuated Fort Lee on the Nolichucky and brought his men and their families to Fort Caswell. Seventy-five fighting men defended the walls.

Old Abram's initial assault failed and he settled into a siege, firing now and then at the fort. About 25 warriors attempting to fire the stockade scattered when James Robertson's sister Ann carried a bucket of boiling wash water to the parapet and poured it on the attackers. Although wounded, she kept it up until the warriors retreated. After about two weeks the siege was lifted. Despite almost two centuries of experience fighting the white man, Indians had not yet learned how to take forts held by determined, well-led garrisons. Their only weapons were ruse and starvation. The Cherokee offensive was a failure. Only Carter's Valley had been cleared of whites, but they would come back, they always did, time after bloody time.

The Americans did not wait long to strike back. In a remarkable example of cooperation, Virginia and the Carolinas staged an offensive against the Cherokees that devastated their country. From South Carolina, from North Carolina, from Virginia, militia columns struck deep into Cherokee country, burning and pillaging towns, storehouses, and crops. No memorable battles were fought, only hopeless skirmishes, for the forces arrayed against them were too formidable for the Cherokees to resist. The earth was scorched. The Virginia column alone, Colonel William Christian commanding, reported that the Indians had left behind "horses, cattle, dogs, hogs, and fowl," and "between forty and fifty thousand bushels of corn and ten or fifteen thousand bushels of Potatoes." The Cherokees, largely a mountain people, were left to face winter without lodges or food. The overwhelming defeat of the Cherokees so discouraged their neighbors to the south, the Creeks, that for the most part they offered little military assistance to the British during the Revolutionary War. The Cherokees were knocked out of the war for six years, and when they rose again a similar campaign, quick and ruthless, by the gifted South Carolina partisan chief Andrew Pickens soon put an end to it.[47]

Dragging Canoe and his followers, however, remained intransigent. In March 1777, he withdrew from the Cherokee Nation with some 500 warriors and their families and settled on Chickamauga Creek, just north of modern Chattanooga, Tennessee. He taunted those who had lost their will to resist as Virginians. He called his people Ani-Yun'wiya—the Real People. The whites called them Chickamauga, a name that would soon command fear and respect.

The smashing American victory in the Cherokee War, both the successful resistance on the Watauga and the Holston and the crushing offensive by the three states, was prelude for further advances by restless American frontier folk. Even as full-scale war was waged by Americans and Britons east of the mountains, frontiersmen pushed out into hostile territory first to reconnoiter, then bringing families to settle. But Indian resistance had not ended. Chickamaugas and Creeks from the south, Chickasaws from the west, Shawnees from the north would bitterly contest the white advance for decades to come—valley by bloody valley. Out of the countless, long-forgotten clashes that took place, which in our time would be described as "incidents," let us look at one that occurred three years before Andrew Jackson's arrival on the frontier, as an example of a not untypical "incident" that reveals the grit and determination of the People of the Western Waters.

Chapter 2

———⚉———

VANGUARD OF EMPIRE

"THAT INDOMITABLE COURAGE, SO COMMON TO WOMAN"

They were nine, probably Shawnee. They had left their horses several days behind them in order to descend to Powell's Valley unseen and unheard. Whites under the leadership of the well-known Virginia frontiersman Joseph Martin had tried to settle this valley in the mountains of southwestern Virginia in 1769. In that year Daniel Boone, headed for Cumberland Gap and his second long hunt to Kentucky, came upon Martin and twenty men clearing land for corn. The crop was never harvested. It was Cherokee land and the warriors drove Martin and his men out of the valley. But if one thing marked the American pioneer, it was persistence. They would not be denied, no matter the toll of death and suffering. Martin and the settlers returned in 1776. Once again the Indians struck; once again the settlers fled northward. At the end of the Revolutionary War they returned, as they always did, and built their cabins and plowed the fields, determined this time to stand their ground.[1]

It was some time in June 1785, just after dark, that the war party stealthily approached the cabin of Archibald Scott at the head of Wallens Creek, a tributary of the Powell River, in Washington County (now Lee County), Virginia. The Scott cabin was on the old Kentucky Trace leading westward to Cumberland Gap, which was approximately fifty miles westward. It was a familiar resting place for pioneers headed for Kentucky, and also the Cumberland settlements in the present state of Tennessee. In 1783 the Washington County Court had appointed Scott "overseer of the road from Powells Valley Station to where it intersects the wagon road at the North Fork of Clinch. . . ." Archibald Scott was described by a neighbor, William Martin, as "a man of more than ordinary consideration in those regions."[2]

It was a hot night. The door had been left open. Inside Archibald and the four children had gone to bed. Mrs. Scott, the former Frances Dickenson, known familiarly as Fanny, was up. William Martin described her as "rather fleshy than otherwise, of good size—good appearance . . . from 25 to

30 years old." Unless otherwise indicated, the quotations below are taken from William Martin's account of Fanny Scott's ordeal.

The warriors came in a rush through the open door. Archibald Scott awakened, rose from his bed, and was "shot and killed." The children were "then dispatched." Frances Scott, who witnessed the sudden destruction of her family, probably would have been killed too had not "one fellow laid hold on *her,* and protected her against the violence of the others."

The Indians plundered the house, taking among other things Frances Scott's saddle. Before leaving the valley they assaulted another cabin, but that family, the Balls, were vigilant and "defended themselves and were not injured."

The war party took Frances Scott with them and left the valley and began traveling in a northwesterly direction over that range of "mountains which give rise to the Cumberland, Kentucky and Sandy rivers." They marched for five days, "still directing their Course towards the Ohio." According to Martin, the men behaved well toward their captive, "were quite civil and kind to her, and would assist her up the mountains." A later account contradicts this and attributes the following statement to Fanny Scott: "To aggravate my grief one of the Indians hung my husband's and children's scalps to his back, and would walk the next before me, in walking up and down the hills and mountains. I was worn out with fatigue and sorrow and they would often laugh when they saw me almost spent, and mimic my panting for breath. There was one Indian more humane than the rest; he would get me water, and make the others stop when I wanted to rest." Whichever account is correct, on the fifth day they reached the horses, put the saddle on one, and mounted Frances Scott on the horse.[3]

The Indians then separated, leaving her with three warriors, one of whom was an old man. She traveled with them for two or three days, when they stopped to hunt. Two men left camp, leaving Fanny with the old man. While he dressed a deerskin, "she took advantage of his inattention and slipped off." She then committed an error common to people who find themselves in unfamiliar woodlands. After walking all night, she found herself in the morning near the camp, and "was much alarmed." Fanny hid near the Indian camp in a canebrake, one of those almost impenetrable thickets of the giant cane (*Arundinaria macrosperma*) of the South, in which whites and Indians alike often hid when pursued. "Through most of the night I heard the Indians searching for me, and answering each other with a voice like that of an owl."[4]

She debated with herself. Having walked in circles during the night, should she give herself up or try again to get home? Between her and Powell's Valley were about a hundred miles of rugged mountain terrain, "interspersed with savages—poisonous reptiles—and ferocious beasts of prey. She had no weapon of defense, not even a knife. No means of subsistence, nor any way to make a fire. Discouraging, however, as was the attempt, she, with that indomitable Courage, so common to woman, determined to make the venture. . . ."

Knowing she might die in the attempt, far preferring that to "savage bondage," Frances Dickenson Scott set out on her quest for freedom, "trusting in God for help."

When she came to the trail they had traveled, this woman of "good sense and good character" turned away, fearing to meet pursuers, and truly entered a trackless wilderness. There was an abundance of berries to eat, but otherwise her diet consisted of one turtle and one small fish. A copperhead bit her on one foot, but it "did not affect her much," and she persevered.

Thirty-three days after she made the decision to flee, Frances Scott "arrived at the settlements, some 50 or 60 miles from the place where taken. . . ." William Martin, who lived in Powell's Valley at the time and to whom Fanny related her adventure "soon after" it ended, wrote that "unreasonable and romantic as was all this, I believe its correctness was never disputed."

Life goes on, we are fond of saying, and it was customary in those days for survivors of frontier tragedies to remarry, for the support of another in a harsh and dangerous environment if nothing else. Frances Dickenson Scott married Thomas Johnson, with whom she had children. It is said, however, that Fanny would never return to the place where she watched the quick, violent deaths of her first husband and their four children.[5]

"AMERICA IS A HONEY OF A PLACE"

This was the breed of people filling in the valleys and invading the lands beyond the mountains. They were the People of the Western Waters, and they were, to use the words of a Creek who knew them well, of "turbulent & restless disposition." Their ethnic backgrounds were overwhelmingly Scotch Irish, English, and German. Among them were also people of Welsh and French descent. But all were on their way to becoming Americans before the Revolution and were now mostly American born and rapidly mixing. To label their society multicultural is to force a current, perhaps ephemeral, enthusiasm on another era. They were ideal frontier people because they knew how to suffer. Some would fall by the wayside, others would turn away from the contest, but most of them, like Fanny Scott, would persevere. Of Indian land tenure they knew little if anything and cared less. America was a "honey of a place" and they meant to make it their own, and if the inhabitants were hostile they could handle that. They were hostile themselves, they knew how to suffer, and they knew how to make others suffer. They had helped take the thirteen colonies away from the British, and now they turned their attention to the lands where the waters ran west, and to its inhabitants, who believed fervently and with the best of reasons that the land belonged to them. Thus the contest, long and savage, resumed.[6]

The frontier folk were demonized as a "pack of beggars" and "white savages" by contemporaries who were comfortable members of the establishment living safely east of the mountains. The planter William Byrd wrote, "I was unlucky, as to be disappointed by my Swiss Colony. In case they should fail me a second time, I will endeavor to supply these places with

Scots-Irish from Pennsylvania, who flock over thither in such numbers, that there is not elbow room for them. They swarm like Goths and Vandals of old & will overspread our continent soon." We shall have occasion to observe other examples of contemporary prejudice against them as our story unfolds. They are demonized in our time, also by people ignorant of peril and privation, as murderous frontiersmen. This kind of intolerance is not unique in history, and its practice crosses racial, ethnic, and cultural lines.[7]

As I have written elsewhere, "Pioneering is a messy business; combined with conquest it is an ugly business and has been since human beings began coveting the property of others." We are dealing with one of history's great folk movements, the greatest of modern times, which began in the seventeenth century and shows no signs of abating. I refer, of course, to the conquest and settlement of North America by Europeans and their descendants for the first three hundred years, and increasingly in our time by Latin Americans, Asians, and other assorted "strangers to our laws and customs," words used to describe my own Scotch Irish ancestors upon their arrival in the eighteenth century.[8]

In my previous book *The Road to Guilford Courthouse,* I also wrote, "We pay little attention today to the moral questions involved in similar folk movements that began before recorded time and have continued since." Our ancestors "were people living under vastly different assumptions than exist in America" at the beginning of the twenty-first century. "The British novelist L. P. Hartley put it well: 'The past is a foreign country; they do things differently there.' To which we may add that the further removed we are from want and danger, the more generous our consciences." Since then I have come across two observations that bear on this matter, one by a well-known American anthropologist whose strong sympathies lie with the Indians who lost their lands to the white invaders, the other by a brilliant historian whose specific intellectual interests lay far from our shores.[9]

Anthony F. C. Wallace, in the *The Long, Bitter Trail,* stated his conviction that nations today must change their way of dealing with "diversity." But he admits that as an anthropologist he "cannot resist seeing events, as well as cultures, in some sort of comparative perspective. One comparative observation is unavoidable. The removal of inconveniently located ethnic groups and their resettlement in out-of-the-way places is, and has been for thousands of years, a common phenomenon in the history of states and empires."[10]

We might take Wallace's point a step further. The impact of conquest can be equally destructive even when displacement does not occur. Europe in the ninth and tenth centuries was under bloody siege from Vikings, Magyars, and Arabs, all uninvited. And who, we may well ask, invited the Mongols to ravage Russia and yoke it to a despotism that so profoundly retarded that unhappy land? Who invited them to strike deep into the Middle East, sack Baghdad in 1258 so terribly that it was centuries before that great and ancient city recovered, and while they were at it destroy Arab civilization and the irrigation system of the Tigris and Euphrates valleys, changing the landscape from agricultural to arid steppes fit only for herding? The Arabs themselves, of course, were hardly shrinking violets when it came to conquest, as attested by their incredible sweep in the space of the seventh century across much of the Middle East, North Africa, and all but two isolated corners of Spain, in that long ago time when dead white Europeans were the victims, or, to use today's fashionable term, the other. For the Muslims, Spain was indeed a "honey of a place," and they meant to make it their own.

Moving southward, in the nineteenth century the unprovoked aggression of the Zulus against their fellow Africans was a brutal imperialism that occurred not so long ago, yet has attracted little attention.

The point, I think, is clear. But before continuing our tale of pioneering and conquest, which is as old as the species, let us not forget that American Indians spawned an imperial society whose blood-drenched sins against their fellow Indians surpass anything found within these pages. They called themselves Mexica, labeled Aztecs by us.

The English historian C. V. Wedgewood, in *Truth and Opinion*, discussed in her usual illuminating style the problems of historical perspective and moral judgments. "Great distances of time," she wrote, "reduce the intensity with which we feel about moral issues. What Cromwell did to the people of Wexford is much closer in time and therefore much more imaginable, and therefore much more distressing, than what the Emperor Theodosius did to the people of Thessalonica. Questions of right and wrong, of humanity and inhumanity ought to be equally significant to the historian whatever the period in which they happen. But it is evident that they are not; few accounts of the September massacres are written without some sign of passion or sympathy on one side or the other, but the story of the Sicilian Vespers can be told with apparent detachment." Perspective is required in order to understand why people acted as they did, which does not necessarily mean approval of their actions. Wedgewood discussed the need for a moral standard to judge all ages, or, as she quotes Lord Acton, " 'In judging men and things, ethics go before dogma, politics and nationality.' "[11]

Like Arabs and Vikings and Mongols and Aztecs before them, frontier Americans were conquerors, and they had the conqueror's self-confidence, convinced that their cause was just. To one of their leaders was attributed the words, "We are the vanguard of civilization. Our way is across the continent." Whether they are James Robertson's words or a later invention is of little moment, for they expressed what the folk had in mind. Restless, aggressive, land hungry, they saw before them millions upon millions of acres that by their lights were unused. Before the Revolution, the Scotch Irish told the provincial secretary of Pennsylvania that "it was against the laws of God and nature, that so much land should be idle while so many Christians wanted it to labor on, and raise their bread." That the Indian inhabitants of the land they coveted thought otherwise was irrelevant to the People of the Western Waters and those pressing behind them in the North American Back Country. They would have that land, they would have it any way they could take it, and if their manner of taking it did not square with first British, then U.S. policy, so be it.

Land and commerce were their beacons. Land from simple dreams of homesteads to visions of vast estates, for some even empires of their own creation. Commerce looked out upon a broader world, its key the mighty Mississippi with the great port at its delta. These are simple concepts, but they bred intricacies within complexities, and there are affairs that remain obscure because they were meant to be.

This fixation on land, from simple farmers to speculators with dreams of grandeur, stemmed from their European heritage and what they saw as an almost empty continent before them. For centuries in Europe land was the solid rock on which men and their families rose to rank and fortune. For an English merchant who had made his pile and yearned for social advancement, the next step was to acquire a country estate, either by purchase or, even better, marriage into the aristocracy. Many proud British families of our time rose from such parvenu backgrounds.

This was the model for eighteenth-century American land speculators, none of whom could claim aristocratic backgrounds in the old country, and in the New World were middle-class strivers whose hunger equaled their Old World predecessors and contemporaries. Farmers might hanker to claw their way into that group, or simply be satisfied with their own patch of rich bottomland. But for all, land was their lodestar. And whatever their dreams, they were people of their times and prisoners of their past, as were the Indians who stood in their way.

These early pioneers were the cutting edge of an irresistible flood of humanity driven by the twin hungers of land and opportunity. As individuals, hunting parties, families, groups, they pushed westward, sometimes overreaching, withdrawing, pushing on again, fighting and bleeding, many dying horrible deaths, with stubborn determination challenging any power to stop them. To deny that this was a people's movement and argue that big land speculators or colonization companies or especially government were the driving forces behind the conquest is to miss the point. For it was not, as some claim, primarily a political movement. It was then as it is today—an unstoppable folk movement. In some cases the organized forces were important factors inducing migrants to come to America and pioneers to move west, just as today our laws invite migration. But once the genie was let out of the bottle, government lost control and became a follower, as a frontier leader noted in 1786: "It is vain to say they must be restrained. Have not all America extended their back settlements in opposition to laws and proclamations?" That government also wanted the land there can be no question. We shall speak to that in the narrative. But the orderly processes favored—indeed, insisted upon—by government, first British, then American, were ignored by the people. Once started the people would do it their way, and they would not be denied.[12]

Frontier folk and high government officials were certainly of one mind on their desire for expansion (a polite word for conquest). But they differed on means. Frontiersmen were forthright in word and deed. High officials usually veiled their desires and actions with high-flown rhetoric. The frontier people were engaged in the dirty work of empire on behalf of those who stayed behind. They were on the firing line, and people on the firing line invariably speak plainly and take a harder stance than those who never stand in harm's way. They could not afford the luxury of grieving for the Indians they killed and drove away. They were too busy grieving for their own dead while awaiting the next onslaught by their increasingly desperate foes, who saw their world disappearing.

It was a long, incredibly difficult, enduring trail they traveled in conditions that ranged from crude to squalid, a trail that has never stopped and has been traveled for three hundred years for the same reason: opportunity denied the travelers elsewhere. We began this chapter with the travail of Fanny Scott. It is fitting that we end it with the words of another woman of endurance. The eighteenth-century Scotch Irishman who said, "America is a honey of a place," was echoed over two hundred years later by Samra Sabir, a young Pakistani woman celebrating in Flushing Meadow Park in New York City with her husband and child for their first-time Fourth of July in America: "everybody wants to come here."[13]

Chapter 3

THE FRONTIER

"THE HOTTEST INDIAN WAR I EVER WITNESSED"

At the end of the Prologue we left Andrew Jackson traversing the great Appalachian range. His migration could not have been pleasant, for travel was then an endurance contest. He and his companions would have first climbed the steep eastern slopes of the Blue Ridge Mountains of North Carolina, then made their way through the high, rugged Asheville plateau, and finally over the mighty Unaka Mountains, consisting of several parallel ranges averaging five thousand feet, before beginning their descent to the great green valley of East Tennessee.[1] He did not leave a record of his journey, but another traveler in that spring of 1788, who sought souls, not position and fortune, recorded his own travail.

The Methodist missionary Bishop Francis Asbury, who crossed the Appalachians sixty times, left North Carolina on 28 April 1788. "After getting our horses shod, we made a move for the Holston, and entered upon the mountains, the first of which I called Steel, the second Stone, and the third Iron . . . they are rough, and difficult to climb. We were spoken to on our way by the most awful thunder and lightning, accompanied by heavy rain. We crept for shelter into a dirty little house, where the filth might have been taken up from the floor with a spade; we felt the want of fire, but could get little wood to make it, and what we gathered was wet. At the head of the Watauga we fed . . . Coming to the river next day we hired a young man to swim over for the canoe, in which we crossed, while our horses swam to the other shore. The waters being up we were compelled to travel an old road over the mountains. Night came on. I was ready to faint with a violent headache, the mountain was so steep on both sides. I prayed to the Lord for help . . . my pack horse would neither follow, lead nor drive, so fond was he of stopping to feed on the green herbage. I tried the lead and he pulled back. I tied his head up to prevent his grazing, and he ran back. The weather was excessively warm. I was much fatigued and my temper not a little tried." When the good bishop finally arrived at the Holston

River, "I was at a loss what to do, but providentially a man came along who conducted me across. This was an awful journey to me, and this a tiresome day, and now, after riding seventy-five miles, I have thirty-five more to General Russell's. I rest one day to revive man and beast."[2]

Jackson, twenty-two years younger than Asbury and undoubtedly full of the keen anticipation of the young, arrived in Jonesborough, Washington County, North Carolina, sometime in the spring of 1788. The town had been founded ten years before and had about sixty log cabins. Tradition related many years later by three old men claimed that Jackson rode into town on a racehorse. Given his love of good horseflesh that would not have been out of character. Attached to his saddle, they said, was a brace of pistols. Given his propensity for violence, they also would have suited his character. His shotgun was with the rest of his belongings on the packhorse that he led. A large pack of foxhounds trailed him.[3]

He and his friends John McNairy and Bennett Searcy were bound for Nashville, the town that would become the base for their legal activities. But some two hundred miles of the wild, rugged, uninhabited Cumberland plateau lay between Jonesborough and Nashville. Hostile Chickamauga and Creek warriors roamed its trails. Individuals and small parties did not venture onto that bloody ground foretold by Dragging Canoe. When enough travelers and settlers bound for the Cumberland had gathered, experienced escorts would guide them through the wilderness. All they could do was wait.

They had arrived at a time of political turmoil approaching anarchy, and during their sojourn in Jonesborough mayhem and massacre erupted on the frontier. Four years before their arrival, in August 1784, settlers of East Tennessee met in convention to declare themselves citizens of the independent State of Franklin. In March 1785 the first assembly of Franklin met in Jonesborough, elected a hero of the Revolutionary War, John Sevier, as governor, and established agencies of government, including new counties.[4]

The founders of Franklin had grandiose geographical ambitions, including within their nascent territory all of East Tennessee from the crest of the Unaka Mountains on the east to the western edge of the Cumberland Plateau; a narrow strip of southwestern Virginia and southeastern Kentucky, including Cumberland Gap; the northwestern corner of Georgia; and the northeastern corner of Alabama's hill country, including present-day Huntsville and the Great Bend of the Tennessee River. The inclusion of the latter alarmed big-time land speculators, who considered the "Bent," as the Great Bend was then called, as the chief prize of their endeavors.

There is no need for us to get bogged down in the intricate history of the State of Franklin, over which arguments about the motivations of the players on both sides still rage. An eminent historian of the period, Thomas Perkins Abernethy, claimed that it was all about land speculation, but Abernethy never saw a speculator he liked, and he saw them everywhere. It is more likely that the major factor behind the establishment of the new state was the strong separatist feelings of the settlers west of the mountains. These feelings would emerge from time to time during critical situations in Tennessee history, especially in the years leading up to and during and after the Civil War. They also appeared during one of the critical periods of Andrew Jackson's life, and we will speak to that at the proper place in the narrative.[5]

We should also note that there were vehement opponents, not only in North Carolina, who refused to recognize Franklin, but also in East Tennessee, and that fierce political arguments led eventually to bloodshed and an attempt to bring John Sevier to trial in North Carolina. Tennessee's first historian, Judge John Haywood, succinctly described events.

"County courts were held in the same counties under both governments, the militia were called out by officers appointed by both; laws were passed by both Assemblies and taxes were laid by the authority of both states. The differences in opinion in the State of Franklin between those who adhered to the government of North Carolina and those who were friends of the new government became more acrimonious every day. Every fresh provocation on the one side was surpassed in the way of retaliation by still greater provocation on the other."[6]

Even worse, the State of Franklin, considered an illegal entity by both North Carolina and the national government, negotiated with the Cherokees the Treaty of Dumplin Creek in May and June 1785, which provided that "all of the lands lying and being on the south side of Holston and French Broad rivers, as far south as the ridge that divides the waters of Little river from the waters of the Tennessee may be peaceably inhabited and cultivated, resided on, enjoyed and inhabited by our elder brothers, the white people, from this time forward and always."[7]

Settlers had already encroached south of the French Broad, and others began pouring in upon the signing of the treaty, and less than a year later some were raising their cabins south of the southern boundary of the cession. Only the State of Franklin recognized the validity of the treaty. North Carolina considered the settlers squatters. More ominous was the attitude of the Cherokees who were not among the handful of headmen who signed away what was not theirs to give. They, too, rejected Dumplin Creek. And in November 1785 the United States signed the Treaty of Hopewell with the Cherokees, which specifically rejected the Treaty of Dumplin Creek and even placed Franklin's capital, Greeneville, in Cherokee Country. This is a good example early on of national versus local interests. The U.S. commissioners at the Hopewell negotiations, led by Benjamin Hawkins, who later will figure prominently in our narrative, and a genuine hero of the Revolution, the highly regarded Andrew Pickens, were anxious to placate the Cherokees in order to thwart what they considered Spanish efforts to bring all of the southern Indians under their control.[8]

The people, however, would not be denied. They were infuriated by the Treaty of Hopewell, and they treated it as a mere scrap of paper. Governments could fulminate and officials order, but for years the frontier people had been moving onto Indian land despite solemn treaty lines. To give only one example, in 1784 Governor Alexander Martin of North Carolina wrote General Joseph Martin, the state's superintendent of Indian affairs, "You will call upon General McDowell and Colonel Sevier . . . to order and drive off those evil minded persons who have intruded and still continue on the Indian lands beyond the French Broad River."[9]

The governor's letter was, if I may be allowed, a dead letter, and the next year, following the Treaty of Dumplin Creek, Joseph Martin reported that the Indians "are in great confusion. The people from Franklin have actually settled or least built houses within two miles of their beloved town of Chota one of their principal towns." Martin, who was writing from Chota, said the Cherokee told him that in treaty talks with Governor Sevier in May "not one of their principal men attended" and the Indians who did "had no power to grant lands" or "to suffer white families . . . actually settled there to remain till they had another talk." Settler attitude was unmistakably summed up by Martin in one sentence: "Since then there has a number of familes moved there and Talk of Building forts and say they will Hold it in Defiance of Every power."[10]

By the time Jackson reached Jonesborough the State of Franklin was almost a corpse. But the affair had helped unleash the demons of border war. That summer that Jackson spent at Jonesborough was described by John Sevier Jr. as "the hottest Indian War I ever witnessed."[11]

In May 1788 a Cherokee whom the whites called Slim Tom went to the home of John Kirk. The Kirk homestead was on Nine Mile Creek on the southwest side of Little River, twelve miles south of present-day Knoxville, and only nine miles from Chota. John Kirk and his son, John Kirk Jr., were away. At home were Kirk's wife, a son, and four daughters. The Kirks and Slim Tom knew each other well. Mrs. Kirk had often fed him, and when on this occasion he asked for food she did not hesitate to give it to him. Slim Tom then left, but soon returned with a party of warriors who fell on the Kirk family members present, killed them all, and left their bloody corpses strewn on the ground outside the cabin.

This was the sight facing John Kirk and his son when they returned. The word was quickly spread. John Sevier collected the militia and they rode south as avenging angels. Among the riders were John Kirk Jr. and one James Hubbert, then forty-seven years old. Hubbert has come down as an Indian-hater who was shaped by witnessing the massacre of his parents by Shawnee warriors when he was a child, and escaping by hiding in a chimney.[12] He was without doubt a hard man, and in the most generous interpretation aggressive toward Indians. Mrs. Mercy Clinkenbeard, who knew Hubbert, recalled that "he was afraid to go out after dark—afraid of the spirits of the Indians he had killed in cold blood."[13] But his complicity in the event described below, accepted as gospel by many writers, is not based on evidence.

Sevier and his riders exacted revenge for the butchery of the Kirk family. Cherokee towns were burned, Indians killed and taken captive. Across the Little Tennessee River from the Cherokee town of Chilhowee the troops camped. What followed next has been a subject of controversy for over two centuries. There are various versions of the sequence of events, in the identities of those present, and of who was to blame. Most of these versions were constructed either without benefit of hard evidence or in contradiction of it. But we know the outline and the terrible ending.[14]

Some friendly and highly respected Cherokee chiefs were in Chilhowee. One, Old Tassel, had been especially conspicuous in his search for peace between Indians and whites, but in war in general and border wars in particular distinctions between the guilty and the innocent are rarely made when each side retaliates for the outrages of the other. Some militiamen began shooting across the river at the house of Abraham, headman of Chilhowee. Under a white flag Abraham and another Indian crossed the river. John Sevier shook their hands, then sent a canoe to bring Old Tassel and another Indian across. Since Sevier was leaving the camp, he ordered a Major Craig to confine the Indians inside a house and guard them. When Sevier left, a militiaman named Robert Pearce told Major Craig to get out of the way or he "would make daylight shine through him." Craig refused, whereupon Pearce told him if he would go after Sevier, and was not gone too long, he, Pearce, would see to the Indians' safety. Why Craig believed Pearce, or whether he decided to wash his hands of the matter, is unknown, but after he left, the other guards were brushed aside.

John Kirk Jr. entered the house, and there can be no mistake about what happened then. Abraham, Old Tassel, and their comrades, without arms, defenseless in the militia camp, one by one were tomahawked to death by John Kirk Jr. Five other men admitted to being present for the bloody deed. Kirk confessed to it when John Sevier's enemies blamed him for not being there, for leaving when he knew the temper of the men he led. On 17 October 1788, Kirk wrote to the mixed-blood John Watts, one of the most important of the headmen of the Chickamauga.

> Sir: I have heard of your letter lately sent to Chucky John [Sevier]. You are mistaken in blaming him for the death of your uncle. Listen now to my story. For days and months the Cherokee Indians, big and little, women and children, have been fed and treated kindly by my mother. When all was at peace with the Tennessee towns, Slim Tom with a party of Sattigo and other Cherokee Indians, murdered my mother, brothers and sisters in cold blood, when childen just before were playful about them as friends; at the instant some of them received the bloody tomahawk they were smiling in their faces. This began the war; and since I have taken ample satisfaction can now make peace except for Slim Tom. Our beloved men, the Congress, tells us to be at peace; I will listen to their advice if no more blood is shed by the Cherokee, and the headmen of your nation take care to prevent such beginnings of bloodshed in all time to come. But if they do not, your people may feel something more to keep up remembrance of.
>
> John Kirk, Jun.
> Captain of the Bloody Rangers[15]

The temper of the militia was also revealed in an incident that occurred shortly thereafter, in which even the hugely popular Sevier's authority was challenged. For John Sevier, though a hard man and relentless foe, was well aware of the damage wrought by the murder of innocents. The men brought into camp Charles Murphy, a mixed-blood interpreter and signer of the Treaty of Dumplin Creek. They insisted Murphy be executed. Sevier refused but was reduced to begging for Murphy's life as a personal favor to him. When the men finally backed off and Sevier freed Murphy, there were still murmurings that "it would be well done to kill any man that would save an Indian."[16]

Men like Sevier also tried to avoid harming noncombatants, but others not only had few scruples in that regard but deliberately committed atrocities on Indian women and children. The following year Joseph Martin described a plan of certain men who had designs on Indian land to appeal to Congress, and that one of them, Alexander Outlaw, was going east to lobby Congress. He then added, "I think it my duty to say the truth of him: Shortly after the murder of the Corn-tassel and two other chiefs, this said outlaw collected a party of men and went into an Indian town called Citico [Settico], where he found a few helpless women and children, which he inhumanly murdered, exposing their private parts in the most shameful manner, leaving a young child, with both its arms broke, alive, at the breast of its dead mother. Those are facts well known and cannot be denied in this country. Mr. Outlaw had done everything in his power to drive the Indians to desperation."[17]

The Cherokee reaction to the murder of Abraham and Old Tassel and the others was massive. Nine hundred Chickamaugas and Overhill Chero- kees and 300 Creek warriors invaded East Tennessee, with elements driving north into Virginia and threatening the Wilderness Trail over Cumberland Gap to Kentucky.

The settlers had to abandon their cabins and hole up in the stations. Colonel Daniel Kennedy described a scene that fits sights familiar to our own century: "The Stations are Chiefly evacuated on the South Side of the French Broad, and the road crowded with Women and Children making their Exeate Numbers of them on Foot, Who have lost all But their Lives only, and Seem Contended to Carry their Tender Babes in their Arms to make their escape."[18]

The fury of the Indians at the deaths of Old Tassel and the other peace- able chiefs knew few bounds. On 8 August Captain John Fain led 31 mounted militia, accompanied by some settlers, across the Little Tennessee River about twenty-five miles south of Knoxville. Near the abandoned Cherokee town of Settico they relaxed to gather apples from an orchard. Indians lying in ambush surrounded them and attacked. Sixteen men including Captain Fain were killed, and 4 wounded. One of the seriously wounded was John Kirk Jr., who survived by hiding in a hollow log. When Captain Nathaniel Evans and his militia command came upon the field they discovered the dead, their bellies sliced open, their hearts ripped out, their privates cut off and stuffed into their mouths.[19]

"LORD JESUS, INTO THY HAND I COMMEND MY SPIRIT"

The bloody tales just related should make it apparent why Jackson and his comrades could not set out across the Wilderness, as the Cumberland Plateau was then called, without a strong escort. And travel by boat on the Tennessee River was also perilous, as the party of Colonel James Brown, bound for Nashville that spring, found to its horror. Colonel Brown's son, Joseph, sixteen at the time, later told the story.[20]

Their boat was strong, with two-inch oak planking above the gunwales and a swivel gun at the stern. Colonel Brown had aboard his wife, two grown sons and three small ones, four small daughters, and several black slaves. Also on board were five young men described as good marksmen: J. Bays, John Flood, John and William Gentry, and John Griffin. They had cleared the Five Lower Towns when they were surrounded by Chickamaugas in canoes. Some of them carried white flags, others claimed protection by treaty. "My father ordered the young men not to fire," Joseph Brown recounted, "as he was coming to an Indian country, and did not wish to break any treaty." Soon over 40 Indians were on board and began robbing them and transferring the plunder to their canoes. "Before they had finished robbing . . . a dirty black-looking Indian, with a sword in his hand, caught me by the arm, and was about to kill me, when my father, seeing what he was attempting, took hold of him and said, that I was one of his little boys . . . The Indian then let me go, but as soon as my father's back was turned, struck him with the sword, and cut his head nearly half off. Another Indian then caught him, and threw him overboard."

Young Joseph Brown's life was initially saved by an old Irishman, a deserter from the British army who had lived with the Cherokees for eighteen years and was married to a French woman, Polly Mallett, who had been captured by the Indians as a young girl. Joseph's brothers, with one exception, and the other men were butchered—shot, tomahawked, stabbed. His mother, a nine-year-old brother, and a seven-year-old sister were taken by Creeks and walked two hundred miles southward. They were eventually purchased from their captors and returned to their people by the great Creek chief Alexander McGillivray, of whom we shall have much to say later in our story. Young Joseph was treated roughly and on at least two occasions his life threatened to the point where he fell to his knees and "cried, like the dying Stephen, Lord Jesus, into thy hand I commend my spirit."[21] But the tomahawks never descended.

About a year after his capture, Joseph heard that John Sevier and his East Tennessee mounted militia had raided into Indian country and taken prisoners and that an exchange had been arranged. He was summoned to Running Water. On his way he found at Nickajack one of his sisters with an Indian and his wife. "The old squaw seemed to think as much of her as though she had been her own child. The little girl was stripped of all her finery, it is true, but she was only five years old, and when I told her I was going to take her to her own mother, she ran to the old Indian woman and caught her round the neck, so that I had to take her by force and carry her twenty or thirty yards; then telling her she should go to see her own mother, I set her down and led her by the hand."

At Running Water "the Head-man of the Upper Towns had come after us." At this point the head man of Nickajack revealed the Indians' knowledge of the whites and where different ones came from, and the Indian from the Upper Towns also revealed the tough, unyielding nature of John Sevier. The Nickajack Indian "grumbled at giving us up, as we, who were taken out of the boat, had come from North Carolina, and did not belong to the Holston settlement. The old Indian who had come for us, said that was all true, but that Little John (their name for Gov. Sevier) was so mean and ugly that he could do nothing with him. This word ugly is their hardest term of abuse. He went on to say that Little John declared he would not let one of their people free unless he got all the whites who were in the nation, naming those taken from the boat particularly."

The Cherokee knew Sevier well, and knew he meant precisely what he said. Several years before, on 28 July 1781, he spoke to them at a council.

> "Warriors and Chiefs, Friends and Brothers.
>
> "I listened to you Talk yesterday. I listened to it with pleasure. I never hated you as a People, nor warred with you on that account. I own I fought with you, but it was for our own Safety & not from any Delight I had in hurting you. I am not afraid to fight with man, but never hurt women and children, they are innocent harmless Beings. It is true that I took some of them Prisoners, but it was only with a View to exchange for our People you have as Prisoners. I have used them well, kept them at my own House, and treated them as my own Children: and you shall have them every one as soon as you bring in our People."[22]

The next day Joseph refused to leave without another sister, age ten, whom he knew was someplace in the Five Lower Towns. A young Indian was sent off immediately but returned at ten o'clock in the morning three days later and announced that the man who had her, thirty miles away, demanded ransom. "There was an old warrior sitting by, his sword hanging on the wall, and his horse standing at a tree in the yard. He rose, and putting on his sword, made this short speech. 'I will go and bring her, or his head.' Sure enough, the next morning, here he came with her; when asked what the Indian said, he replied, 'nothing.'"

Joseph and his sisters were exchanged at Coosawatee on 20 April 1789. "At this time my weight was only eighty pounds. . . ."

We must take note of one more experience of Joseph Brown's before leaving him. On the first day of his captivity he had been with the old Irishman and his wife only fifteen or twenty minutes "when a very large corpulent old woman came in, the sweat falling in big drops from her face, who appeared very angry, and told the old white people that they had done very wrong in taking me away, that I ought to be killed, that I would see everything, and that I would soon be grown and would guide an army there and have them all cut off . . . that I must be killed." The woman's son arrived to kill Joseph, and other Indians appeared for the same purpose, but a combination of the old white couple and Indians opposed to killing him saved Joseph. The reader, however, should store away the old woman's words.

The turmoil on the frontier that year and its principal cause was simply but eloquently summed up by a Cherokee mixed blood, William Elders, on 1 November 1788, in words directed to Joseph Martin in the Cherokee town of Utinaire:

"You were one of the beloved men that spoke for Congress at Keowee [Treaty of Hopewell] three years ago; you then said the [white] people should move off in six moons from that time; but near forty moons are past and they are not gone yet. We well remember, whenever we are invited into a treaty, as observed by us at that time, and bounds are fixed, that the white people settle much faster on our lands than they did before. It must certainly be the case, they think we will not break the treaty, and they will strengthen themselves and keep the lands. You know this to be the case. You told us at the treaty, if any white people settled on our lands we might do as we pleased with them. They come and settle close to our towns, and some of the Chicamoga people came, contrary to our desire, and killed a family; and the white people came and drove us out of our town, and killed some of our beloved men, and several women and little children, although we could not help what the Chicamoga people does. You know that well. We are now like wolves, ranging about the woods to get something to eat. Nothing to be seen in our towns but bones, weeds, and grass."[23]

"YOU HAVE INSULTED ME IN THE PRESENCE OF A COURT AND A LARG AUDIANC"

There is no evidence that Jackson became involved in either the political imbroglio surrounding the State of Franklin or the Indian fighting. Few records exist of his early months over the mountains, and Jonesborough was north of and relatively sheltered from the mutual massacres and desperate actions of that year. The old men remembered Jackson as a sport. A racetrack was one of the first amenities the pioneers had built at the rude frontier settlement of Jonesborough. It was there at least as early as 1780, when Colonel Isaac Shelby rode in to interrupt Colonel John Sevier at a horse race to propose mounting an expedition across the mountains to deal with one of Cornwallis's officers, Major Patrick Ferguson, which ended with Ferguson's death and the shattering of his command in one of the key fights of the Revolutionary War, the Battle of King's Mountain. Tradition has it that Jackson's most passionate interest during his sojourn in Jonesborough was horse racing, in which he was a jockey as well as a gambler. But he had to make ends meet, so he also practiced law, which led to his challenge of one of the most eminent members of the North Carolina bar.

Waightstill Avery (1741–1821), as the reader will recall, was the lawyer in Morganton, on the eastern side of the mountains, with whom Jackson had first wanted to read law. A graduate of Princeton (then the College of New Jersey), a leader of the independence movement in that "hornet's nest" of American Rebels, Mecklenburg County, North Carolina, a state legislator, and North Carolina's first attorney general, Avery was indeed a man of position and distinction. That summer he was attending as usual the district court in Jonesborough, one of North Carolina's three district courts. Years later Avery's son sent James Parton a description of what occurred between his father and Jackson.

"In the trial of a suit one afternoon, General Jackson and my father were opposing counsel. The General always espoused the cause of his client warmly, and seemed to make it his own. On this occasion, the cause was going against him, and he became irritable. My father rather exultingly ridiculed some legal position taken by Jackson; using, as he afterwards admitted, language that was more sarcastic than called for. It stung Jackson, who snatched up a pen, and on the blank leaf of a law book wrote a peremptory challenge, which he delivered there and then. It was as promptly accepted. My father was no duelist; in fact, he was opposed to the principle, but, with his antecedents, in that age and country, to have declined would have been to have lost caste."[24]

The note referred to above has not been found, but the following day, 12 August 1788, Jackson repeated his challenge, his first letter of record.

> Sir. When amans feelings & charector are injured the ought to Seek aspeedy redress; you recd. a few lines from me yesterday & undoubtedly you understand me. My charector you have Injured; and further you have Insulted me in the presence of a court and a larg audianc. I therefore call upon you as a gentlemen to give me Satisfaction for the Same; and I further call upon you to give me an answer immediately without Equivocation and I hope you can do without dinner untill the business done; for it is consistant with the charector of agentleman when he Injures a man to make aspedy reparation; therefore I hope you will not fail in meeting me this day from yr obt st
>
> Andrw. Jackson
>
> P.S. This Evening after court adjourned.[25]

Avery's son wrote that after arrangements were made his father and Jackson met, with their seconds, "in a hollow north of Jonesboro, it was after sundown. The ground was measured, and the parties were placed. They fired. Fortunately, neither was hit. General Jackson announced himself satisfied. They shook hands, and were friendly ever after."[26]

Robert Remini, Jackson's modern biographer, states that they both fired into the air, that "neither had any intention of getting hurt. A solution satisfactory to both sides had been worked out. (Perhaps they agreed to the suggestion of their seconds that the shots be thrown away.)"[27]

Whether they just missed or threw their shots away, Andrew Jackson was a fortunate man. First, he was alive. Second, given public reaction to one of his later duels, which we will cover further along, had he killed or seriously wounded this eminent man, Waightstill Avery, I believe the prospects for a successful career for this young man who had yet to find a powerful patron and establish himself would have been at the least dampened and more likely ruined.

About a month and a half later Jackson left Jonesborough. Not because of the duel. The escort to Nashville was ready to go. After he and John McNairy's arrival in Nashville, the *State Gazette* of North Carolina announced that "notice is hereby given, that the new road from Campbell's Station to Nashville, was opened on the 25th of September, and the guard attended at that time to escort such persons as were ready to proceed to Nashville; that about sixty families went on, amongst whom were the widow and family of the late General Davidson,[28] and John McNairy, Judge of the Superior Court; and that on the 1st day of October next, the guard will attend at the same place for the same purpose."[29]

No documentation exists of Jackson's first march though hostile country. But James Parton accepted a story "which comes to me, in a direct line, by trustworthy channels, from the lips of Thomas Searcy, the clerk of the Superior Court, who rode by Jackson's side."[30] (Searcy's first name was Bennett, not Thomas.)

The guard had pushed hard through what was considered the most dangerous part of the trip, marching thirty-six hours straight, with rest stops lasting no longer than an hour. When they finally made camp, Jackson sat up with the sentinels after everyone else had gone to sleep. He heard an owl hoot at a distance. Suddenly, it was closer. "In an instant he was the widest awake man in Tennessee. All his mind was in his ears, and his ears were intent on the hooting of the owls." He crept to where Bennett Searcy slept.

"Searcy, raise your head and make no noise."

"What's the matter?"

"The owls—listen—there—there again. Isn't that a little *too* natural?"

"Do you think so?"

"I know it. There are Indians all around us. I have heard them in all directions. They mean to attack before daybreak."

As the story continues, all were then awakened, Jackson advised immediate departure. The escort, all experienced guides and woodsmen who had noticed nothing, agreed. All packed up and got quickly on their way. It then seems that an hour after they left some white hunters arrived at their campsite, made their fires, and slept. The Indians fell upon them and killed all but one. The following spring Judge McNairy and a party, without Jackson, returning to Jonesborough camped at the same spot, were attacked by Indians, who killed three. McNairy and the rest fled without horses or belongings.

How do we treat this early tale among many of Andrew Jackson as a leader of frontiersmen? Are we to believe that sixty families, men, women, and children, and all of the others struck camp, which involved taking down tents, saddling mounts, loading packhorses, and took the trail without the surrounding Indians, so attuned we are told to movement and sound, noticing, hearing, and at the very least laying down a harassing fire? His modern biographer saw the story as "appropriate to the Jackson legend, however exaggerated some of its details."[31] That, I think, is the crux of the matter. Some brush with danger probably occurred on the trail and undoubtedly involved Indians, but precisely what it was and Jackson's role happened too long ago and came through too many mouths before it reached Parton and was finally written down that we must treat it as legend. But possibly true. For Andrew Jackson was larger than life, and what we truly know of his accomplishments begs respect for the legends.

On 26 October 1788, one month after leaving East Tennessee, Andrew Jackson arrived in Nashville. It was then eight years old and had a population of a few hundred. Twelve years later, in 1800, the town would number only 345 people. For in those years only the hardy and the foolhardy went to the Cumberland. Nashville and the outlying stations were at the back of beyond, isolated, the targets of several thousand hostile Indians determined to wipe them from the face of the earth.[32]

It was the Cumberland salient, and its founding is a tale worth telling.

Chapter 4

⸺⁂⸺

THE CUMBERLAND SALIENT

"HE GAVE . . . A GLOWING DESCRIPTION OF THE COUNTRY"

The reader will recall from chapter 1 that Judge Richard Henderson, James Robertson, and John Donelson had probably discussed settling the Cumberland area during the Sycamore Shoals treaty conference of 1775. In the winter of 1778–1779 Roberston led eight frontiersmen, his brother Mark and six other white men and one black slave, on a reconnaissance mission to the promised land.

We observed Robertson's key role in the penetration of the Appalachian barrier and the establishment of that "dangerous example," the Watauga Association, and we watched as he sat in council at Sycamore Shoals with Richard Henderson and others and listened to Dragging Canoe's prophetic warning. Now we should briefly pause and consider the stuff of which this man was made. If one were asked to produce a short list of American frontiersmen of the very first rank, the name of James Robertson would demand inclusion. His general obscurity probably stems from his lack of flamboyance. He was a man who went through life performing deeds the like of which epics have been written. But he did it all with a quiet, matter-of-fact blend of courage and competence. An Indian chief with whom he once dealt in council judged Robertson simply but well: "He had winning ways and makes no fuss." Washington's secretary of war, Henry Knox, who generally took a dim view of frontiersmen, had a high regard for his character. His education was limited and he did not write well, and unlike Daniel Boone he did not attract the attention of a John Filson to make him famous. But if giants really did walk the earth in those days he was one of them.[1]

Upon Robertson's return, his daughter Lavinia Robertson Craighead recalled, "he gave such a glowing description of the country through which he had passed that he made up a large party to go and settle on the Cumberland River where Nashville now stands."[2]

Rising in the remote reaches of the Cumberland Mountains in south-eastern Kentucky, the Cumberland River followed a circuitous two-hundred-mile route to the present Tennessee line. The river then snaked southward through the rich lands of Middle Tennessee until it reached French Lick (modern Nashville), where it abruptly turned northwest. After keeping to a relatively straight course as far as modern Clarksville, it dipped briefly south-westerly, then once again turned northwest. Two hundred fifty miles from where it entered Tennessee the Cumberland reentered Kentucky, and after a short passage parallel to the Tennessee River, through Kentucky's western-most alluvial plain, emptied into the bigger, swifter Ohio.

That the goal by land was over two hundred miles in a direct line over the rugged and roadless Cumberland Plateau from the nearest settlements in East Tennessee; that it was a couple of hundred more by the preferred but circuitous Kentucky route; that Dragging Canoe had refused to recognize Henderson's purchase and predicted a dark and bloody time; that a revolu-tionary government waging desperate war against Great Britain could not possibly help them; that East Tennessee settlers fighting the Chickamaugas on their doorsteps and sending expeditions east of the mountains to fight the British had all they could do to save themselves—none of this deterred Robertson and the other pioneers intent on the Cumberland.

They were overwhelmingly white. Slavery in East Tennessee remained negligible, for the system of small-scale agriculture practiced in that largely mountainous country was not suited to massive slave labor. In West Tenness-ee, where the Robertson expedition was headed, whites far outnumbered blacks, both slave and free, during the years with which we are concerned. Later, when cotton became king, the situation would change, and West Tennessee would eventually resemble Mississippi and Alabama in its racial makeup.

But the settlers bound for the Cumberland took slaves with them and by custom and law they would institutionalize a system that in the prophetic words of the Quaker missionary John Woolman, "appeared to me as a dark gloominess hanging over the land; and though now many willingly run into it, yet in future the consequences will be grievous to posterity! I express it as it hath appeared to me, not at once or twice, but as a matter fixed in my mind."[3] This sense of foreboding crossed class lines and walks of life and ranged from the practical danger of controlling large numbers of slaves to the effect of their presence on the white work ethic to the morality of slav-ery. In 1736 William Byrd of Virginia expressed all three concerns.

The traders "import so many negro's hither that I fear this Colony will sometime or other be confounded by the name of New Guinea. I am sen-sible of many bad consequences of multiplying these Ethiopians amongst us. They blow up the pride, and ruin the Industry of our White People, who Seeing a Rank of poor Creatures below them, detest work for fear it should make them look like Slaves . . . Another unhappy Effect of many Negroes is, the necessity of being severe. Numbers make them insolent & then foul Means must do what fair will not. We have however nothing like the Inhumanity here, that is practiced in the Islands & God forbid we ever shou'd. But these Tempers require to be rid with a tight rein, or they will be apt to throw their Rider."

The spectre of a slave uprising haunted Byrd. "And in case there should arise a man of desperate courage amongst us, exasperated by a desperate future, he might with more advantage than Cataline kindle a servile war . . . and tinge our Rivers as wide as they are with Blood. . . . It were there-fore, with the consideration of the British Parliament, My Lord, to put an end to this unchristian Traffick, of makeing Merchandise of our Fellow Creatures. At least, the further importation of them, into our Colonys, should be pro-hibited, lest they prove as troublesome, & dangerous every where, as they have been lately in Jamaica. . . ."

Byrd concluded with a bitter attack on slave traders: "I wonder the Leg-islature will Indulge a few ravenous Traders, to the danger of the Publick safety, & such Traders as would freely sell their Father, their Elder brothers, & even the Wives of their bosomes if they cou'd black their Faces & get anything for them."[4]

Yet Byrd himself was a slaveholder. The ambivalence of his position was shared by most of those slaveholders whose views of the institution ran the gamut from vague misgivings to deep distaste. But they could not make the break. Slavery was a trap for them as well as for their slaves. Their positions and fortunes were tied to the system, and as the decades passed and it became imbedded the possibility of ending the trade and rooting out the evil became so remote that discussion of it was an exercise in futility. But another important reason for their inability to act on their forebodings was their deep-seated belief in the sanctity of private property. It was considered a fundamental liberty.

Byrd uses one word in his letter that in the context is difficult for our twentieth-century minds to contemplate. That word is "merchandise." Slaves were property, as houses and land and livestock were property. They had value; they could be bought and sold. They could, and would, make some men rich, their labor could lighten the burden of people of modest circum-stances. To take away that property, to free the slave, would deny the owner liberty.

A few slaveholders were able to escape this tortured reasoning. One of the most prominent was John Laurens of South Carolina. His father, Henry, a president of the Continental Congress and signatory of the Peace of Paris of 1783, was one of the Low Country's great merchant-planters, and until his retirement from the trade in 1769 had been one of Charleston's two leading slave traders. Despite making much of his fortune from the trade, Henry had serious moral qualms about slavery. But he was never able to resolve them. His son John, however, was made of different stuff and had the optimism of youth. On 12 April 1776 he wrote to his close friend and fel-low South Carolinian, the Tory Francis Kinloch, "I think we Americans at least in the Southern Colonies, cannot contend with *a good Grace,* for Lib-erty, until we shall have enfranchised out Slaves. How can we whose Jealousy has been alarm'd more at the Name of Oppression sometimes than at the Reality, reconcile to our spirited Assertions of the Rights of Mankind, the galling abject slavery of our negroes. . . ." Kinloch replied on 28 April, "I heartily agree with you, but at the same time can not flatter myself that our country men will ever adopt such generous principles."[5]

We know that Kinloch was right, and that John Laurens's was but a cry in the wilderness. Most people undoubtedly never questioned the system. They were like most of us at all times: content with the ways of our fathers, or unwilling or unable to buck the system. If some of our settlers had moral reservations, if the realists among them were aware that this age-old institution of human bondage was a slowly growing moral and political anachronism in a modern world taking shape, hastened along by their own Revolution, they probably did not dwell hard upon it. For our pioneers were gripped by a primal concern that took precedence over all else: survival in a world where death might lurk at every turn in the trail, around every bend in the river.

It is not our purpose to explore the subject of slavery; it has been done by others in monographic detail and will continue ad infinitum as both a legitimate subject of research and commentary and a weapon of the self-righteous. Our obligation is to remind the reader that even in the heroic age all was not well in God's country.

Let us leave it then with perhaps the most telling observation of all, from the sardonic tongue of John Randolph of Roanoke. It was at a time in the nineteenth century when the chattering classes of the West were choked with pity and indignation at the plight of the poor Greeks fighting for their independence from the horrid Turks. A lady was bending Randolph's ear with her sympathy for the struggling Greeks, when in exasperation he turned and pointed at a group of ragged young blacks near her doorstep, and said, "Madam, the Greeks are at your door!"[6]

"I AM DETERMINED TO PURSUE MY COURSE, HAPPEN WHAT WILL"

By the fall of 1779, James Robertson's advance party was ready to move out from Fort Patrick Henry on the South Fork of the Holston River. The contrast then and now is striking. Where the pioneers mounted their horses at the rude frontier fort in October 1779 now stands the huge industrial complex of the Tennessee Eastman Company in Kingsport, Tennessee. The large party of men and boys headed northwesterly over the rugged Cumberland Mountains into Virginia, where they turned west on the ancient Great Warrior's Path and crossed the Clinch and Powell Rivers, through the country where Fanny Scott would begin her travail described in chapter 2. In Powell's Valley they overtook the party of John Rains on its way to Kentucky. But Robertson convinced Rains of the desirability of the Cumberland Valley, and the two parties merged. An early historian of Tennessee thought that one reason behind Robertson's urging may have been that Rains had with him "19 cows, 2 steers, and 17 horses." Rains was given credit for being the first man to introduce domestic livestock into Middle Tennessee.[7]

They climbed by way of the narrow track, three to four feet wide, through Cumberland Gap, where Frederick Jackson Turner urged us to "stand . . . and watch the procession of civilization, marching single file—the buffalo following the trail to the salt springs, the Indian, the fur trader and hunter, the cattle-raiser, the farmer—and the frontier has passed by." Descending to Yellow Creek Valley, the pioneers turned north and followed the Wilderness Road, as if they were heading for the Kentucky settlements. But high in Kentucky, about forty miles south of modern Lexington, they turned again and wound their way southwesterly until they reached the neighborhood of modern Bowling Green, then dropped almost due south for the place on the Cumberland River known as French Lick, later called Nashville. They had come through rough country and heavy snows. It was one of the coldest winters in memory—so cold, recalled an early pioneer, "that its equal in this respect had never been known by the oldest people; and such a winter has not since been felt in this country." The Cumberland River as far south as French Lick would freeze solid. But luck, the toughness and abilities of individuals, and James Robertson's quiet, steady leadership brought them through unscathed. Sometime during Christmas week of 1779 they arrived at French Lick and began preparations to receive their families. They had come about four hundred miles.[8]

Robertson's march, absent a chronicler and singular for its lack of dramatic incident, has been overshadowed by the river voyage of the Donelson party, which included the families of Robertson's men. But that is no reason to describe John Donelson as "inept and unseasoned" and in general nitpick and misrepresent his performance. Donelson, born in Pittsylvania County, Virginia, followed that prestigious colonial occupation of surveyor. Five years before setting out for the Cumberland he was described by a man who knew him "to be about 50 years of age, rather over the ordinary size of man, slightly inclined to be fleshy." He was certainly far from Robertson's equal as a leader and frontiersman, but he was not without stout qualities of his own, and his route was far longer and turned out to be as difficult, if not more so. But let us follow the adventures of Donelson's party and judge his performance for ourselves.[9]

Their intention with the families was to avoid the rigors of the overland route for what would appear to be the less difficult voyage down the Holston to the Tennessee, all the way down that river to the distant Ohio, up the Ohio to the Cumberland, and then to turn east again and go up the Cumberland to French Lick. Their route was not unknown territory to Americans. Traders knew the Tennessee and the Cherokee country. Long hunters, who sought meat and hides for the markets, had penetrated deeply into that wide expanse of territory and had overwintered in the area of French Lick. In April 1779, eight months before the Donelson expedition got under way, the well-known frontiersman Evan Shelby had rendezvoused with 600 men at James Roberston's home on the Holston, from where he led them in pirogues down the Holston and Tennessee on a successful raid against the Chickamauga towns in the vicinity of modern Chattanooga. Eleven towns were burned and plundered. From Shelby and his men Donelson and others certainly had up-to-date information on part of the route. What they did not know was that following Shelby's raid most of the Chickamaugas had moved downriver and established what came to be called the Five Lower Towns, whose precise locations were for several years unknown to the Americans.[10]

Three days before Christmas 1779 of that bitterly cold winter, the flat-boats were launched at Fort Patrick Henry and floated down the Holston. Colonel John Donelson, in his "good boat Adventure," proclaimed their jour-ney into the wilderness as "intended by God's Permssion. . . ." As the Donel-son party rendezvoused downriver with other pioneers, the flotilla would eventually number some forty boats carrying about three hundred people. Almost all of the boats had two families on board, and on one were at least three. Aboard her father's boat was twelve-year-old Rachel Donelson.[11]

Donelson did not leave a description of the boats, but we have infor-mation from other sources to guide us. In 1796 the English traveler Francis Baily left Pittsburgh for New Orleans in a boat "12 feet broad, 36 feet long, and drew 18 inches of water when she had upwards of 10 tons of goods in her." Thus the flatboat was an admirable vessel for navigating the shallow places and shoals so often encountered on the western waters. Baily wrote that "these boats, which may be more properly termed rafts, are built with-out one particle of iron in their composition; they are generally 30 to 40 feet long, and about 12 feet broad, and consist of a framework fastened together with wooden pins, which constitute the bottom of the boat, and to this is fastened a flooring, which is calked to prevent leaking; the sides are about breast high, and made of thin plank; and sometimes there is a rude kind of covering, *intended* to keep the rain out. These boats draw very little water, not enough to sink the framework at the bottom under the water, and generally furnished with a pair of oars, not so much to expedite their progress, as to keep them from the shore when they are driven towards it by the current; and there is a pole projecting from the stern, to steer them with. When they are going down the stream, it is immaterial which part goes foremost; and their whole appearance is not much unlike a large box float-ing down with the current." Baily stated that the Orleans boat he was on could float "according as the stream carried her . . . at the rate of five or six miles an hour; the only attention required was to keep a good look-out . . . and see that she did not drift against the sides of the river. . . ." He left unsaid the danger of rapids and obstructions, of which there were many on the Western Waters.[12]

Flatboats were also relatively inexpensive. Most were built by profes-sional boatbuilders, and in Pittsburgh in 1796 Baily reported that a "boat 40 feet long and 12 feet wide would cost 40 dollars. . . ." The boats of the Donelson flotilla were probably built by professionals at the boatyard next to Fort Patrick Henry. But given the simplicity of their construction, farmers—who have always been jacks of all trades—could and did build them.[13]

John Donelson's journal of their passage is our main source for the voyage and, unless otherwise indicated, all quotations to the end of the chapter are from Donelson's *Journal of a Voyage.*

Their first day on the Holston did not go well, for the water was too low even for their shallow-water craft. They reached the mouth of Reedy Creek, only a few hundred yards downstream, when they were stopped by low water and "most excessive hard frost," Donelson wrote. After delays and difficulties that Donelson does not describe, they arrived at the mouth of Cloud's Creek on the evening of 20 February 1780. There they rested until 27 February, "when we took our departure with sundry other vessels bound for the same voyage. . . ." But the same day Donelson's boat and two others grounded on "Poor-valey shoal . . . on which we lay that afternoon and succeeding night in much distress."

One boat, captained by a man named Stuart and carrying "his family and friends, to the number of twenty eight persons," trailed the flotilla, for Stuart's "family being deseased with small-pox, it was agreed upon between him and the Company that he should keep at some distance in the rear, for fear of the infection spreading." Each night, as the main party put in to shore, a horn was blown to inform Stuart that he, too, should land and make camp. This hard necessity would lead to unavoidable tragedy.

The water rose on the twenty-eighth, but thirty people had to get off Donelson's boat to refloat it, and the craft was damaged and articles lost upon attempting to land on an island. They met several other boats that evening in camp. Following a few uneventful days, an ever-present danger of river navigation struck the boat of a man named Henry. His craft was driven by the current onto the "point of an island" and sunk, "the Crew's lives much endangered, and the whole cargo much damaged. . . ." All of the boats put ashore and the people went to Henry's aid and salvaged his boat: "with much difficulty bailed her out & raised her in order to take in her cargo again."

If this were not enough to contend with, that "same afternoon Reuben Harrison went out a hunting" and got lost. For the rest of that day and night and the following guns and a four-pounder were fired to guide him in and there were "sent out sundry persons to search the wood for him . . . but all without success, to the great grief of his parents and fellow travellers. . . ."

On 4 March the journey continued, for the progress of the entire party could not be jeopardized by the fate of one young man. But Reuben Harrison's father and a few other boats were left behind to continue the search, and at ten o'clock that morning he was found "a considerable distance down the river. . . ."

That day also, at three o'clock in the afternoon, they left the Holston and entered the Tennessee River just above present-day Knoxville and camped ten miles below its mouth. The next day they "cast off and got underway before Sunrise," by noon passed the mouth of the Clinch and "came up with the Clinch river Company, whom we joined and camped. . . ." The Clinch company was led by Captain John Blackmore.[14] The next day a dense fog covered the river and the boats became scattered and the lead boats waited for them. On this day, Monday the sixth of March, Captain Thomas Hutchings's "negro man died, being much frosted in his feet and legs. . . ."

On 7 March wind and river were high and smaller boats were in danger of swamping. They camped at the uppermost of the Chickamauga towns, then uninhabited. That day the wife of Ephraim Peyton, who had gone by land with James Robertson and awaited his wife at the Big Salt Lick, "was here delivered of a child."

The following day occurred the confrontation that though expected and dreaded, nevertheless had not dissuaded them from their purpose, although some would have rated their chances low. In January 1779, three months before Evan Shelby's raid, Patrick Henry referred to Dragging Canoe's Chickamaugas when he wrote to a prominent North Carolina politician, "The navigation of the Tennessee River . . . is rendered unsafe and indeed impracticable so long as these Banditti remain unpunished. Their present situation on the banks of that river gives them command of it." The situation had not changed, despite Shelby's raid. Sixty-four years later Mary Purnell Donelson, wife of John Donelson Jr., who made the journey as a bride, remembered strings of Chickamauga campfires along the banks, and the enticing cries of Indian women and children: "Brothers, how do ye do-o-o-o; come ashore."[15]

The voyagers came to a Chickamauga town on the left bank, whose inhabitants "invited us to 'come ashore,' called us brothers, & shewed other signs of friendship." This induced John Caffrey and Donelson's son to take a canoe they had in tow and paddle toward the beckoning Indians. Meanwhile, the other boats landed on the opposite bank and awaited events. Before Caffrey and young Donelson reached the village, "a half-Breed who called himself Archy Coody with several other Indians jumped into a canoe, met them and advised them to return to the boat, which they did together with Coody and several canoes which left the shore & followed directly after him."

Coody's party "appeared to be friendly," Donelson wrote, and they were allowed on board the boats and given presents, "with which they seemed much pleased." But then the Americans saw canoes putting out on the other side of the river. The Indians in them were armed and "painted with red & black." Archy Coody immediately ordered his companions off the boats. He and one Indian remained with the settlers, whom he told "to move off instantly."

Soon they saw other canoes full of armed and painted Chickamauga warriors "proceeding down the river, as it were, to intercept us." But the boats outran them. Coody and his companion stayed with them "for some time, & telling us that we had passed all the Towns & were out of danger, left us." As we shall see, this was not true, which Coody must have known. But Archy Coody's motivations throughout this incident, in which he first provided timely warning of danger and then misinformed the settlers, remain unknown.

Shortly after Coody left them they sighted another village, also on the south bank of the Tennessee, "nearly opposite a small island." These Indians also invited their "brothers" ashore, and when the boats headed for the opposite channel they called out "'their side was better for boats to pass.'" There were also warriors concealed on the north bank, and Captain John Blackmore's boat, running too close to shore, was fired on and a "young Mr. Payne . . . was mortally wounded." But a much greater tragedy was about to unfold.

Captain Stuart's boat with its load of smallpox victims was still running behind the flotilla. More warriors had gathered at the village after the main party passed, and observing Stuart's "helpless situation . . . intercepted him & killed & took prisoners the whole crew, to the great grief of all the Company uncertain how soon they might share the same fate; their cries were distinctly heard by those boats in the rear." But given the deadly virus the victims carried, revenge would be theirs in the soon-to-be pox-ridden lodges of the Chickamaugas. John Carr wrote, "Though but a small boy at the time, I recollect very well the reports of the great and terrible mortality which prevailed in the Cherokee Nation after the capture of Stuart's boat . . . It was said that, when they were attacked with the smallpox, and the fever was upon them, they took a heavy sweat in their houses for that purpose, and then leaped into the river and died by scores."[16]

And all the while those in the main party saw warriors "marching down the river in considerable bodies, keeping paces with us until the Cumberland mountain withdrew them from our sight, when we were in hopes we had escaped them." They had passed the site of what would become Chattanooga, Tennessee.

Here let us pause and stand on Signal Mountain on the north side of the Tennessee and look far below at the river winding through the canyon of dark, steep, forested slopes, so far down it seems a toy stream. Stand there on a dark, stormy, rain-swept day, black clouds racing overhead, tornadoes sweeping the countryside all around, lightning piercing the distant sky. Stand there and look down and imagine tiny flatboats loaded with hopeful, fearful, determined pilgrims floating down waters shown on early maps as the Cherakee River.

Did they feel puny amid God's awesome work? Donelson, a practical man apparently not given to introspection, does not say. Perhaps he felt it, but in justice he had more pressing matters to consider. Down there, to the south, beyond Signal Mountain, in what came to be called the Narrows, there awaited the Suck and other terrors of the wild river. As they approached it, they would have seen Walden's Ridge looming far above them on the right bank. It was named after Isaac Walden, who in 1761 had led about twenty Virginians on a long hunt into this country, and they had named the range of mountains west of the Clinch River Walden's.[17]

At a point where the mountain "juts in on both sides" and the river narrows to half its usual width a "Whirl or Suck," and what Archy Coody had described to them as the "boiling pot," put the entire expedition in peril. The rapids stretched for about three miles. A half century later a well-known soldier and engineer, Colonel Stephen H. Long, observed that the "usuable channel narrowed to a mere 150 feet, and the rocks jutting into the bed of the river partially dammed it up, and increased the force of the current from an average velocity of 7 miles an hour in this general area to 13 miles per hour."[18]

John Cotton, traveling with his family in a large canoe, had attached his craft with a line to Robert Cartwright's boat, but for safety in the turbulent waters of the narrows, Cotton and his family had gone aboard the boat. The canoe overturned and the Cottons lost their belongings. "The Company pitying his distress concluded to halt & assist him in recovering his property." They found a good landing on the right bank and started to walk back to where the canoe had overturned when "Indians to our astonishment appeared immediately over us on the opposite Cliffs & commenced firing down upon us. . . . " The men ran for the boats, leaped in, and cast off. The Indians lining the cliffs fired down on them all the way through the "boiling pot." Donelson reported only four people "slightly wounded," but he ended this passage with a chilling sentence: "Jenning's boat is missing."

All of the other boats emerged onto a wider river "with a placid and gentle current." But the boat of Jonathan Jennings, with his family, two slaves, and passengers, had run "on a large rock projecting out from the northern shore and partly immersed in water immediately at the Whirl, where we were compelled to leave them perhaps to be slaughtered by their merciless enemies." The flotilla sailed on the rest of that day and the following night.

Thus passed the eventful day of 8 March 1780. East of the Appalachians a large British army had landed in South Carolina and was advancing on Charleston. When the city fell in May the fate of the Revolution itself seemed in question.[19] But of the immediate events leading to that singular contest and its bloody aftermath the Cumberland pioneers, on their daring penetration of hostile territory, for many months would know nothing. They might as well have been travelers on another planet, their overwhelming occupation survival.

On Friday the tenth, at four o'clock in the morning, they were awakened by plaintive cries—"help poor Jennings!" Jonathan Jennings, whom they had undoubtedly given up with his entire party to death or capture, "had discovered us by our fires, and came up in the most wretched condition," and related the following tale, as recorded by Donelson.

"As soon as the Indians discovered his situation they turned their whole attention to him & kept up a most galling fire on his boat. He ordered his wife, a son nearly grown, a young man who accompanied him, & his two negroes to throw all his goods into the river, to lighten their boat for the purpose of getting her off, himself returning their fire as well as he could (being a good soldier & an excellent marksman)." But before finishing his son, the young man, and the black man jumped off the boat. Jennings thought the two older men may have been wounded before jumping.

According to John Carr, the black man drowned; however, the two white men reached shore, stole a canoe, and set out downriver, but were intercepted by "several canoes full of Indians." They were taken to the town, where the young man was "killed and burned," a fate Jennings's son would have suffered had not a trader named Rogers "paid a handsome ransom for him, and saved his life."[20]

Mrs. Jennings and a black woman stuck to their posts and finished unloading the boat. But it would not float off the rock, Donelson wrote, until Mrs. Jennings went into the river and "shoved her off," and almost became a "victim to her own intrepidity on account of the boat starting so suddenly," for it was obviously with difficulty that she clambered aboard as the boat was swept downstream. Donelson wrote that Jennings "made a wonderful escape, for his boat is pierced in numberless places with bullets."

Mrs. Jennings's exploit highlights the toughness and fortitude of these people, a judgment reinforced by the actions of another woman on board the Jennings boat, his daughter, Mrs. Ephraim Peyton, who we noted had given birth to a child the day before. Throughout the frantic attempts to escape the rock, and while under heavy fire, Mrs. Peyton assisted in these efforts, "being frequently exposed to wet & cold then and afterwards," while suffering the tragedy of seeing her newborn "killed in the hurry and confusion consequent upon such a disaster. . . ." Yet, added Donelson in his entry of 10 March, "her health appears to be good at this time, & I think & hope she will do well."

On the morning of the twelfth the sound of cocks crowing alerted them to another Chickamauga town, where they were fired upon but suffered no injuries. At midmorning they sighted Muscle Shoals, several miles of dangerous water, and halted at the upper end on the northern bank of the Tennessee. Here James Robertson was to have left signs that "he had been there & that it was practicable for us to go across by land." A glance at a modern highway map shows what a boon this would have been to the weary travelers. The highway distance between Muscle Shoals, Alabama, and Nashville, Tennessee, is about seventy miles, and in 1780 even the absence of a road would not have deterred them had Robertson left the prearranged signs. "But to our great mortification we can find none. From which we conclude that it would not be prudent to make the attempt, and are determined, knowing ourselves to be in such imminent danger, to pursue our journey down the river."

They ran the much-feared shoals before nightfall, and here we must use John Donelson's descriptive powers and our imaginations, for Muscle Shoals no longer exists. In the twentieth century it was submerged under three lakes created by the dams of the Tennessee Valley Authority. But in 1780 the shoals dropped 134 feet in thirty-four miles[21] and presented a "dreadful appearance to those who had never seen them before. The water being high made a terrible roaring, which could be heard at some distance, among the drift-wood heaped frightfully upon the points of the islands; the current running in every possible direction. Here we did not know how soon we should be dashed to pieces and all our troubles ended at once. Our boats frequently dragged on the bottom. And appeared constantly in danger of striking on the bottom. They warped as much as in a rough sea. But by the hand of Providence we are now preserved from this danger also. I know not the length of this wonderful shoal; it had been represented to me to be 25 or 30 miles: If so, we have descended very rapidly, as indeed we did, for we passed it in about three hours."

Indians fired on them again on 14 March, when two boats got too close to shore. Five men were slightly wounded. That night, upon landing and kindling fires and preparing for rest, their dogs kept up such an "incessant barking" they suspected Indians were sneaking up on them and "retreated precipitally to the boats, fell down the river about a mile, & encamped on the other shore." Given the amusing ending of this affair, one suspects that they panicked. In the morning Donelson "prevailed" upon his son and John Caffrey to recross the river in a canoe and return to the encampment, where they "found an African negro, we had left in the hurry, asleep by one of the fires. The Voyagers then returned and collected their utensils, which had been left" in the wake of their rapid departure.

Their troubles had not ended, but they had run a terrible gauntlet and survived almost whole. Dragging Canoe's warriors had failed. A historian of the Chickamaugas admitted that, but offered an excuse: "Perhaps the major reason was the fact that the entire Chickamauga population had not yet removed to the Chattanooga area. . . ." But three years prior to their encounter with the Donelson party he has some five hundred warriors and their families following Dragging Canoe "to Chickamauga Creek north of present-day Chattanooga,"[22] and obviously by March of 1780 other towns were inhabited on the Tennessee below the modern city. Contrast those numbers with Donelson's party, which had about thirty-one adult white gunmen.

The Chickamaugas had the location and the numbers to stop the voyagers, end their expedition, and render stillborn their invasion of the Cumberland country and occupation of the strategic site at French Lick. They probably failed for the reasons they often failed: their organization for war mirrored their political organization, and their fighting style was designed to minimize casualties. To use modern terminology, they lacked a unified combat command that had the authority to direct the whole toward a common goal, and they failed to use their overwhelming numbers in a mass assault.

For five days the boats "moved on peaceably" along a moderate current through lands "rich, and abundantly covered with Oaks, Walnut, Sugartrees, Hickory, etc." and arrived on 20 March at that point where the Tennessee empties into the Ohio, in the southwest corner of the present state of Kentucky. Their situation was discouraging. The worst Indian danger was behind them, but now they faced hunger and more severe navigational difficulties. Their journey thus far had been downstream, but now they were faced with the exhausting labor of backtracking upstream, first on the Ohio and then the Cumberland.[23]

"Our situation here is truly disagreeable," Donelson wrote. "The river is very high and the current rapid. Our boats not constructed for the purpose of stemming a rapid stream. Our provision exhausted. The crews almost worn down with hunger and fatigue. And know not what distance we have to go or what time it will take us to reach our distination."

So discouraged were some that they resolved to head down the Ohio and then the Mississippi to Natchez. Others turned toward the Illinois country. Among the latter were Donelson's daughter and her husband, of whom he wrote, "We now part, perhaps to meet no more, for I am determined to pursue my course, happen what will."

Donelson and those bound for the Cumberland left the next day, and though it was but thirteen miles to the mouth of that river the current they battled was so swift that they "laboured very hard & got but a little way." The next two days were the same as they pulled up river, "suffering much from hunger & fatigue." And when at three o'clock on the afternoon of the twenty-fourth they came to the mouth of a river flowing into the Ohio and Donelson announced it was the Cumberland, some disagreed. It was too small, they said, although the contemporary geographer Thomas Hutchins described the mouth of the Cumberland as 250 yards wide. Donelson their leader prevailed, for "I had never heard of any river running in between the Cumberland & Tennessee." They turned up the new stream.[24]

The next day, as the river widened and the current proved gentle, the company became encouraged: "we are now convinced," wrote Donelson, "it is the Cumberland." Donelson's own progress was made much easier "from a small square sail which was fixed up on the day we left the mouth of the river. And to prevent any ill effects from sudden flows of wind, a man was stationed at each of the lower corners of the sheet, with directions to give way whenever it was necessary."

Provisions gone, they turned to the land for sustenance. On Sunday the twenty-sixth they "procured some Buffaloe meat; tho poor it was palatable." The next day they "killed a Swan, which was very delicious." On the twenty-eighth more "Buffaloe" fell to their guns. They gathered from the bottomlands along the river herbs "which some of the Company called Shawanee Sallad." But the finest sight of all must have occurred on 31 March when they met Judge Richard Henderson, who was running a survey line between Virginia and North Carolina for the Transylvania Company. Henderson's presence in the wilderness should be of interest to the reader, for it shows that he was willing to risk his life for his speculative gamble. Donelson wrote, "At this meeting we were much rejoiced. He gave us every information we wished. And further informed us that he had purchased a quantity of corn in Kentucky to be shipped at the falls of the Ohio for the use of the Cumberland settlement."

Nevertheless, they still had many days of travel ahead of them, and hard days they were. "We are now out of bread and are compelled to hunt the Buffaloe to preserve life. Worn out with fatigue our progress at present is slow." Although upon their entrance to the Cumberland Donelson had described the current as gentle, five years later another traveler, the young German Lewis Brantz, who would become a leading citizen of Baltimore, wrote of tough going on "waters . . . said to be the quietest of all the western rivers. After passing a day at its mouth, we commenced ascending the stream with the aid of eight oarsmen, but found the current much stronger than we expected; and thus we passed *fifteen days,* laboring harder than galley-slaves, before arriving at Nashville (Nash's Station), which is about two hundred and eleven miles from the mouth of the Cumberland."[25]

On 12 April the Donelson expedition came to the mouth of a small river that flowed in from the north, "by Moses Rentfroe & his company called Red River, up which they intended to settle. Here they took leave of us." Donelson and the others continued to push their weary way up the Cumberland, and on the twenty-third reached the first settlement, Eaton's Station, which had been settled by several families who had come by way of Kentucky.

The Big Salt Lick was a mile and a half above Eaton's, and there, on 24 April 1780, John Donelson wrote the final sentences of his journal: "We have the pleasure of finding Capt. Robertson and his Company. It is a source of satisfaction to us to be enabled to restore to him & others their families and friends, who were entrusted to our care, & who . . . perhaps dispaired of ever meeting again. Tho our prospects at present are dreary, We here found a few log Cabbins which have been built on a Cedar Bluff above the Lick by Capt. Robertson and his company."

They had come a thousand-odd miles and had been four months on the way. They were truly at the back of beyond. Five years later Lewis Brantz observed that "in the civilized portion of the Union, there are at present but few who even know its name."[26]

Chapter 5

⸺❧⸺

UNDER SIEGE

"TAKE CARE THAT WE DON'T . . .
SEND YOU BACK WITHOUT YOUR HEADS"

On or about 7 January 1781 a young man named David Hood was going from Freeland's Station on the Cumberland to Fort Nashborough, about a mile upstream, when he was ambushed by Indians. They were probably Chickasaws. They shot David Hood three times. Then they scalped him. For several hours he lay in the snow where he had fallen, alive but fearing to move before he was sure that the Indians had left. Finally he rose and began heading for Fort Nashborough. But the Indians had not left. He saw them at a distance, watching him. They laughed at him, for they thought the sight of his scalped head funny. Then they shot him again, twice, and left him where he fell.

David Hood lay in the snow all night. He was found the next morning by men from Fort Nashborough, who had followed his blood trail. The men carried him to an outhouse and left him, for if not already dead David Hood, scalped, shot five times, would surely die. The rest of that day, all that night, into the next morning, David Hood lay in the outhouse in his own filth, without a scalp, five bullet holes in him, but he would not die.

He probably would have died had it not been for James Robertson, who could do many things: travel thousands of miles alone through perilous wilderness, establish a settlement deep in hostile country, treat with or fight Indians as the occasion demanded, and a myriad of things necessary for survival on a frontier. Much of what he could do was expected of a seasoned frontiersman. But few could treat properly a scalped man, which James Robertson now proceeded to do for David Hood. He had seen scalps pegged in East Tennessee, and an anonymous French surgeon had taught him how to use a shoemaker's awl to make small holes in the "outer table of the skull, pretty close together." The blood oozing out formed a protective scab under which the terrible wound healed. David Hood's scalp would never be one

65

James Robertson, from the composite portrait by
Washington B. Cooper (Tennessee Historical Society)

for a woman to run her fingers over, and as with many scalping victims who
survived he may never have been the same again in mind or body, but he
lived for several years. James Robertson's son, Felix, born at Freeland's Station the day David Hood was scalped, became a doctor and many years later
described the method of treating a scalped skull.[1]

David Hood's experience is one of the more striking examples of the
daily perils of the Cumberland frontier, especially outside the confines of a
fortified station. The stations were critical in the early history of the Cumberland settlements. On the Tennessee frontier they were usually called stations, and their architecture ranged from mere unfortified lean-tos and cabins

in clearings to stockades with blockhouses at the corners and log cabins inside for living and working. The main purpose of a station was defensive, a refuge from Indian attacks for families living at the station or nearby. A man named Spencer Records, who was a pioneer in Kentucky and Indiana, left a good description of a fortified station.

"In the first place the ground is cleared off, the size they intended to build the fort, which was an oblong square. Then a ditch was dug three feet deep, the dirt being thrown out on the inside of the fort. Logs twelve to fifteen inches in diameter and fifteen feet long, were cut and split open. The ends sharpened, the butts set in the ditch with the flat sides all in, and the cracks broke with the flat sides of others. The dirt was thrown into the ditch and well rammed down. Port holes were made high enough that if a ball should be shot in, it would pass overhead. The cabins were built far enough from the stockade to have plenty of room to load and shoot. Two bastions were constructed at opposite corners with port holes about eighteen inches from the ground. The use of bastions was to rake the two sides of the fort should Indians get close to the stockade so that they could not shoot them from the port holes on the sides. Two gateways were made fronting each other with strong gates and bars so that they could not be forced open. Some forts had a bastion at each corner. Some forts, sometimes called stations, were cabins all set close together, half faced or the roof all sloping one way, with high side out, raised eight feet high and overlaid with split logs. The upper story was over-jutted two feet, and raised high enough to have plenty of room to load and shoot, with port holes both above and below."[2]

Between James Robertson's arrival with the advance party in 1779 and the Cumberland Compact of 1 May 1780, establishing a system of government and signed by 255 free adult white males, the settlers built eight stations dispersed along the Cumberland River and its tributaries: Nashborough, Mansker, Bledsoe, Asher, Stone's River, Freeland, Eaton, and Fort Union. They were all within thirty-six miles of modern Nashville. Eventually, about forty-nine stations were built in six counties in the Central Basin of West Tennessee, many of minor importance, often known by name only, their precise locations unknown. The numbers would fluctuate over the years, and some would be abandoned because they were insufficiently fortified to withstand Indian attacks.[3]

The attacks began that spring of 1780, and the spare reports constitute a dreary litany of the dead, the wounded, the captured. A man named Milligan was the first killed, soon followed by Joseph Hay, a man named Barnard, and another Milligan. Ned Cower was killed, and Jonathan Jennings, who had escaped death on the Tennessee only to die on the Cumberland. Some settlers from Mansker's Station went to Neely's Lick to make salt, which was needed for preserving game, and there William Neely was killed and scalped and his daughter, John Carr wrote, "a very interesting and smart girl, about sixteen years of age," was taken prisoner. She "was with the Indians for a long time," and upon her release "she married in Kentucky, and I am told made an excellent wife."[4]

John Donelson, with his family and others, went eight miles up the Cumberland from French Lick, then three miles south on Stone's River to a lovely stretch of rich bottomland where native white clover grew in abundance and there established a station that he called Clover Bottom. The settlers turned the virgin soil and planted corn and cotton. This was one of the simplest of stations, consisting of lean-tos, and Donelson's wife said that first winter they lived in tents. Of one thing we can be certain: it was an unfortified station. In July 1780 a flood drove them out and the Donelsons and others took refuge at Mansker's Station. The flood probably saved their lives, for stations lacking fortifications were easy pickings for war parties.[5]

Mankser's Station was not immune, however, and in the fall of 1780 Chickamaugas, coming up from their towns on the Tennessee that John Donelson had run his flotilla past, killed David Gion, Patrick Quigley, Betsy Kennedy, John Shockley, and James Lumley. They were killed outside the stations while engaged in working the fields, hunting, or other essential activities. For the settlers could not hole up indefinitely inside stockades. Life had to go on. Although the Donelsons and their neighbors had abandoned Clover Bottom for Mansker's Station, by the fall of 1780 the corn they had planted was ready to be harvested. They needed the crop and were determined to get it. John Donelson, Hugh Rogan, William Cartwright, and others embarked on the Cumberland in two small boats and pushed upstream, past Fort Nashborough at French Lick, and on to Stone's River. At Clover Bottom they harvested the corn and loaded it into the boats. One of the boats started downstream. But Indians had been watching and the boat had gone only a short distance when it was attacked. Abel Gower Sr., Abel Gower Jr., William Cartwright, and John Robertson, brother of James Robertson, were killed. Donelson, Rogan, and the rest escaped to Mansker's Station. The next morning the first boat was found floating on the Cumberland near Fort Nashborough with one of the dead men in it.[6]

This attack so disheartened the settlers at Mansker's that they abandoned the station. Some, including Kasper Mansker himself, moved to Fort Nashborough on the bluffs overlooking the Cumberland, a site located today in downtown Nashville. Others decided to abandon the Cumberland, at least temporarily, and head north for the relative safety of Kentucky. One who went, James McCain, many years later told John Carr "that all who could get horses went to Kentucky." Even Colonel John Donelson removed to Kentucky in November 1780 with his family, including thirteen-year-old Rachel. But Donelson remained active in the affairs of the Cumberland, and as we shall see over the next three years, put his life in jeopardy on more than one occasion and rendered the precarious settlements a signal service.[7]

People on the firing line are often vitally affected by events occurring at a distance of which they may be ignorant and over which they have little if any control. Over two hundred miles west of the tiny stations on the Cumberland another valiant people, the Chickasaws, were in tense disagreement with the state of Virginia over the status of land in western Kentucky. Virginia threatened to destroy the Chickasaws if they persisted in their claim to the land and refused friendship. That was a mistake, for the Chickasaws were "touchy as tinder," as Thomas Nairne described them in 1708. In the spring of 1779 they delivered a blunt warning to the Virginians: "[We] only desire you will inform us when you are comeing and we will save you the trouble of Coming quite here for we will meet you half way, for we have heared so much of it that it makes our heads Ach. Take care that we don't serve you as we served the French before with all their Indians. Send you back without your Heads." The Chickasaws wanted their reply printed in American newspapers, "that all your people may see it and know who it is from, We are men and Warriors and don't want our Talks hidden."[8]

The following spring, as the pioneers on the Cumberland were building stations and planting crops, Virginia built a fort without Chickasaw permission on a site five miles below the point where the Ohio flows into the Mississippi. It was named Fort Jefferson, after the governor who ordered it built. Chickasaw reaction was swift and violent. After six days and nights of attacks and desperate defense by the small garrison, James Colbert, the mixed-blood Chickasaw chief, approached the walls with a surrender demand, was fired upon, and wounded. In a fury the Chickasaws reacted with a tactic rarely used by Indians: a mass frontal assault at night that was repulsed only because of American firepower delivered with artillery mounted on swivels. But it was obvious that Fort Jefferson could not be held, and in June 1781 the garrison was evacuated by water all the way to the Falls of the Ohio (named Louisville in May 1780).[9]

Having made Fort Jefferson untenable, still "touchy as tinder," the Chickasaws turned on the intruders settling on hunting grounds from which the Chickasaws had driven the Shawnees some seventy years before. Recall that during the final leg of the Donelson party's voyage up the Cumberland, the Renfroes and others had peeled off and poled up the Red River. They established a settlement near the modern village of Palmyra, Tennessee, as the crow flies about seventy-five miles west of French Lick. If the Cumberland stations were at the back of beyond, the Red River settlement was in the middle of nowhere. Isolated, few in numbers, it became a bad dream of hopeful pioneers who may have been enticed there by one of the Renfroe's, who had probably been in the area on a long hunt in the winter of 1770–1771. Whatever their motivation in leaving the main party, they would soon regret it. Reports of Chickasaw bands in the area, as well as the killing of Nathan Turpin and another man, so alarmed the settlers that they decided to temporarily abandon their dream and seek refuge at Fort Nashborough. Many fled so hastily that property of value was left behind. One historian claimed that while encamped the first night in the woods, on their way to the Bluffs, the men were reproached for this by several women, and that some men and women turned back the next day to retrieve the property while the others went on to the Cumberland. But John Carr, who heard the tale early from survivors, wrote that the entire party reached Fort Nashborough. It was then, he stated, that some "returned to get their plunder, and to help away those of the settlers whom they had left at the Fort. The lack of horses was the reason, I suppose, why they did not all go off together. Having obtained their plunder, they started back, and at night camped on a small stream, a few miles north of Sycamore Creek."[10]

Chickasaw warriors struck in the morning and killed between twelve and twenty settlers, depending on the source. One woman, the rest of her family dead, was reported to have escaped: "Her clothes were nearly in shreds as she ran through the bushes for twenty miles."[11]

BULLETS WHIZZING "EIGHT INCHES ABOVE HER HEAD"

The Cumberland settlements were caught between Chickasaws coming from the west and Chickamaugas coming from the south. But there was one ingredient lacking: coordination. There is, in fact, no evidence that the Chickasaws and Chickamaugas were even talking to each other. Nevertheless, toward the end of 1780 the situation for the settlements was grim. Many people gave up and retreated to Kentucky, and powder began to run low. Of the original eight stations listed in the Cumberland Compact of 1 May 1780, all but four were abandoned by the end of that year: Fort Nashborough (also known then as French Lick and the Bluffs), Mansker's, Freeland's, and Eaton's. Hunger stalked the diehards. John Cockrill, who had married James Robertson's widowed sister, Ann Johnston, was overcome by the sight of his stepchildren, Mary, Elizabeth, and Charity, trailing their mother around their cabin, saying, "Mother, I'm hungry." John Cockrill said, "I can't stand that; I must have meat or die. So I took up my gun and started. My wife said, 'You better come back; you'll never see the fort again.' I said, the children are starving; I must go. I can see as good as the Indians and I will not follow any path; so they can't waylay me. I went and killed a bear and cut off his skin and, with most of his meat wrapped up in the skin, took it on my back and carried it home. The childen came around as my wife was helping to cut it up. They said, 'Give me a little; I've had nothing for three or four days;' and others said, 'Divide it out; only save some for tomorrow.' Others [Cockrill's neighbors] said, 'My children are starving.' I said, I will go out again tomorrow. Divide it out."[12]

Into the breach stepped the man upon whom all depended. In the winter of 1780–1781, James Robertson made a perilous solo journey to Kentucky to procure powder. He returned with the precious stuff to Freeland's Station on the night of 11 January 1781. Just in time, as it turned out. About midnight he was awakened by noises. He got up to investigate and by the light of the moon saw Indians inside the stockade. They were Chickasaws and they had opened the gate and were stealing horses.[13]

Robertson immediately raised the alarm and the fight began. Children were pushed under the beds, women and girls doused fires and got pails of water ready to foil attempts by the Indians to set fire to the roofs of the cabins, males twelve and up manned portholes. A crescendo of shouts, yells, Indian whoops, barking dogs, bellowing cows, shrieking horses, rifle and musket fire split the air. Charlotte Robertson, James's wife, lay flat with newborn Felix in her arms, bullets whizzing "eight inches above her head." All the confusion and terror of a night encounter reigned. Robertson and the other men finally forced the Indians out of the stockade and closed the gate. The Chickasaws tried to fire the station but failed. The warriors, it was said, howled like wolves.

The fight lasted about three or four hours. Most of the settlers' loss was material: cattle killed, horses run off, fodder stored outside the stockade burned. A Major Lucas and a black slave were killed. One dead Chickasaw was found, and blood trails indicated that several wounded Indians had been carried off.

This was one fight among many, but it reveals a failure of the Indians to take advantage of a most favorable tactical situation. Because of the American failure to mount a sentry, they were able to get over the walls and into the stockade undetected, thus gaining tactical surprise. Then, instead of rushing into the cabins before barking dogs awakened anyone, and tomahawking the men, they wasted time going after the horses. Thus Freeland's Station and the indispensable leader of the Cumberland settlements, James Robertson, survived.

THE DOGS OF WAR

It was now decided by some, including James Robertson and Zachariah White, to leave Freeland's and move a mile upstream to Fort Nashborough. The short dash took the nature of a military movement. All were mounted. Children doubled up with women. A black child rode behind Charlotte Robertson, clinging to her. Packhorses were loaded. With armed men circling the women and children, dogs all around, the whole party went at a gallop. The black child riding behind Charlotte Robertson lost his grip and fell off, but another woman stopped for him and brought him on. If there were Indians in the vicinity, no attempt was made to stop them, and they arrived at Fort Nashborough without mishap.[14]

Fort Nashborough was built by many individuals, but the Buchanans, the Mulherrins, and the Williamses, who had arrived in December 1779, before James Robertson's party, were among the most important occupants. According to one of Lyman Draper's anonymous informants, they were from South Carolina. If that is true, they had probably come north through the Carolina Back Country, at some place crossed the Blue Ridge and then the Unaka Range, and descended into the valley of East Tennessee. Draper's informant reported that they found it "dangerous crossing the mountains for small parties, waited several months when they were augmented to 51 & then started." Among them were John and Alexander Buchanan, John and James Mulherrin, Sampson and Daniel Williams, and Thomas Thompson. Somewhere on the trail they passed Robertson's party. One account states that in their transit through Kentucky the men left the women and children at Clark's Station, near modern Danville, then headed southwesterly and arrived at French Lick "in Decr 1779. The river was frozen over near 220

Charlotte Reeves Robertson (Tennessee Historical Society)

paces wide. They took their abode with the 25 already there." The following fall they fetched the women and children from Kentucky.[15]

The fort built at French Lick was the strongest in the settlements. It was built on the bluffs overlooking the Cumberland, where the steep bank made attack from the riverside unlikely. It was completely stockaded, with the timbers set firmly in the earth and the tops sharpened. The cabins inside were two stories high and had portholes and lookout stations. There was one large gate with a lookout tower for a sentry. The swivel gun, a four-pounder that John Donelson had brought out on his "good boat Adventure," added to Fort Nashborough's strength. One critical feature was a system of troughs that brought water inside the fort from a nearby spring.[16]

The next opportunity of the Indians to deliver a crippling if not mortal blow came that spring when a large force of Chickamauga warriors under Dragging Canoe marched from their towns on the Tennessee against Fort

Nashborough. Opposing them were about 25 adult white gunmen. Although the settlers assumed an Indian presence in the countryside and were on their guard, such a large force was not expected. The night before the attack James Menifee, standing sentry duty, saw an Indian lurking near the fort and fired at him. The rest of the night passed quietly.[17]

Early on the morning of 2 April 1780 the occupants of Fort Nashborough were either preparing for the workday or already engaged in it. Zachariah White, the schoolmaster, was listening to his pupils recite when a number of Indians appeared outside the stockade and attacked. Zachariah grabbed his gun and ran outside and was almost immediately shot and wounded. Old John Buchanan Sr., "tall and spare, blue-eyed, black-haired," was reported to have "killed ten Indians" in a rail pen, although how the old gentleman performed this remarkable feat was left unsaid. The firefight was brief; the Indians retreated downhill and disappeared. The men began what was apparently a prolonged discussion about whether they should ride in pursuit. Sources differ on whether James Robertson approved or disapproved of the tactic, but they finally came to a decision, tightened their cinches, and mounted. Between 20 and 25 men rode out of the fort and headed in the direction the raiding party had taken. Only one man remained in the fort, Zachariah White, whose wound was mortal.

The riders disappeared from sight of the watching women and headed upriver. They had not an inkling of what confronted them. Dragging Canoe was waiting for them with several hundred warriors concealed in a well-planned ambush. About half a mile from the fort half of the Indian force lay hidden from view. They remained hidden and silent as the riders thundered past them. A little farther on Robertson and the others approached a branch where the other half of Dragging Canoe's army was hidden in the brush and cedar stands. This force opened fire on the riders. Robertson and his men reined up hard, jumped out of their saddles, and "treed," as the saying went, each man who survived the initial firing taking post behind a tree to return fire. "At this juncture," wrote John Carr, "the Indians lying between the branch and the fort extended their line to the river, for the purpose of cutting off the retreat of the settlers." The ambush had been perfectly executed: the decoys drawing the riders out of the fort, the first Indian unit allowing them to ride into the trap, the second unit springing it, the white gunmen now taking grievous losses. Peter Gill, John Kesenger, Alexander Buchanan, George Kennedy, Captain Leiper, and J. Kennedy already lay dead on the field, and James Menifee, Kasper Mansker, Isaac Lucas, Joseph Moonshaw, and others were wounded. The little band had suffered at least a 45 percent casualty rate. Robertson and his men faced annihilation, the Cumberland settlements total destruction.

Then it began to fall apart for Dragging Canoe's Chickamaugas. The gunmen's horses panicked and bolted in the direction of the fort. Some of the Indians who had closed the trap halfway between the branch and the fort could not resist the sight of riderless horses complete with tack and their line began to crumble as they chased them in all directions. Meanwhile, it takes little imagination to be aware of the anxiety of the women left at Fort Nashborough. The fighting was out of their sight, but they could hear the firing, the yells, the war whoops, could see gunsmoke rising over the battle-field, and perhaps even the chilling sight of riderless horses with Indians in pursuit. Charlotte Reeves Robertson is credited with then making the crit-ical decision of the fight. The dogs had been locked up so they could not follow the men. Now Charlotte Robertson turned them loose and sent them flying through the gate into battle.

They were big, fierce, mastifflike beasts trained to fight Indians. There must have been dozens of them, for many families had their own packs for hunting and fighting. They boiled down the hill and tore into the first line of Indians and began chewing on them. This gave the gunmen the break they needed to make a desperate retreat for the fort. It was close all the way and took about an hour. The Indians at the branch came on in close pursuit. Ned Swanson was almost at the fort when an Indian caught up with him, shoved the muzzle of his gun up against him, and pulled the trigger. The gun misfired. Swanson grabbed the barrel and they struggled for possession. The Indian recocked, but in the violent struggle the priming powder fell out of the pan. The Indian wrenched the gun away from Swanson, clubbed it, struck Swanson and knocked him to the ground, and then drew his toma-hawk for the coup de grâce. But old John Buchanan Sr., who had regained the fort, rushed out, took aim, shot the Indian dead, and pulled Swanson inside the gate.

Isaac Lucas had also nearly reached safety when a ball hit him and broke his thigh. John Carr wrote, "An Indian rushed up to scalp him. Fortunately, his gun was loaded; and lying upon the ground, he fired, and the Indian fell dead by his side. Great efforts were made by the Indians to drag off their slain warrior, and get the scalp of Lucas. But from the fort they poured death upon them, and finally drove them off and brought Lucas in from his peril-ous situation."

At ten o'clock the Chickamaugas withdrew. There was an attack on the fort that night, but a blast from the swivel gun quickly ended that attempt. The Battle of the Bluffs was over.

We need to analyze this fight, so long ago and long forgotten, for it was critical to the survival of the Cumberland settlements. The settlers had taken a hard blow. Eight dead, several wounded, many of their horses along with bridles and saddles lost, and no one to blame but themselves. They were not greenhorns, they were seasoned borderers well aware of the Indian predilec-tion for using small parties to decoy enemies into well-laid ambushes, and their skill at this tactic. Yet they fell for it and came close to perishing, leav-ing their women and children at the mercy of the enemy and the remaining stations, Freeland's and Eaton's, untenable. For surely the occupants of those two stations would have fled for Kentucky, and would have had good reason to go on their knees and thank their Maker if they got there. One of the key outposts of conquest was almost lost because of a serious tactical error by the men at Fort Nashborough.

But it stood because Charlotte Robertson without hesitation made the right decision, and because the Chickamaugas proved once more that without proper execution the best-laid plans are exercises in futility. The trap was sprung perfectly, but they allowed the prey to escape. We saw the Indians between the gunmen and the fort abandon their positions to chase riderless horses. The other Indians, lying in wait farther on, although heavily outnumbering the whites, failed to overwhelm them quickly in a rush, and then the dogs came and it was too late.

It has been maintained by two modern historians that if the Chickasaws had reinforced the Chickamaugas Fort Nashborough might have been carried, or that 80 warriors from the Overhill Cherokees "arrived too late to bring about the surrender of Fort Nashborough." Neither assertion merits the label of reasonable speculation. No evidence has been presented that the Chickasaws and Chickamaugas ever considered, much less discussed, cooperation. And what possible difference would 80 Overhill Cherokees have made, except to provide more men to chase horses, or for the dogs to chew on? No, these assertions are pure examples of wishful thinking. The real significance of the Battle of the Bluffs is that several hundred Chickamaugas had 20 to 25 white men at their mercy and through their own mistakes and Charlotte Robertson's quick action lost the opportunity to wipe them out and with them the Cumberland settlements.[18]

This is not to maintain that the settlers had not suffered grievous damage. They had lost eight gunmen, close to half of their fighting strength. Many of their precious horses were gone. The attacks had been unrelenting since the previous spring. Family, friends, and neighbors had died violently. The stations had dwindled to three. Now this terrible bloody fight. It broke the will of many, an early source reported: "After this battle a sudden panic seized the people. Most—despairing of being able to accomplish the enterprise of settling the country—determined to remove to Kentucky as a place of safety."[19]

It is said that this decision to leave was taken in council. But one man stood between failure and determination to hang on. "Such a step, however, was violently opposed by Capt. Robertson," wrote John Carr. "He told them it was impossible to get away, because the Indians would waylay and kill them. He reminded them of the hardships already endured by them, and pointed to the beautiful country of which they had thus obtained possession. He urged them to remain another year, in the hope of reinforcements sufficient to put an end to hostilities. Through his influence they agreed to give the settlement the benefit of another year's trial. . . ."[20]

Seventeen eighty-one was a very good year east of the mountains, for on 18 October Lord Cornwallis surrendered to George Washington at Yorktown. But on the Cumberland it was a very bad year, and 1782 brought little respite, especially in the vicinity of Fort Nashborough. Few crops were grown. The "women could not milk the cows or the men go and get a little wood but what they would be shot at." The only source of meat was game, which meant that men had to take the risk to go into the woods.

Some never emerged. People picking berries for sustenance were killed. It was a grim time that went on year after year and never seemed to end. But doom and gloom was not a constant. William Ramsey, arriving from Virginia on Christmas night 1781, entered Eaton's Station and came upon "frolicking and dancing . . . going on in every cabin." And a diplomatic coup that developed gradually lifted the pressure from one direction.[21]

"THE ENGLISH PUT THE BLOODY TOMAHAWK IN OUR HANDS"

In July 1782 an Englishman named Simon Burney escorted by four Chickasaw warriors brought a message from the Chickasaw chiefs to "the Commanders Of Every different Station Between This Nation and the Falls of the Ohio River," that they wished to make peace "for the Bennifitt of our Child[ren]." The Chickasaws had seen the handwriting on the wall. If they were unaware of the precise nature of British defeats at the hands of the Americans east of the mountains, they were quite aware that the Spanish had taken Pensacola and driven the British from western Florida and were once more active in the Mississippi Valley. In its initial reaction Virginia pressed for a land cession, but the Chickasaws were having none of that. The chiefs' message made it quite clear that they were not quite ready to burn all of their bridges: "Youl Observe at the Same Time Our making A Peace with you doth Not Intitle Us to Fall out With Our Fathers the Inglish for we Love them as They were the First People that Ever Supported Us to Defend Our Selves Against Our former Enimys The French & Spanish & All their Indians. & We are a People that Never Forgets Any Kindness done Us by Any Nation." By autumn, however, their diplomacy had taken another tack. They were adamant about not ceding land, but it turned out that the warfare and difficulties between the Chickasaws and the Americans was all the fault of perfidious Albion.[22]

The Chickasaw chiefs explained: "The English put the Bloody Tomahawk in our hands, telling us that we should have no Goods if we did not Exert ourselves to the greatest point of Resentment against you, but now we find our mistake and Distresses. The English have done their utmost and left us in our adversity. We find them full of Deceit and Dissimulation and our women & children are crying out for peace."[23]

But a year passed and nothing happened. Although Chickasaw raids on the Cumberland settlements had stopped early in 1781, a misstep by the Americans might reignite them. The confusion was on the American side and was partly due to the hundreds of miles separating the players and the slowness of eighteenth-century communications by men on horseback riding dangerous trails and traversing great mountain ranges. There was also the problem of coordination between Virginia and North Carolina. A brief description of what ensued should give dwellers in our cyberspace world some idea of the energy, perseverance, and often courage that it took to bring complicated matters to fruition.[24]

In the autumn of 1782 Governor Benjamin Harrison of Virginia offered to appoint John Donelson and the well-known Virginia frontiersman Joseph Martin to enter negotiations for a treaty of peace with the Chickasaws. Both accepted. Then silence. Harrison continued his activities for peace with the Indians, but failed to keep Donelson and Martin informed. John Donelson mounted his horse in late 1782 and made a winter ride eastward over the mountains to see Joseph Martin at his house at the Long Island of the Holston in an attempt to find out what was happening, but Martin had not heard from Harrison, either. Donelson then rode north into Virginia and met on the road Governor Harrison's emissary with commissions and instructions. Returning to Martin's house, Donelson and Martin then rode eastward over the Unaka Mountains and the Blue Ridge and descended to the North Carolina Piedmont town of Hillsborough, where the North Carolina legislature was in session. They found the legislators interested in little else but western lands, and they, too, were soon bitten by the same bug. One of the legislators, the businessman and big-time land speculator William Blount (pronounced "blunt"), who will play an important role in our story, arranged for Donelson and Martin to represent his group in its designs on lands lying north of Muscle Shoals, through which Donelson had made his perilous voyage two years before.[25] That complicated business must not detain us, however, except to note that our two well-traveled frontiersmen once more rode several hundred miles over the mountains and, combining private business with official, met with the Chickamaugas and bought the land north of the Great Bent of the Tennessee for £1,000 in trade goods: "cheap enough," William Blount wrote to Joseph Martin on 26 October 1783.[26]

But what of the Chickasaws? They had been waiting a year for an answer and they were growing impatient. They had written again on 28 July 1783, but this time to Congress. The letter shows their confusion over whom to deal with, and also that they could, if they chose, deal with the Spanish. "The Spaniards are sending talks amongst us, and inviting our young Men to trade with them. We also receive talks from Georgia to the same effect. We have had speeches from the Illinois inviting us to a Trade and Intercourse with them. Our Brothers, the Virginians Call upon us to a Treaty, and want part of our land, and we expect our Neighbors who live on Cumberland River, will in a little time Demand, if not forcibly take part of it from us, also we are informed they have been marking Lines through our hunting grounds: we are daily receiving Talks from one Place or other, and from People we Know nothing bout. We know not who to mind or who to neglect." But although reminding the Americans once more that "we can supply ourselves from the Spaniards," they professed to "being averse to hold any intercourse with them, as our hearts are always with our brothers the Americans."[27]

This was not completely true. There was an American party within the Chickasaw Nation, but also a Spanish party, and the chiefs were tiptoeing through a minefield of fierce passions. The Spanish had an advantage over the Americans: they lacked that insatiable drive for land that made the

Chickasaws rightly suspicious of American overtures. Nevertheless, on 5 November 1783, John Donelson, Joseph Martin, and John Reid finally met with all of the Chickasaw chiefs at French Lick. The Indians complained bitterly about land speculators disguised as hunters, but the question of land was set aside, although it was made clear that the Chickasaws would not cede any land. All agreed that the boundary would be surveyed. The most important result from the point of view of the Cumberland settlers was that peace was declared between Americans and Chickasaws. No longer would the pioneers have to look over their shoulders as they confronted Chickamauga war parties coming from the south. The Chickasaws would continue to be pulled in two directions by the factions within their society, but the peace held, and the words of the dominant pro-American chief, Piomingo, delivered at the end of the conference, reflected reality then and for the future: "Peace is Now Settled, I was the first that proposed it . . . & Am in hope No more Blood [may be] Shed by Either party."[28]

One potential threat had been neutralized, but a danger just as serious was rising to the south, beyond the Chickamauga towns in the powerful Creek Nation, from which came a man who was one of the dominant figures of his time.

Chapter 6

"I Am a Native of This Nation & of Rank in It"

WHAT RIGHT DID GREAT BRITAIN HAVE
TO CEDE IT TO THE AMERICANS?

Far more white blood flowed in his veins than Indian. He was sent by his father to Charleston to study Greek, Latin, and English history and literature with a private tutor. He wrote and spoke English with an ease that escaped most Indians. A war leader but not a warrior, he was honored by the Creeks with the unique title of *Isti atcagagi thlucco,* "Great Beloved Man." Befitting a leader in perilous and turbulent times, he could be ruthless when necessary, as when he ordered the public execution of "three *white men* who had undertaken to lead the faction against him; but he finally crushed the insurgents, and effected his purposes." He wrote of this incident, "Ever Since the Execution of Cor. Sullivan the whole white people in this nation behave remarkably well & live with the Indians very Quietly. Public exmples are sometimes necessary particularly in this Country, as executing one notorious offender, sometimes save the lives of severals. . . ." Of all the great Indian leaders he is probably the least known; in fact, it would not be an exaggeration to refer to him as unknown. Yet one cannot fail to agree with the historian who wrote, "North America has produced no more extraordinary Indian leader than Alexander McGillivray.[1]

He was born on 15 December 1750 on his father's plantation at Little Tallassee, "or Village of the Hickory Trees," on the Coosa River in east-central Alabama, just north of modern Montgomery. He was of Scots-Creek-French ancestry. His father, Lachlan McGillivray, was a Scots trader who left his impoverished Highland home in 1735 for the same reason that most people have come to America, and he did very well indeed. Lachlan McGillivray not only prospered; he became an important man in the Creek Nation.

A key factor in his rise was his marriage to a Creek woman, Sehoy Marchand, daughter of a French officer, probably Captain Marchand de Martel, commander of the Alabama district, and a Creek woman. Creek society was clan based, and Sehoy Marchand belonged to the most prestigious of Creek clans, the Wind Clan. Their society was also matrilineal—that is, descent was traced through the mother's family—thus Alexander automatically became a member of his mother's powerful clan. The boy spent the first fourteen years of his life at Tallassee, and they must have been at least pleasant, and probably idyllic, for when the time came for Alexander to make a choice his direction homeward was unerring. The home under his father and later himself was more than a trading post, for Lachlan also became a planter. Many years later the French adventurer Louis LeClerc de Milford traveled to Little Tallassee with Alexander and wrote, "This habitation seemed very beautiful to me; McGillivray had sixty negroes in his service, each of whom had a cabin of his own, which gave this plantation the air of a little village." In 1791 the American traveler John Pope gave a fuller description of Alexander McGillivray's home and its surroundings.[2]

Pope located "General *McGillivray's* house . . . on the *Cousee* River, about 5 Miles above its Junction with the Tallipoosee. . . ." Upon his arrival, he was informed that McGillivray "had just gone to his upper Plantation, on the same river, about 6 miles distant from his present Residence. Thither I impaired in Company with his Nephew, who supplied me with an *Indian's* stray horse. We had not ridden far, before we unfortunately met the Owner, who, with a menacing Countenance and *sans Ceremonie* seized the Bridle and ordered me to dismount immediately. An Hour's Walk brought me to the Place, where the General was superintending some Workmen in the Erection of a Log House embellished with dormer Windows, on the very Spot where his Father resided whilst a Trader in the Nation. Here are some tall old Apple-trees planted by his Father, which make a venerable appearance, tho' greatly obstruct the Prospect to and from his rural humble Palace." He had "also large Stocks of Horses, Hogs, and horned Cattle. Two or three White Men superintend their respective Ranges, and now and then collect them together in Order to brand, Mark, etc." McGillivray's bountiful fields and herds were matched in his home: "His Table smokes with good substantial Diet, and his Side-board displays a Variety of Wines and ardent spirits."[3]

His mother saw to Alexander's upbringing, for that was the Creek way. Another way was to supplement the education and training he received at the hands of his mother with that of a maternal uncle, and we assume that occurred in Alexander's case. Creek fathers were not expected to become closely involved in this matter. But Lachlan McGillivray was a Scot, and Alexander was literate when, at the age of fourteen, his father took him to Charleston. It was obviously Lachlan who insisted that his son go to that cosmopolitan entrepôt that he might also learn firsthand of the white world and how to deal with it. According to Pope, "Dissipation marked his juvenile Days, and sapped a Constitution originally delicate and feeble." If that is so, Charleston, described by a German mercenary during the Revolution as famous for its "grandiose display of splendor, debauchery, luxury and extravagance," offered every opportunity to a boy from the deep hinterland to indulge his appetites. According to Albert Pickett, who knew McGillivray's grandchildren, in the great city Alexander was placed in school, and a few years later was sent to Savannah to work in Samuel Elbert's countinghouse, and then with Alexander Inglis and Company. While there he lived outside the city on another of his father's plantations. But Alexander did not take to Bob Cratchit's world, and his father took him back to Charleston to study under the boy's cousin, Reverend Farquhar McGillivray, a Presbyterian minister. That, at least, is Pickett's tale.[4]

With the outbreak of the War of the American Revolution in 1775, the McGillivrays, father and son, faced decisions and danger. It was well known on the frontier and in the Carolina and Georgia Back Country that Lachlan McGillivray was a staunch Tory. In Georgia the Rebels put his name at the top of the proscribed list and confiscated property worth more than $100,000. By then he had been in America for forty years. Most of that time he had worked hard in a dangerous environment. Now he was wealthy. Could he think of one good reason why he should risk everything, even his life, if the Rebels caught him? Whatever his reasoning, Lachlan McGillivray, who by then was living in Savannah, went home to Scotland to enjoy his money following the city's surrender to the Americans in 1782. Father and son never saw each other again. In 1777 Alexander went home to Little Tallassee, as ardent a supporter of the Loyalist cause as his father, and British authorities thought well enough of him to make him assistant commissary in the Indian service.[5]

Alexander McGillivray took the field for the British during the war and gave good service, for example, leading a small party of warriors to join the British army in Savannah. But he has never been identified with any battle exploits that define the warrior. Quite the contrary, according to the Frenchman Milford, who married McGillivray's sister. Although Milford's *Memoir* is often overblown and inaccurate, his story of what may have been McGillivray's lone combat experience bears repeating. Milford relates that he persuaded McGillivray to observe the Anglo-Creek force in the field and that just outside Augusta, Georgia, they engaged in a sharp action with the Rebels. "Right at the very beginning of the engagement McGillivray hid in the underbrush, where he remained until nightfall. Winter was then coming on, and he began to feel cold; since we ordinarily fought naked, with the body painted in different colors, he was obliged to do the same when he came to the camp so that he suffered greatly from the cold and could do nothing about it till the engagement was over. He then came out of hiding and courageously went on to the battlefield to despoil one of the Anglo-American dead and wrap himself in the latter's cloak. He rejoined me three days later and said he did not like to witness such affairs, that never again would he be caught in a similar situation, and in fact he left at once. Since then we have often laughed over his terror and the Anglo-American's cloak. When one possesses such executive ability and so many fine qualities as

Alexander McGillivray, one does not need military virtues to be a great man."[6]

Even if Milford's story is either not true or partially true, his final sentence should be taken to heart. The Creeks did not lack for brave warriors. But when it came to "executive ability" and diplomatic skill the nation had only one Alexander McGillivray. When the War of the Revolution ended with the British defeated, and the Peace of Paris signed in 1783 between Great Britain and the independent United States of America, the Creeks had desperate need of a keen intelligence combined with shrewd judgment and cool diplomacy to guide them in a world turned suddenly upside down.

For in place of a relatively benign British imperial administration the Creeks and all other Indians now faced the human version of a plague of locusts that differed from the insect world in that they would never go away. They were not temporary ravagers, they were here to stay and they wanted everything and if you did not give it to them they would take it. And it was now theirs to take, was it not? They had won the war and the British had handed over to them half a continent. Let us take a brief look at that aspect of the peace negotiations and what the Americans won.

One of the most significant, and wisest, diplomatic decisions in American history took place in Paris in the autumn of 1782, when John Adams, Benjamin Franklin, and John Jay decided to ignore their instructions from Congress to consult fully with their French allies, to violate Article 8 of the Franco-American Treaty of Alliance, and negotiate directly with the British peace commissioners. The result was a territorial bonanza for the Americans. The British handed over the western lands from the Appalachians to the Mississippi, from the Canadian border to the thirty-first parallel, which separated those lands from Spanish Louisiana. The parallel, which is the modern Mississippi-Louisiana state line, ran east from the Mississippi River to the modern Alabama-Florida line and on to the Chattahoochee River, which now separates the states of Alabama and Georgia. From there the demarcation line left the thirty-first parallel and ran south to Florida, where the Chattahoochee becomes the Apalachicola; there the line again turned east and followed the present Georgia-Florida line to the Saint Mary's River and down the Saint Mary's to the Atlantic. To bring it even closer to home to the twenty-first-century reader, this vast expanse of country includes all or part of the modern states of Minnesota, Wisconsin, Michigan, Illinois, Indiana, Ohio, Kentucky, Tennessee, Mississippi, Alabama, and Georgia. Of it the Englishman Benjamin Vaughn, who was closely involved in the negotiations, remarked, "It was not worth a cavil." The French, on the other hand, were astounded. "The treaty with America seems to me a dream," the French undersecretary of state wrote to the foreign minister.

When one contemplates what might have been had Spanish hopes or French compromise prevailed, one can only see the balkanization of North America and the ancient feuds of Europe that we witnessed in the twentieth century visited upon its peoples. Spain wanted as much of the territory as it could get, at one point even submitting a map that included most of the

Old Northwest as well as the Old Southwest. France rejected any legal claim of the United States to the territory, and even a historian who defends French conduct during the negotiations "suspects that, given her choice, she would have preferred to have the West left, like Canada, in British hands so as to increase American dependence on the French alliance." The decision of the American commissioners to treat directly with Britain was one of the key factors in gaining this empire beyond the mountains.[7]

There is a problem with this rosy picture, however, and a major problem indeed. Nobody had consulted the Indian nations who lived there and knew in their hearts and minds that it was not England's to give away, nor Spain's to claim, nor the Americans to own. It was theirs, and they meant to keep it, and the strongest military forces from the tall mountains to the mighty river, from the Great Lakes to the Gulf, were also theirs. They were dumbfounded, outraged at the British betrayal, and some wasted little time in looking elsewhere for support and protection from the American juggernaut.

The preliminary peace treaty between Britain and the United States was signed on 30 November 1782. It differed little, and not at all substantially, from the definitive Peace of Paris signed 3 September 1783. Sometime between those two dates Alexander McGillivray learned of the great betrayal. About mid-September 1783, he appeared in Pensacola and met the Spanish governor, Arturo O'Neill, a forty-seven-year-old soldier of Irish birth and parentage who migrated to Spain with his parents and long and loyally served his adopted country.

O'Neill saw before him a tall man, "rather slender, and of a constitution by no means robust," his forehead broad and high, his demeanor grave, his eyes piercing, a man on the eve of his greatest work, a leader of vision and one of the consummate diplomats of his time, hated and admired, feared and respected, his genes mostly white, culturally straddling two worlds, who had chosen his mother's people and would serve them faithfully and brilliantly to the end. McGillivray, O'Neill reported, "had come to solicit the establishment of a trade with them for the purchase of their deer-skins, offering his services to enlist the friendship of the different towns his neighbors. He as well as various other Indians friendly to us will refuse to gather at a congress offered them by the Americans in Augusta and Savannah." O'Neill advised acceptance of McGillivray's proposal, "since in what other fashion can we be assured of the trade and friendship of the Indians, who at present are strongly opposed to the name of Americans?"[8]

In chapter 1 we touched briefly on the Creek political system. At this point we should describe as precisely as possible McGillivray's position in the Creek political hierarchy, the nature of the society in which he operated, and his attempt to change the system to meet changing times.[9]

The modern American political saying "All politics are local" neatly fits Creek society. We have noted that it was strongly clan based. It was also town based. In the eighteenth century there were between fifty to eighty towns among the Lower Creeks situated mainly in Georgia in the Chattahoochee, Flint, and Ocmulgee river valleys, and the Upper Creeks who were separated from their brethren by some one hundred miles of swampy, heavily forested country and lived in towns on the Coosa, Tallapoosa, and Alabama Rivers in central and eastern Alabama. The terms "Lower" and "Upper" Creeks were convenient words coined by whites in colonial times.

We habitually speak of the Creek Confederacy, and it did exist, but in the loosest sense. The Creek Nation was a term common in the eighteenth century and after among whites and Indians, but it was not a nation as we understand the word. Creek loyalty was to the town. A leading scholar of the Creeks described their society "as an assocation of separate, distinct, sovereign, and independent groups . . . a loose gathering of tribes that maintained peace between its constituents and provided both a defensive security and a potential for allied offensive action. But each town retained its autonomy, and there is no known instance of an intertown unity so complete as to suggest the existence of a Creek state."[10] Nor were they Creeks. That word, too, was coined in the late seventeenth century by traders from Charleston. The Creek Confederacy was based on an ancient alliance of peoples who spoke different languages and had different pasts: Cowetas, Cussetas, Tuckabatchees, Alabamas, Koasatis, Hitchiti, Abeikas, and others. Is it any wonder then that factionalism was rife and that it often paralyzed the National Council of the Confederacy? For the National Council was neither conceived as nor intended to be a national body with either legislative or executive powers. In short, it could not coerce the towns to do anything they did not want to do. Alexander McGillivray set out to change that, to bring central authority to Creek government to meet perilous times.

He had the advantages of his own high intelligence and fluency in English, his British appointment during the war as assistant commissary, the prestige of his mother's clan, and the power and influence of his maternal uncle, Red Shoes, a *mico* of McGillivray's tribe, the Koasati. He was never a *mico,* never a member of the National Council. He was too young. But the Creeks had among them many Beloved Men respected for their knowledge and good judgment who were unofficial advisers to *micos* and the National Council, much as American presidents consult with men and women outside government in whom they have confidence. McGillivray fell into this category, but with a difference. He was young for such standing, but his wisdom, accomplishments, prestige, and, it is important to add, control of trade led the Creeks to call him what they called no other: Great Beloved Man. Obviously, he was a cut above the rest, and most of the *micos* followed his advice.

But Creek society was deeply conservative. "No People under Heaven are more attached to, or swerve less from, the Customs of their Ancestors than the *Creeks*," John Pope wrote in 1790. McGillivray also had enemies, and two of them were important headmen. In the upper town of Tallassee, Hoboithle Mico, the Tame King, carried on a campaign of stout resistance to McGillivray and sabotaged his efforts to centralize authority. Eneah Mico, the Fat King of the important lower town of Cusseta, was also adamant in opposing McGillivray. An American agent reported that Hoboithle Mico "with his clan pronounced McGillivray a boy and an usurper," guilty of

Hoboithle Mico, 1790, by John Trumbull (National
Anthropological Archives, Smithsonian Institution)

actions "derogatory to his family clan and consequence." This may refer to
something that McGillivray was able to accomplish that infuriated some of
the *micos*. In time of peace the Creek civil leaders governed the towns. In
wartime, however, warriors with more powers of coercion took over. When
peace came again the warriors stepped aside. McGillivray, however, because
of the continuing emergency situation in which the Creeks found themselves at the end of the American Revolution, managed to change that. The
warriors, especially in the upper towns where he was strongest, retained their
powers at the expense of the civil *micos*. John Pope described the situation
clearly in 1790: "*McGillivray* who is perpetual Dictator, in Time of war sub-
delegates a Number of Chieftains for the Direction of all military Operations; and when the War concludes, they, in Compensation for their martial
Atchievements, are invested by the Dictator with civil Authority which
supercedes the hereditary Powers of their Demi-Kings."[11]

At the same time Creek society was undergoing another radical change. The accumulation of property was foreign to Creeks, and in time of need they generously shared food and other material goods. But decades of exposure to white traders and their foreign ways, and the example set by the traders' mixed-blood children, who were considered Creeks and lived in the nation, had a profound and divisive effect on Creek society. Alexander McGillivray and other Creeks, especially mixed bloods, had adopted the Western system of private property and enterprise. This led to deep inequities and festering resentment that grew over the years. But we should not allow this messy economic change to blind us to one overwhelming fact: McGillivray's goal of a politically unified Creek Nation was the only possible way in which the Creeks might be able to withstand the American invasion. In this McGillivray was a visionary, keenly aware of the price the Creeks would pay for failure to follow his vision. His enemies Hoboithle Mico and Eneah Mico and those who followed them, determined to hew to traditional ways, were reactionaries wed to a system of governance unfitted for the new world in which the Creeks found themselves.[12]

As we noted at the beginning of the chapter, McGillivray resorted to violence to subdue opposing factions. Four white men in the nation died because of their active involvement with Creeks opposed to McGillivray. But he knew just how far he could go, and, to his occasional regret, his fellow Creeks were off limits. With regard to Hoboithle Mico and Eneah Mico, and others of like persuasion, he once wrote to Governor Vizente Manuel de Zéspedes of East Florida, "I lament that our Customs (unlike those of Civilized people) Wont permit us to treat as traitors by giving them the usual punishment." Some will find such methods abhorrent, but they never walked in McGillivray's moccasins as he tried to save a people on the brink of destruction.[13]

At the beginning of the New Year, 1784, McGillivray wrote to O'Neill describing the strong efforts of the Americans to establish trade with the Creeks and "fix this Nation in their Interests which if they are allowed to effect they Will Make the worst use of their Influence & will cause the Indians from being freindly to Spain to become Very dangerous Neighbors." The broad hint was not lost on O'Neill. He forwarded copies of the letter to Josef de Ezpeleta, acting captain general at Havana, and Estevan Miró, governor of Louisiana with headquarters in New Orleans. About a month and a half later McGillivray established direct contact with Miró. He reviewed his talks with Governor O'Neill and discussed trade at some length. He told the governor that he had "offer'd to put the Creek Nation under his Most Catholic Majesty's Protection, as the Americans pretend we are in their Boundary," and that he "had the satisfaction of receiving a most favourable reply from Governor O'Neill, who likewise acquainted me with your Intention of holding a General Congress with the Indians at Pensacola in May next when these matters would be settled." But the primary purpose of the letter seems to have been his wish to let Miró know precisely who he was and what he was capable of doing.

"It is necessary for me to Inform you that I am a Native of this Nation & of rank in it. At the commencement of the American Rebellion, I entered into the British Service & after a long Contest of faithfull Services we have at the Close been most Shamefully deserted as well as every other people that has relied on their honor & Fidelity.

"For the good of my Country I have Sacrificed my all & it is a duty incumbent on me in this Critical Situation to exert myself for their Interest. The protection of a great Monarch is to be preferred to that of a distracted Republic. If I am disappointed in my Expectations, I must as the last necessity embrace the american offers, however disagreeable it may be to my political opinions. I still hope that at our meeting every Matter will be agreeably settled."[14]

McGillivray's reference to his "political opinions" reveals his deep respect for monarchy and his disdain for republicanism. The American experiment was regarded with fear and loathing by Tories and the European establishment, for the republican form of government was as radical and hated in the eighteenth century as communism in the twentieth.

The Spanish had taken to heart McGillivray's candid appraisal of the situation: either the Creeks reach an agreement with Spain or they would turn to the Americans. On 30 May 1784, Miró, O'Neill, and Martin Navarro, intendant of Louisiana, opened a two-day congress with Creek representatives at Pensacola. The resulting Treaty of Pensacola, signed by the three Spaniards and Alexander McGillivray, established a "permanent and unalterable commerce." Spain guaranteed Creek lands that fell within Spanish territory, and if they ever lost their other lands to enemies of Spain, the king agreed to "grant them others, Equivalent, which may be vacant. . . ." About a week after the congress Miró wrote to McGillivray appointing him Spanish commissary to the Creek Nation at an annual salary of 600 pesos. This meant that McGillivray controlled the trade. He had not only been the prime instigator in establishing this relationship with the Spanish, he would run the operation in Creek country. Given the absolute necessity of trade to the Creeks, this put him in a powerful position well beyond his years.[15]

As is always the case in relationships between nations, however, it required constant tending, especially as new situations arose. About 10 July 1785, representatives of the Creeks, the Cherokees, and the Chickasaws met to discuss the new world they faced. The matter had become urgent, for they had "received information that an Envoy has been appointed by his Most Catholic Majesty the King of Spain for the purpose of settling the boundarys of his territorys and those of the United States of America. . . ." Alexander McGillivray was one of the Creek representatives, and it was natural that the chiefs turned to this man who was one of them but also had been educated and trained in the ways of the white world to convey their position to the Spanish envoy in New York, Diego de Gardoqui.[16]

McGillivray got right to the point. The "Cheifs and Warriors . . . have reason to Apprehend that the American Congress . . . will endeavor to avail themselves of the Late treaty of peace between them and the British Nation and that they will aim at getting his Majesty the King of Spain to confirm to them that Extensive Territory the Lines of which are drawn by the Said treaty and which includes the whole of our hunting Grounds to our Great Injury and ruin." He then vigorously contested the right of the United States to "title claim or demand . . . against our lands, Settlements, and hunting Grounds in Consequence of the Said treaty. . . ." And what right did Great Britain have to cede it to the Americans, "as we were not partys, so we are determined to pay no attention to the Manner in which the British Negotiators has drawn out the Lines of the Lands in question Ceded to the States of America—it being a Notorious fact known to the Americans known to every person who is in any ways conversant in, or acquainted with American affairs, that his Britannick Majesty was never possessed either by session purchase or by right of Conquest of our Territorys and which the Said treaty gives away. On the contrary it is well known that from the first settlement of the English colonys of Carolina and Georgia up to the date of the said treaty no tittle has ever been or pretended to be made by his Britannic Majesty to our land except what was obtainable by free Gift or by purchase for good and valuable Considerations.

"We can urge in Evidence upon this occasion the Cessions of Lands made to the Carolinians and Georgians by us at different periods and one so late as June 1773 of the Lands lying on the bank of the River OGeechee for which we were paid a Sum not less than one hundred and twenty thousand pounds Stg. nor has any treaty been held by us Since that period for the purpose of granting any land to any people whatever. . . ."

McGillivray then made quite clear the Indians' outrage, their sense of betrayal at the hands of Great Britain. They, the "Nations of Creeks, Chickasaws and Cherokees" had committed no "act to forfeit our Independence and natural Rights to the Said King of Great Britain that could invest him with the power of giving our property away unless fighting by the side of his soldiers in the day of battle and Spilling our best blood in the Service of his nation can be deemed so."

He mentioned recent encroachments by the Americans, beyond the Oconee River in Georgia, and "Witness the Large Settlement called Cumberland and others on the Mississippi . . . all encroachments on our hunting Grounds." Despite repeated warnings to the Americans to cease and desist, "to these remonstrances we have received friendly talks and replys it is true but while they are addressing us by the flattering appellations of Friends and Brothers they are Stripping us of our natural rights by depriving us of that inheritance which belonged to our ancestors and hath descended from them to us Since the beginning of time."

Having made his case, McGillivray on behalf of the three nations reminded the king that at the congress at Pensacola the Indians had "implored his favor and protection" and that the king "was pleased to express his favorable disposition toward" them. In view of that, and "having the greatest Confidence in the Good faith, humanity and Justice of His Most Greacious Majesty the King of Spain we trust that he will enter into no terms with the American States that may Strengthen their claims or that may tend to deprive us of our Just inheritance."[17]

But in McGillivray's letter of transmittal to Governor O'Neill he once more made equally clear the cold, hard economic realities of the time and place: the importance of the Indian trade and the Indians' dependence upon it, which would take them wherever it was available. The fifth column that we referred to in chapter 1 had wormed its way into the very bowels of Indian society. McGillivray assured O'Neill that the "Nations are exceedingly well Satisfied at the arrival of the Supply of Indian Trading Goods brought by Mr. Panton for the Support of their Nations & they expect that the Trade thus begun will be established on the most permanent footing as was promised them. . . . The supply being now nearly expended, another Importation is become absolutely necessary." But the Americans, he cautioned, "have been using every means in their power to Seduce these Nations from the engagements they have entered into with the Spanish Nation, particularly by offers of a Liberal Trade & which it is Certainly in their power to afford to the Indians. . . ."

He admitted that the Americans were operating under a severe handicap, for the recollection by the Indians of "past Injurys & the Strong Jealousy which Subsists among them lest they Should be deprived of their hunting Grounds (the greatest Injury an Indian can form an Idea of) affords a favorable opportunity of effecting a total Separation of those Nations from the Americans & of establishing an Interest Among them for the Spanish Nation which will not be easily dissolved, and which it is my most ardent wishes to accomplish."

The Spanish, however, should tend to the business and not be complacent. For if the Indians were "not allowed their usual Supplys from this place [Pensacola], necessity must compel them to accept the Friendship of the American States, through which Channel They will be Supplyd with all of their accustomed necessarys to the exclusion of every power on the Continent." McGillivray reminded the Spanish of this on more than one occasion; for example, writing to O'Neill in 1784 that "Indians will always attach themselves to & serve them best who Supply their Necessities." Nothing had changed in this critical aspect of relations between Indians and whites, for the reader will recall Thomas Nairne's even pithier statement of 1708: "They effect them most who sell best cheap."[18]

McGillivray attempted to improve his control of trade by urging the Spanish to allow the British firm of Panton, Leslie & Company, of which he was a silent partner, to supply the Indians from Pensacola, and he eventually succeeded, for Spain was not a manufacturing country, and only Panton, Leslie had access to British goods. Panton, Leslie traders took up residence in all towns loyal to McGillivray, but towns siding with his opponents had difficulty getting resident traders and supplies, including munitions. Daniel McMurphy, an agent from the state of Georgia, wrote from Lower Creek country to Governor O'Neill in protest, for "upon my arrival here I called the principal Indians together & also the Traders requring them to Show their Lycences When I found they had not got any from the State of Georgia, but had a Lycence from Alexander McGillivray. The Said Traders to be Subject to him & no other. . . ." McMurphy tried to arrange for McGillivray's assassination, failed, and fled to Georgia when the Creeks and Spanish came looking for him. It would not be the last time that Georgia tried to kill Alexander McGillivray.[19]

THE AMERICANS "ARE STRETCHING ACROSS TO THE MISSISSIPPI"

The reader by now is no doubt aware that the Americans of that time, especially frontiersmen, were feared and disdained by all who came up against them in North America. Like Goths and Vandals of old, like Arab horsemen sweeping across continents in the name of religion, like the Mongol Horde destroying Islamic cities that never recovered, like Zulu impis unleashing bloodbaths on fellow Africans, the Americans were on their march of conquest. The Creeks called the Georgians *Ecunnaunuxulgee*—"people greedily grasping after the lands of the red people." Governor Zéspedes of East Florida, after observing in the late 1780s the Georgia backwoodsmen who had crossed the St. Mary's River into Spanish territory, reported home that they were "nomadic like Arabs and . . . distinguished themselves from savages only in their color, language, and the superiority of their depraved cunning and untrustworthiness." François Valle, a French Creole of Ste. Genevieve on the Missouri side of the Mississippi, branded them as a "peuple sans loix ni discipline" (people without laws or discipline). Alexander McGillivray was "well Acquainted with the turbulent and restless disposition of our American Neighbourhood," and by 1786, if not sooner, he and most of the chiefs of the Upper Creeks were feeling the pressure all around them. For the Creeks had no hinterland for retreat.[20]

The Georgians lay to the east. To the north were the Cherokees and the Cumberland settlements. Behind them, westward, were the Choctaws and the Chickasaws, and although the Spanish were holding onto Natchez and had posts northward on the Mississippi, the Americans were floating down the great river in increasing numbers seeking land, land, and more land. Between the Creeks and their western neighbors, the Choctaws and Chickasaws, another disturbing development was taking place. Along the Alabama and Tombigbee river systems, Americans were settling in territory claimed by Spain. It had begun during the Revolutionary War with Tory families fleeing South Carolina and Georgia. When William Bartram was traveling with traders from Mobile to the Creek Nation in November–December 1777, "a few days before we arrived at the Nation, we met a company of emigrants from Georgia; a man, his wife, a young woman, several young children, and three stout young men, with about a dozen horses loaded with their property. They informed us their design was to settle on the Alabama, a few miles above the confluence of the Tombigbe." Misfortune descended upon this particular group. Bartram related that a few days later while camped among the Creeks on the Tallapoosa, "late in the evening a young white man, in great haste and seeming confusion, joined our camp, who immediately related, that being on his journey from Pensacola, it happened that the very night after we had passed the company of emigrants, he met them and joined their camp in the evening; when, just after dark, the Choctaws surrounded them, plundered their camp, and carried all the people off captive, except himself, he having the good fortune to escape with his horse, though closely pursued."[21]

More Loyalists arrived after the war. Alexander McGillivray had no problem with the Loyalists and in 1784 encouraged Governor O'Neill to let them settle in West Florida, for they were "people of good Characters," and "men who have been accustomed to Industry, well Skilled in Farming, and raising Stock or any thing in that way, which would soon put that province in a very flourishing Situation & of course become Valuable for its products & Supplys for every kind, whether for the Kings Garrison or shipping."[22]

By 1786, however, Americans of a different sort were arriving, and it was raising alarm bells among the Upper Creeks, as McGillivray explained to O'Neill. They "are proceeding to the head of the Alabamoun River, that falls into the Bay of Mobile & from thence they are Stretching across to the Mississippi. Under such Circumstances we cannot be quiet spectators. We the Chiefs of the Nation have come to a resolution in this last general meeting to take arms in our defence & repel those Invaders of our Lands, to drive them from their encroachments & fix them within their own proper limits." The Creeks meant first to deal with the Georgians who were moving onto the lands between the Oconee and Ocmulgee Rivers. "When this is done we Shall then have leisure to turn our attention to the Lands we possess toward the Mississippi & toward which the americans are moving in numbers of families. That Quarter ought to be well looked after, lest by giving time to them they form Considerable establishments on lands they have no right to, & of Consquence may prove troublesome to remove." He also informed O'Neill that the Creeks had recommended to the Choctaws and Chickasaws to consider these Americans between them "as Common enemies, to take care of and not be duped by their promises." These new settlers would indeed prove troublesome to remove, and as we shall see in the course of our narrative their history is tied directly to the political and military fortunes of a Tennessee frontiersman named Andrew Jackson, to whom we shall soon return.[23]

"THEY KILLED AND SCALPED MY POOR BROTHER"

Despite his deep concern with the Alabama-Tombigbee settlements, McGillivray always vigorously denied accusations that he instigated attacks on them. But he was not at all reticent in claiming credit for his central role in unleashing devastating attacks on the Georgia and Cumberland frontiers. In a letter to Governor Miró he stated that after the chiefs accepted his advice "I then Issued orders and Instructions needful for the occasion & directed them to Collect a Sufficient Number of Warriors & to Set out without loss of time & to traverse all that part of the Country in dispute & whenever they found any American Settlers to drive them off & destroy all the buildings on it but in their progress to conduct themselves with moderation & to shed no blood on no pretence but where Self defense made it absolutely necessary. Neither were they to cross over or within the acknowledged Limits of the States."[24]

The Creeks were well armed for war. On 20 June 1786 Miró informed O'Neill that McGillivray had asked for "five thousand pounds of powder and balls" and that "he would be satisfied now to receive half. . . ." But Miró gave O'Neill precise instructions to make every effort to keep the source of munitions hidden.

"The matter should be handled with the greatest circumspection; therefore I hope that you will prudently find means to deliver these supplies with the fewest possible persons knowing about it. If you know someone in whom you have absolute confidence, I would think it a good method to deposit this ammunition in his warehouse, so that in all events they might seem to have been bought by McGillebray. I recommend the further arrangement that the Indians should come to get them at different times, as from week to week, with only two horses each time, in order that they would appear to have been purchased by different tribes. They should be careful always to take them out at night or at an hour when there probably would be no one in the neighborhood to notice it."[25]

Their powder horns and ammunition pouches filled with Spanish largesse, Creek warriors crisscrossed the land between the Ogeechee and Oconee Rivers in Georgia and expelled the settlers. With the stubbornness fused with fatalism that had marked them from the earliest days, settlers returned in the winter of 1786–1787, and that spring Creek warriors once more cleansed the disputed land of whites. According to McGillivray, "The Americans of Georgia were removed without Injury to their persons. . . ."[26]

Carnage, however, swept the Cumberland country, McGillivray's early protestation to the contrary: "a few were killed at Cumberland which was unavoidable as those people bear extreme hatred & rancour to Indians, & the latter from a Sense of the many Injurys they had Sustained from the Inhabitants there caused them to exceed their orders in Satisfying their revenge." John Carr lists at least eighty-six people killed during the three bloody years, 1786–1788. But instead of reciting names and one shooting and tomahawking and scalping after another, let us put a human face on contested frontiers and follow the adventures of thirteen-year-old William Hall Jr. in the summer of 1787.[27]

On 3 June William and his brother James left the home of their father, Major William Hall, to round up their horses. About a quarter of a mile from the house 15 Indians lay in ambush for targets of opportunity coming from either direction: 10 were hidden behind logs by the side of the road, while the other 5 were fifty yards ahead out of sight by a "gap of the pasture fence." The first group let the boys walk past them, then rose and quietly closed in on their unsuspecting prey. James turned to his brother to suggest using corn to catch the horses, and William then "saw the whole ten hemming us in." The warriors had "their tomahawks in their right hands and their guns in their left." William thought their position hopeless and had decided to surrender, when "the next thing I saw two of them had struck my brother as he turned around, each sinking his tomahawk into his brain one on either side of his forehead." That drove all thoughts of surrender from William's mind. "I sought to dodge the ten, when up rose the other five . . . and as I fled past them I was so near to them, only six or eight feet distant, that some of them raised their tomahawks to strike me down. Dashing into the thickest cane break close by which the road ran, two of them at once rushed after me. Being about thirteen years of age and of couse slimmer than they were, and, with all very active, I soon found that unencumbered with a gun or anything else I could make my way though the cane faster than they could, burdened as they were with their tomahawks and guns. The first mishap that befell me, a grape vine caught me by the neck, threw me over backwards and took my hat off; but recovering myself I still flew onwards, gaining on them at every jump. I feared at last they would cut me off at the point of the ridge which I had to cross to get to my father's house, since the thick cane terminated a little below, and I should be compelled to leave it. Watching one fellow who was running along the hillside where the cane was thickest, as Heaven ordered it, a large tree had fallen right in his path, crushing the cane about in all directions, and forming an insurmountable barrier, thus compelling him to go around at one end or the other. Fortunately, he took down toward me to get around the top and by the time he got to the end of it, for it was a long tree, I had already passed it. . . . They, however, ran me to within one hundred yards of the house. They killed and scalped my poor brother and fled."[28]

Word of the attack spreading quickly, Major James Lynn and 5 men pursued the Indian band, apparently staged their own ambush, and wounded 2 of the warriors. The Indians got away, but lost their guns and packs to the whites. Attached to one of the captured packs was James Hall's scalp.

But young William Hall's summer of travail was not over. Two months later, on 2 August, a report came to Hall's Station that some 30 Indians were in the area. Hall's Station was probably unfortified, and Major Hall decided to remove his family and the rest of the household without delay to nearby Bledsoe's Station, which was about thirty miles northeast of French Lick near modern Castilian Springs. Bledsoe's was described by a contemporary as "an oblong square, and built all around in a regular stockade except at one place, where a large double log cabin stood. This cabin stood in the front line of the fort, the whole being built around an open square. Excepting the open passage between the cabins, the whole was completely enclosed."[29]

The family's flight began that morning. They loaded a sled for the first trip and started for Bledsoe's Station. William's older brother, two young men, and a man named Hickerson went along as guards. While the rest of the household stayed behind packing up, William's sister went with the first group, to stay at Bledsoe's and get things ready for the arrivals. Signs of possible trouble appeared soon after departure. "When about half a mile from my father's house and crossing Defeated Branch, the horses became alarmed, the two I was driving turning around so suddenly as nearly to run over me. I said to the young men that I was sure the horses smelt the Indians, but my brother insisted on going forward." And it seemed he was right, for that trip and two more were made without mishap, with thirteen-year-old William doing a man's work on all of them. The fourth and last trip was made late in the day with the entire household. Five men acted as guards. What happened next remained etched on William Hall's brain over a half century later.

"We packed up when the sun was about two hours high, whites, negroes, and all. I still driving the horses, my little brother behind me on one of them. We had arranged it that we should go ahead as we had been doing all day, the two young men in advance of myself and the sled."

The Indians probably had been watching all day, waiting for the entire household to move out. Forty to 50 warriors lay in ambush for about one hundred yards along the road that the whites and blacks traveled. As the column advanced, William's older brother and Hickerson moved in front of young William's sled. Suddenly "a little dog belonging to my brother showed violent alarm on approaching the top of a very large ash tree that had fallen in the road." William's brother stopped for a moment. William stopped the horses. His brother took "one step towards the tree top," and the world around them exploded into violence.

William "saw a gun poked out from among the leaves, which being fired at once, my brother was shot right through the body with a couple of bullets. He instantly turned and dashed back into the woods and fell dead about one hundred yards off, whilst the Indians . . . rose altogether yelling like demons and charged upon the party." The horses drawing the sled bolted and rammed the sled against a tree, where it overturned. The horses broke free and galloped off. The load was scattered over the ground.

"Hickerson, unwisely, took his stand right in the road instead of treeing, and his gun missed fire, he next attempted to use my gun which he had in his hand, but in the act of firing it he was shot with six or seven bullets, and running a little distance off he also fell and expired." William had jumped off the horse he was riding and "taking my little brother John and my sister Prudence, I ran back and placed them behind the men, who advancing kept the Indians for a few minutes at bay. My mother was mounted upon a large powerful horse and he, scared and quite ungovernable, dashed right along the entire line of Indians whilst she holding to his mane was carried to about a mile distant safely to the fort.

"My father and Mr. Morgan, my brother-in-law, kept the Indians in check until the whites and negroes scattered into the woods and Mr. Morgan was then wounded by the Indians, who flanking around shot him very dangerously in the body." But Morgan managed to escape while William's father temporarily checked the Indian advance. His "heavy rifle" made a report distinct from the Indians' guns. But there were too many Indians for him and "he turned and ran about forty yards, when he fell pierced by thirteen bullets. The Indians scalped him and hastily fled, not stopping to take anything but his rifle and shot pouch and in their haste they did not even pick up the things scattered by the overturn of the sled. . . ."

William in the meantime "had directed my little brother and sister to run back to the house" while he hid behind a tree on a hill overlooking the fight. When he heard his father's rifle, then the scalp yell of the Indians, he made for the fort. But John and Prudence "ran back to the scene of the battle." John found Hugh Rogan's hat and picked it up. When they came to the overturned sled Prudence picked up a small pail of butter, then with the innocence of childhood "thoughtlessly walked on towards the fort, along the road, meeting the men directly who coming from thence. The children were placed in charge of a negro man who took them safely back."[30]

Thus thirteen-year-old William Hall Jr., who would grow up to become a governor of Tennessee, passed the summer of 1787, seeing before his young eyes the deaths of father and two brothers in the savage border war that seemed without end.

Three days later Colonel Anthony Bledsoe wrote to Governor Richard Caswell of North Carolina, reminding him that the last time they had met Caswell had promised "that in case the perfidious Chicamaugas should infest this country, to notify your excellency, and you would send a campaign against them without delay. The period has arrived," Bledsoe stated bluntly, and advised Caswell that he had good reason to believe that Chickamaugas and Creeks were acting together, and he was right. He related the Hall tragedy, which brought the number of settlers killed to "about twenty-four persons in this country in a few months, besides numbers of others in settlements near it." Bledsoe was wondering where the 200 troops were that had been promised by North Carolina. Governor Caswell had informed Bledsoe as early as February 1787 that they would arrive by May. They finally turned up late in the year, 93 rank and file instead of the promised 200. They were infantry, which meant they were of little use in patrolling or pursuit. But as garrison troops parceled out to various stations they were invaluable. And their two-year enlistment term lent reasonable stability to the enterprise.[31]

Before the soldiers arrived James Robertson and others decided to strike back. The pioneers were under strict orders from the government of North Carolina not to take offensive actions against the Indians, for the gentlemen east of the mountains, safe, warm, well-housed, and well-fed, dreaded the possibility of provoking a general Indian war, because Indian wars were disruptive of the normal course of business and public affairs and, above all, expensive. Robertson, a man who believed in the rule of law, had obeyed this prohibition for almost eight years. But for the settlers the provocations had become intolerable. In the summer of 1787 a message for Robertson arrived in Nashville. It was from the staunchly pro-American Chickasaw chief Piomingo, and it contained news that stirred the blood. Two Chickasaw hunters had stumbled onto an unknown Chickamauga village called Coldwater, located on the site of modern Tuscumbia, Alabama, about 125 miles south of Nashville. It was the base for repeated raids on the Cumberland settlements. Besides Chickamaugas, it contained Creeks and Cherokees, and several French traders from the Illinois country who kept the Indians well supplied. The word went out to the scattered stations that gunmen were needed, and about 150 riders gathered at Nashville.[32]

A party of 18 under David Hays cast off from Nashville on boats with provisions for the main group that would travel south by land. Their intention was to rendezvous with the riders in the vicinity of Muscle Shoals. But the boats were ambushed at the mouth of the Duck River. Hays lost 2 killed and 3 wounded and returned to Nashville. James Robertson and some 130 riders, guided by 2 Chickasaw warriors, angled southeast from Nashville to a point on the right bank of the Tennessee near modern Florence, Alabama. That night 7 men swam the river and brought back a large canoe. It had a hole in the bottom but the men patched it with bark. At first light 50 men crossed in the canoe with the arms and ammunition, while the rest plunged into the river and swam the horses over. All reached the south bank without being detected. There were unoccupied cabins on the shore, and a heavy rain coming on; they all took shelter to wait it out, for their guns, the priming powder exposed, would be useless in such weather. When the rain stopped they found a path leading west that in five miles brought them first to a cornfield, then to Coldwater Creek. On the other side of the creek, about three hundred yards from the Tennessee, was the town of Coldwater, containing many cabins. Leaving Captain (John?) Rains and some men on the west bank of the creek, Robertson led the others across and approached the village.

Surprise was total. When the men of the Cumberland were spotted the Indians panicked and ran for the river. Robertson and his men charged and drove the Indians before them. The warriors even left their guns and munitions behind. Some tried to escape across Coldwater Creek. They were shot down by Captain Rains and his men. Three French traders, a white woman, and twenty-six Indians tried to escape in a canoe. A volley killed them all. Seven French traders, including the chief trader, were captured and their merchandise seized. Indian guns, powder, and ammunition, along with other goods, were removed from the cabins for transport. The town was burned to the ground, fowl and hogs slaughtered. The overwhelming nature of the victory can be seen in the failure of the Indians to fire either one shot or inflict one casualty on the Americans.

The victors left the next morning, but not before rewarding their two unerring Chickasaw guides, one of whom was named Taka. The two warriors left for home with new guns and plentiful supplies of munitions and captured merchandise. The French dead were buried. Canoes were loaded with plunder and went off downstream with the French prisoners, guarded by three men. Robertson and the rest followed the river to Colbert's Ferry, located where today's Natchez Trace Parkway crosses the Tennessee, and there rendezvoused with the boats. Robertson released the French prisoners with their spare clothing and ample provisions for their return to the Illinois country. At Colbert's the men of the expedition received one of their sweetest rewards, a luxury hardly known in the Cumberland settlements: the coffee and tea taken at Coldwater was divided equally among all.

Robertson and most of the gunmen then marched overland to Nashville. The canoes, with enough men to guard the plunder, set off down the Tennessee to take the water route via the Ohio and Cumberland Rivers, and on their way they had another adventure. Boats with French traders pushing upriver, loaded with goods and bound for Coldwater, came in sight. The Frenchmen thought the Cumberland party their own and fired their guns in the air in greeting. The Americans paddled quickly into their midst. Their own weapons empty, facing the loaded guns of the Americans, the French traders had no choice but surrender. Their goods were added to the plunder taken at Coldwater and the Americans pushed on for home. At Eaton's Station, all of the merchandise was sold. The money gained was divided among the men who took part in the expedition.

James Robertson, of course, was censured by the comfortable gentlemen east of the mountains. And despite their overwhelming victory, the Cumberland settlers gained little respite from the incessant raids—perhaps a few weeks, a month at most. Bledsoe's Lick, on the far frontier of the Cumberland, where young William Hall saw so much blood spilled, lived up to its reputation as the "Bloody grounds, on account of so many people being killed there and thereabouts. . . ." The five lower Chickamauga towns remained untouched, and from their deep sanctuaries in central Alabama Creek warriors dispatched by Alexander McGillivray came over the Tennessee to wage relentless war against the white invaders. The pressure was unceasing, and the people became desperate. Not enough to flee, despite McGillivray's boast that "the people of the Cumberland are drove over the Ohio River," but desperate enough to seek an accommodation with the great Creek leader.[33]

In the spring of 1788 two emissaries from the Cumberland arrived at Little Tallassee and proposed peace between "this Nation & the Cumberland people," McGillivray wrote. In their discussions with him they made a shocking admission. "They represent that they are reduced to extreme distress by the excursions of our warriors, & to obtain our peace and freindship that they are willing to Submit themselves to any Conditions that I Shall Judge to Impose on them: & thinking no doubt that it would be a greater Inducement to me to favor them they told me that they woud become Subjects to the King [of Spain] & that Cumberland & Kentucke were determined to free themselves from a dependence on Congress, as that body could not & would not protect their persons and property nor enourage their Commerce, So that where there was No Protection, no Submission was due." McGillivray also reported that "Kentucke meant to form a connection with the Brittish of Canada. . . ."

He was noncommittal to their request for his reaction to their proposals, as it was a "Subject that Involved Important politcal questions. . . ."
Robertson, Bledsoe, and others sent with the emissaries "proofs of the purchase of the County of Cumberland . . . by a Virginia Company from the
Northern and Cherokee Indians. My answer to them was that when I held
my first grand Convention these matters Should be discussed & in the
meantime all hostilities Should Cease on our parts, when we agreed upon
Conditions a full peace Should take place." More emissaries from Cumberland came to McGillivray in November 1788 and are "now in my house for
the same purpose" as the first delegation. But they brought with them sweet
inducements. "They bring me Notice that I am Complimented by that State
with a lot & buildings in Nashville, with a large tract of land, & hope to
have the honor of enrolling my name among their Citizens. What think you
of this."[34]

"WE ARE THE MOST COMPETENT JUDGES
OF THE EXIGENCYS OF OUR AFFAIRS"

McGillivray seemed to be at the peak of his power, but enemies were
everywhere, and eternal vigilance and shrewd maneuvering were necessary if
the king of the mountain were to maintain his position. Hoboithle Mico
and Eneah Mico continued their attempts to block his efforts to centralize
authority in the Creek Nation. And fresh problems rose. The overwhelming
military successes of McGillivray's warriors were unexpected and worrisome
to the Spanish. The Creeks were supposed to keep the Americans in check,
not overwhelm them in the case of the Georgians, or discourage them to
the point where the Cumberland settlers approached McGillivrary as suppli-
cants. Was he not their creature after all? Could he become as great a danger to the Spanish as to the Americans? Governor Miró decided that the
answer to both questions was yes, and in early January 1788 he informed
McGillivray that he was cutting back on deliveries of arms, powder, and
lead. Miro also demanded that he seek peace with the Americans. What
came of this demand was for the Spanish also quite unexpected.[35]

At about the same time another development occurred that further
bedeviled McGillivray's relations with the Spanish and increased the divide
between himself and the Lower Creeks. That was the appearance among the
Lower Creeks in Florida of a pretender, although not at first recognized as
such, to McGillivray's authority. His name was William Augustus Bowles. He
was a young, handsome, dramatic adventurer whom McGillivray had met
during the war at Pensacola, where Bowles, a Maryland-born Tory, served in
a Loyalist regiment from which he had either resigned or been drummed
out, depending upon who is telling the story. Upon his arrival in Florida
Bowles announced that he represented an English charitable society that had
learned that the Creeks were short of powder and lead and had sent Bowles
to resupply them. That was a lie. He represented Lord Dunmore, the last
colonial governor of Virginia, now governor of the Bahamas, and John Miller

William Augustus Bowles, ca. 1791, by Thomas Hardy (Photograph courtesy of Kennedy Galleries, Inc., New York)

of the firm of Miller and Bonamy of Nassau, who were out to break Panton, Leslie's monopoly of the Indian trade. Bowles had lived with the Lower Creeks after leaving his regiment, spoke at least one of the Muskogee languages, and had distinguished himself in battle. He seemed the ideal field man. At the time not aware of Bowles's real purpose, McGillivray happily accepted the powder and lead.[36]

This led to problems with the Spanish. Once they got wind of who Bowles represented and what he was up to, they suspected McGillivray of being in league with him, especially given Bowles's nationality and his English backers. Governor O'Neill in Pensacola had already suspected McGillivray of not truly having Spanish interests at heart. The governor admitted in February 1787 that McGillivray "up to the present has been an open enemy of the Americans" and "has been most useful thus far in gaining for us the friendship of the Creeks. But one must not lose sight of the fact that he lives at an extremity of the nations . . . and one must consider that his efforts will always be directed toward the ends that he conceives to favor the Indians his tribesmen. . . ." This was a mild letter. On another occasion he said of McGillivray and Panton, "In view of the passion that these persons profess for Great Britain, I doubt not that in whatever rupture we may have with that nation they will seek to damage us and to disaffect the Creek Indians, who at present are so attached to us." O'Neill's steady drumbeat of charges of disloyalty on McGillivray's part exasperated Governor Miró. "I must say to you that I am greatly embarrassed by the continued distrust that you express on every occasion when you mention these individuals, and always merely with the assertion that they have the British heart [*el Corazon Britanico*], without citing an instance in which by conversation, letter, or in other fashion they have given cause for fear. Continually you propose to me steps to destroy McGillivray's influence with the Indians."[37]

O'Neill, however, did not desist. Shortly after McGillivray accepted the powder and lead from Bowles, O'Neill fired off another accusatory letter to Miró in which he added insults to charges of disloyalty. He sent as enclosures a letter from McGillivray to Miró and a copy of a letter from McGillivray to himself, and wrote, "From them you will see that his and Panton's behavior is exactly what I foresaw and suspected, and it is as much as an unfortunate mestizo and a hide merchant could have the audacity to do." O'Neill repeated contradictory rumors that the courier from McGillivray had brought. But McGillivray was always quite candid with Spanish officials. As for the Americans, he preferred war to negotiation, and wrote to O'Neill, "You may be assured as there is a God & Saints in heaven, that if the Americans get the upper hand in the terms of peace with us that they will use our force directly against the kings territory, & be drawn into all their quarrels & to Support their ambitious Schemes—Concerning this I have wrote to Governor Miró—if my advice is Neglected I can have no blame. Negotiations ought now to be Set aside & the means given to us to Carry our point by force of arms." And in a postscript of a letter to Miró, McGillivray made quite clear that when Spaniards dealt with Creeks they were dealing with equals who had their own interests to protect and that mutual faith between allies was essential. It is a strong piece of writing and deserves our attention.[38]

"It may appear Strange to Your Excellency that the Georgians nowithstanding their distresses Should be so obstinate as not to agree to Just terms of Peace. The reason is that Just as we were on the point to humble them Compleatly, our Support of arms & ammunition given by the royal bounty was Suddenly Stopt from us, & we were unable to exert the Vigour & enterprise necessary to finish the war. Without it an Indian cannot afford to purchase ammunition for war besides providing necessarys for his family. Of course their Mode of war is very Irregular, Carried on by Starts & feeble. I Shall only add that You [encouraged] the origin of our war with the States, Succour & aid was promised us to enable us to defend our rights, a non performance of that engagement on Your part will be Considered by the Cheifs as that You have released yourselves from it. You expect that we Should make no treatys with the States without Your Concurrence, this must be mutual, you Should not take any measures of that kind in which our dearest Interests are so deeply Involved without our Consent. We are the most Competent Judges of the exigencys of our affairs & accordingly make the necessary requisitions to you concerning them, which according to every Idea of good faith ought to be Complyd with by You. You have other resources in View, in case of need, but it is a point of honor with me to be Steady & keep engagements untill released from them by the other contracting pary."[39]

"HE IS NOT VERY DARK . . . AND MUCH OF A GENTLEMAN"

On 30 April 1789, on the balcony of Federal Hall at Wall and Broad Streets in New York City, George Washington took the oath of office as the first president of the United States of America. It was a momentous occasion. The young Republic had abandoned the loosely woven Articles of Confederation, which had failed the test of building a nation that could survive united and strong, and devised a new form of government under a Constitution that has proven sturdy and flexible for over two centuries. Our concern lies with the dramatic change in relations between Americans and the Indian nations.

Under the Articles of Confederation, "The United States in congress assembled shall also have the sole and exclusive right and power of . . . regulating the trade and managing all affairs with the Indians, not members of any of the states, provided that the legislative right of any state within its own limits be not infringed or violated." That was language ambiguous enough for legions of lawyers to march through abreast—and they did. Thus we have watched until now as the states ignored the Confederation and made treaties as they pleased with the Indians. That changed under the Constitution, in which the states lost the power to make any treaties, with other countries or Indian nations.[40]

Washington wasted little time in using his authority to bring peace to the southern frontier. McGillivray was informed by U.S. commissioners hoping to meet with him that "we are now governed by a President who is like the old King over the great water. He Commands all the Warriors of the thirteen great fires." McGillivray, however, held back, especially after Governor Miró promised to support him once again. But Washington and his secretary of war, Henry Knox, did not give up.

Three new commissioners, all distinguished men, were sent out and made their way to Rock Landing in Georgia on the Oconee River. They bore messages of friendship to Cherokees, Choctaws, and Chickasaws, but "the first great object of your commision," their instructions read, "is to negociate and establish peace between the State of Georgia and the Creek Nation. The whole Nation must be represented and solemnly acknowledged to be so by the Creeks themselves." Two thousand Indians appeared, for white men had long been known to dispense gifts at conferences, and no self-respecting Indian ever passed up that opportunity. But the most important man at the

Rock Landing conference was Alexander McGillivray, who arrived with 900 warriors. He was much fawned over by his enemies, the Georgia militia officers present, whom he described as "extremely ignorant and unpolished." When he decided that the terms offered by the commissioners were unacceptable, he told one of them, David Humphreys, that "by God I would not have such a Treaty cram'd down my throat." Then "I decamped without the ceremony of taking leave." A delegation led by General Andrew Pickens, the great South Carolina partisan leader, was sent in pursuit to persuade McGillivray to return. They caught up with him at the Ocmulgee River, where "we had a long conversation, but I would not return" unless Pickens and the other "officers would pledge themselves that the Commissioners would make the Restitution of the Encroacment [the Oconee lands] the Basis to conclude the Treaty upon." The delegation was unable to make such a commitment, "so I remained obstinate to my purpose and came on." He was impressed by Andrew Pickens, however, whom "I take to be a worthy moderate man. We got well acquainted, and I am sure if he had remained in his appointment [as a commissioner], we should have come to some agreement."[41] McGillivray explained why he was able to act in such a high-handed way. "One day before leaving home to go to this treaty, I received a despatch from Governor Miró with favorable report of the benign condescension of our great Protector King Charles IV, conceding us our trade on terms as advantageous as the Americans could or would wish to do, and even better, and confirming the guaranty of protection stipulated in the treaty of peace, friendship and alliance held in Pensacola in '84. These reports made me (to use an Indian expression) stout in my heart and strong in my mouth. Without these assurances I would have been in an embarrassing and painful situation dealing with Lincollen [General Benjamin Lincoln] and Company. . . ."[42]

After McGillivray's departure, there was no reason for a conference, and the commissioners also went home, reporting to Washington that it was all McGillivray's fault. Whatever the president may have believed on that score, he was a realist who knew that McGillivray was the key to peace on the frontier, and he was determined to persevere in his efforts. In early 1790 Washington and Knox sent a lone and trusted emissary to seek out McGillivray in the wilderness and urge him not only to reconsider but to come to New York for negotiations directly with the president and the secretary of war. The man chosen, Colonel Marinus Willett of New York, was a distinguished veteran of the Revolutionary War. Because the new administration's first attempt to negotiate with McGillivray had ended so badly, Willett was dispatched as a private citizen, for Washington wished that "government might not appear to be the agent . . . or suffer its dignity if the attempt to get him here should not succeed." Willett carried with him in addition to Washington's message a letter to McGillivrary from Benjamin Hawkins, a former commissioner to the Creeks and now a U.S. senator. Hawkins emphasized that he was writing "enitirely in my private capacity," and throughout he was most solicitous of McGillivray. But he made equally clear that the choice facing the Creeks was war or peace, that failure to sit down and negotiate was unacceptable, that "if you Strike, the U. States *must punish,* it will then become a Contest of power the events of which may be disagreeable and expensive to the United States, but the result must be ruin to the Creeks."[43]

Willett found McGillivray at the Upper Creek town of Okfuskee on the Tallapoosa River about forty miles northeast of McGillivray's plantation at Little Tallassee, to which they proceeded together. Willett thought McGillivray a "man of an open, generous mind, with a good judgement, and a very tenacious memory." McGillivray was equally impressed with Willett. "This officer during the War was particularly distinguished for enterprise and success, & has since filled respectable offices. I find him just as Genl. Pickens a Candid and Benevolent Character, possessing abilitys but without Show or parade." Willett addressed the Creek National Council on 14 May 1790, urging that McGillivray and a delegation of Upper and Lower Creeks accompany Willett to New York to make a treaty "as strong as the hills and lasting as the rivers." His invitation was accepted, and the Creek spokesman, Hollowing King, told Willett that they would agree to whatever the Great Beloved Man decided.

Whereupon an impressive entourage set out on a thousand-mile journey to New York City. One of them was McGillivray's bitter enemy Hoboithle Mico. Several, including McGillivray, were on horseback. Marinus Willett rode in a sulky. Three wagons contained twenty-six chiefs and warriors. Along the way leading citizens of various towns entertained McGillivray and his fellow Creeks. After a stop in Philadelphia, a sloop awaited them at Elizabethtown Point and took the entire party to the Battery. Their escort up Wall Street was the Society of Saint Tammany in all their marching finery, and they were taken in succession to see Congress in session at Federal Hall, Washington's residence, and then to City Tavern and dinner hosted by the secretary of war, Henry Knox, and the governor of New York, George Clinton. Many well-known people met McGillivray that summer, and they were impressed. Even caustic Fisher Ames paid him a left-handed compliment: "The Indian chief, McGillivray, is here. He is decent, and not very black." The wife of the vice president, Abigail Adams, never one to hand out a compliment lightly, wrote that he "dresses in our own fashion, speaks English like a Native, & I should never suspect him to be of that Nation, as he is not very dark. He is grave and solid, intelligent and much of a Gentleman, but in very bad Health."[44]

Negotiations proceeded throughout the summer, delayed by hard bargaining and McGillivray's frequent illness. They ended on 6 August 1790. The Treaty of New York, signed on 7 August by Secretary Knox, the Great Beloved Man, and twenty-three Creek chiefs, was unique in two respects: it was the first Indian treaty negotiated and signed in the nation's capital instead of Indian country; and it was the first and only treaty signed by the United States from that day to the present that contained secret articles. The Senate consented on 12 August, and the following day at Federal Hall

George Washington, Secretary of State Thomas Jefferson, Secretary Knox, Alexander McGillivray, and his fellow Creeks performed a ratification ceremony before numerous dignitaries that was described by a contemporary reporter as a "highly interesting, solemn, and dignified transaction."[45]

The secret articles, of course, almost immediately became known to the Spanish, the British, and many others. One of them gave McGillivray a commission as brigadier general in the U.S. Army at a salary of $1,200 per year. In return, McGillivray swore allegiance to the United States. Another granted the Creeks annual duty-free imports worth $60,000, through an American port and under McGillivray's control, if their present trading arrangements were interrupted in case of war. In one of the public articles, McGillivray on behalf of the Creeks gave up 3 million acres in Georgia between the Ogeechee and Oconee Rivers, for which he was harshly criticized, especially by many Lower Creeks. But those lands had initially been ceded by Hoboithle Mico and Eneah Mico at the Treaty of Augusta in 1783. Although McGillivray had always denied the validity of that treaty and the other treaties with Georgia, he had to give something in return, and as he pointed out, the land was no longer rich with game because of the proximity of the whites. But excessive interest in the secret articles and the cession of land obstructs our view of the real significance of the Treaty of New York.

It changed the relationship between the Creeks and the American nation, and in this it was a clear victory for McGillivray. No longer could Georgia or any other state or private entity enter into a treaty with the Creeks or any other Indians. The Creeks acknowledged "themselves and all parts of the Creek Nation within the limits of the United States . . . to be under the protection of the United States," and the United States guaranteed to the Creeks "all their lands within the limits of the United States." Furthermore, any non-Indian who "shall attempt to settle on any of the Creek lands . . . shall forfeit the protection of the United States, and the Creeks may punish him or not, as they please." The Creeks, the treaty made clear, could defend themselves against encroachment and the United States was bound by the treaty to support such Creek efforts. In the words of a leading historian of the Creeks and the period, "No longer could the Georgians legally pursue an agressive Indian policy in the hope of deliberately precipitating a frontier crisis from which the United States would then, with all its financial and military power, rescue them at the expense of the Creeks."[46]

"MR. MCGILLIVRAY LIES DANGEROUSLY ILL IN MY HOUSE"

He had wrought well for his people, the Great Beloved Man, but all around him controversy swirled. The Georgians were furious, the Spanish suspicious and unhappy, and the Lower Creeks susceptible to the grandiose plans of William Augustus Bowles, who called himself director general of the Creek Nation, and intrigued to supplant McGillivray. Long on promises, short on delivery, Bowles was a victim of that all-too-frequent human failing called self-delusion. He thought he had it in him to be a great man, and others did, too, but all they got for their faith in him was a fruitless walk down the garden path. His influence among the gullible reached beyond Creek country to the Chickamaugas. David Craig, "a man of Veracity quite well acquainted with the Cherokee chiefs, generally, and their affairs," reported on Bowles's influence from Lookout Mountain, one of the Five Lower Towns of the Chickamaugas.

"At the house of Richard Justice is a painting of Bowles, and two Cherokee chiefs, one each side of him, under which is written, "General Bowles, Commander-in-chief of the Creek and Cherokee nations." There are, also, at his house, a number of dining cards (copper plate) addressed to Bowles while in England, styling him, "commander-in-chief of the Creek nation." This trivial circumstance is mentioned, to show among others that could be added, that Richard Justice, heretofore one of the warmest friends of the United States, now listens, in preference, to Bowles, and adheres to his counsels."

Craig also reported that "near this town . . . lives Moses Price, a sensible half Creek, who can read and write, and who was in England with Bowles. He speaks of Bowles as a very great man; that he can actually procure for the Southern tribes, from England, men and arms to defend them against the United States; and that he can obtain a free port in East Florida to extend trade to them directly from England. He says, while he was in England, he was informed that England, by treaty of peace, did not cede the lands claimed by the Creeks and Cherokees, to the United States, and, consequently, the United States could have nothing to do with the government of them, or their trade."[47]

None of this was true, which makes Craig's report all the more poignant. Yes, Richard Justice and Moses Price and other Cherokees and Creeks were gullible, but if we could walk in their moccasins, watching the invaders growing stronger, their progeny and newcomers sprouting like weeds, forever encroaching on our birthright, in our desperation is it not conceivable that we, too, would fall under the spell of a handsome, personable, smooth-talking adventurer who was as much on the make as any big land speculator?

At no time then or later did the British government grant official recognition to Bowles, and any unofficial encouragement was lukewarm and never came from the top. On this point, even his sympathetic biographer does not offer evidence of Bowles being appointed a British agent.[48] Two weeks after Craig's report the British minister to the United States, responding to urgent queries from American officials, wrote to the U.S. secretary of state in unequivocal terms: "I am directed to assure this Government in the most explicit manner, that the assertion said to have been made by Mr. Bowles, of his pretensions having been encouraged or countenanced by the Government of Great Britain, or of his having been furnished by it with arms and ammunition, are entirely without foundation. The report, also, of his having obtained from the Government of Great Britain any sort of commission as superintendent of Indians, or in any other character, or of his having received authority to promise to the Indians protection and assistance in the recovery of their old boundary with Georgia, or to hold out to them the expectation of English reinforcements in the spring, is equally groundless."[49]

In 1792, Bowles was taken prisoner by the Spanish in New Orleans while under safe conduct, and for the next five years he was sent by his captors to Havana, Madrid, Cádiz, and the Philippines. While being returned to Madrid in 1797 he escaped and got to London. In August 1799 he returned to Florida and at the point where the Flint and Chattahoochee Rivers join to form the Apalachicola he built a post, proclaimed the Indian state of Muskogee, and elected himself its director general. But Bowles had angered too many people, made too many powerful enemies, who finally put aside their own differences to deal with him. In May 1803, with the connivance of his Indian enemies, the American agent to the Creeks, Colonel Benjamin Hawkins, and the Spanish governor of West Florida, Vizente Folch y Juan, he was arrested, handcuffed with cuffs made especially for the purpose, and delivered into his final captivity. He spent two years in a Spanish dungeon in Morro Castle in Havana, and there died in a military hospital in 1805. He was forty-two years old. His career of adventuring and freebooting had no long-term significance for the history of North America. He is of interest only for his colorful career, his role as a spoiler, and as further proof that in turbulent and uncertain times people who otherwise would not even rate a footnote are able to convince others to support their delusions of grandeur.

McGillivray, unfortunately, who had the great abilities Bowles lacked, was cursed with ill health and a weak constitution, "subject to an habitual Head-Ach and Cholic. . . ." Sickness so plagued him throughout his active career that in 1791 he would write, "I am absolutely worn down with the Life I have lived for ten years past. . . ." He was also burdened by his inability to bring to fruition his vision of a unified Creek Nation. Even if he had been hale and hearty, the task was daunting. Enemies abounded, and the extreme conservatism of the Creeks was a mighty weapon in the hands of reactionaries like Hoboithle Mico.

About a year later he informed Panton that the "Cursed Gout seizing me has laid me up these two months nearly. Every periodical attack grows more Severe & longer in Continuance. It now mounts from my feet to my knees, & am still Confined to the fire side. . . ." Gout, fever, rashes, rheumatism, and racking headaches often laid him low. Heavy drinking, a curse of the age, and apparently venereal disease, further "sapped a Constitution originally delicate and feeble." On one occasion he was "Apprehensive that I Shall lose all my finger Nails & tis with much difficulty that I take the pen in my hand to write." In an age when travel was an obstacle course for all, it was sheer torture for McGillivray, and there were times when he was literally unable to leave his home. "I have had a Severe return of Rheumatism which has kept me in torment for some time past. . . ."[50]

In February 1793 he traveled to Pensacola to see his partner and old friend William Panton. He became ill on the way, and on 16 February, seven days after his arrival, Panton wrote to Governor Carondelet in New Orleans, "It is with infinite Concern that I inform Your Excy. that Mr. McGillivray lies dangerously ill in my House of a Complication of disorders of Gout in the stomack attended with perepneaumony and he is so very bad as to leave scarcely any hope of his recovery." Four days later Panton wrote once more to the governor that "now it is my misfortune to announce his death to You which took place on the 17th at 11 OClock at night." He was forty-two.[51]

He was denied burial in the Pensacola cemetery because he was not a Catholic. But he was laid to rest in a better place. A grave was dug in William Panton's garden, and there McGillivray of the Creeks, attended by Panton and white friends who gave him full Masonic honors, and numerous fellow Creeks who, reported London's *The Gentleman's Magazine,* mourned with "loud screams of real woe which they vented in their unaffected grief," said good-bye to the Great Beloved Man.[52]

McGillivray has been criticized for serving two masters, for accepting simultaneously titles and payments from the United States and Spain, because, as one historian wrote, "it was not proper for him, even in his time, place, and situation, to attempt to serve so many paymasters." I respectfully disagree. McGillivray was following traditional Creek foreign policy of playing one power against the other to protect Creek interests. Governor Miró expressed it clearly and succinctly: "I am of the opinion that McGillivray and his chiefs want to keep on the good side of both parties, and that they will maintain themselves in our friendship, the former receiving his pension and the others presents, while at the same time they enjoy all the advantages furnished them by the states."

He left his work undone, and there was nobody to take his place.

The Creeks would never again see his like.

Chapter 7

⎯⎯∞∞∞⎯⎯

THE RISE OF
ANDREW JACKSON

"THE OLD LADY ALWAYS BLAMED HER SON LEWIS"

We last saw the young Andrew Jackson on 26 October 1788 arriving in Nashville. In the few years following his arrival two important events occurred in his life: he fell in love, and he met William Blount. Let us first take up his private life, which eventually became very public.

We noted earlier that during the terrible Indian raids of 1780 Colonel John Donelson moved his family north to Kentucky. By the time Jackson arrived, Donelson had brought them back to the Cumberland. With one exception. His daughter Rachel remained in Kentucky, for she had married Lewis Robards, a member of a prominent Kentucky family. We do not have an image of Rachel as a young woman, only as a short, stout matron who devoted her life to her husband and religion, and though childless raising at least thirteen children. But we should try to put that image aside and picture a vivacious young woman of, to use a phrase common in my youth, pleasingly plump proportions. James Parton described her as "gay and lively," the "best story-teller, the best dancer, the sprightliest companion, the most dashing horsewoman in the western country." She could read and write, she was skilled on the harpischord, and without question in that day and age, beginning as a little girl, Rachel Donelson Robards had learned from her mother the domestic arts. She may also have been a flirt.[1]

By all accounts her husband, Lewis Robards, was another story. He drank to excess, he may have been a wife beater, and he was intensely jealous. Morose and suspicious, he provoked violent arguments with his young wife. They lived with Robards's mother, who took boarders. Among them was John Overton, then studying law, who became a close and lifelong friend of Jackson. Overton put the blame on Lewis Robards. It is true that he made his statement in 1827, during Jackson's first successful presidential

108

Rachel Jackson, by Louisa Catherine Strobel after Ralph E. W. Earl (The Hermitage: Home of President Andrew Jackson, Nashville, Tennessee)

campaign, to counter ugly stories by Jackson's political opponents about the circumstances of his marriage. But according to Parton, Major William B. Lewis, a Nashville resident of high reputation, "spent months in investigating this single affair, and accumulated a mass of evidence in support" of Overton's version. Parton failed to mention that Lewis was an old friend and military and political colleague of Jackson's.

Overton began boarding with the Robards in the fall of 1787. The tension in the household was obvious and growing. Rachel's mother-in-law was deeply distressed. Lewis Robards accused Rachel of being too friendly with a man named Short. Finally, Robards wrote to Rachel's mother that he could no longer live with her daughter and asked that she fetch her. Overton was present when Rachel's brother Samuel arrived to escort her to Nashville.

"I well recollect," Overton wrote, "the distress of old Mrs. Robards, on account of her daughter-in-law Rachel going away, and on account of the separation that was about to take place, together with the circumstance of the old lady's embracing her affectionately. In unreserved conversations with me, the old lady always blamed her son Lewis, and took the part of her daughter-in-law." Overton further related that during his stay in the Robards' home he "never heard any of the family censure young Mrs. Robards . . . but recollect frequently to have heard the old lady and Captain Jouett, who married the eldest daughter of the family . . . to express the most favorable sentiments of her."

Upon finishing his law studies, Overton moved to Nashville, where he boarded with Rachel's widowed mother and renewed his acquaintance with Rachel. It was there that he met and formed his lasting friendship with Jackson, who was also a Donelson boarder. The presence of single men in households was then highly desirable, Overton pointed out, "as a protection against Indians." Rachel was then twenty-one years old. Jackson was also twenty-one—that age when hormones are at full gallop. Both were high-spirited and fun-loving. Both liked to dance. Jackson even then had a presence in a crowd. The chivalry toward women for which he became noted was part of his character then. There is no doubt that a mutual attraction developed. But by no means should we assume an improper relationship. There is absolutely no evidence that either in Kentucky or Tennessee Rachel was unfaithful to Lewis Robards. Nor is there gossip of such behavior. Given the propensity of people to believe the worst when it comes to sex, the absence of gossip is good additional proof that Rachel's faithfulness was without blemish.

Through the good offices of her mother-in-law and Overton, Rachel was reunited with her husband, but this time he came to Tennessee to live with Rachel in her mother's house. Jackson and Overton boarded in a cabin next to the blockhouse where the family lived and took their meals there. Thus Jackson and Rachel were often in close proximity. Robards soon became jealous of Jackson. Overton wrote that "some of his irritating conversations on this subject, with his wife, I heard amidst the tears of herself and her mother, who were greatly distressed." Overton "urged to Robards the unmanliness of his conduct," but to no avail, and the situation soon reached the level of intensity that had prevailed in the Kentucky household. Overton suggested to Jackson that they seek another place to live, but neither knew where to go. Jackson then decided to talk to Robards.

It did not go well. Robards "became violently agitated and abusive, and threatened to whip Jackson. . . ." Jackson refused a test of bodily strength, but if Robards "insisted on fighting, he would give him gentlemanly satisfaction. . . ." In an attempt to defuse the situation, Jackson moved from the Donelsons' to Kasper Mansker's second station.[2] His removal, however, did nothing to improve the situation at the Donelson home. Robards some months later left his wife and returned to Kentucky, and there matters rested for a few years. Our main source for the affair, John Overton, had also moved out of the Donelson household, but sometime after Robard's departure he returned and was thus in a position to observe subsequent developments firsthand.

In the fall of 1790, a rumor had it that Robards intended to return to Nashville and take Rachel back to Kentucky. This caused great distress to both Rachel and her mother. Rachel was "convinced, after two fair trials," wrote Overton, "that it would be impossible to live with Captain Robards," a decision with which Overton and many others in Nashville agreed. He further stated that in the winter of 1791, Rachel's mother told Overton that her daughter had decided to go to Natchez, still occupied by the Spanish but full of Americans, some of whom were friends of the Donelson family. Mrs. Donelson was in accord with her daughter's decision "to keep out of the way of Captain Robards, as she said he had threatened to '*haunt*' her.'" Given the character of Lewis Robards, it was a wise decision. Then Andrew Jackson made a decision that some might consider unwise. He announced his intention of accompanying Rachel.

Rachel was going to travel with old friends of the Donelsons', a Colonel Stark and his family. Stark may have been a man named Robert Stark, who was moving to the Natchez area.[3] Overton heard that Stark had made "urgent entreaties" of Jackson to go along as additional "protection from the Indians" and "that Jackson consented to accompany them. . . ." Jackson later told Overton this was indeed his intention, but assured Overton that as soon as he accomplished his purpose he would return to Nashville and resume his law practice. In the "winter or spring of 1791," Overton wrote, the small party floated down the Cumberland, the Ohio, and the Mississippi to Natchez, whereupon Jackson, after seeing Rachel safe among family friends, returned to Nashville by land via the Natchez Trace in time to attend to business as a lawyer and solicitor general at the Superior Court in May 1791.

Shortly thereafter Jackson and Overton learned that during the winter of 1790–1791 Lewis Robards had been granted a divorce from Rachel by the Virginia legislature through the influence of Robards's brother-in-law, Major John Jouett, then a member of the legislature. That summer of 1791 Jackson returned to Natchez and there, Overton reported, "I understood, married Mrs. Robards. . . ." The couple then returned to the Cumberland and took up residence. The question is, however, who married them? Natchez was governed by Spain, and only Catholic priests were authorized to perform marriages. The Spanish kept careful records, but extensive research by the editors of the Jackson papers in this country and abroad found no record of their marriage. Although Spanish officials did not persecute Protestants and permitted them to practice their religion, Protestant ministers were not authorized to conduct marriage ceremonies, and those who occasionally did perform illegal ceremonies got into trouble, of which there were records. So the question—Who married Jackson and Rachel in Natchez?—remains unanswered, as does a further question that might occur to the skeptical: Were they married?[4]

"COME ON, AND I WILL SAVE YOU YET"

The happy couple settled down on the Cumberland and Jackson continued a promising career. American fondness for litigation is not a recent phenomenon, and there was plenty of work for an ambitious young man with a shingle. In the middle of a struggle for survival on an isolated frontier, life went on, and the age-old problem of creditors and debtors had arisen. Jackson had all the business he could handle from creditors. In one month alone when he first came to the Cumberland he issued seventy writs to debtors behind on their payments. And he was a persistent fellow, which angered many debtors. One man deliberately stepped on his foot, whereupon Jackson showed that the boy who "would not stay throwed" had not changed as a man. He picked up a piece of wood and knocked the man out. Other legal matters also occupied his attention, including land titles and assaults. He was almost constantly on horseback, going back and forth over the wild, dangerous Cumberland Plateau between Nashville and Jonesborough, a distance one way of some two hundred miles.

Between 1788 and 1795, Jackson traveled that route twenty-two times. It started some sixty miles east of Nashville, but about a decade later the English traveler Francis Baily described even that leg of the journey as "scarcely better than a wilderness after you proceed about half-a-dozen miles from the town; for the houses are so far apart from each other, that you seldom see more than two or three in a day." Before his marriage Jackson followed the practice then common of sharing a bed with his roommate, John Overton, when he boarded with the Donelsons. But on the trail *"the custom of the country"* prevailed. When Francis Baily arrived in Nashville in midsummer 1797, in the best tavern in town "we met with good fare, but very poor accomodations for lodgings; three or four beds of the roughest construction in one room, which was open at all hours of the night for the reception of any rude rabble that had a mind to put up at the house; and if the other beds happened to be occupied, you might be surprised when you awoke in the morning to find a *bedfellow* by your side whom you had never seen before and perhaps might never see again. All complaint is unnecessary, for you are immediately silenced by that all-powerful argument—*the custom of the country,* and an inability to remedy it; or perhaps your landlord may tell you that if you do not like it you are at liberty to depart as soon as you please. Having long been taught to put up with inconveniences, I determined for the future to take things as I found them, and if I could not remedy them, to be content. Besides . . . every thing which was beyond a piece of bread and bacon, and the cold hard ground, appeared to *me* as a luxury."[5]

Outside of Nashville food and accomodations for our circuit lawyer and other travelers were even ruder and catch as catch can. Pickings, as they might say on the frontier, were slim. On 3 August 1797 Francis Baily "proceeded the whole of this morning without being able to obtain a morsel of anything to eat. I called at almost every plantation I saw, but they were so poor, or so distressed for provisions themselves, that I could get nothing."

That day Baily settled for a piece of bread obtained at a mill, and felt fortunate as "I sat me down upon a log and made a comfortable breakfast."

Corn bread and butter and milk was a common offering for dinner. Baily's eighteenth-century usage of the word *plantation* should not deceive the reader who might immediately think of Tara and gangs of slaves working in cotton fields. Baily meant settlements in a new country. These were simple farms, often of the crudest sort. A settler might or might not own a few slaves. As Baily wrote, "None of the houses in this part of the world are built higher than the ground floor; and the flooring (if any) is made of very rough boards laid on the ground, sometimes on joists, and sometimes not; but always with great holes between the planks. When I was at this man's [Major Blackamoor, as spelled by Baily, but probably Blackmore] house one of the slaves saw an enormous snake gliding under my bed, and passing through one of these holes in the floor. The Major, to my comfort, told me that they sometimes got into bed, but that they would not hurt me. So soon does custom get the better of these things, that he did not seem to care much about it." Such was life on the frontier in the good old days, and Jackson began riding the circuit nine years before Baily passed through, when the settlements were even sparser.[6]

There are tales of Indian fighting from this period of Jackson's life, but the reports are not of the same quality as those that we have for such men as John Sevier, Evan Shelby, and James Robertson. There is no question that these men were Indian-fighters, yet the evidence for their exploits is matter-of-fact, telling us simply that they were leaders and rode with their men into battle. The Jackson stories, however, appeared many years later and are the stuff of legends. Jackson takes charge! Jackson to the rescue! "Come on, and I will save you yet," he is alleged to have called out on one occasion. They have the ring of stories to fit the larger-than-life leader he became. This is not to deny that he participated in some expeditions, for an able-bodied man on the Cumberland frontier could not have shirked such duty without being shunned by the people. James Robertson would never have formed his high opinion of Jackson had the young lawyer not borne his share of defending the settlements. Stories of cowardice would have circulated and become part of frontier lore. But of all the vicious charges that Jackson's political enemies would later trumpet, not once did they question his courage.[7]

One story does bear repeating. Recalled by Jackson, retold by James Parton, it is only indirectly concerned with Indians, and instead highlights the common rigors and dangers of travel faced by a frontier lawyer riding the circuit. "He came, soon after dark, to a creek that had been swollen by the rains into a roaring torrent. The night was as dark as pitch, and the rain fell heavily. To have attempted the ford would have been suicidal, nor did he dare to light a fire, nor even to let his horse move about to browse. So he took off the saddle, and, placing it at the foot of a tree, sat upon it, wrapped in his blanket and holding his rifle in one hand and his bridle in the other. All through the night he sat motionless and silent, listening to the noise of the flood and the pattering of the rain drops upon the leaves. When the day dawned, he saddled his horse again, mounted, swam the creek, and continued his journey." This, I submit, was the normal course of life for a frontiersman who spent half his days in the saddle following his profession.[8]

"I HAVE THE GOOD OF THIS COUNTRY AT HEART"

Jackson also got involved in those early years in what became known as the Spanish Conspiracy, although, to paraphrase A. P. Whitaker's suggestion, it should be called the Frontier Conspiracy, since it originated not with Spaniards but American frontiersmen, who deceived their own government and Spain's and were the sole beneficiaries. Jackson was not a major player, but his name surfaced early in the carefully kept records of the Spanish colonial bureaucracy. This was another of those shadowy, half-formed conspiracies of the Old Southwest. The intrigue had its genesis in the attempt of Spain to stop the American tide west of the mountains and especially in the Mississippi Valley. As we observed in chapter 6, the Peace of Paris of 1783 between Great Britain and the United States set the U.S. southern boundary at the thirty-first parallel. Spain, however, not a party to the treaty, refused to accept that boundary line and continued to occupy Natchez, which it had seized from the British during the war; contested for several years with the Americans the occupation of Chickasaw Bluffs, the site of modern Memphis, Tennessee; and maintained posts at New Madrid and St. Louis. Spain, in fact, claimed most of the Old Southwest. Their boundary claim followed the Flint River north from the Florida line through western Georgia to its source in modern Fayette County; then in a direct line northward to the Hiwassee River in the northeastern corner of Georgia; it then followed the Hiwassee into North Carolina and westward to its junction with the Tennessee, the Tennessee to the Ohio, the Ohio to the Mississippi, and the Mississippi south to the Gulf of Mexico. In modern terms, the Spanish claimed the western third of Georgia, small slices of North Carolina and East Tennessee, including the site of modern Chattanooga, almost all of Alabama, all of Mississippi, almost the entire western third of Tennessee, and the southwestern corner of Kentucky.[9]

The Peace of Paris, under Article 8, also guaranteed that the Mississippi River "from its source to the Ocean shall forever remain free & open to the Subjects of Great Britain and the Citizens of the United States." This avenue of trade was vital to western exports. But as Spain refused to accept the thirty-first parallel, it also refused to accept the validity of Article 8, and in 1784 closed the Mississippi to American trade. This Spanish action created an uproar in the West. Although at this early date there was little American commerce, the People of the Western Waters were looking to the future.[10]

Western and southern wrath became especially intense in 1786, when the New Yorker John Jay proposed a treaty with Spain that would abandon the right of free navigation on the Mississippi for a generation or more in return for a possible Spanish retreat to the thirty-first parallel and commercial concessions. Congress, in a vote along sectional lines, authorized Jay to negotiate such a treaty. When news of this decision became public the opposition was so intense, especially in the South and the West, that the Washington administration retreated and no treaty was negotiated. But reaction to the congressional vote led to threats of western secession from the Confederation. And the Creek raids begun by Alexander McGillivray's warriors that same year led to even deeper bitterness among westerners. They felt that they were being abandoned by their countrymen, and that they must look to themselves for relief. This, as we saw in chapter 6, led in 1788 to emissaries being dispatched from the Cumberland to McGillivray, offering him citizenship and land, and informing him that they intended to separate from the Confederation and become subjects of the king of Spain. In August of that year, James Robertson even prevailed on the North Carolina legislature to name the Cumberland counties the Mero District, in honor of the Spanish governor, whose name, Miró, the settlers and legislators misspelled. George Washington, who knew the West firsthand, was concerned as early as 1784, for "the flanks and rear of the United States are possessed by other powers—& formidable ones, too," which meant that "the Western settlers (I speak now from my own observation) stand as it were upon a pivot—the touch of a feather would turn them any way." Secession never occurred, of course, and most writers on the subject maintain that was never the settlers' intention. But the West was in ferment, and young Andrew Jackson was caught up in it.[11]

In early 1789, André Fagot, a French trader and Spanish militia captain from St. Louis, arrived in Nashville. His purpose was to establish trade between New Orleans and Nashville, but Indians had captured his last shipment and he was eager to have Daniel Smith, a prominent citizen and brigadier general of the Mero District, to persuade Governor Miró to restrain the Indians. Fagot met Jackson, and later he suggested to Miró that Andrew Jackson, James Robertson, and Daniel Smith "were the chief agents in the intrigue." That Jackson at twenty-one was that important in the scheme is a bit hard to swallow. It is enough to believe that he was involved, and we know that he met with Fagot, for on 13 February 1789, some four months after his arrival in Nashville, he wrote to Daniel Smith on Fagot's behalf. We quote this awkwardly phrased letter in full in order that the reader may contrast Jackson's early appearance into public affairs with his later powerful statements, proclamations, and threats to the Republic's enemies.[12]

> I had the pleasure of seeing Capt. Fargo [Fagot] yesterday who put me under obligations of seeing you this day, but as the weather seems dull and heavy it prevents my coming up; but I comit to you in this small piece of paper the business he wants with you; He expresses a great friendship for the welfare and harmony of this country; he wishes to become a citizen and trade to this country by which means and through you I think he can have a lasting peace

with the Indians; he wishes you to write to the governor [Miró] informing him the desire of a commercial treaty with that country; he then will importune the Governor for a privilege or permit to trade to this country which he is sure to obtain as he is related to his Excellency;[13] then he will show the propriety of having a peace with the Indians for the pirpose of the benefit of the trade of this country; and also show the governor the respect this country honors him by giving it his name; he bears the commission of Captain under the King of Spain which is a honorable title in that country and can in my opinion do a great deal for this; and hopes you will do him the honour as to see him upon this occasion before he sets out for Orleans and I think it the only immediate way to obtain a peace with the savage. I hope you will consider it well and give me a few lines upon the occasion by Collo. Donelson who hands you this as I have the good of this country at heart and I hope also if you will do Mr. Fargo the honor as to go and see him upon the occasion as you go down you will give me a call as I think I could give you some satisfaction on this subject, this Sir from your Very Humble Servant, Andrew Jackson.

As it turned out, Smith did not need an introduction to Fagot. He knew him, and may already have decided to use him as a courier to Miró and for any "particular intelligence" Miró wished to send to the Cumberland. But whatever Daniel Smith may have said to Fagot, when he learned that the Frenchman had told Miró that the Cumberland people planned to secede from North Carolina and become part of the Spanish Empire, he wrote to Miró and denied that Fagot had accurately represented the settlers' intent. There is evidence in letters and statements written in 1789–1790 that at the very least leading Cumberland figures such as James Robertson, and from East Tennessee John Sevier, were flirting with Spain. Their true intent, however, was probably not to join the Spanish Empire but to obtain peace on the frontier and access to the Mississippi by leading Spanish officials to believe that they were ready to break with the eastern states.[14]

One of the conspirators, Dr. James White, spent almost five months in close contact with an able Spanish colonial official who was fluent in English. His name was Manuel Gayoso de Lemos, and he met White in Havana while en route to Natchez to assume his post as its first governor. The two discussed the southern frontier situation, and White prepared for Gayoso a written statement. White was specifically concerned with the State of Franklin, which we discussed briefly in chapter 3, and the plans for that nascent state to expand to both sides of the Tennessee at Muscle Shoals and beyond. The two men traveled together to New Orleans and had plenty of time for protracted discussions. Gayoso was suspicious of White's intentions from the beginning, and from New Orleans he wrote: "Don Diego White is thoroughly republican at heart. The movement that is taking place in the state of Franklin has as its object the establishment of independence rather than a *rapprochement* with Spain. The Franklinites know that it is to their interest to form a connection with this province [Louisiana] and they wish to do so, but they are extremely ambitious and their principal object is to extend their territory so that they may draw near the waters of the Mississippi and Mobile Rivers, in the hope that this advantage will attract many immigrants from other places, and enable them to build an opulent state."[15]

Gayoso read the situation correctly. Flirtation with the Spanish was endemic west of the Appalachians: in East Tennessee, on the Cumberland, and also in Kentucky, where one of the most notorious scoundrels of the early Republic, James Wilkinson, was undoubtedly serious but failed in his attempt to get Kentucky to secede from the United States because the majority of Kentuckians were opposed to separation. But flirtation it remained, holding out enticements in order to get the Spanish to intercede with Alexander McGillivray to stop the raids, and for navigational rights on the Mississippi. Governor Miró, however, had his own plan to neutralize the American threat. He encouraged American settlers west of the mountains to migrate to Spanish territory, take up land grants, swear allegiance to the Spanish monarch, and thus free themselves of the Indian menace and gain unhindered access to the great river and the port of New Orleans. This was a dangerous game, letting the fox into the chicken coop, as Alexander McGillivray had warned on more than one occasion: "I have always spoken of the disposition to usurp that the Americans have if once they are allowed to establish themselves. . . ."[16]

"I INFORMED . . . JACKSON" THAT HE WAS NOT MARRIED

While Jackson performed his legal duties and dabbled in frontier intrigue, the matter of Rachel's first marriage suddenly returned to take center stage in their lives. The reader will recall that in the first section of this chapter we followed John Overton's chronology of Jackson's and Rachel's trip to Natchez in the "winter or spring of 1791," Jackson's return to the Cumberland to attend to his legal work, his receipt of information that the Virginia legislature had granted Robards a divorce from Rachel, and his return to Natchez in the summer of 1791 to marry Rachel. All very well, except for two nagging details. The Virginia legislature had not granted a divorce; it had passed an enabling act authorizing Robards to proceed with his divorce in a Kentucky court. It is strange that neither Jackson nor his close friend Overton, both lawyers, realized this, or sought documentation to back up the information. The other nagging detail is that Overton's chronology of events is almost certainly off by one year. Let us first deal with legalities.

The Virginia legislature gave Robards permission to sue for divorce on 20 December 1790. But Robards sat on the decree for two years before initiating action, and for this behavior there is no explanation, only conjecture. On 24 January 1792, the sheriff of Mercer Country, Kentucky, was ordered to deliver a summons to Rachel to appear in court in Danville, Kentucky, "to answer a charge of adultery exhibited against her by *Lewis Roberts* [Robards]."

There is no evidence that the summons was ever delivered, and given the difficulty and danger of travel between Kentucky and the Cumberland it is a safe assumption that it was not. Robards was granted his divorce on 27 September 1793. According to Overton, he first learned this about December 1793, on his way to Jonesborough to attend the district court there. "I need not express my surprise," he wrote, and "I informed General Jackson of it, who was equally surprised. . . ." This meant, of course, that Jackson and Rachel were not legally married—if they ever had been married—and Overton urged that as soon as Jackson returned to Nashville he procure a license and have the ceremony performed again, "so as to prevent all future caviling on the subject." Jackson, however, stubbornly insisted "that he had long since been married, on the belief that a divorce had been obtained, which was the understanding of every person in the country; nor was it without difficulty he could be induced to believe otherwise." But Overton's arguments prevailed, and upon Jackson's return home he and Rachel were legally married on 18 January 1794. But that is not the end of the story, for we have yet to deal with John Overton's dubious chronology, created thirty-three years later in the heat of a presidential campaign.[17]

The problem is that Overton's account does not fit the evidence.[18] We mentioned the absence of evidence in Spanish records for a marriage in Natchez. The fine-tuned Spanish bureaucracy did, however, record the arrival of the Stark party, with whom Rachel and Jackson traveled, in Natchez on 12 January 1790. This was the date on which Robert Stark, as a permanent migrant to Spanish territory, took the required oath of allegiance to the Spanish monarchy. Yet Overton stated that they went in the "winter or spring of 1791."

On 3 November 1790, a Natchez merchant, George Cochrane, wrote a letter to Jackson that ended, "My best respects wait of Mrs. Jackson." Yet Overton has them marrying in the summer of 1791. Cochrane's letter, however, implies that he knew them in Natchez as a married couple prior to the 20 December 1790 enabling act of the Virginia legislature giving Robards permission to sue for divorce. Cochrane also wrote to Jackson from Natchez on 21 October 1791, "Yours of the 14th April . . . came duly to hand, the only favors I recd. since your departure from this country."[19] This means that Jackson departed Natchez before mid-April 1791 and had not returned when Cochrane wrote his letter. But Overton stated that Jackson and Rachel married in Natchez in the summer of 1791.

Those pesky record keepers, this time American, tripped up Overton once again when the estate of Rachel's father, John Donelson, was probated. The "Inventory, Appraisal, and Division of John Donelson's Estate" was "Made the 28th day of January 1791" by Henry Bradford, Robert Cartwright, and none other than our old friend John Overton. Rachel is listed three times—as Rachel Jackson, some six months before Overton said they were married. How ironic that in this case Overton was one of the record keepers. He had obviously forgotten that role when he wrote his account in 1827.[20]

The evidence suggests a marriage, or at least the beginning of a common law relationship, in the summer of 1790, a full year before Overton's claim, about six months before the Virginia legislature granted Robards permission to sue for divorce, which according to Overton he and Jackson did not learn of until the late spring of 1791. This strong possibility is further strengthened by Jackson's absence from court during the July term of 1790. In Robert Remini's words, "Ten cases came to trial in the July 1790 term in connection with which Jackson had earlier pleaded on behalf of the defendants. In the trials of these defendants Jackson did not appear. For him to fail to follow a client's case through to final disposition was most uncharacteristic. Particularly striking was the large number of cases at this single term. It would take something extremely important to account for his absence."[21]

The evidence is strong that Jackson and Rachel went to Natchez together in January 1790, and at least by the summer of that year entered into an intimate relationship. This is what Jackson's enemies would charge many years later, and they were probably right. But what were these young people to do? Rachel was married to a despicable character who later showed signs of mental instability.[22] He made her life a living hell. He first expelled her from his family household, and later left her. She could not live with him, but divorce in that age was rare and almost always initiated by the husband. What was she supposed to do, enter a nunnery? No, Rachel and Jackson were young, in love, and did what came naturally. And that would have been the end of it if Andrew Jackson had not become a national figure and a presidential candidate. But his political enemies and the press then made the affair into a national scandal that haunted them the rest of their lives. Jackson always swore that vituperative attacks drove Rachel to her grave in 1828.

The most important thing to take away from all of this is the attitude of their friends and neighbors on the Cumberland, who could not have been unaware that Rachel and Jackson had run off together while she was married to another man. On their home turf they were not faulted, and Jackson's career continued steadily upward. An old friend, William B. Lewis, wrote in 1827: "I would ask how it is possible that any man could have been held in such high estimation by a whole community if he had acted as has been alleged? Could any man, so destitute of moral virtue, and even setting at defiance the common dreams of life, no matter what his talents, and acquirements might be, maintain so high a standing? The thing is impossible and the mere supposition of its possibility is a vile slander upon the whole population of this State." Lewis continued his defense in a second letter: "The Genl and Mrs. Jackson both perhaps acted imprudently but no one believed they acted criminally."[23]

Certainly Jackson's transgression did not seem an impediment to one of the most important men in his life. It is now time to turn our attention to one William Blount (pronounced "blunt"), who became precisely what a young, ambitious frontier lawyer needed: a powerful patron.

"STAND BEHIND THE CURTAIN
& GIVE THE NECESSARY DIRECTIONS"

Today William Blount is unknown to all but historians, genealogists, and antiquarians. But he was a mover and a shaker in his day, the central figure in a notorious political scandal, and, in the history of American land speculation, if not the king, a strong claimant for the title. This we can say with certainty about him: America was made for William Blount. . . . Or was it the other way around?

William Blount's passion was colored green. He came by it honestly. Avarice seems to have been a family trait. The Blounts were originally of the English gentry class, but let us not confuse this class with the aristocracy, nor indulge in the fiction that its members who migrated created in North America a colonial aristocracy. We can say that their social status in the old country, between nobility and yeomanry, did give them upon arrival in the new a leg up. In the seventeenth century many of this class, especially younger sons, sought better prospects in Virginia, and in 1664 two Blount brothers arrived and settled in Isle of Wight County. One of them, James, who was William Blount's great-grandfather, four years later moved to the North Carolina Low Country, where he became a member of the establishment. Hard work, manual as well as mental, a sharp eye for commerce, and wise marriages proved a potent combination. By the time William's father, Jacob, was born the Blounts had long been a "family of affluence and leadership." They bought and sold land and slaves, ran gristmills and lumberyards and forges, employed millers and carpenters and coopers and blacksmiths. William Blount's biographer put it neatly: "Land was the theme, but variety the counterpoint."[24]

William Blount (1749–1800) was born on 26 March 1749 in Bertie County, North Carolina, to Jacob and Barbara Gray Blount. When William was a child, his father built a home in Craven County that came to be called Blount Hall. To our eyes it is merely a simple frame house larger than usual, but for its time and place it was impressive, and it was in these surroundings that William Blount grew to manhood, the son of a man of influence. His father was on the grand jury that indicted the North Carolina Regulators, and during the military campaign that followed he was, appropriately, paymaster of the Craven County militia. William accompanied his father upcountry, and presumably was at his shoulder while Jacob kept meticulous accounts of monies paid and weapons distributed, right down to "Capt. Holt's 6 shirts, 2 jackets, 3 prs. Breeches, 2 prs thread stockings to be washed. . . ."

During the American Revolution the Blounts chose the Rebel side and continued to prosper. Jacob was paymaster of the 2nd North Carolina Regiment, William became paymaster of the New Bern District Militia, and by the end of 1776 paymaster of the 3rd North Carolina Battalion of Continentals. The latter appointment is of special interest to us. According to William's biographer, its origin lay in the expected march of the North Carolina Continentals to the northern states, and there lay markets for the

William Blount (Tennessee Historical Society)

Blounts to exploit. For in those days military paymasters, quartermasters, and commissaries engaged in business deals on the side that in our time would get them, if exposed, into a great deal of trouble. Throughout the war William Blount served the cause, reaped rewards well beyond those of front-line officers and men, and paid close attention to connections commercial, political, and matrimonial. In 1778 he married Mary Grainger of Wilmington. She was, of course, of an old family, as prominent as the Blounts.

An incident in 1782, while he was serving as a congressman, well illustrates his keen eye for commercial advantage and his modus operandi.

At the British surrender of Savannah to the Rebels, General Anthony Wayne had agreed that British merchants in the city would have six months to remove their goods. Wayne's commander, Major General Nathanael Greene, approved the agreement, and on 30 December 1782 Congress confirmed it. But Blount, ever alert, had noted an incorrect date in the congressional document, which made its approval "technically invalid." In addition, the six-month grace period was almost over, and rising and falling on the tides of the Savannah River were British merchant ships loaded with goods, ripe for plucking by privateers, and as it turned out the Blounts had long been in the privateering business. On 7 January 1783 William wrote to his brother John Gray Blount, admitting that "a clever Fellow to affect the Seizure is a hard thing to be got," that "he ought to be a Man of Address and Boldness who would not be frighted by Party and one who would understand how to deal with lawyers and judges. . . ." His brother should "imploy who you wish, let the commission be in his Name and all the Business in his Name but take Care that you have a sufficient instrument of writing whereby you will come in for a good share of the profit. . . ." If possible, captures should be "condemned in Georgia either by party, Bribery or any other way . . . & then the British merchants will be the Appealants. . . ." One sentence stands out, for it highlights unmistakably William Blount as a classic behind-the-scenes operator: "it may be necessary for you to go on to Savannah under pretense of some other Business & you may stand behind the Curtain & give the necessary Directions."[25]

When one considers those words of advice to his brother, and then ponders the life of William Blount, one is reminded of John Randolph of Roanoke's observation on Martin Van Buren, who "rowed to his object with muffled oars."[26]

Blount spent the years 1781–1787 as a legislator in either North Carolina or the Congress of the Confederation, and in 1787 he was a delegate to the Constitutional Convention. But he did not seek these offices out of a sense of public duty. The power and influence they brought were meant to further his business and speculative interests. He came to believe in a strong central government, especially one that would supplant scattered state control of the lands beyond the mountains, largely because his business interests increasingly focused on land speculation on a grand scale. He did not, however, neglect other possibilities for profit, for though his name was not included in John Gray & Thomas Blount, Merchants, he was an active silent partner. On his way to the Constitutional Convention in Philadelphia, he stopped in Trenton, New Jersey, for a careful inspection of Robert Morris's ironworks and nail factory. In a letter of 30 July 1787 to his brother John Gray Blount he highly recommended such an enterprise for the Blount interests: "of all Works that I have seen I have seen none more easily done nor none so proper for the employment of Negroes because they may always be kept at the same spot and at the same Work and there's no rainey days & they may be [tasked] and I conceive one Week is quite long enough for any person black or white to learn to make a good Nail."[27]

Blount did not spend much time at the Constitutional Convention, preferring to attend the congressional session in New York to look after his western land interests. If he had any influence in the great work done at Philadelphia, it remains well hidden, befitting a man who rowed with well-muffled oars. His comment on the document is less than memorable but also fits a man careful of what he wrote and said: it would "be such a form of Government as I believe will be readily adopted to the several States because I believe it will be such as will be their respective interests to adopt." Reluctant to put his name on the proposed new instrument of national government—for who knew what North Carolina's reaction would be?—he was persuaded by Gouverneur Morris of New York that it was a mere formality, attesting that the states present were unanimous, and on that basis he signed "without committing himself."[28]

Once the Constitution was ratified and the work of organizing a new national government began, Blount sought election by the North Carolina legislature to the U.S. Senate. But his enemies in the assembly ganged up and not only defeated him but delegated Blount to inform his rival, Benjamin Hawkins, of his victory. To say the least, that did not sit well, but he rowed on, seeing to business and public affairs, so intertwined as to shade where one stopped and the other began. Much of his assembly work concentrated on the West, and one successful piece of work will interest us.

For a new protégé, a promising young lawyer by the name of Andrew Jackson, he secured on 21 December 1789, election with salary as attorney general of the Mero District. On the following day, when the assembly adjourned and most members started for home, William Blount stayed behind and also attempted to take care of himself. It was a small matter, but as his biographer pointed out, "utterly characteristic" of him. He submitted to the clerk of the assembly a chit for mileage, a 750-mile round-trip. He was rebuffed. The clerk stated that Blount "in fact . . . did not travel . . . the miles he charges." Blount was ever marked, as one of his political enemies noted, by "his unvaried attention to two-penny matters." But he would soon score a coup that was no two-penny matter, and his accomplishment would further the career of Andrew Jackson.[29]

Although Benjamin Hawkins had defeated Blount for U.S. senator, the two men remained friendly, and from New York Hawkins urged Blount to "write me freely and confidentially on any of your prospects, I have had occasion to name you once or twice in a manner as you deserve. We shall be embarrassed with the Indian business and shall want some very confidential man in that quarter." Hawkins was referring to the upcoming establishment of the Southwest Territory and the need for a governor. Blount had coveted that job for some months, and by the end of March 1790 he felt "assured" that it was his. But there were strong contenders. Patrick Henry pushed his fellow Virginians George Mason and General Joseph Martin. On paper Martin was an obvious choice. He was a man of wide experience who had spent most of his life on the frontier and had acted as Indian agent for both Virginia and North Carolina, and the governor would also be the chief Indian agent of the territory. But the latter duty was a black mark against him, for he was too solicitous of Indian rights for frontier people, who produced a drumbeat of opposition to his appointment. John Sevier, ever popular on the frontier, was pushed forward by many of his fellow citizens. But Sevier carried heavy negative baggage: his role in the attempted breakaway of the State of Franklin, and massacres of Indians for which he was blamed.[30]

One formidable rival was a hero of the Revolution, General Anthony Wayne. But Wayne was a native of Pennsylvania, not North Carolina, which had ceded to the national government the land in question. This reveals that the Southwest Territory, created on 26 May 1790 for the "Government of Territory South of the River Ohio," in fact included only the land ceded by North Carolina. For Kentucky was governed by Virginia until it became a state in 1792, and the lands south of Tennessee, in dispute between the United States and Spain, were claimed by Georgia, which refused to cede them. This put William Blount in a favorable position and he made the most of it by calling in all the support he could muster. Most of the North Carolina congressional delegation, including the well-regarded Senator Benjamin Hawkins, supported Blount, and the influential Cumberland frontiersman Daniel Smith wrote to congressmen in support of his candidacy. As a Federalist, Blount had the right political credentials, and he knew President George Washington. He was also well versed on western affairs and well liked by its citizens. Everyone knew that he had huge land holdings in the new territory, but that turned out not to be decisive in the choice. On 8 June 1790 William Blount was appointed governor of the Southwest Territory.[31]

He was very pleased, and very candid about his pleasure, and very grateful to those who had pulled strings for him. He wrote to John Steele, "Be pleased to accept my sincere Thanks, for your kind Congratulations on being delivered from my State Enemies and for the very active and friendly part you took in bringing about an Event so much to be wished by me, but independent of these Considerations, the appointment *itself* is truly important to me more so in my opinion than any other in the Gift of the President could have been, the Salary is handsome, and my Western Lands had become so great an object to me that it had become absolutely necessary that I should go to the Western Country, to secure them and perhaps my presence might have enhanced there Value—I am sure my present appointment will—I am so sensible of your Attention to me in procuring this appointment that my Feelings of gratitude surpass what I have language to express of which I hope I shall have it in my power to give you more substantial Proofs by my Actions."[32]

The modern reader, accustomed to shuttle diplomacy and day trips abroad by presidents, should pause and consider once again how long it took to get things done in Blount's day by considering the time that elapsed between the date of his appointment and his arrival west of the mountains. Thomas Jefferson, then secretary of state, dispatched Blount's commission on 15 June; Blount received it in Greenville, North Carolina, on 6 July. He spent the months of July and August preparing for his journey to the frontier. Luggage and cloth for clothing suitable for his new rank had to be ordered from Philadelphia. Horses and equipage had to be bought. He had to raise cash for his trip, for specie was then scarce, and even affluent businessmen were often "without a copper." In order to close accounts—that is, pay debts and collect credits—Blount had to follow the circuit judges on their rounds to Hillsboro, Edenton, New Bern, and Willmington, because it was at the court sessions that businessmen from the respective surrounding areas appeared. To pay his debts he sold slaves. He finally received the congressional act establishing the territory and information on how to set up the new government. Government, as with business, means the production of paper, and a governor without a press is hardly worth notice. At Hillsboro he hired a printer, Robert Ferguson, and the editor of the *Fayetteville Gazette,* who "agreed to cross the mountains as soon as possible with their press."

By early September Blount was ready to set out, but not due west for the mountains; instead he traveled north to Mount Vernon and on 17 September paid his respects to President Washington, who directed him to go on to Philadelphia to take the oath of office from Attorney General Randolph. But Blount saved time by taking the oath on 20 September from Supreme Court justice James Iredell in nearby Alexandria. Finally, on 22 September, he left Alexandria for the Southwest Territory via Winchester and the Shenandoah Valley. On 10 October he stopped briefly to rest at the home of William Yancey on the Upper Holston. There he forwarded news of his arrival, then pushed south to the home of William Cobb, where the Watauga River flows into the Holston, and established his temporary capital. It had taken a few days over five months from his appointment to his arrival in the territory. They not only did things differently in those days, they moved slower.[33]

Blount's was a powerful position. He had no territorial legislature to answer to, and he had sweeping powers of appointment. No lawyer could be licensed without his approval, court officers from clerks to judges served at his will, sheriffs and constables required his approval, all militia officers below the rank of general were appointed by Governor William Blount. It is obvious, therefore, to paraphrase a famous twentieth-century American political observation, that to get along in the Southwest Territory, one had to go along with Governor Blount.[34]

No one was more aware of this than our young man on the make, Andrew Jackson. We do not know when Blount and Jackson met, but within four months of Blount's arrival Jackson received his first appointment from the new governor. On 15 February 1791 Blount appointed Jackson Mero District attorney general, with special instructions to prosecute vigorously white violaters of the treaty with the Cherokees. Jackson's performance in office met Blount's expectations, and on 10 September 1792, the twenty-five-year-old attorney general was given an additional plum: judge advocate of the Davidson County cavalry regiment, commanded by Rachel's brother-in-law, Robert Hays, who two years later as justice of the peace for Davidson County would perform the marriage ceremony that finally, and legally, bound together Rachel and Andrew. The judge advocate's job did not pay much, only "two young Likely second rate cows and calves. . . ." But it was one of the most significant appointments of Jackson's career. It was his entrée to the militia, a key political as well as military institution of the early Republic, and Jackson would eventually make the most of it.[35]

Andrew Jackson was not unaware that he had met his patron, and in 1793 he let his gratitude be known in a letter to a man close to Blount: "Any Transaction of yours or Governor Blount with Respect to my Business will be perfectly pleasing to me as I know from Experience that my interest will be attended to by Each."[36]

Chapter 8

Buchanan's Station and Nickajack

"YOU HAVE GROWN UP SINCE VERY STRONG . . .
WE ARE BUT FEW TO WHAT WE WERE"

Territorial status did not end the bloodletting on the frontier. Dragging Canoe was dead, but the flame of resistance he had helped ignite burned on among the Chickamaugas in the Five Lower Towns. The towns were located in the rugged hill country where the states of Tennessee, Georgia, and Alabama now meet. Lookout Mountain Town lay in the wide valley of Lookout Mountain Creek about fifteen miles south of the Tennessee River, and not much farther than that from modern Chattanooga, Tennessee. The other towns were on the Tennessee. About twelve miles below the Suck, the fearsome navigational hazard that Rachel Jackson had experienced on her father's boat *Adventure,* was the town of Running Water. Three miles below Running Water was Nickajack, and about five miles farther was Long Island Town. They were all on the south bank of the Tennessee, but Crowtown, ten miles below Running Water and about four miles south of modern Stevenson, Alabama, was on the north bank. In 1792 it was estimated that the Chickamaugas could muster 250 to 300 warriors. With some Shawnees who lived among them, and young Creeks unwilling to lay down the hatchet, Chickamauga pressure was unrelenting.[1]

On the Cumberland between 1 January 1791 and 5 November 1792, sixty-two settlers were killed, thirteen wounded, and twenty-two taken prisoner. Among the wounded were James Robertson, shot through both arms while working in his fields, and beside him his son, shot through the thigh. In East Tennessee fifteen were killed, two wounded, and five taken prisoner. During one raid on the Cumberland on 28 February 1792, Elijah Robertson reported that the Indian raiders had revealed a mordant sense of humor.

They killed "James Thompson, and family; also Peter Caffey's family, within about five miles of Nashville." They killed "Mrs. Thompson in the yard, and jumped into the house and killed all the women and children, except two small ones, who they spoke to in English, and told them to grow up, and then they would come and kill them."[2]

Secretary of War Knox was furious with the frontier people, especially John Sevier's followers in East Tennessee, for exhibiting "folly and wickedness" in their utter disregard of the boundary lines established at the Treaty of Hopewell in 1785. But he also recognized in a letter of 4 January 1790 to Washington that the government lacked the means to remove the settlers from their farms south of the French Broad. The president, therefore, instructed Governor William Blount to negotiate a new treaty with the Cherokees. The Treaty of Holston was subsequently signed on 2 July 1791 at White's Fort (modern Knoxville) between Governor Blount and the Cherokees, but it did not include the Chickamaugas, and the Cherokees who signed were dissatisfied with the new land cessions and their annuity. But they had no alternative to signing. The highly respected chief Hanging Maw put it well: "when you first settled on the sea you were young . . . you have grown up since very strong . . . we are but few to what we were. . . ." That winter the Cherokees sent a delegation to Philadelphia, then the national capital, to protest to Secretary Knox both the cessions and the annuity. The cessions stood, their annuity was increased. But neither the original amount nor the increase answered the basic problem that existed between Americans and Indians: the determination of the frontier people to push the Indians off their land, the equal determination of the Indians to defend their country against the invaders.[3]

In late May 1792, Governor William Blount met the Cherokees at Coyatee, about thirty-five miles south of Knoxville, to distribute the increase. On the surface, all was sweetness and light. The Indians prepared a house for the governor's reception, "at which they had erected the standard of the United States upon a pole nearly of the height and size of a liberty pole." Prior to Blount's arrival the chiefs and warriors of the Five Lower Towns, absent the previous year at the Treaty of Holston, had "marched in, painted black, and sprinkled with flour, meaning to show they had been at war, but were then for peace." On 20 May Governor Blount was greeted by about two thousand Indians. He described them as "divided into two lines, extending about three hundred yards each, leaving an open space between for myself and honorary escort to pass. As soon as I entered the space, a firing was commenced in the manner of a feu de joie [musket fire, one man after another firing a round into the air in a continual roar], and handsomely kept up until I had passed through. Shouts of joy instantly followed, and immediately after I had alighted, under the standard of the United States, I was surrounded by the whole number, with countenaces demonstrative of more joy than I had heretofore been a witness of."[4]

After two days of ball playing, eating, whiskey drinking, and "many private talks with the chiefs," Blount addressed the gathering, noting that its purpose was to divide the goods due the Cherokees under treaty provisions. He specifically noted the presence of the chiefs and warriors of the Lower Towns and reminded them that if they had attended the treaty made the year before they would have received a full share of the goods, and "the fault was their own." Then Blount recited a litany of attacks, killings, burnings, and horse stealing by the Indians, demanded that the chiefs "exert yourselves to restrain your young people," adding that he "with difficulty" had restrained the white people "whose relations have been killed from falling on the Indians and taking satisfaction, without regard to age or sex." The chief called Breath, of Nickajack, said that "the people of the Lower towns have been very deaf to your talk, but now we will hear them (he then presented the string of white beads, the usual token of friendship)." But Breath denied knowledge of murders and horse theft: "I tell you truly, I do not know who committed the whole of them; but from the great council of Estanaula you shall be informed of whatever has been done by our nation, and . . . the prisoners in our possession . . . delivered."

It was left that the Indian reply would come from Estanaula, for "there were sundry frontier people present" at Coyatee and Blount feared their reaction if the Indians confessed to killings and theft in an open meeting. But in a private talk with Richard Justice, a mixed blood from Lookout Mountain Town, Blount "expressed great concern for what had happened since the treaty, as did several others, and said, 'they hoped they [the Cherokees] should be able to restrain their young people after the council at Estanaula.'" With regard to Richard Justice, however, recall David Craig's report of the previous March that he had seen a portrait of William Augustus Bowles in Justice's house, and his assessment that Justice, "heretofore one of the warmest friends of the United States, now listens, in preference, to Bowles, and adheres to his counsels." Finally, Blount wrote of two important Chickamauga chiefs, Eskaqua and the mixed-blood John Watts: "The former, who appears to have entered fully into the views of the United States, and the latter, as fully determined to second him, rejoiced much on this auspicious event. They may be said to be champions of peace." Blount's assessment may be said to come under the well-known category of famous last words.[5]

The Cherokee council at Estanaula, 24 June–1 July 1792, produced an extraordinary demand by the Chickamauga chief Little Turkey, who had been at neither the Hopewell nor Holston treaties. Knox described him as the "most influential chief of the Cherokees. . . ." Little Turkey repeated the old Chickamauga insistence that the Cumberland settlers were intruders on the joint hunting grounds of the Creeks, the Cherokees, the Choctaws, and the Chickasaws, "and therefore the Indians "have a right to steal horses and in case of opposition to kill." Had James Robertson, Andrew Jackson, and others seen Knox's reaction to Little Turkey's rejection of what the settlers insisted were their treaty rights, their fury would have surpassed the secretary's. Knox wrote to Washington with regard to the Cumberland, "I have had some doubts whether that part of the line was agreeable to the opinion of the Cherokees generally—and it really appears to me that something will have to be arranged on that subject." Later in this chapter, we will have more to say about the conflict between government attitudes and policy and the driving urge of the People of the Western Waters.[6]

Meanwhile, violence continued on the frontier, despite the new treaty. Four days before Blount set out for Coyatee to meet with the Cherokees and the Chickamaugas, and only about fifteen miles south of his headquarters at White's Fort, Blount reported that two boys named Wells, about eight and ten years of age, "were picking strawberries near their father's door in his view when the Indians six in number came up to them tomahawked & scalped them & went off without making further attempts on the family."[7]

A major disaster occurred on 26 June 1792 on the Cumberland. A station was wiped out. Of some thirty or more settlers gathered there, only about three to seven escaped. Some twenty-five miles northeast of Nashville and north of the Cumberland on the west branch of Bledsoe Creek, Jacob Zeigler had established his station sometime between the fall of 1790 and the spring of 1791. The most important thing to know about Zeigler's Station is that it was a weak station of "three or four families in Cabbins without being Stockaded or fortified in any way, hence it was easy to be taken." On the afternoon of the twenty-sixth a war party estimated at between 30 to 60 Creeks, Cherokees, and Shawnees, the number depending upon the source, fired at men working in a cornfield "adjoining the Station, Killed one and wounded several," according to Silas McBee, who joined the pursuit and related his account half a century later. The men ran to the station and the Indians vanished. At this point the carelessness of the settlers strikes the observer over two hundred years later. We have seen it before and will encounter it again. It is almost a devil-may-care attitude. They lived with danger every day and every night. Constant vigilance was required. But we must remember that the great majority of these men and women were farmers who labored incredibly hard from dawn to dusk and beyond, and in the few hours left them for rest and relaxation they probably succumbed to the all-too-human failing of letting one's guard down at the wrong time.

It is said that the families were sitting up after dark in one of the cabins with the corpse of Michael Shaffer, the man killed in the cornfield that day, and that the fire in the hearth and lighted candles shined through every crack in the wall. No account mentions sentries. The Indians attacked and managed to set on fire a cabin that was filled with flax. One settler burned to death. McBee thought it was Jacob Zeigler. Three others were killed, a few who were hotly pursued escaped either wounded or unhurt, and thirteen were taken prisoner. John Carr reported that Mrs. Zeigler "made her escape with one child, thrusting her handkerchief into its mouth to prevent its crying whilst she fled." Two of her other children were taken. Carr also described the last stand of Archie Wilson: "He had fought bravely, but wounded and finally retreating from the fort, he was brought to bay at about one hundred yards distant. I was there the next day, and the ground was beaten all around, showing the desperate defense he had made. They had broken the breech of a gun over his head in the fight. . . . It was an awful sight."

The pursuit party in which John Carr served "noticed, at each muddy spot . . . passed the tracks of the bare feet of the eight children they had captured," and later "we discovered, by the scraps of dressed skins, that they had made the children moccasins, their feet having doubtless become sore by the hard travelling; and at the next muddy spot, we saw the little foot-prints of moccasins. There was that much kindness in them." It was also probable that the prisoners could be ransomed. With the Indians a day and a half ahead, Carr related, "General Winchester gave us . . . a very sensible speech, and told us that if they were relatives of his who were thus taken, he should prefer to have them taken to the 'Nation,' to having their lives risked by the attempt to take them in action." The prisoners were taken to Running Water Town and the Creek Nation and later ransomed by family and friends.[8]

Women were not always taken prisoner. The following year John Steel and his daughter, son, and brother Robert were ambushed on the road near Greenfield Station. The men in the station heard the gunshots and rushed down the road. John Steel's son was wounded, but he and Robert Steel had escaped. John Steel was killed and scalped. His daughter Betsy, seventeen years old and beautiful, lay on the road scalped and dying. She had obviously fought hard for her life. Her hands, cut and bleeding from grabbing Indian knives, clutched black Indian hair torn from the heads of her killers.[9]

On 15 July 1792 Isaac Pennington and a man named Milligen were killed and a man named McFarland wounded on the road from Nashville to Kentucky. On 31 July, in a peach orchard near Bledsoe's Lick, John Berkeley was wounded and his son John Jr. killed and scalped. The father killed the Indian while he was scalping his son.[10]

But these actions, even the Zeigler disaster, were the usual raids. A far more ambitious strike was being planned by Dragging Canoe's successor, John Watts, described by William Blount as a champion of peace.

"MORE BALLS, MORE BALLS, FIGHT LIKE MEN"

The sky was clear the night of 30 September 1792. A bright moon shined over Buchanan's Station, illuminating stockade and blockhouses, cattle grazing outside, and fields cleared for corn and wheat. In silhouette in the dark forests beyond, some 300 painted warriors lay in wait while their spies crept close to the stockade walls, listened, and peered through portholes to discover whether the inhabitants were alert.[11]

Buchanan's Station was located on Mill Creek, which flows northward into the Cumberland in what are now Nashville's suburbs but was then four miles from the frontier town. We described the arrival of the Buchanan party from South Carolina in 1779, separate from the Robertson party, and their role along with others in building Fort Nashborough, where they lived until 1785. When the North Carolina legislature set aside land for the boundaries of Nashville, the Buchanans and others found their lands within the boundary line and reserved for Revolutionary War veterans. They and other "first comers" who had lost kin defending the fort had to leave. The Buchanans and some other families started over again at Mill Creek. There were some 7,000 settlers on the Cumberland now, but few of the 1779–1780 pioneers were left. Of the 131 who stuck it out and refused to run for Kentucky or return east, 63 were dead by the spring of 1784. It would be interesting to know how many of the 68 survivors were still alive eight years later. Not old John Buchanan Sr., credited with killing 10 Indians in a rail pen and saving Ned Swanson during the battle of Fort Nashborough in 1780. He had moved with the family to Mill Creek, but one day in 1787 somebody carelessly left the stockade gate open and Indians slipped inside and killed and scalped the old man by his hearthside where he was relaxing with his wife, who sank to her knees and begged for mercy, which was granted. An in-law once asked old Mrs. Buchanan "how she felt when she saw her old man she had lived with so long tomahawked in that way; but she gave me no answer, and putting her hands before her face cried so, I thought she would have broken her heart."[12]

Now John Buchanan Jr., described by William Martin, who knew him, as "a thick set man, five feet, six or eight inches tall," was the head of the family, a "good soldier hunter and land Locator, and by the latter business, made himself rich." Martin also found him "dull and uninteresting, not much character, but his wife was a very different character." Sarah Ridley Buchanan, better known as Sally, was the daughter of Colonel George Ridley, who had built Ridley's Station two miles upstream from Buchanan's on Mill Creek. As with the Buchanans, who had been moving on the southern frontier most of the eighteenth century, Colonel Ridley was another example of a deep-rooted American restlessness for the next horizon. He was born in 1737 in Williamsburg, Virginia, at age eighteen had been at Braddock's defeat during the French and Indian War, survived border fights during the American Revolution, settled in the Holston country in 1779, and in about 1790 pushed west again with his family, to the ever-dangerous Cumberland country. Colonel Ridley's son William was killed on 17 April 1788 by that constant companion of soldiers regular or irregular—friendly fire. His daughter Sally was of the stuff of pioneers, the kind of woman needed on the cutting edge of frontiers. She definitely was, as William Martin wrote, an entirely different character than her husband: "She was large, bold, homely, rough, vulgar, industrious, neat, kind, benevolent, highly honorable and much respected by all. She had the physical powers of a man, and one is almost ready to say should have been one. She could stand with both feet in a half bushel measure and shoulder 2 1/2 bushels of corn [150 pounds]."[13]

Sally Ridley Buchanan was a plainspoken woman. On one occasion, Martin reported, General Gaines and his wife called at Buchanan's Station. It was "Scouring day . . . everything was in confusion. She with her [petti]Coats tucked up pretty high, her servant girls were scrubbing the floor when General and his lady stept in. After the usual Salutations of Shaking hands, etc., she exclaimed, 'Well General you have Cotch me with my britches down, but I must do the best I can.'" On the night of 30 September 1792 Sally Buchanan was bigger than her usual two hundred pounds, big with child, probably in her ninth month, for she was due anytime.[14]

Buchanan's Station should not have been caught with its "britches down" that night, even thought the early warning had been canceled and the militia gathered to meet the threat disbanded. The first warnings had come to William Blount from various sources as early as 11 September. Little Turkey wrote nine days earlier from Turkey Town: "I am sorry and ashamed for to tell you, of their proceedings and bad conduct . . . they are determined to go off to war, all of the five lower towns on the Big river; they have and will make war by themselves; you may be assured and believe me, it is not the consent of the whole nation, nor no part of it only them five towns— they agreed amongst themselves." He begged that the other towns be left in peace, "for myself and all the head-men in the nation and talked and done all in our power to have them stopped . . . to have them leave off, and think about nothing but peace, and not to bring war on themselves. . . ."

By the tenth Little Turkey's letter and similar communications from the U.S. interpreters with the Cherokees, James Carey and John Thompson, reached Chota, "where there were a great many Indians, as well as white people from the settlements" gathered for the Green Corn Dance, Blount reported to Henry Knox. The frontiersman James Ore was there and was told by Cherokees that there were 500 hostiles, of whom 100 were Creeks, their apparent destination the Cumberland. Ore made haste to Knoxville with the letters, arriving on the eleventh at three o'clock in the morning. Blount immediately sent a courier with an order to James Robertson to mobilize the Mero District militia. Two days later John Sevier wrote that at Chota he was called by the headmen to the council house and told of the Chickamauga plans and that they had made a formal declaration of war against the United States. That, Blount informed Secretary Knox, "was very unexpected, and has given great alarm to the frontiers. Indeed, I do not find that any thing of the kind has before been done by Indians in so formal a manner."[15]

But then John Watts, Bloody Fellow, and Glass wrote to Blount that there would be no war, that they had stopped the warriors from marching and sent them home. Watts lied, and Blount fell for it. Indian spies even penetrated Blount's home in Knoxville to lull him into confidence, as he admitted later in a report. The Cherokee chief Unacata, "or White Man-killer, . . . came to this place, and stayed with me ten days, immediately pre-ceding the time he set out with Watts for war, ate and drank constantly at my table, was treated in the kindest manner, and made the strongest profes-sion of friendship during his stay, and at his departure." Young Cherokee warriors were recruited by the Chickamaugas to join them, and Blount reported that two of them were John Walker and John Fields, mixed bloods "who have been raised among and by the white people, in whom everybody who knew them had the utmost confidence." John Walker, Blount wrote, was "apparently the most innocent, and good natured youth I ever saw. They were both at the Treaty of Holston and have been repeatedly here since." Blount, to whom intrigue and manipulation were second nature, was hoist on his own petard. On the fourteenth he sent another courier to Robertson ordering him to dismiss the militia.[16]

But Robertson was wary. Two of his own spies, Richard Findelstone and Jonathan Deraque, had come in to warn him that Watts, Bloody Fellow, and Glass were lying, that the Indian force was on the march for the Cumberland. Robertson, encamped with 300 men, declined to dismiss them. And Buchanan's Station, which a contemporary reported many years later "was in a dilapidated condition & would have been easily taken," was immediately repaired. The stockading was rebuilt, "heavy timbers well sunk in the earth," and "new Block-houses" erected, and a "new heavy gate" installed. Robertson, however, could not keep the militia mobilized indefinitely. The march from the Lower Towns to the Cumberland should have taken at the most five or six days, but over two weeks had gone by since the alarm and spies sweeping the countryside for Robertson found no signs of Indians. As we will see clearly later in our narrative, idle militiamen in camp become fractious, a condition that all commanders of militia, even one as highly respected as James Robertson, had to take into consideration. Finally, on 29 September, Robertson dismissed the militia. Fifteen gunmen remained behind to man the stockade walls of Buchanan's Station.[17]

The day the militia left, John Buchanan sent his own spies, Jonathan Gee and Clayton Powell, into the surrounding countryside. They were never heard of again, although Gee's handkerchief and one of Powell's moccasins were later found. Governor Blount later reported that they were killed by John Walker and John Fields, the two young mixed bloods so well trusted by the Americans, who "acted as the advance, or spies in Watts' party. . . ." They may have been the men who reported back to John Watts that Buchanan's Station had been rebuilt and could not be taken. According to John Carr, Watts deployed Indians, undoubtedly mixed bloods, dressed as white men ahead of his main force, and "by these means he decoyed the unfortunate men within reach, and surrounded and killed them." It was said, Carr wrote, that their hearts were cut out.

The bulk of Watts's force consisted of Chickamaugas, augmented by Creeks and Shawnees, and as so often happened to Indians at war they could agree on neither strategy nor tactics. It was this squabbling that apparently slowed their march from the Tennessee. John Watts, the nominal commander, favored striking directly at the heart of the Cumberland Settlements and taking Nashville. But Shawnee Warrior and the Creek chief Talotiskee argued that they should first take Buchanan's Station, and Watts lost the argument. Then they disagreed over tactics. Watts planned to conceal his force under the banks of Mill Creek, wait until the women came out in the morning to milk the cows, then rush the gate. Once again he was right, but a young warrior called him an *"old woman"* and proposed instead to set fire to the rear of the fort. When the people rushed out of the gate, Watts with the main force would be waiting for them. John Watts, an able strategist and tactician, was obviously not a strong personality who could bend men to his will, a trait desperately required given the Indian system of leadership. The young warrior's plan was adopted. William Blount later wrote, "Difference of opinion, as the mode and place of attack, at the rendezvous after they passed at the Tennessee, probably was the cause of the delay; I have no other way to account for it; and it is a rock on which large parties of Indians have generally split, especially when consisting of more than one nation."[18]

Nevertheless, the chance remained that Buchanan's Station could be surprised. The stout new gate was closed and fastened, but no sentries were posted, no lookouts in the blockhouses scanning the moonlit fields surrounding the station. The people sat up late. John McRory was the last to retire, but he "heard the cattle alarmed, looked out a port hole and saw some forty Indians in a squad within a rod or two [5 1/2–11 yards] of the gate, fired at them, and soon all hands were firing." The Indians "immediately returned the fire, and continued a very heavy and constant firing upon the Station . . . for an hour. . . ." James Robertson wrote to Blount in his report: "During the whole time of the attack, the Indians were not more than ten yards from the blockhouses, often in large numbers round the lower walls, attempting to put fire to it. One ascended the roof with a torch where he was shot, and, falling to the ground, renewed his attempts to fire the bottom logs, and was killed." This Indian was a Cherokee mixed blood from Running Water Town, son of a Cherokee man and a French woman. Before he died he is said to have shouted to his comrades "that he was gone but never to abandon the attempt till the fort was taken." His and other attempts to burn the station failed in large part because the new construction was made of green wood that resisted the flames. Meanwhile, Sally Buchanan's efforts were the stuff of legend. "More balls, more balls, fight like men, I'll make you more balls," she is said to have cried out over the din of battle. It is also reported that she repeatedly " 'came amidst the raking fire of bullets singing through the picketing,' a bottle of whiskey in one hand, bullets in her tucked up apron."[19]

Once more the Indian lack of a unified command structure and their deficiency in the tactics and technology of taking fortified places sent a numerically superior Indian force home in defeat. Simple scaling ladders might have made the difference. This was not a unique situation in world military history. On A.D. 9 August 378, in one of history's decisive battles, a Roman army was destroyed and the emperor Valens killed by a Visigothic army on the field of Adrianople. Yet during the following days the victorious barbarian horde met total failure in its attempts to take the city of Adrianople. Siege warfare was beyond them.[20]

Even the sympathetic historian of the Chickamaugas calls the attack on Buchanan's Station a "debacle." Not one casualty had been inflicted on the defenders. But Shawnee Warrior was dead. Talotiskee was dead. John Watts was seriously wounded. James Robertson described the scene in the morning outside the walls. The victors found "much blood, and signs that many dead had been dragged off, and litters having been made to carry their wounded to their horses, which had been left a mile from the station." In their retreat they left behind the signs of a defeated army: "several swords, hatchets, pipes, kettles, and budgets of different Indian articles; one of the swords was a fine Spanish blade, and richly mounted in the Spanish fashion."[21]

The frontier would remain ablaze, small war parties continued to raid, American mounted militia rode in hot pursuit. But the attack on Buchanan's Station was a milestone in the great, unending struggle for North America. It was the last major Indian attack on the Cumberland. The settlers did not yet realize it, but in their patch of country they had won.

"PEACE TALKS ARE ONLY DELUSIONS . . . IN ORDER TO PUT US OFF OUR GUARD"

The lonely struggle of the Cumberland settlers to establish themselves at the back of beyond reveals the profound difference between the federal government and the People of the Western Waters in the means proposed to accomplish a common goal: the removal of the eastern Indians west of the Mississippi. In 1794 Andrew Jackson expressed a sentiment from which he never deviated: "I fear that their Peace Talks are only Delusions; and in order to put us off our Guard; why Treat with them . . . does not Experience teach us that Treaties answer no other Purpose than opening an Easy door for the Indians to pass through to Butcher our Citizens; what Motives Congress are governed by with Respect to their pacific Dispositon towards them I know not. some say humanity dictates it; but Certainly she ought to extend an Equal share of humanity to her own Citizens. . . ." He also raised the specter of separation of the western country if the national government did not afford relief: "Discouraged and breaking and numbers leaving the Territory and moving to Kentuckey, this Country is Declining fast and unless Congress lends us a more ample protection this Country will have at length to break or seek a protection from some other Source. . . ." Almost a quarter of a century later he would write to President James Monroe: "I have long viewed treaties with the Indians an absurdity not to be reconciled to the principles of our Government. The Indians are subjects of the United States, inhabiting its territory and acknowledging its sovereignty, then is it not absurd for the sovereign to negotiate by treaty with the subject." That was the voice of the frontier. It had not changed since the first few families pushed west of Virginia's Blue Ridge in colonial days, risking life and limb for the promised land.[22]

A man who would become Jackson's mortal enemy, John Sevier, was just as candid: if peaceful means did not suffice, the answer was the sword. During the waning days of the breakaway State of Franklin, a man named Samuel Foreman, who was opposed to Sevier and his followers, gave the following deposition: "I heard John Sevier, at a public gathering of people on the French Broad, stand up and inform people that he had received a letter from Colonel Rody, and also one from Colonel Outlaw, informing him that the Assembly of North Carolina had now thrown the people of that country from under their protection, and that they had no other way now but to stand in their own defense. And Mr. Sevier further said, you all well know that the Cherokees have refused selling their lands to us from time to time, and we have no other way now but to take it by the sword, but going into their nation, killing and taking their women and children, destroying their provisions, and by these means we will compel them to give up their lands to us." That, too, was the authentic voice of the People of the Western Waters. Two men who came to loathe the sight of each other, Jackson and Sevier, were as one on the march of conquest.[23]

George Washington and his secretary of war, Henry Knox, had a vastly different approach born of the country's sad experience during the Confederation period. In 1784 the Mohawk chief Aaron Hill, speaking not only for the Iroquois Confederacy "but also in the names of all the other tribes," told U.S. commissioners at Fort Stanwix, "We are free, and Independent, and at present under no influence. We have hitherto been bound by the Great King, but he having broke the chain, and left us to ourselves, we are again free, and Independent." An American commissioner, General Richard Butler, harshly rejected Hill's claim: "It is not so. You are a subdued people; you have been overcome in a war which you entered into with us, not only without provocation, but in violation of most sacred obligations." Butler concluded by informing the chiefs, "We shall now therefore declare to you the conditions, on which alone you can be received into the peace and protection of the United States." In one of those conditions a single sentence clearly described the Indian policy of the United States immediately after the war: "The King of Great Britain ceded to the United States *the whole,* by the right of conquest they might *claim the whole.*"[24]

By the right of conquest. Brave words. Andrew Jackson and John Sevier would have approved. And all very well had the newly independent country the wherewithal to field a large, well-trained, disciplined army to carry out such bold language. But it did not. There was precious little money in the treasury, and even if the necessary funds had been there most of the Founding Fathers had taken in with their mother's milk a deep-seated distrust of standing armies. That feeling had been strengthened by their experiences with the British army in the years leading up to the War of the Revolution, and toward the end of the war by the slightly veiled threat of the American army to march on Congress to claim back pay. Washington had stopped that movement in its tracks, and established once and for all the primacy of civil authority, but that was not at all clear in the years following the war.

The right of conquest doctrine ran up against a solid wall of Indian resistance both north and south of the Ohio, and given the lack of military means to enforce it Congress was forced to back away from threats and bold pronouncements. By the time the new government established by the Constitution took over in 1789, George Washington, Henry Knox, and other high officials of government had resolved on a policy of orderly expansion. Knox knew that the nation lacked the military means to drive the Indians westward

and was unwilling to spend the money for such a purpose. He was also especially sensitive to the opinions of contemporary Europeans and posterity,
writing that "a nation solicitous of establishing its character on the broad basis
of justice, would not only hesitate at, but reject every proposition to benefit
itself, by the injury of any neighboring community, however contemptible
and weak it might be, either with respect to its manners or power. . . ." He
referred to settlers in passing: "Were the representations of the people of
the frontiers (who have imbibed the strongest prejudices against the Indians,
perhaps in consequence of the murders of their dearest friends and connexions) only to be regarded . . . an expedition, however inadequate, must be
undertaken." Upon examination, however, of the "confused state of injuries"
to each side, "both policy and justice unite in dictating the attempt of treating with" the Indians. Thus Knox's policy was the opposite of Andrew Jackson's, who had summed up his position in four short words: "Why Treat
with them? . . ." Knox went further: "The principle of the Indian right to
the lands they possess being thus conceded, the dignity and interest of the
nation will be advanced by making it the basis of the future administration
of justice towards the Indian tribes. . . ."

But then Knox revealed as clearly as any rampant frontiersman the ultimate American goal: "As the settlements of the whites shall approach near to
the Indian boundaries established by treaties, the game will be diminished,
and the lands being valuable to the Indians only as hunting grounds, they
will be willing to sell further tracts for small considerations. By the expira-
tion, therefore of the above period, it is most probable that the Indians will,
by the invariable operation of the causes which have hitherto existed in their
intercourse with the whites, be reduced to a very small number. . . ." In
other words, eventually we are going to get the land, but out of a decent
respect for the opinions of others, and because we do not have the means to
take it by force, we will adopt the reasonable, and less expensive, course of
negotiating treaties, abiding by them, and then negotiating future treaties as
the Indians withdraw and disappear because of the lack of game.[25]

An example of this occurred among the Cherokees about eight years
after Knox wrote and was described by John Sevier: "Red headed Will as I
am informed has already with the whole of his large town left the nation, to
settle on the west side of the Mississippi, and his address and influence will
be the means of number more going after him. This fellow swore, 'that Congress was scratching after every bit of rackoon skin in the nation that was big
enough to cover a Squaws [ass?] that their hunting was nearly over, and after
that their land was the next object.' "[26]

During the first Washington administration there was also a glimmer of
a future policy of weaning the Indians from their way of life. In his third
annual message, Washington recommended "that commerce with them
should be promoted under regulations tending to secure an equitable deportment toward them, and that such rational experiments should be made for
imparting to them the blessings of civilization as may from time to time suit
their conditions."[27]

But Knox, Washington, and others were deluded with regard to the fierce desire of the Indians to keep their lands and maintain their own way of life. As we shall see, efforts to change Indian attitudes toward land tenure and make farmers out of them in the white manner, especially in the South, created terrible divisions in the tribes that would involve frontier whites and become a major cause of an Indian war that surpassed in significance most fought east of the Mississippi and all fought west of the great river. Eastern officials also ran up against another desire as fierce as the Indians': frontier refusal to be reined in by official policy, laws, proclamations, and treaties. Their attitude infuriated eastern officials as it had British colonial soldiers and administrators. As early as 1783, Washington wrote, "To suffer a wide extended Country to be over run with Land Jobbers, Speculators, and Monopolisers or even with scattr'd settlers is, in my opinion, inconsistent with that wisdom and policy which our true interest dictates, or that an enlightened People ought to adopt. . . ." We might add here that George Washington was himself a land speculator, even using military land warrants purchased from Revolutionary War veterans to claim 3,051 acres on the Little Miami River near Cincinnati. By 1790, the year after he became president, Washington's speculative land investments west of the mountains totaled about 52,000 acres.[28]

Henry Knox was no less opposed to the activities of settlers and speculators. We have already taken note of his thought that the legality of the Cumberland Settlements was questionable. In 1788 he reported to Congress on "White Outrages" against the Cherokees by the settlers in East Tennessee south of the French Broad, which he assigned to their "avaricious desire of obtaining the fertile lands possessed by the said Indians. . . ." Which was true. But like modern critics of frontier people, Knox never saw the frontier, never experienced an Indian raid, never felt the hunger within that possessed the People of the Western Waters. His Scotch Irish parents migrated from Ulster to eastern Massachusetts, where Knox grew up, many decades after New England's frontier stage and its own bloody Indian wars. Before the Revolution he was the genteel proprietor of the London Bookstore in Boston. During the war he became chief of artillery and performed with skill and bravery. But the frontier was an alien place to Knox. His main purpose as secretary of war was to maintain peace on the frontier, not to further the immediate desires of the settlers. He once wrote to Major Richard Call, commander of U.S. troops in Georgia, that "the great object . . . is to preserve the peace by conciliating to each other the Creeks and the frontier citizens of that State," and further, while remaining alert and maintaining security for the troops and the country, "you are carefully to avoid every step which may involve the Union in hostilities with the Indians." We should add here that Knox, like Washington, was himself a land speculator, but on a vaster scale. Indeed, he was one of the big operators. In 1791, while Knox was secretary of war and fulminating against western settlers and speculators, he entered into a contract with William Duer, a friend of Alexander Hamilton's, to purchase from Massachusetts two million acres in Maine and was granted exemption from taxes for ten years, an enticement not unfamiliar to modern ears.[29]

The following year Knox let Governor William Blount know in unmistakable terms that an Indian war was unacceptable, and if war should come "it would be considered by the general government as a very great, and by the mass of the citizens of the middle and eastern States an unsupportable evil." Despite his claim, Knox was not speaking for the great mass of people, but for the late-eighteenth-century American chattering classes, such as John Jay, who once wrote to Thomas Jefferson that settling the frontier meant "white Savages" replacing "tawny ones." That was the common opinion of frontier people held by the eastern establishment.[30]

Unlike Knox and Jay, President George Washington knew the frontier intimately, as a surveyor and a militia officer of many years' experience prior to the Revolution. He was well aware of the settlers' need for protection, writing on one occasion to Governor Robert Dinwiddie with regard to settlers on the colonial Virginia frontier, "I see their situation, *know* their danger, and participate in their *Sufferings*; without having it in my power to give them further relief, than uncertain promises. . . . The supplicating tears of the women; the moving petitions of the men, melt me into such deadly sorrow, that I solemnly declare, if I know my own mind—I could offer myself a willing Sacrifice to the butchering Enemy, provided that would contribute to the peoples ease." But like others of his class he also regarded the frontier people with a disdain that he retained to the grave, as "A Parcel of Barbarian's and an Uncooth Set of People." Over forty years later, as president, he again demonstrated his feelings in a letter of 1795: the Indians "are not without serious causes of complaint, from the encroachments which are made on their lands by our people; who are not to be restrained by any law now in being or likely to be enacted."[31]

Ironically, Washington might have been writing about his first American ancestor, his great-grandfather John Washington, firstborn son of an English gentry family fallen on hard times in the old country. John came to America in 1657 when he was about twenty-five, found a friend and patron, a prosperous planter named Nathaniel Pope, married Pope's daughter, and settled on the Tidewater's frontier, the peninsula known as the Northern Neck, between the Potomac and Rappahannock Rivers. George Washington's principal and admiring biographer described that society in two short sentences: "One verb told the story of the proprietorship for almost a century: it was grab, grab, grab. The rest was detail, always interesting and sometimes amusing but detail only." In the early records of Virginia John Washington is described as a "merchant, not a gentleman," but he grabbed, grabbed, grabbed along with his fellow adventurers who had other proud, old Virginia names of Lee and Mason and Allerton and Claiborne.

By 1668 he owned five thousand acres, and by then was certainly accounted a gentleman. By 1675 he was a colonel of militia and became involved in a controversial incident during an expedition in which a number of Susquehanna Indians who had come to parley were murdered—by

Maryland militia, said the Virginians; by Virginia militia, said the Marylanders. John Washington was alleged by a Maryland captain to have said, "What [why] should we keep them any longer? Let us knock them on the head; we shall get the fort today." But the Maryland legislature decided that the Maryland militia was responsible, and a Virginia investigation apparently cleared John Washington, although the matter was not finally settled until 1677. There can be no doubt, however, that John Washington was one of the hard men, who in his day on his frontier grabbed and fought as the frontier people had done from the beginning and would continue to do on successive frontiers. He might with his great-grandson have looked down his nose at the People of the Western Waters, but he would have understood their hunger, and unlike his famous descendant, who benefited by his grabbings, he would have applauded the men who rode with Major James Ore on the Nickajack expedition.[32]

"THE LARGER PORTION SWAM OVER PUSHING THE BOATS BEFORE THEM"

William Blount's position had become increasingly difficult. His superior, Henry Knox, bombarded him with instructions to stay on the defensive, keep the settlers under control and the Indians mollified, and at all costs avoid an Indian war. Knox had not forgotten the twin disasters north of the Ohio, in 1790 and 1791, when American armies had been cut to pieces by the northwestern tribes. Now he was waiting for news of the campaign being mounted by General Anthony Wayne. The last thing the country needed was a major eruption on the southern frontier. The settlers, on the other hand, were not concerned with problems hundreds of miles north of them. They had reached the boiling point and they wanted action and the man on the spot was Governor William Blount. As early as May 1794 James Robertson proposed an expedition against the Five Lower Towns. By this time Blount had come to sympathize with the western point of view, and his feelings were not wholly dictated by his land interests. He had become a westerner. Once a staunch Federalist, his new environment was putting increasing strain on his political loyalties. Blount, therefore, did not discourage Robertson from planning an expedition, and he requested authority from Secretary Knox to order an attack on the Lower Towns.[33]

Knox refused, and that, as it turned out, was unacceptable to William Blount, James Robertson, and others. Once again rowing with muffled oars, Blount and Robertson hatched a plan to attack and destroy the main towns of Nickajack and Running Water without Blount giving Robertson official sanction. Blount obviously could not order an attack, having been ordered by Knox not to take offensive action. General James Robertson, however, after fifteen years of unremitting strain, had tired of official duties. He, therefore, would order the attack, then accept responsibility and resign his office. Blount would huff and puff his official displeasure and accept Robertson's resignation. Robertson's powers of English composition being primitive at best, Blount accommodated his general by writing the letter of resignation himself. He also dispatched Major James Ore from East Tennessee to the Cumberland for what was called a scouting expedition, at the same time placing Ore under Robertson's command. Secretly, a Cumberland settler named Sampson Williams was sent to Kentucky with a suggestion that the aggressive Indian fighter Colonel William Whiteley join the expedition, a suggestion at which Whiteley leaped. When he appeared on the Cumberland, 100 gunmen rode behind him. Robertson himself raised more men. During the summer his scouts had discovered a better route to the towns, and he also had the knowledge of a man who had been there in 1788 as a teenage prisoner and would now accompany the expedition. He was, the reader will recall from chapter 3, Joseph Brown, taken by Chickamaugas when his father's boat was captured, of whom an old Indian woman said at the time "that I ought to be killed, that I would see everything, and that I would soon be grown and would guide an army there and have them all cut off . . . that I must be killed."[34]

On 7 September 1794 some 550 riders under Major James Ore left Nashville and rode southeast toward the Lower Towns. A packhorse carried two cowhides. On the thirteenth, before daylight, the riders from the Cumberland, East Tennessee, and Kentucky reached the Tennessee River, where they left their horses under guard. The cowhides were stretched and made firm with cane or sticks and put in the water. Into them went rifles and ammunition and those men who could not swim, "while the larger portion swam over pushing the boats before them." One-half hour after sunup 230 men were across the river and ready to march. Their guide from this point on was Joseph Brown. His account, that of another participant, Sampson Williams, and Ore's report are our sources for the Nickajack Expedition.[35]

Ore's force was divided into two columns for a circuitous march on Nickajack in order to surround the town. One column still had a ways to go when it met an Indian woman "going out . . . early after horses; she turn and run towards town. They shot her, thinking the sound would alarm less than if she ran into town." The other column thought they had been detected, and the men rushed upon the town before the first column got there. This left a hole in the lines, "through which a large number of Indians Escaped." Nevertheless, "a great many were Killed in the town, perhaps Equally as many more in the river, in their attempt to cross, some in canoes, and others swimming." Surprise was complete. "One of the Indians after the battle asked [Joseph] Brown if the whites had come down from the clouds."

Nickajack had more than two hundred log houses. All were burned. Surrounding the town were fields of potatoes and corn, peach orchards, and melon patches. All were burned. Then Ore's men marched three miles upstream to Running Water and burned it all: town, fields, orchards. When they were finished destroying the two main Chickamauga towns, they recrossed the river in captured canoes. Five days later Ore's expeditionary force rode into Nashville.

At Nickajack and Running Water James Ore and his men broke the Chickamauga will to resist. If that were not enough, General Anthony Wayne's victory on 20 August at Fallen Timbers over the northwestern tribes also affected Chickamauga morale. And James Robertson wrote directly to John Watts, addressing him as "Old Friend," but stressing that if the Chickamaugas continued their raids, "our people will soon return the visit. This I do not tell you as a threat, but you may depend on the truth of it. . . ." That winter John Watts and other chiefs met with Governor Blount and agreed on peace. The Chickamaugas, born of Dragging Canoe's bitter opposition in 1775 to the huge sale of land by his father, Attakullakulla, and other chiefs, returned to the Cherokee fold and thereafter suffered the fate of their nation.[36]

Chapter 9

"When You Have Read This Letter over Three Times, Then Burn It"

In 1796 Tennessee became a state. This was largely the work of William Blount, who saw great possibilities for himself in Tennessee statehood. It would get him out from under the hostile supervision of the new secretary of war, that self-righteous and venemous New Englander Timothy Pickering. Blount's biographer aptly contrasted the two men: "Blount's faults were chiefly those of character, Pickering's those of personality. The former are perhaps more serious, but the latter more often antagonizing." Pickering had also become, through his experience in negotiating earlier in the decade with the Iroquois, extremely sympathetic to Indians. He preached constantly for a policy of conciliation and philanthropy, not confrontation. Those thoughts, of course, were met with derision on the frontier. Pickering became secretary on 2 January 1795, and almost immediately unleashed a barrage of criticism against a man he considered a venal swindler.[1]

Whereupon Blount immediately counterattacked by mobilizing his lieutenants in the territory to undertake various anti-Pickering measures. But his main move represented a 360-degree turn in policy. Heretofore he had maintained firm control over the Southwest Territory and resisted calls for statehood. Situations change, however, and nimble-footed William Blount joined the clamor for statehood and maneuvered to bring it about. Statehood would release him from the hated oversight of federal officials, for he meant to become Senator William Blount of Tennessee, where he would be in a better position to benefit the Old Southwest and oversee and protect his speculative interests.[2]

144

Southeastern United States, 1798

In the midst of all this was Andrew Jackson, not yet a major player, but a full-fledged member of the Blount machine and regarded as a comer who made himself heard. "You have loud Speach," one man wrote to him. By at least the fall of 1795 Jackson was active in promoting his candidacy for Congress, and well before President Washington on 1 June 1796 signed the bill making Tennessee the sixteenth state, men were writing to the young lawyer about his possible election. In an amusing letter, Mark Mitchell, an early settler on the Watauga and a justice of the peace of Hawkins County, offered to help provided Jackson agreed to settle an unknown problem between them: "Your Sise is a gainst you I never knew a man of a Hundred and forty [lbs] in Congress if you would get a pre [pair] of Cloth Over hols, and Ware your big Coat you might pass you have loud Speach; I don't know how the Districts may be Divided if this County is taken in With Cumberland I can do Something and Will do all I can for you if you Offer and I hop you Will—how the Matter Stands betwixt us I will be Damd if I know when i see you We can Settle With Out Fighting. My boy gros Fineley Mrs.

Mitchell Goins me in Comps. to you tell Mrs. Jackson Howday and bleave Me to be your friend."[3]

From his home on the Nolichucky, Joseph Anderson, who would serve as U.S. senator from Tennessee (1797–1815), offered support and suggested some political back rubbing: "My Choice (as well as a number of others) is yourself, and Willm. C.C. Claiborne, your interest here, will by his friends be Supportd, and blended with his; it is our wish, that you may have the same Done for him in Cumberland. From present prospects, he will certainly out poll, either of his opponents. I hope to see you at the Convention, when we will communicate more at large." Anderson ended his letter with more than the usual flourish: "I am Dear Sir, with every Sentiment of most sincere Esteem, your friend and Obedt. Servt." Most of Anderson's letter dealt with business matters, for which he had sent Jackson power of attorney. This is but one example of the wide circle of clients and friends Jackson had made in his seven years on the legal circuit. He was well known on both the Cumberland and in East Tennessee, and he made the most of it.[4]

Jackson was one of the five delegates elected to represent Davidson County at the constitutional convention held in Knoxville from 11 January through 6 February 1796. Two other members were John McNairy, with whom Jackson had ridden over the mountains in 1788, and the indispensable James Robertson. Jackson was not a leading member of the convention, but with McNairy he was one of twenty-two men on the drafting committee to write the state constitution. Of interest to present-day readers will be his position on a requirement that all candidates for public office profess their belief in God, an afterlife, and the "divine authority of the old and new testament." Jackson was prominent in fighting it and getting its final section deleted. Blount's pro-statehood members made up the majority of the convention, and the document produced requested of Congress that Tennessee, the name the convention adopted, be accepted as a state.[5]

Afterward, from the Cumberland, Jackson wrote to his patron: "The people Generally approve of the Constitution, and I shall only add that the Conduct of the members during the Convention has reached this Country; the Conduct of some have verry much detracted from their popularity, but with Respect to yours it has greatly increased. Calumny that fiend to virtue has fled, a calm has arrived, imprections Cease, and Cesar is rendered his due, and if I may hazard an opinion your Election will be unanimous." Blount was elected, but as we shall soon see, calm prevailed for only a short time, and calumny would be flung about with abandon. For Andrew Jackson, however, the course of political events continued onward and upward. Tennessee was allotted only one seat in the House of Representatives, and William Blount decided that his loyal young protégé was the right man for the job. Jackson's close friend John Overton had no doubt of it or that he would be elected: "I must beg leave to congratulate you on your interest and popularity in this country. Your election is certain, and I believe that there is scarcely a man in this part of the Territory that could be elected before you." Whether the latter opinion was correct is of no consequence, for in that fall's election Jackson was unopposed in two districts, and in the Washington District in East Tennessee he received 318 votes to James Roddye's 12. Mr. Jackson was going to Philadelphia as Tennessee's first congressman.[6]

How that must have upset Rachel. For she clung to him desperately throughout her life, resisting each parting with pleas and tears. Although he would spend a good part of that life away from Rachel, Jackson continually maintained his desire to be done with the cares of the world and held before her in his letters the promise of a blissful retirement together.

"My Dearest Heart," he wrote while in East Tennessee on business and also campaigning for the congressional seat, "Tho I am absent My Heart rests with you. With what pleasing hopes I view the future period when I shall be restored to your arms there to spend my days in Domestic Sweetness with you the Dear Companion of my life, never to be separated from you again during this Transitory and fluctuating life.

"I mean to retire from the Buss of publick life, and Spend my time with you alone in Sweet Retirement, which is My only ambition and ultimate wish." After briefly giving her his travel plans and his hopes for an early return, he continued with literary flourishes entirely unsuspected of this fierce warrior. He "could not think of going to bed without writing you. May it give you pleasure to Receive it. May it add to your Contentment until I return. May you be blessed with health. May the Goddess of Slumber every evening light on your eyebrows and gently lull you to sleep, and conduct you through the night with pleasing thoughts and pleasant dreams. Could I only know you were contented and enjoyed Peace of Mind, what satisfaction it would afford me whilst travelling the loanly and tiresome road. It would relieve my anxious breast and shorten the way. May the great "I am" bless and protect you until that happy wished for moment arrives when I am restored to your sweet embrace which is the Nightly prayer of your affectionate husband."[7]

Did Rachel, as we must, take his intention to retire from public life with a large grain of salt?

From Philadelphia and other places where politics and business took him, Jackson wrote to Robert Hays, who had married Rachel's sister Jane, to look after Rachel, and in one letter revealed what every parting must have been like: "I must now beg of you to try to amuse Mrs. Jackson and prevent her from fretting, the situation in which I left her (*Bathed in Tears*) fills me with woe. Indeed Sir, it has given me more pain than any Event of my life."[8]

Jackson's personal problems, however, paled next to the fix in which William Blount found himself, for he was steadily sinking into a financial mire more than embarrassing, and the measure he took to extricate himself put the Senate of the United States into an uproar and prompted powerful men to seek his downfall.

"YOU ARE HEREBY REQUIRED TO ATTEND THE SENATE IN YOUR PLACE WITHOUT DELAY"

Blount's political triumph of 1796 was not mirrored in his huge speculations in land. A speculative frenzy was in full swing in the country. Blount, either on his own account or with his brother John Gray Blount and his business agent David Allison, had bought or committed himself to buy approximately 6,000,000 acres of land, and was involved to at least some extent in his brother's purchase of 1,660,355 acres. Some 4,500,000 acres, slated to be sold by Allison to another speculator, had not been paid for and thus lacked proper title. The cash needed to buy the land was to come from the purchaser, who would not pay until furnished with proof of title. In other words, Allison and the Blount brothers were trying to sell land they did not own. Allison went bankrupt in 1797 and was sent to a Philadelphia debtors' prison, where he died the following year. Bankuptcy among the big land speculators was not uncommon, for in general it was a fool's game they pursued, as the customers were not there. The settlers to whom they hoped to sell the land did not have the hard cash to buy it. Yet the quest for the rainbow continued. We may be excused, I believe, if we compare such frenzied speculation in land with Harry Cohn's classic description of Hollywood: "It ain't a business, it's a racket."[9]

Blount had borrowed to the hilt; there was no more money to be had. In North Carolina he was besieged by creditors and only avoided jail because of his senatorial status. The financial panic of 1797, along with Allison's collapse, brought him to near bankruptcy. In an international development that effected Blount's sadly depleted fortunes, France and Spain entered into a treaty of alliance in 1796, and by October Spain was at war with England. Spain was a mere pawn to France, and all America believed that France's price for alliance would be the cession from Spain to France of Louisiana and West and East Florida. Many Americans thought it had actually happened, and in fact the French government had pressed Spain for the cession only to be rebuffed, but how long could Spain keep France at bay? In place of a Spain growing steadily weaker and unstable a vigorous, revolutionary nation would appear on the Republic's southern border. There was only one way that Blount could climb out of the hole he had dug himself, and that was to sell the land, most of which was in Tennessee. But settlers could not afford it, and who among the big speculators would buy it if the Jacobins of France, the terrifying radicals of the day, were right next door, blocking access to New Orleans and Mobile, and active on the frontier among the still-powerful Creek Nation and the even more numerous Choctaws with whom in the old days the French had maintained good relations?

Then came a possible solution to Blount's problems in the person of a "hardy, lusty, brawny, weather-beaten" adventurer by the name of John Chisholm. As Blount had turned around his political fortunes, could he not now reverse his spectacular financial decline? Thus did William Blount, businessman and speculator, enter the grand game of international intrigue. The result came to be known as the Blount Conspiracy.[10]

John Chisholm was an American Tory who had served with British forces during the Revolutionary War and had been a prisoner of the Spanish after their reconquest of East and West Florida. That experience had given him a hatred for the Dons (Spanish noblemen or gentlemen). He stayed in America after the war and engaged in various occupations: trader, innkeeper, merchant, Indian interpreter, and agent among the Indians for the governor of the Southwest Territory, William Blount. In November 1796, Chisholm journeyed to Philadelphia as interpreter for some twenty Creek chiefs on a visit to President George Washington. Chisholm and a number of other Old Southwest Tories had decided that if they were going to remain in America it was time to apply for citizenship, and Chisholm took the opportunity of his stay in Philadelphia to present their petitions to the new secretary of war, James McHenry. McHenry's reception of the petitions was cool. Whether this prompted Chisholm to immediately proceed with a plan he had conceived is unknown, but given his nature he probably intended the other all along.

Put simply, Chisholm's plan, as he explained it to the British minister to the United States, Robert Liston, was to overthrow Spanish rule in East Florida, using Indians and British supplies as well as naval assistance in the form of a privateer. It has been suggested that Chisholm may have been sent to Liston by Blount, who preferred to keep his distance, but there is no evidence for it. Liston remained noncommittal while he communicated Chisholm's scheme to his superiors in London. Chisholm was undoubtedly, as described by a contemporary, "enterprising, resolute, and well acquainted" with the Old Southwest, but he threw the first rule of intrigue, reticence, to the winds. He liked to talk and drink, and he drank much and apparently told almost everybody he came into contact with about his plan. The word spread far and wide—in Philadelphia, on the frontier, in Natchez, even in Europe. A warning to Madrid came from the Spanish ambassador in Paris as early as December 1796. While visiting Chisholm in his quarters, John Rogers, a fellow frontiersman and interpreter also accompanying Indians to Philadelphia, saw several papers describing the plan strewn about. Rogers, who was definitely not interested, advised Chisholm as he left "to take care that he did not get hanged."[11]

In December Chisholm also told his former employer, William Blount, who had just returned to Philadelphia. Blount, desperate to find a way out of impending ruin, immediately took such an interest that Chisholm later complained that Blount stole his plan. Certainly, Blount enlarged what he called Chisholm's "petty enterprise" and began masterminding the intrigue, although Chisholm remained involved. As it should be with conspiracies, solid proof is lacking, and changes may have occurred along the way, but it appears that Blount planned a three-pronged invasion of the Floridas and Louisiana by American frontiersmen and Indians with the support of the British navy. Frontiersmen from New York and Pennsylvania with British allies from Canada would take New Madrid and the lead mines on the Red River. Chisholm would lead Indians and the old Tories living among them against Pensacola. The greatest prize of all was reserved for none other than William Blount, senator turned warrior, who assigned to himself command of Tennessee and Kentucky frontiersmen allied with Indians for a descent on New Orleans. A British fleet would assist operations at Pensacola and New Orleans. Afterward, rewards would be handed out: the British would get Louisiana, the United States the Floridas. New Orleans would become a free port and navigation rights on the Mississippi would be guaranteed to both countries.[12]

Blount was so concerned about the danger of France gaining control of the Gulf Coast and blocking American access to southern waters and the great world beyond, thus preventing the economic development of the southern frontier, that he was prepared to give up further American expansion westward—if he had ever envisioned the wings of the eagle stretching from the Atlantic to far Pacific shores. It has been suggested that concentration on his less-than-sterling character and his desperate financial condition blind us to the political realities of the time. This approach argues that Blount entered into the conspiracy because the Washington administration, which had been politically and militarily active north of the Ohio, had done little in the Old Southwest that lent confidence to its American inhabitants that the administration cared for their interests. For them there were no Anthony Wayne and regiments of regulars. Their fate rested with themselves. On one front they met the challenge and triumphed over the Chickamaugas and stood fast against Creek raids without assistance from the national government.

True, Thomas Pinckney had negotiated with Spain in 1795 the Treaty of San Lorenzo. Under its terms Spain agreed that the boundary line between American territory and Spanish territory would begin at the thirty-first parallel and proceed east on the line given to the United States by Britain in the Treaty of Paris of 1783. Spain further agreed that for a period of three years U.S. citizens could deposit goods at New Orleans for transshipment without paying duty. But since then Spain had dragged its feet in implementing the terms and, despite diplomatic pressure, was still occupying Natchez, although in 1798 the Spanish would finally evacuate the town and retreat below the thirty-first parallel.

In further defense of national policy, we must also stress that the British in Canada, in concert with the northwestern tribes, were considered a far greater threat to expansion than the southern Indians and Spain in its Gulf borderlands. Spain was weak and growing weaker, and it was thought that their territories, under pressure from a burgeoning American frontier population, now some 300,000 west of the mountains, would eventually fall like ripe fruit. Jefferson had put it well about a decade earlier: "Our confederacy must be viewed as the nest from which all America, North & South, is to be peopled. We should take care too, not to . . . press too hard on the Spaniards. Those countries could not be in better hands." Jefferson added a caveat that spoke directly to Blount's fear: "My fear is that they are too feeble to hold them till our population can be sufficiently advanced to gain it from them piece by piece." That time that Jefferson feared now seemed to have arrived, thus William Blount's decision to act. But as to his motivation, would he have been so concerned about the economic and political stability of the Old Southwest were he not facing financial ruin?[13]

Whatever moved Blount to roll the dice with everything resting on it, once he made the decision he got busy setting the machinery in motion, while John Chisholm's tongue was equally busy telling anybody who would listen what the conspirators were up to. From his house on Chestnut Street Blount dispatched messages far and wide. Chisholm continued his talks with the British minister. But Liston could not commit even if he wanted to and decided to send Chisholm to London to see the foreign secretary, Lord Grenville. He was supposed to sail on 19 March 1797, and wrote to the Tennessee frontiersman John McKee, "I now steer for foreign Climes . . . to be plaine Jack—I will conquer or be Damnd." But he was not aboard ship when it sailed, and when Robert Liston found him that night in, of course, a tavern, he was revealing all to a group of Frenchmen. A few days later Liston made sure Chisholm sailed for England. While Chisholm was on the high seas, Lord Grenville replied to Liston's reports, informing the minister that the government had rejected the scheme because it would violate American neutrality. Grenville let Chisholm cool his heels in London for several weeks before giving him the same message. Thereupon John Chisholm, who had sworn to "conquer or be Damnd," vanishes from our story and history.[14]

Unaware that the British would have nothing to do with the conspiracy, Blount arrived in Tennessee in April 1797 to personally inform coconspirators of the plan and its status. But in late April he received word that President John Adams had called a special session of Congress to convene on 15 May. Thus he could not travel on to visit various people and discuss privately the grand enterprise. So he wrote several letters, one of which, double-sealed, was quite uncharacteristic of this man who had once advised his brother to "stand behind the Curtain & give the necessary Directions." James Carey was an agent of the Southern Indian Department who had reported to Blount when the latter had been governor. He was then stationed at Tellico Blockhouse on the Little Tennessee River. Blount gave the letter to his partner in an ironworks, James Grant, to deliver to Carey, and Grant faithfully carried out the task. We need to quote extensively from this once famous letter of 21 April 1797.[15]

> Amongst other things that I wished to have seen you about, was the business Captain Chesholm mentioned to the British Minister last Winter in Philadelphia.
>
> I believe, but am not quite sure that the plan then talked of will be attempted this fall; and if it is attempted, it will be a much larger way than then talked of; and if the Indians act their part, I have no doubt but it will succeed. A man of consequence has gone to England about the business, and if he makes the necessary arrangements

as he expects, I shall myself have a hand in the business, and probably shall be at the head of the business on the part of the British. You are, however, to understand, that it is not yet quite certain that the plan will be attempted; yet, you will do well to keep things in a proper train of action, in case it should be attempted, and to do so, will require all your management. I say require all your management, because you must take care in whatever you say to [John] Rogers, or anybody else, not to let the plan be discovered by [Benjamin] Hawkins, [Silas] Dinsmore, [James] Byers, or any other person in the interests of the United States or Spain.

If I attempt this plan, I shall expect to have you, and all my Indian country and Indian friends, with me, but you are now in good business I hope, and you are not to risk the loss of it by saying anything that will hurt you, until you again hear from me.

Once again Blount stressed the need for secrecy, although he was committing a serious breach of security: "I have advised you, in whatever you do, to take care of yourself. I have now to tell you to take care of me too; for a discovery of the plan would prevent the success and much injure all the parties concerned."

In the penultimate sentence he gave Carey his final instruction: "When you have read this letter over three times, then burn it."

James Grant, who may have known the letter's contents and was present when Carey read it, urged Carey to burn it. Did Carey burn it? Of course not. In fact, Blount had badly misjudged Carey's loyalty and neglected to take into account one of the man's personal vices, for it was a hard-drinking age and James Carey loved his bottle. Carey had taken an oath of loyalty to the United States and later stated that he was torn "between my regard for Governor Blount and what might possibly be my duty with regard to the letter." Or, as Blount's biographer suggested, was it love of liquor that led to disaster? Carey showed the letter to James Byers, one of the men Blount had specifically warned him against, and it was charged that Carey was drunk when Byers took possession of the letter and showed it to David Henley, a War Department agent and an enemy of Blount. Henley copied the letter and sent the copy to George Washington. As word of the letter spread on the frontier, Blount's adherents took alarm, as did Byers, who quickly left Tennessee with the letter and rode hard for Philadelphia. By mid-June the letter was in the hands of Secretary of War McHenry and his predecessor, now secretary of state and Blount's fierce enemy from his latter days as governor, Timothy Pickering.

Blount was not immediately confronted with the letter. He had been unable to keep his conspiracy a secret, but the government kept well hidden the unmasking of it while further evidence was gathered and President Adams and his advisers decided what to do about Senator William Blount. The Spanish minister, Carlos Martínez de Yrujo, spoke to Secretary Pickering of information received from Louisiana about an Anglo-American plot.

Pickering could truthfully reply that the United States was not involved in any plot with Britain. Robert Liston could just as truthfully tell Pickering, who asked him about Blount's involvement, that Britain was not involved in the conspiracy, for by then he had received Grenville's letter rejecting the plan. Some believe that Pickering, an ardent Anglophile, did not want the letter to become public and thus damage Anglo-American relations. Whatever Pickering's wishes, President John Adams made the decision.

On 3 July 1797 the Senate was debating the mind-numbing subjects of consular salaries and taxes on parchment. Bored, William Blount decided to leave for a while. Outside on the steps he met the president's secretary, Samuel B. Malcolm, with a message to the Senate from President Adams. Blount asked him what it was. Malcolm replied that it was confidential and that he could not reveal its contents. A while later Blount returned to find that consular salaries and parchment taxes had been shelved. The Senate was in a high state of excitement. As Blount took his seat all eyes were riveted on him. But he remained ignorant of the cause, until a motion was made for a certain letter to be read, and thus it was that Senator William Blount had to sit in his chair and listen to the words of his letter to James Carey. When the clerk finished the Senate's presiding officer, Thomas Jefferson, asked Blount if he had written the letter. A pale William Blount replied that he had written to Carey about that time but he could not be sure that the letter read was the one. He requested a copy of the letter and a day's delay in proceedings in order to examine his papers. The request was granted, and then Blount stood and left the chamber, all eyes riveted on him.

There is no need for us to go into the details of ensuing congressional investigations and hearings and impeachment and trial proceedings. When the matter became public, which took only a few days, the uproar equaled any cause célèbre of our time. It was the Watergate of the late eighteenth century. Blount did not appear the following day, nor did he appear as ordered on the fifth before a Senate committee, instead sending a letter by Senator William Cocke of Tennessee that was equivocal at best. Thomas Jefferson sent Blount a command: "Sir, you are hereby required to attend the Senate in your place without delay." But the messenger could not find Blount, who had hired a boat to take him to Ocracoke Inlet in North Carolina. Officers went to apprehend him; they almost caught him, but they did not know Blount by sight and he slipped away. But they got his trunks that were full of his papers, which were sent to the Senate committee.[16]

Panic had led to his attempted flight. Now he calmed down as much as anybody can who has been so devastatingly compromised and decided to fight back. He appeared in the Senate on 7 July with two Philadelphia lawyers. When he was asked if he had written to Carey he refused to answer. During the proceedings word came that the House of Representatives had impeached Blount—the first and last U.S. senator to be impeached. The following day, 8 July 1797, while he grimly watched and listened from his seat in the chamber, William Blount became the first senator to be expelled from the Senate. The vote was twenty-five to one, the lone dissent being on a procedural matter. And on or about that date an action was entered against him in federal district court on the charge of disturbing the "peace and tranquillity of the United States." There was also the possibility that he was in violation of the Neutrality Act, an act still on the books and little changed from its enactment in 1794. The judge immediately issued a warrant for Blount's arrest.[17]

A U.S. marshal had been waiting in the wings with the arrest warrant while the Senate debated Blount's expulsion. As he considered his position, Blount had second thoughts about staying to fight. His instinct told him, as one of his ruder Tennessee constituents might have put it, to git. After the Senate was through with him, he somehow evaded the marshal and other pursuers. At least by daybreak on Sunday, 9 July, William Blount was riding hard southward, for the Shenandoah, and the road to Tennessee, and home.

About six miles north of Staunton, Virginia, where the land begins its long rise to the great mountains, he was recognized by a rider heading south, who informed people in Staunton. A posse immediately set out to capture him, but they had no more luck than the marshal in Philadelphia. He went first to North Carolina to fetch his wife, but she was too ill to travel. Although not well himself, Blount pushed on alone to Knoxville. As he approached the capital of his adopted state he was met by volunteer cavalry and "a large concourse of citizens" who escorted him into town, where he was welcomed by the citizens. He was safe in Tennessee. Federal agents sent to arrest him could find no one to join them in a posse, and had they attempted to take him into custody it is likely that their persons would have been in peril. Such was the primitive state of law enforcement in those days. He might have been reelected to the U.S. Senate had he chosen to run, but he wisely chose not to. To complete his term, the Tennessee legislature elected Jackson's friend Joseph Anderson, who ran unopposed and would remain in the Senate until 1815. Then the legislature punished the other senator, William Cocke, for voting to expel Blount from the U.S. Senate and terminated his tenure in office. Cocke ran for reelection, but William Blount, disgraced elsewhere but still a power in Tennessee, decided that it would not come to pass. He later wrote his brother that "it was as certain as the Decrees of Heaven that Cocke would not be elected a Senator." The Blount forces put forward a man whom Blount had earlier described as a "valuable and highly respected member of Congress." It was by a vote of twenty to thirteen that the legislature on 26 September 1797 elected to the U.S. Senate Blount's faithful lieutenant Andrew Jackson.[18]

One would think that William Blount's sudden fall from power and his dismal financial plight would have at least sobered the old speculator. Besides, his health was poor. He had lost thirty pounds and he frequently suffered from chills and fever. A physician friend lived in his home to care for him. Yet he persevered in his quest for riches, and his methods had not changed. He spread rumors by way of agents and letters to Carolina newspapers of Indian raids, title problems, and lack of water in the Cumberland. All of which was meant to depress land prices so he, with his slim purse, could afford to buy. The man was incorrigible. But in Tennessee, for the majority, he could do no wrong. He was elected to the Tennessee Senate and became president of that body. And on 13 January 1798 he escaped conviction by the U.S. Senate when it ruled that senators are not civil officers and therefore cannot be impeached.

Blount remained active in Tennessee politics and, of course, the land game, for prices would rise, he knew they would, and then all would be put right. But on 15 March 1800 he caught a bad cold while up nights tending a child sick with malaria. Then a violent chill struck him, then fever, and he became delirious. On 21 March he lost the ability to speak. In the words of his biographer, "Two large tears coursed down his stricken face, and he turned his face to the wall and died."[19]

So passes William Blount from our story. Of his life he might have observed, as that worldly monk Fra Paolo Sarpi said of himself, "I never *never* tell a lie, but not the truth to everybody," had he possessed the Venetian's wit.[20]

Chapter 10

⊶⊶⊷

Major General
Andrew Jackson

"THE INJURY DONE MY PRIVATE CHARECTOR
AND FEELINGS REQUIRES REDRESS"

William Blount lived long enough to give Andrew Jackson the boosts the young man needed to begin his climb up the greasy pole. That Jackson was ambitious is an understatement. He especially revealed it in his campaign to be elected major general of the Tennessee militia at the age of twenty-nine, which led to a dangerous feud with one of the most popular and powerful men in Tennessee. The position had been held by the Revolutionary War hero and renowned Indian fighter John Sevier, but when Tennessee became a state in the summer of 1796, Sevier was elected its first governor and had to relinquish direct command of the militia. Sevier objected to Jackson's candidacy. It has been suggested that Jackson's youth and military inexperience, and perhaps Sevier's jealousy of his popularity, may have led to Sevier's objections. That Sevier led a clique not allied with the Blount machine also probably influenced Sevier's decision to back a man named George Conway. The brigadier generals and field officers of the various districts were the electors, and at the meeting of the Mero District officers, which Jackson attended "as a private citizen," as he put it, Joel Lewis read a letter from Sevier supporting Conway's candidacy. Jackson objected to Sevier's attempt to influence the voting as an "unconstitutional act," but he did not do it privately. Instead, his temper got the better of him and he rose at the meeting and delivered some heated remarks about Sevier that the latter described as "Scurrilous." Sevier wrote letters to James Robertson and Joel Lewis in which he called Jackson a "poor pitiful petty fogging Lawyer. . . ."[1]

Jackson rose to the occasion. "Those Sir," he wrote to Sevier, "are Expressions, that my feelings are not accustomed to, and which my conduct

156

John Sevier, 1790–1792, by Charles Willson Peale (Tennessee Historical Society)

through life by no means merits, and which, Sir, I will not, tamely submit to." He finished his letter by laying the groundwork for a challenge, stating that Sevier's "Conduct requires an Explanation and the Injury done my private Charector and feelings requires redress. An answer to this letter is expected." Sevier, who was in Nashville then, replied in more measured tones that he was not a stranger to "calumny," and that "I have had too many attacks on my own character, to be desirous of attacking that of any other Citizen. rest assured then Sir, Any observations I made in the letters you have quoted, were not bottomed on malice; they were the language of A man who thought himself highly injured, and if it betrayed a little imprudence I will here add that like yourself when passion agitates my Breast I cannot view things in the calm light of mild philosophy."[2]

A few days later a matter that could have led to a duel had been smoothed over. Mutual friends, especially James Robertson and William C. C. Claiborne, had raised voices of sanity, and the two men exchanged friendly letters in which Jackson suggested a personal meeting to which Sevier agreed, and Sevier on his part expressed the wish that a reconciliation would lead to "the future existence of not a nominal but real friendship." But it was not to be. The seeds of what became a deep and undying enmity between the two men had been planted and awaited only fertilization.[3]

The incident did not prevent Jackson from performing well on behalf of Sevier on at least one occasion as a congressman. Although he did not really possess the legislative temperament, he showed skill and determination in getting Congress to pass a bill reimbursing Tennessee militia led by Sevier in a 1793 raid against the Cherokees. Because it was an offensive action, and therefore not authorized by the administration and in direct opposition to its policy, the administration refused to pay for it without congressional approval. We can assume that he lobbied his fellow congressmen. When he rose in the House to speak he was restrained but convincing, maintaining that "some of the assertions" of Henry Knox, who had been secretary of war at the time, "were not founded in fact," and trusted "it would not be presuming too much . . . from being an inhabitant of the country, he had some knowledge of the business." He insisted that the "measures pursued on the occasion alluded to were both just and necessary. When it is seen that war was waged upon the State, that the knife and the tomahawk were held over the heads of women and children, that peaceable citizens were murdered, it was time to make resistance."[4]

The following day he received the recognition of the Speaker and rose once more in the well of the House in defense of his argument that the entire expenses of the expedition should be paid. He pointed out that the "rations found for the troops had already been paid for by the Secretary War." But it is what he had to say with regard to militia and its duty to obey superior officers that is of interest to us: "As the troops were called out by a superior officer, they had no right to doubt his authority. Were a contrary doctrine admitted, it would strike at the very heart of subordination. It would be saying to soldiers, 'Before you obey the command of your superior officer, you have a right to inquire into the legality of the service upon which you are about to be employed, and, until you are satisfied, you may refuse to take the field.' " This is very interesting in light of Jackson's future career. Robert Remini quite correctly points out that there were basic principles here that went to the heart of Jackson's concept of military behavior: "They had to do with authority and responsibility, subordination and obedience, discipline and loyalty. Jackson's ideas were strict and allowed no room for compromise: Soldiers obeyed orders properly authorized and government supported and defended their soldiers regardless of the expense or the risk of embarrassment."[5]

But we need to look further into Jackson's concept of military subordination in light of the times in which he lived. General Sevier, commander of the militia, had been ordered into the field by proper civilian authority of the Southwest Territory; therefore, officers and soldiers of the militia had no recourse but to obey and follow him. The reader should note that I have been careful to use the word *militia*. These were not regular troops. They were part-time soldiers, mostly farmers, called out in time of emergency. Here we should review the words of Jackson's boyhood *beau sabreur* (dashing cavalryman), the Revolutionary War partisan hero William Richardson Davie, who after the war described clearly and succinctly the peculiar nature of militia: "in those times [it] was absolutely necessary" for the officers to explain to their men what was intended and obtain their approval, and in this case (the 1780 Hanging Rock action) the militia "entered into the project with great spirit and cheerfulness." Jackson would discover that "those times" had not passed. As we saw in the Prologue, Jackson had been at Hanging Rock and other militia actions in the Carolinas. Had he pondered on what he saw as a boy, officers haranguing the men to obtain their approval, and decided that for him it was unacceptable? Whatever his musings, his rigid ideas on discipline and authority in the field would in not too distant a time lead to situations incredible to behold and further controversy in his strife-filled life.[6]

He got his way with Congress. Robert Rutherford of Virginia thought there was no need to discuss the matter further since Jackson had explained it in "so fair a light." James Madison of Virginia also supported him. Jackson chaired a Select Committee on Claims, which recommended reimbursement of $28,816.85, and without debate the House approved payment. It was a job well done. Tennessee would not forget it.[7]

"YOU HAVE HELD ME UP TO PUBLICK ODIUM UPON FALACIOUS INFORMATION"

But that session of Congress was his last in the House. As noted in the previous chapter, in September 1797 he defeated William Cocke in the senatorial election and returned to Washington that winter as Senator Andrew Jackson. At the same time two friendships were shattered, and he eventually challenged one of those former friends to a duel. The cooling of his friendship with John McNairy, his old friend from Salisbury days, with whom he had come over the mountains, began for reasons unknown, but it progressed rapidly when Jackson concluded that McNairy was too close to John Sevier, who had been McNairy's houseguest on the Cumberland when Chucky John and Jackson exchanged their first angry letters. The matter with William Cocke began with a letter from Jackson objecting in violent language to Cocke's making public a private letter from Jackson. That letter has never been found and its contents are unknown, but the real reason for the quarrel was probably Cocke's resentment of his electoral defeat by Jackson, which prompted him to release Jackson's letter. Jackson was in a fury: "Sir the baseness of your heart in violating a confidence reposed in you . . . will bring down the indignation of the thinking part of mankind upon you & the thunderbolt you were preparing for me will burst upon your own head. . . ." That was in early November 1797, and the conflict was still raging the following June when Jackson wrote to Cocke, "I have now to say that you have held me up to publick odium upon falacious information, and that this odium must be wiped away by some act of publick notoriety." He called upon Cocke to either make "reparation of the injury you have done me . . . or to meet and give me such satisfaction as is due from one Gentleman to another. . . ."[8]

Once again wise old James Robertson, assisted by Robert Hays, had by then stepped in, cooled things down, and got both men to agree to arbitration by a panel of brother Masons. But Jackson's sense of honor—perpetually worn, it seems, on his sleeve—promised future disputes that would end far more seriously than any to date and do grave harm to both his body and his reputation. He remained, as Thomas Nairne observed of the Chickasaws, "touchy as tinder."

"HE COULD NEVER SPEAK ON ACCOUNT OF THE RASHNESS OF HIS FEELINGS"

Jackson was in a black mood that winter of 1797–1798, which he spent in Philadelphia as a senator. We cannot definitely know the reasons for it. Rachel's hysteria whenever he left her certainly weighed heavily upon him. He was also in serious financial trouble. For like so many Americans Andrew Jackson was not immune to the lure of getting rich through speculation in land.

His difficulties began in 1794 when he and John Overton entered into partnership to buy and sell 50,000 acres of Tennessee land. Jackson went to Philadelphia in 1795 to sell that land, as well as 18,750 acres on behalf of the family of the late John Rice. In Philadelphia three weeks passed before he found a buyer in the person of William Blount's business agent and Jackson's friend from his early years in Tennessee, David Allison, who offered Jackson twenty cents an acre for all the land. But there was one problem. Allison was not offering cash, only three promissory notes. Jackson did not see this as a problem, accepted the notes, then endorsed them and used them to purchase supplies from two Philadelphia firms for a store he planned to open on the Cumberland in partnership with his brother-in-law, Samuel Donelson. A few months later, back in Tennessee, he received shocking news from one of the Philadelphia firms, Meeker, Cochrane & Company. Allison could not meet payment on the promissory notes, and Meeker, Cochrane was taking "this early opportunity to make Known . . . that we shall have to get our money from you. . . ." In January 1796 Jackson received a similar letter from John B. Evans & Company. Jackson was obviously shocked, for he would later admit that he had no idea when he signed Allison's notes he "stood security for the payment" of the notes, "or that Mr. E expected me to do so, or then contemplated such a thing." This revelation has to shock us. The man was a lawyer. How could he not have known? But apparently he did not.[9]

To meet his obligations Jackson had to sell his store to James Robertson's brother, Elijah, for 33,000 acres of land. He immediately sold the land to James Stuart, whose agent was William Blount, for $0.25 per acre. Of the proceeds, $2,800.00 was to be paid to the Philadelphia firms within sixty days and the balance within two years. Then, incredibly, in February 1796, only one month after hearing the bad news from John B. Evans & Company, Jackson again began buying land all over Tennessee, and when he arrived in Philadelphia in June he had 30,000 acres to sell. And who did he offer it to? David Allison and William Blount. And he accepted from Allison, who already owed him $20,000, two notes for the new sale in the amount of $5,676.73. The reader will recall that David Allison finally went officially bankrupt in 1797 and died in debtors' prison the next year, leaving Jackson without a cent that he was owed. It took Jackson years to climb out of the hole he had dug for himself.[10]

We have skimmed the surface of Jackson's financial transactions to help explain his depression during the winter of 1797–1798, and also to satisfy ourselves that Jackson lacked the Midas touch. His gifts lay elsewhere. In the meantime, he was still serving his apprenticeship in the world of men and affairs, and in that respect not doing at all well in the U.S. Senate, which was full of men with famous names and presided over by the vice president of the United States, and president of the Senate, Thomas Jefferson.

James Parton wrote of Jackson's senatorial career, "His record is a blank." The exaggeration is only slight. The difference between his performance in the Senate and his tenure in the House is striking. He rarely spoke in the Senate, and of that we will soon give a famous man's opinion. He did see to the interests of his constituents, and Tennesseans thought well of him for that. Whenever Senate action on William Blount came up, he did what was expected and supported his patron. He also met two men who would reappear in his life some years hence: Aaron Burr, who would tempt Jackson in joining his delusion, whatever it was, and Edward Livingston of New York, a member of the powerful Hudson River Valley clan. Jackson and Livingston were as unlike as two men could be, but they formed a friendship that lasted to the grave, and at the most critical period of Andrew Jackson's life Livingston would serve his friend and his country faithfully and well. It is tempting to speculate that the well-born, well-educated, highly cultivated Livingston saw then that the thirty-year-old frontiersman, for all his rawness and foibles, was no ordinary man.

Thomas Jefferson then thought otherwise, if we can believe Daniel Webster. Webster and the historian George Ticknor visited Jefferson at Monticello in December 1824. It was the year of Jackson's first run for the presidency, which he lost to John Quincy Adams. Both Webster and Ticknor were Adams supporters. Webster wrote down what he saw and heard at Monticello, and according to him Jefferson said, "When I was President of the Senate, he was Senator, and he could never speak on account of the rashness of his feelings. I have seen him attempt it repeatedly, and as often choke with rage. His passions are no doubt, cooler now; he has been much tried since I knew him; but he is a dangerous man."[11]

Jefferson, of course, was nothing if not contradictory, and the year before Webster's visit he wrote to Jackson, "I recall with pleasure the remembrance of our joint labors while in the Senate together in times of great trial and of hard battling. Battles indeed of words, not of blood, as those you have since fought so much for your own glory and that of your country. With the assurance that my attamts [attachments] continue undiminished, accept that of my great respect and consdn." Perhaps the best perspective on the Webster affair came from Jefferson's grandson: "I can not pretend to know what my grandfather said to Mr. Webster, nor can I believe Mr. Webster capable of misstatement. Still, I think the copy of the portrait incorrect, as throwing out all the lights and giving only the shadows."[12]

So we are left knowing that Jackson may or may not have been speechless with rage when he tried to address the Senate, and the sure knowledge that other than taking care of his constituents Jackson's Senate career was barren of accomplishments and promise. But his narrow vision of senatorial responsibility did not mean that he was ignoring the larger world. In a letter to James Robertson, his prediction on what was about to happen to Great Britain could not have been further off the mark, but it is of interest to us for what it reveals about Jackson—his burning hatred of England, and his admiration for the man who would become emperor of the French: "France . . . is now turning her force towards Great Britain. Boneparte with 150,000 troops anured to conquer is ordered on the coast and called the army of England. do not then be surprised If my next letter Should announce a revolution in England. Should Boneparte make a landing on the English shore, Tyranny will be Humbled, a throne crushed and a republick will spring from the wreck—and millions of people restored to the rights of man by the conquering arm of Boneparte."[13]

William Blount may have planned a coup on the Gulf Coast in cooperation with Great Britain, but Jackson was steadfast in his disdain of England and support of revolutionary France. While Jackson was serving in the House, and referring to the long-forgotten, undeclared naval war with France (1797–1801) that dominated the administration of John Adams, he wrote to John Sevier, "I am sorry to see our Country by the Conduct of our Government involved in such a situation with the republick of France, who are now struggling to obtain for themselves the same Blessings (liberty) that we fought and bled for, we ought to wish them success if we could not aid them. How the present differance with France may terminate is for wiser politicians than me to Determine." Jackson's concern with foreign affairs was echoed by Sevier and other leaders on the frontier, who, though far removed from the maelstrom that was then Europe, were well aware of its effect on the young republic. Sevier wrote, "Should a rupture happen between the United States and any of the Beligerent powers, we should find in all the southern tribes inveterate enemies. The traders of every description would conceive it their interest to divert the attention and intercourse of the Indians from the United States to a quarter where they could recommence their trading as usual, by which means enhance a profit to themselves who alone they think entitled to it."[14]

Writing from Knoxville, William C. C. Claiborne worried about both French and British high-seas assaults on American shipping that refused to "respect our Flag." But he, like Jackson, favored France and the rise in Europe of republicanism, referring to France as that "gallant . . . nation who have established a free Republic on the overthrow of Tyranny, and risen Superior to the Attacks of Combined Europe. Proud Austria has at length sued for peace, and owned a Conqueror; Bonaparte had been the able nego-ciator, what the dictates of reason and Justice, could not effect, his sword has forced; and I hope, this is only a prelude to the final downfall of Kingship and Priestship which have for so many ages held the world in Chains."[15]

"I LOOKED HIM IN THE EYE, AND I SAW SHOOT"

Jackson, unhappy in his present situation, unsure of himself in a job for which he was at that time obviously unsuited, decided that he could observe the outside world as well from Tennessee as from Philadelphia. In April 1798 he received a leave of absence from the Senate and returned to Nashville, where he immediately resigned his seat, "believing that another [Daniel Smith] would better serve the people of Tennessee in the capacity of sena-tor. . . ." But he was finished with neither politics nor public office. Either he or someone else broached the proposition that Andrew Jackson was well suited to become a judge on the Tennessee Superior Court, whereupon the Blount machine, still well-oiled and functioning within the state, went to work. Blount wrote two letters to Governor John Sevier, in early July and mid-August 1798, and in late August Sevier wrote to Jackson that "you will please Consider yourself as Already appointed." How often in the years to come, we wonder, did John Sevier wish that he had never written that letter?[16]

The new judge was a lawyer who had not known that endorsing a promissory note and purchasing goods on the strength of it left him liable, a lawyer whose knowledge of the law was not, shall we say, finely tuned. But for the six years that Jackson served, according to Parton, "Tradition reports that he maintained the dignity and authority of the bench, while he was on the bench; and that his decisions were short, untechnical, unlearned, some-times ungrammatical, and generally right." After all, states Parton, "the cases that came before the courts of Tennessee at that day were usually such as any fair-minded man was competent to decide correctly." And a man of Jackson's temperament would neither shilly-shally nor stand for it by windy lawyers. On one occasion he dispatched fifty cases in fifteen days. Andrew Jackson would have agreed that justice delayed is justice denied. He also did not hes-itate when necessary to enforce the law himself outside the courtroom, which led to an incident that became part of Tennessee folklore. There are variations of the story, but the main thread is believable because it is pure

Jackson. It was woven together by James Parton, from whom the following is taken.[17]

Russell Bean was a Jonesborough gunsmith described by Colonel Isaac T. Avery, who knew him, as the "most perfect model of a man, for strength and activity, I ever saw; perfectly fearless, and, when excited, desperate. . . ." About the time that Jackson arrived in Tennessee, Bean had returned from a year's absence to find his wife in a tavern rocking a newborn baby in a cradle. Bean, who was not a drinker, went out and got drunk. Then he took the baby from the cradle and, said Avery, "cut off its ears close to its head." He was convicted, branded on the hand, and sentenced to a year in jail. He broke out his first night and performed prodigious feats in helping to put out a fire that threatened to destroy Jonesborough, whereupon John Sevier, then governor of the breakaway State of Franklin, pardoned him.

Leaping forward several years to Jackson's tenure on the bench, we find Russell Bean still haunted by his wife's infidelity and involved in some sort of altercation with the seducer's brother. Jackson was holding court in "a shanty at a little village" and ordered the sheriff to bring Bean to court. Bean was in the street armed with pistol and knife and refused to be taken. The sheriff returned and so informed Jackson, who said, "Summon a posse, then, and bring him before me."

But Bean told the sheriff and his posse that he would "shoot the first skunk that come within ten feet of him." They backed off, and the sheriff reported to Jackson that Bean could not be taken. One can easily imagine the effect that this had on Jackson's temper. "Mr. Sheriff," he said, "since you cannot obey my orders, summon me; yes sir, summon me."

"Well, judge, if you say so, though I don't like to do it; but if you will try, then I suppose I must summon you."

Striding toward the door, Jackson said, "I adjourn this court for ten minutes."

Bean was in the middle of the street, cursing loudly, brandishing his weapons, "vowing death and destruction to all who should attempt to molest him."

With a pistol in each hand, Jackson advanced on Bean and came up to him eyeball to eyeball. "Now, surrender you infernal villain, this very instant, or I'll blow you through."

Bean meekly handed over his weapons and allowed the sheriff to lead him off. Later he was asked why, after holding off the sheriff and his posse, he had allowed himself to be taken by one man?

Because, Russell Bean said, when Jackson "came up, I looked him in the eye, and I saw shoot, and there wasn't shoot in nary other eye in the crowd; and so I says to myself, says I, hoss, it's about time to sing small, and so I did."

As Parton observes, the story "is a growth, rather than an invention, each period contributing some little addition to the delightful whole." And as our story progresses we will observe situations packed with drama in which other men in other places could say, with Russell Bean, "I looked him in the eye, and I saw shoot."

"GREAT GOD! DO YOU MENTION *HER* SACRED NAME?"

It was during Jackson's judicial tenure that the smoldering feud with John Sevier broke into the open. It began with his revelation of the Glasgow land frauds. In October 1797, while on his way to Washington to serve in Congress, Jackson was told by a man named Charles Love of a group of speculators who were forging North Carolina military land warrants for land in Tennessee, which they meant to sell. Love told Jackson that he had actually observed warrants being signed at the house of William Terrell Lewis Jr. in Nashville by a militia officer, Major John Nelson, who "was very much intoxicated," and in "this State of Intoxication, signed nearly five hundred." Lewis then sent for another militia officer, a captain Phillips, and told him that "to enable a number of Soldiers to obtain their just Rights," a Captain had to "countersign the papers." Lewis had furnished the "Table with old Peach Brandy & Loaf Sugar . . . a large Bowl of Apple Toddy was made, and Phillips pressed to drink, which he did very freely." The "Brandy further press'd, & Phillips becoming very much intoxicated, he was induced . . . to sign nearly five hundred." Charles Love was astonished, and questioned an employee of William Tyrell, Lewis's partner in fraud, who "jocosely informed him *that he had drawn nearly all of them:* meaning the Certificates."[18]

Jackson investigated, found that the accusation was true, and in December gave a written statement that was forwarded to Governor Samuel Ashe of North Carolina. An investigation was launched that traced the fraud to the office of James Glasgow, the secretary of state of North Carolina. Glasgow was the father-in-law of Rachel's brother, Stockley Donelson, and Jackson was horrified when he learned that Stockley was deeply involved in the fraud. When Jackson revealed what he knew, he had not the "most distant Idea that such practices was countenanced by Either Donelson or Glassco, but sir Even had I suspected this, my duty would have impelled me to have made the communication that I have done." His sense of duty, however, did not impel him to reveal what else he knew. Jackson had discovered that Governor John Sevier might also be involved. Yet he kept the information to himself. After all, Sevier was a frontier hero, one of the leaders of a key victory of the Revolutionary War, the Battle of King's Mountain, Indian fighter par excellence, a man whom Tennessee would elect and reelect governor several times. Who knew when this information might come in handy? For Jackson still hungered for command of the Tennessee militia. Better to bide his time, keep his cards close to his vest, maintain civil relations with the old war horse, and wait for the opportune moment.[19]

It was not long in coming. Major General George Conway, who had defeated Jackson for command of the militia in the previous election in 1796, died in 1801. An election to replace him was scheduled for 5 February 1802. Sevier, having served the three consecutive terms as governor allowed by the Tennessee constitution, decided it was time for him to once again lead the militia. For who else in Tennessee commanded his wealth of experience in organizing for war and leading men into battle? Imagine his consternation, then, when Jackson, the "poor pitiful petty fogging lawyer," rose in opposition. We can even sympathize with Sevier's all-too-human resentment of Andrew-come-lately, who had apparently participated in skirmishes with Indians but had not taken part in either memorable sieges or deep strikes into Indian country, of which Sevier was a veteran many times over. But in the six years since his defeat Jackson had done his homework, stroked those who needed stroking, made friends and gained clients throughout the state, as congressman and senator delivered for his constituents, and showed in such incidents as the Bean affair that he had stomach. He had received from the influential King's Mountain veteran David Campbell assurances that other men of influence saw no conflict in Jackson's holding judicial and military offices at the same time. Jackson was also a popular man and a born leader. Recall his time reading law in Salisbury, when it was he who led the young blades on their highjinks. Recall also the high regard in which he was held by men quite different from him, such as Edward Livingston and James Robertson. Jackson, despite his lack of experience in matters martial, had become a formidable candidate.[20]

Sevier was also formidable, and the race went down to the wire. In Mero, Jackson's home district, Sevier lost by only five votes. The final vote throughout Tennessee was seventeen votes for Jackson, seventeen for Sevier, and three for Jackson's friend and adviser James Winchester. The tiebreaker was held by the governor, who happened to be Jackson's old friend Archibald Roane. It has been alleged by some writers that on the day Roane cast his vote Jackson gave him the evidence of land fraud that he had collected against Sevier. He did hand it over, whether on that day or later is not clear. In any case, Roane voted for his friend. Sevier bottled his fury and waited.[21]

The importance of this election to Andrew Jackson's career and the history of the United States cannot be overestimated, as will be made clear as we pursue our tale.

The year after the militia election, Roane came up for reelection, and Sevier, foiled by Jackson and Roane in recovering his militia rank, challenged Roane. Whereupon Roane released his evidence of Sevier's alleged complicity in land fraud. An explosion of indignation followed, especially after 27 July 1803, when Jackson came into the open in the pages of the *Knoxville Gazette* and charged Sevier with fraud. Sevier replied in the same paper on 8 August denying the charge and making his own charge of political motivation on the part of Jackson. As a judge Jackson had to travel the circuit, and in East Tennessee Sevier's champions were alerted. Jackson was told that a mob was waiting for him in Jonesborough. He was ill with a high fever when he arrived and had to be assisted from his horse. He was lying on a bed in a tavern when a friend came in and told him that a Colonel Harrison and a "regiment of men" had gathered in front of the tavern to tar and feather the judge. Lock your door, his friend urged. Instead, Jackson threw it wide open, and said, "Give my compliments to Colonel Harrison, and tell him my door is open to receive him and his regiment whenever they choose to wait upon me, and that I hope the Colonel's chivalry will induce him to *lead* his men, not follow them." Upon receiving Jackson's message, Harrison and his "regiment" quietly melted away and Jackson had no more trouble in Jonesborough.[22]

In Knoxville, however, violence could not be contained once unforgivable words had been uttered. On 1 October 1803 Jackson was in Knoxville to hold court in the public square, which was packed with people, when he came face to face with Sevier. The old warrior ripped into Jackson, unloading torrents of abuse and vituperation. Just who, asked Sevier, did Jackson think he was to challenge a man of his standing? Jackson replied that he had given many services to the state of Tennessee, only to be met with laughter and sarcasm from Sevier, who offered a definition of Jackson's services that struck like a lightning bolt: "I know of no great services you have rendered the country, except taking a trip to Natchez with another man's wife."[23]

Jackson froze. He must have paled. Sevier had crossed the line, he had stepped onto holy ground.

Jackson screamed. "Great God! Do you mention *her* sacred name?"

Pistols appeared, shots were fired, an innocent was grazed, people fled in all directions. Friends of both men leaped in and stopped the confrontation before a riot ensued. But after that there would be no turning back, no mending of fences. The next day Jackson wrote Sevier and challenged him to a duel with pistols, describing Sevier's "ungentlemanly expressions, and gasgonading conduct" as the "ebulitions of a base mind goaded with stuborn proof of fraud, and flowing from a source devoid of every refined sentiment, or delicate sensation." Sevier accepted, provided that the duel was held outside Tennessee, which had outlawed dueling. Jackson refused. Sevier had taken the "name of a lady into your poluted lips" in Knoxville and he would pay for it in Knoxville. When Sevier did not reply, Jackson published his challenge in the *Knoxville Gazette* and proclaimed Sevier a "base coward and poltroon."

We could go on and describe further details of two grown men behaving like jackasses out of an exaggerated sense of honor, of a meeting of the two antagonists and their followers on the road that turned into a comic opera fracas with injury to neither man. But time presses and we must turn to other matters. Let us leave it with two results of this bitter enmity, one amusing, the other of importance to Tennessee politics that in time would indirectly effect the nation. "Great God" became for a while the favorite expression of impressionable young men of Knoxville. The important result was the impetus given to a nascent Tennessee sectionalism that would harden over the decades. The Jackson-Sevier feud did not begin the split between East Tennessee and the rest of the state. The Cumberland Settlements and the rest of West Tennessee, poorer and less populous than the eastern counties, had early resented East Tennessee's dominance. But the feud hastened a feeling that would come to its fullest fruition in the Civil War. Much earlier it would also affect Jackson at a critical period of his military career.[24]

"YOU HAVE MADE A NOBLE BARGAIN FOR YOURSELVES"

In the election of 1800 Thomas Jefferson defeated John Adams for the presidency. The Federalists were appalled. The barbarians were no longer at the gates. They were inside the walls and astride the throne, and one of them was a Jefferson follower by the name of Andrew Jackson. Three years later that fierce Federalist Fisher Ames wrote, "What can be expected from a country where Tom Paine is invited to come by the chief man, as Plato was by Dionysius; where the whiskey secretary is Secretary of the Treasury; and where such men as the English laws confine in gaol for sedition, make the laws and unmake the judges?" Yet despite the bitterest political enmities that make ours today pale in contrast, despite predictions of disaster, a peaceful transfer of power took place and endured from the party of Hamilton to the party of Jefferson. Such an event, not common in the world, was one of the happy milestones in the unfinished march of American democracy and political stability. But that is another subject. Our interest is the elevation to power of an American icon who was the high priest of unbridled American expansion, and how he used and bent the political power given to him in furtherance of that cause.[25]

It is not my purpose to enter the current debate over Thomas Jefferson, but a brief statement of my general opinion is in order. Jefferson was an idealist who did not have the luxury of standing above the fray, offering unsolicited advice to participants in the trenches of political warfare. As a practicing politician, Jefferson had to deal with the real world of imperfect human beings and institutions, and he has been flayed by purists ever since for being unable to perform the impossible: always merging his ideals with the reality of the world he was very much a part of. He is well known for contradicting himself, and it has laid him open to the charge of hypocrisy. But this is a common human failing, and when we are dealing with a man like Jefferson, who in his lifetime turned out a Niagara of words, we must expect major inconsistencies. So let us take him as we find him.[26]

In his Indian policy Jefferson talked a good game, but his eloquent words kept getting ambushed by his obsession: the conquest of North America. Sometimes he even threw in the rest of the Americas. He agreed with the policy devised by Washington and Knox, and wanted to move even faster in civilizing Indians—that is, making farmers in the American manner out of them—and assimilating them into a wider white culture. In December 1808 he told visiting Delawares, "You will unite yourselves with us, and join in our great councils and form one people with us and we shall all be Americans. You will mix with us by marriage. Your blood will run in our veins and will spread with us over this great island." He repeated this in similar words over the years. There is no reason to believe that Jefferson did not mean what he said, at least at the time he said it, but he either did not understand or ignored two fatal flaws in his concept of a union of two peoples: most Indians did not want to give up their way of life, and most whites did not want to merge with Indians and become one people, and the feeling was intense on both sides.[27]

Thomas Jefferson, ca. 1791, by Charles Willson Peale (Independence National Historical Park)

At other times the pretty words were replaced by duplicity. Jefferson suggested to William Henry Harrison, governor of the Indiana Territory, that to promote exchanges of land, "which they have to spare and we want, for necessaries, which we have to spare and they want, we shall push our trading uses, and be glad to see the good and influential individuals among them run in debt, because we observe that when these debts get beyond what the individuals can pay, they become willing to lop them off by a cession of land. At our trading houses, too, we mean to sell so low as merely to repay us cost and charges, so as neither to lessen or enlarge our capital. This is what private traders cannot do, for they must gain; they will consequently retire from the competition, and we shall thus get clear of this pest without giving offence or umbrage to the Indians. In this way our settlement will gradually circumscribe and approach the Indians, and they will in time either incorporate with us as citizens of the United States, or remove beyond the Mississippi

River." If the Indians chose war, Jefferson was quite clear as to their fate: "Should any tribe be fool-hardy enough to take up the hatchet at any time, the seizing the whole country of that tribe, and driving them across the Mississippi as the only condition of peace, would be an example to others and a furtherance of our final consolidation."[28]

Jefferson has been scored by critics for the policy described in the previous paragraph, but over the long run the nation ended in Jefferson's debt. The frontier people could not be reined in and were moving too fast, even if his highly dubious assimilation theory, given enough time, would have worked; and the foreign danger weighed heavily upon him. Jefferson believed that the United States was the world's last best hope against European monarchies and Napoleonic despotism. In 1800, in the secret Treaty of San Ildefonso, Napoleon forced Spain to return New Orleans and Louisiana to France. By the time Jefferson wrote to Harrison he knew of the transfer. Furthermore, on 16 October 1802, before physical transfer to France had occurred, the Spanish intendant at New Orleans revoked the right of American deposit of duty-free goods at New Orleans. It was not lifted until April 1803, and in the interval westerners were in an uproar. Jefferson feared reassertion of French control in the Mississippi Valley, a fear that had a firm base in reality, for there can be no doubt that Napoleon envisioned a new French empire in America. The danger then of a carving up of the North American continent between the United States and European powers was real. Jefferson could not foresee the monstrous twin tyrannies of the twentieth century, fascism and communism, but his overriding goal of occupying the continent, however disastrous it was for the Indians, placed the United States in the twentieth century in the position to assume the leading, and indispensable, role in defeating those evil empires of our time.

Jefferson made his purpose clear in his letter to Harrison: "Combined with these views [of the Indians], and to be prepared against the occupation of Louisiana by a powerful and enterprising people, it is important that, setting less value on interior extension of purchases from the Indians, we bend our whole views to the purchase and settlement of the country on the Mississippi, from its mouth to its northern regions, that we may be able to present as strong a front on our western as on our eastern border, and plant on the Mississippi itself the means of its own defense."[29]

With the French in mind, Jefferson urged quick action on Indian land cessions: "The crisis is pressing: whatever can now be obtained must be obtained quickly. The occupation of New Orleans, hourly expected, by the French, is already felt like a breeze by the Indians. You know the sentiments they entertain of that nation; under the hope of their protection they will immediately stiffen against cessions of lands to us. We had better therefore, do at once what can now be done." In closing, Jefferson added fuel for the severest critics of his Indian policy: "I must repeat that this letter is to be considered as private and friendly. . . . You will also perceive how sacredly it must be kept within your own breast, and especially how improper to be understood by the Indians. For their interests and their tranquillity it is best they should see only the present age of their history."[30]

Matters moved very quickly that spring of 1803. Upon Jefferson's instructions the American minister to France, Robert Livingston, had been negotiating with Napoleon's foreign minister, Talleyrand, for New Orleans and West Florida. But France's situation had changed. A French army of reconquest in Haiti had been decimated by yellow fever and fierce guerrilla warfare carried out by black revolutionaries under the brilliant Toussaint-l'Ouverture. The French commander, General Leclerc, who was Pauline Bonaparte's husband, was dead of fever. The regiments that would have taken possession of Louisiana were wasted remnants. Napoleon's interests shifted elsewhere. He was preparing to go to war again on the European continent and needed money. On 11 April he ordered all of Louisiana offered to the Americans. A few hours after Napoleon announced his decision, Livingston received what may have been the surprise of his life: "M. Talleyrand asked me . . . whether we wished to have the whole of Louisiana." A couple of days later Livingston was joined by Jefferson's ambassador plenipotentiary for the negotiations, James Monroe. Neither American had instructions for what to do if all Louisiana were offered, for nobody, including Jefferson, expected such a thing. Are we not fortunate then that Robert Livingston and James Monroe were operating in a precyberspace age, before micromanagers could intervene and probably ruin the deal? For they decided on their own to accept Napoleon's offer. Jefferson had constitutional qualms about the purchase and thought for a time that it required an amendment to the Constitution, but fortunately he managed to overcome his doubts. As he later put it himself, "It is incumbent on those who accept great charges to risk themselves on great occasions," adding, "to lose our country by a scrupulous adherence to written laws, would be to lose the law itself. . . ."[31]

The consequences of the Louisiana Purchase are staggering. In one fell swoop, for a total sum of $15 million the United States doubled its size—some 828,000 square miles at about three cents an acre. It now controlled both banks of the Mississippi almost to its source in Minnesota. Within the boundaries would be created the states of Arkansas, Missouri, Iowa, South Dakota, Nebraska, Minnesota, Oklahoma, Kansas, North Dakota, and Montana, most of Louisiana, almost half of Colorado, and over half of Wyoming. The heartland now seemed secure. The French retreat from North America meant that the United States would be spared a struggle for empire between powerful European antagonists into which it would inevitably have been drawn, its fate entwined with the stubborn quarrels of ancient foes. Instead, the nation now faced southward in Florida an outpost of a Spanish empire sapped of vitality, for whom the word *conquistador* was but a memory. The best description of the purchase occurred when Robert Livingston asked for its precise boundaries, and the brilliant but cynical Talleyrand replied, "I can give you no direction. You have made a noble bargain for yourselves, and I suppose you will make the most of it."[32]

Jefferson tried to make the most it, stating that "we have some claims, to extend on the sea coast Westwardly to the Rio Norte or Bravo [Rio Grande to Americans], and better, to go Eastwardly to the Rio Perdido, between Mobile & Pensacola, the ancient boundary of Louisiana." But Texas is another tale. And American insistence that much of West Florida was included in the Louisiana Purchase rested on such flimsy evidence that even the French ambassador to the United States, Louise-Marie Turreau, a tough soldier who lacked all of the usual qualifications for diplomacy, in a meeting with the Spanish ambassador and James Madison, neatly got the better of the U.S. secretary of state.

"But General," said Madison, "we have a map which probably carries to the Perdido the eastern limit of Lousiana."

Turreau replied, "I should be curious to see it, sir; the more because I have one which includes Tennessee and Kentucky in Louisiana." And if that were not neat enough, he added, "You will agree that maps are not titles."[33]

Jefferson and the nation could be well satisfied with what was obtained, especially as the transaction did not meet the highest standards of legality. Under the terms of the secret Treaty of San Ildefonso (1 October 1800), France could not sell or otherwise dispose of the territory without first offering to return it to Spain. This is an important point we must keep in mind as our story progresses, for it was why the British refused to recognize the legality of the Louisiana Purchase, even though it was not then in a position to do anything about it. But Bonaparte was not a man to be bothered by a scrap of paper, and Spain got the news of the purchase via the rumor mill. Under the Constitution of the United States Jefferson, normally the strict constructionist, did not have the right to buy Louisiana. But this man of boundless imagination, fortunately not hamstrung by legions of lawyers, accepted what Livingston and Monroe brought him. Therefore, to the establishment of the University of Virginia, to the Virginia Statute of Religious Liberties, to his role in drafting the Declaration of Independence, we must add another star to his firmament. Had Napoleon not in his imperious way decided to sell Louisiana, had Jefferson lacked the vision and boldness to grasp the opportunity, the various scenarios of what might have been range from dismal to nightmarish.[34]

"CLAIBORNE WILL NOT FILL THAT OFFICE"

Jackson was enthralled with the purchase. He wrote to Jefferson that it was "an event which generations yet unborn in each revolving year will hail the day" and ended his letter, "Accept sir of the unanimous congratulations of the citizens of Mero, on the Joyfull event of the cession of Louisiana and New orleans, every face wears a smile, and every heart leaps with joy." And when he received an alert that the militia might have to march on New Orleans to ensure that the Spanish did not contest the cession to the United States, Major General Andrew Jackson did not hesitate. His general order to the militia stated that the conduct of the Spanish government and the "hostile appearance and menacing attitude of their Armed forces . . . make it necessary that the militia under my Command, should be in complete order and at a moments warning ready to march." But it was not to be. The Spanish complained bitterly of the illegal nature of the sale but bowed to reality, and American regulars soon hoisted the flag in New Orleans.[35]

Denied military glory, Jackson decided that he should be the choice to govern the Territory of Orleans and began a vigorous, wide-ranging campaign to get the appointment. He got the entire Tennessee congressional delegation to send a petition to President Jefferson recommending Jackson for the job, and he approached important Jeffersonian Republicans to further his cause. On his way to Philadelphia to buy goods for his store, he traveled by way of Washington to continue his lobbying efforts. He knew that Jefferson was at Monticello and could have stopped on the way, but he could not bring himself to approach the great man directly, for "it might be construed into the conduct of a courteor, and my vissit might have created such sensations in his mind, I therefore passed on without calling. of all ideas to me it is the most humiliating to be thought to cringe to power to obtain a favour or an appointment—feelings calculated to bend to those things are badly calculated for a representative Government, where merrit alone ought to be the road to preferment."[36]

In Washington, Jackson learned that there was "not a hint who is to be appointed Governor of New Orleans," but he had "reasons to conclude that Mr William [Charles Cole] Claiborne will not fill that office." He also had "reasons to believe" that preference would be given to a person fluent in French if one could be found, which Jackson thought a proper qualification "provided it is accompanied with other necessary ones." He then claimed that "I never had any sanguine expectations of filling the office. If I should it will be more than I expect." Why then did he lobby so hard and detour to Washington? To see the sights? No, when he wrote those words he may by then have learned that he would not get the appointment. It went to the man Jackson had predicted would not get it, his old Tennessee colleague and now governor of the Mississippi Territory, the twenty-eight-year-old William Charles Cole Claiborne, who was not Jefferson's first choice. But when James Monroe turned it down and Lafayette also declined, the selection of Claiborne was obvious. He was of Jefferson's class, an attribute Jackson especially could not claim; he was an experienced territorial governor; he was in place as provisional governor of Louisiana, having gone to New Orleans with the troops for the takeover ceremony; and, perhaps most important, during the tense election of 1800 he had kept Tennessee in Jefferson's corner. He was also a better choice than Jackson. New Orleans was a political minefield, "a position," wrote one historian, "which would have tried the soul of any man." Jackson in that office would have been in a perpetual rage, as Jefferson undoubtedly realized, having observed his performance in the Senate.[37]

Jackson was furious over his rejection, and in turn he rejected Jefferson. Denied a position he thought that he deserved, although we must admit our failure to see any visible qualification for the office, Jackson was about to enter a barren period in his life in which he engaged in reckless acts that threatened to banish him to political and social purgatory.[38]

Chapter 11

CONSPIRACY AND BLOOD

"I LOVE MY COUNTRY AND GOVERNMENT"

Jackson resigned his judgeship in 1804. He needed to make money, and the bench did not pay enough. He did not resume his legal practice; instead, he turned to commerce to relieve his debts and opened a dry goods store in partnership with others. One of his partners, John Coffee, was a big, strong man whose name and future became closely linked with Jackson. Like Jackson, Coffee was of Scotch Irish ancestry. He left North Carolina with his widowed mother and the rest of the family in 1797 and crossed the mountains to the Cumberland, where he eventually married Rachel's niece, Mary Donelson. His main occupation was land surveyor, one of the most useful and prestigious in early America. John Coffee was brave, steadfast, and loyal, and as we shall soon see he possessed another skill that would serve Jackson and the nation well in perilous times.[1]

Jackson may have been in financial trouble in this first decade of the new century, but he impressed people he met. One woman retained a vivid memory of him. "It was in 1808, when I was a girl of sixteen, that I first saw General Jackson. It was in East Tennessee, at the house of Captain Lyon, whose family myself and another young lady were visiting. We were sitting at work one afternoon, when a servant, who was lounging at the window, exclaimed, 'Oh, see what a fine, elegant gentleman is coming up the road!' We girls ran to the window, of course, and there, indeed, was a fine gentleman, mounted on a beautiful horse, an upright, striking figure, high jack-boots coming up over the knee, holsters, and every thing handsome and complete." The stranger entered the house, "where we girls were sitting as demurely as though we had *not* been peeping and listening. We all rose as he entered the room. He bowed and smiled, as he said: 'Excuse my intruding upon you, ladies, in the absence of Captain Lyon. I am *Judge Jackson*. I have business with Captain Lyon, and am here by his invitation. I hope I do not incommode you.' We were all captivated by this polite speech, and the agreeable manner it which it was spoken. Soon after, Captain Lyon entered, accompanied by two officers of the army. . . . We had a delightful evening. I remember Jackson was full of anecdote, and told us a great deal about the early days of Tennessee . . . The party broke up the next morning, and we saw Judge Jackson ride away on his fine horse, and all agree that a finer looking man or a better horseman there was not in Tennessee."[2]

Jackson's store prospered for a while, but eventually failed. Debt burdened him to the point were he and Rachel were reduced to living in a two-story log blockhouse on the site where their grand house, the Hermitage, now stands. But as interesting as all this may be, it is not our business and we cannot tarry. For on 29 May 1805, a then famous man came to Nashville and stayed with the Jacksons for five days. His name was Aaron Burr, and he was up to no good. But Andrew Jackson was taken with the charming, cultivated easterner. A man who knew Burr from boyhood left a good physical description of him. He was a small man, five feet six inches, "his figure . . . well-proportioned, sinewy, elastic . . . his head was not large, but . . . well proportioned. His forehead was high, protruding, but narrow directly over the eyes, and widening immediately back. The head was classically poised on the shoulders; his feet and hands were peculiarly small; the nose was rather large, with open, expanding nostrils; and the ears so small as almost to be a deformity. But the feature that gave character and tone to all, and which made his presence felt, was the eye. Perfectly round, not large, deep hazel in color, it had an expression which no one who had seen it could ever forget. No man could stand in the presence of Col. Burr, with his eyes fixed on him, and not feel that they pierced his innermost thoughts. There was a power in his look—a magnetism, if I may be allowed the expression—which few persons could resist." Later observers in Alabama confirmed this, telling the historian Albert Pickett that Burr's "eyes were peculiarly brilliant . . . 'they looked like stars.' " But "when addressing ladies," his boyhood friend said, "uttering some pleasantry or witticism, the smile around his mouth was literally beautiful, and his eyes would lose their piercing look, and become tender and gentle." Which was quite in character, for Burr did love the ladies.[3]

He was also an excellent conversationalist, his friend testified, with a "voice not powerful, but round, full, and crisp, and though never loud, was tender or impressive as the occasion required. His elocution in conversation was perfect, always precisely suited to the occasion, and the style of thought, to which he was giving expression. His language was terse, almost epigrammatical, and he rarely indulged in illustrations or metaphor; his words were always the most apt that could be used, and he had command of a vocabulary which would make Roguet of the Thesaurus envious. His manners were polished, his motions graceful and easy, yet he never for a moment lost his dignified and noble bearing." He was, in other words, a man well equipped to convince others that his schemes were sound and his prospects promising.[4]

Portrait of Aaron Burr and a View of Richmond Hill, by
Francis S. King (Print Collection, Miriam and Ira D.
Wallach Division of Art, Prints and Photographs, The New
York Public Library, Astor, Lenox and Tilden Foundation)

Well born, well educated, well connected, a veteran of the Revolutionary War to boot, a world of opportunity lay open to the young Aaron Burr.
But he wasted it all, for one vital ingredient was lacking—character. Alexander Hamilton was Burr's bitter enemy, but even taking that into account we
must agree with his judgment that Burr was "a man whose only political
principal is to *mount at all events* to the highest legal honours of the Nation
and as much further as circumstances will carry him." Aaron Burr was a classic example of a political adventurer who toyed with the loyalties and emotions of his followers as a libertine toys with his conquests, and the analogy
is apt, for his fleshly weaknesses were notorious.[5]

But what was Burr doing on the Cumberland? To be sure, the Indian danger had passed, and there were signs of growing gentility and affluence, but it was still a new, raw country, as travelers would attest for decades to come. Yet a promising country for those bold enough to take her on. One's fortunes, political and otherwise, might be recouped in the West, and of all men, Burr's fortunes were at the nadir.

In the presidential election of 1800, the Jeffersonian Republicans intended Thomas Jefferson as their candidate for president, and Aaron Burr as their candidate for vice president. But at that time there was a flaw in the Constitution's electoral college system: each elector voted for two men, but with no indication of which candidate was his choice for president and which for vice president. When the votes were counted Jefferson and Burr each had seventy-three votes, and that threw the election into the House of Representatives, which voted by state delegations. Although Burr was obviously the vice presidential candidate, he refused to either step down or pledge to resign the presidency if chosen. The Federalists saw a chance to do mischief, and many of them preferred Burr to their archenemy, Jefferson. On the thirty-sixth ballot sanity prevailed among just enough congressmen for Jefferson to be elected. But the affair ended with Burr scorned by Jeffersonian Republicans and many Federalists alike. Even his very sympathetic biographer referred to his "baffling behavior during the presidential election of 1800," which is the kindest interpretation one can put on the affair.[6]

Now distrusted and scorned by both parties, Burr sealed his fate on 11 July 1804 when he shot and mortally wounded Alexander Hamilton in a duel in Weehawken, New Jersey. Burr himself acknowledged that Hamilton's death "has driven me into a sort of exile, and may terminate in an actual and permanent ostracism," and he was close to the truth. Eight years had to pass before he could appear publicly in New York State, and a New Jersey grand jury indicted him for murder. A little less than two months after the duel, the British minister to the United States, Anthony Merry, produced the first concrete piece of evidence of Burr's Conspiracy, in a secret letter in cipher to the British foreign minister, Lord Harrowby: "I have just received an offer from Mr. Burr . . . to lend his assistance to His Majesty's Government in any Manner in which they may think fit to employ him, particularly in endeavouring to effect a Separation of the Western Part of the United States from that which lies between the Atlantick and the Mountains, in its whole extent."[7]

Eight months later, before Burr's first trip west, Anthony Merry wrote again in secret to Lord Harrowby that "Mr. Burr . . . has mentioned to me that the Inhabitants of Louisiana seem determined to render themselves independent of the United States & that the Execution of their Design is only delayed by the Difficulty of obtaining previously an Assurance of Protection & Assistance from some Foreign Power and of concerting & connecting their Independence with that of the Inhabitants of the Western Parts of the United States, who must always have Command over them by the Rivers which communicate with the Mississippi.

"It is clear that Mr. Burr (altho he has not as yet confided to me the exact Nature & Extent of his Plan) means to endeavour to be the instrument for effecting such a Connection." Burr then told Merry that the inhabitants of "French or Spanish Origine," as well as the People of the Western Waters, preferred the "Protection and Assistance of Great Britain to the Support of France," but that if the British turned away they would apply to the French, "who will, he had every reason to know," eagerly grasp the opportunity. Unfortunately for us, and for generations of historians who have tried to decide what the adventurer actually meant to do, "Mr. Burr observed that it would be too dangerous and even premature to disclose to me at present the full Extent and Detail of the Plan he had formed. . . ."[8]

That is a very brief background for Burr's visit to the Jacksons'. He had pushed off from Pittsburgh in a luxurious flatboat for his first trip west, had left it at Louisville, and proceeded overland through Kentucky and Tennessee to Nashville, getting the lay of the land and the temper of men of influence. That is why he stopped at Jackson's, to confer with one of West Tennessee's leading citizens and the commander of its militia. There is no evidence that he discussed separatism with Jackson, and in 1806, when Jackson was told that separating the West from the Union was Burr's intention, he immediately separated himself from Burr and wrote warning letters to Governor Claiborne in New Orleans and to Daniel Smith, senator from Tennessee. We should note here that Burr's contemporaries—and historians since—were at odds as to what precisely Burr had in mind. If we accept Anthony Merry's letters to Lord Harrowby as accurately reporting Burr's intention, then in 1805 he indeed aimed at separation of the western states and territories. Burr denied this in a letter to William Henry Harrison, and after his return east from his reconnaissance mission he probably gave up hope of separation for the time being, but he seems not to have cast it aside.[9]

Between mid and late November 1805, Burr had a two-hour meeting with Thomas Jefferson at the White House. On 1 December Jefferson received an anonymous letter: "You admit him at your table, and you held a long and private conference with him a few days ago *after dinner* at the very moment he is meditating the overthrow of your Administration . . . Yes, Sir, his abberations throughout the Western States *had no other object*. A foreign Agent, now at Washington knows since February last his plans and has seconded them beyond what you are aware of . . . Watch his connexions with Mr. M[err]y and you will find him a British pensioner and agent. . . ."

On 5 December another anonymous letter came to Jefferson, announcing the arrival in New York of the Venezuelan patriot and revolutionary Francisco de Miranda. "This event forms a link in Burr's manouevres. His instructions like those of Burr come from the same source. The same plans, or others similar in their tendency are to be offered to you. . . . Although ostensibly directed against a foreign power [Spain], the destruction of our Government, your ruin and the material injury of the Atlantic States are their true object."[10]

Many pieces of the jigsaw are missing, and if they were not it wouldn't have been much of a conspiracy. Some believe Burr wanted only to live peacefully on his lands in the Orleans Territory. Still others maintain that his real purpose was an invasion of Mexico with thousands of American frontiersmen. Whatever Aaron Burr had in mind, and I personally believe that Anthony Merry was an accurate reporter, it is not what Burr intended, but Andrew Jackson's connection with the adventurer and its effect on his career, that is of interest to us. For Burr, in the final analysis, is a minor character in American history, whereas Jackson is one of its major figures.[11]

Jackson provided a flatboat for Burr to float down the Cumberland to the Ohio to rendezvous with his own craft and journey on to New Orleans. Upon his return east he stopped once more at Nashville, this time for eight days in August 1805, and once again was a guest at Jackson's modest home. Jackson arranged a ball in Burr's honor, and James Parton spoke to a "few persons living at Nashville who remember this famous ball; remember the hush and thrill attending the entrance of Colonel Burr, accompanied by General Jackson in the uniform of a Major General; and how the company looked intently on while the two courtliest men in the world made the circuit of the apartment, General Jackson introducing his guest with singular grace and emphasis. It was a question with the ladies which of the two was the finer gentleman."[12]

During Burr's 1805 visits with Jackson the two men discussed the position of the Spanish in North America, and apparently Jackson believed that Burr's aim was not disunion but the expulsion of Spain from North America, including Mexico. He told Jackson that the secretary of war, Henry Dearborn, was secretly allied with him. The following March Burr wrote to Jackson from Washington with specific requests: "I am glad to learn that you have had your division reviewed; but you ought not to confine your attention to those men, as officers, who accidentally bear commissions—your country is full of fine matterials for an army and I have often said that a brigade could be raised in W. Ten. which would drive double their number of frenchmen off the Earth. I take the liberty of recommending to you to make out a list of officers from Colonel down to Ensign for one or two regiments, composed of fellows fit for business & with whom you would trust your life and your honor." Note that Burr is asking Jackson to bypass officers in whom he lacks confidence and prepare a special officer corps for duty in the field, a move that would be unusual under normal circumstances. He continued: "If you will transmit to me this list, I will, in case Troops should be called for, recommend it to the department of war and I have reason to believe that, on such an occasion, my advice should be listened to." The final sentence is absurd. He had no intention of submitting the list to the War Department, and had he the temerity to offer advice it would have been rejected. But the list, which has never been found, was prepared. In 1828, John Coffee said that Jackson, James Robertson, and "sundry others of the old respectable citizens" met in Nashville and drew up the list, "and as I supposed sent it on to" Burr.[13]

Burr reappeared at Jackson's home on 24 September 1806 and stayed for a few days. He was now in the final stage of his scheme, meaning to rendezvous downstream with a large armed force and descend the Mississippi for whatever purpose he had in mind at that point. He contracted with Jackson to build five large boats and stock them with provisions. Burr was again lionized in Nashville at a round of banquets. On 4 October Jackson issued an Order to Brigadier Generals of the 2nd Division that began, "The late conduct of the Spanish Government, added to the Hostile appearance & menacing attitude of their armed forces already incamped within the limits of our government, make it necessary that the militia under my command, should be in complete order & at a moments warning ready to march." Jackson was straining at the leash to make war on the Dons, and his appetite for conquest was huge. On the same day he wrote to James Winchester that he had no doubt seen in the newspapers "that the negociation for the purchase of the Floridas have failed. The certain consquence is war. . . ." He hoped "that at least, two thousand Volunteers can be lead into the field at short notice. That number commanded by firm officers and men of enterprise, I think could look into Santafe and Maxico" and "give freedom and commerce to those provinces and establish peace, and a permament barrier against the inroads and attacks of foreign powers on our interior—which will be the case so long as Spain holds that large country on our borders." In addition to his arguments on behalf of national security, there was a personal element for all involved. "Should there be a war this will be a handsome theatre for our entrerprising young men, and a certain source of acquiring fame."[14]

The following day he wrote to the president, Thomas Jefferson, enclosing a copy of his order and offering three regiments for duty: "In the event of insult or aggression made on our Government and country from any quarter, I am so well convinced that the publick sentiment and feeling of the citizens within this state, and particularly within my Division, are such . . . that I take the liberty of tendering their services . . . and at one moments warning after your signification that this tender is acceptable, my orders shall be given. . . ." Jefferson's judicious reply of 3 December thanked Jackson and informed him that the questions of war or peace were under consideration. So matters stood until early November, when a man named John A. Fort came to stay at Jackson's house.[15]

"About the 10th of November," Jackson wrote, "a Capt Fort called at my house and after a stay of a night and part of a day he introduced the subject of the adventurers—and in part stated that their intention was to divide the union. I sternly asked how they would effect it. he replied by seizing (New orleans) & the bank shutting the port, conquering Mexico, and uniting the western part of the union to the conquored country. I perhaps with warmth asked him how this was to be effected, he replied by the aid of the Federal troops, and the Genl at their head. I asked, if he had this from the Genl, he said he had not. I asked him if Colo. Burr was in to the scheme he answered that he did not know nor was he informed that he was: that he barely knew Colo. Burr, but never had any conversation. I asked him how he knew this and from whom he got his information, he said from Colo. [John] Swartwout, in New York." Swartwout was the brother of Burr's confederate Samuel Swartwout, and with this knowledge, Jackson wrote, "it rushed into my mind like lightning that Burr was at the head.[16]

Making war on the Spanish was one thing, treason quite another. For Jackson loved his country. As he wrote to George Washington Campbell, "Should you ever hear that I am embarked on a cause innimicable to my country believe it not. should you hear, that treasonable intentions have come to my knowledge, And that I have been silent believe them not." Almost immediately after he heard Fort's story, Jackson wrote in dramatic language to the governor of Orleans Territory, William C. C. Claiborne: "Indeed I fear treachery is the order of the day. This induces me to write you. Put your Town in a state of Defense organize your Militia, and defend your City as well against internal enemies as external . . . I fear you will meet with an attack from quarters you do not at present expect. Be upon the alert—keep, a watchful eye on our General [Burr's coconspirator Major General James Wilkinson, commander of U.S. forces on the lower Mississippi]—and beware of an attack, as well from your own Country as Spain, I fear there something rotten in the State of Denmark. you have enemies within your own City, that may try to subvert your Government, and try to separate it from the Union. You know I never hazard ideas without good grounds, you will keep these hints to yourself. but I say again be upon the alert. your Government I fear is in danger, I fear there are plans on foot inimical to the Union. Whether they will be attempted to be carried into effect or not I cannot say but rest assured they are in operation or I calculate badly. beware of the month of December. I love my Country and Government, I hate the Dons. I would delight to see Mexico reduced, but I will die in the last ditch before I would yield a part to the Dons, or see the Union disunited."[17]

Aaron Burr's scheme, whatever it was by the time he floated downstream from Nashville, collapsed with a whimper. His legions of adventurers turned out to be pitifully few. On 6 February 1807 Governor Claiborne declared him a fugitive from justice. Burr tried to flee with one companion to Spanish Florida riding "a small tackey of a horse" and disguised in the rough clothes of a river boatman. After traveling some two hundred miles of wilderness, he was recognized and taken into custody on 19 February in Alabama, not far north of the junction of the Alabama and Tombigbee Rivers, by Lieutenant Edmund Pendleton Gaines of the U.S. Army, who had with him a sergeant and three men. Taken to Richmond, Virginia, he was tried for treason and acquitted, but his public career was over.[18]

Jackson's link to Burr, although not treasonous, would bedevil him on more than one occasion and seriously threaten his thirst for military acclaim. It was only natural for people to suspect that he was involved. Burr had been more than once a guest in Jackson's home. Jackson had been most attentive to him, had introduced him to the leading men on the Cumberland, and had sold him boats which Burr had taken on his final descent of the Western Waters in quest of power, fortune, and glory. No wonder there were whispers, no wonder slightly veiled suspicions appeared in newspapers. And Jackson did not help himself by his extravagant conduct during Burr's grand jury hearings in Richmond. Jackson was subpoenaed to testify and on 12 May 1807 left Nashville for Richmond. He was "more convinced than I ever was before, that *treason* was never intended by Burr; but if ever it was, you know my wish is, and always has been, that he be hung." His testimony before the grand jury on 25 June was straightforward, and he told of Burr's denial to him of treason. But it was not what he said inside the courthouse but outside that got him into trouble.[19]

Loudly and clearly, Jackson let it be known that he believed General James Wilkinson the villain and Burr the innocent. He was so out of control that Burr's defense lawyers decided to forgo his testimony at the jury trial, which also enraged him. The grand jury foreman, John Randolph of Roanoke, wrote to James Monroe that Jackson "does not scruple to say that W[ilkinson] is a pensioner of Spain, to his knowledge, & that he will not dare to show his face here." Jefferson was informed on 14 June by George Hay that "General Jackson, of Tennessee, has been here ever since the 22nd. denouncing Wilkinson in the coarsest terms in every company." If that were not conspicuous enough, James Parton reported that people still living when he wrote were present when Jackson "harangued the crowd in the Capitol Square, defending Burr, and angrily denouncing Jefferson as a persecutor." Official Washington would not forget, especially James Madison, secretary of state, whom Parton claimed "took deep offense" at Jackson's conduct. And Madison would succeed Jefferson as president.[20]

"I SHOULD HAVE HIT HIM, IF HE HAD SHOT ME THROUGH THE BRAIN"

One would think that Jackson had enough on his hands during this period: planning to humble the Dons, scrambling to sever his links to Burr, and continuing his efforts to climb out of debt and rebuild his fortunes. But his violent nature and hair-trigger sense of honor simmered, heated up, and finally boiled over in an outburst that shocked even frontier Tennessee. And all over a horse race that never took place.

Jackson was a lover of good horses and devoted to their breeding and training, as well as betting on them at the track. In May 1805 he bought for $1,500 five-year-old Truxton, a racer out of impeccable breeding. In November of that year a match race was scheduled between Truxton and Captain Joseph Erwin's Ploughboy. The mile-long racetrack was at Clover Bottom on Stone's River, where, we recall, Colonel John Donelson and his family, including Rachel, had first settled in the grim year of 1780. The stakes were $2,000 to be paid on the day of the race in promissory notes then due. If either side forfeited, $800 in notes due would be paid. Ploughboy went lame the day before the race. The list of notes was held by Erwin's son-in-law,

Charles Dickinson, who "selected out of them such as he had rather part with" and gave them to Erwin, who handed them over to Jackson. But Jackson "objected saying he thought he ought to have Choise of the Notes & ask'd me for Mr. D's List of Notes." Dickinson produced the list, Jackson selected the notes he wanted, and the gentlemen went their separate ways.[21]

Until Jackson heard that Charles Dickinson had committed the unforgivable: making disparaging remarks about Rachel in front of others. The only evidence for the story came from Sam Houston and other friends of Jackson who told it several years later to James Parton. There is no mention of it in contemporary sources. According to Houston, Jackson confronted Dickinson with the charge. Dickinson denied it, but said if it were true he must have been drunk when he said it. Their conversation seemed to settle the matter and they parted. Dickinson, who was also a lawyer, was said to have been well connected, had many friends, was amiable enough, and not usually given to insulting others. But he was also young, somewhat wild, and given to loose, vulgar talk when drunk. Sam Houston told Parton that Dickinson insulted Rachel a second time in a Nashville tavern. The news of the second transgression reached Jackson. Instead of seeking out Dickinson, Jackson went to Captain Erwin and urged him to exert control of his daughter's husband. "I wish no quarrel with him," Jackson is reported to have said, "he is *used* by my enemies in Nashville, who are urging him on to pick a quarrel with me. Advise him to stop in time." But it seems that the enmity grew, and by January 1806 "there was the worst possible feeling between them."[22]

Although Jackson and Dickinson were the principals, their respective friends gossiped and bore tales back and forth. This led to the heated involvement of other persons. The charge was made in public by Jackson's friends that the promissory notes delivered to Jackson upon the forfeiture of the horse race were not notes due, as agreed upon and which Jackson had chosen. This meant that Jackson could not immediately claim his forfeiture of $800. A friend of Dickinson's, a young lawyer named Thomas Swann, who had recently come from Virginia with excellent letters of recommendation, became involved as a talebearer. Without getting bogged down in who said what to whom and where and when, this phase of the dispute led to Jackson calling young Swann a "damn'd Lyar!" Naturally, that was reported to Swann, who wrote Jackson on 3 January that "the harshness of this expression has deeply wounded my feelings; it is language to which I am a stranger, which no man acquainted with my character would venture to apply to me, and which should this information of Mr. Dickinson be correct I shall be under the necessity of taking proper notice of." It was not a challenge, but the groundwork had been laid, and Swann put Jackson on notice that "I shall expect an answer."[23]

Jackson's answer on 7 January is interesting, for he treated Swann like a young stranger whose maturity was questionable and reserved his insults for Dickinson: "*when the base, poltroon and cowardly assassin tale bearer, will always act in the dark back ground* you can apply the Two latter to Mr. Dickinson, and see which best fits him, and I write it for his eye—and the latter I *emphatically intend for him."* Jackson added that he was about to depart for Southwest Point (modern Kingston, Tennessee), but Dickinson could expect that "I will furnish him with an anodine as soon as I return." Three days later Dickinson replied. After reviewing his version of events, he concluded with his own insults and revealed a sense of humor, although whether Jackson saw it as such is questionable: "As to the word *Coward, I think it as* applicable to yourself as anyone I know and I shall be very glad when an opportunity serves to know in what manner you give your Anodines and hope you will take in payment one of my most moderate Cathartics. Yours at Command."[24]

Dickinson left on a previously scheduled trip to New Orleans before Jackson received his letter, but in his absence Jackson did not lack for an offended opponent. Poor young Swann refused to bow out of a dispute that was between Jackson and Dickinson. For Swann was a gentleman, which means little today, but then it was an important badge of rank. Those who claimed it had a highly developed sense of honor, and this particular gentleman had been called a "damn'd Lyar." It was not only outrageous, it was quite unacceptable. "Think not that I am to be intimidated by your threats," Swann wrote to Jackson. "No power terrestrial shall prevent the settled purpose of my soul. The statement I have made in respect to the notes is essentially correct: The torrent of abusive language with which you have assailed me is such, as every gentleman should blush to hear; your menaces I set at defiance, and now demand of you that reparation which one gentleman is intitled to receive of another: My friend the bearer of this is authorized to make compleat arrangements in the field of honor." Young Swann, without doubt to his great good fortune, would be denied satisfaction. Jackson ignored the challenge, instead telling Swann's friend and messenger, Nathaniel A. McNairy, that he did not know Swann to be a gentleman. But he did promise to cane him. A few days later Jackson, accompanied by John Coffee, came upon Swann in Winn's Tavern, walked over, and whacked him "a very severe blow" with his cane. He would have struck him again, but he got his feet tangled and almost fell into the fireplace. Swann reached inside his coat. Jackson thought he was pulling a pistol and drew his own. People scattered. But Swann's hand came up empty, and instead of getting shot he suffered Jackson's well-refined vituperation. According to Coffee, Swann fled, although Swann said that he once again demanded satisfaction.[25]

Swann then published his version of events in the *Impartial Review and Cumberland Repository* of 1 February. It included his challenge and the charge that "the ingenious General had discovered another pretext to shield himself from the dangers of an equal combat—'he did not know me to be a gentleman.'" James Robertson was in Nashville, and upon reading Swann's statement he wrote that day to Jackson. Robertson's purpose was to stop Jackson from behaving like a jackass and getting himself into a scrape that could have mortal consequences. Thus we can allow for a certain amount of flattery. But the letter also reveals not only Robertson's liking of Jackson but a recognition that Jackson was not an ordinary man, that within him was a capacity to perform extraordinary deeds. Quoting from it also gives us the opportunity to witness once again Robertson's deeply imbedded common sense, and to enjoy once more his delightful spelling.[26]

He began by apologizing for his intrusion into the matter and trusts Jackson "will pass it over as an Errore of one who wishes you well from the bottom of my hart. . . ." He stresses that "when I vew your superiour compacity I see thare is no Comparrison who is and may be most yousefull in Sociaty." Robertson hopes that Jackson will "not suffer pation to git the upper hand of your good Sence." For "Should yuou fall, your tallance are lost to your County, besides the Erreperable loss your Famuley and friends myst sustane and on the other hand, were you to Resque your life and in defening it take the life of your Fellow mortal, might this not make you miserable so long as you lived. . . ." Robertson drove home his last point by reminding Jackson of the effect on Aaron Burr's life of his killing of Alexander Hamilton.

Robertson then got to the heart of the matter:

> will you pardon me my friend when I tell you that I have bin longer in this world than you have and ought to have heard the opinions of people more than you have, and do heare the fals honer of dueling Redeculed by most of thinking perons and I assure you that your friends do think a man of your standing ought to say but littel about duling . . . young hot heded persons to be in the fashion of the presant age, may talk of killing there fellow Creater, and do not Reflict that they are doing an act that will not be in thare power to Repare . . . I cannot find whare aney honer is attached to dueling. if I had aney doubt of being in your frendship, I should not have taken the liberty to trobel you with sentiments on this subject, but as I have from the Earlys acquaintance bin attached to you and the long acquaintanc and Frendship I have formed with the Famuley you are conected with makes it my dutey to give you my opinion.

Robertson hastens to add that he has no doubt of Jackson's bravery and would not have written if he had, and therefore "once for all let me tell you, that you will have more than ten to one which will applaud your prudance in avoyeding a duel, your acquaintances think your pation is such, that if you were to git into a duel I assure you it is my opinion you would have a full sheare of the blame attached to your self."[27]

Could a man have received better advice?

Did Jackson heed it?

Of course not.

On 15 February Jackson replied to Swann through the pages of the *Impartial Review,* a long statement that included letters from Robert Hays and Robert Butler on why Swann was not a gentleman. But it had the unintended consequence of bringing about a duel between John Coffee and Nathaniel McNairy, the young man who had delivered Swann's challenge to Jackson. Jackson dismissed Swann as the "puppet and lying valet for a worthless, drunken, blackguard scoundrel," that is, Dickinson. Jackson then wrote of McNairy: "This young man has either a vicious habit of deviating from the truth, or a natural weakness of memory, either of which is equally pernicious to society . . . It is difficult to find an appropriate epithet for a character who descends to state falsehoods, where the honor of a man is at stake. . . ." Jackson finished with McNairy by referring to a duel McNairy had fought with Jackson's friend John Overton, noting that "the squire's conduct is in perfect unison with a recent act on the field of honor; he fired before the word; it was declared to be an accident; and this prevarication, or whatever you may please to call it, I suppose he will declare to be another."[28]

McNairy, of course, could not let this go unanswered, for he was a gentleman. His reply, published in the *Impartial Review* on 22 February, was laced with sarcasm and challenged Jackson to "come out . . . risk yourself for once on equal terms . . . The risk is not great when you consider that your opponent will be under the impression that he has come in contact with the *brave, magnanimous, invincible and honorable Major General Andrew Jackson,* of Tennessee, *but not commander of the navies."* But then he also scored Coffee: "Let this suffice as a relish for the *gentleman General* until I shall have time to answer the charges exhibited by the *braggadocio General;* espcially as it regards his honorable certifier, Mr. Coffee, who was under the necessity of being sworn, because he is not only *honorable, but religious."*[29]

John Coffee immediately challenged McNairy, Dueling being illegal in Tennessee, they met on 1 March across the state line in Kentucky. In view of what had happened at the McNairy-Overton duel, the seconds discussed but ruled out shooting either man who might shoot before the word "fire" was given, "but should either of them fire before the word, they would be *disgraced,* which they must well know." Major Robert Purdy, Coffee's second, said that after the pistols were loaded "I then cautioned them to be careful not to fire before the word." After Coffee and McNairy had taken their positions, Purdy once more cautioned both men on that specific point. Then Purdy and George Bell, McNairy's second, took their positions, each carrying a loaded pistol. Major Purdy wrote, "I proceeded to give the word, 'Make Ready,' at which time both the gentlemen raised their pistols, and appeared perfectly calm and deliberate. I then proceeded to count, 'one,' and about the word 'two,' Mr. McNairy fired, and shot Mr. Coffee through the thigh. Mr. Coffee fired immediately after; but I am clearly of opinion it was in consequence of the wound he had received, that extracted his fire."

Major Purdy was incensed. He cocked his pistol and approached McNairy and told him "that he ought to be shot" and were it not for the agreement reached between himself and George Bell "I would shoot him." McNairy said it was an accident. Purdy said "that accidents of this kind on the field were inadmissable." Coffee was a bit warm himself. He walked up to McNairy and said, "Goddamn you, this is the second time you have been guilty of the same *crime."* Major Purdy, shocked by Coffee's language on the field of honor, "told Mr. Coffee to desist; that this was an improper place to have words." George Bell suggested another fire. Only, Purdy said, if McNairy took back everything he had written about Coffee and agreed to have "this day's transaction to be published, which I supposed he would not do." Purdy was right. McNairy refused, and the parties went their separate ways.[30]

Thus matters stood until May 1806. Coffee had fought McNairy, and James Robertson and others had intervened and actually prohibited Swann from replying to Jackson's published statement. A second race between Truxton and Ploughboy was scheduled for early April and took place, with Truxton winning easily. Then, in May, Charles Dickinson returned trom New Orleans and immediately took up the original quarrel by publishing a letter in the *Impartial Review*. He declared Jackson "(nowithstanding he is a major general of militia in the Mero District) to be a worthless scoundrel, 'a paltroon and a coward.' A man who, by frivolous and evasive pretexts, avoided giving the satisfaction, which was due to a gentleman whom he had injured. This has prevented me from calling on him in the manner I should otherwise have done, for I am well convinced that he is too great a coward to administer any of those Anodynes, he promised me in his letter to Mr. Swann."

Dickinson's letter, written on the twenty-first, was published on 24 May, but Jackson got wind of it on the twenty-second and asked John Overton's brother Thomas to ride into Nashville to the newspaper office and get a look at it. Thomas Overton returned and told Jackson, "It's a piece that can't be passed over. General Jackson, you must challenge him." Whereupon Jackson decided to see for himself and rode into town and was shown the letter by Thomas Eastin, publisher of the *Impartial Review*. The next day Thomas Overton delivered to Charles Dickinson a letter from Jackson, which was relatively short and, also in contrast to the lengthy missives spawned by this affair, restrained. Jackson wrote, "I hope, sir, your courage will be ample security to me that I will obtain speedily that satisfaction due me for the insults offered, and in the way my friend who hands you this will point out. He waits upon you for that purpose, and with your friend will enter into immediate arrangements for this purpose."[31]

They met on 30 May 1806 in Kentucky. Charles Dickinson was reputed to be the best shot in Tennessee, and since a week passed between Jackson's challenge and their meeting, there was plenty of time for wagers to be made. James Parton was told that the odds were against Jackson. Dickinson was even said to have been one of the bettors. Dickinson had a young and beautiful wife, who apparently did not know of the impending duel, and on the morning he left home for the field of honor he told her he had business in Kentucky. "Good bye, darling," Dickinson said to his lovely young wife, "I shall be *sure* to be at home tomorrow night." He and his party, described by James Parton as "half a dozen of the gay blades of Nashville," were a merry group as they rode north. Dickinson displayed his marksmanship on the way, on one occasion at twenty-four feet firing four balls upon command into a space "that could be covered by a silver dollar"; and near a tavern he severed a string at the same distance, left it hanging, and told the landlord, "If General Jackson comes along this road, show him *that!*"[32]

Jackson, however, with his second Thomas Overton, was all business on the way. The rules for the duel as established by Overton and Dickinson's second, Hanson Catlett, were simple: "the distance shall be 24 feet, the parties to stand facing each other with their pistols down purpendicularly. When they are ready, the single word fire, to be given, at which they are to fire as soon as they please. Should either fire before the word given, we pledge ourselves to shoot them down instantly." These rules, different than for the Coffee-McNairy duel, may have been made to avoid premature firing, but they also meant that one man might knock down the other before his opponent had a chance to fire. Jackson and Overton mulled over the question: fire first, or wait for Dickinson's first shot. They agreed that Dickinson, a fine marksman, would probably move fast and fire quickly, despite anything Jackson could do. Jackson was sure he would be hit, and he did not want his shot spoiled by the impact of Dickinson's bullet. So the decision was made. Let Dickinson fire first, take the hit, and if he was still on his feet take his own shot. Jackson said once, "I should have hit him, if he had shot me through the brain."[33]

They met just north of the Red River in Kentucky on bottomland covered with poplars. It was early, before breakfast, the morning bright. Hanson Catlett won the choice of position, Overton of giving the word. The duelists took their positions, facing each other, twenty-four feet apart, their pistols held downward at their sides. Overton asked if they were ready and each man replied, "I am ready." Overton at once called out fire.

Dickinson quickly raised his pistol and fired, as Jackson and Overton had predicted. Overton saw a puff of dust rise from Jackson's frock coat. Jackson raised his left arm and held it tightly across his chest. He clenched his teeth. Then he raised his pistol.

Dickinson could not believe Jackson was still on his feet. He stepped back a few paces and called out, "Great God, have I missed him?"

Overton, pistol in hand, shouted an order to Dickinson. "Back to the MARK, sir!" Dickinson returned to the mark.

Jackson took careful aim and squeezed the trigger. The hammer stopped at half cock. He pulled the trigger back again to full cock, squeezed it, and fired. Dickinson staggered. His friends rushed to him and seated him carefully on the ground, his back resting against a bush. His pants were red. They removed his clothes and found the wound. The ball had struck him below the ribs, passed almost through his body, and lodged just under the skin above the opposite hip. Blood gushed from him.

Thomas Overton walked over and looked at Dickinson, then went to Jackson, and said, "He won't want anything more of you, General." Overton and the surgeon then escorted Jackson from the field, but they had gone only about one hundred yards when the surgeon noticed that one of Jackson's shoes was filled with blood.

"My God! General Jackson, are you hit?"

"I believe that he has pinked me a little."

Dickinson had more than pinked Jackson. His ball had struck home, breaking a rib or two and lodging near the heart and left lung along with cloth and pieces of dirt. It would stay there for the rest of his life, giving Jackson extreme pain and causing occasional bouts of pulmonary hemorrhaging. But Dickinson was not to know, Jackson ordered; not even in his death agonies was he to be given the satisfaction of knowing that he had hit Jackson.[34]

Dickinson was carried to a nearby house where he had stayed the night before and laid upon a mattress that quickly became sodden with his blood. His agony lasted the day and into the evening. He "uttered horrible cries all that long day. At nine o'clock in the evening he suddenly asked why they had put out the lights." Five minutes later he died, cursing Jackson's ball still inside him. His beautiful young wife, who had been called to his side, was too late and met on the road his party of gay young blades, now silent as they escorted a "rough emigrant wagon" that carried her handsome young husband's corpse.

Shock and anger swept Nashville as the news circulated. A large crowd attended Dickinson's funeral, which was described by the *Impartial Review* in the most sorrowful tones, condemning the act which took the life of an "amiable man and a virtuous citizen" who had fallen "victim to the barbarous and pernicious act of dueling." The loss to his wife and infant child "is above calculation."

Seventy-three of Dickinson's friends demanded more. In a memorial they urged the editor of the *Impartial Review* to drape the next issue in mourning as a mark of respect and regret. The editor, Thomas Eastin, agreed, but Jackson heard of it and wrote Eastin demanding that since the paper was a public vehicle the public had a right to know who had signed the memorial. Eastin decided that was only fair. Twenty-six of the number then removed their names from the memorial before it was published, presumably because they dared not risk the general's wrath.

Jackson's reputation suffered severely, and one wonders if, as he recuperated at home, he remembered James Robertson's prophetic words: "if you were to git into a duel I assure you it is my opinion you would have a full sheare of the blame attached to your self." Coming only a few years after his clash with John Sevier, Jackson's name was blackened among many throughout Tennessee. James Parton went so far as to insist that "it is certain that at no time between the years 1806 and 1812, could Jackson have been elected to any office in Tennessee that required a majority of the voters of the whole State. Almost any well-informed Tennessean, old enough to remember those years will support me in this assertion." Admitting that Jackson had a large circle of friends, Parton also asserted that beyond that circle "there existed a very general impression that he was a violent, arbitrary, overbearing, passionate man."

The assertion is probably right. The description is certainly correct.

Chapter 12

───∞───

OLD HICKORY

"WAR NOW! WAR FOREVER! WAR UPON THE LIVING!
WAR UPON THE DEAD!"

"A more sagacious or a more gallant Warrior does not I believe exist. He was the admiration of every one who conversed with him."[1]

The writer was the very able British general Isaac Brock, who died in battle against the Americans. The subject, who would also die in battle against the common foe, became a legend in his own time—Tecumseh, war chief of the Shawnees.

While Andrew Jackson struggled to overcome debt and public reproach, Tecumseh and his brother Tenskwatawa, called by the whites Shawnee Prophet, were in a life-and-death struggle to create a confederacy of all the eastern tribes to stop the advance of the American frontier and roll it back. As war approached between the United States and the northwestern tribes, and between the United States and Britain, in July 1811, Tecumseh left the place called by the whites Prophetstown, located on the Wabash River in modern Tippecanoe County, Indiana. He traveled south on a vital mission to convince the southern tribes that survival in the face of the American juggernaut demanded unity and a concerted effort in alliance with the British to drive the Americans from their lands. The makeup of his party symbolized his dream. They were twenty: six Shawnees, six Kickapoos, six Winnebagos, and two Creek guides. Tecumseh himself was the son of a Shawnee father and a Creek mother.[2]

Tecumseh first stopped among the Chickasaws, but those fierce warriors rejected his call that they join the Indian confederacy, wait until the time was right, and then rise in unison against the Americans. The long-ago diplomatic efforts of James Robertson, the peace with the Americans negotiated twenty-eight years before at Nashville by John Donelson and others, held firm against Tecumseh's eloquence. Besides, the northwestern tribes were the Chickasaws' hereditary enemies. In the early years of the eighteenth century France had recruited warriors from the north against the Chickasaws to support the French attempt to seize control of the entire Mississippi Valley, and in the final decade of that century Chickasaw warriors had enthusiastically joined General Anthony Wayne in his campaign in Ohio and Indiana that ended in victory at Fallen Timbers. The Colbert family, mixed-blood descendants of the early Charleston trader James Logan Colbert, were pro-American and in ascendancy among the Chickasaws. Their answer to Tecumseh's plea that they use their influence among their people to join the cause was a flat rejection. Tecumseh saw the futility of his mission among them and did not tarry.

Pushing farther south he next called upon the numerous Choctaw Nation to join his cause. A famous Choctaw warrior, Hoentubbee, passed on to his son Charley the uniform appearance of Tecumseh and his party. They "all were armed, dressed, and painted alike. Their arms were rifles, with tomahawks and scalping knives in their belts. Their dress was a buckskin hunting shirt, a cloth flap, with buckskin leggings and moccasins profusely fringed and beaded. All wore garters below their knees. Their hair was plaited in a long cue of three plaits hanging down between the shoulders, while each temple was closely shaven. The heads of all, except Tecumseh, were adorned with plumes of hawk and eagle feathers. Tecumseh wore, depending from the crown of his head, two long crane feathers, one white the other dyed a brilliant red . . . the white feather was an emblem of peace—peace among the various Indian tribes. The red feather was a war emblem—war to their enemies, the Americans. They wore silver bands on each arm, one around the wrist, one above and one below the elbow, and a few wore silver gorgets suspended from their necks. Around the forehead of each, encircling the head, was a red flannel band about three inches wide, and over this a silver band. Semi-circular streaks of red war-paint were drawn under each eye, extending outward on the cheek bone. A small red spot was painted on each temple, and large red spot on the centre of the breast."[3]

Their finery, and the dances they performed, may have impressed the Choctaws, but their message did not. The Choctaws had never gone to war against the United States, and they were not at that time under the severe pressure of white settlers felt by the northwestern tribes and their neighbors the Creeks. As Tecumseh made his way through what is now the state of Mississippi, he was followed by the highly influential and pro-American chief Pushmataha, whose countermessage was clear and delivered with equal fervor. The Choctaws had always been at peace with the Americans. To break that peace and go to war would be a disaster for the Choctaw people. They would be ruined, Pushmataha insisted, and he prevailed. Like the Chickasaws before them, the Choctaws as a people turned the great Shawnee away. To the east, however, in Alabama, where the indispensable Alexander McGillivray had once woven his diplomatic magic on behalf of his people, Tecumseh found fertile ground. For the Creeks were a people in crisis.

The peace forged by McGillivray at the Treaty of New York in 1790 had held, but during the two decades that had passed a subtle decline in Creek fortunes had worked its cancerous way. They were literally surrounded by

Pushmataha, ca. 1824, by Charles Bird King (The Warner Collection of Gulf States Paper Corporation, Tuscaloosa, Alabama)

the enemy. Eastward the pressure from Georgia remained as always unrelenting, although tempered somewhat by a federal presence. On the north Tennesseans were established well south of Nashville, as far as the Tennessee River at Muscle Shoals. To the west the settlers on the Alabama and Tombigbee that many years ago Alexander McGillivray had warned against, and for whose expulsion he had sought in vain in a joint action with the Choctaws, had multiplied and seemed firmly established. Southward danger also loomed. The Spanish still held Pensacola, but their hold on Mobile and West Florida west of the Perdido River was tenuous at best, as rebellious American frontiersmen kept up the pressure and the U.S. government made clear its insistence that the area was part of the Louisiana Purchase. From that sector the Creeks could expect from Pensacola occasional supplies only, certainly not armed intervention from a Spain devastated at home by French occupation and a cruel guerrilla war against Napoleon's armies.

The Creeks' unfavorable geographical position was exacerbated by the unceasing efforts of the influential American Indian agent Benjamin Hawkins, a proponent of Jefferson's policies, to change their way of life from warriors and hunters to farmers and herders. If that were not drastic enough, the Creeks were also importuned to cast aside their age-old system of common ownership of land and adopt the white man's concept of private property, in which each Indian family would own its own farm and be able to buy and sell land as whites did.

Hawkins was clear in his purpose: "The plan I persue is to lead the Indians from hunting to the pastoral life, to agriculture, household manufactures, a knowledge of weights and measures, money and figures." Benjamin Hawkins was a decent, honorable, well-meaning man, and his arguments for Creeks to become like whites would have made sense in that better world that no human has ever experienced. But in the real world, the world of the American frontier, where two peoples of diametrically opposed cultures contested the land, the American policies pushed upon the Creeks by Hawkins were a concoction for disaster. Generally, the Lower Creeks on the Chattahoochee and eastward were amenable to Hawkins's arguments. But the Upper Creeks in south-central Alabama were generally opposed. And within each group there were those who opposed the majority. Many mixed bloods adopted white ways with enthusiasm, but others were fiercely nativist, and from them would appear leaders who bitterly fought against abandonment of the old ways. The terrible irony, and tragedy, of all this was that those establishment Americans responsible for the so-called civilizing policy never cleared this critical program with the settlers they governed, who wanted no part of Indians, civilized or otherwise, in their backyard.[4]

Another, immediate, factor in Creek unrest was the opening in 1811 of the Federal Road that sliced through the entire Creek Nation. The road ran southwest from Fort Wilkinson near Milledgeville, Georgia, then the state capital, to Fort Stoddert, just north of Mobile in the Mississippi Territory. Soldiers, travelers, post riders, and, even more ominously for the Creeks, migrants began using the road with increasing frequency. The sight of migrant wagons rumbling daily through their country to the Alabama and Tombigbee settlements behind them produced emotions among the Creeks ranging from nervousness to fury. American plans to open another road through the nation, from Tennessee to Mobile, increased their agitation.[5]

Are we surprised then that the resulting strains within Creek society produced intense passions that lay just beneath the surface? The Creeks were a people at odds with themselves when Tecumseh arrived among his mother's people with his powerful message of liberation and rejuvenation.

At Tuckabatchee, about two and one-half miles below the falls of the Tallapoosa River and some thirty miles east of modern Montgomery, Alabama, the Creek National Council was in session when Tecumseh and his followers arrived. As Tecumseh had marched east and spoken to the Creeks in the towns of Autauga and the Hickory Ground, people had flocked to hear him, and when he arrived in Tuckabatchee several young Creek warriors were in his entourage. About five thousand Creeks, and assorted whites and blacks, were there to witness the great Shawnee's entrance into town. One of the white men was Benjamin Hawkins, who was attending the council. At the end of the first day of the council Tecumseh led his northern warriors into the town square.

> They were entirely naked, except their flaps [breechcloths] and ornaments. Their faces were painted black, and their heads adorned with eagle plumes, while buffalo tails dragged from behind, suspended by bands which went around their waists. Buffalo tails were also attached to their arms, and made to stand out, by means of bands . . . They marched round and round in the square; then approaching the Chiefs, they cordially shook them, with the whole length of the arm, and exchanged tobacco, a common ceremony with the Indians, denoting friendship. . . .[6]

But Tecumseh would not speak while Benjamin Hawkins was in town, and it was only after the agent's departure that he appeared in the great round council house and announced his purpose in a speech that lasted about an hour. There is no copy of his speech. We are dependent upon oral tradition, upon faded memories, upon the pens of nineteenth-century historians who interviewed witnesses. One was the Mississippi historian J. F. H. Claiborne, whose main source was the well-known southern frontiersman Sam Dale, who claimed to have been present when Tecumseh delivered his thundering oration. Dale's story has been vigorously disputed by subsequent historians, who maintain that Tecumseh, renowned for his chivalry, opposed to the slaughter of women and children and the torture of prisoners, could never have spoken the words attributed to him. It has also been argued that Dale, a white man, would not have been allowed to be present. Others have accepted Dale's account. What all agree upon, however, are Tecumseh's eloquence, and his passion, and the fervor of his belief in his cause. Thus Tecumseh as presented by Sam Dale through J. F. H. Claiborne.[7]

"Every thing," Dale recalled, "was still as death; even the winds slept, and there was only the gentle rustle of the falling leaves." Then Tecumseh lashed out at the once mighty Creeks.

> Accursed be the race that has seized on our country and made women of our warriors . . . The Georgians trembled at your warwhoop, and the maidens of my tribe, on the distant lakes, sung the prowess of your warriors, and sighed for their embraces . . . Now your blood is white; your tomahawks have no edge; your bow and arrows were buried with your fathers.
>
> Oh, Muscogees, brethren of my mother, brush from your eyelids the sleep of slavery; once more strike for vengeance, once more for your country! The spirits of the mighty dead complain. Their tears drop from the weeping skies. Let the white race perish! They

TECUMTHA.

Tecumseh (National Anthropological Archives, Smithsonian Institution)

seize your land; they corrupt your women; they trample on the ashes of your dead! Back, whence they came, upon a trail of blood, they must be driven. Back! back, ay, into the great water whose accursed waves brought them to our shores! Burn their dwellings! Destroy their stock! Slay their wives and children! War now! War forever! War upon the living! War upon the dead! Dig their very corpses from the grave. Our country must give no shelter to a white man's bones!

Whether Dale's memory and Claiborne's transcription were accurate is of little consequence. For whatever Tecumseh said, the effect on many Creeks was electrifying. Civil strife among the Creeks over adoption or rejection of the white man's ways had been brewing for years. Now it heightened, feelings hardened, became bitter, and harsh words between Creeks became commonplace. Tecumseh returned north to find that his brother Tenskwatawa had, contrary to Tecumseh's instructions, been drawn into battle by William Henry Harrison and met disastrous defeat at Tippecanoe. But that neither halted nor slowed the course of events in the South, where an eruption that would change the history of North America was in the making. In the meantime, international affairs that would bear directly on the fortunes of both the Creeks and Andrew Jackson had come to a head. On 18 June 1812, the United States and Great Britain went to war.

"A COMBINATION OF HYPOCRITICAL POLITICAL VILLAINS"

Our concern is not with the causes of the War of 1812 but its results for the Old Southwest, although below we will briefly touch upon causes. It has been called the forgotten war and the unnecessary war. Wits tend to poke fun at it. Americans largely ignore it. The British have truly forgotten it, and why not, for at the same time they were engaged in a life-and-death struggle with Napoleon. For them the fight with their former colonists, who had not yet become "the cousins," was a sideshow. For Americans at the time, however, it was critical, because on the whole they did very badly and were lucky to get out of it whole.

Probably the main overall cause of the war was British interference in American affairs. This took several forms. British Orders in Council regulated neutral trade with Europe, giving British warships the right to stop American merchant ships, board them, and seize contraband. This infuriated Americans. Their blood also boiled over impressment, the British practice of boarding American vessels and removing from them crewmen whom they claimed to be deserters from the Royal Navy. British encouragement of Indian unrest in the Northwest was another form of interference that brought American indignation to a fever pitch, as did similar encouragement, real and imagined, of unrest among the southern tribes. All of these actions led to a feeling by Americans that England did not take the United States seriously. Were they or were they not an independent nation free of their former master?[8]

Jackson was ready. He had been ready for a long time. What good was it to be a major general of militia without a war to fight? He and his fellow frontiersmen were literally chafing at the bit. With war obviously approaching, Congress authorized President Madison to enlist 50,000 volunteers. Jackson was ecstatic, and on 7 March 1812 he issued a thundering order to his 2nd Division entitled *"Volunteers to arms!"* His urgency leaps off the pages, his words are unrestrained Jackson in fine form, and his reasons for going to war are an encapsulated history lesson.[9]

"Citizens! Your government has at last yielded to the impulse of the nation. Your impatience is no longer restrained. The hour of national vengeance is now at hand. The eternal enemies of american prosperity are again to be taught to respect your rights, after having been compelled to feel, once more the power of your arms.

"War is on the point of breaking out between the united states and the King of Great Britain! and the martial hosts of america are summoned to the tented fields."

How could the young men of America refuse to volunteer for the field? he asked. Compulsion was out of the question. For "another and nobler feeling should impell us to action. *Who are we? and for what are we going to fight? are we the titled Slaves of George the third? the military conscripts of Napoleon the great? or the frozen peasants of the Russian Czar? No, we the free born sons of america; the citizens of the only republick now existing in the world; and the only people on Earth who possess the rights, liberties, and property which they dare call their own."*

Having warmed up, Jackson got to the heart of the matter and also took the opportunity to state precisely what he thought of European aristrocrats, kings, and a certain general turned emperor. Modern readers who would scoff at his language should set aside their late-twentieth-century mind-set and remember they are now in that foreign country we call the past, when Jackson's words would have been understood and applauded by his audience.

> *For what are we going to fight?* To satisfy the revenge or ambition of a corrupt and infaturated Ministry? to place another and another diadem on the head of an apostate republican general? to settle the ballance of power among an assasin tribe of Kings and Emperors? 'or to preserve to the prince of the Blood, and the grand dignitaries of the empire' their overgrown wealth and exclusive privileges? No: such splendid atchievements as these can form no part of the objects of an american war. But we are going to fight for the reestablishment of our national charector, misunderstood and vilified at home and abroad; for the protection of our maritime citizens, impressed on board British ships of war and compelled to fight the battles of our enemies against ourselves; to vindicate our right to a free trade, and open a market for the productions of our soil, now perishing on our hands, because the *mistress of the ocean* has forbid us to carry them to any foreign nation; in fine, to seek some indemnity for past injuries, some security against future aggressions, by the conquest of all the British dominions upon the continent of North america.
>
> "Here then is the true and noble principle on which the energies of the nation should be brought into action: *a free people compelled to reclaim by the power of their arms the rights which god has bestowed upon them, and which an infatuated King has said they shall not enjoy.*"

And while they were at it they might march north to that will-o'-the-wisp of early America upon which much blood and treasure would be wasted. Jackson became positively lyrical over the possibility of conquering alien territory: "Should the occupation of Canada be resolved upon by the general government, how pleasing the prospect that would open to the young volunteer while performing a military *promenade* into a distant country, a succession of new and interesting objects would perpetually fill and delight his imagination the effect of which would be heightened by the war like appearance, the martial music, and the grand evolutions of an army of fifty thousand men."

How could a young fellow resist? But just in case, Jackson had not finished: "To view the stupendous works of nature, exemplified in the falls of Niagara and the cataract of Montmorence; to tread the consecrated spot on which Wolf and Montgomery fell, would of themselves repay the young soldier for a march across the continent."

Not that such motives were needed. "But why," Jackson concluded, "should these inducements be held out to the young men of america? They need them not. animated as they are by an ambition to rival the exploits of Rome, they will never prefer an inglorious sloth, a supine inactivity to the honorable toil of carrying the republican standard to the heights of abraham."

Having done himself well in prose, Jackson waited impatiently for government's call to the colors. But it did not come. Instead, the secretary of war wrote a short, polite letter to the governor of Tennessee noting Jackson's "tender of service," which was "received by the president with peculiar satisfaction, and in accepting their services He cannot withhold an expression of His admiration of the zeal and ardor by which they are animated." Pretty words conveying nothing. For the president was James Madison, who had not forgotten Jackson's performance at the Burr trial in Richmond, nor his support of James Monroe as candidate for president over Madison himself. Ever since the Burr trial Jackson had been anti-Jefferson and anti-Madison, and in his inimitable style had not minced words. Now it was payback time. Jackson and his volunteers twiddled their thumbs in Tennessee while others marched on Canada. Jackson could only write letters to friends and more "Division Orders" to his idle troops, and on 31 July he turned their sights from Canada to the Gulf. That spring six settlers, including five children, had been massacred by Creek followers of Tecumseh where the Duck River flows into the Tennessee. This and other incidents inflamed the frontier and ignited Jackson's short fuse. He fully expected to lead an expedition against the Creeks, publishing in a newspaper an account of the incident and finishing with a ringing appeal: "Citizens! hold yourselves in readiness: it may be but a short time before the question is put to you: *Are you ready to follow your general to the heart of the Creek nation?*"[10]

On 8 July, the day the article appeared, Jackson held a council of war with his officers "which will determine the date of our movments against the Creeks." But the federal government had no intention of launching an invasion of Creek country. The governor wrote Jackson that the secretary of war "has observed entire silence as to that part of my letter which recommended that the Creeks should by order of the General Government be soundly drubed. I cannot account for silence on that head." The answer, of course, was national concerns taking precedence over regional needs. With a major war against a powerful enemy on its hands, Washington's policy was to rely on their Creek Indian agent Benjamin Hawkins to keep matters under control in Creek country and punish hostile elements by sending friendly Creeks against them. For Jackson the solution was to strike deep and hard, once and for all. "I know your impatience," he wrote to the volunteers, that "you burn with anxiety to learn on what theatre your arms will find employment. Then turn your eyes to the South! Behold in the province of West Florida, a territory whose rivers and harbors, are indispensable to the prosperity of the Western, and still more so, to the eastern Division of our State. Behold there likewise the asylum from which an insidious hand incites to rapine and bloodshed, the ferocious savages, who have just stained our frontiers with blood, and who will renew their outrages the moment an English force shall appear in the Bay of Pensacola. It is here that an employment adapted to your situation awaits your courage and your zeal: and while extending in this quarter the boundaries of the Republic to the Gulf of Mexico, you will experience a peculiar satisfaction in having confered a signal benefit on that section of the Union to which you yourselves immediately belong."[11]

In October 1812 Jackson's deepest desire was realized. Washington ordered the governor of Tennessee to call out 1,500 volunteers to march south and assist in the conquest of that old Anglo-American dream, La Florida. There were, however, two hitches. By excluding from the order any mention of Jackson and his division, Washington made clear to the governor that the command could go to somebody other than Andrew Jackson. Had the governor still been Jackson's mortal enemy John Sevier, history might have been changed. But Sevier had been governor for three consecutive terms, and the Tennessee constitution prevented him from running for a fourth term. The new governor was named Blount, and he is often confused with the better-known William Blount. But his first name was Willie (pronounced "wily"). He was a half brother of William, and a friend and political ally of Jackson. Willie Blount ignored the order's implication. Jackson also publicly ignored the slight, as well as the unwelcome prospect of leading his volunteers to New Orleans and placing them and himself under the command of a man he loathed, the commander of U.S. forces on the Gulf, James Wilkinson. He believed, he wrote to Willie Blount, that the orders from the secretary of war were meant "either to exclude me from the command—or if I did command by an apparent willingness and condesension on my part to place me under the command of General Wilkinson." He would not forget it, but for the time being he would set it aside: "There appears something in this thing that carries with it a sting to my feelings that I will for the present suppress." For "viewing the situation of our beloved country at present . . . I will sacrafice my feelings, and lead my brave Volunteers to any point your excellency may please to order all I ask is that we may be ordered to a stage where we may pertake of active service, and share the dangers and laurels of the field."[12]

Governor Blount ordered Jackson to muster troops on 10 December 1812 in Nashville and to requisition boats and supplies. Jackson gathered about him able officers he trusted. With one exception, they would follow him faithfully through good times and bad. Instead of the 1,500 volunteers the government had requested, some 2,000 to 2,100 gathered in Nashville. Jackson divided them into three regiments of approximately 700 men each: two infantry and one cavalry. He gave command of one infantry regiment to hot-tempered Thomas Hart Benton, then thirty-one years old, whom Jackson knew from the legal circuit and who would eventually become a powerful national figure. Thirty-seven-year-old William Hall, a staunch Jackson loyalist, led the other infantry regiment. To command the cavalry Jackson appointed his most gifted officer, the hulking, forty-year-old John Coffee, 6 feet and 216 pounds, to whom Jackson once wrote, "I have no friend on earth who possesses more of my affection than you." He made the able and faithful twenty-four-year-old William Carroll, a future governor of Tennessee, his brigade inspector. His twenty-eight-year-old deputy assistant quartermaster, William Berkeley Lewis, was a well-born Virginian who remained a Jackson loyalist through thick and thin. One of his aides, twenty-eight-year-old John Reid, a strikingly handsome young man, was another transplanted Virginian who was recommended to Jackson by Thomas Hart Benton. He became a fast friend and valuable biographer of Jackson.[13]

On 7 January Jackson ordered Coffee to march the cavalry overland to Washington in Mississippi Territory, where he should await the arrival by water of Jackson and the two regiments of infantry. One regiment of the latter cast off at 12:30 P.M. on the eighth, and the other was marched to Robertson's Landing, six miles below Nashville, to meet other boats. Thomas Hart Benton reported that "It is impossible to describe to you the enthusiasm with which the men committed themselves to the stream. I looked in vain for a single countenance which was not animated with joy." Benton led the second regiment on their march to Robertson's Landing. "Never," he wrote, "did men go forward with greater alacrity; it was necessary continually to repress their ardor, and direct them to march slower." Rachel sent Jackson a miniature. "I shall wear it near my boosom," he wrote, and thanked her "for your prayers" and "for your determined resolution, to bear our separation with fortitude. . . ." And so Andrew Jackson drifted down the Cumberland with his little army, forty-five years old and in his prime, a general who had never been to war but was sure in his heart that he had what it took to do the job and was not hesitant in expressing it. He wrote to the secretary of war "that I am now at the head of 2,070 vounteers, the choicest of our citizens, who . . . will rejoice at the opportunity of placing the American eagle on the ramparts of MOBILE, PENSACOLA, AND FORT ST. AUGUSTINE, effectually banishing from the southern coasts all British influence."[14]

The one-thousand-mile voyage down the Cumberland to the Ohio, then to the Mississippi and on to Natchez and the rendezvous with John Coffee and his cavalry regiment, took thirty-nine days and was relatively uneventful, even though it was one of the coldest winters in memory, with large masses of ice causing delays on the Ohio. One boat was stove in by an obstruction and sank, but the men were saved. A Methodist preacher, Learner Blackman, chaplain of the army, much beset by "ungodly officers" and "profane swearing . . . among the soldiery and likewise among the officers," had a minor run-in with Jackson after Blackman "prayed [and] talked with the sick men," apparently preparing them to meet their Maker. For shortly "the Gen. in presence of the Col. and Lieutenant Col. of the first Redgement examined me a little to know how I talked to the sick signified that it would be highly improper to tell a person he would die if Simtoms were unfavorable. I let him know on that point that I should be independent & that I should do as I thought best." Jackson's reply is unrecorded, but Blackman provided a clue when he wrote, "I find the Gen cannot bare much opposition. He is a good General but a very incorrect Divine."[15]

A pesky preacher, however, was the least of Jackson's problems. General Wilkinson in New Orleans was aghast at the thought of his enemy Jackson joining his command, and beginning on 22 January he began bombarding Jackson with letters repeating "my desire, that you should halt in the vicinity of Natchez. . . ." In New Orleans there was no lodging or food for his troops, no forage for the horses. Stay where you are, insisted Wilkinson, who also professed to "have been left without information respecting your destination or instructions. . . ." Until late March Jackson and Wilkinson exchanged reasonably polite correspondence. But on 15 March Jackson received a letter from another quarter that came like a shot out of the blue. It was from the new secretary of war, John Armstrong, dated 6 February 1813.[16]

"The causes for embodying & marching to New Orleans the Corps under your command having ceased to exist, you will on receipt of this Letter, consider it as dismissed from public service, & take measures to have delivered over to Major General Wilkinson, all articles of public property which may have been put into its possession.

"You will accept for yourself & the Corps the thanks of the President of the United States."

Jackson's fury left him quivering. When Wilkinson read his copy of the letter, he correctly predicted, "This order will come like a thunder clap on Jackson." It was reported to him that "when the Genl. read this he flew into a passion & damned himself if he would disband them till he had marched them back to Tennessee and if the Q. Master and contractor would not furnish them with the needful supplies he would take them." For Jackson, however, his reply to Armstrong, written the day he received the secretary's order, was relatively restrained, although its sharp edge led Thomas Hart Benton to suggest that it be toned down. Jackson refused. "If it was intended by this order," he wrote, "that we should be dismissed eight hundred miles from home, deprived of arms, tents and supplies for the sick—of our arms and supplies for the well, it appears that these brave men, who certainly deserve better fate and return from their government was intended to be sacrificed." He finished by taking a swipe at criticism of militia, which had failed so badly in the North: "believing as I do that it is such patriots as I have the honor to command that our country and its liberties are to be saved and defended—that a well organized militia is the bulwark of our Nation—I have no hesitation in giving the lie to the modern doctrine that it is inefficient to defend the liberties of our country, and that standing armies are necessary—in time of peace. I mean to commence my march to Nashville in a few days at which place I expect the troops to be paid and the necessary supplies furnished by the agents of Government while payment is making, after which I will dismiss them to their homes and families."[17]

What Jackson did not know was that Congress had balked at the administration's plans to invade the Spanish territory of East Florida. It did authorize occupation of Spanish West Florida, which American officials had always thought part of the Louisiana Purchase, but left that to the forces under Wilkinson's command. But Armstrong's brief, dismissive letter with its one-line thank-you had failed to explain all of this to Jackson. Would it have made a difference if he had? Probably not. For Jackson saw things in personal terms. This outrage had not happened, as James Parton reasonably pointed out, because of the government's "inexperience, and the difficulty of directing operations at places so remote from the seat of government." And John Armstrong's belief that because of the severe weather his order would catch up to Jackson before he had gone far could be nothing but a lie. No, there were malevolent forces abroad plotting against him, Andrew Jackson, and his brave volunteers.[18]

Jackson threw restraint aside in private letters to friends. This "extraordinary order," as he described it, "this new incumbent . . . must have been drunk when he wrote it or so proud of his appointment as to have lost all feelings of humanity & duty . . . It is time for the people to recollect, that Sempronius in the Roman Senate cried out that he was for war, when he was in the act of betraying his country." He became excited, very excited. "I shall march them to Nashville or bury them with the honors of war, should I die I know they will bury me. And as soon as I arrive the necessary inquiries of intended sacrifice of the whole of this detachment wil be made & the publick will be able to judge how far certain friends representatives & men in office are the friends or traitors to their country. The history of all *Barbarous Europe* cannot furnish a parallel." His anger even increased on the march home as he asked, "is this the reward of a virtuous administration to its patriotic sons—or is it, done by a wicked minister, to satiate the vengeance, of a combination of hypocritical Political Villains, who would sacrifice the best blood of our Country to satiate the spleen of a Villain who their connection with in acts of wickedness they are afraid to offend."[19]

On 25 March 1813 the volunteers, led by their fuming general, turned northward onto the Natchez Trace and set out for home. Denied the glory he sought on the field of honor, Jackson resolved as only he could to conduct the return in proper military manner. They had left home as an army; they would return as an army, not as a mob. Without pay, without proper supplies, burdened by the sick and the lame, the long columns wended their way along the dark, narrow Trace. Many generals at this point would have lost control of their troops, especially these troops, not a regular among them, but militia well known for lack of discipline and rowdy behavior that could easily turn ugly. The irony of this entire affair and the long march home is that it made Andrew Jackson's reputation as a leader of men at war, even though they had not seen combat. What we have glimpsed throughout our story now appears full blown in all its magnificence. Willpower. A willpower that defies description, that has been called superhuman in its tenacity. He would not allow indiscipline, he would not allow straggling, and he marched with his men, all five hundred miles. He had three horses. He gave them to the sick. He ordered his officers to give up their horses. They walked, like their general. Day after day he walked with his men. He was everywhere up and down the columns, no task beneath him. Stern when necessary, gentle as a woman when dealing with the sick, Andrew Jackson took his men home. For "it is my duty," he wrote to Rachel, "to act as a father to the sick and to the well and stay with them untill I march them into Nashville."[20]

His men repaid him handsomely, for they were quick to note something about Jackson that placed him above other men. James Parton put it well: "Jackson had the faculty, which all successful soldiers possess, of completely identifying himself with the men he commanded; investing every soldier, as it were, with a portion of his own personality, and feeling a wrong done to the least of them as done to himself. They saw, indeed, that there was a whole volcano of wrath in their General, but they observed that, to the men of his command, so long as they did their duty, and longer, he was the most gentle, patient, considerate and generous of friends." And so they watched him on that trek that fell three days shy of one month, and a soldier remarked that he was tough, and another soldier added tough as hickory, and it filtered through the ranks, and thus was born the familiar name that became a badge of honor to a man who deserved it: Old Hickory.[21]

"NOW, YOU DAMNED RASCAL, I AM GOING TO PUNISH YOU"

In the hearts of his troops, in the esteem of the public, Jackson was born again. The dreadful duel that felled Charles Dickinson, if not forgotten, retreated to the dim recesses of memories. The *Nashville Whig* made it official: "Long will the General live in the memory of the volunteers of West Tennessee for his benevolent, humane, and fatherly treatment to his soldiers; if gratitude and love can reward him, General Jackson has them. It affords us pleasure to say, that we believe there is not a man belonging to the detachment but what loves him. His fellow-citizens at home are not less pleased with his conduct. We fondly hope his merited worth will not be overlooked by government."[22]

Government not only overlooked Jackson, it returned his transportation drafts. Jackson should bear the expense of the expedition. This was disastrous. It would ruin him. Thomas Hart Benton, who was going to Washington on business of his own, agreed to take a letter of appeal from Jackson to the secretary of war. Jackson was fortunate in his messenger, for on this mission Benton displayed an ability to maneuver in the halls of power that would later mark his distinguished public career. He neatly found his way through the bureaucracy, expedited the procedure, and in a personal meeting convinced Secretary Armstrong that Congress need not be involved. Armstrong then appointed an agent to audit and approve Jackson's accounts. All seemed well. Jackson had come home a hero, and he was not going to be ruined financially. Then, in another of the foolish affairs that he seemed unable to avoid, his actions threatened to throw it all away.[23]

It began with an argument, in which Jackson at first was only indirectly involved. The young man he had made his brigade inspector, William Carroll, had promise and winning ways, and Jackson had promoted him rapidly and paid him "marked attentions," to use Parton's words. This, combined with his efficiency as brigade inspector and what some thought were his superior manners, created envy among many junior officers. During the march home from Natchez a quarrel of unknown origin rose between Billy Carroll and Littleton Johnston, and Johnston challenged Carroll to a duel. Carroll twice refused the challenge on the ground that Johnston was not a gentleman, whereupon Jesse Benton, Thomas Hart Benton's brother, stood in for Johnston and issued his own challenge. This Carroll could not ignore, for Jesse Benton was considered a gentleman. Upon the army's return Carroll found himself so unpopular that he was unable to find a second in Nashville. He then rode out to the Hermitage and asked Jackson to second him. Jackson wisely declined. He was too old, he told Carroll; it would not be judicious of him to act as a second at his age. Carroll should find a man nearer his own age. Carroll argued that if this were an ordinary quarrel he would not have asked Jackson. But he told Jackson some young men, jealous of his close relationship with Jackson, were conspiring to "run him out of the country."[24]

Conspiracy? Run Billy Carroll out of the country? Jackson's ears pricked up.

No, no. Not as long as Andrew Jackson had anything to say about it. Jackson saddled his horse and rode to Nashville. Not, it must be emphasized, to stoke the fire, but to put an end to this foolishness. He went to Jesse Benton and had a talk with that quick-tempered young man. The "laws of honor," he told Benton, did not call for a challenge by him. Jesse Benton apparently relented, and Jackson thought that he had smoothed things over. But Carroll's enemies egged Benton on. He once again became hostile, and demanded that his challenge be accepted. Given his age, his station, the esteem in which he was now held, Jackson should have insisted that both men come to their senses, should have made it clear that he would have nothing to do with a duel. Instead, he agreed to second Billy Carroll on the field of honor.

Old men to whom James Parton spoke in mid-nineteenth-century Tennessee told him that the Billy Carroll–Jesse Benton duel was still treated as a standing joke. What followed from it, however, was not a joke.

They met at six o'clock in the morning on 14 June 1813. The standard distance between duelists was usually about thirty feet. But Jesse Benton was reputed to be a crack shot, whereas Billy Carroll had little shooting experience, so he insisted the distance be shortened to ten feet. As the man challenged, he had that right. At ten feet they stood with their backs toward each other. Jesse's second called them to the ready. Then he shouted "Fire!" In one motion Jesse wheeled, presented himself in profile, squatted, and fired. Billy fired. His ball raked Jesse's jutting buttocks. Jackson later argued that just prior to the face-off, when "J. Benton observed that he did not perfectly understand how they were to wheel, did I not get up & shew them how they were to wheel, did I not explain to them that they were to wheel erect . . . and did not Major Carrol wheel erect as shewn by me." Jesse's second agreed that he had, "but I did not under stand that the right of Stooping was prohibited as They fired."[25]

Billy Carroll was hit in the thumb. Jesse was laid up for several weeks with his bottom wound. One can imagine the hilarious tavern talk about the nature of Jesse Benton's wound. But there the matter should have ended. Thomas Hart Benton, however, became enraged when he heard that while he was rescuing his general from financial ruin, Jackson had been a party to his brother's humiliation. Like Jackson, Tom Benton was "touchy as tinder." He began speaking about Jackson in public in offensive terms and issuing wild threats of revenge. Gossips repeated them to Jackson. The two men exchanged threatening letters that stopped short of challenges but created an atmosphere in which latent violence needed only a spark. Jackson's ire rose as Benton's wild accusations in public places were repeated all over Tennessee. He refused to stand by and see his hard-won reputation shredded by young Benton's charges. Finally he had enough. He swore that the next time he saw Thomas Hart Benton he would horsewhip him. "On sight," his close friend John Coffee added. Soon all Nashville knew it. Thomas Hart Benton knew it. All awaited the dreadful meeting.[26]

On 3 September 1813 Thomas Hart Benton and his brother Jesse, whose bottom had healed sufficiently for him to sit a horse, rode into Nashville. They usually stayed at the Nashville Inn on the public square, where Jackson always put up, but in order to avoid Jackson they went to the City Hotel, which was also on the square. It was a vast, rambling building with wide piazzas. That evening Jackson and John Coffee also rode into town and stopped at the Nashville Inn. About nine o'clock the next morning Coffee suggested they walk over to the post office, which was diagonally across the square from the Nashville Inn, on the same side as the City Hotel. Jackson wore a short sword and carried a loaded pistol in his rear pocket. In one hand he carried, as always, a riding whip. Coffee also carried a pistol. On the way Coffee looked over at the hotel and saw Tom Benton standing in the doorway glaring at them.

"Do you see that fellow?" Coffee asked.

Without looking over, Jackson said, "Oh, yes, I have my eyes on him."[27]

Jackson and Coffee fetched their mail at the post office. When they came out, instead of retracing their way across the square they turned right and walked down the sidewalk past the City Hotel. As they got closer they saw Jesse Benton standing near his brother. When they drew abreast of the hotel entrance, Jackson suddenly turned and faced Tom Benton with his riding whip in his right hand.

"Now, you damned rascal, I am going to punish you. Defend yourself."[28]

Tom Benton reached into his breast pocket. Jackson quickly drew his pistol and aimed it and advanced on Benton, who retreated. Jackson continued to walk toward Benton, who kept backing up. They walked that way down a hallway through the hotel to the rear piazza. Tom Benton turned onto the piazza. Jesse Benton, meanwhile, had taken a different route into the hotel and emerged from the bar into the hallway at just that moment behind Jackson. He had in his hand a pistol loaded with two balls and a slug. He raised it and fired at Jackson from behind. The slug hit Jackson in the left shoulder and shattered it. One ball missed, the other struck Jackson in the arm and lodged near the bone. The shock knocked Jackson down over the entry. As he fell he fired at Tom Benton, but missed. Then he was prostrate and helpless. Blood poured from his wounds.

Tom Benton fired twice at Jackson lying on the floor. He missed. Jesse had a second pistol and was going to fire at Jackson again when a bystander intervened and prevented him. At that point John Coffee came running into the hallway, saw his general lying at Tom Benton's feet, drew his pistol, and fired at Tom. Coffee missed, too. Then he grabbed the pistol by the barrel and rushed at Benton with the intention of clubbing him. Benton stepped back and tumbled down a flight of stairs. Coffee then rushed to aid Jackson.

Jackson's friend Stockley Hays, as big as Coffee, ran into the hallway, took in the scene, then rushed at Jesse Benton and tried to run him through with a sword cane. The point hit a button and broke. Big, strong Stockley Hays grabbed Jesse and threw him to the ground, drew his dirk, and stabbed him several times in both arms. Jesse got his hand on his second pistol and pressed the muzzle to Hays's body and pulled the trigger, but the weapon misfired. By that time several people had gathered and the two men were pulled apart. The gunfight at the City Hotel was over.

Jackson was carried to the Nashville Inn. Blood gushed from him. The doctors of Nashville gathered to work on him, but before they could stop the bleeding two mattresses were soaked through. With one exception, they recommended amputation of Jackson's left arm. But just before he fainted Jackson gave an order, and it was obeyed: "I'll keep my arm." He also kept the ball within his arm for almost twenty years.[29]

While the doctors worked on Jackson and his friends hovered, the Benton brothers paraded in the square for about an hour loudly telling their account of the fight. Tom Benton's voice boomed around the square with insults. But in the view of public opinion the Benton brothers had tangled with the wrong foe at the wrong time. Jackson's new stature was not lessened by the gunfight, and Tennessee proved too small to hold both the general and the Benton brothers. "I am literally in hell here," Thomas Hart Benton wrote not long after the fight. He went home to Franklin, Tennessee, entered the U.S. Army as a lieutenant colonel, and after the War of 1812 migrated to Missouri, where he entered politics and in time became a towering national figure of his time, a spokesman for the West and free land. His strong-minded daughter Jessie, who inherited many of her father's characteristics, became a writer and married the explorer and would-be president, John Charles Frémont. In 1823 Senator Thomas Hart Benton of Missouri and Senator Andrew Jackson of Tennessee met in Washington for the first time since the gunfight. They saw eye to eye on politics, and there the two men shook hands, put the past behind them, and became close political allies.[30]

Jesse Benton drifted to Texas, where he took part in the Texas War of Independence, and later established himself on a plantation in Louisiana. He cursed Jackson to the end of his days, and he never forgave his brother for making up with the archfoe.

Jackson remained in bed for nearly three weeks. He was in a terrible physical state: pale, weak, racked by intense pain, his left arm useless. The cauldron that was the Creek Nation was bubbling furiously and threatening to boil over at any time. But Jackson lay incapacitated at the Nashville Inn and later at the Hermitage. It was obvious to all who saw him that he would be unable to command in the field. All one had to do was look at him. It appeared that Jackson's failure to quench his violent passions had ruined his chances to achieve the military glory he hungered for.

Chapter 13

∽∾∽

MASSACRE

"THE MOST EXTRAVAGANT DELUSIONS PREVAILED UPON THE COOSA"

Even before Jackson's gunfight at the City Hotel, fighting had begun between hostile Creeks and Americans from the Tombigbee River settlements in southern Alabama. They had been precipitated by the bitter hostilities within the Creek Nation. Prophets had appeared among those Creeks who had been mesmerized by Tecumseh's appearance among them, and they had built a nativist religion that preached rejection of white culture. To use the felicitous words of Albert James Pickett, "The most extravagant delusions prevailed upon the Coosa. . . ." For the prophets claimed supernatural powers. One, the mixed-blood Josiah Francis, was said to disappear for days under water, then mysteriously reappear, which left his followers in awe. He also claimed that he met daily with the Creek supreme being, the Giver of Breath, who taught him all the different languages he would need to conduct business. Thus this man who could neither read nor write pretended to write a letter in Spanish, of which he was totally ignorant, to the governor at Pensacola requesting arms. He explained the contents of the letter in great detail to his envoys, then sent them off with the letter for delivery. Later the envoys said they thought the letter was full of "crooked marks," not anything resembling writing, but they feared to disobey and carried out their mission. The Spanish governor looked at the paper and became angry, whereupon the Creek messengers repeated what Josiah Francis had told them. The governor then laughed over the incident and told them he had a mind to send back a letter with similar markings informing Josiah Francis that he had no arms—and indeed, none was sent.[1]

Josiah Francis also introduced among his followers a dance taught to him, he said, by the Giver of Breath. The dance could break out at the most unexpected times, as it did in the summer of 1813, when, Josiah Francis's brother-in-law, the mixed-blood Sam Moniac, met on the road Tustennuggee Emathla, called by whites High-Headed Jim and Jim Boy. High-Headed

208

Jim was described as remarkably handsome, well over six feet, with a "commanding air." He was six feet eight inches, recalled one man, "and in every way admirably proportioned." Dr. A. B. Clanton of Mississippi, who knew him, said that "in his person he was the beau ideal of a hero," and "beyond all comparison the finest looking man" he had ever seen. When Sam Moniac encountered High-Headed Jim that summer of 1813, "he shook hands with me, and immediately began to tremble and jerk in every part of his frame, and the very calves of his legs would be convulsed, and he would get entirely out of breath with the agitation." What a sight it must have been, that handsome giant of a man unexpectedly breaking into a dance as if suddenly demented.[2]

The Creeks were no more immune to such delusions and emotional behavior than other people, and as amusing as these incidents are, they are basically tragic, for they show a people caught between cultures, desperate to grasp something in which to believe. The old ways, the ways of their ancestors, were rapidly crumbling before the American avalanche, and it is in such times that the voice of the irrational seems rational. On a smaller scale, we see it in our own secular age with the appearance of cults promising salvation in the midst of confusion and disbelief.

It was in this ground, the seeds long planted and now full grown into luxuriant if bitter plants, that the sparks occurred that set off the conflagration. On 26 March 1812, a band of Indians led by a chief named Mamoth, who appeared to be drunk, attacked a party of whites traveling on the Federal Road to the Mississippi Territory and killed an old man named Thomas Meredith Sr. On 25 May the American agent to the Creeks, Benjamin Hawkins, reported to the secretary of war that a man named William Lott had been murdered "without the least provocation." These incidents occurred within the Creek Nation, but the violence had spread.[3]

We referred in the previous chapter to the Creek massacre of six settlers, including five children, in Tennessee where the Duck River flows into the Tennessee River. This was the incident that inflamed Tennesseans and convinced Andrew Jackson that he and his division would be sent against the Creeks. It was committed by eleven Creeks under Little Warrior, who in 1811 had accompanied Tecumseh on his return north. On their way home the next year, on 12 May 1812, the Creeks attacked the Crawley cabin. Mrs. Martha Crawley's husband, John, a riverboat man, was away. With her, in addition to her three children, was a Mrs. Manley, who had come to the Crawley cabin with her two older children "to lie in." Mrs. Manley's new baby was seven days old. A man named Hays was also there. When the Indians attacked, Martha Crawley stated that she "saw them coming, heard their hellish screams. . . ." She slammed the door shut and tried to hold it against them but the Indians "burst it open upon her and flung round so as to hide her behind it." Mrs. Manley was wounded, but survived. Her new baby was killed. Then the Indians killed the two older Manley children. Then they killed one of Martha Crawley's children in the cabin and another in the yard. They also killed Hays. As Martha Crawley looked on, "Another little child, her own, she saw hide itself in the cellar." When the Indians finally saw Martha she caught hold of one and "begged her life of him." They took her with them southward to an Upper Creek town on the Black Warrior River. There they "dug a grave for her."[4]

There are different versions of Martha Crawley's rescue. William Henry, who was in St. Stephens, Mississippi Territory, when Martha was brought in, wrote at the time that an Indian woman in charge of Martha let her go the night before she was to die. While she wandered in the forests and swamps of Alabama, the *mico* of the town, who was "disposed to be peaceable," bought Martha from her captor and then sent several young men to search for her and return her to her people. They found Martha Crawley "after two or three days, half starved and half naked," and took her to St. Stephens.[5]

But the incident that brought matters to a head occurred farther north in February 1813, near the junction of the Ohio and the Mississippi Rivers, and was reported on 5 March by James Robertson, then the U.S. agent to the Chickasaws: " 'Seven families have been murdered near the mouth of the Ohio, and most cruelly mangled, shewing all the savage barbarity that could be invented. One woman cut open, a child taken out and stuck on a stake.' " These were Creeks who had been delegated by the *micos* on a mission of peace to the Chickasaws. Two chiefs were with them, and one was the same Little Warrior who was implicated in the killings at the Crawley cabin on Duck River. Hawkins was outraged and in no uncertain terms told the Creeks what they must do. This act, he wrote to the *micos* of the Upper Creeks, was "not done by thoughtless wild young men, but deliberately, by a party under the command of two chiefs; and what makes it still worse, by chiefs sent by the Creek nation on a public mission of peace and friendship to the Chickasaws, with the nation's talks and letter from the assistant agent and the Creeks—a great nation, in peace and friendship with the United States, and daily giving assurances to me of their determination to remain so. It now becomes my duty to inform you, this murderous outrage must be settled immediately, and in a friendly way. You must . . . apprehend the two chiefs and their associates, and deliver them to me, or some officer of the United States commanding on the frontiers, to be punished according to the laws of the United States. This you are bound to do, by the eighth article of the Treaty of New York. Nothing less than this will satisfy the Government of the United States. Let me hear from you, as soon as you get together. This affair will not admit delay. The guilty must suffer for their crimes, or your nation will be involved in their guilt."[6]

Hawkins's demand was more than a spark, it was a torch thrown onto dry tinder, for it prompted a string of events that set off the Creek Civil War.

The *micos* responded to Hawkins in their meeting at Tuckabatchee on 16 April 1813, when they ordered out men to find the killers. But the instructions to the *micos* to capture and deliver to Hawkins the guilty parties for judgment under the laws of the United States proved impossible to carry out. As the *mico* Big Warrior wrote, they "could not be taken alive, for they fought until they were killed. This is the case with all of them: for they all

Benjamin Hawkins (Courtesy of the North Carolina Division
of Archives and History)

fight till they drop. The laws of the white people are, that they can take your
people alive; but ours is not so: it is different from ours."[7]

And so it was. The important Lower Creek mixed-blood William McIntosh and another chief led the avenging party. Nimrod Doyle, assistant agent
to Benjamin Hawkins, went with them and shortly afterward wrote a report.
The searchers had information that their prey had split into two groups, and
that Little Warrior and some were at the Upper Creek town called Hickory
Ground, on the Coosa River four miles downstream from Alexander McGillivray's old plantation at Little Tallassee, and two miles north of where the
Coosa and the Tallapoosa form the Alabama. The searchers also split into two
groups. McIntosh's party marched all night and at first light surrounded the
house where the culprits lay. The door was barred and McIntosh's men
could not break it in. A brisk firefight began. From inside came the shouts

of the Tuskegee warrior who boasted that "he had killed and eaten white people, and he had killed and cut open the white woman near the mouth of the Ohio." McIntosh's men set the house on fire. The Tuskegee warrior died in the flames. Two others who came to the door were pulled away from the fire, then tomahawked. Another two tried to run; one was killed, and one got away. Little Warrior was on the other side of the Coosa. Three Creeks, including one whom the whites called Captain Isaacs, were sent after him. He was found in a swamp the next day and finally forced out into the open. At ten o'clock on the night of the twenty-fifth Little Warrior was cornered and killed.[8]

The relentless pursuit continued. Nimrod Doyle reported that after one culprit was tracked down and fired on his pursuers, he "drew his knife and tomahawk, defended himself, and the warriors shot three balls through his body. He fell, retained the power of speech till next day, and died. He said he had been to the Shawanese helping of them, and had got fat eating white people's flesh. Every one, to the very last, called on the Shawanee General Tecumseh. This fellow had been five years with the Northwestern warring Indians, and after he was wounded, told the town people, the nation would be ruined for killing him, and not taking the Prophet's talk."[9]

Doyle told of two Indians who killed and robbed a white man "on the road near the Wolf warrior's path . . . One of the murderers, upon returning from Pensacola, with a saddle belonging to the murdered man, got a little drunk, and said, the master of this saddle I have left on the road dead, and have a heap of money, hard money and papers . . . The Chiefs sent two parties after them, one they found and killed at Immokfau [Emuckfau] . . . Their uncles went with the warriors and pointed them out. . . ." The second man was actually arrested, but when his captors were attempting to tie him up, "he slipped out a knife to defend himself, when a warrior standing before him with a knife in his hand, cut across his belly, let out his guts, and killed him."[10]

The National Council had met Hawkins's demand. "We have killed eight for the murder at the Ohio," Big Warrior wrote; "two for the murder at the Wolf-path; one for last year, for the murder at the Duck River; in all eleven, since the 16th of this month [April]."[11]

The hostiles had become known as Red Sticks, for the color of the war clubs they carried, and as such they would go down in history. The execution of Little Warrior and his comrades was for them the final straw. They vowed to execute the executioners, and they lost little time in retaliating. The new religion had swept through the Upper Creeks and gained many adherents who struck back at those who would follow white man's ways. "The prophet's party," Hawkins reported, "have destroyed, in several places of the Upper towns, all the cattle, hogs, and fowls. They have moved out of their towns into the woods, where they are dancing 'the dance of the Indians of the lakes.' " This was a change for the Creeks, who always danced the war dance after war, not before, which is another indication of the influence of the great Shawnee. Plots were made to kill *micos* and warriors who had accepted the counsels of Benjamin Hawkins. A campaign of terror spread throughout Upper Creek country. Hawkins wrote that "Letecau, a Prophet, eighteen years of age . . . went up to Coosa, with eight young followers, sent an invitation to the chiefs of his native town to come, and witness for themselves, his magical powers. They went accompanied by a crowd of both sexes. The Prophet ranged them in a line on the bank of Coosa River, and directed them to sit down, made his circle in front, and began 'the dance of the Indians of the lakes.' After exerting themselves for some time, the Prophet gave the war-whoop, attacked, and killed three of the chiefs, wounded the fourth. The others took to the river, swam over, went up and recrossed to their towns, collected their warriors, sent after the murderers, and found them dancing. One chief went into their circle; they knocked him down with their war clubs, and put him to death with bows and arrows. The warriors put the party to death, and scalped the Prophet."[12]

In the small village of Okfuskee, Hawkins wrote, the Red Sticks killed five chiefs and slaughtered almost all of the cattle. Mrs. Grayson, a white woman who had been invited by the headman "to teach the women to spin and weave, had much of her stock, her loom, and web of cloth destroyed. . . ." The friendly Creeks referred to in the previous paragraph went there and killed all the Red Sticks. But the Red Sticks were gaining the upper hand. Mrs. Grayson removed to Hillabee, the home of her husband's family, where she had lived for twelve years and had been "universally esteemed." But the Red Sticks caught up with her and she "was stripped of all her clothing, except the shift and petticoat on her back, and all her cattle and hogs. . . ." Mrs. Grayson was a lucky woman to lose only her belongings. Everywhere dead livestock rotted. In the cattle range of Tuckabatchee the stench continued for fifteen miles. Towns were destroyed, people slaughtered.[13]

Benjamin Hawkins reported that "the declaration of the prophets is, to destroy every thing received from the Americans; all the chiefs and their adherents who are friendly to the customs and ways of the white people; to put to death every man who will not join them; and, by those means, to unite the nation in aid of the British, and Indians of the lakes, against their white neighbors, as soon as their friends, the British, will be ready for them."[14]

At the individual level the choices were stark. On one occasion Red Sticks confronted two mixed bloods who were returning from "trading in beef cattle." The message was simple: join us or die. The situation of one of the mixed bloods, Sam Moniac, was typical of civil war, anytime, anyplace. While he had been absent in Pensacola his brother and sister joined the Red Sticks and stole some of his horses and other livestock and thirty-six black slaves. Now he confronted another Red Stick, his brother-in-law, Josiah Francis. According to Thomas Woodward, "Moniac boldly refused and mounted his horse. Josiah Francis . . . seized his bridle; Moniac snatched a war-club from his hand, gave him a severe blow and put out, with a shower of rifle bullets following him." The other mixed blood, William Weatherford, also known as Red Eagle, whom we shall soon encounter in one of the war's more dramatic incidents, decided to stay. Again according to Woodward, Weatherford disapproved of their course of action, believing "that it would be their ruin; but they were his people—he was raised with them, and he would share their fate." What evidence we have for Weatherford—as is usual with Indians, it is shadowy—presents him as a humane man, so when he maintains that one of his reasons for joining the Red Sticks was to use his influence to lessen the bloodshed and horrors of war, we tend to believe him.[15]

The Red Sticks also got on to the trail of the Upper Creek *mico* Captain Isaacs, whom we just met as one of Little Warrior's executioners. He had gone north with Tecumseh and listened to Tecumseh's brother, the Prophet, and had talked to British agents and officers in Canada. He had become a prophet himself and related to the people wondrous tales rivaling, if not surpassing, those of Josiah Francis and other Creek prophets. He may have been an opportunist. Thomas Woodward called him "one of the most cunning, artful scamps I ever saw among the Indians." His fame among people increased and aroused the jealousy of Josiah Francis and another important prophet, Paddy Walsh. They plotted against him and finally declared him to be "a diabolical witch." He was proscribed and sentenced to death by fire. But some of his people did not forsake him and warned him, and with these followers Captain Isaacs fled, taking with him his town's precious supply of powder and lead. With other Upper Creeks escaping the wrath of the Red Sticks, Captain Isaacs sought safety in the fortified town of Tuckabatchee, and with its *mico,* Big Warrior.[16]

Big Warrior was another of the Upper Creek headmen who had rejected the message of the Red Stick prophets. He did it not out of love for the Americans. He probably had various reasons of which we are unaware as to why he chose to stay loyal, even at the risk of his life. But certainly an important reason was his economic stake in the Federal Road. Big Warrior was a striking figure, a large man, as his name implies, with purple tattoos all over his body. He also had something in common with William Blount, for though he operated on a smaller scale, his acquisitive nature rivaled Blount's. He owned much property and slaves. To gain his cooperation on the Federal Road, Big Warrior was in effect given control of it: he collected the profits from all the taverns on the road, plus the tolls from bridges and ferries. His fate had the Red Sticks caught him would have been unpleasant indeed.[17]

Yet Big Warrior had no desire to cede Creek lands to the Americans. He would have no truck with the Red Sticks, and he was happy to get rich, but now he liked things as they were, with enough travelers on the Federal Road to keep filling his purse but no flood of whites onto Creek lands. Which is why a passage in one of Benjamin Hawkins's letters disturbed him. Hawkins wrote, "As we are now in possession of Mobile, you will soon see people from Tennessee coming down Coosa, with their produce to market; when you see that, you will see you are friends, and you may go that water path yourself, to Tennessee or Mobile." Hawkins continued in this vein, the clear message being that the waters belong to all. But the Creeks did not want the Coosa to belong to all, and they did not feel that they needed an invitation to use it, for they owned it.[18]

Big Warrior replied that they had done what Hawkins asked, knowing that if they did not Hawkins had said "we should lose our land to the Chattahoochee, and to Coosa waters. The chiefs thought it best to save their land, and they did all in their power, and punished all they could: that no nation was to come and cross in our land by land or water, to bring trouble in our rights. Now, you white people have large, and a great many people to surround us; you have told us that there was no enemy to come and disturb us; that if you saw any, you would be able to keep them back; that nothing should fret the nation. Now, Colonel Hawkins, you say you are a friend to the nation, and one of the old chiefs; if any people of any nation should use the waters of the Coosa, it will bring trouble on us, and I hope you will inform the people of Tennessee, and Cherokees, of these talks; that if any thing should happen, I shall tell you I have told you of it. I have stated this to you; the nation was obliged to give up the public road, and they knew that would bring trouble on them, and since that, the nation have spilt blood, and we had to give satisfaction. If they have give up the waters of the Coosa, it will hurt the feelings of the Creeks; it will not do. You thought you would mention this waters to them, to bring trouble on them, and destruction at once; you mean to destroy us, on these waters, in trying to make use of it, when we don't allow of it."[19]

And because he had done what he was asked to do, Big Warrior found himself hunkered down inside his town of Tuckabatchee, while outside throngs of Red Sticks howled for his scalp. The first full-scale Red Stick assault on the town was thrown back with heavy losses. For several days they kept attacking without success. The powder and lead brought inside by Captain Isaacs probably made the difference. The Red Sticks settled in for a siege to starve out the defenders. Big Warrior then got word out to Benjamin Hawkins requesting help. Hawkins sent Joseph Marshall, son of an English father and a Creek mother, with a large force of Lower Creeks from Coweta on the Chattahoochee River, near modern Columbus, Georgia. Marshall's relief column got through the hostile camps on the river and made it into Tuckabatchee. Two days later the Red Sticks once more launched a general assault. But the defenders behind their fortifications poured a fire on the attackers so devastating that some laid on the ground and feigned death. "Braver ones," wrote George Stiggins, "lay down and rolled over to the pickets and tried to cut their opponents down." But their valor was in vain, and the Red Sticks retreated. Joseph Marshall lost an eye that day. The defenders decided to attempt a breakout, and the next day, accompanied by their women and children and aged, they struck out. George Stiggins described it for us.[20]

"Women and children, mixed with armed men, marched out of the fort in a line for the river and crossed it. The men in the rear, stripped to their naked bodies and painted red, black, or white, were ready and willing to fight for their wives and children. Their determined manner must have dampened the ardor of the hostiles, for they never molested them or pursued them on the road. So they had no interruption in their escape to Georgia." As Stiggins also notes, the heavy Red Stick losses probably was another reason the escape turned into just a long walk in the woods.[21]

At first the Red Sticks were divided between whether they should direct their hostility only toward Creeks who followed the white man's way, or also toward whites. The latter opinion soon gained ascendancy. To maintain, therefore, that what happened next was American interference in internal Creek affairs is naive at best. The Americans closest to the action, the settlers on the Tombigbee and Tensaw Rivers, would have been derelict had they not taken measures to stop the ability of the Red Sticks to wage war against them, which was precisely the Red Sticks' aim. That they made a hash of it is beside the point.

"STARVED ALMOST TO DEATH, AND BEREFT OF THEIR SENSES"

With the Red Stick attack on Tuckabatchee there could be no doubt that a full-blown Creek Civil War had begun. It was only a question of time before the entire southern Alabama frontier was set ablaze, and that time was near.

The Red Sticks were desperate for guns, powder, and lead, and the place to get them was Pensacola. Had not Tecumseh told them that? Had not Little Warrior brought with him from Canada a letter from British officers for delivery to Pensacola? That letter, they were convinced, requested the Spanish to arm the Creeks. It did not, but the Red Sticks were not to know that. And the Spanish governor of West Florida, Mauricio de Zuniga, had asked the Indians to come to Pensacola. Given everything else the Red Sticks knew, or thought they knew, that could mean only one thing—the arms and ammunition were ready. Thus Red Stick wishful thinking and Spanish confusion prompted some 300 to 350 Red Stick warriors led by Peter McQueen, Josiah Francis, and High-Headed Jim to make the trek to Pensacola, leading unladen packhorses to carry the munificence they were about to receive. They were received in a friendly manner by the new governor, Don Mateo González Manrique. The governor had not yet come around, as he would, to full cooperation with the Indians, but he feared their rage and possible violence against his small garrison if he turned them away empty-handed. So he gave them food and blankets, some lead, and a thousand pounds of gunpowder. But he not only refused to give them guns; he would not even repair their broken guns. The Red Sticks became so furious and unruly that Governor González Manrique called out the garrison and militia, which quieted things down. Some Pensacola merchants either sold or gave the Indians other supplies, among which may have been some guns. Some of the Red Sticks led by High-Headed Jim then loaded everything on their packhorses and departed, while the others lingered in Pensacola.

It was only afterward that González Manrique and his superiors all the way up the chain of command to Madrid decided on a policy of arming the

Indians. Their reasoning was basic and correct. They knew that the Americans were determined to take Florida, and they feared an attack. Spain, a dim shadow of itself during the Age of Conquistadors, ravaged by the Napoleonic Wars, could not successfully defend its territory. The British might help it, since they were allies against Napoleon and had gone to war with the United States on 18 June 1812. But who could trust the British? The Indians, however, hated the Americans and had a huge stake in the imperial outcome in the Old Southwest. They were the best allies the Spanish had. But all of this took place months after the departure of High-Headed Jim and part of the Red Stick force with a pitifully small supply of lead and only a thousand pounds of powder to work their will among their people and take on the Americans to boot.[22]

Those Americans knew exactly what had happened in Pensacola and acted with dispatch. American spies in Pensacola also reported that the Red Sticks were planning to attack the settlements on the Tombigbee and Tensaw Rivers north of Mobile during their return. American authorities, therefore, decided to attack McQueen's Red Sticks and capture the munitions. Colonel James Caller, the senior militia officer on the frontier of what is now southern Alabama, called out the militia and began his march eastward. Other militia companies joined him along the way, including one commanded by Captain Sam Dale, one of the most famous frontiersman of his time, whose celebrated canoe fight will be described in a later chapter. Caller finally gathered around him about 180 whites, mixed bloods, and full bloods. One company was commanded by a highly regarded mixed blood, Captain Dixon Bailey, who was one of the Creeks educated in Philadelphia under the provisions of the McGillivray-Knox Treaty of New York of 1790. The militiamen were well mounted and armed with rifles and shotguns. Sam Dale carried a weapon unusual for the time, a double-barreled shotgun. An eyewitness described Colonel Caller "as wearing a calico hunting shirt, a high bell-crowned hat and top boots, and riding a large fine bay horse." A fine figure of man, it might be said, leading a fine body of men. But Caller's command had a problem, and it was critical: that old militia bugaboo, lack of discipline.[23]

On the morning of 27 July 1813, the command was reorganized and an unusual number of field officers were elected: one lieutenant colonel and four majors, all of whom were now happy men, as their military aspirations had been met. Colonel Caller then led his men down the old Pensacola Road. At about eleven o'clock that morning scouts who had been sent out returned to report that Red Sticks were only a few miles ahead, camped in a low pine barren enclosed by a bend in Burnt Corn Creek. It was High-Headed Jim's packhorse train. High-Headed Jim later told Thomas Woodward that he had less than 100 men. When discovered by the American scouts they were cooking and eating, at unguarded ease. What a perfect situation, thought the American officers; we shall take them by surprise. The Creek camp on the low ground was at the foot of a low range of hills that formed a semicircle before the camp. The attackers could come down the

Tustennuggee Emathla, known as High-Headed Jim or Jim Boy, 1820s, by Charles Bird King (National Anthropological Archives, Smithsonian Institution)

hill in front of the camp and get within gunshot before being detected. The Creek Civil War was about to become the Creek War.

The militia made their way to the rear of the hill directly in front of the Red Stick camp and dismounted. It seems that the officers failed to take the rudimentary step of providing a guard for the horses, and just let the men dismount and see to their horses as they pleased. The Americans then went over the hill, filtered down through the woods toward the Creek camp, and opened fire. Taken completely by surprise, the Creeks fought back for a while, then fled in total confusion to the bank of the stream. Some of the militia pursued them and may have driven them across the creek. Had the bulk of the American forces done the same and pressed the attack, the fight might have turned out differently. But the sight of the loaded packhorses was a far greater temptation than pushing one's luck in battle, and most of the Americans busied themselves leading the animals off. Colonel Caller and his newly elected field officers obviously did not have the situation well in hand.

The Red Sticks, observing the now disorganized nature of the American force, noticing the few men facing them on the line, with whoops and cries rushed forward brandishing guns, war clubs, and tomahawks. The troops who had just driven the Indians from the camp now became the chased. Colonel Caller could not stop them, so he ordered a retreat to the foot of the hill, where they could regroup and continue the fight. But the men who had stayed behind to plunder took one look at their retreating comrades, stared in horror at the onrushing Indians, felt their blood chill at sound of the enemy's terrible, high-pitched shrieks, and Caller's command fell apart. Panic reigned supreme among most of the militia. Some men even swung aboard the Indians' packhorses and galloped off. Efforts by some of the officers to stem the rush to safety were fruitless. Terror had gripped most of their men. There was no holding them.

About 85 men commanded by Captains Dale, Bailey, and Smoot fought for an hour in open woods at the foot of the hill. Dale took a ball in his side that ricocheted inside him and ended up near his backbone, but he was a tough customer and fought on as long as he could. But they, too, were finally forced to withdraw, and the battle ended in a rout, with men escaping in small bands or alone, many on foot. Most of their horses had scattered, or been commandeered by the plunderers, or captured by the Red Sticks. In many cases it was every man for himself and the devil take the hindmost. The Creeks pursued them for about a mile, but the Americans excelled in speed afoot and outdistanced the scalping knife.

Colonel Caller and Major Wood, having lost their horses, fell behind and were soon alone in the woods and lost their way. Finally, when they did not return, men were sent to search for them. Fifteen days after the fight, Caller and Wood were found, Albert Pickett wrote, "starved almost to death, and bereft of their senses." Colonel Caller had lost his fine hat and top boots and his pants, but he had retained his calico shirt and his drawers. The experience drove Major Wood, one of the newly elected field officers, to the life of a drunkard. For many years Caller and others suffered ridicule for their roles, and few men who served at Burnt Corn would afterward boast of it.[24]

As was often the case of these frontier clashes, losses on both sides were minimal. Two dead and 15 wounded for the Americans, who thought 10 to a dozen Indians had been killed and 8 or 9 wounded. The Red Sticks had lost their precious powder and lead, but they had won something valuable, yet at the same time dangerous. Their morale soared. They had won the fight. Against a superior force, armed largely with clubs, tomahawks, and knives, with only thirteen guns among them, according to George Stiggins, they had not only prevailed, they had run the Americans off the field. Which meant, of course, that the Americans were obviously cowards. Thus the Red Sticks, already gripped by religious fervor and a deep and abiding hatred of the white man and his mixed-blood allies, assumed a state of mind dangerous for any people.

"EVERY MAN PAINTED RED OR BLACK
AND STRIPPED TO THE BUFF"

American authorities in the Mississippi Territory realized that they now had an Indian war on their hands and sent out warnings to the settlers that they should fort up, as that old frontier term went. One of the main stations was Fort Mims. Many of its defenders were mixed bloods, including Dixon Bailey, who had fought so valiantly at Burnt Corn. The Red Sticks, seeking revenge, decided to go after Fort Mims in strength.[25]

The fort was built by well-off mixed bloods and whites who united for a common defense. It was located about one mile from the Alabama River in modern Baldwin County, Alabama, about twelve miles north of Stockton and forty miles north of Mobile. A wealthy mixed blood, Samuel Mims, who had started off as a packhorse man in the deerskin trade, had a large home there. The fort was built around the home, which occupied ground in the middle of the fort. The rectangular stockade enclosed one acre and contained about a dozen buildings. There were two large gates, western and eastern, and on the southwest corner an unfinished blockhouse. Into this acre in August 1813 there crowded some 300 souls: whites, mixed bloods, blacks, and some friendly full bloods. There were about 100 children. Of the total 120 were Mississippi Territorial Volunteers commanded by Major Daniel Beasley. Upon his arrival, Beasley, a lawyer with little if any military experience, took command of Fort Mims. On 7 August Brigadier General Ferdinand L. Claiborne, commander of the Mississippi territorial militia, rode into Fort Mims on an inspection tour and ordered Major Beasley "to strengthen the picketing, build two more block-houses, respect the enemy, to send scouts out frequently. . . ." The pickets may have been strengthened, but the blockhouses were not built. Yet Fort Mims was strongly built, with a large garrison, and it was common knowledge that Indians were rarely able to take well-defended forts.[26]

The Red Sticks, meanwhile, were gathering for the assault. Their nominal leader was Paddy Walsh, but the real commander was William Weatherford, also known as Red Eagle. We have seen that Weatherford was opposed to the Red Stick cause, but may have joined them partly to use his influence to lessen the horrors of war. But there was probably a more immediate reason: blackmail. In his temporary absence on a journey to Pensacola, his wife's family had taken his wife, his children, and his property to a Red Stick town. Weatherford went there and saw no chance of escaping with them, for his feelings were well known and the Red Sticks kept him under strict surveillance. At the same time, Weatherford was highly regarded by all for his intelligence and judgment. He was the son of a Georgian, Charles Weatherford, while his mother, Sehoy, was a half sister of Alexander McGillivray. He had, according to Pickett, a "fine form" and commanding personal presence, with eyes "large, dark, brilliant and flashing." Strangers meeting him knew "that they were in the presence of no ordinary man." Which is no doubt why Peter McQueen, Paddy Walsh, and other Red Sticks, when they were certain that they had the necessary leverage over him, turned to Weatherford for advice on how to take Fort Mims and in the end put him in actual command of the Red Stick force.[27]

The presence of a large Red Stick army on the Tombigbee did not go unobserved or unreported. On 23 August a Choctaw Indian reported seeing a large party of hostiles. While the Red Stick force lay at a deserted plantation just south of modern Claiborne, Alabama, and planned the attack, a captured black slave escaped and made his way to Fort Mims, where he told what he knew of the hostiles and their intentions. But after a few quiet days, the Indians not appearing, the slave was declared a liar. The Red Sticks, meanwhile, 750 of them, were on the move. They had only fifty miles to go but moved slowly, taking four days. They were seen by many people, who rode in to Fort Mims and reported the news. The Indians were on the direct road to Fort Mims, they said, so many "they could only see one end of them in single file." But their reports were not taken seriously, for Major Beasley, ignoring General Claiborne's prudent advice to "respect the enemy," refused to believe that Indians would attack such a well-garrisoned fort.

On 29 August 1813 the Red Sticks stopped about six miles from Fort Mims to rest and cool off from the terrible heat and humidity that afflicts the Deep South at that time of year. They spotted two scouts some three hundred yards away. The scouts were talking freely to each other, and from their relaxed manner appeared to be unwary. They failed to pick up the Red Stick trail and were allowed to return unmolested to the fort. Later that day the Red Sticks followed the path of the scouts to within three-quarters of a mile of Fort Mims, where they made a quiet, and almost certainly cold, camp for the night.

The same day two young black slaves were sent out of Fort Mims to tend cattle grazing a few miles away. They soon rushed back, breathless and terrified, and said they had seen 24 painted warriors. The next day Major Beasley sent a report on the incident to General Claiborne: "Two negro boys . . . told that they saw a great number of Indians painted, running and hallooing on towards Messrs. Pierce's Mill." Beasley sent Captain Hatton Middleton with 8 to 10 horsemen "to reconnitre & ascertain the strength of the enemy . . . but the alarm has proved to be a false one. What gave some plausibility to the report of the negro boys at first was some of Mr. Randon's negroes who had been sent up to his plantation for corn and reported his plantation to be full of Indians committing every kind of Havoc; but I now doubt the truth of that report." Major Beasley added that he was most pleased at the reaction of his troops when the alarm was given: "when it was expected every moment that the Indians would appear in sight, the soldiers very generally appeared anxious to see them." Incensed by what he considered a false alarm, Beasley had one of the slaves tied up and whipped hard.[28]

That night Weatherford picked two men he trusted in time of peril and took them with him on a reconnaissance of Fort Mims. Security was so lax that the three men were able to sneak right up to the stockade and peer through the portholes, which were four feet high and four feet apart along the entire diameter of the fort. Although Weatherford could see little in the darkness, which was punctuated by a few lights here and there, he and his comrades could not help but notice from the manner of the inhabitants and their casual conversations that they did not seem to have been alarmed by anything that had occurred in the neighborhood of the fort. We can also reasonably speculate that the three men saw the fort's Achilles' heel—the east gate was partially open. Sand had either blown or washed against it, making it difficult to close, and Major Daniel Beasley had done nothing to rectify the situation.

What was wrong with Beasley? Was he a fool? He was not a trained or experienced soldier, but one does not need to be either to know that fort gates are kept closed and secured when trouble is brewing. Such a simple security measure comes under the heading of common sense. Nevertheless, nothing was done about the gate. General Claiborne sent an express on the twenty-ninth warning Beasley and "enjoining the utmost circumspection." If Thomas Woodward's *Reminiscences* are accurate, a clue to Beasley's conduct was offered by the mixed-blood Jim Cornells, who rode into Fort Mims on the morning of 30 August. He had seen Indians, and "the Fort would be attacked that day," he told Beasley. But the major, Cornells said, was drunk. Cornells "had only seen a gang of red cattle," Beasley said, to which Cornells replied, "That gang of red cattle would give him a hell of a kick before night." Cornells then rode away from Fort Mims. William Weatherford, watching from concealment, saw and recognized Jim Cornells entering and leaving the fort and allowed him to ride to safety. If Albert Pickett's informants recalled correctly, Beasley also decided that morning to flog the other slave who had reported sighting painted Indians the previous day. The one who had been whipped the day before was again sent out to tend cattle, again spotted Indians, but wary of being whipped again fled to Fort Pierce, a smaller defensive work about one mile from Fort Mims.[29]

Meanwhile, in a ravine four hundred yards from the east gate, under an already high, hot Alabama sun, Red Eagle and some 750 Red Stick warriors lay on the ground, "Every man painted red or black and stripped to the buff. . . ." The prophet Paddy Walsh had come up with an excellent idea. They would rush forward silently and surround the fort and take charge of all of the portholes, thus enabling them to fire at the unprotected defenders inside while they were shielded by the stockade. But being a prophet, he added to his plan a recipe for suicide. Four men whom he, by magic, would make bulletproof would rush through the partially open gate and engage the enemy. If they emerged unscathed, that would be an omen for success.[30]

Inside the fort, 30 August 1813, the noon drum beat for dinner. The Red Sticks mistook its meaning and thought they had been discovered. They rose as a body and charged across the 400 yards of open ground. The only sounds they made were their breathing and the pounding of their moccasins on the earth. At the partially open east gate the sentry was looking over the shoulders of two men playing cards. Inside, people were getting ready to eat. The Red Sticks came on, fanning out to surround the fort, undiscovered . . .

300 yards . . . 200 yards . . . 150 yards. Finally, at 100 yards somebody spotted them and shouted, "Indians."

Pandemonium ensued. The four warriors who believed they had been made bulletproof by Paddy Walsh's magic raced through the open gate. Three were immediately shot down and killed. The fourth turned and fled, unwilling to trust further the prophet's magical powers. But the Red Sticks outside had taken control of the portholes and were firing through them. Balls whistled through the fort striking men, women, and children. Major Beasley ran to the east gate and tried to close it, and there paid the ultimate price for his incredible negligence. The sand was too high to close the gate, and as Beasley frantically struggled with it the shrieking, painted warriors were upon him. They clubbed and tomahawked him and knocked him to the ground, where he died.

A large group of Indians then ran into the fort and engaged the soldiers, who under the direction of Captain William Jack, Lieutenant Peter Randon, and Captain Dixon Bailey were trying as best they could to organize resistance. But there was no continual line of defense in the largely open area of the fort. Men were scattered in groups at various points, and we can be almost certain that early on there was no possibility of a coordinated defense. Casualties were heavy from the beginning. Captain Hatton Middleton, who had seen no signs of Indians the day before, died at the outset with all of his men defending the eastern section of Fort Mims. More Indians rushed into the fort. The dozen or so houses inside and some old picketing afforded protection, and from these points the men fought back fiercely enough that the Red Sticks withdrew from inside of the fort for almost an hour. But according to George Stiggins, escaped black slaves serving with the Red Sticks urged them on and the Indians once again entered the fort.

It was Red Stick control of the portholes outside and fire inside that determined the fate of Fort Mims, its garrison, its women and children. The Red Sticks began setting fire to the buildings. As the blazes grew higher and hotter, people were forced out. Some did not make it. Many women and children were burned alive. Imagine the scene. To the sound of guns and the yells and shouts of fighting men were added crackling flames and the shrieks of burning innocents. Samuel Mims's house was full of women and children, and around it danced young, screaming Red Stick prophets. Building after building had to be abandoned to the flames, and those who could, finally escaped to the loom house and its vicinity, where the final stand was made under the leadership of the gallant mixed blood Captain Dixon Bailey.

Albert Pickett interviewed survivors years later and described the horror that followed. Women fetched water from the well and reloaded guns. Dixon Bailey's sister-in-law, Mrs. Daniel Bailey, became so incensed at the behavior of a Sergeant Matthews, who cowered against a wall, trembling, that she stabbed him with a bayonet. But all was in vain. By about five o'clock in the afternoon, the loom house was "full to overflowing. The weak, wounded and feeble were pressed to death and trodden underfoot." People were "herded too close to defend themselves, and like beeves in the slaughter-pen of the butcher, a prey to those who fired upon them." A few Spanish deserters from the Pensacola garrison knelt by the well, made the sign of the cross, and awaited the tomahawks. Others attempted escape by cutting through the stockade and running for the swamps, and in some cases those who made it hid for days before reaching sanctuaries. For those in the loom house who survived the flames but had been unable to escape, the final horror awaited. "The bastion was broken down, the helpless inmates were butchered in the quickest manner, and blood and brains bespattered the whole earth. The children were seized by the legs, and killed by beating their heads against the stockading. The women were scalped, and those who were pregnant opened, while they were alive, and the embryo infants let out of the womb." Some of the wounded were thrown into the fire. One account has Dixon Bailey cutting his way out of the fort but dying of his wounds in the swamp next to a cypress stump. Another claims he died inside the fort and that his sister, standing near his body, was asked by a Red Stick, "What family she was of? She answered, pointing to her brother, I am the sister to that great man you have murdered there; upon which they knocked her down, cut her open, strewed her entrails around."[31]

William Weatherford knew what his warriors would do if they won. Yet he begged them to spare the women and children, and for his humanity threatening gestures were made against him, war clubs raised, and he turned away from a scene where he knew dear friends awaited an awful fate. "His eyes refused to see the mangled end," George Stiggins wrote. "He turned for his horse, mounted him abruptly, and rode off . . . without deigning to look back."[32]

Of the some 300 people inside Fort Mims on the day of the attack, about 250 died in and around the fort. Some escaped, the rest were taken prisoner. The four hours of fighting had also taken a heavy toll on Red Sticks. A burial party found at least 100 of their dead. George Stiggins wrote that a head count by town *micos* came up with 202 Red Stick dead out of the 750 who took part in the assault.

Three weeks after the fall of Fort Mims, General Claiborne sent Major Joseph P. Kennedy with a strong detachment to the site for the purpose of burying the dead. When they looked up they saw a sky dark with buzzards. When they looked down they saw hundreds of dogs running wild, feasting on the carcasses of the dead. Major Kennedy directed his men to dig two large pits for burial. To General Claiborne he wrote: "Indians, negroes, white men, women and children, lay in one promiscuous ruin. All were scalped, and the females, of every age, were butchered in a manner which neither decency nor language will permit me to describe. The main building was burned to ashes, which were filled with bones. The plains and woods around were covered with dead bodies. All the houses were consumed by fire, except the block-house, and a part of the pickets. The soldiers and officers, with one voice, called on Divine Providence to revenge the death of our murdered friends."[33]

Divine Providence was waiting, but not in godly form. It was off to the north, in the Cumberland country, in the guise of a tall, fierce man whose eyes could blaze with fury, racked now with terrible wounds, his body thin to the point of emaciation. Andrew Jackson well understood the word *revenge,* and he thirsted for it.

Chapter 14

⬥

"TIME IS NOT TO BE LOST"

"I AM DETERMINED TO PUSH FORWARD IF I HAVE TO LIVE ON ACORNS"

On Saturday, 18 September 1813, Enoch Parsons, a Tennessee state legislator and one of Jackson's oldest friends, arrived in Nashville and found the public square full of people being harangued by speakers. Talk of war was in the air, and Enoch Parsons wrote that "the talking part of a war was never better performed." Parsons was invited to speak, but "I declined the distinction. . . ."[1]

On Monday, the twentieth, the legislature met to consider the emergency. Enoch Parsons wrote the bill "to call out 3,500 men, under the General entitled to command, and place them in the Indian nations, so that they might preserve the Mississippi territory from destruction, and prevent the friendly Indians from taking the enemy's side, and to render service to the United States until the United States could provide a force." At that time Jackson had been in bed seventeen days, recovering from the terrible gunshot wounds suffered in the Benton fight. He asked if Parsons would come to see him, and after adjournment that day Parsons visited Jackson in his bedroom. He found Jackson "minutely informed of the contents of the bill. . . ." Parsons told him it would pass and become law on Wednesday, "and I mentioned that I regretted very much that the General entitled to command the forces of the State, was not in a condition to take the field. To which General Jackson replied:

"'The devil in hell, he is not.'

"He gritted his teeth in anguish as he uttered those words, and groaned when he ceased to speak. I told him that I hoped I was mistaken, but that I did not believe that he could just then take the field. After some time I left the general. Two hours after, I received fifty or more copies of his orders, which had been made out and printed in the mean time, and ordered the troops to rendezvous at Fayetteville. . . ."

Few people if any thought Jackson fit for field duty. James Robertson wrote to him that "I am so ounderfully uneasy to heare the plan of the cam-

226

paign against the creeks, and who commands. I cannot harber the smallest hopes that you will be able."[2]

Either that evening or the next day Parsons asked Jackson's principal physician, a Dr. May, "if he thought General Jackson could possibly march. Dr. May said that no other man could, and that it was uncertain whether, with his spunk and energy, he could; but that it was entirely uncertain what General Jackson could do in such circumstances." When Jackson left for the field in early October Dr. May accompanied him a ways and after three or four days returned to Nashville. Enoch Parsons asked him "how the General had got along," and Dr. May told him "that they had *to stop the General frequently and wash him from head to foot in solutions of sugar and lead to keep down the inflammation;* and that he was better, and he and his troops had gone on."

"The devil in hell, he is not," Jackson had told Parsons, and he meant it. Physical weakness and extreme pain were just other obstacles to be overcome.

To return to Jackson's order that Enoch Parsons had seen, on the day that Jackson received his own orders from Governor Blount, 24 September, he recalled to duty his division of 2,000 "Volunteer infantry and militia" and ordered the men to rendezvous on 4 October at Fayetteville, eighty miles south of Nashville. The opening paragraph of his order was lurid.[3]

"Brave Tennesseans!

"Your frontier is threatened with invasion by the savage foe! Already do they advance towards your frontier with their scalping knifes unsheathed, to butcher your wives, your children, and your helpless babes. Time is not to be lost. We must hasten to the frontier, or we will find it drenched in the blood of our fellow-citizens."

Further on, between details of mobilization, a one-line paragraph stood alone and assured his troops that he, Jackson, would be undeterred by his wounds:

"The health of your General is restored. He will command in person."

Command he would, and he had far more in mind than just defending the frontier. His strategy was far-seeing and boded ill for Creeks and foreigners standing in the way of the American people in their long march to the Gulf. It did not require a detailed explanation. On the contrary, he described it to a correspondent briefly, simply, clearly, and with unmistakable determination: ". . . I am anxious to reach the center of creek country, and give them a final blow, and then strike at the root of the disseas pensacola."[4]

Could he do it, though? He was a general who had never led an army into battle, had neither trained for nor studied the art of war. One of the most successful generals in the Revolutionary War, the architect of victory in the South, Nathanael Greene, had also been untried. But he was a studious man, and by the time he went to war he was steeped in its history and literature and proved able to learn from his mistakes as well as apply in the field what he had learned in the study. *Studiousness,* however, is not a word one associates with Andrew Jackson, and a blunder deep in Indian country could well be a general's last. Despite the willpower and leadership qualities he had exhibited on the trek from Natchez, that movement was closer to a peacetime maneuver than a wartime march, for there had not been an enemy in sight. But now he meant to fight his way through some five hundred miles of wilderness in which, wrote a soldier from a previous war in the American wilderness, there were no roads, no supply depots, no hospitals, no "good towns to retreat to in case of misfortune," where "there is no refreshment for the healthy, nor relief for the sick. A vast inhospitable desart, unsafe and treacherous . . . where simple death is the least misfortune which can happen to them."[5]

Disasters were not uncommon. Two seasoned but plodding veterans of the Revolution who never should have held independent field commands, Brigadier General Josiah Harmar on the Maumee in 1790, and Major General Arthur St. Clair on the Wabash in 1791, had led American armies to bloody debacles in the Ohio country. Harmar never had control of his mixed army of regulars and Kentucky and Pennsylvania militia. He kept sending out detachments that kept getting cut to pieces by warriors under that fine Miami tactician Little Turtle. March discipline was sloppy. In one incident a mounted column of 100 men were stretched single file for about half a mile just before they rode into an ambush. During the army's retreat Harmar, who never got near any of the fighting, allowed his column to get strung out on the march, a perfect situation for disaster. He was saved by a two-hour lunar eclipse that so unsettled the superstitious Indians that their force broke up and went home.

St. Clair's defeat on 4 November 1791 was total, the worst ever suffered by a major American force in an Indian war, far surpassing Custer's overpublicized, overanalyzed blunder on the Little Bighorn. Little Turtle's warriors, only 700 strong, overran and shattered St. Clair's 1,450 regulars and militia. Over 600 were killed and some 300 wounded, and the slaughter extended to the camp followers and their children. Over 50 of the 200 to 300 women were killed, some of them "cut in two, their boobies cut off, and burning with a number of our officers on our own fires." One survivor left for all time an indelible picture of the debacle on the Wabash: the soldiers' "freshly scalped heads were reeking with smoke, and in the heavy morning frost looked like so many pumpkins [in] a cornfield in December." Simple death had eluded them.[6]

Closer in time to Jackson's expedition, on 21 January 1813, another regular and Jackson's friend Brigadier General James Winchester of Tennessee, who was serving under William Henry Harrison in the Old Northwest, committed more serious errors than we have either space to list or time to consider. Winchester lost to a British and Indian force a battle that under a good combat commander could have been won, suffered about 350 killed out of 850, and surrendered the rest at River Raisin in southeastern Michigan. Drunken Indians massacred at least 30 wounded men after the surrender. American officers reported that "the savages *were suffered to commit every depredation upon our wounded; many were tomahawked, and many were burned alive in the houses.*"[7]

The Prussian officer Karl von Clausewitz, who was a field soldier as well as a thinker, pointed out "that ideas in war are generally . . . simple" and apparent. It is, he continued, the "ability to choose the most promising, the acuteness which can pierce a cloud of obscure relations, and by the application of judgement can decide among them on an instant, these may more properly be considered the cardinal virtues of a commander. . . ." On that score, Jackson had correctly identified the problem and the solution when he stated that he meant to invade the heart of Creek country, crush the hostiles, then go on to strike at Pensacola and prevent either the Spanish or the British from encouraging and arming the Creeks. His strategy could not have been simpler, and it cannot be faulted, although it did foresee the invasion of sovereign territory. We should point out that others also had the same aim in mind, but as we shall see none possessed Jackson's single-minded devotion to attaining his goal.[8]

How to accomplish it, though? Here Clausewitz, who saw war close up, is once again our guide. "The chief thing, however, is the relative difficulty of the execution. In war all is simple; but the most simple is still very difficult. The instrument of war resembles a machine with prodigious friction, which cannot, as in ordinary mechanics, be adjusted at pleasure, but is ever in contact with a host of chances. War is, moreover, a movement through a dense medium. A motion easy in the air is difficult in water. Toil and danger are the elements in which the mind has to act in war. . . ."

Which leads us back to our original question: Could our inexperienced amateur pull it off? Could Jackson's simple idea, expressed in one sentence, survive the difficulties and complexities of operations in the field? Would luck, or what Clausewitz called "a host of chances," the vital partner of successful generals, be with him?

Jackson revealed early his instinctive understanding of the need for good intelligence when he wrote to John Coffee, "Correct information is all important before we make a movement with our whole force. . . ." Rumors as to Creek intentions abounded, and they all flowed into Jackson, who had to analyze them: the Creeks and Spanish were gathering to attack Mobile, or the Creeks with their families were preparing to cross to the western bank of the Mississippi; or they were about to descend on Huntsville and the Tennessee frontier. He dismissed all of them: "These various rumours, are in my oppinion created by Briitsh agents to amuse & distract us and draw our attention from their true point of attack. I am inclined to believe that they will never abandon their nation untill they are severely Drubed."[9] He directed the faithful Coffee, who was already in the field with his cavalry and mounted infantry, to "keep me well advised. . . ." Whatever British agents may or may not have been doing, Jackson was right that the Creeks would not stray far from home, and then only on raiding expeditions. He would have to go in after them. He also decided to start a rumor of his own in hopes it would confuse the Indians. He wrote to Coffee to spread word that Coffee's company was on its way to Mobile.[10]

Coffee had established Camp Coffee near Huntsville, Alabama (then part of Mississippi Territory). There he ran into what would become by far the most critical element of the campaign. Food . . . and the severe shortage of it.

Jackson has been criticized for plunging into the wilderness without careful advance planning and the establishment of forward supply depots.[11] The charge is true, and generals who take risks with supply—or to use its military term, logistics—place themselves and their commands in jeopardy. Clausewitz criticized Napoleon for taking logistical risks in 1812 with his Grande Armée on its march to Moscow. Clausewitz, who was with the Russian army during the campaign, stressed that the master's failure was a major contribution to the French disaster in Russia. Had Napoleon adopted "more precaution and better regulations as to subsistence, with more careful consideration of the direction of his marches, which would have prevented the unnecessary and enormous accumulation of masses on one and the same road, he would have obviated the starvation which attended his advance from its outset, and have preserved his army in a more effective condition." Clausewitz continued, "If Wilna, Minsk, Polozk, Witebsk, and Smolensko, had been strengthened with works and sufficient pallisades, and each garrisoned with from 5000 to 6000 men, the retreat would have been facilitated in more than one respect, especially in the matter of subsistence . . . If we consider that the army would also have both reached and quitted Moscow in greater force, we may conceive that the retreat would have lost its character of utter destruction."[12]

I would not dream of ranking Andrew Jackson anywhere near Bonaparte, although it must be said that Jackson's generalship is often underrated. But the criticism of Jackson overlooks realities peculiar to the man, the system of supply and transport then in use, and, most important of all, the troops he had to wage the campaign with.

Jackson was still bedridden, recovering from his terrible wounds, when the news of Fort Mims arrived. When he mounted and rode south to war he was pale and weak, one arm still in a sling. He had hardly time to prepare himself for the rigors of campaigning, much less oversee the detailed planning that in the best of all possible worlds should have been done. Flour and suitable corn were in very short supply in Tennessee. A hard-charging governor might have made a difference, but Willie Blount was not that man. John Coffee gauged him correctly when he wrote, "I fear very much the energies of our Governor." In addition, the commissary system in those days rested solely on private contractors, and the company hired to supply the army, Read, Mitchell & Company, should have had several months' notice for the gathering of provisions and supplies. But no one could have anticipated the bombshell of Fort Mims that aroused the warlike passions of Tennesseeans.[13]

Those passions provide the key to the necessity for immediate action. If one meant to conquer the Creeks and move on to cleanse the stables with the fighting men available, militia and volunteers, their passions had to be taken advantage of immediately, lest they cool while the humdrum activities of the commissariat moved at measured pace. These part-time citizen soldiers proved the truth of Franklin's maxim of idle men being "mutinous and quarrelsome." The ever-present propensity of militia on campaign to become unruly, disobedient, even mutinous, when not kept active cannot be underestimated. Lolling about in camp for extended periods waiting for action was a recipe for serious trouble. That militia might not perform well in action was another problem, as we will see on more than one occasion. But to allow them to be idle invariably meant a breakdown of what little discipline they possessed and the crumbling of their morale.

As for setting up forward supply depots, who was going to move ahead of the main army and build roads and depots in the wilderness? Jackson and his men would have to do that themselves as the campaign progressed.

Jackson was not unaware of the critical nature of supply and transport. He wrote about it often and cast a wide net to find food for his troops. But the system of private contracting to supply military forces was basically flawed. Even if contractors were given enough advance notice and government loans to buy supplies, there was no guarantee that they would deliver in an expeditious manner or even meet their obligations. Jackson's aide-de-camp, Major John Reid, wrote clearly on the frustrations of commanders in the field:

"Unfortunately . . . it is a misfortune that will always continue, so long as the present mode is persisted in . . . nor did complaints on the subject cease, even to the close of the war. Great as was the evil, no adequate remedy was at hand; nor was it confined to any particular section; but in all directions, where our armies moved, were complaints heard, and their operations frustrated, through the misconduct of contractors. An advancing army, already having within its reach decided advantages, is made to halt, and to retrograde, or starve."

The only recourse for government was another exercise in frustration, with which we in the twentieth century in other contexts are all too familiar. Major Reid continued: "The remedy is to sue the contractor; and after twelve or eighteen months of law, a jury decides how far he has or has not broken his covenant. In the mean time, the government has lost the most decided advantages—advantages which, had they been secured, might have saved millions of treasure, and thousands of lives."[14]

Despite this serious roadblock, Jackson's determination to get at the enemy, and his confidence in himself, drove him where ordinary commanders would have feared to go. He arrived at Camp Blount near Fayetteville in the late afternoon of 7 October 1813, and at nine that evening he wrote to John Coffee, "I lament that on my arrival here, I did not find either so many men as I had expected, or them so well equipped. This evil however I shall endeavour to remedy as speedily as possible. . . ." His troubles on that score were far from over, but he did not tarry. On the ninth he ordered Coffee to ride with 700 men to the headwaters of the Black Warrior River, where there were believed to be several Creek towns, and reconnoiter. Two days later he wrote to Rachel, at six o'clock in the morning, "I write in great

The Creek War, 1813–1814

haste and in the Bustle of a hasty movement, owing to an express recd. from Colo Coffee this morning one o'clock." This was Coffee's letter advising Jackson of an impending Creek attack. On the thirteenth he informed Rachel, from Camp Coffee near Huntsville, "I reached this camp on yesterday. Colo. Hays no doubt advised you of my sudden departure from Camp Blount, we marched thirty miles in Eight hours & 20 minutes."[15]

In his reconnaissance Coffee and his mounted troops had crossed the Tennessee at Ditto's Landing (modern Whitesburg, Alabama), ten miles south of Huntsville, and ridden southwesterly deep into hostile country. He took with him a mixed-blood son of John Melton, an Irishman who had married a Cherokee and may have been a pirate on the Tennessee River. Young Melton "said he knew not the road," Coffee wrote. But Melton showed Coffee a path that the column took, and on the third day Coffee met James Russell, a scout Jackson had also ordered out on 9 October with the mission of determining Indian strength. Russell told Coffee he was on the right path and that a village across the river was the main town on the Black Warrior. Coffee was not convinced and pushed on. He came to another deserted village, where, he reported to Jackson, he "got about 100 bushels of corn, burnt the houses, and proceeded eight miles further, come to the main Black Warrirs town. . . ." The town was possibly on the site of modern Tuscaloosa,

Alabama, and if that is so it meant that by modern highway distances Coffee had led his 700 men approximately 140 miles from Ditto's Landing.[16]

The main town was also empty, with "fresh signs of One or two Indians, and no other signs." Coffee gathered more corn, "in the whole about 300 bushels . . . burnt their town or counsel house and about 50 other buildings. . . ." Coffee decided it was "not adviseable to go further in search of villages where no other spoils can be had than such as we have found, and having no pilot or even any one that ever had been in the country . . . having been two days out of rations the most of the men living on parched corn, I have determined to meet your army. . . ." In closing, Coffee "must beg that you will order provisions put in a State of readiness for my men when we come up with you."[17]

In the meantime, Jackson had crossed the Tennessee at Ditto's Landing and made camp on a high bluff, where he stayed a week, training the troops and waiting for supplies. Then a young Creek, Selocta, came into camp. He was the son of Chennabee, a friendly *mico* who had sent warriors east to serve with General John Floyd and his Georgia militia, a part of the overall campaign against the Creeks whose activities we will follow in the course of the narrative. Chennabee lived on Natchee Creek, near the present Talladega, Alabama, which will also soon become familiar to us. Young Selocta had come to urgently solicit Jackson's "speedy movement, for the relief of his father's fort, which was then threatened by a considerable body of the war party, who advanced to the neighborhood of Ten Islands, on the Coosa." This was on the eighteenth. The next day he sent off a reply to Chennabee, urging him to "hold out obstinately" and guaranteeing "I will come to your relief." He promised—and it is well that his hungry militiamen did not see this letter—that "if one hair of your head is hurt, or of your family or of any who are friendly to the whites, I will sacrifice a hundred lives to pay for it. Be of good heart, & tell your men they have nothing to fear." Then, true to his nature, Jackson did not hesitate. That same day the army marched.[18]

But to his astonishment he discovered that the private contractor was unable to supply him on the march. Only a few days' rations were available. Jackson dismissed the contractor and appointed others, hoping for the best. For it was inconceivable to him that the campaign could stop because of the mere shortage of food. The enemy was in the field. The army must march, find him, engage him. And march it did, his aide-de-camp John Reid wrote, with considerable exaggeration, "army and baggage wagons over several mountains of stupendous size, and such as were thought almost impassable by foot passengers. . . ."[19]

The army hacked its way upriver through the roadless wilderness of the rugged north Alabama hill country, keeping close to the Tennessee. On 22 October Jackson reached a point on the south bank twenty-four miles from Ditto's Landing, where the Tennessee dipped farthest south, in the general vicinity of today's Guntersville Dam. There, at the mouth of Thompson's Creek, he built a stockaded supply depot that he named Camp Deposit, for it was here that he expected supplies could most easily come either down-river or upriver.[20]

But it was unlikely that there was much food in a "State of readiness" when Coffee's column, returned from its long scout, arrived at Camp Deposit on 24 October. That day Jackson wrote to the commander of the 7th Military District headquartered in New Orleans, Brigadier General Thomas Flournoy, a lawyer from Georgia whose historical obscurity is merited. "After having encountered every difficulty that can possibly arise from the want of Supplies, & from the ruggedness of mountains, I have at length reached this place." Then he got to the heart of the matter and revealed his keen awareness of the critical importance of logistics to a military campaign. "What I dread . . . infinitely more than the fact of the enemy, is the want of supplies. Can you, by any exertion, procure me supplies of bread stuff & have it forwarded upriver? No service you could render me would be so important, nor impose upon me so lasting an obligation."[21]

Nevertheless, the following day, 25 October, he broke camp and marched south.

Four days later, during his march to the Ten Islands of the Coosa, near modern Ohatchee, Alabama, he wrote to the governor that he had been forced to stop for a day to scrounge for "some small supplies of corn." But the governor should know that although there were terrible difficulties they were not insurmountable: "Indeed Sir we have been very wretchedly supplied. Scarcely two rations in succession have been regularly drawn. Yet we are not despondent, whilst we can procure an ear of corn a piece, or anything that will serve as a substitute for it we shall continue our exertions to accomplish the objects for which we were sent out."[22]

But what had sent him plunging with hardly any rations for six days over the rugged Raccoon and Lookout Mountains into the heart of Creek country? It was more intelligence of the enemy gathering some fifty miles south of his position on the Tennessee, brought to him by two runners sent by Pathkiller, principal chief of the Cherokee Nation and a faithful ally of the Americans who recruited warriors to serve under Jackson. He lived in Turkey Town on the Coosa River, in Cherokee County, one mile south of modern Centre, Alabama. His letter of 22 October was written by another, perhaps the mixed-blood John Lowry, since Pathkiller was illiterate and signed the letter with his mark: **X**. It contained the "substance of a Talk I had with two of the hostile Creeks who were sent as messengers from the alabama warrior," who was probably Peter McQueen. Pathkiller wrote that a Creek army had been raised and "three nights ago . . . had crossed the coosee river and the[y] would take the musle shoal path . . . and on the return of the army, they Intended to attack old Chenibee and I am advised to be causious how I acted."[23]

Pathkiller was singularly unimpressed by the warning given him. He told Jackson that "about fifteen or sixteen of my people have arrived to Join your army, more will arrive today untill the[y] all come. . . ." He also had "spys out constantly, and send out two for Twenty four hours Tour . . . my son was one of the spys. . . . I have sent two other spys out this morning. . . ."[24]

Jackson answered immediately, thanking Pathkiller for the information, urging that he continue "constantly to keep out, as spies, some of your men, in whom you can confide," and informing him that he would break camp and "take the nearest rout to the Ten-Islands. It will give me great pleasure, if I can fall in with that party of the hostile Creeks who were sent against our frontiers. I think it will be the last of their adventures." Jackson's final sentence is another reminder for us that his own hostile intentions were directed not just at hostile Creeks: "It is time that *all* our enemies should feel the force of that power, which has indulged them so long, & which they have, so long, treated with insult."[25]

Insufficient supplies and short rations and his own debilitated health would not be allowed to stand in the way of this iron determination to punish the enemies of the Republic, all of them, and sweep them from the land. To his close friend and quartermaster, William Berkeley Lewis, he wrote on the eve of his march into hostile country, "I am determined to push forward if I have to live on acorns."[26]

"WE SHOT THEM LIKE DOGS"

As he went over the mountains to the Coosa, Jackson built a road. It would have been primitive, a quick, rough clearing of timber and underbrush to allow men and wagons to make their way. Near Ten Islands on the Coosa, fifty miles south of Camp Deposit, he made a temporary camp. There he expected to be joined by Brigadier General James White, who led the 1,000-man advance of Major General General John Cocke, commanding the troops from East Tennessee. He had been ordered by Governor Blount to merge his command with Jackson, who would then command the entire force. Jackson expected them daily, and also anticipated that Cocke would bring ample provisions with him.

A few days prior to his arrival at the site of Fort Strother, Jackson had been met by the friendly Creek *mico* Chennabee, who had with him two hostile Creek prisoners. Jackson was told that 1,000 Creek warriors were sixteen miles away ready to engage him. The information was thought to be false, and the army marched on, and indeed at that time the 1,000 proved to be a phantom Indian army. Soon, however, solid intelligence came in that thirteen miles east of Jackson's camp, at the town of Tallushatchee, were some 200 hostile warriors. Jackson turned to the formidable Coffee and his horsemen. Take 900 men, he ordered Coffee, and "attack and disperse them."[27]

With an Indian guide preceding, Coffee and his men rode four miles up the Coosa River, forded it at some fish dams, and camped. Rising very early on the morning of 4 November, Coffee rode to within a mile and a half of Tallushatchee and arrived before dawn. There he divided his force into two columns and ordered them to encircle the town "by uniting their fronts

General John Coffee (The Hermitage: Home of President
Andrew Jackson, Nashville, Tennessee)

beyond it." Masked by the night, Coffee's cavalry and mounted infantry set
out. That many men riding through the woods in the dark so close to the
town could not pass unnoticed. The enemy "began to prepare for action,
which was announced by the beating of drums, mingled with yells and war
whoops." One hour after sunrise Coffee ordered the ranger companies of
Captain Eli Hammond and Lieutenant Patterson to deploy within the circle
of horsemen, begin the action, and entice the warriors toward the waiting
host. This tactic, a feigned retreat, was not unlike that used repeatedly and
successfully by Genghis Khan's Mongol cavalry in their sweeping campaigns,
beginning in the thirteenth century, that carried them from inner Asia across
Russia into eastern Europe and south to the heartland of the Islamic Middle East and the horror of the sack of Baghdad.

Major John Reid described the action in his history. Hammond and
Patterson advanced until they came in sight of the town. Their men opened
fire. The Creek warriors "made a violent charge." The rangers retreated, the

warriors pursued. But coming upon Coffee's main body they met a general fire and were "charged in their turn." As they did so often to the whites, now the tactic was turned upon them. Nine hundred men began closing the noose. The Creeks retreated to their cabins, "where an obstinate conflict ensued, and where those who maintained their ground persisted in fighting, as long as they could stand or sit, without manifesting fear, or soliciting quarter."[28]

The warriors fought to the death, the Americans obliged them. "We shot them like dogs," wrote David Crockett, who was there.[29]

Lieutenant Richard Keith Call was sickened by the slaughter. "We found as many as eight or ten dead bodies in a single cabin. Some of the cabins had taken fire, and half consumed human bodies were seen amidst the smoking ruins. In other instances dogs had torn and feasted on the mangled bodies of their masters. Heart sick I turned from the revolting scene."[30]

Andrew Jackson wrote to Rachel, "Coffee . . . has executed this order in elegant stile. . . ." And to Governor Blount, "We have retaliated for the destruction of Fort Mims."[31]

One hundred eighty-six warriors, all that were in town, died at Tallushatchee. Coffee lost 5 killed and 41 wounded. He was upset because women and children were killed when troops ran into cabins in pursuit of warriors and killed everybody inside, but no figures were given. He returned to Fort Strother with 84 women and children as prisoners. One of the children, a ten-month-old boy lifted from the breast of his dead mother, Jackson sent to Rachel, to be brought up with their ward, Andrew Jackson Donelson. The boy, Lyncoya, lived at the Hermitage until his death from tuberculosis just before he turned seventeen.[32]

Tallushatchee showed the ability of the Americans to penetrate over rough, inhospitable terrain into Creek country and strike hard at the hostiles. The lesson was not lost on several Creek towns. But the fight at Tallushatchee also displayed a determination equal to Jackson's, that of a gallant, besieged people ready to defend to the death their native heath.

THIS "FAUX PAS OF THE MILITIA"

On the north bank of the Coosa, at Ten Islands, Jackson proceeded to build a stockaded fort with blockhouses as a supply depot and place of refuge in the event of misfortune. He named it Fort Strother. Once that was done he wanted to push on, but he would have to leave troops behind to protect his rear and any supplies that might reach him; thus he was anxious to unite with the East Tennessee troops. General White with his 1,000-man advance was only twenty-five miles away, with the friendly Cherokees at Turkey Town, also on the Coosa. On 4 November Jackson sent him an express letter urging him to come forward and to bring with him all the supplies he could get his hands on. But to wait for White meant an idle militia army, which had always led to trouble as the men, who lacked the constraints on behavior of disciplined regulars, grew bored and chafed at camp duties and what they considered petty restraints on their freedom to do what they wished. The difficulties of leading militia had driven officers wild with frustration from the earliest days. The Reverend Joseph Doddridge, born in 1769, grew up on the Pennsylvania and Virginia frontiers and left one of the best descriptions of this thankless duty, and his words will prepare us for Jackson's coming travails. The officers "could advise but not command. Those who chose to follow their advice did so to such an extent as suited their fancy and interest. Others were refractory and thereby gave much trouble. These officers would lead a scout or campaign. Those who thought proper to accompany them did so, those who did not remained at home. Public odium was the only punishment for their laziness or cowardice. There was no compulsion to the performance of military duties, and no pecuniary award when they were performed." Yet in the absence of a large standing army, which the nation neither wanted nor could afford, the militia in Doddridge's time and Jackson's, and for decades to come, necessarily made up the bulk of American forces for frontier conflicts and full-scale war.[33]

On the seventh, Jackson sent another courier off to White with yet another request to hurry, for he wished to leave White and his men at Fort Strother while he marched on. He did not then know that on the morning of the same day, about thirty miles south of Fort Strother, Red Eagle and 1,000 Creek warriors had surrounded the friendly Creek town of Talladega, on the site of the present town of the same name. According to Albert Pickett, the early historian of Alabama, the siege was so tight that it seemed nobody could get through the lines. But the story was passed down that a warrior slipped through the lines of besiegers wearing the skin of a large hog, "grunting and apparently rooting, until he slowly got beyond the reach of their arrows. Then, discarding his swinish mantle, he fled with the speed of lightning to Jackson. . . ." Another early writer declared the story "all a hoax," which seems to happen to good stories with alarming regularity. But somebody, somehow, got through, for Jackson's aide, Major John Reid, wrote that on the same evening a "runner arrived from Talladega" with the news and said the hostiles were "in great numbers, and would certainly destroy it, unless immediate assistance could be afforded." Jackson later wrote to Rachel that the runner arrived at five o'clock in the afternoon and informed him that the hostiles "had there collected first to destroy the creeks forted there and next to give me battle." Telling Jackson that was like waving a red flag in front of a fighting bull. And he could ill afford not to go the immediate relief of imperiled allies. Had he not promised Chennabee? There was no sign of General White and his column, so he sent a messenger to meet him and guide him to Fort Strother, to "protect it in his absence."

Then, never one to vacillate, Jackson marched at midnight.[34]

He left the sick and wounded and the baggage and a small garrison to protect them until White's arrival. His force consisted of 1,200 infantry and 800 cavalry and mounted infantry and probably about 20 Cherokee allies. They crossed the Coosa one mile above Fort Strother, a movement that took several hours, for the river at that point was 600 yards wide, its bed uneven and strewn with rocks. Each mounted man took one foot soldier behind him, and then some 400 horses had to be sent back across the river for the rest of the infantry.

The march discipline of this self-taught, backwoods general should be of interest to us, for more than one white army marching in long, straggling columns had been surprised and cut to pieces in the wilderness. Jackson, wrote Major Reid, "used the utmost circumspection to prevent surprise; marching his army, as was his constant custom, in three columns, so that, by speedy manoeuvre, they might be thrown into such a situation, as to be capable of resisting attack from any quarter." What Reid meant was that the army could quickly form a square upon command, thus presenting a front to every side. In this manner the army marched toward Talladega and "on the night of the 8th lay within 6 miles of the enemy."

Into the night Jackson sent three scouts, two Indians and a white man who had long been a Creek captive and was now acting as Jackson's interpreter. They returned from their dangerous mission about eleven o'clock with news that Red Eagle's warriors were "posted within a quarter of a mile of the fort, and appeared to be in great force; but they had not been able to approach near enough to ascertain either their numbers, or precise situation."[35]

Not an hour later, to Jackson's utter consternation, a runner from Turkey Town brought a bombshell from General White.

"My dear Genl.

"I was on my march to meet you at the Ten Islands when I recd. a positive order from Majr. Genl. Cocke to alter my rout & form a junction with him near the mouth of Chatuga, which I hav done. And am sorry so many disappointments have taken place, that our junction has not sooner been formed. I presume Genl. Cocke will in future confer with you he having taken the command."[36]

Major Reid described Jackson's reaction to White's letter as one of "astonishment and apprehensions. . . ." But had Jackson seen General Cocke's letter to White his fury would have been terrible to behold. Cocke wrote: "I understood that General Jackson had crossed the Coosa and had an engagement with the Creeks. I called a council of the officers here. I stated the case—put the question. 'Shall we follow General Jackson?' which was decided unanimously in the negative. The next question. 'Shall we cross the Coosa here, and proceed to the Creek settlements on the Tallapoosa?' which was unanimously decided in the affirmative. I want the East Tennessee troops together. I leave it to your discretion whch side of the Coosa you come up; but you must form a junction with me. It is the unanimous wish of the officers and men also. if we follow Gen. Jackson's army we must suffer for supplies, nor can we expect to gain a victory. Let us, then, take a direction in which we can share some of the dangers and glories of the field."[37]

At least two historians, James Parton in the nineteenth century and Robert Quimby in the twentieth, have defended Cocke on the ground that lack of supplies in both armies made a junction unwise, and that this was the reason for Cocke's decision to recall White. Or as Parton put it, why "add

twenty-five hundred hungry men to twenty-five hundred starving men"?
On the face of it, the argument appears irresistible, for the want of supplies
in both armies was real. But take a second look at Cocke's words. He mentions the subject of supplies only once while reiterating his primary concern: keeping the East Tennessee troops together and leading them to
victory. Reading Cocke, then sniffing the air, one catches the unmistakable
stench of Tennessee sectionalism.[38]

The irresponsibility of Cocke's design is not really surprising, being yet
another example not uncommon in those times of militia officers doing as
they pleased, even though they might jeopardize the common cause. In this
case, had a commander other than Andrew Jackson suffered Cocke's outrageous behavior the campaign against the Creeks might have ended before it
had hardly begun.

Determined to persevere despite General White's withdrawal, fearful that
somehow the enemy before him might slip away and attack Fort Strother,
Jackson decided to seek battle without delay. By four o'clock on the morning of 9 November 1813 the army was in motion. Four hundred yards in
front of the main force Colonel William Carroll led a company of artillerists
armed with muskets, two companies of riflemen, and one company of spies.
His orders were to start the action, but then "to fall back on the centre." The
main force of infantry marched in the usual three columns, and behind them
came the cavalry, also in three columns, with flankers out on both sides. By
7:00 A.M. they had arrived within a mile of the enemy and deployed into
order of battle. Two hundred fifty cavalrymen under Lieutenant Colonel
Robert Henry Dyer (ca. 1774–1826) took position in the rear of the center
as a reserve. The rest of the cavalry and the mounted infantry were ordered
to advance on both wings and, as Coffee had done at Tallushatchee, encircle
the enemy by "uniting the fronts of their columns, and keeping their rear
rested on the infantry, to face and press towards the centre, so as to leave
them no possibility of escape." The infantry was ordered to advance by companies, General William Hall's (1775–1856) brigade on the right, General
Isaac Roberts's (1761–1816) brigade on the left.[39]

The advance continued. For the first time in his life, Andrew Jackson
was about to command troops in battle.

About one hour after deployment, Major Reid wrote, Colonel Carroll's
van "received a heavy fire, which they instantly returned with much spirit."
Carroll, after forcing out the Indians who had fired on him from their place
of concealment, followed orders and moved his command back toward the
center. The warriors, "screaming and yelling hideously," charged in the direction of General Roberts's brigade. Their numbers and yells panicked a few
companies, which "fled at the first fire." Jackson, who had posted himself
properly, where he could see the action and exert command and control,
sent an order by a staff officer to Lieutenant Colonel Edward Bradley (d.
1829), commanding 1st Regiment, Volunteer Infantry, to move his regiment
into the breach. Incredibly, Bradley declined. He had occupied a hill and
refused to move from it until attacked by the enemy. Jackson then ordered

Colonel Dyer's reserve to dismount and engage the charging warriors. Although there were at least "three indians for one white man," Dyer and his men "met them like Bull dogs," wrote Jackson, who was eight yards from the action, "and at two fires repulsed them killing 27 on the spot." The companies that had fled took heart and rejoined the line.[40]

The action then became general. The Indians went from one part of the closing American lines to another. They were repulsed by the mounted infantry. But Colonel Bradley's obstinancy, if that is what it was, had left a hole in the circle. And Lieutenant Colonel John Allcorn, commanding a regiment of volunteer cavalry, had circled too wide and left, reported Major Reid, "a considerable space between the infantry and the cavalry." Through these gaps most of the warriors fled to the hills three miles away, where "pursuit and slaughter" ended.[41]

Had the circle been closed, the Creek War might have ended at Talladega. Jackson was chagrined at the escape of the bulk of the enemy's force. But he was also exultant. The siege had been lifted; 299 Red Stick warriors lay dead on the field, and the rest were in disarray and fleeing for their lives. Well might he praise Colonel Carroll's advance, on whom "too much praise cannot be bestowed . . . for the spirited manner in which they commenced and sustained the attack," nor upon Colonel Dyer's reserve "for the gallantry with which they met and repulsed the enemy." Despite the failings of a few and the "faux pas of the militia," he was right to report that "officers of every grade, as well as privates, realized the high expectations I had formed of them, and merit the gratitude of their country."[42]

He must also have been pleased with his own "rookie" performance as a combat commander. He had moved through hostile country ready for action; with adaptations he had wisely used Coffee's tactic at the Tallushatchee encirclement; he had seen his amateur troops execute the maneuver well, if not flawlessly; and at the moment of crisis he himself, in the heat of the action, had acted quickly and coolly to restore his line. And his own casualties were only fifteen killed in action and eighty wounded, several of whom later died. All of this in an endeavor notoriously susceptible to things going wrong, beyond the control of the best commanders, which suggests that in this action luck, that essential ingredient marking all successful generals, had also been on his side.

But there was still that nagging problem we call logistics that would not go away. Everybody was hungry. From the grateful Creeks of Talladega, who would certainly have perished had not Jackson and his men come to their rescue, Jackson bought with his own money what "they could spare, from their scanty stock" and gave it to the soldiers who, wrote John Reid, "were almost destitute." Jackson wrote to Rachel upon his return to Fort Strother, saying that "we were out of provisions, and half starved for many days. and to highten my mortification when we returned here last evening had not one mouthfull to give the wounded or well; but that god that fed moses in the wilderness in the night brought us a partial Supply. a small quantity of meat and meal was brought in by the contractor. we had been fed on parched corn half our time one third fasted, and about a third had bread & beef. I hope for better times."[43]

He would hope for longer than he probably thought. He was on the brink of one of the great crises of his career. He was terribly worn by the debilitating effects of dysentery and wounds. He felt the weight of a responsibility that most would be unable to bear.

He confessed to Rachel, "My mind for want of provision is harrassed. My feelings excoriated with the complaints of the men."[44]

Chapter 15

─∞∞∞─

MUTINY

"YOU SAY YOU WILL MARCH. I SAY BY THE ETERNAL
GOD YOU SHALL NOT MARCH . . ."

There now occurred a series of episodes that verge on comic opera but drove the general to distraction. Upon the army's return to Fort Strother on the evening of 11 November, the men found that no fresh supplies of food had arrived. There were some cattle captured from the Creeks and purchased from the Cherokees, and the animals were slaughtered. Jackson took for himself and his staff only the offal, which had been thrown away when the steers were butchered, and of which Major Reid wrote, "Tripes, however, hastily provided in a camp, without bread or seasoning, can only be palatable to an appetite very highly whetted; yet this constituted, for several days, the only diet at headquarters, during which time the general seemed entirely satisfied with his fare."[1]

Not so the men. They grumbled and plotted. Discontent and homesickness spread. According to Major Reid "a few designing officers, who . . . hoped to make themselves popular" not only encouraged but took part in whisperings and murmurings and meetings in tents to discuss grievances, all of which led to a determination "to abandon the camp." Supplies trickled in, but were not sufficient to quell a rising movement among the men to take matters into their own hands. Several militia officers submitted petitions to Jackson urging that he march the entire division back to the settlements in order to meet the provisions being forwarded and to allow the men to outfit themselves properly for the campaign. Jackson was absolutely opposed. He would never have returned to Fort Strother after Talladega if General White had shown up with his 1,000 men, he would have pushed on from Talladega, deeper into Creek country in order to bring the main Red Stick force to bay. He used every conceivable argument to convince the army to remain in the field, from dubious promises that provisions were on the way and expected daily, to stern calls to duty and honor.[2]

243

But words would not dissuade them. Learning that the militia intended to march home, that morning Jackson deployed the volunteers in front of the men. Faced with force, the militia returned to camp. The following day there occurred what Major Reid described with admirable restraint as "a singular scene." It had, in fact, elements of comedy and madness. The volunteers who the day before had stopped the militia from going home now decided they would go home, whereupon the militia answered Jackson's call to turn back the volunteers, who returned in "peace and quietness to their quarters." Major Reid speculated that one reason for the militia action was to pay back in kind those "who had so lately thwarted their own" desires. But there continued what Jackson described as a "turbulent & mutinous disposition" that led him to assemble a meeting of his officers and address them. He praised their achievements and extolled their patriotism, sympathized with their situation, and spoke of provisions that he expected the next day. He also reminded them that to quit now after important victories would have "dreadful consequences." And what of the wounded who cannot be moved? Were they to be abandoned? Was the army so bereft of humanity that it would even consider leaving behind "our brave, wounded companions . . . ?" He reminded them, "To be sure, we do not live sumptuously; but no one has died of hunger, or is likely to die. . . ." Which was quite true. Major Reid felt that the men's sufferings, although severe, "were by no means so great as they themselves represented. . . ." If they were really starving, staring death in the face, they would have begun to eat their horses, and it never came to that.

Jackson concluded without bombast or hyperbole, simply but eloquently:

> I have no wish to starve you, none to deceive you . . . if supplies do not arrive in two days, we will all march back together, and throw the blame of our failure where it should properly lie; until then, we certainly have the means of subsisting; and if we are compelled to bear privations, let us remember that they are borne for our country, and are not greater than many—perhaps most armies have been compelled to endure. I have called you together to tell you my feelings and my wishes; this evening, think on them seriously; and let me know yours in the morning.[3]

The next morning the officers of the volunteers announced their decision that the army should march back immediately, but the militia officers had decided to give Jackson his two days. Jackson compromised by ordering General William Hall to march his volunteer brigade back to Fort Deposit, resupply it, then escort the provisions coming on to Fort Strother. But one of Hall's two regiments, feeling challenged by the militia decision to stay, said they, too, would stay on. So the matter was temporarily settled. Jackson did not like what he had been forced to do, and only spoke of his feelings to his confidants: "I was prepared to endure every evil but disgrace; and this, as I never can submit to myself, I can give no encouragement to in others."[4]

The two days passed, without the appearance of supplies, but from at least one quarter good news arrived. A letter carried by a slave of an old Scots trader named Robert Grierson arrived from Hillabee, a Creek town about sixty miles southeast of Fort Strother. The Creeks of Hillabee had been violent hostiles, Grierson informed Jackson, and had committed "outrageous depredations on me and my family for five months past," including burning his house and possessions and murdering one of his mixed-blood sons. But Talladega had changed their minds, and they had come to Grierson "begging me to offer to your Excellency terms of pacification with the United States. The glorious action you obtained" at Talladega "has such a good effect on their passions" that "the Hillabees from this day forever offer to lay down their arms, and to join in peace and amity with the United States of America, & ever to evade every hostile measure that may be offensive to the interest and peace of the said United States Government; together with any other proposition your Excellency may see cause to enjoin them to."[5]

Jackson replied immediately upon receipt of Grierson's letter. His was the stern position of the victor. He would demand "indubitable proof of their sincerity. Let all those who were lately our enemies & now wish to become our friends" return all prisoners and property taken from "whites or friendly Creeks. Let them deliver up all Instigators of the present war" and "meet me on my arrival with a flag and furnish my army with such provisions as they have to spare." But a further proof of sincerity was demanded: "Let them unite their forces with mine in prosecuting the war against those who still hold out & then they may expect my hand in friendship. The terms upon which a final peace will be granted them will greatly depend upon their conduct in the meantime." Jackson announced his intention "to carry a war of destruction through every part of the Creek nation that remains unfriendly," and ended with a solemn and frightening promise: "I will shew them what kind of reliance is to be placed on these prophets & those who instigated this war. Long shall they remember Ft. Mims in bitterness and tears."[6]

Governor Blount thought Jackson's reply "very good," but suggested attaching other conditions that reveal the sweeping intentions of the frontier people, "to wit, that we shall at any time in future be at liberty to navigate their rivers unmolested, to improve the beds of these rivers, build places of deposit for produce, Garrisons, etc; and open roads through their country and travel them without passports, just as we do thro' our own settlements." Which meant that in fact, if not in law, Creek country would become at the very least an American dependency.[7]

But not until he was able to set things right with his victorious but increasingly rebellious army could Jackson continue to punish the enemy with "bitterness and tears." Time had run out, he had to make good on his promise. But he did not want to abandon Fort Strother to the Creeks. Major Reid reported that in his despair he called out, "If only two men will remain with me, I will never abandon this post." Whereupon Captain John Gordon (1763–1819), in civilian life a hotel operator and merchant, in war the commander of a company of scouts, responded, "You have one, general, let us look if we can't find another," and immediately began with the help of Jackson's staff to raise volunteers to the number of 109.[8]

Jackson marched out of Fort Strother that day, 17 November, with the rest of the army. But he knew something the troops did not know. He had made quite clear to them that if they met supplies on the way they would turn about, return to the fort, and continue the campaign. And lo and behold, ten to twelve miles north of Fort Strother the army met 150 head of cattle and 9 wagons of flour. Jackson invited the troops to eat their fill, which they promptly did. Then he ordered them to return to the fort. The discontent began as murmurings in the lines, but it soon became something far more serious than the ageless prerogative of soldiers to express among themselves their disgust with their officers, their conditions, and a regimented life that civilian soldiers despise. One company, oblivous to orders, began marching north, Jackson was told. He immediately pursued them.

About a quarter of a mile ahead he came upon General Coffee and a few soldiers and some of his staff. He formed them in a line across the road. If the mutineers continue to march, he ordered, shoot them. The sight of Jackson tall on his horse and a solid line of men across the road with arms at the ready "threw the deserters into affright, and caused them to retreat precipitately to the main body," Major Reid wrote. It is also reasonable to speculate that Jackson had a few things to say to them. "His ability in swearing," wrote James Parton, "amounted to a talent. Volleys of the most peculiar and original oaths, ejected with a violence that can not be imagined, scared and overwhelmed the object of his wrath. Aware of his powers in this respect, he would feign a fury that he did not feel, and obtain his ends through the groundless terror of his opponents." On this occasion, however, if he did explode, I think we can infer that his fury was real.[9]

The crisis apparently over, Jackson left Major Reid writing dispatches, returned to the main body, and rode alone among the men. And discovered that the matter had not ended. It was, in fact, worse. The entire brigade had decided to go home. Jackson snatched a musket and placed himself, alone, on the road in front of the mutinous troops. His left arm was still in a sling, so he had to rest the barrel on the neck of his horse, the muzzle pointed directly at the front line of sullen soldiers. He yelled at them. "You say you will march. I say by the Eternal God you shall not march while a cartridge can sound fire."[10]

General Coffee and Major Reid galloped up and took post beside him. Two companies were gathered behind Jackson and ordered to fire when he fired. Once more the mutineers looked into the blazing eyes and terrible countenace of Andrew Jackson and like Russell Bean almost certainly saw "shoot" should they cross him. Once again that remarkable will to proceed against all odds prevailed. The brigade backed off, and agreed to return to the fort. Major Reid believed that if it not been for Jackson "at this critical moment, the campaign would for the present have been broken up, and would probably never have been re-commenced."[11]

"MILITIA BECOMES RESTIVE ON LYING AT ONE PLACE"

With the crisis apparently ended and the troops on their way back to Fort Strother, Jackson went on to Fort Deposit and then to Ditto's Landing. His logistical problems had to be corrected lest the entire enterprise be ruined. For that to happen Jackson felt he had to meet with his contractors and impress upon them in his own inimitable style the urgency of the matter and the necessity for regularity in the system. On the way he wrote to General Cocke of the East Tennessee troops to inform him of the supply situation, the urgency of Cocke joining his column with Jackson's, "600 men at least with as little delay as possible," and the news that the Creeks of Hillabee had sued for peace and the terms offered by Jackson.[12]

But it was too late for the Hillabees. Cocke's failure to coordinate operations, his quest for glory independent of Jackson, had returned the Hillabees to a hostility they would retain to the bitter end. On the day that Jackson wrote, General James White's detachment, under orders from Cocke, had attacked Hillabee at dawn. Sixty-four warriors were killed. Twenty-nine warriors and 227 women and children were taken prisoner. Cocke reported that "I did not loose one man killed or wounded," and that Jackson could rely upon his appearance at Fort Strother on 12 December, sooner if possible. James Parton maintained that when Jackson received Cocke's letter he expressed "grief and rage," but as the editors of Jackson's *Papers* point out, there is no record of this, and in his correspondence with Cocke and General Pinckney he either did not condemn the attack or ignored it. The affair presents, in fact, a minor historical puzzle.

Cocke had written to Jackson earlier, on 14 November, reporting that he had sent a detachment to destroy Hillabee. Jackson replied on the sixteenth without mentioning that expedition. He did not receive until the seventeenth Robert Grierson's letter with the Hillabee peace overture, to which Jackson replied that day. Nowhere in the record does Jackson express alarm about Cocke's raid against the Hillabees at the very time that they were offering to lay down their arms. Why? The late Robert Quimby thought it likely that Cocke's letter of the fourteenth with news of the raid, coming at a time when the mutinous behavior of the troops at Fort Strother were pressing upon Jackson, and the implications revealed with the arrival of Grierson's letter on the seventeenth—the critical day of the troop crisis—failed to register with Jackson and members of his staff. In other words, Jackson and his officers did not put two and two together. I find that unlikely. If any man could handle unrelenting pressure and keep more than one ball in the air at the same time it was Jackson. In any case, replying to Cocke on the sixteenth he took time to deliver a relatively stern if civil lecture on the injury Cocke's decision to recall White had done to Jackson's plans and thus the common cause. And immediately upon receipt of Grierson's letter of the seventeenth, seeking peace for the Hillabees, he had replied with his terms for surrender. Yet on the eighteenth, on his way to Ditto's Landing, he wrote Cocke explaining in some detail the Hillabee suit for peace and the terms he had offered. It is indeed a mystery, and one for which there seems to be no answer.

At Ditto's Landing Jackson sat down with his contractors and discussed the critical subject of supply and the necessity of introducing a regularity to the system heretofore lacking. He bore a good share of the blame because of his hasty strike into Creek country, but his successes had at least balanced his early inattention, and had he dallied, a scenario inimical to the American cause might have arisen. There are times in war when commanders must set aside the book and follow their instincts.

In Jackson's discussions with the contractors, wrote Major Reid, the "most effectual means in his power were taken with the contractors for obtaining regular supplies in the future. They were required to furnish, immediately, thirty days' rations at Fort Strother, forty at Talladega, and as many at the junction of the Coosa and Tallapoosa; two hundred pack horses and forty wagons were put in requisition, to facilitate their transportation. Understanding, now, that the whole detachment, from Tennessee, had, by the president, been received into the service of the United States, he persuaded himself that the difficulties he had heretofore encountered, would not recur, and that the want of supplies would not again be a cause of impeding his operations. He now looked forward with sanguine expectations, to the speedy accomplishment of the objects of the expedition."[13]

Jackson then set out on his return ride. At Fort Deposit he encountered a "spirit of mutiny and revolt" among the volunteers that was only "restrained by an animated address of the general," who "succeeded, once more in restoring quietness to the troops." Jackson then headed south over the Lookout and Raccoon Mountains to Fort Strother. He had left in charge there Colonel William Carroll, who wrote to him on 20 November that "very early on the morning of the 18th," the day after Jackson had left with the army, Carroll and his 109 men had begun completing the stockading of the fort, which they almost finished, for "we had no lazy man, our own safety made us industrious."

Carroll also informed Jackson of a problem of command. When Generals William Hall and Isaac Roberts returned they argued over who should command and agreed to share the position. Carroll thought Jackson had placed Hall in command, but observed that Hall "is a gentleman and would cede any thing for the benefit of the service." He also reported that a soldier had killed and scalped an Indian some distance from the fort, and that the scouts had found "where an Indian had been the night before," and that all agreed he was a Creek spy. But Carroll reported a more pressing problem than petty bickering between generals and a lone Indian who may have been a spy. "My dear Genl," he reminded Jackson, "militia becomes restive on lying at one place, have nothing to do." In order to avoid difficulty, Carroll begged "leave to suggest the propriety of stating a time to them, when you think the campaign will terminate."[14]

THE TALLAPOOSA "WAS CRIMSONED WITH THEIR BLOOD"

The overall campaign continued. While Jackson struggled with the maddening difficulties of commanding fractious militia, the Georgians had marched against the Creeks from the east. They were plagued by the same shortage of provisions and lack of a proper system of transport and supply that bedeviled Jackson. Their activities deserve attention, and will also give us the opportunity to discuss the strategy adopted by the Creeks to meet these deep thrusts into their country.

Despite his present embarrassment and inability to continue the offensive, Jackson's victories at Talladega and Tallushatchee had forced the Red Sticks to reconsider their position. According to the mixed-blood George Stiggins, their success at Fort Mims and subsequent raids had brought them "a vast number of horses" and other booty, and had made them overconfident. "They . . . concluded that the time had arrived, spoken of by Tecumseh and repeatedly confirmed by their own prophets, that there was to come a time when the Indians would have sole possession and undisturbed range of all their lands and country. No white man would dare put his foot thereon without their permission. Such was decreed by the Great Spirit, and it must come to pass and so remain."[15]

Jackson's deep strikes and his continuing presence in their country had disabused them of that comfortable opinion. And escaped slaves told them "that great preparations were being made, in men and provisions, in Mississippi and Georgia for an invasion," although it was not expected "until towards the spring of the ensuing year." George Stiggins, a twenty-five-year-old mixed blood then living in Creek country, in a manuscript probably written prior to 1836, described the strategy the Red Sticks forged to meet the threat. They "had begun to be more cautious and to think how they might evade a total annihilation of their nation, and to pay more attention to their scattered dwellings and move them so as to make their situations more dense and to better their concerns of war. They had seen the impropriety of having a war at the door of every town and the repelling of the foe to be done alone by the warriors of each town attacked. They saw that even their largest towns would be inevitably overthrown when brought singly into contact with a well equipped army of white people, that their small towns in their present local situations would fall one by one and be an easy prey to the invader, until the nation would be consumed piecemeal. So the conclusion in the debating councils of their prophets and head warriors was that certain towns should be selected and different bodies at particular places of natural strength should be formed; those different stations or encampments would be strong enough to contend with and repel any invading army that might attack them."[16]

In other words, the Red Sticks decided to concentrate their forces in a few towns where the terrain would favor them. Their strategy would face its first test when militia from Georgia under General John Floyd crossed the Chattahoochee River and marched west.

At this point we might pause and orient the modern reader by means of a current highway map of Alabama. Jackson's fights with the Red Sticks and the operations of the Georgians took place in a large, roughly triangular area bordered on the north by Interstate 59 between the Georgia line and Birmingham, Alabama; on the west by Interstate 65 between Birmingham and Montgomery, Alabama; on the south by Interstate 85 and U.S. 80 between Montgomery and Phenix City, Alabama, across the Chattahoochee from Columbus, Georgia; and on the east by the modern Alabama-Georgia line. The operations on the Alabama River, under the Mississippi militia general Ferdinand L. Claiborne, took place southwest of our rough triangle, but we will orient ourselves when we arrive at that point.

General Floyd had begun gathering his forces in Georgia in September 1813. He faced the same supply and transport problem as Jackson, and for the same reasons: failure to begin gathering supplies early and the uncertain and inefficient system of using civilian contractors. But unlike the Tennessean, Floyd remained at Fort Hawkins on the Ocmulgee River, across from modern Macon in central Georgia, until mid-November. In the meantime another Georgia militia officer, Major General David Adams, led a "Body of Five hundred mounted Infantry" to the northward and engaged the Creeks in a number of skirmishes that culminated in his burning the Red Stick town of New Yauca[17] and the disruption of their food supply. And about the first of October the Red Sticks lost more towns and crops to fire at the hands of friendly Creeks led by William McIntosh, Big Warrior, and Little Prince.[18]

Floyd finally marched for the Chattahoochee, even then admitting that "the means and risk of regular supplies is my greatest dread." On the other side of the river, below modern Phenix City, Alabama, he built Fort Mitchell as a base for supplies and to fall back upon in time of need. By late November he was approaching Autosse, one of the towns chosen by the Red Sticks as a place of defense, "where they were in the habit of organizing war parties and dispensing provisions." George Stiggins claimed that it held about 1,000 warriors. Autosse was sixty miles west of Fort Mitchell, located on the left bank of the Tallapoosa River at the mouth of Calabee Creek, about twenty miles above the point where the Tallapoosa met the Coosa near modern Wetumpka, Alabama. Floyd had 950 Georgia militia and some 300 to 400 friendly Indians. But his guide on the approach was a white man, Abram Mordecai, a Jewish trader who had been in the Autosse area for about twenty-eight years. Among his many experiences in Indian country, in 1802 he seduced a married Creek woman; in retaliation, Creek men beat him insensible, cut off his ear, destroyed his boat, and burned his cotton gin.[19]

Red Stick scouts had been following Floyd's progress and estimated that he would arrive at Autosse at noon on 29 November 1813. They got the day right, but the hour wrong. Abram Mordecai showed that he had intimate knowledge of Creek terrain as well as Creek women, and he led Floyd's army unerringly the final miles in the dark and brought them to Autosse at first light. A Creek "who had camped out for an early turkey hunt, came running into the town and announced the near approach of a large army of white people." Floyd described the morning as "calm, clear, and intensely cold; the field appeared covered with snow from the intense cold."[20]

According to Stiggins, the head man of Autosse, Coosa Micco, and one of the principal prophets, Te-wa-sub-buk-le, had been discussing for three or four hours whether to await Floyd's attack or to attack the Americans while they were on the march, when the turkey hunter ran in with the news that the whites were almost on their doorstep. They had talked too long, the decision had been taken from them. But the Indians did not panic. Stiggins wrote that "as the Indians had long expected it, they were not dismayed or surprised. There was an instant order for the infirm old men to cross the river with the women, children, and Negroes and disperse them into places of safety. . . . If they succeeded in repelling the foe, of which they had no doubt, they would send word to return."[21]

Floyd planned an attack somewhat similar to that first used by Coffee at Tallushatchee, with two columns advancing on opposite sides of the town and surrounding it. But he did not include a column to penetrate the center and then feign a retreat in order to draw the Creeks in a charge against waiting guns. Nevertheless, it was a good plan. The Creek allies were directed to cross the Tallapoosa and block any attempt at escape in that direction. Then began the hitches that one can expect in battle.[22]

As the sky grew lighter Floyd saw to his surprise that a second town lay about five hundred yards below Autosse. Why hadn't Abram Mordecai told him of it? Was it a new village? Whatever the case, Floyd quickly modified his plan. He directed his left column to extend its advance so as to encompass the lower town as well as Autosse. But the area was too large, the troops too few. Then the friendly Creeks, who by then should have been across the Tallapoosa, began falling back on the main body. River too deep, water too cold, they said. Pickett is so unkind as to suggest that "fear, in all probability, was the main cause," but also admits that the Creeks from Coweta under McIntosh fought bravely upon rejoining the main force.

It was a hard fight marked by heavy fire. James Tait, who was there, wrote, "Then, for the first time, was heard to resound on the remote banks of the Tallapoosa the dreadful noise of contending armies." John Floyd told his daughter that "the rolling pillars of smoke issued by the devouring flames preying on the savages' dwellings, in addition to the columns produced by the regular discharge of our artillery and the lighter sheets, produced by the discharge of small arms, were in various figures fantastically floating in the air." Their horses were shot from under Floyd's two aides. Floyd caught a round in a kneecap. The warriors of Autosse pressed forward, advancing on the Americans. The American artillery had been unlimbered, infantry was readied for the charge, and in the end it was grapeshot and bayonets that decided the issue. The cannons boomed. The infantry charged. The Creek line broke. A leading Red Stick, Old Tallassee King, mounted and waving a war club, tried to rally the warriors. He was swept from his horse by grapeshot and killed. Another important leader, Autossee King, was also killed.[23]

A runner from the lower town reached Coosa Micco and told him that Te-wa-sub-buk-le was dead and his warriors in retreat. "On hearing this," Stiggins wrote, "Coosa Micco mounted his horse and sped to the lower-town warriors to try to repair the damage. But the cause was scarcely retrievable; the greater part of them were retreating. . . . They were in a panic after they had been charged by the horsemen. Coosa Micco rallied and stopped some of them," but they were unwilling to close with the Americans. Coosa Micco then tried to turn the American left flank at the rear, "hoping to cause the warriors to rally and fight." But the Americans always presented a solid front. The warriors ran for the canebrakes. Stiggins wrote that this convinced Coosa Micco "that he was whipped and overcome. He himself was badly wounded in two places from bullets and chopped across the cheek by a sword, and his horse shot through the neck and body. Being very faint from loss of blood, Coosa Micco dismounted at length and went into the reed brake and gave up Autosse town to the conquerors."

The warriors fled to thickets and canebrakes and into the caves in the bluffs overlooking the river. Massive American fire was directed at the warriors taking refuge on the bluffs. The Tallapoosa, wrote Floyd to his daughter, "was crimsoned with their blood."[24]

The Red Stick old men, women, and children who had been hidden in the woods were not taken, but they were seen by Floyd, "as thick below the bank as fiddlers, of all sizes, perfectly naked, scampering, and screeching, in every direction." Most of the warriors escaped due to the American attempt to surround both towns and the failure of the friendly Creeks to cross the river. The Red Sticks lost about 200 dead, if you accept Albert Pickett, but according to Stiggins the "hostiles supposed that they lost probably eighty men and more than a hundred wounded." Autosse was destroyed by an artillery barrage and fire, to the number, wrote Pickett, of about four hundred buildings, "some of which were of fine Indian architecture and filled with valuable articles." George Stiggins wrote that "their complete defeat, and burning of their town, broke up the hostile settlement in the Autossees. It gave them a complete scare and set them to rambling. Many of them took up quarters in the Othlewallee camps. Some made their way with their families to inaccessible places in the swamps or the forest, and others went to Pensacola for safety among the Spaniards." But not all scattered. Many would be brought together at a new stronghold, to roll the dice again and perhaps prevail, a place not far northward at a lovely turn on the Tallapoosa called Horseshoe Bend.

Floyd lost 11 killed and 54 wounded, including himself. Once again an American army had penetrated Creek country and inflicted serious damage on the Red Sticks. Unlike Jackson, however, Floyd did not stay. As he had planned, he turned his army around and marched the sixty-odd miles back to Fort Mitchell on the Chattahoochee, where in addition to his painful and serious wound he had also to contend with those twin devils supply and transport. There we will leave him, for it will be another two months before the Georgians reappear. We now move on to the American column coming up from the south, along the river called Alabama.

"NOW FOR IT, BIG SAM"

It should not surprise us to learn that the southern column was also short of supplies. But that was not its only problem. Operations in lower Alabama and Mississippi were plagued by wounded feelings and a military turf war. Brigadier General Thomas Flournoy—to whom, we recall, Jackson had written pleading for supplies—was a regular army officer and commander of 7th Military District with headquarters in New Orleans. His district included the Mississippi Territory and the states of Louisiana and Tennessee. Unfortunately, the Creek nation, which extended into much of western Georgia, overlapped Flournoy's district and 6th Military District commanded by Major General Thomas Pinckney with headquarters in Charleston, South Carolina. If that were not enough to contend with, Flournoy, a brigadier general, was outranked by a militia general operating in his district with whom we are well acquainted—Major General Andrew Jackson. That would simply not do.

Even under the best of circumstances it is foolish, to say the least, to try to run a war with a dual command. Given Flournoy's personality and the communications nightmare then existing, to pursue the Creek War in such a manner was an invitation to disaster. Secretary of War John Armstrong solved both problems by leaving Brigadier General Flournoy in place and in command of every aspect of his district except prosecution of the Creek War. That he turned over to Major General Pinckney, who would command all American armies in the field. Since the British were tightly blockading the Atlantic and Gulf Coasts, and Creek country was too dangerous for couriers, messages from Washington to Flournoy had to go overland through Tennessee to the Mississippi and then downriver to New Orleans. Thus General Flournoy did not know that Pinckney had been given responsibility for the war when he made his own plans to send a force against the Creeks.[25]

The commander of the southern column was a militia officer, Brigadier General Ferdinand Leigh Claiborne, whom we met in connection with the disaster at Fort Mims. He was the brother of another man we have met and who will later figure again in our tale, the governor of Louisiana, William Charles Cole Claiborne. General Claiborne's motley force of some 1,000, including militia, volunteers, and 150 Choctaw warriors, marched from St. Stephens on 12 November and headed eastward for a point on the Alabama River called Weatherford's Bluff. It was during this march that there occurred an incident that bears telling. Its main protagonist was Captain Samuel Dale (1772–1841), whose contributions to the westward movement have been overlooked, for like James Robertson he lacked a John Filson, without whom Daniel Boone might have become the subject of footnotes.

Sam Dale, as he was widely known, was born to Scotch Irish parents in Rockbridge County, Virginia. His father was of a wandering disposition and moved first to the Clinch River on the frontier in Washington County, where he engaged in the border fighting of the time; and from there in 1784 to another frontier farm in the neighborhood of Greensboro, Georgia, approximately sixty-five miles east of modern Atlanta. The Dales and their eight children were forced to leave their farm and take refuge in Carmichael's Station, which was fiercely attacked by Creeks. About this time both parents died. Leaving his brothers and sisters on the farm, and a "steady old man in my place on the farm," Sam Dale joined a Captain Foote's "troop of horse" and was engaged in several actions toward the end of 1794, in which, wrote Pickett, he "displayed those traits which so distinguished his subsequent career—vigilance, perseverance, energy, and dauntless courage."[26]

Dale provided us with a brief but clear word picture of the mounted frontier irregular of those days: "our accoutrements were a coonskin cap, bearskin vest, short-hunting shirt and trowsers of homespun stuff, buckskin leggins, a blanket tied behind our saddle, a wallet for parched corn, coal flour, or other chance provision, a long rifle and hunting-knife."[27]

Another man who knew Dale well, Thomas S. Woodward, left a capsule description of his character: "he was honest, he was brave, he was kind to a fault, his mind was of the ordinary kind, not well cultivated, fond of speculation and not well fitted for it; a bad manager in money matters and often embarrassed . . . was very combative, always ready to go into danger; would hazard much for a friend and was charitable in pecuniary matters, even to those he looked down upon as enemies." For those who consider the terms *frontiersman* and *Indian-hater* synonymous, Woodward must disappoint, for he states that although Dale "knew very little about Indian character," he "entertained a good feeling for that persecuted people. So soon as he had an enemy in his power he was done, and would sympathize with and for him, and at times would cry like a child."[28]

Thus we see that Sam Dale had qualities vital for a successful Indian-fighter, but none that led to success in politics or the marketplace.

Dale became a trader among the Creeks and Cherokees and a guide for migrant parties going to the Mississippi Territory. He established a trading house in Jones County, Georgia. As we saw earlier, he claimed to have been at Tuckabatchee the night Tecumseh called upon the Creek Nation to rise against the American invaders. By the time of the Creek War Sam Dale was one of the best-known frontiersmen in the Mississippi Territory. He was in his prime then, forty-one years old, a big man, over 6 feet and some 190 pounds of bone and muscle. Big Sam, the Indians called him.[29]

The action in which Big Sam figured may seem insignificant in the larger scheme of things, but in Indian and partisan wars especially small actions involving handfuls of men are often of significance well beyond their size. This one became part of the lore of the Old Southwest, stiffened American morale in the lower Mississippi Territory when it was badly needed, and brings modern Americans, who see war at 20,000 to 30,000 feet as the norm, face to face with the reality of conquest. Let us follow, then, in all of its grim detail, the Great Canoe Fight of 12 November 1813.[30]

Dale had been ordered out by Colonel Joseph Carson to engage Red Stick war parties and drive them east of the Alabama. He had 30 Mississippi volunteers and 40 militiamen from Clarke County, now in Alabama. On 11 November they recovered two canoes that had been hidden in the cane by Caesar, a free black who marched with them. At dusk they used the canoes to cross to the east bank of the Alabama, where they camped. The next morning, 12 November, "when the sun made its first appearance over the tall canes," Dale led most of his column up the east bank. On the river the canoes stayed parallel with them. They were manned by Caesar and seven other men. Dale put nineteen-year-old Jeremiah Austill, a sinewy, erect, 6-feet 2-inch, 175-pounder, in charge of the canoes.

Austill (1794–1879), described by Albert Pickett, who knew him, as having "piercing . . . dark brown eyes," was a daring and formidable fighter. Born in South Carolina, he had spent his early years among the Cherokees at their Georgia agency, where his father, Captain Evan Austill, spent seventeen years as an official. Shortly before joining Dale's command, young Austill had proven his mettle. He had made a solo night ride of forty miles with a dispatch for General Claiborne, over what was described by a man who followed that route several decades later in daytime as "a wild, long, lonesome road." Then he turned and retraced his way with Claiborne's orders.[31]

When Dale's column reached the farm of Dixon Bailey, Sam Dale crossed in one of the canoes, searched the ground, and "discovered fresh signs of the mysterious foe, with whom he was so well acquainted." Almost as soon as Dale returned to the east bank Austill saw a canoe filled with Indians, who quickly retreated into the tall cane when Austill paddled toward them. A few minutes later some Indians on horseback charged Dale's land party, but the Americans stood fast and delivered a fire that drove them off with one killed and several wounded. Dale then ordered his men to cross to the west bank, for the cane and vines along the east bank of the river had become too thick for passage.

The ferrying took several trips. While Dale and 10 other men waited their turn they took the opportunity to make a fire for boiling beef and roasting potatoes. Just as Caesar returned in the small canoe for them, the men on the west bank cried out that Indians were approaching from the land side. Dale and the others quickly took cover under the bank of the river, from where they saw an extraordinary sight. It was described by Pickett, who interviewed at least 2 of the participants, Jeremiah Austill and Gerard Creagh. Down the river came 11 warriors in a "large flat-bottomed canoe," probably a pirogue. They were naked. Their bodies were painted in a "variety of fantastic colors, while a panther-skin encircled the head of the chief, and extended down his back. . . ." The Indians "glided gently down the river, sitting erect, with their guns before them."

The Indians on the land side had retreated, so Dale and the others turned their fire on the Indians in the pirogue, who promptly returned fire.

They lay in the bottom of the pirogue, showing only their heads as they fired. Then two of them cautiously slipped over the side and swam downstream toward the east bank, holding their guns above the water. Jeremiah Austill and James Smith immediately went in pursuit. Smith was then twenty-five, a well-proportioned man of 5 feet 8 inches and 165 pounds. He was said to be a man of "great prowess," a daring frontiersman always ready to serve in time of need.

There now occurred one of those comic reliefs that for those engaged only become funny afterward. Austill's buckskin leggings had become full of water. As he ran with Smith after the two Indians his leggings fell to his feet, tripping him, whereupon he tumbled over the bluff. Smith, meanwhile, stopped, took aim at one of the Indians in the water, and shot him in the head. The Indian rolled onto his back and sank. The other Indian gained the bank, climbed to the bluff, and ran. Austill had by then pulled up and fastened his leggings and climbed to the bluff and pursued, and almost became the victim of friendly fire. A round "passed just over his head," he told Pickett. It had come from the rifle of Lieutenant Gerard Creagh, whose vision had been obscured by the tall cane. This incident stopped Austill's pursuit of the Indian. Whether he had some choice words for Creagh is unrecorded.

While this side action was transpiring, Captain Dale called out an order for the larger canoe on the other side of the river to be manned for the purpose of capturing the rest of the Indians, who continued to float down the Alabama. Eight men jumped in and paddled for the pirogue. Getting close, seeing that the 9 Indians left were enthusiastic for a fight, they changed their minds and returned to the west bank. Pickett says this exasperated Dale, which one suspects is a mild description of Big Sam's reaction. In any case, he immediately called for volunteers to follow him and jumped down the bank and into the small canoe paddled by Caesar. Jeremiah Austill and James Smith, who had returned, were on his heels. The others wanted to go, but there was no room.

Caesar paddled toward the hostile canoe. At twenty yards the 3 white men stood to fire a volley, but only Smith's priming was dry, and he missed. Caesar kept paddling. The distance narrowed. The chief in the panther skin recognized Dale. "Now for it, Big Sam," he said. They were the only words the combatants spoke to each other. Then the canoes closed and the primitive pounding began.

The chief put his gun to Austill's breast. Austill swung at him with an oar. The chief dodged the blow and hit Austill on top of the head with his gun. Dale and Smith then brought their rifles down on the chief's head with such force, Pickett wrote, that he fell "to the bottom of the canoe—his blood and brains bespattering its sides." Dale had hit the chief so hard the stock broke from his rifle and he continued the fight with the barrel. Austill, still on his feet despite the chief's blow, quickly killed 2 warriors with his clubbed rifle and Smith did the same to 2 others. The gallant Caesar kept the canoes closely locked "with a mighty grasp," which enabled "Dale . . . and the others, to maintain a firm footing, by keeping their feet in both canoes." Caesar maintained his "mighty grasp," unable to protect himself but steadfast throughout.

The remaining Indians and the 3 frontiersmen swung at each other with abandon, while on shore Dale's command shouted encouragement. An Indian with a war club knocked Austill down. As he lay across both canoes, another Indian raised his club to deliver the death blow. But Dale, Pickett wrote, "buried his heavy rifle barrel deep in the warrior's skull." Austill got up, wrested away another Indian's club, and with it knocked the warrior into the river.

The fight was over. It could not have lasted more than a few minutes. Sam Dale, Jeremiah Austill, and James Smith, with the critical support of Caesar, had killed 9 Red Sticks in a stand-up, hand-to-hand fight. Eight of the bodies lay at their feet. As their comrades on the bank cheered "loud and long," one by one they picked up the dead warriors and "cast them into the bright waters of the Alabama, their native stream, now to be their grave," Albert Pickett recorded. Emptied of the dead, "the Indian canoe presented a sight unusually revolting—several inches deep in savage blood thickened with clods of brains and bunches of hair."

"IT WAS AWFULLY CURIOUS TO SEE A MAN AND HORSE FLY THROUGH THE AIR"

On 16 November, four days after the Great Canoe Fight, General Ferdinand Claiborne's main force arrived at Weatherford's Bluff, rafted across the river the next day, and immediately began constructing a stockaded fort, which took about ten days and upon completion was called Fort Claiborne. It was on the site of the present Claiborne, Alabama. Claiborne's operations occurred within a rough V-shaped area starting just north of Mobile, where Interstate 65 and U.S. 43 diverge, the former heading for Montgomery, the latter toward Tuscaloosa; this large area contains the Alabama River from Montgomery to its junction with the Tombigbee north of Mobile to form the Mobile and Tensaw Rivers flowing into Mobile Bay.

On the twenty-eighth Claiborne was joined by Colonel Gilbert Russell and 3rd Regiment of U.S. Infantry, which General Pinckney had ordered General Flournoy to release to Claiborne. This increased his force to about 1,200 men. On 13 December Claiborne finally marched north along the Alabama. His goal, about one hundred miles away, was the Red Stick town of Ekonachaka, called by the whites the Holy Ground. It lay on a bend of the Alabama River about two miles north of the modern village of White Hall, which is some fifteen miles west of Montgomery.[32]

The Holy Ground was one of the most important Red Stick towns, a place of refuge and a storehouse for arms and provisions. But it also had magical powers. Had not the mixed-blood Red Stick prophet Josiah Francis so declared? It was consecrated ground, he told the people, protected all around by invisible "wizard circles" that would strike dead any white man who tried to enter. Thus spoke the prophet Josiah Francis, who, it is said, had an emergency route out of the Holy Ground—just in case.[33]

At a point about twenty miles south of the Holy Ground, Claiborne halted and built Fort Deposit. Leaving behind 100 men to guard his cannon, supplies, and the sick, lame, and lazy, Claiborne marched for the Holy Ground on 23 December. The town was well situated for defense on a high bluff overlooking the river and surrounded by wooded ravines. The approaches were fortified with stakes. Claiborne advanced in three columns. The first unit to come under fire was Colonel Joseph Carson's Mississippi Territory Volunteers, whereupon Colonel Gilbert Russell's regulars, 3rd U.S. Infantry, came to their support and charged with the bayonet. That broke the Creek will to fight. Colonel Carson called out to his volunteers, "Boys, you seem keen! Go ahead and drive them!" The action does not deserve to be called a battle. When the "wizard circles" failed to strike the whites dead, Josiah Francis and his followers fled by way of his escape route. Only William Weatherford (Red Eagle) and 30 warriors and some black slaves put up the semblance of a fight, and of course they were too few.

Seeing the futility of further resistance, and with no gaps in the advancing American lines, Weatherford galloped for the river on a swift gray horse named Arrow. According to his brother-in-law, George Stiggins, he rode to a bluff fifty or sixty feet above the river, let Arrow see it, then rode back thirty yards, and with the reins in one hand and his rifle in the other, touched Arrow with his spurs and off they went. "Weatherford said he seemed to go straight forward for more than thirty feet, then turned nearly head down and kept a curving flight until he struck the water. Man and horse separated long before they touched the water; then they swam ashore together, gun and all unhurt." From the opposite bank Weatherford watched as a comrade, a mixed blood named McPherson, took the same leap and also made it to shore safely. Weatherford "said it was awfully curious to see a man and horse fly through the air like a cormorant or fish eagle when he pounces on a fish."

That is the story of Red Eagle's amazing escape from the Holy Ground, and I leave it to the reader whether to accept it or reject it. William Woodward, in his *Reminiscences,* maintained that the "bluff-jumping story" was pure fiction, but Woodward was something of a killjoy when it came to good stories. The important thing is that Weatherford escaped. How he did it is irrelevant, and I shall continue to treasure my boyhood vision of Red Eagle and Arrow soaring through the air above the Alabama while pursuing Americans gaped in amazement.[34]

As at Autosse, the old men and the women and children had been hidden across the river in the woods. None was taken. The Creeks lost only 33 killed, of whom 21 were Indians and 12 black slaves of the Creeks. Because one American unit failed in its assigned mission to block the way, all the other warriors escaped, with their wounded. Claiborne lost one man killed and 20 wounded. It had been a skirmish, not a battle. But important, nonetheless. Another American army had marched into the heart of Creek country and defeated a Red Stick force and sent it fleeing. Another Creek town and those in the surrounding area would go up in flames after being plundered. Claiborne gave the Holy Ground to the Choctaws to sack. The whites found two things that infuriated them. In the middle of the public square was a tall pole on which hung 300 white and mixed-blood scalps taken at Fort Mims. Men and women, infants, the old and the young. The other was a letter from González Manrique, the governor of Pensacola, to the chiefs of the Creek Nation. The chiefs had offered to take and burn Mobile. No, the governor wrote, Spain wanted to recover the city without damage. "I hope that you will not put in execution the project which you tell me of, to burn the town: Since those houses and properties do not belong to the Americans but to the Spaniards." He also congratulated them on their victory at Fort Mims.[35]

General Claiborne, victorious, nevertheless found himself in the same fix as other American generals in the Creek War. The army had run out of food. Terms of enlistment were soon to expire. The army returned downriver to Fort Claiborne, and in January 1814 the men were mustered out and went home. Colonel Gilbert Russell and his 3rd Infantry stayed on, but General Flournoy, in a snit over being superseded by General Pinckney, either refused to cooperate or delayed cooperation. Colonel Russell's design of another major offensive by way of the Black Warrior and Cahaba Rivers floundered for that and other reasons, not the least of which was getting lost and running out of provisions deep in Indian country. On their retreat to Fort Claiborne, the troops were forced to eat several of their horses to survive. Colonel Russell offered his best horse to the common pot.[36]

There was now only one general and his army remaining in Creek country, and by the standards of reasonable people they should not have been there. Floyd and Claiborne had done good work, but neither possessed the demonic will that drove Jackson. His position, however, had grown even worse than when we left him, and it is now time to return to a highly irritated Old Hickory and his equally ill-tempered army.

"DEATH BEFORE DISHONOR"

Upon Jackson's return to Fort Strother he found the work on the fort well done, but the troops, in Major Reid's words, had not lost "their deep-rooted aversion to further prosecution of the war." Pessimism temporarily overcame Jackson when he contemplated the attitude of his army. On 3 December 1813 he wrote to the Presbyterian preacher and missionary Gideon Blackburn, "Perhaps I was wrong in belie[ving that] nothing but death could conquer the spirits of brave men." Perhaps he was confusing them with himself.[37]

Food at that point was not a problem. "Nothing is more difficult," Major Reid wrote, "than to re-animate men who have . . . lost their spirits . . . inspire with new ardour, those in whom lately it has become extinct." Men who had used the shortage of food as an excuse to go home, "when they were no longer hungry, began to clamour, with equal earnestness, about their term of service."[38]

This was even more serious than supply shortages. The volunteers had signed up for one year. That year would be up on 10 December 1813. They contended that their time spent at home after the Natchez expedition, on call for possible service, counted as time served. Not so, said Jackson. Time served ended when they went home upon their return from Natchez and did not begin again until they were recalled to duty for service against the Creeks. In case he lost this argument, Jackson sent the ever-loyal Colonel William Carroll and his aide, Major Robert Searcy, back to Tennessee to try to raise more men for either six months or the duration of the campaign. At the same time he exhorted others to help in this endeavor. To Gideon Blackburn he revealed his intention: "by the 15th of this month at farthest I shall recross the Coosa, & recommence my operations."[39]

Jackson also urged General Cocke to join him by 12 December with 1,500 East Tennessee troops, and expressed surprise and concern "to hear that your supplies continue deficient. In the name of God what is [Barclay] McGee doing & what has he been about. Every letter I receive from the governor assures me I am to receive plentiful supplies from him, & takes for granted, that they have hitherto been regularly furnished. Considering the generous loan he obtained for this purpose, & the facility of procuring bread-stuff in E. Tennessee & transporting it by water to Ft Deposit it is wholly unaccountable that not a pound of it has ever arrived there." But Jackson assured Cocke that "I shall have beef & pork sufficient, I think, for our armies; & I have forty waggons in requisition for the transportation of bread-stuff. I have also ordered the purchase of 200 pack horses for the purpose of facilitating the conveyance.

"My contractors are directed to furnish with all practicable dispatch thirty days rations at Fort Strother—forty days at Talladega, & forty days at the junction of the Coosa & Tallapoosa." Nevertheless, he urged Cocke to pass on to McGee Jackson's requirement that he "furnish at Ft Deposit in twenty days, all the bread-stuff he can procure."

Jackson also informed Cocke that he had learned of Floyd's action at Autosse through a friendly Creek, James Fife, who had told him that the Red Sticks were successful: "if it be correct would form an additional reason for our forces being speedily united; and for a speedy movement afterwards."[40]

But the situation at Fort Strother put all plans for offensive action in abeyance. The mood had become ugly. He wrote to Rachel on 9 December, "I am sorry to say that my Volunteer infantry, in whom I had so much confidence . . . are about to disgrace themselves by a mutinous dispostion in the face of an enemy, but the officers are more to blame than the men. . . ." That evening, wrote Major Reid, General Hall had "hastened to the tent of Jackson, with information that his whole brigade was in a state of mutiny, and making preparations for moving forcibly off." Jackson reacted immediately.[41]

Hall's brigade was ordered to parade on the west side of the fort without delay. The artillery company was called out. Two cannon were loaded and primed, one in front of the brigade, one behind. The militia was deployed on a hill blocking the road to Tennessee and ordered to use force to prevent Hall's brigade from departing. Major Reid described what happened. "The general rode along the line . . . and addressed them by companies, in a strain of impassioned eloquence." He spoke of their good conduct in the past and the "esteem and applause it had secured them," but also "to the disgrace which they must heap upon themselves, their families, and country, by persisting, even if they should succeed, in their present mutiny." There was, he told them, only one way to succeed—"by passing over his body." If they did, "he should perish honourably, by perishing at his post, and in the discharge of his duty."

He finally said to them: "I have done with intreaty, it has been used long enough. I will attempt it no more. You must now determine whether you will go, or peaceably remain: if you still persist in your determination to move forcibly off, the point between us shall soon be decided. "

Nobody spoke. Nobody moved.

Jackson, Major Reid wrote, "demanded an explicit and positive answer."

Nobody spoke. Nobody moved.

Jackson ordered the gunners to light their matches. He remained in front of 1st Brigade, in the line of fire, "which he intended soon to order," wrote Major Reid.

First Brigade believed it. The murmur of "let us return" was heard along the line. Then the officers came forward to Jackson and agreed to return to their quarters.[42]

It was, he later wrote to Rachel, "a scene that created feelings better to be Judged of than expressed."[43] But it was not over. Readers who expect to hear that after this dramatic scene in the wilds of the Mississippi Territory 1st Brigade shouldered arms and marched off behind their general against the enemy will be disappointed. Jackson had faced them down, but he soon learned that their ardent desire to go home had only been postponed and that they could not be counted upon. He thereupon made the wise decision to "rid himself, as soon as possible, of men whose presence answered no other end, than to keep alive discontents in his camp." One final appeal to their pride and patriotism was read to them on the thirteenth by Major John Reid. One man, Captain Thomas Williamson, agreed to stay, and for "this act of patriotism," Jackson wrote to Rachel, "he was huted at by Colo. [Edward] Bradly," commanding officer of the 1st Regiment. Jackson thereupon issued an order to General Hall to march the brigade to Nashville and report to Governor Blount.[44]

Jackson's world seemed to be collapsing. On the twelfth General Cocke had finally marched into Fort Strother with the 1,500 East Tennessee troops. Fifteen hundred men whose terms of service, General Cocke informed General Jackson, would expire by respective units on the twenty-third and twenty-ninth of December and the fourteenth of January. Jackson wrote to Governor Blount that "they were detemined to go home the moment there times were out, and one regt. had swore that if they were marched and in front of the Indians and had their guns up with their fingers on the trickers and their times would that moment expire they would take down their guns and not fire, but march directly home." Could they possibly have made themselves any clearer? Jackson did not even bother to argue with them. Keeping Colonel William Lillard's 2nd Regiment, not due for discharge until 14 January, to help protect the fort, Jackson issued an order for the other regiments to march home without delay.[45]

A crushing disappointment was the attitude of one of the army's best units, John Coffee's volunteer cavalry. Jackson had sent them to Tennessee to get fresh horses and winter clothing. They were to return by 8 December. But in Huntsville they met General Hall's 1st Brigade of volunteers marching home and decided that they should be treated no differently. Not only did they refuse to return, they behaved in an unruly manner. Colonel Coffee, who was in Huntsville recovering from a severe illness, was mortified. He rode after his men and pleaded with them. But in vain, he reported to Jackson. "I am really ashamed to say any thing about the men of my Brigade."[46]

Of course, Jackson still had the some 600-man militia brigade commanded by General Isaac Roberts. Or did he? They had enlisted for three months. During that time they had been taken into federal service, of which the tour of duty was six months. Careful explanations of the difference had no effect on them. They had enlisted for three months, their term was up on 4 January 1814, and then they would go home. The matter was referred to Governor Blount for a decision. Blount agreed with the militia: they were not liable for service beyond 4 January, and on that day all but one company marched for home, leaving Jackson with one artillery company, two small companies of spies, and the East Tennessee regiment whose term of service expired on the fourteenth.[47]

Governor Blount's action in this matter was overshadowed by a blow he delivered that seemed to herald the end of Jackson's dream. On 22 December he wrote to Jackson that it was time to evacuate Fort Strother and abandon the campaign. It was time to come home. Since he as governor was not authorized to call up more troops, all they could do was await instructions from Washington. To do otherwise would be a "fruitless endeavour."[48]

During these months of one frustration after another, of constant tension, the specter of failure staring him in the face, did Jackson awaken every night in the wee hours of the morning, unable to fall asleep again, consumed by the awful possibilities? It is a fair speculation, given the experience of a future American commander. Following the American disaster at Pearl Harbor on 7 December 1941, Admiral Chester Nimitz was appointed commander of the Pacific Fleet with the assignment of repairing and rebuilding the fleet and leading it against the victorious Japanese navy. Nimitz told a British historian, A. L. Rowse, that "during the period of crisis and suspense, he found that he regularly woke at 3 A.M. and could not go to sleep again. He began his working day at 7 A.M., took a swim in the afternoon, went to bed regularly at 11 P.M., then woke again at 3 A.M." The morning after he received the news of the great American naval victory off Midway Island in June 1942, Admiral Nimitz "slept soundly until 9:30 A.M., when he had to be awakened. . . ."[49]

However Jackson dealt with the pressures of those months, he was not about to knuckle under to Governor Willie Blount. An ordinary general, burdened by crushing disappointments and seemingly insurmountable obstacles, in constant pain from old wounds and racked by chronic dysentery, abandoned by his political chief, would have evacuated Fort Strother and gone home. But Jackson, James Parton wrote, was "of that temper which gained new determination from other men's despair." For he was not an ordinary man. He was a man possessed. Perhaps by demons. We cannot know. But literally a man possessed by such an indomitable will to succeed that it approaches, perhaps reaches, the superhuman. He defied Blount in Alabama as he had defied Armstrong at Natchez. But in Alabama the stakes were far higher. They involved life and death. As the year 1813 drew to a close, he sat down one night and replied to Blount's advice that he throw in the towel in a letter that is one of the most remarkable documents of his career. James Parton thought it was "the best letter he ever wrote in his life. . . ."[50]

Blount's letter was a recommendation. Jackson treated it as such.

> If you would preserve your reputation, or that of the state over which you preside, you must take a straight-forward, determined course; regardless of the applause or censure of the populace, and of the forebodings of the dastardly and designing crew, who, at a time like this, may be expected to clamour continually in your ears. The very wretches who now beset you with evil counsel, will be the first, should the measures which they recommend eventuate in disaster, to call down imprecations on your head, and load you with reproaches. Your country is in danger. Apply its resources to its defense! Can any course be more plain?

Jackson used a historical incident, probably Isaac Shelby's role in the 1780 King's Mountain campaign,[51] to drive home his point: "How did the venerable Shelby act, under similar circumstances. . . . Did he wait for orders, to do what every man of sense knew—what every patriot felt—to be right? He did not; and yet how highly and justly did the government extol his manly and energetic conduct! and how dear has his name become to all the friends of their country!"

He then spelled out the governor's responsibilities.

> I consider it your imperious duty, when the men, called for by your order . . . are known not to be in the field, to see that they be brought there; and to take immediate measures with the officer, who, charged with the execution of your order, omits or neglects to do it. As the executive of the state, it is your duty to see that the full quota of troops be constantly kept in the field, for the time they

have been required. You are responsible to the government; your officer to you. Of what avail is it, to give an order, if it be never executed, and may be disobeyed with impunity. Is it by empty orders, that we can hope to conquer our enemies, and save our defenceless frontiers from butchery and devastation? Believe me, my valued friend, there are times, when it is highly criminal to shrink from responsibility, or scruple about the exercise of our powers. There are times, when we must disregard punctilious etiquette, and think only of serving our country.

How could Jackson retreat when his commanding officer, General Pinckney, "has ordered me to advance, and form a junction with the Georgia army; and, upon the expectation that I will do so, are all his arrangements formed, for the prosecution of the campaign"?

Retreat? "I will perish first. No, I will do my duty: I will hold the posts I have established, until ordered to abandon them by the commanding general, or die in the struggle—long since I have determined, not to seek the preservation of life, at the sacrifice of reputation."

Finally, he gave his political boss a lecture and a promise. You do not, he stated, defend the frontiers "by loitering on the frontiers . . . they are to be defended, if defended at all . . . by carrying the war into the heart of the enemy's country. All other hopes of defence are more visionary than dreams. What then is to be done? I'll tell you what. You have only to act with the energy and decision the crisis demands, and all will be well. Send me a force engaged for six months, and I will answer for the result, but withhold it, and all is lost—the reputation of the state, your's, and mine along with it."[52]

There he rested his case, determined to stay where he was.

He had written earlier that month to Rachel, "My heart is with you, my duty compels me to remain in the field . . . you know my motto, I know you approve of it—that is death before dishonor."[53]

Chapter 16

They "Whipped *Captain* Jackson, and Run Him to the Coosa River"

"Men . . . entirely unacquainted with the duties of the field"

On the fourteenth day of January of the New Year, 1814, the ever-loyal Billy Carroll marched into Fort Strother with about 800 recruits who had signed up for sixty days. It was the same day on which the term of service ended for the regiment of East Tennessee troops, so it meant that Jackson would not be left with only two companies of spies and the artillery company. The reader will recall that Colonel Carroll had been dispatched to Tennessee to raise men for six months' service. But the men refused to enlist for that long a period. It was sixty days or nothing. And instead of being infantry, which was wanted, they were mounted, which meant feeding two mouths instead of one—the man and his horse. But a weightier concern overcame these objections. Considering it essential to have men in the field, Carroll accepted them on their terms. Jackson was dubious, as there was no state or federal law allowing for only two months' service, but when had Jackson allowed himself to be dissuaded by, as he had written to Governor Blount, "punctilious etiquette"? And to reject them would not look good for a general who kept pleading for troops. In late December General Pinckney, writing from his field headquarters at Fort Hawkins, Georgia, although sympathizing with Jackson's situation, urged that if he had enough men Jackson should "mount temporary expeditions against such of the Enemy's Towns or settlements as are within striking distance. . . ." This is what Jackson now had in mind, a raid against the Red Sticks that would create a diversion for General Floyd's column from Georgia.[1]

265

But the new men were raw recruits. Untried, untrained, and, being volunteers, definitely undisciplined. Would one dare march them deep into hostile country? Yes, one would, if one's name was Andrew Jackson.

And he wasted no time. On 15 January, the day after their arrival, Jackson sent the volunteers across the Coosa to graze their horses. Jackson joined them the next day, he reported to General Pinckney, with the "artillery company, with one six pounder, one company of infantry of forty-eight men; two companies of spies commanded by Captains Gordon and Russell, of about thirty men each; and a company of volunteer officers, headed by General Coffee . . . making my force, exlusive of Indians, nine hundred and thirty." The little army marched on the seventeenth for Talladega, where they arrived on the eighteenth. There they were joined by 200 to 300 friendly, but badly armed, Creeks and Cherokees. The Indians, Major Reid reported, were discouraged by the small size of Jackson's force. And well they might be. Major Reid presented the situation facing Jackson briefly and clearly: "Seldom, perhaps, has there been an expedition undertaken, fraught with greater peril than this. A thousand men, entirely unacquainted with the duties of the field, were to be marched into the heart of an enemy's country, without a single hope of escape, but from victory, and that victory not to be expected, but from the wisest precaution, and most determined bravery." One authority on Jackson's campaigns has stated that it was probably the only time in the Creek War that an outnumbered American force took the offensive against the enemy. But Albert Pickett, who interviewed many of the participants, including Indian veterans, claimed that "we are enabled to state, with confidence, that the force of the Red Sticks, in these battles, did not exceed five hundred warriors, for the larger body had assembled below, to attack Floyd, while others were fortifying the Horse-shoe, and various other places." Whatever the Indian numbers, Reid was basically correct, given the unstable nature of Jackson's force, in labeling the expedition fraught with peril.[2]

But Reid concluded that despite the extreme danger "to march was the only alternative that could be prudently adopted." How else could a diversion be mounted for General Floyd, who was again in the field with his Georgia militia? Jackson had also received information that weakly garrisoned Fort Armstrong on the Coosa River in modern Cherokee County, Alabama, was in danger from hostile Creeks who were uniting their forces. That rumor was confirmed at Talladega, where he received a letter from Colonel William Snodgrass, commandant at Fort Armstrong, that the intended attack was no longer in doubt. He also received there an express from General Pinckney informing him that General Floyd would leave Coweta on the Chattahoochee and march to Tuckabatchee and establish himself. General Pinckney recommended to General Jackson, Major Reid wrote, that "if his force would allow him to do no more, that he should advance against such of the enemy's towns, as might be within convenient distance" and harass them. There was also the thought constantly in the minds of all officers, and which General Pinckney actually used as a reason

Major John Reid (The Hermitage: Home of President
Andrew Jackson, Nashville, Tennessee)

for action, that idle militia meant trouble. These were men who had to be
kept occupied, lest they become a mutinous rabble. For all of these reasons,
Major Reid insisted, if Jackson "could have hesitated before, there was now
no longer any reason to do so."[3]

One reason for Jackson's decision to plunge into the wilderness with
raw militia was not mentioned by Major Reid. That was his fiercely aggressive nature. Andrew Jackson was a fighter with an instinct for battle. I would
not use the word rash, although others have, and it is a good subject for
debate, over drinks by the fire while winter storms rage outside. Jackson
knew, to use Major Reid's words, that it was an expedition fraught with
peril. But imbued with his fighter's nature, and his supreme self-confidence,
Jackson dared that from which other men shrank. He had been doing it successfully against great odds since the war began. Why should he stop now?

On 19 January Jackson's little force left Talladega and headed in an east-
erly direction for the Tallapoosa River, "near the mouth of a creek called

Emuckfaw," where it was thought the large Red Stick force was gathering prior to advancing on Fort Armstrong. Of the troops on this march, Major Reid noted that "their ardour to meet the enemy was not abated," and he left a classic description of green troops before they tasted battle: "Troops unacquainted with service are oftentimes more sanguine than veterans. The imagination too frequently portraying battles in the light of a frolic, keeps danger concealed, until, suddenly springing into view, it seems a monster too hideous to be withstood."[4]

A "BOLD & FEROCIOUS ATTACK"

The night of the twentieth the army camped at Enitachopko, about twelve miles from Emuckfau Creek. There Jackson took stock of his situation, especially of how few of his men he could count upon in a crisis, which he later reported to General Pinckney: "Here I began to perceive very plainly how little knowledge my spies had of the country, of the situation of the enemy, or of the distance I was from them. The insubordination of the new troops, and the want of skill in most of their officers, also became more and more apparent. But their ardor to meet the enemy was not diminished; and I had sure reliance upon the guards, and upon the company of old volunteer officers, and upon the spies, in all about one hundred and twenty-five." Only 125 men of whose steadfastness he was sure. But that did not deter him.[5]

On the next morning, 21 January, the army marched toward the Tallapoosa. About two o'clock in the afternoon Jackson's spies spotted two Red Sticks and tried to catch them, but they got away. Late in the day "I fell in upon a large trail, which led to a new road, much beaten and lately traveled." It was obvious that they were close to the gathering of a large force of hostiles. A night engagement, especially with his unruly if enthusiastic volunteers, was unthinkable. Better to make a secure camp and use the darkness for reconnoitering by his skilled Indian and white spies. Choosing the best site available, on a rise overlooking Emuckfau Creek, Jackson "encamped in a hollow square, sent out my spies and pickets, doubled my sentinels, and made the necessary arrangements before dark for a night attack." The night stillness was broken about ten o'clock when a picket fired at three Indians and killed one, whose body was found the next morning. About an hour later the spies slipped out of the darkness into the camp. The Red Sticks in a large number were about three miles away, they reported, and "from their whooping and dancing, seemed to be apprized of our approach. One of these spies, an Indian, in whom I had great confidence, assured me that they were carrying off their women and children, and that the warriors would either make their escape, or attack me before day." Jackson quite wisely decided to await events on the defensive, to go on the offensive only if the Indians failed to attack in the morning.[6]

The Red Sticks hit Jackson's left flank at "dawn of day," when it was still difficult to tell friend from foe. The unit engaged was commanded by Colonel William Higgins. Jackson wrote to Rachel, "My troops tho raw met their bold & ferocious attack with firmness and undaunted resolution." General Coffee and Colonels William Carroll and James Sittler mounted and "flew to the point of attack" and encouraged and animated the men. When it became light enough "to discover and distinguish our enemies from our friends," Jackson was told that the "part of the line where the battle waxed hottest was verry much thinned being many wounded, whereupon he ordered his only reserve, "about forty raw infantry" under Captain Larkin Ferrell, to reinforce the line. Then the whole line led by Coffee charged. Jackson's Indian allies joined in. The Red Sticks were routed. The pursuit continued for two miles. Twenty-four Red Sticks were confirmed killed.[7]

Jackson then wanted to move immediately against the enemy's encampment with his whole army, but he could not march at once because he had several wounded who could not be left behind unprotected. When the attacking force returned to the line, Jackson detached Coffee with 400 men and the friendly Creeks and Cherokees to attack and burn the hostile encampment. But if it was fortified, as had been reported, they were not to attack until the artillery could be brought forward. Coffee found the report to be true and returned for the six-pounder. It was a wise move that Jackson called "providential." About 1 P.M., some thirty minutes after Coffee's return to the main body, the Red Sticks struck again, this time on the right flank, to the accompaniment, wrote Major Reid, of "prodigious yelling."[8]

Coffee immediately asked Jackson if he could take 200 men and turn the enemy's left flank. Jackson as quickly agreed. Gathering his force from several units, Coffee moved out. Being where he belonged, at the head of his men, he was unaware that many were not as eager as he to engage the enemy. "Those in the rear," wrote Major Reid, "availing themselves of the circumstance, continued to drop off, one by one, without his knowledge, until the whole number left with him, did not exceed fifty." Nor did Jackson realize this. Coffee continued to advance and found the hostiles well concealed on a "ridge of open pine timber, covered with a low undergrowth. . . ." Coffee ordered his men to dismount and charge on foot. Jackson at the same time ordered 200 friendly Indians to attack the enemy's right flank. The charge was delivered by the gallant fifty with vigor. The hostiles were swept off the piney ridge. But Coffee was shot through the side, and his brother-in-law and aide-de-camp, Major Alexander Donelson, Rachel's blood nephew, was shot through the head and killed.[9]

The attack that led to Sandy Donelson's death, Jackson wrote, was "as a faint to draw my attention from that point . . . they intended to attack. . . . " Which was, once again, Jackson's left flank. But he had alerted the officers there, and when the firing began he rode immediately to that part of his line and again ordered in Captain Ferrell's reserve company as reinforcement. The Red Sticks' main force, which had been concealed, suddenly "made a violent onset on our left line," wrote Major Reid. The American line held fast. The Red Sticks kept up for some time a "quick and irregular firing, from behind logs, trees, shrubbery, and whatever could afford concealment. . . ." Then Colonel Carroll ordered a charge described by Major Reid:

"the whole line . . . by a most brilliant and steady movement, broke in upon them, threw them into confusion, and they fled precipatately away, and they were overtaken and destroyed in considerable numbers: their loss was great, but not certainly known."[10]

While this was going on Coffee, himself severely wounded, his men outnumbered, was engaged in heavy fighting on the right. The 200 Indians Jackson had sent to assist him had deserted him when they heard the firing beginning on the other side of the square and had joined the fighting and the chase there. Coffee saw that trying to drive the Indians from the cane-brake in which they had taken refuge would produce heavy casualties, so he ordered a withdrawal. According to Major Reid, this was meant to entice the Indians out of the canebrake, and it worked. The Red Sticks emerged from "their hiding places, and rapidly advanced upon him." Whereupon Cof-fee turned on them and a "severe conflict commenced, and continued about an hour, in which the loss on both sides was nearly equal." Coffee's situation was becoming critical. He had several dead and wounded, the survivors were exhausted. But Jackson was aware of Coffee's peril, and as soon as the pur-suit on the left ended and he had closed his lines, he sent the mixed-blood James Fife with 150 friendly warriors to Coffee's assistance. Immediately Coffee ordered a charge and the Red Sticks were routed. The pursuit went on for three miles. Forty-five Red Sticks were left dead on the field.[11]

The Battle of Emuckfau was over. If Major Reid was correct, Jackson had been lucky. His aide wrote, "The Indians had designed their plan of operations well, though the execution did not succeed. It was intended to bring on an attack at three different points, at the same time; but a party of the Chealegrans, one of the tribes which compose the Creek confederacy, who had been ordered to assail the right extremity of our front line, instead of doing so, thought it more prudent to proceed to their villages, happy to have passed, undiscovered, the point they had been ordered to attack. But for this, the contest might have terminated less advantageously." Thus fortune, the ever-present handmaiden of victory, had shone on Jackson, while the old Indian problem of command and control had struck again.[12]

But Jackson's position was not enviable. He had twenty-three litter cases, and in an Indian war the wounded could not be left alone or under light guard while an army advanced. The horses were starving. But at least as important was Jackson's knowledge that he had gone as far as he could with his sixty-day volunteers. His men, he wrote to Rachel, "in some degree began to be panic struck," a judgment that did not make it into his official report to General Pinckney. Evidence that it was almost certainly true is offered by Major Reid, who observed their behavior: "Having brought in and buried the dead, and dressed the wounded, preparations were made, to guard against an attack by night . . . by ordering a breast-work of timber around the encampment; a measure the more necessary, as the spirits of our troops, most of whom had never before seen an enemy, were observed visi-bly to flag, towards the evening. Indeed, during the night, it was with the utmost difficulty the sentinels could be kept at their posts, who, expecting, every minute, the appearance of the enemy, would at the least noise, fire and run in."[13]

The next morning Jackson decided he had done all he could and ordered preparations for a return to Fort Strother. The army moved out at 10:30 A.M., 23 January.

THE "MONSTER TOO HIDEOUS TO BE WITHSTOOD"

The soldiers made litters for the wounded out of the hides of horses killed in the fighting. One was occupied by John Coffee. Jackson's "march was slow but cautious. I expected another attack. I had a harycane [an area of trees blown down by a windstorm][14] to pass, I wished to avoid an attack there. . . ." Although signs of pursuit were evident, the army proceeded safely and by end of day reached the south bank of Enitachopko Creek, in the direction of the ford the troops had crossed on the way in. There Jackson ordered a breastwork thrown up "with the utmost expedition, and every arrangement made to repel their attempts" either during the night or in the morning.[15]

But the Red Sticks did not appear, and this made Jackson suspect their real intention. He had observed on the approach march to Emuckfau that the ford was an ideal place for an ambush. Major Reid left us an excellent description. The ford was deep, "the banks rugged, and thickly covered with reeds. . . . Near the crossing place was a deep ravine formed by . . . two hills, overgrown with thick shrubbery and brown sedge, which afforded every convenience for concealment, whilst it entirely prevented pursuit." Early on the morning of the twenty-fourth Jackson sent out a few pioneers (road builders) to find a another crossing place downstream. Six hundred yards from the old ford they found a place that exactly suited Jackson, "to draw the enemy after me over a peace of ground, that I could slaughter the whole of them." Major Reid described it: "a handsome slope of open woodland led down to the new ford, where, except immediately on the margin of the creek, which was covered with a few reeds, there was nothing to obstruct the view." Jackson ordered a new road cut, and when it was ready he carefully ordered the army for the march downstream and the expected fight with the Red Sticks.[16]

Jackson's army marched in its accustomed three columns. He had, he stated, confidence in his rear guard: the right rear guard commanded by Colonel Nicholas Tate Perkins, the left by Lieutenant Colonel John Stump. The inspector general, Billy Carroll, commanded the center rear guard and was also overall commander of the rear. A plan of battle had been drawn up. Jackson reported to Pinckney that he had laid out the "manner in which the men should be formed in the event of an attack on the front or rear, or on the flanks," and he had "particularly cautioned the officers to halt and form accordingly, the instant the word should be given." If the attack came from behind, Colonel Carroll's center rear guard was to turn, deploy into line of battle, and hold its position. The right and left rear guards would then face outward and swing around as if shutting doors on either side and attack the flanks and rear of the enemy. Meanwhile, the Red Sticks, who had been laying in ambush in the defile at the old crossing, had learned that Jackson was marching downstream and came on in hot pursuit.[17]

The army began crossing Enitachopko Creek. Jackson was approximately in the center of the long columns, from where he could exert control in any direction. The advance and part of the flank columns and the wounded had crossed and the "last litter was advancing up the bank." The guards and gunners, "my little Spartan band," with the six-pounder were about to enter the water. Then the alarm gun sounded in the rear and the shrieks of the attacking Red Sticks split the morning air. They first hit the company of spies commanded by Captain William Russell. There were, Russell later reported, "upwards of 500 indians in view." Russell's little company returned fire and withdrew in an orderly manner upon the main rear guard. While this was happening, Jackson, who had been in the act of crossing, ordered Major Reid to first form a line to protect the wounded, then to turn the left rear guard on its hinge and swing the door shut. Jackson rode back toward the right rear guard to do the same and thus surround the attacking Indians. Lieutenant Robert Armstrong, commanding the guards, ordered them to form and unharness the six-pounder. Colonel Carroll ordered the center rear guard to turn around and deploy. So far officers and men were reacting smoothly.[18]

Then the militia panicked. Without breastworks from which to fight behind, they saw the "monster too hideous to be withstood." The right and left rear guard columns, wrote Jackson, "broke like Bullocks with their Colos. at their head" and stampeded for the crossing. The left column literally ran over the guards trying to unharness the gun and "threw several of the guards into the creek. . . ." From a smoothly operating machine the army had in seconds been thrown into confusion. The panic became infectious. Billy Carroll's center rear guard ran for the creek. When the dust cleared from their heels Carroll was left with 25 men willing to stand and fight. Jackson screamed at the men to turn and rejoin the few stalwarts on the south bank, but in vain. The comedy of war, always so close to the surface, occurred when "I attempted to draw my sword, it had become hard to draw, and in the attempt I had like to have broke my left arm." The left rear guard poured across the creek like sheep running from wolves and got mixed up with the advance. The bulk of the army was in such a state of panic and confusion that it was impossible to straighten out the mess in time to deal with crisis at the rear. The army's fate, Jackson's fate, rested with the only men whom he could be sure of: Captain Russell's company of spies, the guards and gunners, and the old volunteer officers, joined now by the 25 men who had stayed with Billy Carroll, perhaps 150 in all to face several hundred Red Sticks pressing upon them.

Others, singly and in small groups, began to hasten to the sound of the guns. General Coffee had chosen to leave his litter and mount that morning in anticipation of trouble. He rode into the action, wrote Major Reid, "with his usual calm and deliberate firmness." Dr. John Shelby, the hospital surgeon, rushed to the point of combat and joined the fight. The adjutant general, James Sittler, immediately recrossed the creek and rode to the gunners. They were commanded on that day by Lieutenant Robert Armstrong. He sent most of his men to the top of the rise "under a most galling fire," Jackson reported to Pinckney, to defend a position while Armstrong and a few others wrestled the six-pounder to the top. "The most deliberate bravery was displayed by Constantine Perkins and Craven Jackson of the artillery," Jackson wrote in his official report. In the confusion the rammer and the picker had been left behind. But there was no time to be lost. Perkins used his musket as a rammer, and Craven Jackson the ramrod of his musket as a picker to puncture the flannel cartridge through the touchhole, then primed with a musket cartridge. While this was going on Lieutenant Armstrong was hit and fell, calling out that the cannon must be saved. Captain Hamilton fell, mortally wounded, and by his side Bird Evans. Two other men fell. Captain Quarles, leading the 25 militiamen who had stayed, was shot in the head and later died. But a salvo of grapeshot was fired to good effect on an enemy who, despite its overwhelming superiority in numbers at that particular location, was apparently reluctant to close with the Americans and engage hand to hand.[19]

The tide turned. Captain Gordon and his company of spies, who had been with the advance, rushed across the creek and tried to outflank the Red Sticks. Friendly Indians filled the ranks and joined the fight. Jackson, wrote Reid, was in the thick of it. "In the midst of a shower of balls, of which he seemed unmindful, he was seen performing the duties of subordinate officers, rallying the alarmed, halting them in their flight, forming his columns, inspiring them by his example." The six-pounder boomed again and another whiff of grape swept the field. At that, wrote Jackson, "this Spartan band charged and broke the enemy. . . ." Officers and men from privates to colonels and Indian allies charged together. Billy Carroll was there, and the militia colonel who did not run that day, Colonel William Higgins, and sixty-five-year-old Colonel William Cocke, who had enlisted as a private, joined in the "pursuit of the enemy with youthful ardor, and saved the life of a fellow soldier by killing his savage antagonist." The Red Sticks dropped their packs, abandoned their dead, and ran as the American militia had earlier run. The pursuit went on for about two miles. For both actions, Emuckfau and Enitachopko, 189 dead Creek warriors were found, while Jackson lost only 20 killed and 75 wounded, of whom 4 died. The march resumed and continued unmolested, not a hostile to be seen or heard. On the twenty-seventh they arrived at Fort Strother.[20]

Many years later Red Stick *micos* and important warriors who had fought at Emuckfau and Enitachopko told Albert Pickett that they had "whipped *Captain* Jackson, and run him to the Coosa River." Jackson, on the other hand, sent a positive report to General Pinckney, but what else would we expect? To paraphrase and expand to all periods the observation of a Canadian archivist, who was referring to generals of the eighteenth century, generals write for two reasons: to cover their asses or toot their horns.[21] Jackson was no exception. "All the effects which were designed to be produced by this excursion, it is believed to *have* been produced," he wrote. "If an attack was meditated against Fort Armstrong, that has been prevented. If General Floyd has been operating on the east side of the Tallapoosa, as I suppose him to be, a most fortunate diversion has been made in his favor." His most important accomplishment came toward the end of his report: "The enemy's country has been explored, and a road cut to the point where their force will probably be concentrated when they shall be driven from the country below."[22]

So who was right? The Creeks did stop Jackson from burning their town and forced him to return to Fort Strother. But they did not defeat him in the field, and at Enitachopko Creek they failed to take advantage of Jackson's vulnerable tactical situation: an army in the middle of crossing a body of water. Had the Creeks been well armed with rifles and muskets and powder, and we know they were not, they could have wreaked havoc. But the "could haves," like the "ifs," of history don't count. Only results matter. Armed for the most part as they were, with bows and arrows, war clubs, spears, and knives, they could only have seriously damaged and possibly routed Jackson's army by overwhelming with sheer numbers in a mass frontal assault Jackson's tiny Spartan band. That without doubt would have increased the panic of those who had bolted to sheer hysteria. But that was rarely the Indian way of fighting, which is not to denigrate their skills or their bravery, which they often demonstrated. They just did it differently. But if they were to overcome the Americans and preserve their homeland, they would need to do more than harass armies on the march.

Jackson was convinced that he would have crushed the Red Sticks at Enitachopko had it not been for the "cowardly conduct" of the two militia officers who had led their men in wild flight: Colonel Nicholas Tate Perkins, commanding 1st Regiment of West Tennessee Volunteers, and his second, Lieutenant Colonel John Stump. "They ought to be shot," he wrote Rachel. "They were the cause of the death of several brave men." He wasted no time in seeking their punishment. Both officers were arrested and charged with disobeying orders, cowardice, and abandonment of their posts. In their subsequent courts-martial (27–30 January), Perkins was acquitted and returned to his command, but Stump was found guilty and cashiered.[23]

Back home in Tennessee the militia officers who had either deserted with their men or rejected Jackson's pleas to stay on regardless of terms of service had been busy spreading stories about his dictatorial ways and alleged drunkenness. Jackson was outraged, especially by the charge of drunkenness: "the fiend is not in human shape that dare say to me that he has saw me intoxicated in camp or anywere else since I left Nashville." He left his opinion of the slanderers in vivid terms: "as to those vile slanderous vipers, I despise them as the crawling worm that rolls through the slime untouched, unnoticed by any." He would not be deterred. "I shall do my duty. And with the blessing of kind providence will conquor my enemies both foreing and domestick. . . ."[24]

Providence in one form took the shape of a man whose good opinion was of crucial importance to Andrew Jackson: Major General Thomas Pinckney. As James Parton noted, eastern papers may have taken little notice of obscure skirmishes in far-off barbarous places involving a backwoods general who was less than obscure. But General Pinckney was well pleased with Jackson's performance. He wrote to the secretary of war, John Armstrong, "I take the liberty of drawing your attention to the present and former communications of General Jackson. Without the personal firmness, popularity, and exertions of that officer, the Indian war, on the part of Tennessee, would have been abandoned, at least for a time, as will appear by reference to the letters of Governor Blount heretofore transmitted. If government thinks it advisable to elevate to the rank of general persons than those now in the army, I have heard of none whose military operations so well entitle him to that distinction."[25]

Pinckney was referring to making Jackson a general in the regular army. Unfortunately, at that particular time there were no vacancies. While we let that and other matters brew, we need to see whether Jackson's diversion did indeed help General John Floyd in his second march into Creek country.

"MAN IS BORN TO DIE"

Floyd was having the usual problems that drove the generals of early America to distraction. By late December he had recovered sufficiently from his wound suffered at Autosse to again take the field, but he lacked provisions, and the term of enlistments of his troops ended on 22 February 1814. If he was to mount another campaign, he would have to move quickly. The maddening thing about all of this was that the provisions were available. But not where Floyd needed them. For the private contractors and the state of Georgia were mired in a contract dispute. Floyd's army was at Fort Mitchell, just west of the Chattahoochee River. The Georgia frontier was at Fort Hawkins, near present-day Macon, approximately one hundred miles east of Fort Mitchell. The contractors insisted that the contract called for delivery to the frontier, and they would not take one step past it. Floyd argued that they should deliver to wherever the army was. And the army was starving. And the friendly Lower Creeks, whose fields had been destroyed by the hostiles, were also hungry and expected to be fed by Floyd, and if they were not they might change sides. If that were not enough pressure on him, General Pinckney was pushing Floyd to take the field.[26]

By mid-January Floyd felt he had enough supplies to march and proceeded forty-one miles west of the Chattahoochee and built Fort Hull, about five miles southeast of modern Tuskegee, Alabama. Four days later, on 25 January, the 1,100 Georgia militia and volunteers, and 600 friendly Creeks under William McIntosh, the well-known mixed blood, headed west, their goal the Upper Creek town of Tuckabatchee. The reader will remember that Tecumseh had there made his speech to the Creek Nation. And from there Big Warrior, Captain Isaacs, and their people had been driven by the Red Sticks. The town was on the west bank of the Tallapoosa just below modern Tallassee, Alabama, roughly only fifteen miles northwest of Fort Hull as the crow flies. Floyd's progress, however, did not go unobserved.[27]

A swift runner brought the news to the Red Stick prophet Paddy Walsh. The Georgians were on the move and they had artillery with them. Runners were immediately dispatched to the Red Stick towns for their fighting men to rendezvous at the Othlewallee camps. There was a determination to meet and destroy Floyd's army, and now the Red Sticks had at least some means beside hand weapons to go into battle. Following the destruction of the Holy Ground, Red Eagle with an escort of 390 mounted men had gone to Pensacola to seek powder and lead from the Spanish. The Spanish governor turned them down, but from British and other sources they got a small amount of supplies—three horse loads of powder and lead—and returned to the nation.[28]

In the meantime, Floyd's progress was slow. The army marched only three miles on the twenty-fifth before making camp. Apparently Floyd expected an attack that night, for the men, both whites and Indians, were geared for one. But the night passed quietly. Early the next morning the army set out once more, and again moved slowly. Seeing that the supply wagons were slowing his progress, Floyd decided to send them back to Fort Hull. He turned the army around and escorted them about half a mile to a point near Calabee Creek, which flows northwesterly in modern Macon County, Alabama, and empties into the Tallapoosa. On high ground bordered by swamps, called Chuseekna Wockna, or the "spike horn bucks' bed," Floyd stopped and made camp on 26 February 1814.[29]

While Floyd marched and countermarched and did not seem to be able to decide what to do, almost 1,300 Red Stick warriors, stripped for battle and painted red, had answered Paddy Walsh's call. The night of 26 February they marched to the west bank of Calabee Creek and stopped about one mile from Floyd's camp. There a question was raised by some: What was the plan of attack? Whereupon Paddy Walsh, Red Eagle, High-Headed Jim, and William McGillivray, who was no relation to Alexander McGillivray, and was by some called Bit Nose Billy McGillivray, sat down to work out tactics. Paddy Walsh, described by George Stiggins as a very short and ugly man, but also a "great natural orator, both persuasive and commanding" and "deep in his manner of reasoning," proposed a night attack after the Americans retired. They knew that Floyd's camp was laid out in two squares. Walsh proposed that the warriors creep as close as possible on all sides, then rush the camp from all directions. He meant to close with the enemy. If the fighting was still going by daylight and going well, they would maintain the action. If they had not done serious damage by then, they would retreat from the camp and end the fight. High-Headed Jim agreed with Paddy Walsh. Red Eagle and Bit Nose Billy dissented.[30]

It seemed to them that the thought of preparing a possible retreat before the battle began would imbue the warriors with a sense of defeatism. Red Eagle agreed on a night attack, but with a significant difference. The white commanding officers, he said, always have their quarters in the center of camp. He proposed what is called in military parlance a forlorn hope; that is, a unit assigned a perilous mission. Three hundred men led by Paddy Walsh would attack suddenly in a rush and tomahawk their way into the center of the camp, kill all of the white officers, then fight their way out. At the same time the rest of the Red Sticks would charge the whites all around the camp. Red Eagle stressed that white soldiers were accustomed to fight at the direction of their officers, and without them they would fall into confusion. Thus the prospect was good that the other ranks, deprived of leadership, would lose all cohesion and bolt for the woods and home.

It was a good plan, but it set off a dramatic scene between the actors. Paddy Walsh and High-Headed Jim vehemently objected, describing the plan as a "measure of insanity and desperation, a sure and unnecessary sacrifice of three hundred men." Walsh was especially incensed at Red Eagle's generous choice of him to lead the forlorn hope. In effect, he said thanks but no thanks for a job that seemed designed to sacrifice him and that neither Red Eagle nor McGillivray "dared undertake."

What a scene it must have been. Four angry men, their hardening features lit by a dancing campfire, other Indians crowding around listening, as what had begun as debate descended into fierce, insulting argument. Red Eagle and Bit Nose Billy jumped to their feet, infuriated at this public challenge to their courage. Both said they were willing to undertake the mission. George Stiggins wrote, "They said they were convinced that man is born to die and that he could lose his life but once." Volunteers were called for. Few stepped forward. According to Stiggins, the reluctance was due to Paddy Walsh's opposition, for he was one of the most important prophets. Red Eagle, however, considered the rejection of his advice and his offer to lead the forlorn hope a public insult, told Walsh to "fight his cautious half-fights," mounted his horse, and with his followers rode for home.

So much for battle planning by committee.

"CHEER UP BOYS, WE WILL GIVE THEM HELL WHEN DAYLIGHT COMES"

During the night the Red Sticks stealthily filtered into the swamps surrounding Floyd's camp. No alarm was raised. At 5:20 on the morning of the twenty-seventh Creek warriors rose and in the darkness rushed forward, screaming their war cries. Their close presence came as a complete surprise to the Americans. Half-dressed men suddenly awakened, groped for shoes and weapons. The Red Sticks drove in the pickets and sentinels. For a while all was confusion. One party of American pickets, commanded by Captain John Broadnax, was cut off from the main force. Fighting desperately, and assisted by some valiant Uchee Indians under the mixed-blood Timpoochy

Barnard, Broadnax and his men reached the lines. Most of the Indian allies, however, according to Pickett and Stiggins, remained within the lines and were inactive during that stage of the battle.[31]

"Cheer up boys, we will give them hell when daylight comes," Floyd called out. But hell was needed then, and it came in the form of artillery booming in the dark. The fight for the two guns became critical. A large number of Red Sticks crawling under the fire got to within thirty feet of the guns before they were discovered. The guns were depressed and grapeshot sprayed the Indian ranks. The battle was won in front of the guns. At daybreak, keeping his cavalry in the center as reserve, Floyd ordered a bayonet charge, and it was the Red Stick lines that broke. Then the cavalry charged and it became a rout. Two rifle companies and the friendly Indians joined in the pursuit.[32]

The Red Sticks lost an estimated 40 to 50 killed and an undetermined number wounded, including a badly hurt Paddy Walsh. Bit Nose Billy McGillivray, although smarting from what he considered Walsh's insult, stayed, fought, and ran. The friendly Indians committed the usual atrocities on the dead enemy—slicing them open, cutting off privates, ripping out a heart and parading it around. They had great sport with a corpse they kept putting on a horse. Every time it fell off they shouted, "Whiskey too much."[33]

Floyd lost 17 killed and 132 wounded. He also lost his army. Although they had beaten off the attack, the fight lowered militia morale close to the breaking point. Mutiny was in the air. They were short-timers, their term of service up in less than a month, and they wanted to go home. Floyd also had many wounded to care for. He retreated to Fort Hull, where he wanted to remain until replacements of South Carolina militia recruited by General Pinckney arrived. But when the men threatened to march back to Georgia on their own en masse, Floyd gave in and led them all the way to Milledgeville, then the state capital, for discharge. He left in charge at Fort Hull a regular army officer, Colonel Homer V. Milton, with a unit of regulars from 3rd U.S. Infantry and 140 militia who had volunteered to stay behind.[34]

George Stiggins claimed that the defeat at Calabee was a fatal blow to the Red Sticks. Except as individuals and small bands, the Red Sticks from the southern towns on the Tallapoosa never again took the field. Paddy Walsh gave up the organized fight. On the other hand, although repulsed at Calabee Creek, they had knocked the Georgians out of the war. And the Upper Creek hostiles who had met Jackson at Emuckfau and Enitachopko were bloodied but unsubdued. Thus the issue was unresolved. Only one general remained in the field, a general who had never left the field since he took it, despite trials and calamities that would have broken the will of most. Once again, then, we return to the further adventures of Old Hickory and his rowdy, disputatious Tennessee citizen soldiers.

Chapter 17

⊶⊷

Horseshoe Bend

"PUNISHMENT MUST AWAIT EVERY INDIVIDUAL
OF THE ARMY, THAT DISOBEYS ORDERS"

On 6 February 1814 an event occurred that had a major impact on the Creek War. Thirty-ninth U.S. Infantry, thirty-six-year-old Colonel John Williams commanding, marched into Fort Strother. The previous year, when ordered to disband his troops in Natchez, Jackson had passionately defended militia. In the Creek War, however, all too often militia behavior had not squared with his stern ideas of duty and discipline. Now that situation would change. Now Jackson had regulars, 600 strong, not only to fight the Red Sticks but to enforce discipline upon volunteers and militia.

Thirty-ninth was made up mostly of native-born Americans of English and Scotch Irish descent recruited in Knoxville and the surrounding area. Its term of service was one year. General Pinckney had assigned the 39th to Jackson in late December 1813, but it had not arrived in time to join the raid at Emuckfau. In its ranks was a twenty-one-year-old third lieutenant who would become a fast friend of Andrew Jackson, a governor of Tennessee, and later the first president of the Republic of Texas—Sam Houston (1793–1863). Thirty-ninth Infantry would quickly become the backbone of Jackson's army. [1]

Around this hard core of disciplined troops the army would be filled out with new volunteers and militia units that would either obey orders or suffer the consequences. For Jackson's stinging letter of 29 December to Willie Blount, which we quoted at length at the end of chapter 15, had lit a fire under the governor. He had almost immediately called up 2,500 men from West Tennessee for three months' service and ordered them to rendezvous at Fayetteville on 28 January 1814, at which time their term of service would begin. He also instructed General John Cocke to obey Jackson's orders to raise a brigade in East Tennessee. [2]

High commanders felt Jackson's determination to brook no resistance, no interference, with his goal of crushing the Red Sticks and foiling Spanish and British machinations on the Gulf Coast, real or imagined. General Isaac Roberts made the mistake of siding with his men in their dispute with Jackson over that perennial militia issue, terms of service. General Roberts was arrested on 19 February, tried by a court-martial on 23–28 February, convicted, and cashiered.

On 2 March Jackson received a letter from Brigadier General George Doherty, an old King's Mountain veteran, commanding the East Tennessee Brigade on its way to join Jackson at Fort Strother, which revealed in the middle of a war fierce personal rivalry and the equally fierce Tennessee sectionalism. Doherty informed Jackson of his men's uneasiness, which he "attributed to their remaining so long in a state of inactivity, [and which] as you know, Sir, is a never failing cause in the minds of the militia. . . ." But upon further investigation Doherty was astonished to learn that Major General John Cocke, who had failed to cooperate with Jackson on his first foray into Creek country, had come among Doherty's brigade and become the "chief instigator of their mutinous resolutions." Doherty charged that Cocke told the men " 'that the quota of six months men from E. Tennessee was not in proportion to that of West Tennessee.' " When the men asked him "whether he would go on in command," Cocke said " 'he would not, for if the men were taken to Jackson, they would be placed in a situation he did not like to mention, which he could not endure to witness, as it would not be in his power to extricate them.' " Cocke warned the men that Jackson now had regulars under his command and "would turn his artillery upon them," that he would take them all the way to Mobile and make them serve there, that he " 'would compel them to serve six months—nine months—and a year if he chose.' " Confessing that "I am at a loss" to explain General Cocke's actions, General Doherty concluded that Cocke "has used every exertion to diffuse anarchy and revolt among the troops from the Colonel down to the cook. I was about to take rigid measures with him, when this morning he left camp for home and I am happy he is gone, for during his stay the camp was in incessant confusion."[3]

Jackson was furious, but he was not sure whether he had the authority to arrest Cocke. He was determined to see him punished, however, and set the machinery in motion. He sent copies of General Doherty's letter to General Pinckey and Governor Blount and demanded of the governor the "immediate arrest of Majr Genl. John Cocke for disobdience of orders—Mutiny—Exciting mutiny & not suppressing the same—for unmilitary—unofficer like, & ungentlemanly conduct." Cocke was arrested and charged in Tennessee. Unlike Isaac Roberts, John Cocke was an important Tennessee politician, and he was eventually acquitted of all charges. But he was also no longer in the field to bedevil Jackson.[4]

Once again General Cocke has his defenders. James Parton disputed General Doherty's report, insisting that the "really *guilty* persons in this affair were those who, from misunderstanding General Cocke's designs, or from enmity to him, conveyed to General Jackson reports of his conduct, which were either totally false or monstrous exaggerations." Robert Quimby also found Cocke ill-used in this affair, but admitted that "his usefulness in the war, however, was destroyed."[5] What "usefulness"? one is tempted to ask. Even if Cocke were falsely accused, a rough justice had removed from the war a militia officer who had been troublesome from the start and had little if anything to offer the cause.

Another pressure was exerted upon Jackson during this period in which he was preparing for what he hoped would be the final push. We quoted extensively from his letter of 28 January to Rachel in which he described the actions at Emuckfau and Enitachopko. That letter, vivid in its description of battle, and with its news of the death of Rachel's nephew Sandy Donelson, had almost driven the poor woman around the bend. One wonders why he felt compelled to present so much detail and in such stark terms.

> My Dearest Life
> I receved your letter by Express Never shall I forgit it I have not slept one night sinc What a dreadful scene it was how did I feel I never Can disscribe it I Cryed aloud and praised my god For your safety how thankfull I was—oh my unfortunate Nephew he is gone how I Deplore his Loss his untimely End—My Dear pray let me Conjur you by Every Tie of Love of friend ship to Let me see you before you go againe I have borne it untill now it has thrown me Into such feavours I am very unwell—my thoughts is never Diverted from that dreadfull scene oh how dreadfull to me—o the mercy and goodness of Heaven to me you are spared perils and Dangers so maney troubles—my prayers is unceasing how Long o Lord will I remain so unhapy no rest no Ease I Cannot sleepe all can come home but you I never wanted to see you so mutch in my life . . . I must see you pray My Darling never make me so unhapy for aney Country . . . you have now don more than aney other man Ever did before you have served your Country Long Enough you have gained maney Laurels you have Ernd them . . . *you* have been gone a Long time six months . . . oh Lorde of heaven how Can I beare it . . . Let it not be long from your Dearest friend and faitfull wife untill Death.

Jackson replied firmly on 21 February 1814: "I have this moment recd. your letter of the 10th Instant, and am grieved to think the pain my absence occasions, but when you reflect, that I am in the field, and cannot retire when I please, without disgrace I am in hopes that your good sense, will yield to it a little while with resolution and firmness. . . ." Then he returned to the business at hand.[6]

As Jackson prepared his new army for what he hoped would be the final strike against the Red Sticks, there occurred an incident that would follow him beyond his military career into national politics. He had written to Billy Carroll that "punishment must await every individual of the army, that disobeys orders. . . ." He meant it. General Roberts and General Cocke would soon be arrested and face courts-martial. Four of Roberts's captains—

Samuel B. Patton, James Harris, James H. Pickens, and Pleasant Nelson—were arrested, tried, and convicted for desertion, mutiny, and other offenses. Since Roberts was considered the main culprit, they were given light sentences. But the lesson of speedy action and punishment was not lost on the army. Nor was the fate of Private John Woods of James Harris's company. The reader is warned that the only documentation for the affair is Jackson's General Order, which does not go into details. I have followed Parton, who may have embroidered with regard to particulars or been misled by informants; but the outline and ending are unquestioned.[7]

It was late February on one of those raw, rainy days that people unfamiliar with the South do not associate with that part of the country. John Woods, a bit shy of his eighteenth birthday, was on guard duty. He had not eaten that morning and he was hungry as well as cold. The officer of the guard gave him permission to go to his tent and fetch his blanket. In the tent he found his breakfast ready and sat down to eat instead of returning to his guard post. Bones and other garbage and trash littered the ground around the tent, and the officer of the day, observing the mess, ordered the men present to clean it up. His order included Woods, but the boy continued to eat his breakfast. The officer spoke sharply to him. Woods explained that he was on guard duty, to which he was about to return, and that he had been given permission to leave his post, whereupon the officer once again spoke sharply, ordering him to return immediately to his post. Woods refused. The officer of the day again ordered him to his post. An argument ensued. Woods, who had been in the army about a month and was not inured to military discipline, again refused and began arguing with the officer. The dispute between the two became louder and angrier. Young Woods was in a fury. The officer turned to soldiers standing by and ordered them to arrest Woods. Grabbing his weapon, Woods swore he would shoot the first man who tried to arrest him.

Enter Jackson. He was told that a soldier was threatening mutiny. He rushed from his tent. "Which is the damned rascal? Shoot him! shoot him! Blow ten balls through the damned villain's body!" Woods had been persuaded by comrades to give up his weapon by the time Jackson reached the tent. Woods was then shackled and confined in the camp of 39th Infantry.[8]

Apparently nobody expected what then came to pass. Nobody, that is, except Jackson. When militiamen were involved in such incidents, the worst that happened was dismissal from service and being drummed out of camp. But for months Jackson had endured the tumultuous and mutinous disposition of the militia, which had seriously threatened his ability to remain in the field and prosecute the campaign. At Talladega he had seen the disobedience of his orders by a militia officer enable the bulk of the Red Sticks to escape. At Enitachopko the blind panic of militia columns could easily have resulted in disaster. He was determined that such conduct, such rebellious attitudes, had to end, that the army must know that he would not flinch from the ultimate penalty, that each soldier must realize his fate should he engage in mutinous behavior.

John Woods was tried by court-martial, and before and during the trial Jackson made his purpose clear to all who cared to listen, including the five officers who made up the court. "A fellow has mutinied, and I expect he will have to be shot," Jackson told an officer. And during the trial, as he paced up and down nearby, the court could hear him say, "Be cautious, and mind what you are about; for by the eternal God, the next man that is condemned, I won't pardon; and this is a hearty, hale young fellow." If the report of what he said is true, then Jackson was urging the court to convict Woods and condemn him to death, and also suggesting that he would pardon Woods but not the next man to be condemned.[9]

The trial was held in the open on 12 March 1814. The prisoner's dock on which John Woods sat was a log. The proceedings probably did not take long. Private John Woods was found guilty of "disobedience of orders, disrespect to your commanding officer, and mutiny," and condemned to die by firing squad. Some pleaded to the general for mercy. The prisoner's youth was stressed. It was also brought to his attention that John Woods provided the main support for his aged parents. Jackson was unbending, writing that "however as a man he may deplore your unhappy situation, he cannot as an officer, without infringing his duty, arrest the sentence of the court martial." On 14 March the army was drawn up to witness an execution few had believed would happen.[10]

John Reid summed up Jackson's position:

> The execution . . . produced, at this time, the most salutary effect . . .
> A fit occasion was now presented to evince, that although militia, when at their fire-sides at home, might boast an exemption from control, yet, in the field, these high notions were to be abandoned, and subordination observed . . . The execution was productive of the happiest effects; order was produced, and that opinion, so long indulged, that a militia-man was for no offence to suffer death, was, from that moment, abandoned, and a strict obedience afterwards characterized the army.[11]

"IT WAS DARK BEFORE WE FINISHED KILLING THEM"

Jackson and the army, about 3,500 strong, moved out for Red Stick country the day John Woods was executed. Four hundred fifty men were left at Fort Strother to secure the base and relay supplies. Previous reconnaissance had shown that the Coosa could be navigated to Three Islands, located where Cedar Creek joined the Coosa in the southwestern corner of present-day Talladega County, not far from the modern village of Talladega Springs. Jackson therefore decided to move by land and water. Upon his return from the Emuckfau raid, he had used the time remaining for the militia, who were soon to be discharged, to build flatboats. In these boats Colonel John Williams and the officers and men of the 39th Infantry, along with equipment and provisions, would float down the Coosa to Three Islands, while Jackson with the militia and volunteers marched overland to the rendezvous. The distance from Fort Strother to Three Islands was less than the commuting distance for millions of Americans today, only some fifty-five miles as the crow flies. But there were no roads. The army had to build one as it marched. And Colonel Williams and the 39th struggled down the Coosa through low water. Jackson's force reached the rendezvous point on 21 March, eight days after its departure from Fort Strother, but Colonel Williams's flotilla had finally grounded on shoals about a mile and a half upstream. Some of the supplies were unloaded and transferred to pirogues, enabling the lightened boats to float down to the mouth of Cedar Creek where, Jackson reported, "they are now safely harboured." On the "point of land between the mouth of Cedar Creek, & the Coosa River," Fort Williams, named after the commander of the 39th, was built as a supply base and a refuge in case of misfortune. The site now lies under the waters of the Coosa River.[12]

On the day he arrived Jackson also sent out a detachment "to scour the countryside" for signs of hostiles, but during a two-day scout they found only "fresh trails of small stragling parties, who had, probably, been sent out to gather the remains of their stock." At the same time the army was joined by several hundred Indian allies—mostly Cherokees, but also Lower Creeks under William McIntosh—"to partake in the war." Jackson found them a "very serious tax on my provission-stores . . . & the very moment I can rid myself of them with a good grace, & without leaving improper impressions on their minds, I shall certainly do so. At Emuckfau I must find or make a pretext for discharging the greater part of them; & perhaps the whole, except my guides." His judgment, however, was premature, and he would soon have reason to be grateful for their attachment to the army.[13]

The reader will recall that on 22 January, the day the action at Emuckfau was fought, General Coffee reconnoitered the nearby Red Stick town and had found it too strong to attack. It was fifty-two miles southeast of Fort Williams. Through his excellent intelligence service, which was largely the work of friendly Indians, Jackson knew that the Red Sticks were still there and gathering in force. The town, Tohopeka, was located in a large bend of the Tallapoosa River once called by the Creeks Cholocco Litabixee (Horse's Hoof). The Americans called it, as they still do, Horseshoe Bend.

Leaving a garrison at Fort Williams, and taking provisions for eight days, on 24 March Jackson headed for Horseshoe Bend with an army of about 3,300 men: the 600 regulars of 39th Infantry; some 2,100 Tennessee militia and volunteers, consisting of a regiment of East Tennessee infantry under twenty-eight-year-old Colonel Samuel Bunch, and General John Coffee's West Tennessee brigade, half of whom were mounted; the artillery company with two fieldpieces; two companies of Jackson's faithful spies, one commanded by fifty-six-year-old Captain William Russell (1758–1825), the other by twenty-year-old Lieutenant Jesse Bean (1794–1845); and about 600 Cherokee and Lower Creek allies.[14]

Cautiously, marching in the usual three columns with scouts out, Jackson took three days to cover the fifty-two miles to Horseshoe Bend. Both sides were well informed of the other's presence. Neither side made any effort to avoid battle. On the night of the twenty-sixth the American army camped in its usual fortified square near the site of the Emuckfau action, variously given as three to six miles from the bend. At Tohopeka that night, among the Red Sticks, three prophets, their gyrating bodies outlined by campfire, danced the Dance of the Lakes, taught them by the Shawnees.

Early the next morning the American columns began their final approach march. At 6:30 A.M., a short time after they moved out, Jackson detached John Coffee with 700 cavalry and mounted infantry and most of his Indian allies: 500 Cherokees under Colonel Gideon Morgan Jr. (1778–1851) of Knoxville and 100 Creeks commanded by Major William McIntosh (1775?–1825) of Coweta. Coffee's mission, Jackson wrote, was to cross the river below the bend "& to surround the bend in such a manner, as that none of them would escape by attempting to cross the river." Coffee later reported that "I crossed the Tallipoosey river at the little Island ford about three miles below the bend, in which the enemy had concentrated, and then turned up river bearing away from its clifts." While Coffee moved his force into the blocking position, Jackson and the rest of the army marched toward the neck of the horseshoe.

The bend of the Tallapoosa had created a peninsula of about one hundred acres bordered on three sides by the river. The neck, or open end, of the horseshoe stretched for some four hundred yards between the riverbanks. Opposite the downstream side of the neck, where the river broadened, was a fifteen-acre wooded island. Coffee ordered Lieutenant Jesse Bean and forty riflemen "to take possession of the Island . . . to prevent the enemy's taking refuge there. . . ." The distance over the water from the peninsula to the island was about forty yards.

The rear of the peninsula was on low ground bordering the Tallapoosa, and there the town called Tohopeka was situated about one hundred yards from the river, clearly visible from the opposite bank. Along the river's bank on the whitish-brown sands deposited by annual floods were scores of dugout canoes, probably hollowed out from sycamore logs, ready for a quick evacuation of the peninsula should the need arise.

The name Tohopeka comes from the Creek word *tohopki,* meaning fortified place or fort, but afterward whites gave it the spelling by which it has come down to us. It was a new town built that winter of 1813–1814 for refugees from the many Red Stick towns destroyed by the American armies. There were about three hundred log huts housing about 1,350 people, of whom by Indian testimony some 1,000 were warriors. The rest were non-combatants: women, children, the aged. Since it was just settled there were no gardens. The refugees had to make do with the stores they had brought with them, and what wild game the hunters could find.

Stand today at the site of Tohopeka, a beautiful place on the low ground, nestled in the bend of the brown waters of the Tallapoosa. Behind the town the land rose about fifty feet to an overlook—what in those parts passes for high ground—and undulated toward the neck of the bend, the target of Jackson with his main force. Look across the river at the opposite bank and hilly woods to which the Red Sticks hoped to escape if necessary. That bank was the destination of John Coffee and his detachment of Tennessee riflemen and Cherokee and Creek allies—1,300 strong. Coffee wrote in his battle report, "When within half a mile of the village the savage yell was raised by the enemy, and I supposed he had discovered and was about to attack me. I immediately drew up my forces in line of battle in an open hilly woodland, and in that position moved on towards the yelling of the enemy—previous to this I had ordered the Indians on our approach to the bend of the river to advance secretly and to take possession of the bank of the river and prevent the enemy from crossing on the approach of your army in his front."

At the neck of the horseshoe most of the Red Stick warriors gathered behind a defensive work that spanned the neck from bank to bank, and for which Jackson expressed admiration in a report to General Pinckney: "It is difficult to conceive of a situation more eligible for defense than the one they had chose, or one rendered more secure by the skill with which they had erected their breast work, it was from five to eight feet high, and extended across the point in such a direction, as that a force approaching it would be exposed to double fire while they lay in perfect security behind. A cannon placed at one extremity could have raked it to no advantage."

The breastwork was made of "large logs laid one above the other," reported Billy Carroll, and ran across the open ground in some sort of zigzag fashion that allowed the Red Sticks to deliver enfilading fire against attacking infantry trying to climb the walls. It was double-walled, with the space between probably filled with dirt except where portholes had been cut through the logs for firing. One account describes three rows of firing ports, the lower for men lying down, the middle for those kneeling, and the top ports for standing gunmen. At both ends of the wall the ground descended steeply, as it still does, toward the river, and these steep descents, wrote Major Reid, who was there, "were covered by the trees that had been felled from their margin," which must have appeared as a tangled blowdown left in a forest following the passage of a severe windstorm. Elsewhere on the high ground, from the breastwork to where the land descended to the refugee town, Major Reid reported that "brush and timber . . . lay thickly scattered over the peninsula," providing as did the tangled trees on the cliffsides fall-back fighting positions should the Americans succeed in forcing their way over the breastwork.

It was indeed a formidable position. It would have been even more formidable had the Red Sticks been well armed, but as throughout the Creek War they were short of firearms, powder, and lead. Of the estimated 1,000 warriors, only about 330 carried muskets or rifles. The rest were armed with bows and arrows, spears, and war clubs. In fighting spirit, however, imbued with a grim determination to prevail or die in defense of their homeland, they were even more formidable than the breastwork they waited behind and watched from as Jackson's main force filed onto the field. On a knoll about fifty to seventy-five yards behind them and to the right, but in full view of the field of battle, the three prophets who the night before had danced the Dance of the Lakes danced again. They shrieked as they danced, cursing the white enemy, calling upon the warriors to be brave. Their bodies were painted black. Each wore his badge of office, an entire cow's tail dyed bright red fastened to an arm, the thick end at shoulder height, tail end tied to the wrist, the long cow hairs dangling below the hand, waving in the morning air as they danced. The wore cloth turbans adorned with bird feathers. On the other side of the breastwork, Jackson deployed the main force to the steady beat of the drums, while the black-painted prophets on their knoll danced and shrieked, and the gods of war waited to reap their own.

About to begin was one of the most important, yet least well-known, battles ever fought in North America. In strategic importance many better-known battles pale beside Horseshoe Bend. Custer's defeat in Montana sixty-two years later does not even deserve to be mentioned in the same breath with Horseshoe Bend.

Jackson placed his two guns, a six-pounder and a three-pounder, on a height now called Gun Hill opposite the left side of the breastwork, which was about 80 yards away, with the far side about 250 yards from the guns. The gunners were commanded by Captain Joel Parrish. Looking at the breastwork from Jackson's position, 39th Infantry was drawn up behind and to the left of the guns, 300 yards from the enemy's position. Next to them, according to Colonel Carroll, was Colonel Samuel Bunch's regiment of East Tennessee infantry. Well behind the main line of battle the rest of Jackson's Tennessee militia was drawn up in reserve. At 10:30 A.M. the guns began to pound the breastwork.

To no avail. For two hours the guns roared while marksmen on both sides took potshots at each other. Seventy rounds of solid shot were fired. They either bounced off the front wall or, Jackson wrote to Rachel, "passed through the works without shaking the wall." Colonel Carroll confirmed the failure of the small field guns to make an impression upon the double-walled, dirt-strengthened breastwork: "the artillery tryed to batter the logs down but without effect." Stalemate seemed to be in the air. Then, during the bombardment, came the unplanned tactical move that changed the nature of the battle. To better savor what happened, we should remind ourselves of Jackson's letter to General Pinckney written from Fort Williams, in which he said of his Indian allies, "the very moment I can rid myself of them with a good grace, & without leaving improper impressions on their minds, I shall certainly do so."

On the other side of the river the 600 Cherokee and Creek allies with Coffee were in the act of carrying out his order "to take possession of the river" on their side of the Tallapoosa. They were moving through the open woodland "when within a quarter of a mile of the river, the firing of your cannon commenced, when the Indians with me rushed forward with great impetuosity to the river bank." Coffee halted his cavalry and mounted gunmen and kept them "in order of battle, expecting an attack on our rear from the Oakfuskee villages, which lay down the river about eight miles below us." Meanwhile, the allied Indians on the riverbank, listening to Jackson's bombardment, within sight of Tohopeka, could hardly contain themselves, and soon found their ardor for battle uncontainable. Coffee wrote,

> The firing of cannon and small arms in a short time became general and heavy, which animated our Indians, and seeing about one hundred of the Warriors and all the squaws and Children of the enemy running about among the huts of the Village, which was open to our view, they could no longer remain silent spectators, while some kept up a fire across the river (which is about one hundred & twenty yards wide) to prevent the enemy's approach to the bank, others plunged into the water and swam over the river for canoes that lay at the other shore in considerable numbers, and brought them over. . . .

A Cherokee called Whale, showing unerring tactical instinct, was the first warrior to plunge into the river under his comrades' covering fire. A few others followed him. The canoes they brought over were used to transport other Cherokees and Creeks. Coffee reported that Captain William Russell "with part of his company of Spies was amongst the first that crossed the river. . . ." The allied Indians and a handful of white riflemen advanced on Tohopeka. To replace the now unguarded riverbank Coffee sent 230 of his 700 white troops "to be posted around the bend on the river bank, whilst the balance remained in line to protect our rear."

Jackson, blasting away without effect, first became aware that some of his troops were across the river when smoke began to rise above Tohopeka. The allied Indians were setting fire to Tohopeka's log huts. They and the riflemen drove the 100-odd Red Stick warriors out of the town onto the high ground and, Jackson wrote to Pinckney, "advanced with great gallantry towards the breast work & commenced a spirited fire upon the enemy behind it." They were too few to advance farther, and in fact were in danger of being overwhelmed, but their presence made Jackson aware that Coffee was in control of the near bank of the Tallapoosa. Jackson recognized the decisive moment and seized it.

"I now determined to take their works by storm," he reported to General Pinckney. "The men by who this was to be effected, had been waiting with impatience to receive the order, & hailed it with acclamation."

The 39th's drummer, fourteen-year-old Zachariah Turnage, beat the long roll. The regulars under Colonel John Williams shouted and charged by heads of sections with bayonets fixed. They were supported by Colonel Samuel Bunch's East Tennessee infantry. Indulging in hyperbole, Jackson claimed that "the history of warfare furnishes few instances of a more brilliant attack." But the charge was indeed spirited, and according to Major Reid both the regulars charging into their first battle and the militia "advanced with the intrepidity and firmness of veteran soldiers." The fighting at the breastwork lasted eight minutes, Colonel Carroll reported, as men on both sides fired at each other through the portholes. Jackson reported a "tremendous fire from behind" the works. Then all six feet, two inches of the regiment's first major, Lemuel P. Montgomery (1796–1814), leaped atop the breastwork and called for his men to follow. A Red Stick warrior shot Montgomery in the head and killed him instantly. But Montgomery's deed encouraged the men to follow suit and the regulars began pouring over the breastwork and engaging the Red Sticks hand to hand. Third Lieutenant Sam Houston leaped into the melee brandishing his sword. He was an over-size target at six feet, five inches. A Red Stick shot him high in the thigh just below his groin with a barbed arrow. Another officer wrenched the arrow from his body. Blood poured from Houston's thigh. A surgeon stopped the bleeding and dressed the wound. Despite the incredible pain he must have been in, Houston returned to the fight only to be later shot twice, in the right arm and right shoulder. He wrote that "arrows, spears, and balls were flying, and swords and tomahawks [were] gleaming in the sun."

From the knoll, shrieking at the tops of their voices, the three prophets raced down the incline and joined the melee. But their efforts and their spells could not stem Jackson's troops. The Red Sticks retreated, Major Reid wrote, and "concealed themselves amidst the brush and timber, that lay thickly scattered over the peninsula, whence they continued resistance, and kept up a galling and constant fire. . . ." Once more the bayonets were called upon, once more the Red Sticks were driven from their positions. Scores of dead and wounded were now sprawled about the killing ground.

Desperate now, the Red Sticks began to scatter. Some got through to the bank where they had beached their canoes, only to find them no longer there. On the opposite bank they could see part of Coffee's command prepared to resist any effort to escape in that direction. Yet they tried. But Coffee reported that "[Captain Eli] Hammonds company of Raingers took post on the river bank on my right and during the engagement kept up a continued and destructive fire on those of the enemy that attempted to escape into the River and killed a very large proportion of those that were found dead under the bank as well as many others sunk under water."

Lieutenant Jesse Bean and the 40 men of his company of spies, who had been sent by Coffee to the island off the western end of the neck, did more of the same. Coffee reported that "many of the enemy did attempt their escape to the Island, but not one ever landed, they were sunk by Leut. Beans command ere they reached the bank." All around the bend it was a turkey shoot—or a turtle shoot. Forty-seven years later a veteran of the battle, John Campbell of East Tennessee, a private in Colonel John Brown's 2nd Regiment of Volunteer Mounted Gunmen, recalled that "the Indians had felled trees into the river. In the effort to escape they would crawl out on these, when Coffee's men would pick them off, and they would drop like turtles into the water." Coffee, not given to metaphors, put it plainly: "Attempts to cross the river at all points of the bend was made by the enemy, but not one escaped very few ever reached the bank, and that few was killed the instant they landed."

Farther up the peninsula, where Major Reid could see the fighting, the remaining Red Sticks, driven by relentless bayonets from the brush and timber on the high ground, "leaped down the banks, and concealed themselves along the cliffs and steeps, which were covered by the trees that had been felled from their margin. From these secreted spots, as an opportunity was afforded, they would fire, and disappear. General Jackson, perceiving that any further resistance would only involve them in utter destruction, sent a flag, accompanied by an interpreter, to propose them to surrender, and save the further effusion of blood. Whether the proposal were fairly explained, none but the interpreter can know; at any rate, instead of being accepted, as was fully expected would be the case, it was answered by a fire, which wounded one of the party."

Jackson ordered the action continued. The six-pounder and the three-pounder were brought forward and fired into the tangle of trees on the banks, but without effect. The Red Sticks were neither cowed nor rendered incapable of further resistance. For them it was either fight to the death or escape. Jackson was determined to prevent the latter, and as for the former, he gave them their wish. Major Reid wrote, "Lighted torches were now thrown down the steeps, which, communicating with the brush and trees, and setting them on fire, drove them from their hiding places, and brought them to view. Thus the carnage continued" as the soldiers on top of the banks picked off the Red Sticks as the warriors climbed out of the tangle to escape the flames.

"It was dark before we finished killing them," Jackson wrote.

Chapter 18

"We Have Conquered"

"I CAN NOW DO NO MORE THAN WEEP
OVER THE MISFORTUNES OF MY NATION"

If the Creek War was not quite over, only mopping up remained. The Red Stick defeat was overwhelming. On the field lay 557 dead warriors. Of those who tried to flee by the river, John Coffee estimated that "from the report of my Officers as well as from my own observation, I feel warranted in saying that from Two hundred & fifty to three hundred of the enemy was buried under water and was not numbered with the dead that was found." The figure of between 800 and 900 Red Stick dead is not an exaggeration. Jackson thought only 15 or 20 escaped, but a Red Stick estimate of some 200 escaping during the night, probably by quietly swimming down the Tallapoosa, may be closer to the mark. In the morning 16 warriors discovered in the tangle on the banks were called upon to surrender, refused, and were killed. Nobody described Horseshoe Bend better than Andrew Jackson: *"The carnage was dreadfull."*[1]

All of the prisoners except four wounded warriors were women and children. The Red Sticks had literally fought to the death. The women and children, variously estimated at 250 to 350, were later turned over to the friendly Indians. One of the wounded warriors while being tended looked defiantly at Jackson and asked, "Cure 'im, kill 'im again?" Impressed by the young warrior's "manly behavior," Jackson sent him to the Hermitage and arranged to have him learn a trade. The young man married a black woman and eventually set up his own business.[2]

Jackson's casualties were trifling in contrast, although not trifling to those who suffered them. The adjutant general's final count was 32 American dead, 99 wounded. The friendly Cherokees had 18 killed and 36 wounded, the friendly Creeks 5 dead and 11 wounded.[3]

One of the main reasons for the massive Red Stick defeat in the Creek War was the condition of their armaments. From beginning to end they were poorly armed, and the Americans could be thankful that was the case. As Frank Owsley has pointed out, perhaps no more than one in three or four Red Stick warriors had a gun, and quite often they lacked enough powder and lead. Logistics and a hostile terrain were the chief problems faced by the Americans. Of the two, logistics was by far the more important, and it was staggering. Only Jackson among the American commanders in the field overcame it, and at times he did it as only he could, by simply ignoring it and pushing on and insisting that his army push on, too. His performance was magnificent, and that also spelled a critical difference between the Americans and the Red Sticks.[4]

Of the Red Stick leaders not one can be called a strategist or tactician. William Weatherford, the storied Red Eagle, is often presented as an exception, but we only know that he fought at Fort Mims, where sheer American negligence guaranteed victory to anybody. At Calabee Creek, against Floyd and his Georgians, Red Eagle's tactical advice was excellent but ignored. So we have little on which to judge him. We can, however, judge the others, and their strategy of waiting for the Americans to attack them was disastrous. The one occasion in which the Red Sticks attacked Jackson's army while it was on the march, at Enitachopko Creek, where they had at a critical moment the overwhelming advantage in numbers, was lost because of supreme valor and leadership by the Americans and the Indian failure to quickly push their advantage to hand-to-hand combat. At Horseshoe Bend the Red Sticks committed the folly of situating themselves on a peninsula and allowing the Americans to surround them.

The Indian genius at war was as guerrillas, or partisans, dealing the sudden strike, the quick withdrawal, only to appear once again, swift and unexpected, visiting terror and panic upon the enemy. Their great victories over Harmar and St. Clair north of the Ohio came when they attacked American armies on the march, not when they holed up in towns and allowed the Americans to come to them, surround them, annihilate them. To allow that was inviting a debacle, and that is what they got. Some might argue that the Americans were too many and too well armed for the old tried-and-true Indian tactics to have made a difference, that the Red Sticks might have held out longer but in the end the Americans' vastly superior numbers and better weapons would have prevailed. But that is to ignore the rest of our story, and a development on the Gulf Coast that could have made a crucial difference to the final outcome. We shall get to that shortly.

Leadership, then, was also critical, and on that score the Red Sticks failed the test, while Americans had in Andrew Jackson one of the great wartime commanders in their history.

The Battle of Horseshoe Bend has been called one of the great American victories of the War of 1812. One of America's leading diplomatic historians, Bradford Perkins, labeled the Creek War itself the most important victory of the war, a judgment that cannot be faulted, for it destroyed Creek military power on the Gulf Coast before the British intervened and came calling with arms and unchallenged naval power and a strong, veteran army. But that, and Jackson's response, are the major subjects of the rest of this book.[5]

In the meantime, Jackson thought one more battle against the Creeks would be necessary, on the Hickory Ground near Alexander McGillivray's old haunts. Before leaving Horseshoe Bend, however, he had the American dead weighted down and buried in the river, for after the fight at Emuckfau the Red Sticks had dug up the American dead and scalped and stripped them. Some dead Indians at Horseshoe Bend were found in the clothing of those American dead.

The army then marched for Fort Williams and arrived there on the afternoon of 31 March. On 2 April, Jackson paid tribute to his "Fellow-Soldiers," who had "entitled yourselves to the gratitude of your general & of your country," so much so that he ordered that an "extra ration be isued to the troops." His purpose in what was a long proclamation was to maintain their pride and common enthusiasm for a mission unfinished, and to "ward off," wrote John Reid, "that despondency from his ranks, which had once proved so fatal to his hopes." And he did not risk idleness among the militia and volunteers by tarrying at Fort Williams. He marched with eight days rations on 7 April and proceeded down the west bank of the Tallapoosa, headed for the old French Fort Toulouse at the confluence of the Coosa and the Tallapoosa. The army was unopposed and the torch liberally employed. Empty Creek towns went up in flames. Indians fled before the Americans. *Micos* from the hostile towns came in to surrender. Jackson directed them to take their people north of Fort Williams and settle. That way they would be removed from easy access to the Spanish and the British in Florida. As he marched, Jackson once more ran into the problem of shortage of food, and also the prickly jealousies of regular officers.[6]

Colonel Homer Virgil Milton, commanding regulars and Georgia militia, was operating on the lower Tallapoosa in the vicinity of old Fort Toulouse. Soon after leaving Fort Williams Jackson sent a message to Milton requesting a rendezvous between the two forces on 11 April, and alerting him to how much food Jackson had and "the reliance I placed . . . upon what I should be able to obtain from him." Even though the two armies were not far apart, Milton did not reply until the fourteenth. He told Jackson "that he would send a small supply to the friendly Indians who had accompanied me, & that *tomorrow* he would *lend* me some, for the remainder of my troops; but that he felt himself under no *obligation* to furnish any." The armies were then three miles apart, and Milton's message was clear: Jackson might be a major general, but a militia major general, whereas Colonel Homer Milton was regular, and there lay all the difference. Jackson described the incident to General Pinckney, and he included a veiled threat with regard to Colonel Milton. On the fifteenth, "Captain Gordon of the Spies . . . returned; bringing two thousand rations, & a note from the Colo., stating that they were sent, not because I had *ordered* them but because my men were destitute. His unwillingness to obey my orders (tho in the neighbourhood) until a junction is actually formed, & his apparent wish to postpone that event as long as possible, are a little singular & will be noted."[7]

Milton's jealousy and petty behavior became academic on 21 April when General Pinckney arrived at Fort Jackson, then being built on the site of old Fort Toulouse, and took command of all American forces in the field. Jackson had arrived on the eighteenth, hoisted the American flag, and on that day began clearing the ground for the erection of Fort Jackson. Detachments were sent out to sweep the countryside and break up parties of hostiles. But John Coffee wrote to his wife that "the Indians have all fled, they are running in all directions, numbers are arriving in and begging forgiveness, some are running towards Pensacola, while others are hiding in the swamps. . . ." And Creek *micos* who kept arriving to seek peace informed Jackson that the Red Sticks who meant either to continue the fight or refused to live under American rule had fled to the Gulf Coast and Spanish sanctuary.[8]

The *micos* were right, but Jackson was not satisfied. He wanted Weatherford. Where was he? Where was Red Eagle? Bring him in, he demanded of the *micos*. Learning of this, Weatherford disdained flight, scorned being brought bound before the conqueror. Alone he penetrated the American lines at Fort Jackson and rode unmolested to Jackson's tent, where he stood before the stern general and identified himself and said he had come on behalf of his people to seek peace. Jackson was astonished and replied that had Red Eagle been brought to him a captive he would have known what to do to him. The other leaders—Josiah Francis, Paddy Walsh, Peter McQueen, and High-Headed Jim—had fled to Pensacola, but this fearless, fine-looking man standing before him had ridden in of his own accord. Jackson was obviously impressed, both by what he saw and what he heard.[9]

"I am in your power," Red Eagle said, "do with me as you please. I am a soldier. I have done the white people all the harm I could; I have fought them, and fought them bravely: if I had an army I would yet fight, and contend to the last: but I have none; my people are all gone. I can now do no more than weep over the misfortunes of my nation."

Jackson replied that if Weatherford wanted to continue fighting he would be allowed to leave and join those Red Sticks still hostile, but if taken, his life would be forfeit. If it were peace he sought, however, "he might remain where he was, and should be protected."

Red Eagle chose peace, for he had no choice. This nephew of the great Alexander McGillivray told Jackson, "There was a time when I had a choice, and could have answered you: I have none now, even hope has ended. Once I could animate my warriors to battle; but I cannot animate the dead. My warriors can no longer hear my voice: their bones are at Talladega, Tallushatchee, Emuckfaw, and Tohopeka." He maintained that "if I had been left to contend with the Georgia army, I would have raised my corn on one bank of the river, and fought them on the other; but your people have destroyed my nation, You are a brave man: I rely upon your generosity." Then he admitted that whatever terms Jackson enacted, "it would now be madness and folly to oppose."

Some present called for his execution, but Jackson, so often simplistically described as an Indian-hater, silenced that talk. He was clearly taken with the man. Thomas Woodward wrote, "I have heard Gen. Jackson say that if he was capable of forming anything like a correct judgement of a man on a short acquaintance, that he pronounced Weatherford to be as high-toned and fearless as any man he had met with—one whose very nature scorned a mean action." And as Robert Remini points out, keeping Weatherford alive to persuade other Red Sticks to lay down their arms and come in was the wiser course. William Weatherford survived those terrible times of trouble for his people, when relatives of those butchered at Fort Mims would gladly have killed him. He never again took up arms against the Americans, and spent his remaining years in prosperous retirement, finally honored and respected by his former enemies, on his plantation in Monroe County, Alabama, where he died in 1826. A fine horseman from a family noted for owning superb horses, on various occasions he visited another lover of good horseflesh, his friend Andrew Jackson, at the Hermitage, and is reported to have trained horses there.[10]

"WE HAVE ADDED A COUNTRY TO OURS"

General Thomas Pinckney was delighted with Jackson. Their backgrounds could not have been more different; the one a spottily educated Back Country orphan, the other from one of South Carolina's most prominent Low Country families. But Pinckney, a veteran of the Revolution, recognized a winner when he saw one, knew that Jackson was the man most responsible for the sudden humbling of the Creek Nation. His praise for Jackson and his troops overflowed, and in the middle of what white men would consider a howling wilderness he gave a banquet for Jackson and his officers. The following day, Jackson reciprocated.[11]

But now it was time for the militia and volunteers to go home, and on 21 April 1814, the day he received Pinckney's orders, Jackson had the regiments swung into line and headed north for Tennessee. He addressed them and praised them anew twice on the way, at Fort Williams, and later at Fayetteville, Tennessee, where the West Tennessee troops had rendezvoused the previous fall and were now honorably discharged by the general who had led them to victory. The bad times were left behind. What you have accomplished, he told his soldiers, "will long be cherished in the memory of your General, and will not be forgotten by the country which you have so materially benefited." Now it was time for Jackson to go home.

The day before his arrival in Nashville, he was met on the road by some citizens who joined his entourage. The word spread. Jackson is coming. Four miles from town the crowds began, hundreds of them, cheering their hero. How times had changed. He was taken to the courthouse where Felix Grundy delivered a welcoming address, as did the students of Cumberland College. Then it was on to Bell Tavern where, according to the *Nashville Whig* of 16 May, all "partook of a collation prepared for the occasion." Jackson then delivered a fine speech, acknowledging their greetings with heartfelt thanks on behalf of his officers and soldiers for all they had endured, and then adding something else, words that go far in explaining just what he saw as the purpose of the war.

> We have conquered. We have added a country to ours, which, by connecting the settlements of Georgia with those of the Mississippi Territory, and both of them with our own, will become a secure barrier against foreign invasion, or the operation of foreign influence over our red neighbors in the South. . . . How ardently, therefore, is it to be wished that government take the earliest opportunity, and devise the most effectual means, of populating that section of the Union.

Then once more a tribute to his men, especially those who had paid the ultimate price: "In acquiring these advantages to our country it is true we have lost some valuable citizens, some brave soldiers. But these are misfortunes inseparable from a state of war; and while I mingle my regret with yourselves, that the sons of Tennessee who fell contending for their rights have approved themselves worthy of the American name—worthy descendants of their sires of the Revolution."

All may not have forgiven him, but their voices were still or muted. For most of the People of the Western Waters, Jackson was the hero of the hour. He was primarily responsible for the giant step that put them so much closer to their cherished goal of taking the land, all of it, which was his goal as well, for he was one of them and would continue to be one of them into his grave.

Washington's eyes were also on Jackson. At last, in a war that had produced one humiliation after another, as incompetent generals left ruined reputations in the wake of that folly called the conquest of Canada, at last, a general who knew how to win. Even the Madison administration had to put aside its hostility toward this tempestuous, outspoken frontiersman and give him his due. And it all happened with rapid-fire action. A vacancy in the army lists had appeared with the resignation of Major General Wade Hampton. "Something ought to be done for Gen. Jackson," Secretary of War John Armstrong wrote to President Madison, who was then at Montpelier, his home in Virginia. Madison agreed and told Armstrong to send him, Madison, the necessary papers. Armstrong, who often acted as an independent operator, ignored Madison and on 22 May 1814 wrote to Jackson offering him the rank of brigadier general in the regular army, a brevet, or temporary, rank of major general, and command of 7th Military District, replacing Brigadier General Thomas Flournoy. Seventh was in Jackson's backyard: Louisiana, Tennessee, Mississippi Territory, and most of the Creek Nation. Jackson was unhappy that Armstrong had not offered him the permanent rank of major general, which was his rank in the Tennessee militia, but he did not quibble about accepting a commission in the U.S. Army. On 8 June he accepted.

Then, on 28 May, ignoring Madison's intention to at least discuss the matter, Armstrong wrote to Jackson offering him the permanent rank of major general, a vacancy created by the resignation of William Henry Harrison. Jackson accepted on 18 June. Now not even the Homer Virgil Miltons of this world would question his authority. Jackson's awareness of the importance of his promotion is revealed in a letter to Rachel: "I have wrote to my friend John Hutching to have you a god pair of horses procured, and I wish your carriage well repaired or exchanged for a new one—you had better visit Nashville and make this erangement with the carriage maker your self—you must recollect that you are now a Major Generals lady—in the service of the U.S. and as such you must appear, elegant and plain, not extravagant—but in such stile as strangers expect to see you."

Even more important, with his new rank came his own military district, and the opportunity in those days before rapid communications, and the ability of distant superiors to micromanage events, to put into effect his goal, his people's goal, to rid the Old Southwest of all enemies foreign and domestic.[12]

"OLD MAD JACKSON"

By the Creeks he had been given a new name: Sharp Knife. By the time he got through dealing with them at Fort Jackson they also called him "Old Mad Jackson."[13]

While the hero basked in the admiration of his fellow westerners and gave Rachel the tenderness and attention she deserved, General Pinckney and Benjamin Hawkins proceeded under Secretary Armstrong's instructions to discuss the terms of a peace treaty with the Creeks. The People of the Western Waters viewed their appointments with deep suspicion. They demanded a draconian settlement that would include a large cession of land. The American terms, however, were quite generous, and the source lay in Washington, not at Fort Jackson, for the peace commissioners followed Armstrong's instructions almost to the letter. The only change Armstrong made was in a brief follow-up letter to Pinckney of 20 March in which he stated that the treaty "should take a form altogether military, and be in the nature of a capitulation, in which case the whole authority . . . rests with you, exclusively, as commanding general," which left Benjamin Hawkins in the role of an adviser.[14]

Jackson had different ideas, and paramount among them was the security of the nation against foreign foes. Spain, a mere shadow of its former greatness, still held East Florida, but the colony was prey to whoever took it first. Many Red Sticks had fled there, and the British were on the threshold with arms and ammunition. The simplistic notion that Jackson was an Indian-hater and a land-grabber satiating bigotry and greed reveals a prejudice against him and the People of the Western Waters as deep as racial and ethnic prejudice. In a letter to Colonel John Williams, commander of 39th Infantry, who had made known his alarm at the terms offered the Creeks, Jackson made his thoughts quite clear: "I answer that the country west of the Coosee and North of the Allabama, is a valuable country and might endemnify the government fully for the expence of the war. But sir, this cannot be the only object of government. The hostile Creeks have forfeited all right to the Territory we have conquered, and while Justice to the friendly part of the Nation require that they should be left in the peaceable enjoyment of their towns and villages with a sufficient appendage of woodland, humanity dictates, that the conquered part of the nation should be alloted sufficient space for agricultural purposes."

Then Jackson got to the nub of it, repeating, but in more detail, what he had told the citizens of Nashville: "Still the grand policy of government ought to be, to connect the settlements of Georgia with that of the [Mississippi] Territory and Tennessee, which at once forms a bulwark against foreign invasion, and prevents the introduction of foreign influence to corrupt the minds of the Indians. The settlements should be so formed as to separate the strength of the creek nation, and the settlement of the whites between them would always keep them peaceable and faithful."

After outlining his boundary proposals, Jackson stated, in language rarely if ever used in Washington by men who wanted the same thing but shrank from candor, that after telling the Creeks where they might live, "the balance rightfully belongs to the United States by conquest . . . and afford a settlement from Georgia to the Mobile and from Tennessee to the southern limits of the United States." Thus we have come full circle, from the years immediately following the Revolution, when the United States announced ownership by right of conquest but had not the means and force to back it up, to the greatest Indian-fighter of all pronouncing right of conquest from a position of overwhelming strength. And once he was given the chance, he wasted little time in making it official.[15]

In late April 1814 General Pinckney withdrew from the peace commission before terms were settled. He wished to return to Charleston and his own 5th Military District and prepare the Carolina coasts for any British military onslaught. On 24 May Armstrong wrote to Jackson informing him that President Madison wished him to proceed to Fort Jackson and "consummate the arrangements committed to Major Gen. Pinckney in relation to the hostile Creeks." Armstrong enclosed a copy of his instructions to Pinckney.

On 26 June Jackson left home and rode south. By then he had already received ominous news. From the Mississippi Territory had come a report that the British had landed at the mouth of the Apalachicola River with "twenty thousand stand of arms and a large quantity of ammunition." The writer was inclined to discount the information because of the huge amount of guns involved, but that was the only piece of incorrect intelligence. For on 10 May 1814 Captain Hugh Pigot, commanding HMS *Orpheus,* had given the order to drop anchor off the mouth of the Apalachicola. Aboard Pigot had two thousand muskets and supplies of ammunition. He also had with him a white trader from Jamaica by the name of George Woodbine, who knew many of the Creek and Seminole *micos* and could also interpret. Woodbine so impressed Pigot that he made the young man an officer of Royal Marines. It was Woodbine to whom Pigot handed over the two thousand muskets and powder and lead to arm the refugee Red Sticks.[16]

The excellent American intelligence service, from civilians and military alike, poured information into Jackson's headquarters as he once more rode south. Similar reports had gone to Washington, but Amstrong was inclined to dismiss them. Jackson was more realistic. The day after he left home he wrote to Armstrong from Murfreesboro, Tennessee, "At this place I met a corroboration of the account that 300 British had landed and are fortifying at the mouth of the Apalachacola, and are arming and exciting the Indians to acts of hostility against the United States. Whether these rumors are founded in fact, or not, we ought at least to be prepared for the worst." If true, he concluded, will Washington authorize him to deal with the problem by marching upon Pensacola? "If so I promise the war in the south a speedy termination and British influence forever cut off from the Indians in that quarter." About two weeks later, a few days after his arrival at Fort Jackson, he wrote a civil but firm letter to the governor of Pensacola, Don Mateo González Manrique: "I trust sir, that no foundations for these reports exist; I trust, that the officers of the Spanish government at Pensacola and its vicinity have had more regard for the *interests* of Spain and the *rights* of the United States, than to permit the violation of a neutrality important to the American people." González Manrique, who could do nothing about the British, thought the letter impertinent and insulting. He would soon have far more than strong letters to complain about.[17]

So would the Creeks. For Jackson had succeeded to General Pinckney's authority as sole American negotiator. Benjamin Hawkins would be there, but only as an adviser. Summoned by the general, the Creeks gathered at Fort Jackson on the appointed day, 1 August 1814. If they did not come, warned Jackson, "Destruction will attend a failure to comply with these orders." Jackson followed Armstrong's instructions to Pinckney with regard to five matters. The United States would have the right to build roads wherever they thought necessary through Creek country, to freely navigate all of its rivers and streams, and to build military posts and trading houses wherever they wished. Creek trade and communications with foreign nations would be regulated by the United States, with such restrictions as deemed necessary. Finally, the Creeks must surrender the prophets and other instigators of the war identified by the United States. That was the easy part. There was a sixth stipulation, listed by Armstrong but stretched to its limits by Jackson and a source of controversy into our own times.[18]

Armstrong had written that the Creeks must also cede land to indemnify the United States for the expenses of the war. Jackson enforced this with a vengeance. After all, this was a capitulation, and he had inherited Pinckney's exclusive authority of "making and concluding the terms. . . ." He was determined that the Creeks would never again rise and to block easy access to them by any foreign government. North of the Alabama River he left the Creeks a slice of country in the eastern part of Alabama measuring some 150,000 square miles. But from the heart of the Creek Nation, from all of the Creeks, friendly and hostile, Jackson carved a huge swath through central and southern Alabama of what he reckoned was 23 million acres: approximately three-fifths of what is now the state of Alabama, and one-fifth of Georgia. He was taking more than half of what had been the original Creek Nation. The swath began in northern Alabama, descended southward all the way to the thirty-first parallel at the Louisiana line, then turned east and followed today's line between Alabama and Florida and then Georgia and Florida to the St. Mary's River. Thus the Creeks no longer owned land contiguous to Spanish Florida, land that Jackson wanted quickly populated with a "preference right to those who conquered it at two dollars per acre of three hundred and twenty acres," for then, he asserted, "it would be quickly settled by a hardy race that would defend it."[19]

This was but part of a grander scheme that with the Creek cession marks Andrew Jackson as a man of his time and place, when the young nation was at war with a powerful foe as close to American territory as a day's march, when eventual American control of the Gulf Coast and retention of Mobile and New Orleans were by no means certain. Even before the Creek cession he was thinking ahead to further cessions by all of the southern tribes, which would

> therefore extend our settlements to the Mississippi to cut off all communications of the Southern tribes with that of the North, and give to our citizens perfect safety in passing through their country. We must give them [the various tribes] a fair compensation for a surrender of their rights. Our national security require it and *their* security require it: the happiness and security of the whole require this salutary arrangement. It must be done, and they shall be endemnified Either in money or land gained by the Creek conquest. Now is the time to obtain it and it ought and must be had. This then will give strength to the southern section of the United States, both in the councils of the nation, and against foreign invasion and foreign influence. . . .[20]

Thus the harsh nature of his final stipulation dictated to the Creeks. The friendly *micos* were in shock. They were allies. Their people had died fighting beside Jackson's soldiers against a common enemy. How could he do this to them? They listened with stony faces to Old Mad Jackson deliver the terms, and then they retired to their councils and discussed at length this unbelievable demand, and rejected it. They appealed to Hawkins, but he could do nothing. When they returned to once more face Jackson, it was Big Warrior who rose to speak eloquently of all they had been through together. The Creeks had divined Jackson's purpose and his fears, and Big Warrior tried to set the general's mind at ease. He admitted that when "we were young and foolish" the Creeks had joined the British during the Revolutionary War, but "the British can no more persuade us to do wrong; they have deceived us once, they can deceive us no more." If the British "offer me arms, I will say to them, You put me in danger, to war against a people born in our own land." Big Warrior repeatedly emphasized this point: "If the British advise us to do anything, I will tell you, not hide it from you. If they say we must fight, I will tell them, No!"[21]

Major Reid reported that the faithful Selocta, he whose fidelity had been proven from the beginning of Jackson's campaign, "who had marched and fought with" the Americans in all their battles, then rose before the assemblage. He said that "he was not opposed to yielding the lands lying on the Alabama, which would answer the purpose of cutting off any intercourse with the Spaniards; but the country west of the Coosa, he wished to be preserved to the nation." He made a personal appeal to Jackson, reminded "him of the dangers they had passed together; and of his faithfulness to him, in the trying scenes through which they had gone."[22]

All in vain. Hawkins's presence made not a whit of difference, nor would his anguished pleas to Washington later on behalf of his charges. Jackson had made up his mind and would not budge, and nobody would overrule him. Whatever arguments the Creeks came up with he rejected. Finally, tired of the wrangling, he said, "Those who are opposed to it shall have leave to retire to Pensacola. Here is the paper: take it, and show the President who are his friends. Consult and this evening let me know who will sign it, and who will not. I do not wish, nor will I attempt, to force any of you; act as you think proper."[23]

That was his final word. The *micos* capitulated. For what choice had they? It is estimated that 3,000 Creeks (15% of the population) died during the war. The Upper Creek country, towns and fields and storehouses, was a smoldering ruin, burned either by the Red Sticks or the Americans. And facing them was the conqueror they truly feared, whom neither the Creeks nor the other southern Indians would ever forget. Several years later a traveler was sitting in his tent on the banks of the lower Mississippi. This man had gray hair worn in the manner of Jackson. Six drunken Indians came up to his campfire. One attempted to enter the tent. The traveler grabbed him by the neck and sent him head over heels, whereupon the others took hold of their knives and rifles and "made for me. Seeing my pistols cocked and pointed in the direction of the two foremost, a pause was made, accompanied by silence; when one, who had been too drunk to come up with the rest, rose upon his feet, and stretching out his arm, and pointing at me with his finger, said, in a loud voice, '*Jackson!*' That moment knives were put up, and rifles lowered, and I became the object of a general gaze. Shortly after, they all, in tolerable quiet, left the ground."[24]

Chapter 19

‎——✦——

"I Act without the Orders of Government"

"I owe to Britain a debt of retaliatory vengeance"

Once the Creeks had signed, Jackson did not tarry. On 11 August, two days after the signing ceremonies, he set out for Mobile with 3rd Regiment of U.S. Infantry, about 500 strong. The date is significant. On the same day, in Paris, Napoleon abdicated and began his journey to Elba. This meant that England, freed of the Corsican's threat, would be able to turn much of its attention to the war in America and supply the veteran troops needed to teach the upstarts across the Atlantic a long overdue lesson.

Jackson left behind at Fort Jackson Colonel Philip Pipkin, whose regiment of West Tennessee militia, along with one company of 44th U.S. Infantry, garrisoned the posts Jackson had built during the Creek War. England was now the main enemy, and he meant to deal with it in a forthright manner, for the nation—and for himself. Harking back to the terrible trials of his boyhood in South Carolina during the War of the Revolution and the loss of his entire family, he had written to Rachel a week earlier, "I owe to Britain a debt of retaliatory Vengeance. Should our forces meet I trust I shall pay the debt."[1]

That enemy was now busily engaged in preparing for an assault on Mobile, preparatory to moving against New Orleans and the Lower Mississippi Valley. Let us take a brief look at this British plan for conquest.[2]

The British aimed a two-pronged attack on the United States. From the north a large British army under Sir George Prevost was to invade northern New York from Canada by way of Lake Champlain and occupy a large slice of America's northern borderlands that would be held hostage during the peace negotiations. A small amphibious force under General Robert Ross, designed to raid Atlantic Coast cities, may have been meant as a diversion for the Gulf Coast campaign. On the Gulf Coast, which had few inhabitants and even fewer defenders, the British planned to arm Creeks, Seminoles, Choctaws, and Chickasaws and, in alliance with them, land troops for a campaign to capture Mobile before taking New Orleans. Early plans envisioned pushing northward up the Alabama River and capturing the recently built American forts, and also up the Mississippi deep into the Mississippi Territory, with dreams of detaching the South from the Union. Although the 10,000-man northern thrust was uppermost in the mind of Lord Bathurst, secretary of state for war and colonies, the Gulf Coast offensive became paramount following the decisive American naval victory on Lake Champlain and General Prevost's abysmal failure at Plattsburgh, New York. The northern front was once more stalemated.

In the Chesapeake country, however, General Robert Ross and Admiral George Cockburn, with 4,500 men, had scored signal and humiliating victories over the Americans, despite their subsequent failure to take Baltimore. On 24 August 1814, at Bladensburg, Maryland, the American rout was so precipitate that the battle became known as the "Bladensburg Races." At 8:00 P.M. that evening the victorious British troops marched into Washington and began burning and looting. The fires burned all night, and the "sky was brilliantly illuminated by the different conflagrations," wrote the young British officer George Robert Gleig, whose further adventures in America will enhance the narrative.[3]

But General Ross was killed in action during the assault on Baltimore. Until his replacement was appointed, his deputy, Major General John Keane (1781–1844), took temporary command. This change in command will have a critical effect on our story. Meanwhile, the highly experienced and aggressive Vice Admiral Sir Alexander Inglis Cochrane (1758–1832) was moving ahead with his plans for the Gulf Coast offensive. Cochrane was an enthusiast for using not only Indians but also escaped black slaves, organized into British army units, to raid the Georgia frontier, thus tying down the Georgia militia, and to act in concert with British troops for the assault on Mobile. Three thousand troops were envisioned for the attack. Most important to the entire operation, Cochrane planned to have brought from England large numbers of shallow-draft boats, each to carry naval guns and 100 men. No matter what approach to New Orleans the British finally adopted, these craft were vital to navigate the shallow rivers, lakes, and sea approaches on the Gulf Coast and its hinterland.

At this point readers who recall from school days the notable American naval victories earlier in the War of 1812 might well ask why we have not mentioned the danger to any British invasion fleet from American warships. The answer is simple. There was no danger. There was no American naval force capable of challenging British seapower. From Passamaquoddy Bay in Maine along the length of the Atlantic Coast, in the Gulf from the Keys to the Mississippi and beyond, Britannia ruled the waves. The intrepid and skillful actions of *Constitution* and *United States* and other Yankee ships of the line in 1812 were memories. American ships and American seamen still sailed, still dared, but they were few, and annoyances only, mostly privateers sailing distant seas looking to cut out lone prizes. The British sailed American waters with impunity, put troops ashore where they wished, when they wished.[4]

We have already discussed Captain Pigot's landing in May at the mouth of the Apalachicola, where he distributed arms to the Indians. But we need to say a bit more about the good captain as well as the English trader George Woodbine, in whom Pigot placed great confidence and received the information on which he based his report to Admiral Cochrane of 8 June 1814. Pigot reported that there were some 2,800 Creeks anxious to ally themselves with the British, and another 1,000 hiding in the swamps near Pensacola. The Choctaws would also side with the British, Pigot said. And he claimed that there were 800 Baratarian privateers under the Lafitte brothers based at Barataria Bay, about thirty miles south-southwest of New Orleans, who could be persuaded to assist British forces. It was also Pigot who recommended the indirect approach of advancing from Mobile to Baton Rouge by land and cutting off New Orleans from relief. The British then expected the city to fall like a ripe plum. Pigot's optimism was intoxicating for minds conditioned to accept it. On 20 June Cochrane wrote to London that "three thousand British Troops landed at Mobile where they would be joined by all the Indians with the disaffected French and Spaniards, would drive the Americans entirely out of Louisiana and the Floridas." Cochrane would make one important change to Pigot's recommendation. Instead of a land approach to Baton Rouge, he planned to transport the troops against New Orleans in shallow-draft boats along the coast from Mobile to Lake Pontchartrain, immediately north of the city. From there the British could either strike overland to Baton Rouge, some seventy miles westward, or directly at New Orleans, four miles to the south.[5]

While awaiting London's response, Cochrane sent into the field a highly decorated officer of the Royal Marines, Brevet Major Edward Nicolls (1779–1865), to whom Cochrane gave the local rank of lieutenant colonel to impress the Indians and others. Nicolls brought with him another two thousand muskets, two cannon, and two thousand swords, for Woodbine and Pigot felt that the Indians would make excellent cavalrymen. His assignment was to train the Indians, scout the Gulf Coast, and find the best approaches to New Orleans. Nicolls, an Anglo Irishman, was described as an "impatient, blustering," but "brave officer well known in the European wars." Cochrane put a Scot, the "mild and gentlemanly" Captain Sir William Henry Percy (1788–1855) of HMS *Hermes,* in command of all British naval ships in the Gulf and ordered him to support Nicolls.[6]

Nicolls had been refused permission to land at Pensacola by the Spanish captain general in Havana, but he was "determined to land at Pensacola, with or without leave," reported an anonymous informer from Havana. With 100 Royal Marines he arrived at the Apalachicola in mid-August 1814. Leaving some men and provisions there, he sailed to Pensacola. There the Spanish governor, González Manrique, on his own authority, asked for British help against the attack he expected from the Americans. Nicolls did not hesitate.

He immediately landed, was given occupation of one of the forts defending the city, and ordered Captain Percy to bring the rest of the marines from Apalachicola. That day, with Spanish approval, the Union Jack as well as the banner of Castile and Leon flew over Fort San Miguel. The British, commanded in the Gulf by confident, aggressive officers from Admiral Cochrane on down, their contempt for their foe heightened by the disgraceful American performances at Bladensburg and Washington, began preparations to capture Mobile, which they planned as their base for conquest.[7]

In a manner reminiscent of proclamations issued by British officers during the Revolutionary War, Nicolls issued his own from Pensacola on 29 August: "Natives of Louisiana! on you the first call is made to assist in liberating from a faithless, imbecile government, your paternal soil: Spaniards, Frenchmen, Italians, and British, whether settled or residing for a time in Louisiana, on you, also, I call to aid me in this just cause: the American usurption in this country must be abolished, and the lawful owners of the soil put in possession." Note that Nicolls used the words "American usurption." This gives us the opportunity to remind the reader that Great Britain had never recognized the legality of the French sale of Louisiana to the United States. In its eyes, Spain was still the rightful owner, a legal position, we must admit, with which it is difficult to argue. But Nicolls was not through. "Inhabitants of Kentucky," the proclamation continued, "the whole brunt of the war has fallen on your brave sons; be imposed upon no longer, but either range yourselves under the standard of your forefathers, or observe a strict neutrality. . . ."[8]

At the same time, Nicolls and Captain Percy were attempting to recruit Jean Lafitte and his Baratarian privateers. Nicolls wrote to Lafitte reminding him that England and France were now friends and called upon him, "with your brave followers, to enter into the services of Great Britain, in which you shall have the rank of captain; lands will be given to you all, in proportion to your respective ranks, on a peace taking place, and I invite you on the following terms." One of those terms was to "cease all hostilities against Spain, or the allies of Great Britain." Nicolls sent Captain John McWilliams of the Royal Marines aboard the sloop *Sophie,* Captain Nicholas Lockyer commanding, to deliver the message to Lafitte.[9]

While Nicolls and Percy laid the ground for invasion, London made a decision and wrote to Admiral Cochrane in August that his plan had been accepted. He could have Ross's force from the Chesapeake reinforced by 2,100 men from Europe. Later the ministers in London would decide on an even larger army. The rendezvous time and place was set for November 1814 at Negril Bay, Jamaica. London had chosen December as the time for invasion because of the murderous climate of the Gulf Coast. Admiral Cochrane, who was spoiling for a fight with the Americans, must have been ecstatic when he received the word from London. He had written in July, "I have it much at heart to give them a complete drubbing before Peace is made, when I trust their Northern limits will be circumscribed and the Command of the Mississippi wrested from them."[10]

In the meantime, on 22 August one of those Americans whom Cochrane yearned to drub, a backwoods general with a personal score to settle and of whom the British knew little if anything, arrived in Mobile. Jackson had drifted down the Alabama, passing "vast quantities of most excellent bottom and high lands bordering this river throughout its whole distance." By the rivers, the Alabama and the Mobile, the distance from Fort Jackson was about 420 miles. Even before leaving Fort Jackson he had ordered Colonel Richard Sparks of 2nd U.S. Infantry at Mobile to restore Fort Bowyer. The fort was located thirty miles south of the city across Mobile Bay, on what was then known as Mobile Point (now Fort Morgan), a spit of land at the very end of a barrier beach at the outer reaches of Mobile Bay. Fort Bowyer, of which no physical trace exists, commanded the main ship channel to the bay. It had been built in 1813, but was abandoned as indefensible when the totally inexperienced and inept General Thomas Flournoy commanded 7th Military District. But it was key to the defense of Mobile, and both Jackson and the British saw Mobile as the key to the defense of the Gulf Coast and the approaches to New Orleans. As Jackson disembarked on the wharf at Mobile, he met Major William L. Lawrence (d. 1841). Major Howell Tatum (1753–1822), who was in Jackson's party, recorded in his "Journal" that Lawrence was preparing to sail for Fort Bowyer with 160 men, "cannon & military stores" to restore and garrison the fort. Lawrence sailed that same day, Tatum wrote, and after "encountering, & surmounting many difficulties, from unfavorable winds and weather," finally landed on Mobile Point and got to work. He had little time left.[11]

Jackson's wound from the Benton fight continued to plague him, as he told Rachel the day after his arrival in Mobile: "My arm has broke, and has been running for some days, and has become painful, I entertain some fears, that it will rise and break in the underside. . . ." But as during the Creek campaign, mere physical disabilities could not be allowed to hinder the mission. Meanwhile, the rumor mill was working overtime. Reports of incredibly large British forces poured into Jackson's headquarters, and he had earlier that month received gloomy reports from Governor Claiborne of Louisiana on the state of arms, discipline, and loyalty among the New Orleans militia. A source at Pensacola reported that 5,000 British troops had landed at the Apalachicola. Jackson wrote that 10,000 men would reach Pensacola on 27 August, "that 14 sail of the line, large transports and 25,000 of Lord Wellington's Troops had reached Bermuda—and that the emperor of Russia had offered england 50,000 Troops to aid her and Spain to conquer and divide America," and "there is no doubt . . . at least 35,000 British and Spanish troops on the coast & at Pensacola."[12]

Wild exaggerations, of course, but the British were obviously preparing a major buildup, and Jackson's forces immediately at hand were few. Secretary of War Armstrong still refused to believe the British would mount a major effort on the Gulf. Events, however, soon brought Armstrong face to face with reality.

Captain Sir William Percy, twenty-six years old and imbued with the optimism of youth and his class, decided that with the forces at hand Fort Bowyer could be taken. Major Nicolls of the Royal Marines, though an intrepid and aggressive officer, was not so sure, feeling that he did not yet have enough men. How ironic that "mild and gentlemanly" Percy pushed for action while the "impatient" Nicolls advised caution. But Percy persisted, and Nicolls finally agreed. He became ill and traveled on HMS *Hermes,* placing Captain Robert Henry of the marines in charge of the land force, which was meant to take Fort Bowyer from the rear while the navy battered it from seaward. On paper it was a good plan, especially as Fort Bowyer had been built only for defense against a naval attack. Without getting too technical, Fort Bowyer was a semicircular redoubt made of pine and earth, four hundred feet long, facing the sea in a southwesterly direction at the tip of the narrow spit of land. It was an excellent site, commanding the entrance to Mobile Bay. But it was small, only eleven of its guns were mounted for action, and it was not constructed to be defended from a land attack from behind. In other words, it was in miniature an early Singapore.[13]

The land force under Captain Henry got to within eight hundred yards of Fort Bowyer's rear on the afternoon of 14 September. According to Nicolls, it consisted of 60 Marines and 180 Indians. Captain Henry ordered the twelve-pounder and the howitzer he had with him to open fire, but Major Lawrence, commanding the garrison, reported that the British fire "was silenced by a few shot," whereupon Captain Henry decided to pull back and wait for Captain Percy's warships to silence Fort Bowyer's guns.[14]

Percy's squadron had four vessels: the ships *Hermes* and *Carron,* and the sloops *Sophie* and *Childers.* Against Fort Bowyer's 11 guns and 158 men, the ships altogether carried 78 guns and 600 men. Percy was in the vicinity of the fort by 12 September, but could not approach because of contrary northerly winds. The entire squadron finally got across the bar and by four o'clock on the afternoon of 15 September 1814 "were under full Sail, and with an easy and favorable breeze standing directly for the Fort. . . ." Major Lawrence wrote, "At 4 P.M. we opened our Battery, which was returned from two Ships, and Two Briggs; as they approached. The Action became General at about 20 minutes past 4 and was continued without intermission on either side untill 7. . . ." The fort and Percy's squadron were "enveloped in a blaze of fire and smoke." During this action Captain Henry of the marines assaulted the rear of Fort Bowyer but was repulsed, and thereafter contented himself with hurling most of his howitzer rounds into the fort. At 5:30 P.M. Captain Percy's ship, the *Hermes,* had her bow cable shot away and drifted into a position in which the fort's guns were able to rake her stem to stern and severely damage her. Percy managed to get her back into action, but she was too badly damaged to be effective, and when he cut her anchor cables to withdraw she proved to be unseaworthy. The *Hermes* was set on fire by the crew and abandoned. She drifted along the front of Fort Bowyer to the eastward, and at 10 P.M., wrote Major Lawrence, "we had the pleasure of witnessing the explosion of her Magazine."[15]

Percy's overconfidence had resulted in a British debacle, and the following day his three remaining vessels stood out to sea and sailed away. Fort Bowyer's determined garrison with eleven effective guns, at least three of which were put out of action during the bombardment, fired between 400 and 500 rounds and sent proud Albion scurrying back to Pensacola. The British lost 23 killed and 47 wounded. Ten later died of their wounds. Major Edward Nicolls, aboard the *Hermes,* was wounded three times and lost his right eye. In the fort Major Lawrence reported 4 killed and 5 wounded, although an officer and about a dozen men were badly burned when loose cartridges exploded. Lawrence wrote that the "Surgeon reports one Man lost: owing to the want of Surgical Instruments as he was compelled to amputate his arm with a Razor. The Man shortly after expired."[16]

Jackson was told that the explosion of the *Hermes* had been Fort Bowyer blowing up and immediately began preparations to retake the fort. When he learned the truth he rolled out the hyperbole: "the gallant Lawrence, with his little spartan band, has given them a lecture that will last for ages." That the ages are fickle is obvious, for who outside the realm of specialists and buffs remember this hot little action? But it should be remembered. The expedition itself was a serious British error in judgment, and their tactical defeat was significant, because it set back their strategy for taking Mobile and opening the way for either a sweep to the Mississippi or a direct advance on New Orleans. But Jackson believed they would be back, for Mobile's importance was obvious, and he did not intend to wait for the next British move. The British attack had been launched from Pensacola, and this gave Jackson another justification to satisfy a hunger that had been building for years on the Western Waters.[17]

At the outset of the Creek War, we recall, Jackson had been anxious to "strike at the root of the disseas pensacola," and he was now straining at the leash to do just that: "would the government only say the word, we would soon have a frolic," he wrote three days before the Battle of Fort Bowyer. And to the governor of Pensacola, González Manrique, who had written to the Creeks congratulating them on their victory at Fort Mims, he had sent threatening, bloodcurdling letters, accusing him of harboring Josiah Francis, Peter McQueen, and "others forming that Matricidal band for whom your christian bowels seem to sympathise and bleed so freely." He rounded this off with a splendid passage in which he demanded that Spain

> restrain the Tomahawk and Scalping knife, or the head which excites their use shall feel the sharpness of their edge. I know that head. I am well advised of the head, which has . . . furnished and excited the use of these savage implements. But it is not on defenceless women and children that retaliation will be made but upon the head which countenanced and excited the barbarity. He is the responsible person and more barberous than the savage whom he makes his instrument of execution. An Eye for an Eye, Toothe for Toothe, and Scalp for Scalp.[18]

A few weeks later, replying to a letter from the Spanish governor, Jackson wrote, "Your Excellency will in future be pleased not to view me as a diplomatic character (unless proclaimed by the mouths of my cannon), and withold your chimerical insulting charges against my government for a Ear more inclined to listen to slander than mine."[19]

At the same time he was bombarding Secretary of War Armstrong with letters asking permission to attack Pensacola. When James Monroe replaced Armstrong, Jackson pressed him for the go-ahead: "I beg leave to refer to my former letters as to the necessity of having possession of Pensacola, and confidently hope to receive instructions relative thereto." But an American minister had just been appointed to Spain, and the Madison administration, Monroe advised Jackson, preferred to make representations to Spain "thro' the Ordinary channels of communication than that you should resent it by an attack on Pensacola." Further, "I hasten to communicate to you the directions of the President, that you should at present take no measures, which would involve this Government in a contest with Spain."[20]

That was clear enough. But not quick enough. Even before Monroe had put pen to paper, Jackson had decided to act on his own authority. From Mobile on 20 October, he wrote a private letter to the ever-faithful John Coffee, who was on his way to a rendezvous north of Mobile with his mounted volunteer infantry: "I shall move the troops from here the moment I can get the supplies on the way and hear of your arival at Mims Ferry— give your strength as early as possible—say nothing about the intended attack on P———a I shall see you shortly adieu." On 23 October, two days after Monroe had written, Jackson and his staff left Mobile at three o'clock in the afternoon to rendezvous with the reinforcements he had summoned. They were on the march south and east from Tennessee and the Mississippi Territory. Orders were left for 3rd U.S. Infantry and one company of 44th Infantry at Mobile to follow the general as soon as possible.[21]

On the twenty-sixth, Jackson wrote to Monroe from Pierce's Fort, about a mile from the tragic ground of Fort Mims, stating that "as I act without the orders of government, I deem it proper to state my reasons for it." He advised the new secretary of war that because of Spanish conduct "I have been induced to determine to drive the British and Indian force from that place, possess myself of the Barancas [a Spanish fort guarding the entrance to Pensacola Bay] . . . and all other points that may be calculated to prevent a British fleet from entering Pensacola Bay. This will put an end to the Indian war in the South, as it will cut off all foreign influence." It is doubtful, given his moral certainty of the justice of his cause, and the complete backing he would have from his fellow westerners, that Jackson worried overly about the reaction in Washington. Madison may have thought it wiser to deal through official channels, but Madison also wanted the Spanish and British out of Florida as much as Jackson, and any move that would weaken the Spanish grip would please him, even if he did not admit it publicly. Besides, Jackson's secretary at the Treaty of Fort Jackson, the New Yorker Charles Cassedy, had reported to him on 23 September that on the strength of a conversation with Monroe he was convinced that no retribution would be forthcoming with regard to the Spanish "if it should be necessary to notice them in a hostile manner."[22]

During the final week of October fighting men of the Western Waters rendezvoused north of Mobile at the new supply base of Fort Montgomery, which was located three miles east of the Alabama River and about a dozen miles north of where it joined the Tombigbee: Coffee's Tennessee Mounted Volunteers, Lieutenant Colonel Thomas Hinds's Mississippi Dragoons, Colonel Joseph Carson's mounted gunmen from the Mississippi Territory, a company of West Tennessee Rangers, and 1st Regiment of West Tennessee Militia. To these were added some 520 regulars: 3rd Infantry and one company of 44th came up as ordered from Mobile, and a second company of 44th arrived on the last day of the month from Nashville. Two companies of 39th Infantry were added to 44th for command purposes. The little army was nicely rounded off by more Mississippi fighting men whom the British had confidently thought would be with them: 700 Choctaw warriors commanded by Major Uriah Blue (d. 1836) of 39th Infantry and Major Joseph Pulaski Kennedy of Mississippi Territorials. The Choctaws, Jackson wrote, "have been out and have killed seven of the hostile Indians, which has animated them; and I have no doubt but through these I will make the whole nation faithful to us."[23]

Some 4,100 strong, the army marched at 2:00 P.M., 2 November 1814, for Pensacola, about eighty miles away. Before and during this march and subsequent events, Jackson was provided with solid intelligence from Thomas H. Boyles, an American who lived in Spanish territory: "His residence in this country, and knowledge of its geography, proved of considerable advantage to the Commanding General." The tight security that always marked Jackson's marches prevailed, with scouts under an experienced woodsman, Jesse Bean, forming the advance. The Choctaws and Coffee's horsemen acted as flankers. The army advanced through the flat, piney woods of the Gulf Coast for five uneventful days and on 6 November appeared before the town.

Pensacola was not much of a town, with only two streets leading to a square. But it had three strong forts: San Miguel in town, and about nine miles south of town, guarding the approach to the finest harbor on the Gulf Coast, San Carlos de Barrancas and Santa Rosa. Jackson wrote a note to Gonzáles Manrique demanding "possesion of the Barancas and other fortifications, with all the munitions of war." Should the governor refuse, "let the blood of your subjects be upon your own head. I will not hold myself responsible for the conduct of my enraged soldiers and warriors." Jackson sent Major Henry D. Peire of 44th Infantry under a flag of truce to deliver his terms to the governor. But Peire and his party were fired on five times and returned to the American lines. Spanish officers later told Jackson that it was the British marines who fired on Major Peire's party. The American army then pitched camp about two miles west of Pensacola. Soon after dark a captured Spanish sergeant was sent into town with a note of protest from Jackson. After more coming and going that night by emissaries, at 7:00 A.M.

on the seventh Jackson received from González Manrique a letter refusing surrender of the forts, for "duty prevents me from agreeing to it."[24]

As soon as he received the governor's reply, Jackson prepared to storm the town. The Spanish were vastly outnumbered, totaling about 500 regulars in the town and the forts, with Gonzáles Manrique controlling perhaps 288 men in the town, and some 500 militia. They had been described by an American in July as "without subordination or discipline; a most spiritless corps, commanded by an old set of lazy pot-gutted officers. The effective militia are about 500, a mere calico generation without principle or love of country. . . ." The Spanish, however, had one advantage: many of them were behind fortress walls.[25]

Jackson decided to take the town by surprise. Fort San Miguel was on the west side of Pensacola, in front of the American camp. And seven British warships were anchored in the harbor in a position to shell an American advance from the western side. Jackson wrote, "I calculated they would expect the assault from that quarter, and be prepared to rake me from the Fort, and the British armed vessels seven in no. that lay in the bay. To cherish this Idea I sent out part of the mounted men to shew themselves on the west whilst I passed in rear of the Fort undiscovered to the East of the town, when I approached within a mile I was in full view. . . ."[26]

Beginning at nine o'clock on the morning of 7 November, three thousand men made the flank march of some three miles in three columns. Upon entering the town the sand in the street became so deep the artillery accompanying the regulars became bogged down. The regulars left the gunners and their pieces behind and pushed down Centre Street. Before them they saw two pieces of Spanish artillery loaded and "manned for their reception." The guns boomed and the Americans returned a "heavy fire" of musketry. Captain William Laval (1788–1865) and his company of 3rd Infantry immediately charged with the bayonet. Jackson's "pride was never more heightened, than viewing the uniform firmness of my troops, and with what undaunted courage the[y] advanced, with a strong fort ready to assail them on the right seven British armed vessels on the left, strong Blockhouses, and batteries of cannon on their Front, but the[y] still advanced with unshaken firmness, entered the Town, when a battery of two cannon was opened up upon the centre column composed of the regulars with ball & grape and with a shower of musquetry from the houses and gardens, the battery was immediately stormed by Captain [William] Lavall & company & carried, and the musquetry was soon silenced by the steady & well directed fire of the regulars." The other columns had kept pace with the regulars, including the Choctaws, who "advanced to the charge with equal bravery."[27]

That was the end of it. The Battle of Pensacola turned out to be a skirmish lasting minutes at the cost of 5 Americans killed and 10 wounded and 14 Spaniards killed and 6 wounded. Pigot's thousands of Indian allies were conspicuous only by their absence. They had no desire to meet Jackson again. Jackson wrote that same day to Willie Blount that González Manrique himself appeared with a white flag of surrender before two volunteer officers, "beged for mercy, and surrendered the Town & Fort unconditionally, mercy was granted and protection given to the citizens and their property." But the commander of Fort San Miguel refused to honor the surrender and permit American troops to enter. Scaling ladders were called for and Jackson was ready to storm San Miguel when the commander finally bowed to the inevitable and surrendered close to midnight. The British had lobbed some balls into town without effect during the day. The delay, however, allowed them to withdraw across the bay to Forts San Carlos de Barrancas and Santa Rosa. The next day, 8 November, they took aboard the Spanish garrison of Barrancas and sailed away. A short time later a tremendous explosion destroyed Barrancas. Santa Rosa was also blown up.[28]

Jackson was criticized for the Pensacola expedition then, and since, on the grounds that he had invaded sovereign territory and that it was militarily unnecessary. Neither criticism stands up under scrutiny. Since Spain was helpless in enforcing its neutrality, Jackson was justified in driving out the British, and he was careful to claim precisely that, not conquest, as his purpose. Diplomacy aimed at getting Spain to do what it was incapable of doing was a fool's errand, and even if there had been hope of success the problem could not wait for the slow grind of negotiations and proposals and counterproposals. As for its military justification, the Pensacola coup, together with the successful defense of Fort Bowyer, finished the dim threat of the Creeks and the Seminoles joining the British offensive and left unthinkable future cooperation between the British and the Spanish. With regard to its effect on British operations, Admiral Cochrane also disagreed with the armchair generals regarding the loss of the use of Pensacola as a serious setback to his plans. "The attack made by the Americans upon Pensacola has in great measure retarded this service," he wrote, by which he meant his Gulf offensive. He dropped his plans to use Mobile as a base for his offensive and turned to the far more difficult task of striking directly at New Orleans. But that left Jackson with a problem. The city was not prepared for an attack. As one of Jackson's ruder constitutents would have put it, time was a-wastin'.[29]

With the fortifications defending Pensacola's harbor destroyed, there was no need to remain, so Jackson returned the city to the Spanish, with a flourish, in a communication to González Manrique: the "enemy having disappeared and the hostile creeks fled to the Forest, I retire from your Town, and leave you again at liberty to occupy your Fort." The army marched on 10 November and on the thirteenth reached the Boat Yard on the Tensaw River north of Mobile. There Jackson spent three days regrouping. Major Uriah Blue, with about 1,000 mounted gunmen and 53 Choctaw volunteers under the famous chief Pushmataha, was detached to scout the country north and east of Pensacola, "to pursue the fugitive Creeks into the Seminole towns, and destroy them and their crops." It was Blue's unheralded operations that finally ended the Creek War of 1813–1814.[30]

Jackson still felt that Mobile was a possible target, and he would therefore order Fort Bowyer strengthened and leave behind in defense of fort and town two precious regiments of regulars. But he was also aware that New

Orleans loomed large in British operational plans. John Coffee and most of his brigade were ordered to the vicinity of Baton Rouge, where there was corn to feed their horses, in order to "cover New Orleans, until the militia from West Tennessee, and those from Kentucky reach that point. I have ordered the Dragoons from the Mississippi Territory to a half-way point between this and New Orleans to be foraged (there being no longer any supplies in this quarter). This squadron can be ordered to either point [Mobile or New Orleans] at which their services are most wanted."[31]

All this while his health was wretched. His wounded arm, which he had complained about in August, had improved a month later, when he wrote Rachel, "I have the pleasure to inform you, that since the bone came out of my arm which I sent you, it is healling and strengthening verry fast, I hope all the loose pieces of bone is out, and I will no longer be pained with it." But before the march to Pensacola "I was taken verry ill, the Doctor gave me a dose of Jallap & calemel, which salavated me, and there was eight days on the march that I never broke bread—my health is restored but I am still verry weak." He needed Rachel. "It is my wishes that you Join me . . . as Early as possible. I shall endeavor in a day or two to send on some of my young friends to accompany you to New orleans." He asked that she bring with her from the farm "Beacon, flower and Vegetables, for they will add "much to our good living and oeconomy."[32]

Sickness and pain having never deterred him, Jackson then dropped down the river to Mobile, arriving on 19 November. The following day two companies of 44th Infantry were sent on to New Orleans by sea. Jackson left on 22 November for the same destination, but by land, reporting to Monroe that "I travel by land to have a view of the points at which the enemy might effect a landing."[33]

While Jackson was en route, on 26 November HMS *Tonnant* (80 guns), flagship of Vice Admiral Sir Alexander Inglis Cochrane, and three other vessels weighed anchor in Negril Bay, Jamaica, and put to sea, destination New Orleans. With Cochrane was Major General John Keane, still filling in as commander of British land forces aimed at New Orleans. The next day the fleet followed, an armada of warships escorting troop transports loaded with 5,498 British and West Indian regulars, some of them serving in storied regiments: Sutherland Highlanders, six companies of Rifle Brigade, King's Own, Royal North Britain Fusiliers. The invasion fleet's departure was described by eighteen-year-old Lieutenant George Robert Gleig, a thrice-wounded veteran of a year's combat in the Peninsula and France:

> It is impossible to conceive a finer sea-view than the general stir presented. Our fleet amounted now to upwards of fifty sail, many of them vessels of war, which shaking loose their topsails, and lifting their anchors at the same moment, gave to Negril Bay an appearance of bustle such as it has seldom been able to show. In half an hour all the canvass was set, and the ships moved slowly and proudly from their anchorage, till having cleared the headlands, and caught

the fair breeze which blew without, they bounded over the water with the speed of eagles, and long before dark, the coast of Jamaica had disappeared.[34]

As the proud British invasion fleet bounded eaglelike over the waves, Jackson arrived in New Orleans on the morning of 1 December "after a tedious journey through incessant rains and high waters." Gaunt and sallow, his clothes as worn as the man, he nevertheless carried himself as straight as a ramrod, and when he spoke to the dispirited citizens, assembled to greet him in a city where defeatism was as thick and rank as the surrounding swamps, they felt that they beheld their savior. For him, he told them, the choice was simple. Victory or death. There were no alternatives. He invited them to join him.[35]

Chapter 20

"To Arms!"

"WHY MADAM, HE IS A PRINCE"

Jackson had never commanded in such a situation. He was accustomed to dealing with people of predominantly Scotch Irish, English, and German descent whose language was English, whose political heritage was British. But New Orleans was a polyglot city of some twenty-five thousand people sharply divided along racial, ethnic, and class lines and unaccustomed to republican government. A French city graced with Spanish architecture, its dominant French population was divided into two often warring groups: the *ancienne population,* or ancient French, also known as Creoles, who were American-born descendants of the first children born in the territory to European settlers; and the foreign French, who were relatively recent refugees from France or Saint-Domingue (modern Haiti). The word *Creole* has many myths attached to it, but let us dismiss one immediately. In the words of a close student of New Orleans, the Creole "was no more an aristocrat than he was an Ottoman Turk."[1]

Then there were the Spanish, the Germans, the Portuguese, the Italians, and the Irish, to list only the whites, for there was also a big black population, mostly slave but including a large group of free blacks. If they were native to the mainland, blacks were also Creoles, as were Spanish descendants of native-born settlers. But the subject of who was and was not a Creole is a complex, testy, and often bewildering subject that is not part of our story, so we shall leave it at once, adding only a tale that is both funny and sad. Mixing had produced a kaleidoscope of color: mulattoes, quadroons, and octoroons, that led to outbursts such as the New Orleans housewife who called quadroon women "*Heavens, last, worst gift* to white men."[2]

One more group rounded out this rich but often unsettling stew: the Americans, newcomers like the foreign French and their bitter opponents for political power. The contest was between them, one historian has said, with the Creoles left in the dust.

315

One of those Americans was Jackson's old friend from congressional days in Philadelphia, Edward Livingston. John Randolph of Roanoke, who had something to say of just about everybody who was anybody, said of Livingston, "He is a man of splendid abilities but utterly corrupt. He shines and stinks like a rotten mackerel by moonlight." Livingston had been mayor of New York City when one of his agents absconded with funds. Although not personally involved, and despite Randolph of Roanoke's opinion of him, Livingston took the blame, sold his property, and eventually paid back all the money. He had left the East for New Orleans to rebuild his financial and political fortunes. There, after the death of his first wife, he had married a Frenchwoman from Saint-Domingue, described by a man who knew her as the "young and fascinating widow" Louise Davezac de Castera, and was well on his way to reestablishing himself. Jackson needed a guide to the intricacies of New Orleans society and its power structure, and it was the intelligent, well-educated, urbane Livingston who provided it. Livingston became his aide and private secretary, and was at Jackson's side to advise and interpret during the tense weeks ahead.[3]

Jackson had begun well on the day of his arrival with his heartening talk to Governor William C. C. Claiborne, Mayor Nicholas Girod, Commodore Daniel Patterson of the U.S. Navy, and other notables. They sensed, these men of widely different backgrounds, that an uncommon man had come to lead them. He then proceeded to his headquarters, a three-story brick building at 106 Royal Street. A crowd assembled outside and insisted he speak to them. He stepped onto the balcony, and by the time he finished talking this group, too, had taken heart from the unquenchable fire within him.

Edward Livingston had sent word to his wife that General Jackson would dine with them at their home that evening. The news was received with some consternation, as Mrs. Livingston had scheduled a dinner party that included some of the leading women of the city. News that they would be joined by the wild backwoodsman from Tennessee was unsettling, to say the least. One of the fashionable ladies at the dinner party told James Parton that Jackson, erect and bronzed from years of exposure, entered the Livingston home in his "uniform of coarse blue cloth and yellow buckskin" and high dragoon boots. He made a graceful bow to the roomful of ladies, who had all risen, "as much from amazement as from politeness," then greeted his hostess and took a seat next to her. The fashionable ladies were astonished at his graceful deportment, his ease in their presence. At dinner he spoke to them about the expected invasion in a manner that suggested he was born to such company and relieved their anxieties. Louise Davezac Livingston later pronounced judgment: "Erect, composed, perfectly self possessed, with martial bearing, the soldier stood before them. One whom nature had stamped a gentleman." The feeling was universal. When Jackson and Edward Livingston left, the guests turned to their hostess and spoke as one: "Is *this* your back woods-man? Why madam, he is a prince."[4]

Jackson next reviewed in the Place d'Armes, now the well-known Jackson Square, the New Orleans militia, commanded by Major Jean Baptiste

Edward Livingston, by P. C. Coqueret after John Vanderlyn
(New York State Office of Parks, Recreation & Historic
Preservation, Clermont State Historic Site)

Plauché. Some of its members were said to be battle-tested veterans of the
Napoleonic Wars. Although there were definitely British sympathizers in
New Orleans and its environs, the British expectation that the Creoles
would desert the American cause en masse was as delusional as their hopes
for massive Indian assistance. Neither the Creoles nor the foreign French had
any love for the British, and they were horrified at the burning and looting
of Washington and the sufferings at Hampton, Virginia, on 25 July 1813 at
the hands of a British raiding party, which was described by a British officer: "every horror was committed with impunity, rape, murder, pillage: and
not a man was punished." We can be certain that these tales had gained in
the telling by the time they reached New Orleans. In addressing its inhabitants Jackson played on the historic antipathy between French and English.[5]

It may be difficult for the modern reader, caught in an age of cynicism,
to contemplate the effect that Jackson's arrival, manner, and fiery words of

determination had upon a populace wanting desperately to resist but unable to organize, stuck in factional wrangling and turmoil. As one of its leading Creole citizens, Bernard Marigny, later reflected, "The desire to fight was not sufficient. There was among them a sense of uneasiness, arising from a defect of organization." There was no one, Marigny continued, with the "energy necessary to give great impulse to the population of Louisiana." Then Jackson announced from Mobile that he was "hastening to the defense of our State," and the effect was electric, his arrival awaited with eager anticipation. "Never," wrote Marigny, "was a general received with more enthusiasm. His military reputation, his well-known firmness of character contributed to call forth a spontaneous movement. From all quarters, the cry was 'to arms!' "[6]

Élan alone, of course, would not stop the British. Of the New Orleans militia, enthusiastic but few, there were five companies, each in distinctive and splendid uniforms; but they numbered on paper only 700 and in fact probably fielded less than 500. They were manned largely by Creoles, but one company, the Louisiana Blues, had many Irishmen and was commanded by an expatriate Irishman, Captain Maunsell White, who had married into the French community. But Coffee and Hinds were near Baton Rouge and northward awaiting only the order to march, and Billy Carroll was floating down the western waters from Tennessee with about 3,000 volunteers. Somewhere behind Carroll was General John Thomas with 2,300 Kentuckians. Carroll and Thomas, however, had a serious problem: there were not enough arms for all of the men, with Thomas's situation especially bad. So contrary to legend and song, hundreds of men were floating for New Orleans without enough arms, powder, and lead. In November the War Department had ordered the Pittsburgh arsenal to ship five thousand muskets with flints and other equipment, including three hundred thousand cartridges, to New Orleans with the "least possible delay." Whereupon the quartermaster hired a flatboat instead of a steamboat and sent the guns and equipment on their meandering way with a flatboat owner who made stops along the rivers to conduct his own business.[7]

There was another New Orleans militia unit, the battalion of free men of color, and Jackson did not ignore it. Governor Claiborne had written to him in August recommending the "Battalion composed of chosen men of Colour" that had been "organized under a Special *Act* of the Legislature. . . ." On 21 September, while still in Mobile, Jackson responded enthusiastically and sent to these men, through Claiborne, an address calling upon them to rally to the nation, promising them equal pay and the same 160 acres per man that whites would get, and guaranteeing they would not be exposed to improper comparisons or unjust sarcasm." In his letter of transmittal he expressed to Claiborne his determination to use them and his reasoning:

> Our country has been invaded, and threatened with destruction. She wants Soldiers to fight her battles. The free men of colour in your city are inured to the Southern climate and would make excellent Soldiers. They will not remain quiet spectors of the inter-

esting contest. They must be either for, or against us—distrust them, and you will make them your enemies, place confidence in them, and you engage them by Every dear and honorable tie to the interests of the country who extends to them equal rights and privileges with white men.

Claiborne replied that although he had no problem with Jackson's aim, "I have deemed it *best* to postpone giving publicity to your address. I must not disguise from you the fact, that many excellent citizens will disapprove the policy, you wish to observe towards the free people of Colour; the Battalion already organized, limited as it is, excites much distrust, and I should not be surprised, if at the insuing legislature, an attempt should be made to put it down." He pointed out that the Louisiana constitution forbade putting free blacks on an equal footing with whites. What it boiled down to, as Claiborne's letter makes clear, is that those "excellent citizens" were terrified at the thought of any blacks being armed, for if afterward they were allowed to stay in Louisiana, "with a Knowledge of the use of arms, & *that pride of Distinction,* which a soliders pursuits so naturally inspires, they would prove dangerous." Claiborne did not mention that some of the white fear was based on the slave uprisings of 1811.

Jackson would have none of that. The free men of color would serve under white officers, as was the custom, but otherwise on an equal footing with the white units. This was the first lesson to the people of New Orleans that if necessary, Jackson would ride roughshod over any obstacle. His address was published, and upon his arrival in the city he also reviewed the two battalions of free men of color. When an assistant paymaster had the temerity to question his authority to enlist blacks, thunder rolled and lightning struck. "Be pleased," Jackson wrote to him, "to keep to yourself your opinions upon the policy of making payments of the troops with the necessary muster rolls without inquiring whether the troops are white, black, or tea."[8]

Having established his bona fides and won the hearts and minds of most of both sexes, as well as disturbing some, Jackson turned to the watery environment that was as strange to him as its human occupants. It must be said that from the outset geography favored Jackson. New Orleans was situated about a hundred miles from the mouth of the Mississippi. Seventy-five miles below New Orleans, where the river bends at a sharp angle, was Fort St. Philip, which had been neglected but was the key to river defense. Colonel Arthur P. Hayne (1790–1867), whom Jackson had sent ahead to survey the city's defenses, was working hard to bring Fort St. Philip and other river defenses to a higher state of repair and readiness. Eighteen miles south of New Orleans was an S-turn in the river called the English Turn. It was guarded on the left bank by Fort St. Leon. Here sailing ships were even more vulnerable because the winds that brought them up the river were head on when they tacked into the first turn, forcing them to wait for favorable wind conditions under the guns of the fort. Merchant vessels were sometimes held up for days.

New Orleans and Environs, 1815

Jackson found, however, that he could get "no correct information . . . respecting the Topography of any part of this country, even from the best informed persons of the Country, or City. It appeared that scarcely any person had made enquiry further than the limits of his own possessions, and many had failed to acquire even that knowledge, or if they possessed it, did not choose to communicate it, least it might lead to a discovery of some smuggling passage into the Lakes, from the river." Jackson, therefore, his military engineer wrote, "adhering to his constant practice of seeing everything himself, as far as practicable," decided to do his own reconnaissance.[9]

On 4 December accompanied by his aide, Major John Reid, Commodore Daniel Patterson, commanding U.S. naval forces in the Gulf, his topographical engineer Major Howell Tatum, and two other engineers, Jackson boarded a gunboat to go downriver and inspect its defenses. The other engineers were Major Arsène Lacarrière Latour and Captain Lewis Livingston, Edward Livingston's son. Jackson, upon Edward Livingston's recommendation, had appointed Latour principal military engineer of 7th Military District, and named as his assistant engineers young Lewis Livingston and Henry

Boneval Latrobe, who was the son of Benjamin Henry Latrobe, architect of the U.S. Capitol.

Described as a "little sharp looking frenchman," Latour (1778–1837) was born to the minor nobility in the village of Aurillac in the Auvergne. His world had been destroyed by the French Revolution. But he survived and became an architect, studying in Paris under Charles Percier, who designed the Arc de Triomphe and additions to the Louvre and the Tuileries. Latour went to Saint-Domingue in 1802 to recover his wife's estate and found himself in the middle of one of history's bloodiest revolutions. Two of the French army's military engineers had died of yellow fever and the third was too sick to perform his duties. Desperate, the French commander, General Donatien Rochambeau, offered the newcomer an appointment to the Corps of Engineers in December 1802 and Latour accepted. On 29 November 1803, bottled up in the fortress city of Le Cap and facing certain terrible retribution from the black revolutionaries surrounding the city, Rochambeau surrendered what was left of the French army to the blockading British naval force. Somehow Latour got off the Island and to the United States by May 1804, but we know not how or when. Nor do we know when he first came to Louisiana. By early 1806 he obtained an appointment to design a city plan for Baton Rouge. Between then and the time he met Jackson he practiced architecture in New Orleans and also obviously learned the lay of land and water surrounding the city. In 1812 he became a citizen of the United States. He is especially important to us because of his indispensable history of Jackson's Gulf Coast campaign, published in 1816: *Historical Memoir of the War in West Florida and Louisiana in 1814–15.*[10]

Jackson could depend upon Major Latour's accurate maps of New Orleans and the Gulf Coast surrounding it, made earlier in the century in collaboration with another engineer, perhaps as an agent of the French government. And it was Latour who provided the information Jackson could not get elsewhere: the possible routes the British could take to approach the city.

During his inspection of the river route Jackson found Fort St. Philip in good state, but ordered the demolition of the barracks there, probably because they were a fire hazard, and more artillery mounted. He also ordered the construction of two additional batteries, one across the river about nine hundred yards upstream and the other on the same side as Fort St. Philip one-half mile upstream. Time caught up with the defenders before these batteries could be built, but Fort St. Philip was already strong, and even if ships got past it "strongly built" Fort St. Leon at the English Turn was formidable. In Major Tatum's opinion only "a few batteries of heavy cannon erected at different points, would destroy every Armed Vessel that dared to attempt the ascent, as it is impossible to round this Turn without the assistance of different winds, the waiting for which would prove their utter destruction . . . unless a land force can first gain possession of them. This would be a difficulty not easily surmountable with any thing like an equal force, as the opposing . . . army on either side of the river have the advantage of occupying excellent places for erecting strong lines of defence running from the river, back to impenetrable swamps." And at Fort St. Leon Jackson found just that going on: Louisiana militia "erecting a line of defence from the river, back to the Swamp" for a small battery to assist the defenders of the fort. In other words, strong forts on the river combined with tricky navigational hazards and little room for maneuver on either water or land made an invasion up the Mississippi hazardous. Added to that, the British would not be able to get their big ships of the line across the shallow bar at the mouth of the river.[11]

Jackson returned to New Orleans from his river inspection tour on the night of 9 December. The next day he wrote Governor Claiborne and asked him to set in motion approval by the legislature to draft slaves from the plantations to begin digging the planned river defense lines, reminding him that "with vigor, energy, and expedetion, all is safe, delay may loose all."[12]

Another possible invasion route seventy miles west of the mouth of the river was by way of Barataria Bay, thence toward the city by various bayous. But none of these bayous could be dared without guides, and they were the three Lafitte brothers' Baratarian privateers who used the bayous leading from the bay to smuggle loot and slaves to New Orleans for sale. In the previous chapter we left the British trying to recruit the Baratarians. But the Lafitte brothers had no intention of entering British service if they could work out a deal with the Americans. One important reason for their attitude was British insistence that they give up raiding Spanish commerce, which was their main occupation. How, then, was a poor privateer to make a living?

Jean Lafitte told Captain Nicholas Lockyer of HMS *Sophie,* who had arrived at Barataria with the British offer on 3 September, that his unexpected appearance and the "confusion" arising from it prevented an immediate answer to the British request. But "if you grant me a fortnight, I would be entirely at your disposal at the end of that time." But the very next day Lafitte sent Major Edward Nicolls's letter of 31 August seeking to recruit the Baratarians and other papers to Jean Blanque in New Orleans. Blanque immediately turned over the papers to Governor Claiborne. Three days later Lafitte sent to Blanque as further proof of his patriotism and desire to serve the cause an anonymous letter from Havana warning of British plans. But Claiborne thought Jean Lafitte's offer a trick to get him to release one of his brothers, Pierre, and other Baratarians from jail for smuggling and evasion of customs duties. The Americans considered the Baratarians pirates and had determined to destroy them. Despite what they knew of the British offer to the Lafittes and their followers, on 16 September Commodore Patterson and a small U.S. naval force destroyed the Baratarian headquarters and depot. Lafitte and most of his men got away on the best ships, but Patterson had done considerable damage and captured eighty privateers and hundreds of thousands of dollars' worth of Baratarian loot. Yet the Lafitte brothers still refused to join the British and held out for a U.S. pardon in exchange for service, and there essentially matters stood until Jackson's arrival in December.[13]

Jackson wanted nothing to do with "those wretches," and he would not bend on the issue, even though the privateers had cannon that could be used in defensive positions and were themselves skilled gunners. Claiborne tried to reason with him. Jackson turned him away. Edward Livingston was Jean Lafitte's legal adviser. According to the merchant Vincent Nolte, Lafitte and others often appeared in New Orleans and "paraded arm in arm with Livingston's brother-in-law," and when they were arrested for smuggling and other crimes "Livingston and his brother-in-law always managed to get them released." But now not even Livingston could sway Jackson. Almost the entire New Orleans establishment pleaded with Jackson to change his mind, but this probably made him dig in his heels even deeper. Then the important Creole leader Bernard Marigny conferred with U.S. District Judge Dominick Hall, and the two men devised a scheme involving legislative resolutions and the court's decision to release the prisoners and suspend legal action against the Baratarians for four months. This gave the Lafitte brothers the opportunity to come to New Orleans and arrange to confront Jackson.[14]

Jean Lafitte faced Jackson on the corner of Rue Royale and Rue St. Philip. We know that Jackson was an impressive figure, but so was Lafitte. Over six feet, elegant, well dressed, fluent in French, English, Spanish, and Italian. Other writers have remarked on the similarity of this confrontation and Red Eagle riding boldly into Jackson's camp to face the conquering general. There is no record of their exchange, but according to Major Latour, Lafitte offered Jackson ammunition, cannon, seasoned gunners to man them, and his maps and knowledge of the country. Jackson liked bold men and bold actions. He accepted, and thus into his army entered some 800 seasoned fighting men who knew just about all there was to know about handling big guns.[15]

The southern approach to the city was now covered. Neither Jackson nor the British gave serious consideration to the western approach via Bayou La Fourche, which was long and narrow and easily obstructed. Just east of the Mississippi were the Rivière aux Chenes and Bayou Terre aux Boeuf, which ended near the English Turn, but this route was also long, narrow, difficult, and easy to defend. The best possibilities lay east and north on two large bodies of water that came close to New Orleans: Lake Borgne to the east, and Lake Pontchartrain immediately north of the city. Both were accessible from the sea if one had the proper watercraft, and as we know, Admiral Cochrane had requested shallow-draft vessels from England. At the end of Lake Borgne dense cypress swamps and wet prairies separated water's edge from the narrow strip of dry land that ran along the Mississippi northward. If the British managed a landing at that point and got to dry land, they would only be about ten to twelve miles from the city. But Jackson had been advised by Latour and undoubtedly others that "if the canals and bayous on both sides of the Mississippi above and below New Orleans" were obstructed and observation posts established, passage by the enemy would be extremely difficult. Jackson issued clear and unequivocal orders to three officers for this work to be done, as in the following: "Major General Villeré will without delay obstruct the passage from the Lakes Borgne Ponchatrain & Maurepas to the Mississippi, and station at every important point a guard or post of

observation, & report regularly to Head Quarters every occurrence of importance." Villeré was authorized to requisition labor and supplies from all persons in his district to accomplish the job.[16]

On 11 December Jackson turned to a well-known commercial route
along which he thought the invasion was most likely to come—Lake Pontchartrain via Bayou St. John, to within two miles north of the city. From
Lake Borgne there are two narrow passages to Lake Pontchartrain. Northeast
of New Orleans was the well-traveled Les Rigolets, which would be close to
the anchorage of the British fleet. Passage required shallow-draft vessels, as
maximum water depth was eight feet. Rigolets was guarded by Fort Petites
Coquilles, which was surrounded by an open morass, giving it good protection from assault. But it had neither gun platforms nor a parapet, and its
magazine was open, thus unprotected. But it was considered by the Americans a strong position, able to repel an attack in combination with Commodore Patterson's gunboats. Later, well after the British arrived and action
had commenced, the fort was "reinforced by several heavy pieces of cannon"
and more men.[17]

The other passage from Lake Borgne to Lake Pontchartrain lay southwest of Petites Coquilles. It was called Chef Menteur and was "150 paces
wide and has not more than five feet of water on the bar," according to
Major Howell Tatum, who visited the site with Jackson. An enemy force
could either proceed through the channel into Lake Pontchartrain and on to
Bayou St. John, or land from the channel onto the Plain of Gentilly, which
was really a peninsula between the lakes with a road leading almost due west
twenty-four miles to New Orleans. But serious problems faced any attacker.
One mile into Chef Menteur, a site at the mouth of Bayou Sauvage commanded Chef Menteur and the Gentilly road, and there Jackson ordered a
battery to be built. Marsh prairies believed to be impassable for large bodies
of troops dominated the landscape, so what was left, wrote Major Tatum, was
a road "between Bayou Savage & the impenetrable swamps on each side . . .
so narrow" that a column of troops "could not move one mile at any time
without being within the fire of an ambuscading force. The roads were too
deep for the passage of artillery, and the woods too thick and brushy for the
exercise of the bayonet. . . ."[18]

It seemed, therefore, that all of the invasion routes had been covered.
Jackson was also confident where the British invasion fleet would appear,
and early warning depended upon the U.S. Navy.

Given the watery nature of the countryside, and the importance of
seapower to control it, one would think that Commodore Daniel Patterson's
naval force would have been formidable. Quite the contrary. The New
Orleans Station had been neglected by the Navy Department throughout
the war and was regarded by officers stationed there as outright banishment.
Promotion comes from being in the thick of the action, and from the outset glory was reserved for northern waters. Officers yearned for transfers to
the blue-water navy, to speed over the waves with their feet planted firmly
on the quarterdecks of graceful frigates and close with the enemy in single-

ship actions. But pleas to the secretary of the navy by midshipmen and lieutenants were largely fruitless. They were destined to meet the British in graceless gunboats nicknamed "Jeffs," for the president who thought they were the answer for seapower, along with one ship, two schooners, and a sloop.[19]

Commodore Patterson had under his command only six gunboats, the ship *Louisiana,* which was under repair, the armed schooners *Carolina* and *Seahorse,* and the sloop *Alligator.* Gunboats were shallow-draft sailing vessels, but their designs and sails differed widely. They ranged from fifty to seventy feet long and sixteen to twenty feet wide. The hold had a depth of six feet. They were armed with either a 24- or 32-pounder at the bow, mounted or on a pivot, and two 12-pound carronades (short cannon) on either side, although a few more guns could be carried. In the fall of 1813 the secretary of the navy ordered Patterson to replace his gunboats with boats that could be rowed as well as sailed, but Patterson had not carried out his instruction. When under sail, the guns had to be stowed in the hold to maintain seaworthiness. The recoil when the guns were fired made the boats roll excessively.[20]

Shortly after 5 December Patterson received an anonymous letter from Pensacola informing him that a large British fleet, including Admiral Cochrane's flagship, was off Pensacola. He immediately ordered five gunboats and *Seahorse* and *Alligator* to Lake Borgne to act first as advance pickets to report the British arrival, and then to fall back into Les Rigolets to help defend Fort Petites Coquilles. The gunboats carried a total of twenty-three guns and 186 men. *Seahorse* had one 6-pounder and 14 men, *Alligator* one 4-pounder and 8 men. The little force was commanded by Lieutenant Thomas Ap Catesby Jones.[21]

A "BRILLIANT AFFAIR"

HMS *Tonnant* and her escorts dropped anchor off the Chandeleur Islands southeast of New Orleans on 8 December 1814. The rest of the fleet arrived the next day. HMS *Seahorse,* Captain James Gordon commanding, spotted the five American gunboats while scouting the area. On 12 December the fleet moved northward a short distance to an anchorage between Ship Island and Cat Island near the mouth of Lake Borgne. Between those dates Lieutenant Jones sighted the British fleet and sounded the alarm. On the twelfth, observing the large size of the British armada, Lieutenant Jones found it "no longer safe or prudent for me to continue on that part of the lakes . . . I therefore determined to gain a station near the Malhereux Islands as soon as possible, which situation would enable me to oppose a further penetration of the enemy up the lakes, and at the same time afford me an opportunity of retreating to the Petite Coquilles if necessary." Some of the lighter British vessels pursued Jones, but they all ran aground, proving the critical importance of shallow-draft vessels in the watery environs of New Orleans. But with regard to naval matters London had been as parsimonious as Washington. Admiral Cochrane's plea for shallow-draft sailing vessels of the Dutch type had been rejected as too expensive to procure in Europe and he was advised to get them in the West Indies. But he had not been able to get anywhere near the number he needed.[22]

This meant that the troops had to be landed, wherever the British meant to land, in open ships' boats powered by oars, and in Admiral Cochrane's own words, that was not possible until Jones's "formidable flotilla was either captured or destroyed." Wasting no time, Cochrane went after Jones with his sailors' brawn and sweat. On the night of the twelfth, the day the fleet moved to its new anchorage, he ordered lowered into the water forty-five launches and barges powered by oars, armed with forty-three guns, and carrying 1,200 sailors and marines. In command was Captain Nicholas Lockyer, detached from HMS *Sophie.* All that night the British sailors rowed for Lake Borgne.[23]

At 10:00 A.M. on the thirteenth Lieutenant Jones observed Lockyer's boats heading for Pass Christian. When they gained it at 2:00 P.M. and did not disembark troops but continued on, Jones correctly assumed that his little flotilla was their target. The lake was uncommonly low because of a westerly wind that had been blowing for several days, and in the deepest channel three boats "were in 12 or 18 inches less water than their draught" and went aground. By throwing overboard all unnecessary articles, and with the help of the flood tide that started coming in at 3:30 P.M., they got under way and Jones headed for the Rigolets and Fort Petites Coquille.[24]

In the meantime, USS *Seahorse,* commanded by Sailing Master William Johnson, was anchored in Bay St. Louis, engaged in either loading supplies from the shore or destroying them to prevent them from being taken by the British. She carried one 6-pounder and 14 men. At 3:45 P.M. three British boats were dispatched from Lockyer's force to take USS *Seahorse.* But they were discouraged by a few rounds of grape and pulled out of range until they were joined by four other boats, when the attack was resumed. But Sailing Master Johnson had chosen a good position for assistance by a battery of two 6-pounders on the shore, and after a sharp thirty-minute action the British once again pulled away, this time with one boat damaged and casualties. But Johnson, cut off from Jones's flotilla, decided to abandon ship and destroy it along with the supplies on the shore. At 7:30 P.M., USS *Seahorse* blew up.

Lockyer, meanwhile, continued to chase Jones. At one o'clock on the morning of the fourteenth, Jones later reported to Patterson, his wind "entirely died away, and our vessels become unmanageable, came to anchor in the west end of Malheureux Island's passage." By daylight there was still no wind. The Americans, without oars, could not move, only prepare to surrender, abandon and destroy the boats, or fight. The British boats, "about nine miles from us at anchor . . . soon got in motion and rapidly advanced on us. The want of wind, and the strong ebb-tide which was setting through the pass, left me but one alternative; which was, to put myself in the most advantageous position, to give the enemy as warm a reception as possible."

Jones had his gunboats "form a close line abreast across the channel, anchored by the stern with springs on the cable. . . ." There, unable to move without wind, the gunboats awaited the British assault.[25]

About 9:30 A.M. USS *Alligator,* with one 4-pounder and 8 men, Sailing Master Richard S. Sheppard commanding, attempted to come up from the southeast and join Jones's flotilla, but it was attacked and captured by the British. At 10:00 A.M. Lockyer told his men to eat breakfast. Thus refreshed, the sailors began rowing again at 10:30 with the boats in line abreast. They rowed against a strong current of about three miles per hour. But that same current drove American gunboats No. 156 and No. 163 out of line and one hundred yards in advance of the others. When the British were within range the American long guns opened up, "but without much effect, the objects being of so small a size." At ten minutes to eleven the British began firing, at which time, Jones wrote, "the action became general and destructive on both sides." At 11:49 Gunboat No. 156, commanded by Lieutenant Jones, was attacked by three boats and an attempt made to board her, but Jones reported that they were driven off with the loss of two boats sunk and nearly every officer killed or wounded, and that "a second attempt by four boats "shared almost a similar fate."[26]

But superior numbers eventually told. The British sailors had been rowing for thirty-six hours, but their endurance and ardor paid off when "about noon," Lockyer wrote, "I had the satisfaction of closing with the commodore. . . ." The action was brief but furious. Most of the officers and men of Lockyer's boat were killed or wounded, "myself among the latter, severely. . . ." Jones received a severe shoulder wound and was forced to turn over command to George Parker, a master's mate. But the British sailors and marines led by the twice-wounded Lockyer cut their way through the boarding nets and were soon fighting on the deck. Other British boats converged on Jones's gunboat, and by 12:10 P.M. the British had taken the deck and turned the guns onto the other American gunboats.[27]

By 12:40 P.M. it was all over. The gunboats had fallen into British hands and would be used by them. Jones reported his losses in killed and wounded as slight in contrast to the British, but his estimate of their losses, 300, was grossly exaggerated. Captain Lockyer's return listed 17 killed, 77 wounded. Jones and his men had gone down fighting and that was to their credit, and they had bought Jackson time. But it was still a defeat. The roots lay in errors of judgment and execution long before the fight on Lake Borgne. Washington's refusal to spend the money necessary to maintain an adequate naval defense in the Gulf, and its disregard until it was too late for New Orleans's safety, were the principal reasons for what happened that day. And Patterson's disregard of his instructions to provide vessels that could be rowed as well as sailed guaranteed defeat once the weather turned against Jones.

It was, Admiral Cochrane wrote to the Admiralty, a "brilliant affair," and we must acknowledge the dogged British pursuit and their gallant assault. But the affair was a disaster for Jackson. Now there was no force on Lake

Borgne to keep him informed of British activities and probable intentions. Would they try to go through Les Rigolets, subdue Fort Petites Coquilles, and continue into Lake Pontchartrain and land their forces only four miles north of New Orleans? Would they land at Chef Menteur and march on the city via the Gentilly road? Would they go elsewhere? Jackson did not know. His usually reliable intelligence system had broken down at a critical place, at a crucial time.[28]

Chapter 21

"I WILL SMASH THEM, SO HELP ME GOD!"

"THOSE WHO ARE NOT FOR US ARE AGAINST US,
AND WILL BE DEALT WITH ACCORDINGLY"

Jackson learned of the loss of the gunboats upon his return from reconnoitering the Chef Menteur area. His response was to send urgent word to John Coffee waiting near Baton Rouge, and to Major Thomas Hinds and his Mississippi Dragoons higher up the Mississippi. The messages were clear. I need you. Make haste. The first order went out from Robert Butler, Jackson's adjutant general, on the fourteenth, the day the gunboats were taken, for Coffee to march immediately to New Orleans. Jackson wrote two days later:

> I need not say to you, to reach me by forced marches, it is enough to say, that Lord Cochrane is on our coast with about eighty sail great and small, and report says he has taken all our gun Boats in the lakes. I have still a hope it is not true, notwithstanding a naval officer reports he saw the engagement & saw the gun Boats strike.
>
> I am astonished that the T. & Kentucky Troops are not up. If heard from, please to detach an express, to them to proceed night and day untill the arive—and notify the commander of the Detachment of the regular Troops to proceed without delay to this place. In great haste . . .[1]

Jackson's first order reached Coffee at 8:00 P.M. on 16 December. Coffee replied at four the next morning that "by exertion shall move my command this morning at sun rise, no time will be lost by me untill I reach New Orleans, I think we will reach you in four days. . . ." Coffee was camped on the Mississippi at the mouth of Sandy Creek, twenty miles north of Baton Rouge and a hundred miles from New Orleans. He had reached Sandy Creek on 9 December after a nightmarish march from the point north of Mobile where he had left Jackson following their return from Pensacola. It was, he wrote to his wife, "worse than any I have ever experienced, the line of march was parallel with the Sea Coast, and distant from it generally forty or fifty miles, crossing all the little Rivers that are very numerous in this Country, having the whole, to Swim, Bridge or Ferry; it rained on us twenty days Suckcessively and heavier rain than you ever saw."[2]

Coffee's march had left "my arms in bad condition, and now I have no time to examine into their state, but I know we have from 2 to 4 hundred that are not good," he wrote Jackson. "If I could be furnished with muskets, and Cartridge Boxes to that amount I should be glad, it would be well to have the Boxes filled with cartridges before my arrival, all my powder has been destroyed by the rains on the march to this place, furnish us with the best rifle powder that can be had." Yet despite these problems, "my command are in fine spirits," and if they could reach Jackson in time they would give the British a "warm reception."[3]

If Coffee and his horsemen, who were accustomed to rough cross-country marches in wild and semiwild environments, found the going "worse than any I have ever experienced," what effect would it have on thousands of British soldiers strung out through prime ambush country described by Coffee as "mud, water, and brush"? This was the route recommended by Captain Pigot in the summer. Admiral Cochrane had chosen instead an approach by water. But without shallow-draft vessels, with the Mississippi heavily defended and the bayous obstructed and guarded by Jackson's orders, Cochrane and Major General Keane might have no other alternative.[4]

Both sides, then, were facing serious problems. Jackson might have breathed a bit easier if he had known that at 10:00 P.M. on 13 December Billy Carroll's flatboats loaded with Tennesseans had arrived at Natchez, "after a prosperous Voyage of 18 days from Nashville." Carroll wrote to Jackson that he had stopped there to rest his troops, who were "much fatigued by incessant duty," and give them "an opportunity of Washing their Cloathes. . . ." He had intercepted a keelboat with "about 1400 stand of arms and ammunition," which was probably part of the shipment from Pittsburgh. The guns were badly needed, for a "great number" of Carroll's men were "badly armed, and many others are not armed at all. . . ." He planned to remain at Natchez two days at the most, then "fall down to Baton Rouge" and await the return of his messenger "and your orders."[5]

Jackson also worried about "seditious reports" in New Orleans spread by "British emissaries . . . amongst you, that the threatened invasion is with a view to restoring the country to Spain from a supposition that some of you would be willing to return to your ancient government—believe not such incredible tales—your government is at peace with Spain. It is the vital enemy of your country, the common enemy of mankind, the highway robber of the world, that threatens you, and has set his hirelings amongst you with this false report to put you off your guard, that you may fall an easy prey to him. Then look to your liberties, your property, the chastity of your wives and daughters. Take a retrospect of the conduct of the British army at Hampton and other places where it has entered our country, and every bosom which glows with patriotism and virtue, will be inspired with indignation and pant for the arrival of the hour when we shall meet and revenge these outrages against the laws of civilization and humanity."

He then urged citizens to track down the spreader of "this unfounded report," for "the rules of war annex the punishment of death of any person holding secret correspondence with the enemy creating false alarm or supplying him with provision, and the general announces his unalterable determination to execute the martial law in all cases which may come within his province." We can be sure that he meant, precisely, every word of it. Do not disappoint me, he warned them, for then "he will separate our enemies from our friends. Those who are not for us are against us, and will be dealt with accordingly."[6]

At the same time the streets were full of sailors whom Commander Patterson desperately needed to man USS *Carolina* and USS *Louisiana,* but they would not serve. Patterson asked Governor Claiborne to propose to the legislature that habeas corpus be suspended so he could impress the men he needed. The legislature refused, offering instead to pay $24 per month to sailors who enlisted. Jackson was disgusted. A city in peril obviously required drastic action on his part.[7]

The day after his proclamation to the citizens, 16 December, he took the necessary step and placed the city and environs under martial law. New Orleans became an armed camp, the military in control, Jackson the sole arbiter of enforcement. His General Order to the citizens of New Orleans read:

> Every individual entering the city will report at the Adjutant General's ofice, and on failure will be arrested and held for examination. No person shall be permitted to leave the city without a permission in writing signed by the General or one of his Staff. No vessel, boat or other craft will be permitted to leave New Orleans or Bayou St. John without a passport in writing from the General (or one of his staff) or the commander of the naval forces of the United states on this station. The street lamps shall be extinguished at the hour of nine at night, after which period, persons of every description found in the streets, or not at their respective homes without permission in writing as aforesaid and not having the countersign shall be apprehended as spies and held for examination.

He only bent on one of the above conditions, rescinding on 2 January 1815 at the request of the mayor the order to extinguish street lamps at nine o'clock every night.[8]

Jackson was preparing to fight.

"A CONFIDENT ANTICIPATION OF SUCCESS
SEEMED TO PERVADE ALL RANKS"

So were the British. The day after Jackson proclaimed a state of martial law, Admiral Cochrane and General Keane began moving the troops off the transports to an advance base where they would be poised to invade the mainland. The fleet weighed anchor and advanced into the lake and soon "ship after ship ran aground," reported eighteen-year-old Lieutenant George Robert Gleig. Once more the sailors of Cochrane's fleet were called upon. The troops had to be rowed thirty miles to the jump-off base, "no very agreeable prospect," Lieutenant Gleig wrote, for the soldiers would be cramped in one position the entire way. That, however, "was but a trifling misery. . . ." The weather changed, the heavens opened up. "Instead of constant bracing frost, heavy rains, such as an inhabitant of England cannot dream of, and against which no cloak will furnish protection, began." The sailors rowed the troops ten hours in the open boats, and the only thing for which the sailors could be thankful as they took up the long row back to pick up the next contingent was that they did not have to leave the boats.

For what passed for a forward base was Isle aux Pois (Pea Island), a miserable swamp that passed for an island in Lake Borgne at the mouth of the Pearl River, of which Lieutenant Gleig wrote, "it is scarcely possible to imagine any place more completely wretched." There was one small piece of firm ground at one end, the rest was the domain of waterfowl and also "abounded in dormant alligators." The British troops perched and endured without tents or huts or shelter of any sort, the island devoid of fuel to make fires, munching on salt meat and ship's biscuits and drinking "a small allowance of rum," while heavy rains of the sort that had drenched Coffee's men on their westward march to the Mississippi now tormented them. Worse followed, Gleig noted: "To add to our miseries, as night closed, the rain generally ceased, and severe frosts set in; which, congealing our wet clothes upon our bodies, left little animal warmth to keep the limbs in a state of activity. . . ." Many of the black soldiers of the West Indian regiments, "to whom frost and cold were altogether new, fell fast asleep, and perished before morning."[9]

Yet Gleig thought the sailors' "hardships were experienced in a four-fold degree. Night and day were boats pulling from the fleet to the island, and from the island to the fleet . . . many seamen were four or five days continually at the oar." In fact, the transfer took five days, from 17 to 22 December, which reveals the enormity for Jackson of the loss of the gunboats. On Lake Borgne he was blind, without a clue as to what the British were doing.[10]

At present they were wet, cold, and miserable, but despite their travail Gleig reported that morale among troops and seamen remained high, in large part due to keen anticipation of what awaited them in New Orleans. "From the General, down to the youngest drum-boy, a confident anticipation of success seemed to pervade all ranks; and in the hope of an ample reward in store for them, the toils and grievances of the moment were forgotten." Much of their confidence sprang from the tales told them by American deserters, who claimed "there were not at present 5,000 soldiers in the State," that the populace that remained would join them when they appeared, allowing a "speedy and bloodless conquest." The deserters also spoke of the wealth of the city, "the rich booty which would reward its capture," and although Gleig does not mention it, how could the storytellers, with sly grins and chuckles and pokes and nudges, have failed to describe for men who had been without women for a long time the fabled beauties of New Orleans.

They were, Gleig wrote, "subjects well calculated to tickle the fancy of invaders, and to make them unmindful of immediate afflictions, in the expectation of so great a recompense."[11]

"THE PLACE WHERE WE LANDED WAS AS WILD AS IT IS POSSIBLE TO IMAGINE"

Admiral Cochrane and General Keane wasted no time in pushing on. They had already decided on the invasion point. Cochrane's first choice by way of Les Rigolets into Lake Pontchartrain had been abandoned. The lack of shallow-draft vessels would mean an even longer row by Cochrane's sailors, under the guns of Fort Petites Coquilles, and the American prisoners from the gunboats had told the British whopping lies about the strength of the fort: 500 men and forty guns, they said. Probably from fishermen and deserters, the British had learned of a bayou close to the city called Bienvenue. They were undoubtedly also told by fishermen who lived at its mouth that contrary to Jackson's orders, it was unobstructed and unguarded. On 18 December, while the troops were still being ferried to Isle aux Pois, Cochrane and Keane sent Lieutenant John Peddie of the quartermaster's corps and Captain Robert Spencer of the navy to reconnoiter Bayou Bienvenue.[12]

The mouth of Bayou Bienvenue was in the northwest corner of Lake Borgne, thirty miles due west of Isle aux Pois. Thirty to forty Spanish and Portuguese fishermen lived in a village on a "tongue of land" at the mouth of the bayou, and it was they who provided guides and information for the two British officers. Bayou Bienvenue was a considerable body of water, 110 to 150 yards wide, and navigable for vessels of a hundred tons up to twelve miles from its mouth. It was surrounded by cypress swamps and prairies. The latter were described by Major Latour. The land between the bayous, being lower than their banks, "form what are called *trembling prairies,* which are at all seasons impassable for men and domestic animals," while "ordinary prairies are passable" only at "times of great drought, and in low tides. . . ." Thus the vital importance of the bayous to reach the narrow strip of dry ground that ran along the Mississippi to New Orleans. A short distance from the fishermen's village, Bayou Mazant forked southwest from Bayou Bienvenue, and not far from its end it linked up with the Villeré Canal, which led to the plantation of the militia general Jacques-Philippe Villeré. Jackson had ordered him to obstruct the passages to the Mississippi and post a guard at every critical point. For reasons that were never explained, and, as

Major John Reid wrote, "nowithstanding the General's most positive orders," Villeré and his son had failed to obstruct the route leading to their own plantation. And that was the route along which Lieutenant Peddie and Captain Spencer were led by three of the traitorous fishermen. The officers, themselves disguised as fishermen, not only penetrated Villeré's plantation grounds, they walked to the bank of the Mississippi and tasted the water. Lieutenant Peddie and Captain Spencer had come about fifteen miles from the mouth of Bayou Bienvenue, and as they drank the waters of the great river they were only some twelve miles from New Orleans.[13]

On 21 December, after Peddie and Spencer had returned to the fleet with their report, a twelve-man American militia guard arrived in the fishing village at the mouth of Bayou Bienvenue. They had been sent by General Villeré's son, Major Gabriel Villeré, who was stationed with militia at the Villeré plantation. There was only one fisherman in the village. The others were with the British on Isle aux Pois, preparing to act as pilots for the invaders. The sergeant in charge of the guard sent a few men in a boat out on the lake, but they saw nothing. That night a sentry was posted while the others slept in one of the cabins. At daybreak on the twenty-second three men went two miles out on Lake Borgne, but again saw no signs of the British. This was repeated without success every two hours, and as darkness approached, three Americans arrived who had paddled a pirogue from Chef Menteur without spotting any British force. Once more a sentry was posted for the night.

The British sailors had to have been very quiet at the oars as they rowed the troops across Lake Borgne. Cochrane and Keane had not hesitated once Peddie and Spencer reported on the route. At 10:00 A.M. on 22 December an advance light brigade, Colonel William Thornton commanding, boarded the boats to be rowed to Bayou Bienvenue, thirty miles from Isle aux Pois. The commander of the ground forces, Major General John Keane, was with them. Their fishermen pilots guided them unerringly across the water. The brigade consisted of 85th Regiment of Foot (Bucks Light Infantry), 3rd Battalion of 95th Regiment of Foot (Rifle Brigade), rocketeers, and 100 sappers and miners, with 4th Regiment of Foot (King's Own) in support—1,600 strong. About 11:30 a torrential rain wet everybody through. Water collected ankle-deep in the bottoms of the boats, which were too crowded to allow bailing. When the rain finally stopped, a frigid north wind and sharp frost must have made some of the men wonder why they had ever agreed to accept the king's shilling.

A little after midnight the American sentry at the fishermen's village raised the alarm. He had heard a noise. The guard turned out under arms. "By the last gleams of the setting moon," Major Latour wrote, "they perceived five barges full of men, with some pieces of artillery, ascending the bayou. . . ." Given the disparity in numbers, the guard prudently hid behind a cabin. When the barges passed they scuttled to their boat in order to get away across the lake, probably to Chef Menteur, and raise the alarm. But they were spotted, and before they could push away, the barges had turned and hemmed them in. All but four of the guard were taken, and they ran in different directions into the prairies. Three of them wandered that night and the next day, unable to find their way because of the height of the grass, got turned around, and finally blundered into the village from which they had run and were captured. The fourth man, named Rey, wandered for three nightmarish days through canebrakes and over trembling prairies, bayous, and lagoons until finding friendly faces, and by then everybody in New Orleans and the environs knew what had happened.[14]

It was a strange environment through which the British advance made its way, best described a few days later by Colonel Alexander Dickson.

> The Creek has a great many turns and reaches in it, and the whole way up is covered on each side by high Reeds, it is of good breadth for four or five Miles, and then narrows so much, and is so shallow, that the boats cannot row for want of room, and pushed through the Mud by means of the Oars shoving against the bank. About a mile above the Huts [Cochrane's headquarters] there are two broad Creeks, one running into the Marsh to the right [upper Bienvenue], and the other to the left [Bayou Mazant], and all the way up there are on both sides a number of little Channels or inlets, full of water, which would render moving along the bank impossible, even when it is hard enough. From the landing place to Head Quarters [Villeré's plantation] is about 2½ Miles, the road being nothing more than a very bad and boggy path along the bank of a little Canal or Bayoue, which extends from the Creek nearly to the Misissippi, and is navigable for Canoes to within 1000 yards of the river. . . . The Road for the distance of ¾ of a mile from the landing place is through Reeds and the ground Consequently very boggy, it then enters a thick wood about 1¼ miles across . . . the Wood is generally of Cypress trees growing closely together, and full of thick Brush and Palmettos, the bottom being swampy with deep holes interspersed, full of water, it is therefore in every respect impracticable. From the edge of the woods to Villeré's plantation the distance is about half a Mile of tolerably good and broad road, and from the Plantation to the bank of the river is about 300 yards.[15]

By daylight on the twenty-third of December, a date to keep in mind, the British advance had reached the head of Bayou Mazant, where the troops disembarked. Lieutenant Gleig described it: "The place where we landed was as wild as it is possible to imagine. Wherever we looked, nothing was to be seen except one huge marsh, covered with tall reeds. . . ." There they rested for a few hours while sappers and miners cut a way "through several fields of reeds, intersected by deep muddy ditches, bordered by a low swampy wood." Then, according to Major Latour, although Lieutenant Gleig does not mention it, before setting out for Villeré's plantation and the Mississippi, "the British colours were displayed at the top of a tree, while the band played *God Save the King*. . . ." Can this really be true? Was this approach not meant as a clandestine movement to take the enemy by surprise?[16]

The regiments of the advance marched through canebrakes and small bayous from the head of Bayou Mazant to the mouth of the Villeré Canal. From there to the edge of the woods was about one mile, and from the edge to the east bank of the Mississippi about two miles. If "God Save the King" was really played, only birds, alligators, and other denizens of bayous and swamps heard it, for around noon the first troops, moving at the double, surrounded General Villeré's plantation house and took all of its occupants by surprise: the general, his son Gabriel, and a company of militia. But in a moment of British carelessness, Major Gabriel Villeré leaped out a window and ran for the swamp. Several shots were fired at him but missed. He headed north and got to the de la Ronde plantation, where he found Colonel Denis de la Ronde. The two men rowed across the Mississippi to the west bank, secured horses, and hastened north toward New Orleans to raise the alarm.

Major General Keane established British headquarters at the Villeré plantation house, a simple one-story building surrounded by a covered gallery, or porch. The regiments were marched about one mile north and bivouacked, their right flank on the road, their left on the east bank of the Mississippi. General Keane reported that "in this situation I intended to remain until the boats returned for the rest of the troops to the vessels, some of which grounded at a great distance."[17]

Armchair generals have been arguing about that decision ever since. Some think Keane should have pushed on at once to New Orleans, which was held by a small number of American troops. The city, they say, was ripe for plucking. One student has written that the boldness of the approach march, placing the advance at the end of a long and hazardous line of supply and communications, should have been matched by "bold execution." Colonel William Thornton, commander of the advance brigade, urgently pressed to immediately march on the city. But Keane, his critics maintain, was inexperienced and indecisive, and rejected Thornton's advice, thus losing a golden opportunity. Yet he was neither. Keane had served during the capture of Martinique from the French in 1809, under Wellington at Vitoria had led a brigade of the Iron Duke's famous 3rd Division, and had fought during the final year of the Peninsula campaign and into France. Nor did he have the reputation before or after, during a long military career, of being indecisive. Indeed, he had a reputation for recklessness; in fact, Lieutenant Gleig described him as "a young and dashing officer." Keane was faced with two problems: he was in a precarious position, and he suffered from a total lack of accurate military intelligence. He did not know how many troops Jackson had or where they were. Spies, deserters, prisoners, and others had given numbers ranging from 4,000 to 20,000. There were American troops behind him at the English Turn and elsewhere, but he did not know where or how many. Keane also had a third problem, of which he was ignorant, but it was the biggest problem confronting him. He had not a clue, nor

did anybody in the expedition, of the nature of the opponent he faced—
the man the French would come to call Napoléon des Bois (Napoleon of
the Woods).[18]

"SHOCKING AND DISGUSTING SIGHTS"

"I will smash them, so help me God!" Jackson said when he first learned of
the British landing. It was then between one-thirty and two o'clock in the
afternoon. He did not hesitate. He would attack. Not tomorrow. Tonight.[19]

The alarm gun boomed. An order was sent to Major Jean Baptiste
Plauché, commanding the uniformed battalion of city volunteers stationed
four miles north at Bayou St. John, to return immediately to New Orleans.
The battalion double-timed all the way. John Coffee's mounted Tennessee
riflemen had arrived on 20 December after a three-day forced march of 135
miles. His pace had been so fast about 400 men who could not keep up
straggled in on the twenty-first. That was the day Billy Carroll arrived with
his Tennesseeans and the arms and ammunition he had intercepted on the
way. Coffee and Carroll were camped four miles north of New Orleans on
Robert Avart's plantation. "Not a moment was lost," wrote John Reid, "in
putting a part of genl Coffee's Brigade consisting of about 800, & the 7th &
44 Regts in motion to attack the enemy in his first position."[20]

On the morning the British landed, Jackson had sent his two senior
engineers, Major Latour and Major Tatum, to investigate reports that British
ships had been sighted off Bayou Terre aux Boeuf. They left New Orleans at
11:00 A.M., and when they got close to the de la Ronde plantation they met
fleeing people who told them the British had taken the Villeré plantation.
Major Tatum immediately turned his horse and rode for New Orleans to
inform Jackson, while Major Latour carried out some valuable reconnaissance. Approaching within rifle shot, Latour observed the deployment of the
British advance brigade and estimated them at between 1,600 and 1,800.
Then he rode for New Orleans.

By the time Latour returned, many riders—including Major Villeré and
Colonel de la Ronde—had reached Jackson with the news, but Latour's
information alerted Jackson that Keane's force was undoubtedly an advance,
and perhaps a diversion. He still suspected an attack by way of Chef Menteur and put Governor Claiborne in command of three regiments of Louisiana militia, stiffened by Carroll's Tennesseeans, and posted them on the Plain
of Gentilly. Commodore Patterson was at Bayou St. John examining batteries the navy had erected there when he was told of the British landing. Patterson immediately returned to town and boarded USS *Carolina*, Captain
John D. Henley commanding. Henley cast off and "dropped down" the Mississippi "with the current." At 6:30 P.M. Jackson got word to Patterson
through Edward Livington asking him "to anchor abreast of the enemy's
camp . . . and open a fire upon them." In this action the *Carolina* carried one
long twelve-pounder and a number of light twelve-pound carronades.[21]

Jackson and his assault force marched out of a fearful city, south along the east bank of the Mississippi. He had between 1,600 and 2,000 men. They marched "about one hour after dark (a fine moonlight night)," wrote John Coffee. By 7:00 P.M. they were close to the British camp. Their approach was so quiet the British pickets were quite unaware of their presence. In the enemy camp exhausted soldiers slept, arms stacked, warming fires burning brightly. Contempt for their foe overcame the alertness to danger required of every soldier in the field. For as Lieutenant Gleig wrote, "As the Americans had never yet dared to attack, there was no great probability of their doing so on the present occasion." Thus the overconfident British rested, while in front them Jackson's men moved stealthily into position.[22]

Jackson and Coffee had reconnoitered together, and Jackson had decided on a plan of attack. On his left he placed Coffee with his now dismounted Tennessee Volunteers, to which he attached Beale's Orleans Rifles. In the center, left to right, were some Choctaw warriors, Major Louis D'Aquin's 2nd Battalion of free men of color, Major Plauché's uniformed city battalion, 44th Infantry, and 7th Infantry along the river on the right. Also on the right was Jackson's artillery, two 6-pounders protected by 7th Infantry and a marine detachment. Coffee's mission was to penetrate deeply into the British lines, then wheel, turn the British right flank, and drive all before him toward the river while Jackson's center and right drove straight ahead. Any night operation, even in our times with its instant communications, is very risky, even with well-trained and experienced troops. Jackson's center was filled largely by militia whose experience was mostly on the drill field. Yet he was determined to proceed and smash the enemy.

On USS *Carolina,* Captain Henley and Commodore Patterson had a good view of the British bivouac, outlined as it was by campfires described by Lieutenant Gleig as "made to blaze with increased splendour. . . ." About 7:30 P.M. the British could also see the *Carolina* as she maneuvered into position. Repeated hailings by sentries went unanswered, so they fired several musket rounds at her, but all remained quiet on the *Carolina.* Captain Henley got the ship close to the British shore, dropped anchor, and ordered the sails furled. The *Carolina* was swung broadside toward the east bank. About 8:00 P.M. Lieutenant Gleig heard somebody aboard "cry out in a commanding voice, 'Give them this for the honour of America.' The words were instantly followed by flashes of her guns, and a deadly shower of grape swept down numbers in the camp."[23]

The British artillery of the advance brigade was too light to duel with the naval guns. Heavy musketry was fired against the *Carolina* to no avail, and the Congreve rockets, wrote Gleig, "made a beautiful appearance in the air; but the rocket is an uncertain weapon, and these deviated too far from their object to produce even terror among those against whom they were directed." There was nothing to do but hunker down, with many soldiers finding shelter under the levee that rose above the Mississippi's waters, and there they "listened in painful silence to the pattering of grape shot among our huts, and to the shrieks and groans of those who lay wounded beside them." By 9:00 P.M. British return fire had been suppressed.[24]

By then, Gleig wrote, the young moon was "totally obscured with clouds," the British fires grew dull, and except when the *Carolina's* gun flashes lit up the sky "not an object could be distinguished at the distance of a yard." Then the night was split with a "fearful yell; and the heavens were illuminated on all sides by a semi-circular blaze of musketry." Jackson's ground attack had begun as, he reported to Monroe, "Coffee's men, with their usual impetuosity, rushed on the enemy's right and entered their camp, while our right advanced with equal ardour."[25]

All of the confusion of combat heightened by night fighting ensued. Coffee and his Tennesseeans, along with Beale's Orleans Rifles, attacked on the left and eventually wheeled right for their drive to the river. But the words are neater than reality. Beale's Rifles, made up of lawyers and merchants, became separated from Coffee's Tennesseeans, drove deep into the British camp, and took many prisoners, but eventually ran into British reinforcements and lost half their own number as prisoners. The militia in the center also attacked, but they fell behind the regulars and their line became a crescent. Seventh Infantry preceding the artillery on the levee road ran into eighty men of the veteran Rifle Brigade under Captain William Hallen. These men fought with tenacity. Captain Hallen was seriously wounded and lost half of his men killed and wounded and was probably forced from his initial position, but the riflemen refused to be driven from the field. Next to them, however, elements of 7th Infantry along with 44th Infantry drove hard against Bucks Light Infantry and sent them reeling in confusion. Jackson was in the thick of it, as close as pistol range, rallying men who were confused or beginning to bend, performing those acts required of a general at desperate moments. The merchant Vincent Nolte, no friend of Jackson, was there that night fighting with the New Orleans uniformed militia, and wrote later that in the charge of the militia "who had not yet smelled powder . . . Jackson's example spurred us on," along with "careless ignorance of what awaited them." On the British side Colonel William Thornton also exposed himself to death to rally and direct the troops. General Keane paid him a handsome tribute. "To Colonel Thornton I feel particularly grateful; his conduct on the night of the 23d, I shall ever admire and honour. He headed his brigade in the most spirited manner, and affored it a brilliant example of active courage and cool determination."[26]

To re-create precisely that night action is impossible. In the dark one saw nothing, heard only the roar of muskets, the dull thud of rifle butts against skulls, the screams, shrieks, and curses of men enraged, frightened, frenzied, the shouts of officers and sergeants trying to bring order out of chaos. "All order was lost," Lieutenant Gleig wrote. "Each officer, as he was able to collect twenty or thirty men round him, advanced into the middle of the enemy, when it was fought hand to hand, bayonet to bayonet, and sword to sword, with the tumult and ferocity of one of Homer's combats." Friend and foe mingled on the field, often not knowing who was in front or behind or beside them. Friendly fire claimed Americans and Britons.

Fog rolled in. Jackson broke off the attack. The British from Lieutenant Gleig to General Keane claimed that the Americans, appalled by the drubbing they were taking, fled the field and "did not again dare to advance." Lieutenant Gleig, while admitting "the combat had been long and obstinately contested," claimed the "victory was decidedly ours; for the Americans retreated in the greatest disorder, leaving us in possession of the field." Jackson for his part claimed "there can be but little doubt that we should have succeeded on that occasion, with our inferior force, in destroying or capturing the enemy, had not a thick fog . . . occasioned some confusion among the different corps. Fearing the consequences, under this circumstance, of the further prosecution of a night attack with troops then acting together for the first time, I contented myself with lying on the field that night. . . ."[27]

Does it matter, the technical question of who won or lost, who held the field? Casualties were roughly the same: the British lost 46 killed, 167 wounded, 64 captured; the Americans 26 killed, 115 wounded, 74 captured. But neither do statistics tell the story. Jackson's attack was a master stroke that disrupted the British timetable, shook their self-confidence, and swelled the morale of American troops and civilians alike. Lieutenant Gleig and his comrades had been rudely disabused of their conceit that Americans would not fight. Gleig wrote, "Instead of an easy conquest, we had already met with vigorous opposition; instead of finding the inhabitants ready and eager to join us, we found the houses deserted, the cattle and horses driven away, and every appearance of hostility. To march by the only road was rendered impracticable, so completely was it commanded by the shipping. In a word, all things had turned out diametrically opposite to what had been anticipated; and it appeared, that instead of a trifling affair more likely to fill our pockets, than to add to our renown, we had embarked in an undertaking which presented difficulties not to be surmounted without patience and determination."[28]

Two days after the night action, John Reid wrote that a British major—probably Major Samuel Mitchell of Rifle Brigade—taken prisoner that night observed that it was "obvious that *these Yankees* fight very differently from those at Washington City." What the backwoods general accomplished with his mixed bag of militia and regulars, combined with the devastating fire from the *Carolina,* was remarkable. He had dared that from which average generals shrink, and he and the men he led that night deserve our kudos.[29]

Many who remained on the field were past caring who won or lost. Lieutenant Gleig walked the battlefield looking for an old friend and comrade from whom he had become separated during the fighting. During his search this young veteran of the savage fighting with Wellington's army in Spain came across "shocking and disgusting sights . . . wounds more disfiguring or more horrible, I certainly never witnessed." Many men he saw "had met their death from bayonet wounds, saber cuts, or heavy blows from the butt ends of muskets; and the consequence was, that not only were the wounds themselves exceedingly frightful, but the very countenances of the dead exhibited the most savage and ghastly expressions. Friends and foes lay together in small groups of four to six . . . such had been the deadly closeness of the strife, that in one or two places, an English and American soldier might be seen with the bayonet of each fastened in the other's body."[30]

Of the hospital, he wrote: "It is here that war lose its grandeur and show, and presents only a real picture of its effects." He listened to prayers, groans, shrieks, and curses, saw some men who had lost their senses. Among the officers, all "personal acquaintances of my own," he saw one who had "received a musket ball in the belly, which had pierced through and lodged in the back bone." He "was in the most dreadul agony, screaming out, and gnawing the covering under which he lay."[31]

Lieutenant Gleig found his friend on the field, "lying behind a bundle of reeds . . . shot through the temples by a rifle bullet so remarkably small, as scarcely to leave any trace of its progress." Gleig wept over the body of his friend, then had him conveyed in a cart to British headquarters at Villeré's plantation, "and having dug for him a grave at the bottom of the garden, I laid him there as a soldier should be laid, arrayed, not in a shroud, but in his uniform. Even the very privates, whom I brought with me to assist at his funeral, mingled their tears with mine. . . ."[32]

Chapter 22

∽∾∞∾∽

BEAUTY AND BOOTY

The next day, Christmas Eve 1814, in the faraway city of Ghent, Belgium, American and British commissioners signed a treaty of peace. This has led many to believe that the continuing clashes between the two armies were exercises in futility, a useless waste of lives. Such is not the case, for the war would not end until the treaty was ratified by each country, and a battlefield coup by the British prior to ratification could change minds in London. We must therefore continue our tale.

Jackson wanted to attack the next morning. He ordered General Carroll to leave his position guarding the Gentilly road and bring 1,000 men to join the attack. But at a midnight meeting others, especially Edward Livingston, argued vehemently against it, and this is one of those occasions when a fighting general's instincts were wrong. He had been right the night before, but a daylight attack was quite another matter. It was one thing for militia to attack regulars by surprise at night, but to attack lines of bayonet-wielding British regulars who they can see was not what militia was trained to do.[1]

"The onset of the bayonet in the hands of the valiant is irresistible," Gentleman Johnny Burgoyne wrote in 1777, and that state of affairs was still true in the War of 1812 whenever American militia faced British regulars in open-field combat. On 12 September 1814, as British forces marched on Baltimore, American militia stood their ground and exchanged volleys with advancing British infantry. Lieutenant Gleig, who was there, wrote that the Americans "maintained themselves with great determination, and stood to receive our fire till scarcely twenty yards divided us. . . ." Then came the moment of truth, bayonet time: "we pushed on at double quick, with the intention of bringing them to the charge." Gleig could not "recollect on any occasion to have witnessed a more complete rout. Infantry, cavalry, and artillery, all huddled together, without the smallest regard to order or regu-larity. The sole subject of anxiety seemed to be which should escape first from the field of battle . . . numbers were actually trodden down by their countrymen in the hurry of flight."[2]

Jackson could not risk that. Cool reason, prodded by Livingston's pleas and John Coffee's reports that the rest of the British army was streaming into Keane's camp, overcame the warrior's passion to smash them, by God. He ordered a withdrawal of two miles to the Rodriguez Canal on a plantation owned by Ignace de Lino de Chalmet. There he set his men to work digging and building a mud rampart. He left behind Major Thomas Hinds and his Mississippi Dragoons, along with the Feliciana Dragoons from the Baton Rouge area, to patrol no-man's-land and gather intelligence on British movements.

Keane sat where he was. It has been suggested that when the British gained the ground next to the river they meant to immediately mount a coup de main—a bold, vigorous, surprise attack—and capture New Orleans before Jackson had a chance to consolidate his forces. This is speculation, however, for on the twenty-third, the day he had gained the dry ground at Villeré's plantation, Keane certainly did not act as a commander intent on a coup de main. He probably would have marched on the city once all of his troops were ashore had not Jackson attacked him in his camp and left him worried and cautious.

Matters were taken from Keane's hands on Christmas Day 1814, when the commanding officer of the expeditionary force finally caught up with his army. Lieutenant General Sir Edward Michael Pakenham (1778–1815) was an Anglo Irish soldier of wide experience and desperate battles, having entered the army in 1794 at age sixteen. He had been in several actions in Europe and the West Indies, and was wounded while commanding 64th Foot at Saint Lucia. But his major experience in war began in 1809 when he was posted to the Peninsula and joined Wellington, who had married Pakenham's sister Catherine. At Busaco and Fuentes d'Onoro he commanded 7th Fusiliers and Cameron Highlanders. It was at Wellington's great victory at Salamanca, where he commanded 3rd Division, that Pakenham made his name and was mentioned in dispatches by breaking the French center. Wellington, spotting a gap in the French lines, turned to him and said, "Now's your time, Ned," and Ned responded as directed. Wellington wrote, "I put Pakenham to the third division . . . and I am very glad I did so, as I must say he made the movement which led to our success . . . with a celerity and accuracy of which I doubt if there are very many capable, and without both it would not have answered its end." Then Wellington tempered his praise and at the same time made a telling comment on his senior officers: "Pakenham may not be the brightest genius, but my partiality for him does not lead me astray when I tell you that he is one of the best we have." The New Orleans expedition was Pakenham's first independent command.[3]

Immediately upon his arrival, Lieutenant Gleig wrote, Pakenham "proceeded to examine, with a soldier's eye, every point and place within view.

Of the American army nothing could be perceived, except a corps of observation, composed of five or six hundred mounted riflemen, which hovered along our front, and watched our motion." All that Pakenham could really see was the flat, monotonous terrain, the river on his left, the woods and swamps on his right, and the *Carolina* and the *Louisiana,* which kept lobbing shot into the British camp. It was a wretched position. His supply line stretched some eighty miles to the fleet anchored outside Lake Borgne. He had no good intelligence as to how many men Jackson had or where they were. That he was unhappy with what he found is a reasonable assumption. But tradition unsupported by evidence has it that Pakenham was not only unhappy but also gave vent to his feelings loudly and clearly enough that it filtered down to junior officers and other ranks. He is supposed to have said that an immediate and rapid advance upon the city should have begun on the twenty-third upon the capture of Villeré's plantation. Which he may well have done. But there is no record that he said it. Nor is there any evidence that he distrusted Admiral Cochrane and blamed him for the unenviable position the army was in. All is speculation, and in this case unreasonable and a waste of time. What we do know is what Pakenham did, and his first move was to pick up what General Keane had started and go after the two American vessels.[4]

A battery of nine guns had been brought from the fleet to the camp by backbreaking labor of the sailors and gunners: four 6-pounders firing shrapnel, two 5½-inch howitzers, and 5½-inch mortars. Even more ominous were two 9-pounders firing hot shot, which was simply an early incendiary made of balls of round shot heated red hot in portable field furnaces. Premature explosion in the barrels of guns was prevented by loading the powder charge, then a dry wad on top of the charge, then a wad of wet straw or clay on top of the dry wad, before ramming home the hot shot. Colonel Alexander Dickson (1777–1840), who had arrived with Pakenham, was in command of the guns. He had been Wellington's chief of artillery in the Peninsular War and would command the guns again at Waterloo. Dickson was widely acknowledged to be one of the leading artillerists of his time. But he made a mistake in his first engagement on American soil. Pakenham also wanted to silence USS *Louisiana,* which was anchored about a mile upstream from the *Carolina.* Doubtful that the guns Dickson had at hand could reach the *Louisiana,* Pakenham wanted to wait for four naval 18-pounders. But Dickson talked him out of it, and when the bombardment began the *Louisiana's* boats towed her upstream well out of range.[5]

Dickson's battery began firing at the *Carolina* at daylight on 27 December. The *Carolina* was anchored close to the opposite bank, and only one of her guns, a long 12-pounder, had the range to reach the British battery. "The air being light, and at north, rendered it impossible to get under way," reported the *Carolina's* skipper, John Henley. Dickson's second hot shot "lodged in the schooner's main-hold under her cables," where the crew could not get at it, and set the ship afire, "which rapidly progressed. . . ." Shortly after sunrise, Henley wrote, "the vessel in a sinking situation, and the fire increasing, and expecting every moment that she would blow up . . . I reluctantly gave orders for the crew to abandon her . . . a short time after I had succeeded in getting the crew on shore, I had the extreme mortification of seeing her blow up." What Henley did not mention in his report was that two of the guns were saved when, if we can take Major Howell Tatum literally, they were "thrown on shore" by the explosion. Henley had only one killed and six wounded, and some of his gunners would be added to the line that Jackson was building. USS *Louisiana*, meanwhile, heavier and better gunned than the *Carolina*, had anchored across the river from Jackson's line, where she could deliver enfilading fire against attackers.[6]

At this point we should examine the defensive position Jackson was building, which Major Latour called Camp Jackson but has since come to be called Line Jackson. The Rodriguez Canal, an old, partially overgrown mill-race, was seven miles south of New Orleans and formed the boundary between the Chalmette plantation to the south and the Macarty plantation to the north. Jackson chose it because it was the narrowest strip of dry land between the Mississippi on his right and the cypress swamp on his left. According to Jackson's topographical engineer, Major Howell Tatum, the distance between the river and the "thick, and almost impenetrable swamp" was about 600 yards. Since then, only about 180 feet of riverbank has been lost from erosion and the building of a larger levee. If we put out of our minds the highway and railroad tracks running out of the city, the few modern buildings and a cemetery, and distant signs of the petrochemical industry, what we see today if we stand behind the earthworks is essentially what Andrew Jackson and his troops saw: flat terrain leading southward with unobstructed fields of fire, for Jackson had ordered all buildings torn down, which was done within 500 to 600 yards of Line Jackson. If Pakenham was determined to attack Jackson, he would have to come straight across those open fields.[7]

Jackson had the canal deepened and widened and partially filled with water. The earthworks behind it, made largely of mud anchored by cypress logs, were raised shoulder high for men behind it but seven to eight feet from the bottom of the canal. Jackson ordered Major Latour to open the levee and flood the ground in front of the canal. Major Barthelemy Lafon did the same south of the British camp, but this attempt to surround the British with water failed when the river went down, although it did leave the ground soggy. Some four days of digging by slaves and soldiers, including reluctant Creole militia who were not accustomed to manual labor, served to create a formidable line of defense. And none too soon, for on 28 December Pakenham, as they liked to say in those days, put his army in motion.[8]

The British had been kept awake most of the night by American snipers, of whom we will have more to say later. But according to Lieutenant Gleig, the army was in a "merry mood." He described the scene as the columns, preceded by skirmishers, moved forward: "It was a clear frosty morning, the mists had dispersed, and the sun shone brightly upon our arms . . . it was impossible to guess, ignorant as we were of the position of his main body, at what moment opposition might be expected. Nor, in truth, was it a matter of much anxiety. Our spirits, in spite of the troubles of the night, were good, and our expectations of success were high; consequently many rude jests were bandied about, and many careless words spoken."[9]

On the British right, next to the swamp, Pakenham's second in command, Major General Samuel Gibbs, led King's Own (4th Foot), Royal North Britain Fusiliers (21st Foot), East Essex (44th Foot), and 5th West India Regiment. On the left, by the river, Major General Keane commanded Bucks Light Infantry (85th), Sutherland Highlanders (93rd Foot), 3rd Battalion of Rifle Brigade (95th Foot), and 1st West India Regiment. Keane's artillery consisted of two 6-pounders, two 9-pounders, and a howitzer. Total strength was between 5,500 and 6,000 men. Jackson then had almost 3,300 men in his lines. According to Pakenham's assistant adjutant general, the advance was meant "to reconnoitre the enemy's position, or to attack if we saw it practicable." Today it is called a reconnaissance in force.[10]

The American militia dragoon patrols from Mississippi and Feliciana withdrew before the advancing British columns. As the British drew closer they could see the American lines. By then Jackson had five artillery pieces in place. Two were twenty-four-pounders. Jackson had asked for volunteers to work them, and the sailors from the sunken *Carolina,* commanded by naval Lieutenants Otho Norris and Charles E. Crawley, "instantly volunteered." Jackson's lines were nearly complete on the right, near the river, but on his left they had not reached the swamp and according to the British consisted only of an abatis (felled trees imbedded at an angle in the ground with sharpened ends pointing outward) and rudimentary earthworks behind. This was the weak point of the American defense. Three days earlier, Edward Livingston had reported to Jackson that Jean Lafitte recommended that "our line to afford a Complete protection ought to be extended *thro* the first wood, to the Cypress swamp & the Canal Extended that Distance as they may otherwise turn our left." If that was done, Lafitte considered the cypress swamp impassable. But according to the British, by the night before their advance Jackson's left only "touched the woods."[11]

General Keane's column by the river came in sight of Jackson's lines when it moved past the still burning Chalmette plantation house at a distance of some seven hundred to eight hundred yards. Keane ordered his artillery to engage. Meanwhile, at about 7:30 A.M., Commander Patterson had seen the American patrols withdrawing and ordered USS *Louisiana,* Lieutenant Charles B. Thompson commanding, into enfilading position in front of Jackson's lines and cleared for action. At 8:25 A.M. one of Keane's 9-pounders and the howitzer began firing on the *Louisiana,* while the two 6-pounders and the other 9-pounder engaged the five guns on Jackson's line. The ship replied in kind and Jackson's guns, including the two big 24-pounders, joined in. Lieutenant Gleig has been accused of exaggerating the effects of the American fire, but he was there and his description bears repeating. The fire "striking full into the midst of our ranks, occasioned terrible havoc. The shrieks of the wounded . . . the crash of firelocks, and the fall of such as were killed, caused at first some little confusion; and what added to the panic, was, that from the houses beside which we stood, bright flames suddenly burst out." The Americans were using hot shot as well as round and grape shot. A tremendous cannonade mowed down our ranks, and deafened us with its roar; while two large chateaux and their outbuildings, almost scorched us with the flames, and blinded us with the smoke which they emitted."

The *Louisiana's* performance was exemplary, and especially striking as the crew was "composed of men of all nations (English excepted) taken from the streets of New Orleans not a fortnight before the battle; yet I never knew guns better served," Patterson wrote, adding that Lieutenant Thompson "deserves great credit for the discipline to which in so short a time he had brought such men, two-thirds of whom do not understand English."

The British infantry was ordered to take cover as best they could, which meant a knee-high wet ditch with high rushes growing on its bank that provided some concealment, if not cover. There they huddled while the unequal artillery duel continued. According to Gleig, "two of our field-pieces, and one field-mortar, were dismounted; many of the gunners were killed; and the rest, after an ineffectual attempt to silence the fire of the shipping, were obliged to retire." Sailors from the fleet saved the dismounted guns by braving the American fire, lifting the heavy pieces, and carrying them out of range. But not without loss. Commander Patterson reported that "I distinctly saw, with the aid of my glass, several shot strike in the midst of the men (seamen) who were employed dragging it away." This occurred about 1:00 P.M., when the British fire began to slacken. American counterfire silenced the British guns by 3:00 P.M., and an hour later the *Louisiana,* from which eight hundred shot had been fired at the enemy, ceased fire. In the entire exchange one of her crew had been slightly wounded by shrapnel. The British suffered 40 to 50 casualties. Keane's infantry, after spending the day in a wet ditch, was gradually withdrawn and by twilight mustered out of range of the American guns.

In the meantime, on Jackson's left General Gibbs's column, spearheaded by the gallant and aggressive Colonel Robert Rennie of Royal North Britain Fusiliers, was out of sight of the *Louisiana* and at extreme range for its guns. The line here was defended by Tennesseeans: Coffee's volunteers and Billy Carroll's militia. Rennie with the vanguard moved through the woods on the edge of the swamp. He described the woods as "very boggy, deep, thick, and difficult to penetrate through." Rennie's men exchanged fire with Coffee's skirmishers, who gradually withdrew. General Carroll ordered Colonel James Henderson with 200 Tennessee militia to enter the swamp and then move to his right and attack Rennie's flank. Henderson apparently misunderstood his orders and moved obliquely away from the swamp and ran into Rennie. In the ensuing fire Henderson and 3 of his men were killed and the detachment withdrew. Jackson by then was aware of the danger and ordered Captain Pierre Jugeant and his Choctaw warriors, of whom there were probably some 60 by then, into the swamp to do the job botched by Henderson. The Choctaws took Rennie under heavy fire. But Rennie was convinced then and always that he could have turned Jackson's left, thus endangering the whole line. Despite the many historians who agree, we are dealing here with another of those pesky ifs of history so dear to the hearts of second-guessers. We must admit, however, that Jackson had received due warning from Lafitte, through Livingston, that the line should be extended to the swamp.[12]

Pakenham, having witnessed the shambles made of Keane's advance, decided to take a look himself and with Colonel Dickson rode across the field to his right, dismounted, and got close enough to survey Jackson's line. Lieutenant Peter Wright climbed a tree and reported that the ditch in front of the rampart was filled with water and the woods too thick to allow the turning of Jackson's line on the left. Without investigating further, Pakenham ordered General Gibbs to withdraw. Colonel Rennie is reported to have been furious.

Jackson then took Lafitte's advice and extended and strengthened the line through the woods and then, to cover their flank, bent it to the left at right angles in the cypress swamp as far as it was thought an enemy might appear. The ground in front was cleared of underbrush to give Coffee's riflemen a clear field of fire. The terrain was so soggy in the woods from incessant rain that earthworks were not continued. Instead, a rampart was built that was proof against musketry only, as the ground for an attacker was unsuitable for artillery. It was described by Major Latour as a "double row of logs, laid one over the other, leaving a space of two feet, which was filled up with earth." From where the woods began to the end of the line, Latour wrote, "the ground was so low, and so difficult to be drained, that the troops were literally encamped in water, walking knee deep in mud; and the several tents were pitched on small isles or hillocks, surrounded with water or mud." Later a number of Coffee's men died of illnesses brought on by the wet, unhealthy conditions.[13]

At the same time, Jackson had grave problems, both official and personal. First, where were the Kentuckians? Reporting to Monroe on the day's action, Jackson wrote, "The Kentucky troops have not arrived; & my effective force, at this point, does not exceed 3000. Theirs must be at least double. . . ." Second: "We are very deficient in arms. Those who having descended the river having come without their necessary accoutrements. There is also a great scarcity of flints." Third: "One other evil (& it is the greatest) I mention with pain: we are greatly deficient in experienced officers." Fourth, in a letter to Monroe he admitted to being mortal: "My constitution having suffered considerably by exposure may at length fail; & to provide against such an event I could wish that some experienced officer were sent on to take command of the forces, when I shall be unable to do justice to it." But who? For there was no one. Major General Edmund Pendleton Gaines, a very competent career officer, had been ordered to New Orleans, but his arrival was over a month away.[14]

Ill and exhausted he might be, but a new problem arose that infuriated him. It was prompted by the action on the twenty-eighth and the precautions Jackson was taking by building second and third lines behind his main line—just in case. All of this made the Louisiana legislature restive, and as legislators are prone to do when matters are taken out of their hands and they feel helpless, they meddled. The Speaker of the state Senate, an influential planter and friend of James Monroe with the unforgettable name of Fulwar Skipwith, was curious, as he spoke to Robert Butler, Jackson's adjutant general, who was on duty in the city. What, he wondered, were the commanding general's intentions should he be driven from his lines and forced to retreat through and beyond the city? Why do you ask? Butler inquired. Well, Fulwar Skipwith said, as related by Major Reid, it's rumored that if Jackson were forced to retreat he "had it in contemplation to lay the city waste. . . ." The legislature would like to know if this was indeed what the general had in mind, in which case "they might, by offering terms to the enemy, avert so great a calamity." Butler immediately reported the conversation to his chief.

Nothing could have been better designed to provoke Jackson's ire. Weakness on the home front? Betrayal from behind? Property before honor and country? At the beginning of the action on the twenty-eighth, as Jackson was "riding rapidly" toward his threatened left flank, one of his volunteer aides, a New Orleans lawyer named Abner Lawson Duncan, hailed him with news from Governor Claiborne that the legislature meant to turn over the city to the British. Jackson was incensed, although a few days later in a letter to the Louisiana General Assembly he said that he did not believe what he had been told. But he also admitted that he sent an order via Duncan for Governor Claiborne to investigate, and if it were true there was only one way to deal with the legislature: "blow them up," he called out to Duncan. Later he reprimanded Duncan on the "impropriety of delivering such a message publicly in the presence of the troops."[15]

The affair blew over, but we need to examine Jackson's intentions were he driven from his lines. Would he have torched the city, applied a scorched earth policy, rendered a British victory hollow? Vincent Nolte wrote in his *Memoirs,* "Jackson had openly declared that he would imitate the example of the Russians at Moscow, and consign the whole city to the flames, should he not be able to defend it, for he was determined the English should reap no profit from their success." James Parton reported that Jackson told a committee of the legislature that if the "fate of war drive me from my line to the city, they may expect to have a very warm session." When asked directly by his longtime confidant John Henry Eaton of his intentions, Jackson replied, "I should have retreated to the city, fired it, and fought the enemy amidst the surrounding flames . . . Nothing for the comfortable maintenance of the enemy would have been left in the rear. I would have destroyed New Orleans, occupied a position above on the river, cut off all supplies, and in this way compelled them to depart the country." Knowing Jackson by now as we do, can there be a doubt in our minds that is precisely what he would have done?[16]

Pakenham, in the meantime, had decided on the advice of his chief engineer, Colonel John Fox Burgoyne, bastard son of Gentleman Johnny Burgoyne, who had lost a British army at Saratoga during the American Revolution, and his artillery commander, Colonel Alexander Dickson, to treat the American line as a defensive position to be besieged by breaching it with artillery and silencing its guns prior to an assault. Burgoyne and Dickson had served with Wellington and were highly regarded by the Iron Duke. But the big siege guns were somewhere on the Atlantic and Pakenham had no idea when they would arrive. He therefore asked Cochrane to send him heavy naval guns from the fleet and the admiral ordered his long-suffering sailors to jump to it. We lack the space and time to describe the movement of the big cast-iron guns weighing up to forty-eight hundred pounds, but we must pause for a moment to pay tribute to what was an incredible feat by Cochrane's sailors in moving the monsters sixty miles across Lake Borgne and then through bayou, swamp, and boggy ground. It is another reminder that in addition to being bloody and dirty and often sheer madness, war is sometimes just prolonged hard labor.

While the British sailors lifted and hauled and strained, Jackson kept improving his defenses and adding to his artillery. By 1 January 1815 he had thirteen guns in place in time for Pakenham's grand gunnery show. In addition, Commander Patterson's suggestion to Jackson that a redoubt (a small, enclosed defensive work) be established across the river to provide flanking fire was approved. There Patterson mounted a 24-pounder from the New Orleans arsenal and two 12-pounders taken off the *Louisiana*. This gave Jackson a total of sixteen guns, although one small brass carronade on the far left of his line was of little service.

By 1 January Pakenham and his artillery commander were ready—or rather, Packenham was ready. Colonel Dickson was unhappy with the lack of suitable equipment and materials to mount the guns, and there was also a shortage of ammunition, all of which had to be brought from the fleet. But field expediencies, as soldiers say, had overcome the severe obstacles he faced, although many of the gun mountings were jerry-built. Yet he had more guns than Jackson, a total of twenty-four, ranging from three-pounders to eighteen-pounders plus a howitzer and three mortars. Two of the eighteen-pounders were positioned to challenge the *Louisiana* if she appeared, but she did not, as Commander Patterson explained: "I did not drop the *Louisiana* down within the range of their shot, having learnt from deserters that a furnace of shot was kept in constant readiness at each of their batteries to burn her; and the guns being of much greater effect on shore, her men were drawn to man them, and I was particularly desirous to preserve her from the hot shot, as I deemed her of incalcuable service to cover the army in the event of General Jackson retiring from his present line to those which he had thrown up in his rear."[17]

Thick fog obscured the fields on New Year's Day until sometime between 9:00 and 10:00 A.M., when the British opened fire and immediately made a mistake. Instead of finding the range and concentrating on the American batteries and ramparts, they wasted much of their precious ammunition on the Macarty plantation house, where Jackson had his headquarters. "In less than ten minutes," wrote Major Latour, "upwards of one hundred balls, rockets and shells struck the house, and rendered it impossible to remain there." Jackson and others were inside at the time, but came out unscathed. The sudden and fierce bombardment took the Americans by surprise, but Jackson's gunners were as seasoned as the British and they quickly settled down into their polished routines of serving the guns and returning fire. With a big difference. They first fired for range, and when they had it, unleashed their own bombardment and eventually silenced one 7-gun battery and might have done the same to the main British battery had the contest continued. The British failed to achieve their two main objectives: silence the American artillery and breach the defense line.[18]

It has been suggested that Pakenham should have launched an infantry assault against Jackson's left at the time of the bombardment. This is a reasonable position to take, but that is about all one can say since Pakenham did not do it and we will never know whether it would have been successful. Fire slackened by 1:00 P.M. and ended at 3:00 P.M. Under cover of night the British guns were withdrawn. The effect on British morale was severe. Privates to high officers were, as Lieutenant Gleig wrote, "not only baffled and disappointed, but in some degree disheartened and discontented." An officer who was there described Pakenham as being "much mortified at being obliged to retire the army from a second demonstration and disposition to attack. . . ." Rear Admiral Sir Edward Codrington, who was also present, wrote to his wife that the gunners had fired too high. "Such a failure in this boasted area was not to be expected, and I think it is a blot in the artillery escutcheon. We have by this allowed the enemy to increase our difficulties and gain spirits; and the harrassing job of withdrawing the guns half-buried in the mud, occasioned by the pouring rain of that night, wore down the whole army as well as the Johnnys [sailors] who had the heavier part of that severe duty to perform."[19]

The British damaged some American positions and blew up two powder caissons. But overall, Wellington's proud gunner, Colonel Alexander Dickson, had been outgunned by Jackson's U.S. regulars, New England seaman, Baratarian privateers, and recycled French gunners from Napoleon's armies.

Pakenham now decided to wait until the arrival of reinforcements being brought by Major General John Lambert. Jackson was also waiting for reinforcements. Finally, on the evening of 2 January, Brigadier General John Adair, adjutant general of the Kentucky reinforcements, arrived at Jackson's headquarters. The 2,300 Kentuckians were camped above New Orleans. Their arrival, however, proved to be a deep disappointment to Jackson. He wrote the next day to Monroe, "Not more than one third of them are armed, &

those very indifferently. I have none here to put into their hands, & can, therefore, make no very useful disposition of them." An assiduous search of the city was made and enough weapons were found to arm another 400 Kentuckians, but most of them remained unarmed. So much for the mythical hordes of Kentucky riflemen at New Orleans so beloved of story and song.[20]

The two armies sat facing each other for almost a week. Jackson continued to strengthen his line. The British repaired their damaged artillery and made preparations to act on Admiral Cochrane's suggestion to transfer some troops to the west bank of the Mississippi and attack on that side in conjunction with a main assault against Jackson on the east bank. Jackson had also sent Louisiana militia to the west bank, and he would send some of the armed Kentuckians after their arrival. He placed in command on that side of the river the inept Louisiana militia general David Bannister Morgan, who by no means should be confused or connected in any way with the great Daniel Morgan of Revolutionary War fame. Major Latour was assigned to build defensive works for Morgan.

Jackson continued to wage every night a little war that the British found ungentlemanly. From the start, groups of Coffee's Tennessee riflemen and Jugeant's Choctaws had slipped between the lines after dusk and made life miserable for the British troops. They would fire upon an outpost of men sitting around a campfire and wake up the whole camp as the alarm was raised and the troops called to arms. Then it would grow quiet and the troops would lay down to sleep and firing would break out in another direction and they would go through the whole routine again. Lieutenant Gleig wrote, "Thus was the entire night spent in watching, or at best in broken and disturbed slumbers, than which is nothing more trying, both to the health and spirits of an army." The shrieks of the Choctaws when they took a sentry's scalp were especially unnerving. This was not how things were done in Europe, where two armies facing each other in an inactive state respected the safety of outposts and sentries and officers. Lieutenant Gleig told of English and French sentries being within twenty yards of each other without harm coming to either. "But the Americans," wrote Gleig, "entertained no such chivalric notions." While granting the logic of the American belief that an enemy was an enemy no matter where situated or in what mode, to Gleig and his comrades "it appeared an ungenerous return to barbarity." All night, every night, this kind of harassment went on. British losses were few, but Gleig admitted that it "occasioned anxiety and uneasiness throughout the whole line."[21]

Lambert arrived with Pakenham's reinforcements on 6 January. The fresh troops consisted of Royal Fusiliers (7th Foot) and Monmouth Light Infantry (43rd Foot), and numbered in all about 1,640 men. Both were veteran regiments of many desperate battles against the French in Portugal and Spain. Pakenham then held a council of war at which it was decided to launch a grand infantry assault on Jackson's line. Preparations were begun immediately.

Cochrane's sailors, of course, got the tough job of hauling forty-seven boats on the night of 7 January from the end of Villeré's Canal to the Mississippi for the transportation of the west bank force. Rumors of what the British were up to filtered to the Americans during the week, and on the seventh definite intelligence of British intentions was passed to Jackson. This force was commanded by Colonel William Thornton and was about 600 strong: Bucks Light Infantry, Royal Marines, part of 5th West India, and 200 sailors.[22]

Pakenham's plan differed from the reconnaissance in force of 28 December in that a full-scale infantry assault was scheduled against Jackson's lines for the morning of 8 January, in coordination with Colonel Thornton's attack up the west bank. General Gibbs was once again given the wing skirting the swamp, General Keane the left wing along the river. Newly arrived General Lambert would command the reserve.[23]

General Keane's columns consisted of about 1,600 men. Of these, the light companies of Royal Fusiliers, Monmouth Light Infantry, Sutherland Highlanders, and 100 men of 1st West India Regiment, commanded by Colonel Robert Rennie, were assigned to push fast along the levee and attack and take an unfinished but dangerous redoubt that was being built just in advance of the American line to provide enfilading fire along the front of the line. The aggressive Rennie, who had fumed on the twenty-eighth because Pakenham had not let him attack and try to turn the American left, was the perfect commander for the mission. Next to Rennie's little force General Keane would advance with the bulk of the Highlanders and the rest of 1st West India with discretion to support either Rennie or Gibbs, depending upon the circumstances. Preceding Keane's main force were some skirmishers from 95th Rifles.

The bulk of Rifle Brigade, however, 300 strong and reinforced by some troops of East Essex, were assigned to skirmish in front of Gibbs's column on the right. Gibbs's spearhead was 250 men of East Essex (44th Foot), Lieutenant Colonel Thomas Mullens commanding. The regiment's mission was critical. The engineers had prepared six long ladders with planks attached to them, ten small ladders, and bundles of fascines made of sugarcanes. Fascines are large bundles of sticks, cane, or whatever usable material is at hand to be used in filling ditches—in this particular case, to fill in the Rodriguez Canal at the point of attack to help the troops cross it. The long ladders covered by planks were also for that purpose, and the small ladders were for scaling the parapet. The order given to Colonel Mullens on the night of 7 January was explicit: "The officer commanding the 44th Regiment must ascertain where these requisites are, this evening, so that there may be no delay in taking them forward tomorrow to the old Batteries," a point 650 yards from Line Jackson, which the skirmishers would occupy by daylight.[24]

Behind East Essex, King's Own and Royal North Britain Fusiliers would join in the main attack aimed at Billy Carroll's Tennesseeans stationed just left of Jackson's center. Gibbs detached the light companies of his regiments and 100 men of 1st West India into the woods to his right to protect his own flank and attempt to outflank Coffee's Brigade. Once the Americans were driven from their line, these elite troops would lead the chase.

In the center, as the reserve, Pakenham placed General John Lambert with 14th Light Dragoons, who had no horses, Royal Fusiliers, Monmouth Light Infantry, and 5th West India, the latter three minus their light companies, which were assigned elsewhere.

Jackson's order of battle had changed little from 1 January. The advanced redoubt that Colonel Robert Rennie and his elite light companies would aim at was garrisoned by a company of U.S. 7th Infantry, Lieutenant Andrew Ross commanding; its two 6-pounders positioned to support the line with enfilading fire were served by a detachment of U.S. 44th Infantry, Lieutenant Louis de Marant (or Meant) commanding. Behind the redoubt, and within Jackson's line, were thirty riflemen of Thomas Beale's New Orleans Rifles, who held the extreme right of the line. Moving left, next to these riflemen and seventy feet from the river, was Battery No. 1: two brass 12-pounders served by U.S. regular artillerymen, Captain Enoch Humphreys commanding, and a 6-inch howitzer by dismounted militia dragoons commanded by Major Henri de St. Geme. The rest of U.S. 7th Infantry, Major Henry Peire commanding, and minus two companies posted to Fort St. Philip, held the line between Batteries 1 and 2. Battery No. 2 had a 24-pounder served by some Yankee sailors from the sunken USS *Carolina,* Lieutenant Otho Norris, U.S.N., commanding. U.S. 7th Infantry also held the line between Batteries 2 and 3. Battery No. 3 contained two 24-pounders manned by Baratarian privateers commanded by Captain Dominique You (born Alexandre Frederic Lafitte, oldest brother of the famous Jean Lafitte) and his cousin (whom he called "uncle") Renato Beluche, who had been born in New Orleans at 632 Dumaine Street. Dominique, born in Port-au-Prince, Saint-Domingue, was a casting director's dream for a pirate captain: just shy of five feet, four inches but built like a large rock with shoulders broader than average, eyes black and flashing, scarred by severe powder burns on the left side of his face, and jutting from the middle of it all a fierce hawk nose. But he was reputed to be a likable fellow.[25]

The space between Batteries 3 and 4 were held by Major Jean Plauché's battalion of uniformed New Orleans militia companies, and Major Pierre Lacoste's battalion of free men of color. Battery No. 4 held the biggest killer, the naval 32-pounder served by more New Englanders from the *Carolina,* Lieutenant Charles E. Crawley commanding. More free men of color, Major Louis D'Aquin's battalion of Saint-Domingue refugees, were posted between Batteries 4 and 5. Battery No. 5 was manned by regular U.S. gunners serving two 6-pounders, a Colonel Perry and Lieutenant William C. Kerr commanding. U.S. 44th Infantry, Captain Isaac L. Baker commanding, which apparently filled in a gap up to Battery No. 5, manned the line between Batteries 5 and 6. Battery No. 6, with a brass 12-pounder, was a foreign French operation commanded directly by Lieutenant Etienne Bertel, whose superior was General Garrigues Flaujeac. All of the infantry and artillery listed until now were under the overall command of Colonel George Ross, command-ing officer of 7th Infantry.

The center and left center of Jackson's line had only two batteries, No. 7 and No. 8, which was probably why Pakenham was planning to direct his assault there. The troops manning the line were Billy Carroll's Tennesseeans. Battery No. 7 held a long brass 18-pound culverin and a 6-pounder served by U.S. regular gunners commanded by Lieutenants Samuel Spotts and Louis Chaveau. Battery No. 8 held a small brass carronade, but it gave little service because of a faulty carriage. A corporal of U.S. artillery commanded some of Carroll's militia who served this gun. In reserve behind General Carroll's Tennessee militia was Brigadier General John Adair's armed Kentuckians.

To the left of Battery No. 8, in their hellhole of water and mud, were John Coffee's Tennessee Volunteers, who had no idea when they left Ten-nessee that they would end up as aquatic troops. And beyond them, in the cypress swamp, were Captain Pierre Jugeant and his Choctaws.

How many men did Jackson have on the line, including Adair's Ken-tuckians? That depends on which authority you consult. Latour, who was there, recorded 3,519. Jackson, who of course was also there, said 4,045. A recent "best judgement" of one authority is between 4,200 and 4,400. So let us say that Jackson had somewhere between 3,500 and 4,500 men on the line and engaged. There were a few other small units available, but we will ignore them, as we will the horde of unarmed Kentuckians whom Jackson placed behind his second line.[26]

Jackson had enough intelligence from various sources of British activity to know that almost certainly the attack would be launched on the eighth. He also foresaw that despite obvious British designs on the west bank, it was on the east bank that the main assault would come. Observations, deserters, and prisoners had led him to these conclusions. He was awakened at 1:00 A.M. on 8 January by a courier with a message from Commander Patterson at his enfilading battery on the west bank. General David Morgan had told Patterson that he expected the main attack to be directed against him. Jack-son sent the courier back with a message to Morgan that he was wrong and could have no more men. Then he awakened his officers and told them that their day had begun.

Jackson rode his lines. He went to his old and faithful friend Coffee first, comrade from Emuckfau and Enitachopko and Horseshoe Bend, and in the terrible fight with the Bentons. Then he rode east toward the river, first to another old comrade, Billy Carroll. He probably addressed many of the Tennesseeans by name, for Robert Remini has remarked that it was remark-able how many Tennessee soldiers Jackson knew by name. Militia, regulars, American, French, white, black, other rich shades of the Gulf Coast, he rode his lines and spoke to them. They were in good spirits, ready to fight, con-fident of victory. He stopped at Dominique You's battery and they enjoyed a cup of coffee together. What a conversation to eavesdrop on. Jackson rode his lines and surveyed what was really quite a remarkable sight, one that would not be seen again until our times: Tennessee and Kentucky militia and U.S. regulars largely of Anglo-Saxon stock; the battalions of free men of color; St. Domingue-born Dominique You's mixed bag of Baratarian privateers; Louisiana white Creoles; and foreign French. A multiethnic, multiracial, multireligous American army commanded by a Scotch Irish orphan from South Carolina's Waxhaws. It was a multiculturalist's dream team.

On the British side the regiments were assembled at 4:00 A.M. and moved out to their jump-off points. Pakenham rose an hour later. It was Ned's time once more, but now as an independent commander over three thousand miles away from the master's guiding hand.

What does one do when everything seems to be going wrong? By the time Pakenham arose Thornton and his men should have been on the west bank, moving ahead to neutralize Patterson's enfilading battery. But Thornton had not even left the east bank. The labor involved in getting the boats to the Mississippi had been greatly underestimated. Colonel Dickson wrote, "It is hardly possible to express the fatiguing nature of this work, and the exertions made to overcome the difficulty, the parties of seamen etc. employed being obliged to work in a deep Mud in which they frequently Sunk up to the Middle." Pakenham was surprised to learn that Thornton had not left and considered calling off the west bank attack. He finally ordered it to proceed, but remarked that "Thornton's people will be of no use whatever to the general attack."[27]

Problems also kept dogging Colonel Dickson's artillery. The forward batteries were still unfinished by 2:30 A.M., and two hours later they were reported to be "not half finished." With Pakenham was his assistant adjutant general, Harry Smith, who thirty-one years later would lead the final charge at the Battle of Aliwah, India, and once and for all defeat the Sikhs. In his autobiography, Smith said that he urged Pakenham to withdraw the skirmishers and postpone the attack until later in the day. Pakenham declined. "I have twice deferred the attack. We are strong in numbers comparatively. It will cost more men, and the assault must be made." Smith continued: "While we were talking, the streaks of daylight began to appear, although the morning was dull, close and heavy, the clouds almost touching the ground."

"'It is now too late,'" Pakenham said.[28]

At his signal a rocket soared into the sky. Upon sighting it the skirmishers of 95th Rifle Brigade rose 650 yards from Jackson's line and moved out. The Americans saw the rocket, too, and got ready.

The night before, Lieutenant Colonel the Honourable Thomas Mullens, third son of Lord Ventry, commanding 44th Foot, violated the old rule that if you want something done right, do it yourself. He did not personally inspect the location of the vital ladders and fascines. He delegated that to Lieutenant Colonel Johnston, who also did not look for himself, but asked the engineers and returned to tell Mullens that they were at the advanced battery. But they were not. They were in a redoubt five hundred yards behind the battery. On the morning of the eighth Mullens and his regiment stopped for about ten minutes at the very redoubt where the ladders and facines were, only a few feet away. The engineering officer, Captain Henry Tapp, was assigned to distribute them to the regiment's grenadier company and supervise their placement. But apparently Tapp was asleep inside the redoubt, and when Mullens and the regiment moved on he was still snoring. At the advanced battery Mullens went in search of the ladders and fascines. Forty-five minutes passed before he finally learned where they were, and after a searing rebuke of Colonel Johnston he sent another officer with 300 men to return to the redoubt five hundred yards in the rear and fetch them. But the operation was by now botched. The men became strung out along the British line of march, and when firing began many dropped their bundles and began firing back. This caused more confusion in Gibbs's column because there were British troops ahead of them.

But the attack proceeded. When the rocket went off Battery No. 6 in Jackson's line fired at Gibbs's column. The British troops "gave three cheers," Latour wrote, "formed in close column of about sixty men in front, and advanced nearly in the direction of Battery No. 7. . . ." They were carrying fascines and some carried ladders. "A cloud of rockets preceded them, and continued to fall in showers during the whole attack." Batteries 6, 7, and 8 opened an "incessant fire," but the red-coated column advanced in "good order." Then Billy Carroll gave the order to fire and his Tennesseeans joined in with muskets and rifles, and then John Adair's Kentuckians in reserve came up and joined them.[29]

Kentuckians became mixed with the more numerous Tennesseeans. A Kentucky soldier reported that the "smoke was so thick" the dawn was like darkness. He wrote that "our men did not seem to apprehend any danger, but would load and fire as fast as they could, talking, swearing, and joking all the time." After the first volley "every one loaded and banged away on his own hook." The massacre of Kentucky militia at River Raisin in Michigan in 1813 seared the memories of many, and a Lieutenant Ashby shouted at the advancing British, " 'We'll pay you now for River Raisin! We'll give you something to remember the River Raisin!' When the British had come up to the opposite side of the breastwork, having no gun, he picked up an empty barrel and flung it at them. Then finding an iron bar he jumped up on the works and hove that at them. At the height of the action our Kentucky soldier saw another officer, Captain Patterson, an Ulster-born Scotch Irishman, jump "upon the breastwork and stooping a moment to look through the darkness as well as he could, he shouted with a broad North of Ireland brogue, 'shoot low, boys! shoot low! rake them—rake them! They're comin' on their all fours.' "[30]

The British column, Major Latour wrote, was "soon thrown into confusion. It was at that moment was heard that constant rolling fire, whose tremendous noise resembled rattling peals of thunder." The officers and sergeants did what they always did best, lead by example, and for a while the troops pushed on. Battery No. 7 at "every discharge opened the column, and mowed down whole files," but those behind stepped over their dead, dying, and shrieking comrades and marched on. But they also "shared the same fate." For twenty-five minutes the firing from the American line never slackened. It became a firestorm, more than mortals could bear. The column broke. A few platoons got to the canal but no farther. Some ran to the shelter of the woods. The rest withdrew four hundred yards to a ditch before they stopped.[31]

Across the field with Keane's column, Captain John Henry Cooke watched the light companies of Highlanders, Fusiliers, and Monmouth come up without packs. Cooke wrote that the Highlanders had their "blankets slung across their backs." They wore only the "shells of their bonnets, the sable plumes of real ostrich feathers brought by them from the Cape of Good Hope, having been left in England." Cooke hailed Lieutenant Duncan Campbell, a fine-looking twenty-year-old veteran of "many bloody encounters in Spain and France." Where were they going? Cooke asked. "I be hanged if I know," Campbell replied. Cooke reminded him of the American cannon at short range and advised that he "take off his blue pelisse coat to be like the rest of the men. "No," Campbell said gaily, "I will never peal for any American."[32]

On the levee with the light companies, Colonel Robert Rennie drove in the American pickets of the advanced battery with his usual dash. Rennie and his men leaped over the ditch, climbed the parapet, and jumped down into the battery. Major Tatum charged that the garrison's company of 7th U.S. Infantry fled "in a state of confusion disgraceful to its commander," while Major Latour claimed that the British killed the garrison, "who bravely defended their post at the point of the bayonet, against a number much superior, and continually increasing." A British officer backed Latour, writing that the redoubt had been defended with honor. Whatever the case, Beale's Rifles, a unit made up of lawyers, merchants, and other civilians, now went to work. Rennie climbed the parapet to cross over toward Jackson's line, but met a rifleman by the name of Weathers who shot Rennie through the eye and killed him. The rest of Rifles, joined by 7th Infantry, made a charnel house of the inside of the redoubt, firing down on British soldiers packed into a small space. Batteries 1 and 2 swept the levees clear. Most of Rennie's men ended up either dead or prisoners, while the rest fell "back in disorder, leaving the road, the levee, and the brink of the river, strewed with its dead and wounded."[33]

Returning to the British right, beyond Gibbs's main column the light companies and the West Indians in the woods advanced on Coffee's Tennesseeans. Major James Sinclair, commanding the light company of Royal North Britain Fusiliers, later reported that "after pushing through the wood, with great difficulty, we approached that part of the enemy's lines we formerly found unprotected. A tremendous fire of grape and musketry was opened on us which killed and wounded a great many men, and we found, with all our effort, that on this part of the line it was impossible to make any impression." The elite British light troops withdrew, carrying with them their mortally wounded commander.[34]

General Gibbs and his officers, however, had rallied the main column. The soldiers dropped their packs and followed their officers back into the storm. The big guns on Jackson's line boomed and that long roll of musketry began once again. Like Major Latour, Captain John Henry Cooke heard it and marveled. For the "echo from the cannonade and musketry was so tremendous in the forests, that the vibration seemed as if the earth was cracking and tumbling to pieces, or as if the heavens were rent asunder by the most terrific peals of thunder that ever rumbled; it was the most awful and grandest mixture of sounds to be conceived . . . each cannon report was answered over a hundred fold, and produced an intermingled roar surpassing strange . . . this phenomenon can neither be fancied nor described, save by those who can bear evidence of the fact. And the flashes of fire looked as if coming out of the bowels of the earth, so little above its surface were the batteries of the Americans." Harry Smith, after a lifetime of soldiering in America, India and Africa, said in his autobiography that he had never seen a column of men receive such destructive fire.[35]

General Keane sent the Highlanders to Gibbs's support. He feinted forward first, then directed the column to march obliquely across the field in front of Jackson's lines. The great war pipes added to the din as the Scots marched stoically toward the maelstrom. Lieutenant Colonel Robert Dale led them. At 150 yards the American line erupted with round shot, grape, musketry, rifle fire, and buckshot, described by Lieutenant Charles Gordon, who marched into it, as a "most destructive and murderous fire . . . along the whole course and length of their line in front, as well as on our left flank. Not daunted, however, we continued our advance which in one minute would have carried us into their ditch, when we received a peremptory order to halt—this indeed was the moment of trial. The officers and men . . . mowed down by ranks, impatient to get at the enemy at all hazards yet compelled for want of orders to stand still and neither to advance or retire. . . ."

It was magnificent, but was it war? Colonel Dale was killed there, where he stood awaiting higher orders. Lieutenant Gordon was hit, and as he was carried off the field he heard one of Pakenham's staff officers call out, "93rd! Have a little patience and you shall have your revenge."[36]

Gibbs's column was broken. They could stand no more and began to flee, Major Latour wrote, "in the utmost confusion." Panic gripped them, "a panic," wrote Colonel Alexander Dickson, "which no exertions could restore. . . ." Their officers struck them with the flats of their swords, but that was preferred to the death that surrounded them, which they could see on the faces of so many fallen comrades.[37]

Pakenham rode to where generals belong in times of crisis, to the critical point, in this case the head of Gibbs's column. Captain Sir John Maxwell Tylden of the 43rd was with him. They could make out the Americans on the breastwork of Line Jackson. Tylden wrote that General Gibbs rode up to them and admitted to Pakenham, "Sir Ed., I am not able to make these men move on. They will not follow me." Pakenham's reaction was to spur his horse forward. He was in the middle of it trying to rally soldiers to return to the fight when grapeshot shattered his knee and killed his horse. Major Duncan Macdougall leaped from his horse and helped Packenham get up and onto the horse. Pakenham was then shot in the arm, but carried on. Major Macdougall took the reins and led the horse forward into the hell the Americans had created for the British army. Packenham raised his hat and called out, "Come on, brave 93rd!" Then he was shot in the spine and could no longer carry on. He was carried from the field. It had been Ned's time once again, but it had ended badly and now it was time to die, which he did, before his comrades could lay him down in the shade of an old oak tree.

Shortly after Pakenham was carried off General Gibbs was hit and he, too, was carried off the field and remained in agony until released by death the next day. General Keane was shot in the groin and also taken from the field. The British army was down to one general, John Lambert, commanding the reserve, and the colonels had hardly fared better. Rennie was dead. Dale was dead. Other colonels commanding regiments were either dead or down. Major John Whittaker of Royal North Britain Fusiliers actually made it to the top of the parapet before he was shot and killed and fell back into the ditch. Some of the Fusiliers, a stubborn lot, were in the ditch trying to climb the slippery mud wall of the parapet by driving their bayonets into it to use as steps.

All in vain. Gibbs's column was no more. Out of the smoke men ran wildly to the rear. "Regiments," wrote John Henry Cooke, "were shattered, broke, dispersed—all order was at an end." He saw Lieutenant Duncan Campbell, who had marched gaily to battle, "running about in circles, first staggering one way, then another, and at length fell on the sod helplessly upon his face, and in this state several times recovered his legs, and again tumbled, and when he was picked up he was found to be blind from the effects of grape-shot that had torn open his forehead . . . While being borne insensible to the rear, he still clenched the hilt of his sword with a convulsive grasp, the blade thereof being broken off close to the hilt with grape-shot, and in a state of delerium and suffering he lived for a few days."[38]

The Highlanders broke last. They had taken terrible punishment. John Coffee wrote, "Before they reached our small arms, our grape and canister mowed down whole columns, but that was nothing compared to the carnage of our rifles and muskets." Sutherland Highlanders had 545 casualties out of some 1,000 who made that mad diagonal march across New Orleans's bloody field. Upon his arrival on 6 January, John Henry Cooke had asked General Gibbs's brigade major what had stopped them up to then, for these were men who had stormed real fortresses in Europe. "Bullets stopped us—bullets—that's all," was the answer. The assessment still held.

"For an hour," John Reid wrote, "the most tremendous fire & small arms was kept up, that I am sure was ever witnessed in America. Twice the enemy were repulsed from our very entrenchments & twice returned to the assault. At length, cut to pieces, they were forced to retire from the field, leaving it covered with the dead & the dying."[39]

Our anonymous Kentucky soldier left the best account of the field. "When the smoke had cleared away . . . like a sea of blood. It was not blood . . . but the red coats in which the British soldiers were dressed. Straight out before our position, for about the width of space which we supposed had been occupied by the British column, the field was entirely covered with prostrate bodies. In some places they were laying in piles of several, one top of the other. On either side, there was an interval more thinly sprinkled with the slain; and then two other dense rows, one near the levee and the other towards the swamp."

The Kentuckian could see a dead horse about two hundred yards off. He said he had no doubt he could "have walked on the bodies from the edge of the ditch to where the horse was laying, without touching the ground."

The guns had stopped, but the field of honor—as battlefields were once called—was neither quiet nor still. The Kentuckian saw "some laying quite dead, others mortally wounded, pitching and tumbling about in the agonies of death: Some had their heads shot off, some their legs, some their arms. Some were laughing, some crying, some groaning, and some screaming. There was every variety of sight and sound."

Some had not been hit. "A great many had thrown themselves behind the piles of slain, for protection. As the firing ceased, these men every now and then jumping up and either running off or coming in and giving themselves up."[40]

Of the approximately 5,300 British soldiers in the attacking columns and reserve, 2,037 became casualties: dead, wounded, missing. Jackson lost 7 killed, 6 wounded.

"Surely Providence had a hand in this thing," John Coffee wrote. "I have seen many affairs," Captain Sir John Maxwell Tylden confided to his "Journal," "and some severe ones, but I never saw so melancholy, heartbreaking business as this." He was so devastated that it was three days after the battle before he could bring himself to write down what he had seen. To John Henry Cooke it did not seem real: "The fire of the Americans from behind the barricades had been indeed most murderous, and had caused so sudden a repulse that it was difficult to persuade ourselves that such an event had happened—the whole affair being more like a dream, or some scene of enchantment, than reality."[41]

It was no dream. The Battle of New Orleans was one of the most important ever fought in the New World, and its effect on world affairs was not insignificant. It effectively ended the British threat to Young America. It rendered irrelevant London's and anybody else's opinion on the legality of the Louisiana Purchase. It ended any hopes the Creeks may have had that their disaster at Horseshoe Bend and their humiliation at the Treaty of Fort Jackson could be reversed. It made certain that before too long Spain would lose the rest of Florida. The United States had proven to the world that it had come of age and was here to stay.

Major General Sir Edward Michael Pakenham's naked, disemboweled corpse was scrunched into a hogshead that was then filled with rum. Thus preserved, he was shipped home for burial and oblivion. On that terrible field on which he died, on the eighth day of January 1815, a president was made who would give his name to an age.

Andrew Jackson, architect of the great victory, had saved New Orleans, Louisiana, the Gulf Coast, and set the stage for the taking of the rest of Florida. He had led the People of the Western Waters to the promised land and sealed it by humbling proud Albion. He had collected his "debt of retaliatory Vengeance," seared in his memory from those hard, bitter boyhood days in the Waxhaws.

Jackson had been able to do that because he was cut from a different mold. His was the mold the times and the goal demanded.

EPILOGUE

"VIVE LE GÉNÉRAL JACKSON!"

The action on the west bank went badly for the Americans and Jackson was partially to blame. He had put the inept General David Bannister Morgan in charge, and then did not give him first-class troops to defend his positions. The result was a rout of the Kentuckians and the capture of Commodore Patterson's redoubt where the big guns had been mounted to provide enfilading fire across the river against Pakenham's main force. But as we know, Colonel William Thornton's British force on the west bank was late, very late, and Patterson's guns had done their work and been spiked before the British got to them. By then, across the wide Mississippi, Pakenham's regiments lay shattered, routed, stopped by grape and canister and bullets: "bullets—that's all." The west bank effort was all too late, Thornton's success rendered academic by Jackson's stunning victory on the east bank. Second-guessing would have the only British general on his feet, John Lambert, reinforce Thornton and exploit the west bank victory. But arguments over what might have been serve only to remind us that the ifs of history don't count. Lambert was more the realist than later observers. His decision to withdraw was almost immediate, and by 18 January the British camp was empty. The battered army was withdrawn in stages along the bayous, and on 27 January Cochrane's weary sailors made their final long row across Lake Borgne to the fleet, whereupon anchors were weighed and the tall ships sailed away. Jackson, watching, waiting, ever alert, made the right decision and let Lambert go unmolested.

The British then did what they probably should have done in the first place. They took Fort Bowyer in order to set the stage for the capture of Mobile. But then came word that the war had ended. Once again the British were too late. As they had been too late in coming to arm and support the Creeks before Jackson smashed them. As they had been too late in marching on New Orleans when they had the advantage of surprise, thus allowing Jackson to seize the initiative. Once again the proud, depleted regiments boarded Cochrane's ships and sailed away, this time for England and home, and never again would they return. Never again would a foreign army threaten the American mainland. Jackson had seen to that.

Many in the defeated British army would fight again, on the eighteenth of June 1815 at Waterloo. The British would remember Waterloo and forget New Orleans. Not the Americans. They knew what it meant to Young America. All the humiliations of the war, the grave threat to American territorial integrity, were stricken from the national memory and replaced by the magic word—New Orleans. For there they had smashed "Wellington's *invincibles*," there they had sent fleeing the "conquerors of the conquerors of Europe." Throughout the land pride swelled for the accomplishment of American arms. In far-off Boston the *Yankee* boasted for all: "we have unqueened the self-stiled Queen of the Ocean," and "we have beaten at every opportunity, *Wellington's Veterans!*"[1]

Myths would arise from the great victory, as they always do, but this we can say with certainty: the United States came of age that day. The roots of America and Americans as a distinct nation and people were already well established before the Revolution, but the world demanded proof, to borrow Lincoln's words, that they would long endure. On the field at Chalmette, Jackson and his army of mixed Americans gave that proof and set the tone for a national mood that exulted in being American. What Crèvecoeur had in mind in *Letters from an American Farmer*, that American, that "new man," would emerge full blown, and its foremost embodiment was the Hero, Andrew Jackson.[2]

For he truly became the Hero, and his fellow Americans would amply reward him despite more stormy controversies. He did not lift martial law in New Orleans until the thirteenth of March, long after it was necessary, and in the interim actually jailed and then exiled a federal judge, Dominick Hall, who had dared issue a writ of habeas corpus. The citizens of the city rightly chafed under the rigors of prolonged military rule When he was president his enemies would accuse him of yearning to become King Andrew, but they were wrong. He was not a European military adventurer. He simply did what he so often did, out of the tempestuousness of his nature and his stern sense of duty. He went too far. When he received from Washington official notification of the ratification of the Treaty of Ghent, he immediately raised martial law.

He explained his actions in reply to a statement by the officers of the Uniformed Battalions of New Orleans praising his leadership.

> Whenever the invaluable rights which we enjoy under our own happy constitution are threatened by invasion, privileges the most dear, and which, in ordinary times, ought to be regarded as the most sacred, may be required to be infringed for their security. At such a crisis, we have only to determine whether we will suspend, for a time, the exercise of the latter, that we may secure the permanent enjoyment of the former. Is it wise, in such a moment, to sacrifice the spirit of the laws to the letter, and by adhering too strictly to the letter, lose the *substance* forever, in order that we may, for an instant, preserve the *shadow*?[3]

That was no man on a white horse.

Judge Hall returned and put Jackson on trial for contempt of court, found him guilty, and fined him $1,000. Jackson paid the fine.

Citizens of New Orleans knew who had saved them, and for most all was forgiven. *"Vive le Général Jackson! Vive le Général Jackson!"* they shouted when he walked out of court that day, They surrounded his carriage and unhitched the horses and pulled it to his quarters. Crowds gathered along the way and Jackson stopped twice at coffeehouses to address the throngs and speak directly and eloquently to the vital issue.

> Considering obedience to the laws, even when we think them un-justly applied, as the first duty of a citizen, I did not hesitate to comply with the sentence that you have heard pronounced. I shall soon leave you, my fellow-citizens; and I entreat when you recollect the services I have been so fortunate as to render you in the field, that you will not forget the example I have given this day of a respectful submission to the administration of justice. Defend your constitution and your country, as you have done, against all open attacks in war, and when peace returns, support the civil authority by an exact obedience to its decrees. If my example can teach you this useful lesson I shall not regret the sacrifice it has cost me.[4]

One general, George Washington, established the primacy of civil author-ity during the Revolution. Another general, Andrew Jackson, on the thirty-first of March 1815, reconfirmed it.

Another storm loomed on the horizon. "We are far from acknowledg-ing that Florida belongs to the King of Spain," the British Board of Trade had written in 1730, and their successors in the United States had precisely that in mind as they gazed southward at the sparkling waters of the Gulf. One historian explained the American hunger for Florida as an "absurd con-cept that the American frontier should lie along the Gulf Stream." Another wrote, "One of the more curious aspects of Jefferson's and Madison's admin-istrations was their unhesitatingly predatory attitude towards the Florida's, even though Spain and the United States were officially at peace."[5]

Curious? Absurd? What strange judgments. What better boundary between nations than a great body of water? To have left the "sick man of Europe"—to borrow a phrase from another time—in place in Florida, un-able to control the Indians, at the mercy of the great predatory powers of Europe—that would have been beyond curious, that would have been absurd as well as irresponsible.

How to take it, though, from a nation with whom we were at peace without abandoning on the surface at least the behavior expected of a civi-lized nation? The United States had a perfectly competent officer in the field, General Edmund P. Gaines, who had been ordered by Jackson into Florida on a raid to take British-designed Negro Fort, which was situated sixty miles below the U.S. border on a cliff commanding the Apalachicola

River. The stout fort, containing nine artillery pieces and magazines well stocked with British powder, lead, muskets, carbines, and other stores, was a haven for escaped slaves and a number of hostile Choctaws who thought they had an alliance with the British, although there were no British troops in Florida. A squadron of U.S. Navy gunboats supporting Gaines's command destroyed Negro Fort and killed 270 of its 334-man garrison of blacks and Choctaws when a round of hot shot blew up the fort's biggest powder magazine.

On top of this disaster, the British government once more abandoned the southern Indians, just as they had done in 1783 following the Revolutionary War. Cold reasons of state took precedence: good relations with the United States and the safety of Canada. But the Spanish remained, and welcome as the destruction of Negro Fort was to the United States, it was not the answer to what the nation really wanted. Monroe and others knew the answer and it was simple. Turn Jackson loose.[6]

The Hero of New Orleans has been flayed by critics for actions that were, admittedly, outrageous, but he was carrying out the veiled policies of President James Monroe, who could not openly admit what he was up to. In December 1817, the secretary of war, John C. Calhoun, ordered Jackson to take command of the forces in the field and "terminate the conflict" with the Indians in Spanish territory. Calhoun wrote a little later to the governor of Alabama that Jackson was "authorized to conduct the war as he thought best."[7]

But Jackson well knew what Washington was up to, realized the delicacy of the situation, and asked Monroe for authorization to proceed to the real goal. Give it to me "through any channel," he wrote, "that the possession of the Floridas would be desirable to the United States, & in sixty days it will be accomplished." In a carefully phrased letter actually written before Jackson's, Monroe gave his general the green light. The Seminoles were the first order of business, but "possibly you may have other services to perform, . . ." Monroe continued. "This is not a time for you to think of repose. Great interests are at issue, and until our course is carried through triumphantly & every species of danger to which it is exposed is settled on the most solid foundation, you ought not to withdraw your active support from it."

"Other services to perform . . . Great interests are at issue." Come now, Mr. President. Surely you were not writing about an Indian War.[8]

Jackson knew precisely what Monroe meant. He wrote to Andrew Jackson Donelson, "Whether any other service than putting down the seminoles may detain me on the Southern frontier, time can only unfold." He eventually gathered an army of some 3,000, including friendly Creeks under General William McIntosh. There were hundreds of miles of marching but little fighting with the Seminoles, who stayed out of Jackson's way as he burned towns and food supplies from the Apalachicola to the Suwannee. On the way he occupied the Spanish post of St. Mark's, writing to its commander, "I deem it expedient to garrison that fortress with American Troops untill the close of the present war," a "measure . . . justifiable on that universal principal of self defence. . . ." The Spanish commandant objected, but of course

Jackson paid him no heed. He marched in with his troops, hauled down the Spanish flag, and ran up the Stars and Stripes.[9]

He caught the Red Stick prophet Josiah Francis and hanged him. He caught two British subjects, Alexander Arbuthnot and Robert Ambrister, and had them tried by special courts-martial as "exciters of this Savage and Negro War. . . ." Arbuthnot was hanged, Ambrister shot. Jackson announced, "I hope the execution of these two unprincipled villains will prove an awful example to the world, and convince the Government of Great Britain as well as her subjects that certain, if slow retribution awaits those unchristian wretches who by false promises delude & excite a Indian tribe to all the horrid deeds of savage war." Then he marched on Pensacola.[10]

The Spanish governor, José Masot, bombarded Jackson with dire warnings if he continued his operations in Florida. On 23 May 1818 he wrote, "If you will proceed contrary to my expectations I will repulse you force to force." The next day Jackson and his troops occupied Pensacola without serious incident. Governor Masot and his troops were allowed to depart for Cuba. Jackson reported to Calhoun that the articles of capitulation "with but one condition amount to a complete cesion to the u States of that portion of the Floridas hitherto under the government of Don Josse Massot." He then issued a proclamation setting up a provisional government for Florida. The commanding officer of U.S. 4th Infantry, Colonel William King, was appointed civil and military governor of Pensacola.[11]

Outrageous? Of course. And far more than the Monroe administration, if not Monroe himself, expected. Jackson had destroyed what little Spanish rule was left in Florida and established a provisional American administration. Would Washington have the wit and nerve to seize the opportunity? An angry Spanish ambassador fulminated, but that was the only weapon available to Spain. The British Parliament steamed over the executions of Arbuthnot and Ambrister and the press demanded action, but the king's ministers decided otherwise. Only at home did Jackson face real trouble. A heated cabinet debate ensued in Washington on whether the general should be censured. A furious John C. Calhoun wanted to go further: Jackson's conduct should be "the subject of investigation by a military tribunal," he wrote to John Quincy Adams. That meant a court-martial. But America's greatest secretary of state, alone of the cabinet, did not flinch. Adams argued that "if the question is dubious, it is better to err on the side of vigor than of weakness—on the side of our officer, who has rendered the most eminent services to the nation, than on the side of our bitterest enemies, and against him." For Adams, as visionary as Thomas Jefferson in his concept of a United States stretching to the Pacific, was then in negotiations with the Spanish ambassador, Don Luis de Onís, for the boundary of the Louisiana Purchase west of the Mississippi River. Jackson's unofficial conquest of Florida did more than shock the Spanish, it paralyzed them. More than one writer has commented that the Spanish were terrified of Jackson. He was as audacious and as ruthless as Napoleon. The southern warrior Jackson provided Adams with his hammer and the Yankee statesman used it well.

On 22 February 1819 the Adams-Onís Treaty, also known as the Trans-continental Treaty, was signed. For $5 million Spain relinquished all of East and West Florida. On the west the Sabine River, today's Louisiana-Texas line, was established as the U.S.-Spanish border. West of the Mississippi Adams negotiated the boundary of the Louisiana Purchase and pushed it to the Pacific Ocean at the forty-second parallel, today's California-Oregon line. Spain stalled and did not ratify the treaty until 24 October 1820. At St. Augustine the following year, on 10 July 1821, the Spanish flag was lowered over the stone fortress of Castillo de San Marcos, never to reappear. After some three hundred years of exploration, conquest, and colonization, Spain vanished from the eastern half of North America.[12]

Jefferson, Adams, Jackson. On a modern map of the United States the names of those three men are writ large. Two men of intellect, and the in-dispensable man of action with the demonic will who made their visions possible.

"THE WEST IN THEIR EYES"

"The various tribes . . . possessed valor without conduct, and the love of freedom without the spirit of union. They took up arms with savage fierce-ness, they laid them down, or turned them against each other, with wild inconstancy; and while they fought singly, they were successively subdued."[13]

The words were written in the eighteenth century by Edward Gibbon. He was describing the failure of the "various tribes of Britons" to unite against the Roman invaders in volume one of *The History of the Decline and Fall of the Roman Empire*. But he might as well have been writing about the Indians of North America. For despite the brief alliances forged by Pontiac in the early 1760s against the British, and Little Turkey in the Ohio Coun-try in the 1790s against the Americans, the failure of Tecumseh to rally the southern tribes in 1811 to a massive pan-Indian cause was the norm.

The majority of Americans, on the other hand, were united in their determination to take the continent. Sharp differences between Yankees and southerners were already apparent, but it would take another half century for political failure to be succeeded by the maelstrom of civil war, and by then the war with the Indians was essentially over. Noises of separation by some on the Western Waters were hollow. New England Federalists openly threat-ened secession during the War of 1812, but that crabbed minority lacked the political power to carry out its threats. Party conflict was fiercer than any we have known in our time, yet the political system that was developing sur-vived stroke and counterstroke, slander and calumny, while the pillars of con-stitutional government were firmly embedded. And throughout, all Americans kept their steady gaze and fierce hunger on far Pacific shores and all that lay between. They would have it. All of it. It was their destiny.

Against this resolve, this mystic sense of mission; against the increasingly sophisticated political and administrative systems that backed it up; against this greatest of modern folk movements, the Indian cause was lost. Edward

Gibbon's description of the ancient Britons perfectly fit the American Indian. One by one, the tribes succumbed to the legions of invaders.

Reverend Timothy Flint, who knew the invaders well, knew their hunger and their restlessness, believed that they had "the West in their eyes." He was aware that migration arose from "mixed motives." But he also knew that "There is more of the material of poetry than we imagine diffused through all the classes of the community. And upon this part of the character it is, that the disposition to emigration operates, and brings in aid the influence of its imperceptible but magic power . . . The notion of new and more beautiful woods and streams, of a milder climate, deer, fish, fowl, game, and all those delightful images of enjoyment, that so readily associate with the idea of the wild and boundless license of new regions; all that restless hope of finding in a new country, and in new views and combinations of things, something that we crave but have not. I am ready to believe, from my own experience and from what I have seen in the case of others, that this influence of imagination has no inconsiderable agency in producing emigration."[14]

"My father loved a border life," wrote the future physician and naturalist Gideon Lincecum, "and the place he had purchased on the Ocmulgee, as the people had already commenced settling on the opposite side of the river, was no longer looked upon as a border country. He sold his place and was soon equipped and geared up for the road, and so was I. I had been reared to a belief and faith in the pleasure of frequent change of country, and I looked upon the long journey, through the wilderness, with much pleasure."

The party of twenty-six people, including ten slaves, set out from western Georgia on 10 March 1818. "We had good horses and wagons and guns and big dogs . . . I felt as if I was on a big camp hunt.

"The journey, the way we traveled, was about 500 miles, all wilderness, full of deer and turkeys, and the streams were full of fish, We were six weeks on the road, the most delightful time I had ever spent in my life. My brother Garland and I "flanked it" as the wagons rolled along and killed deer, turkeys, and wild pigeons and at nights, with pine torches, we fished and killed a great many with my bow and arrows, whenever we camped on any water course. Litte creeks were full of fish in that season."[15]

Thirty years later Gideon Lincecum decided to move on to Texas.

For distant horizons always beckoned. Close your eyes and watch them. Watch as they gather the family, load belongings on the wagons and hitch the horses and set out, with the sons and the big dogs ranging on the flanks.

The West in their eyes.

NOTES

ABBREVIATIONS

ASPFR   *American State Papers . . . Commencing March 3, 1790, and Ending March 3, 1815,* Class I, Foreign Relations, 6 vols. (Washington, D.C.: 1832, 1834)

ASPIA   *American State Papers . . . Commencing March 3, 1790, and Ending March 3, 1815,* Class II, Indian Affairs, 2 vols. (Washington, D.C.: 1832, 1834)

Arnow, *Flowering*   Harriet Simpson Arnow, *Flowering of the Cumberland* (New York: 1963)

Arnow, *Seedtime*   Harriet Simpson Arnow, *Seedtime on the Cumberland* (Lexington, Ky.: 1983)

Brown, *Amphibious Campaign*   Wilburt S. Brown, *The Amphibious Campaign for West Florida and Louisiana, 1814–1815: A Critical Review of Strategy and Tactics at New Orleans* (University, Ala.: 1969)

Buchanan, *Road to Guilford Courthouse*   John Buchanan, *The Road to Guilford Courthouse: The American Revolution in the Carolinas* (New York: 1997)

Carr, *Early Times*   John Carr, *Early Times in Middle Tennessee* (Nashville: 1958)

Carter, *Territorial Papers*   Clarence E. Carter and John Porter Bloom, eds., *Territorial Papers of the United States,* 27 vols. (Washington, D.C.: 1934–)

Caughey, *McGillivray*   John Walton Caughey, *McGillivray of the Creeks* (Norman, Okla.: 1938)

Draper Mss.   Draper Manuscripts (State Historical Society of Wisconsin)

ETHS   East Tennessee Historical Society

Folmsbee et al., *History of Tennessee*   Stanley J. Folmsbee et al., *History of Tennessee,* 4 vols. (New York: 1960)

GHQ   *Georgia Historical Quarterly*

Gleig, *Narrative*   George Robert Gleig, *Narrative of the Campaigns of the British Army at Washington and New Orleans . . . . in the Years 1814 and 1815* (London: 1826)

Griffith, *McIntosh and Weatherford*   Benjamin W. Griffith, *McIntosh and Weatherford, Creek Indian Leaders* (Tuscaloosa, Ala.: 1998)

H&B, *Creek War*   H. S. Halbert and T. H. Ball, *The Creek War of 1813–1814* (Tuscaloosa, Ala.: 1995)

Jackson Papers   Andrew Jackson, *The Papers of Andrew Jackson,* vol. 1; ed. Sam B. Smith and Harriet Chappell Owsley; vols. 2– ed. Harold Moser et al. (Knoxville: 1980–)

JSH   *Journal of Southern History*

Latour, *Historical Memoir*   Arsène Lacarrière Latour, *Historical Memoir of the War in West Florida and Louisiana in 1814–1815,* expanded edition; ed. Gene A. Smith (1816; reprint, Gainesville: The Historic New Orleans Collection and University Press of Florida, 1999)

LHQ   *Louisiana Historical Quarterly*

Masterson, *Blount*   William H. Masterson, *William Blount* (Baton Rouge: 1954)

MVHR   Mississippi Valley Historical Review

Nolte, *Memoirs*   Vincent Nolte, *The Memoirs of Vincent Nolte* . . . (New York: 1934)

Owsley, *Borderlands*   Frank L. Owsley Jr., *Struggle for the Gulf Borderlands: The Creek War and the Battle of New Orleans, 1812–1815* (Gainesville, Fla.: 1981)

Parton, *Jackson*   James Parton, *Life of Andrew Jackson*, 3 vols. (New York: 1861)

Pickett, *Alabama*   Albert James Pickett, *History of Alabama, and Incidentally of Georgia and Mississippi, from the Earliest Period* (Charleston, S.C.: 1851)

Quimby, *U.S. Army*   Robert S. Quimby, *The U.S. Army in the War of 1812* (Lansing, Mich.: 1997)

Ramsey, *Tennessee*   James Gettys Ramsey, *The Annals of Tennessee to the End of the Eighteenth Century* (Chattanooga: 1926)

R&E, *Jackson*   John Reid and John Henry Eaton, *The Life of Andrew Jackson* (University, Ala.: 1974)

Reilly, *British at the Gates*   Robin Reilly, *The British at the Gates: The New Orleans Campaign in the War of 1812* (New York: 1974)

Remini, *Jackson*   Robert V. Remini, *Andrew Jackson and the Course of American Empire, 1767–1821* (New York: 1977)

Remini, *New Orleans*   Robert V. Remini, *The Battle of New Orleans* (New York: 1999)

Rogers, "Survey"   Stephen T. Rogers, "1977 Historic Site Survey" (Nashville: 1978)

Stiggins, *Creek History*   George Stiggins, *Creek Indian History* . . . (Birmingham, Ala.: 1989)

"Tatum's Journal"   Howell Tatum, "Major Howell Tatum's Journal while Acting Topographical Engineer (1814) to General Jackson," ed. John Spenser Bassett (October 1921–April 1922)

THQ   Tennessee Historical Quarterly

VMHB   Virginia Magazine of History and Biography

Williams, *Franklin*   Samuel Cole Williams, *History of the Lost State of Franklin* (Johnson City, Tenn.: 1993)

Woodward's Reminiscences   Thomas S. Woodward, *Woodward's Reminiscences of the Creek, or Muscogee Indians* . . . (Mobile, Ala.: 1965)

PROLOGUE

1. James Parton, *Life of Andrew Jackson*, 3 vols. (New York: Mason Brothers, 1861),vol. 1, pp. 73–74, who got Mrs. Susan Smart's story "from her intimate friends to whom she was in the habit of telling it."

2. I have described the Scotch Irish at more length in *The Road to Guilford Courthouse: The American Revolution in the Carolinas* (New York: John Wiley & Sons, 1997), pp. 85–89. Overall I stand by it, but although the eighteenth century immigrants from Ireland were overwhelmingly Protestant and non-Celtic, I probably underestimated the number of Irish Catholics among them. As a corrective to this particular point, and for its sheer erudition, the reader with a serious interest in the subject should read David Noel Doyle, *Ireland, Irishmen and Revolutionary America, 1760–1820* (Dublin: Mercier Press, 1981). I am indebted to Michael Montgomery for bringing my attention to this excellent and, sadly, out-of-print book. For a conspicuous example of an Irish Catholic on the frontier in a sea of Scotch Irish and English Protestants, see Canetta Skelley Hankins, "Hugh Rogan of Counties Donegal and Sumner: Irish Acculturation in Frontier Tennessee," in Carroll Van West, ed., *Tennessee History: The Land, the People and the Culture* (Knoxville: University of Tennessee Press, 1998), pp. 56–79.

3. Robert V. Remini, *Andrew Jackson and the Course of American Empire, 1767–1821* (New York: Harper & Row, 1977), pp. 2–5 and the accompanying notes, is the place to start for readers interested in the details of Jackson's sparsely documented early years. For ownership of the land, see "Deed from Thomas and Sarah Ewing, 17 December 1770, *The Papers of Andrew*

Jackson, vol. 1, ed. Sam B. Smith and Harriet Chappell Owsley (Knoxville: University of Tennessee Press, 1980–), pp. 3–4; Parton, *Jackson,* vol. 1, p. 49, is the source of the quotations.

4. Remini, *Jackson,* pp. 5–8, for Jackson's education and Remini's thoughts on the subject.

5. Parton, *Jackson,* vol. 1, pp. 64–66.

6. Ibid., p. 64; G. R. Elton, *The Practice of History* (1969; reprint, London: Fontana Press, 1987), p. 39; Michael Paul Rogin, *Fathers and Children: Andrew Jackson and the Subjugation of the American Indian* (1975; reprint, New Brunswick, N.J.: Transaction Publishers, 1991), pp. 42–45; Arthur Schlesinger Jr., *The Age of Jackson* (Boston: Little, Brown, 1945), pp. 40–41 and n. 20, for observations and citations on Jackson's "rages."

7. John Reid and John Henry Eaton, *The Life of Andrew Jackson,* ed. Frank L. Owsley Jr. (1817; reprint, University: University of Alabama Press, 1974), p. 11.

8. Parton, *Jackson,* vol. 1, p. 70; Buchanan, *Road to Guilford Courthouse,* pp. 80–85, 89, for a description of this action.

9. Buchanan, *Road to Guilford Courthouse,* p. 84, for this incident.

10. Marquis James, *Andrew Jackson, Border Captain* (Indianapolis: Bobbs-Merrill, 1938), p. 20; Parton, *Jackson,* vol. 1, p. 72; Remini, *Jackson,* p. 17, for a judicious assessment of Davie's possible influence on Jackson; for readers interested in pursuing Davie, a forgotten figure worth remembering, see *The Revolutionary War Sketches of William R. Davie,* ed. Blackwell P. Robinson (Raleigh: North Carolina Department of Archives and History, 1976), and Blackwell P. Robinson, *William R. Davie* (Chapel Hill: University of North Carolina Press, 1957); for descriptions of actions and other events in which Davie figured, see Buchanan, *Road to Guilford Courthouse,* pp. 186–190 and passim.

11. "Jackson's Description of His Experiences during and Immediately Following the Revolutionary War," in *Jackson Papers,* vol. 1, p. 5.

12. Ibid.

13. Remini, *Jackson,* p. 19; Thomas Sumter to Nathanael Greene, 13 April 1781, in Dennis M. Conrad et al., eds., *The Papers of Nathanael Greene* (Chapel Hill: University of North Carolina Press, 1976–), vol. 8, pp. 91–92; "Jackson's Description of His Experiences," p. 5.

14. Remini, *Jackson,* pp. 20–21; R&E, *Jackson,* p. 12; *Jackson Papers,* vol. 1, p. 9 n. 4.

15. R&E, *Jackson,* p. 7 and note.

16. "Jackson's Description of His Experiences," pp. 5–6.

17. Ibid., p. 7.

18. Parton, *Jackson,* vol. 1, pp. 94–95; Remini, *Jackson,* p. 24.

19. Rogin, *Fathers and Children,* p. 46 and passim.

20. "Jackson's Description of His Experiences," p. 7.

21. Parton, *Jackson,* vol. 1, p. 96.

22. Ibid., pp. 97–98; Remini, *Jackson,* pp. 27–28.

23. Parton, *Jackson,* pp. 104–109, for the escapades, as recalled by people in Salisbury in the mid-nineteenth century.

24. R&E, *Jackson,* p. 14; Remini, *Jackson,* pp. 28–29; ibid., pp. 98–99.

25. Parton, *Jackson,* p. 101.

26. Remini, *Jackson,* p. 31.

27. *Jackson Papers,* vol. 1, pp. 10–11; ibid., pp. 33–34.

CHAPTER 1. BEGINNINGS

1. Katharine E. Holland Braund, *Deerskins and Duffels: Creek Indian Trade with Anglo-America, 1685–1815* (1993; reprint, Lincoln: University of Nebraska Press, 1996), pp. 28–29; for the daring and resourceful Woodward, see the sketches in the *Dictionary of American Biography (DAB)* by Verner Crane, and the new *American National Biography (ANB)* by Joyce E. Chaplin; for the quotation, see "Diary of Anthony Allaire, of Ferguson's Corps," in Lyman C. Draper, *King's Mountain and its Heroes* (Cincinnati: n.p., 1881), n.p..

2. William Bartram, *Travels and Other Writings: Travels through North and South Carolina, Georgia, East and West Florida; Travels in Georgia and Florida, 1773–74; A Report to Dr. John Fothergill; Miscellaneous Writings,* ed. Thomas P. Slaughter (1791, 1943; reprint, New York: Library of America, 1996), pp. 355–356.

3. Ashe quoted in Verner W. Crane, *The Southern Frontier, 1670–1732* (1929; reprint, Ann Arbor: University of Michigan Press, 1956), p. 111; Braund, *Deerskins and Duffels,* p. 29; Peter A. Coclanis, *The Shadow of a Dream: Economic Life and Death in the South Carolina Low Country, 1670–1920* (New York: Oxford University Press, 1989), p. 1.

4. Charles Hudson, *Knights of Spain, Warriors of the Sun: Hernando de Soto and the South's Ancient Chiefdoms* (Athens: University of Georgia Press, 1997), an excellent book, is the latest attempt to trace de Soto's route.

5. For the benefit of younger readers, I should explain that *fifth column* was once a well-known term, originally heard on 16 October 1936 during the Spanish civil war. As General Franco's rebel army advanced on Madrid, to sow consternation among the defenders one of his generals announced on the radio that four columns were advancing on the capital and a fifth column was already inside the city preparing to rise. Ernest Hemingway used the term as the title of a play (1938). In the late 1930s and during the Phony War of 1940, it was widely claimed that German fifth columns were subverting the defenses of the Western democracies. The term was used in a similar manner during the Cold War, and recently in connection with the Kosovo crisis, in Misha Glenny, "When Victors Become a Threat," *New York Times,* 6 April 1999, p. A27.

6. Crane, *Southern Frontier,* p. 35; Herbert Eugene Bolton, "Spanish Resistance to the Carolina Traders in Western Georgia, 1680–1704," *Georgia Historical Quarterly* 9:2 (June 1925), pp. 115–130.

7. Crane, *Southern Frontier,* pp. 44–46; Dawson A. Phelps, "The Chickasaw, the English, and the French, 1699–1744," *Tennessee Historical Quarterly* 16:2 (June 1957), pp. 117–133.

8. For Nairne, see Crane, *Southern Frontier,* pp. 168–169; Crane's sketch in *DAB,* Alexander Moore's in *ANB;* and especially the editor's introduction in Thomas Nairne, *Nairne's Muskhogean Journals: The 1708 Expedition to the Mississippi River,* ed. Alexander Moore (Jackson: University Press of Mississippi, 1988), and included in this publication, *Thomas Nairne's Memorial to Charles Spencer, Earl of Sunderland,* 10 July 1708, pp. 73–79. I have also read with profit an unpublished paper by Gregory H. Nobles, "Thomas Nairne, Indian Agent: The Explorer-Promoter as Intercultural Mediator in Anglo-America," delivered at the annual conference of the Omohundro Institute of Early American History and Culture, 7 June 1997.

9. Randolph to the Board, 16 March 1698, in Alexander S. Salley Jr., *Early Narratives of Carolina, 1650–1708* (New York: Scribner's, 1911), p. 206.

10. Quoted in Crane, *Southern Frontier,* pp. 74–75.

11. Thomas Nairne, *A Letter from South Carolina, 1710,* in Jack P. Greene, ed., *Selling a New World: Two South Carolina Promotional Pamphlets* (Columbia: University of South Carolina Press, 1989), pp. 52–53; *Nairne's Muskhogean Journals,* p. 76; Witold Rodzinski, *A History of China,* 2 vols. (Oxford: Pergamon Press, 1979, 1983), vol. 1, p. 157.

12. For action against the Spanish, a good, brief account is in David J. Weber, *The Spanish Frontier in North America* (New Haven: Yale University Press, 1992), pp. 141–146; Board of Trade quoted in Crane, *Southern Frontier,* pp. 252–253.

13. Amy Turner Bushnell, "Patricio de Hinachuba: Defender of the World of God, the Crown of the King, and the Little Children of Ivitachuco," *American Indian Culture and Research Journal* 3 (July 1979), pp. 13–14, 16; the quotations are in Mark F. Boyd et al., *Here They Once Stood: The Tragic End of the Apalachee Missions* (Gainesville: University of Florida Press, 1951), pp. 79, 81–82.

14. Boyd, *Here They Once Stood,* p. 94.

15. Arrell M. Gibson, *The Chickasaws* (Norman: University of Oklahoma Press, 1971), pp. 221–225; *Nairne's Muskhogean Journals,* pp. 49–50.

16. *Nairne's Muskhogean Journals,* p. 75; Hudson, *Knights of Spain, Warriors of the Sun,* pp. 120–144; Weber, *Spanish Frontier in North America,* pp. 118 (for an estimate of Apalachee numbers), 144, 419 n. 21; Peter H. Wood et al., eds., *Powhatan's Mantle: Indians in the Colonial Southeast* (Lincoln: University of Nebraska Press, 1989), p. 52, for another estimate of Apalachee numbers; James W. Covington, "The Apalachee Indians Move West," *Florida Anthropologist* 17 (December 1964), pp. 221–225.

17. David H. Corkran, *The Creek Frontier, 1540–1783* (Norman: University of Oklahoma Press, 1967), p. 56.

18. Ibid., pp. 53–54; Braund, *Deerskins and Duffels,* pp. 33–34; Walter Edgar, *South Carolina: A History* (Columbia: University of South Carolina Press, 1998), pp. 99–100.

19. Crane, *Southern Frontier,* pp. 168–169; *Nairne's Muskhogean Journals,* pp. 20–21; Charles Hudson, *The Southeastern Indians* (Knoxville: University of Tennessee Press, 1976), pp. 254–257, for torture in general.

20. Edgar, *South Carolina,* pp. 100–102; Corkran, *Creek Frontier,* pp. 58–60; Wood, *Powhatan's Mantle,* p. 61, for estimate of Cherokee warriors in 1715.

21. Edgar, *South Carolina,* p. 101; Corkran, *Creek Frontier,* p. 59.

22. Edgar, *South Carolina,* p. 100.

23. Johnston to the Secretary of the Society for the Propagation of the Gospel, 19 December 1715, quoted in Crane, *Southern Frontier,* p. 179 n. 54.

24. Corkran, *Creek Frontier,* p. 65; and especially Daniel H. Thomas, *Fort Toulouse: The French Outpost at the Alabama on the Coosa* (Tuscaloosa: University of Alabama Press, 1969), which is a relatively brief but clear discussion with an informative introduction by a specialist, Gregory M. Waselkov.

25. *Nairne's Muskhogean Journals,* p. 75.

26. For England's lead, see the discussion in J. Leitch Wright Jr., *The Only Land They Knew: American Indians in the Old South* (1981; reprint, Lincoln: University of Nebraska Press, 1999), pp. 109–110.

27. This brief paragraph, touching upon a complex situation, is based on the discussion in Corkran, *Creek Frontier,* pp. 61 ff; Wilbur R. Jacobs, ed., *The Appalachian Indian Frontier: The Edmund Atkin Report and the Plan of 1755* (1954; reprint, Lincoln: University of Nebraska Press, 1967), p. 38, for the British quotation; Thomas, *Fort Toulouse,* p. x, for the French quotation.

28. *Chicken's Journal, 1725,* in Newton D. Mereness, ed., *Travels in the American Colonies* (New York: Macmillan, 1916), pp. 111–113; Corkran, *Creek Frontier,* pp. 226–227; Gage to Lord Hillsborough, 10 October 1770, in Clarence Edwin Carter, ed., *The Correspondence of General Thomas Gage with the Secretary of State, 1763–1775,* 2 vols. (New Haven: Yale University Press, 1931), vol. 1, p. 278.

29. Quoted in Crane, *Southern Frontier,* pp. 199–200.

30. Jacobs, *Appalachian Indian Frontier,* pp. xvii, xxix; James Adair, *Adair's History of the American Indians,* ed. Samuel Cole Williams (1930; reprint, New York: Argonaut Press, 1966), p. 270.

31. Jacobs, *Appalachian Indian Frontier,* pp. xxxv–xxxvi.

32. For the eighteenth-century migrations, see Bernard Bailyn, *Voyagers to the West: A Passage in the Peopling of America on the Eve of the Revolution* (New York: Knopf, 1986); David Hackett Fischer, *Albion's Seed, Four British Folkways in America* (New York: Oxford University Press, 1989), esp. "Borderlands to Back Country," pp. 605–782; Marianne S. Wokeck, *Trade in Strangers: The Beginnings of Mass Migration to North America* (University Park: Pennsylvania State University Press, 1999); for loosening ties with Britain and the continuity between the colonial era and the American Revolution and beyond, see the clear, concise essay by Jack P. Greene, "The American Revolution," *American Historical Review* 105:1 (February 2000), pp. 93–102.

33. Gage to Lord Halifax, 8 June 1765, in Carter, *Correspondence of General Thomas Gage,* vol. 1, p. 61; see Gordon S. Wood, *The Radicalism of the American Revolution* (New York: Knopf, 1992), pp. 22–42, for an excellent discussion of eighteenth-century class structure and the wide social gulf separating gentlemen and John Adams's "common Herd of Mankind" (p. 27).

34. Bernard Romans, *A Concise Natural History of East and West Florida,* ed. Kathryn E. Holland Braund (1775; reprint, Tuscaloosa: University of Alabama Press, 1999), p. 123.

35. Quoted in Ian K. Steele, *Warpaths: Invasions of North America* (New York: Oxford University Press, 1994), p. 246.

36. "The Proclamation Line of 1763," 7 October 1763, in Henry Steele Commager, ed., *Documents of American History,* 7th ed. (New York: Appleton-Century-Crofts, 1963), pp. 47–50; Washington to William Crawford, 21 September 1767, in Consul W. Butterfield, ed., *Washington-Crawford Letters: Being the Correspondence between George Washington and William Crawford, from*

1767 to 1781, Concerning Western Lands (Cincinnati: Robert Clarke, 1877), pp. 3–4; for the inability of the British army to enforce the proclamation, and for frontier attitudes, see, e.g., Thomas Gage to Lord Shelburne, 10 October 1767, 22 January 1768, and 12 March 1768, in Carter, *Correspondence of General Thomas Gage,* vol. 1, pp. 152, 157, 165.

37. At the time the Holston was thought to join the Tennessee several miles below modern Knoxville; it was not until the late nineteenth century that the Tennessee's beginning was officially set at the confluence of the Holston and the French Broad Rivers: see James R. Montgomery, "The Nomenclature of the Upper Tennessee River," ETHS *Publications* 51 (1979), pp. 151–162.

38. Stanley J. Folmsbee et al., *History of Tennessee,* 4 vols. (New York: Lewis Historical Publishing, 1960), vol. 1, p. 103; unless otherwise indicated, my discussion of the East Tennessee settlements is based on Folmsbee, vol. 1, pp. 101–114.

39. Cora Bales Sevier and Nancy Sevier Madden, *Sevier Family History* (Washington, D.C.: privately published, 1961), pp. 524–527; Nancy Sevier Madden to the author, 3 September 1999.

40. "Felix Walker's Narrative of His trip with Boone from Long Island to Boonesborough in March 1775," in George Washington Ranck, *Boonesborough: Its Founding, Pioneer Struggles, Indian Experiences, Transylvania Days, and Revolutionary Annals; with Full Historical Notes and Appendix,* Filson Club Publication, No. 16 (Louisville, Ky.: J. P. Morton, 1901), p. 162.

41. Robert E. Corlew, *Tennessee: A Short History,* 2nd ed. (Knoxville: University of Tennessee Press, 1990), p. 48; see esp. Folmsbee et al. *History of Tennessee,* vol. 1, pp. 107–108, for Brown's version and a different, Cherokee, version of the Nolichucky lease.

42. Quotations in Folmsbee, et al. *History of Tennessee,* pp. 108–109; Corlew, *Tennessee: A Short History,* pp. 48–49; with regard to authority, see the excellent discussion in Wood, *Radicalism of the American Revolution,* pp. 155–159 and passim.

43. Samuel Wilson's Deposition, 14 April 1777, *Calendar of Virginia State Papers and Other Manuscripts,* vol. 1: *1652–1781,* ed. William P. Palmer (1875; reprint, New York: Kraus Reprint, 1965), vol. 1, pp. 282–283.

44. Dragging Canoe's description in Colonel Brown's Notes, 20 June 1844, Draper Mss. 5 XX 52 (Reel 117); Samuel Wilson's Deposition, p. 283.

45. Unless otherwise indicated, the ensuing events are based on James H. O'Donnell III, *Southern Indians in the American Revolution* (Knoxville: University of Tennessee Press, 1973), pp. 34–53; Philip M. Hamer, ed., "Correspondence of Henry Stuart and Alexander Cameron with the Wataugans, *MVHR* 17 (December 1930), pp. 451–459; Philip M. Hamer, "The Wataugans and the Cherokee Indians in 1776," ETHS *Publications* 3 (1931), pp. 108–126; Samuel Cole Williams, *Tennessee during the Revolutionary War* (1944; reprint, Knoxville: University of Tennessee Press, 1974), pp. 35–60; James P. Pate, "The Chickamauga: A Forgotten Segment of Indian Resistance on the Southern Frontier," Ph.D. diss., Mississippi State University, 1969, pp. 59–81.

46. Williams, *Tennessee during the Revolutionary War,* p. 39.

47. Christian to Patrick Henry, 27 October 1776, quoted in O'Donnell, *Southern Indians in the American Revolution,* p. 48.

CHAPTER 2. VANGUARD OF EMPIRE

1. William Martin to Lyman Draper, 7 July 1842, Draper Mss. 3 XX 4 (Reel 116), for the number of Indians and their approach; John Mack Faragher, *Daniel Boone: The Life and Legend of an American Pioneer* (New York: Henry Holt, 1992), p. 77.

2. There are several accounts of this incident. Unless otherwise indicated, I have chosen to follow that given in Martin to Draper, 7 July 1842, largely because his recounting is restrained, and also because Frances Scott described her experience to him "soon after" her return. Another account is "Narrative of Mrs. Scott's Captivity," Draper Mss. 10 DD 39 (Reel 83), from information furnished by John Kobler, an elder over the Holston circuits, who presided at Frances Scott's funeral on 9 May 1796. But his account apparently passed through at least one other person before being written down, and the story of the intervention of

"Providence" in the guise of a "little bird of a dove color near to my feet" which persisted in guiding her in the right direction does not lend confidence to this recounting. Other accounts are in the captivity literature then popular and published in various places, most of which are described in *Early American Imprints*. The location of the cabin and Scott's appointment as overseer are in Hattie Byrd Muncy Bales, comp., *Early Settlers of Lee Country Virginia and Adjacent Counties* (Greensboro, N.C.: Media, 1977), vol. 2, p. 474.

3. The contradictory account is in "Narrative of Mrs. Scott's Captivity."

4. Ibid.

5. Bales, *Early Settlers of Lee County*, p. 475.

6. For "turbulent & restless disposition" see Alexander McGillivray to Vizente Manuel de Zéspedes, 22 May 1785, in John Walton Caughey, *McGillivray of the Creeks* (Norman: University of Oklahoma Press, 1938), p. 87.

7. Charles Woodmason, *The Carolina Backcountry on the Eve of the Revolution: The Journal and Other Writings of Charles Woodmason Anglican Itinerant*, ed. Richard J. Hooker (Chapel Hill: University of North Carolina Press, 1953), pp. 60–61; William Byrd to Mr. Collenson, 18 July 1736, *VMHB* 34:4 (October 1928), p. 354.

8. Buchanan, *Road to Guilford Courthouse*, p. 206.

9. Ibid.

10. Anthony F. C. Wallace, *The Long, Bitter Trail: Andrew Jackson and the Indians* (New York: Hill & Wang, 1933), p. vii.

11. C. V. Wedgewood, *Truth and Opinion: Historical Essays* (New York: Macmillan, 1960), pp. 43, 47.

12. For a contrary view see Gregory H. Nobles, *American Frontiers: Cultural Encounters and Continental Conquest* (New York: Hill & Wang, 1997), pp. 14–15 and passim; David Campbell to the Governor of North Carolina, 30 November 1786, quoted in Randolph C. Downes, "Cherokee-American Relations in the Upper Tennessee Valley, 1776–1791," ETHS *Publications* 8 (1936), p. 43.

13. *New York Times*, 5 July 1999, p. B1.

CHAPTER 3. THE FRONTIER

1. Folmsbee et al., *History of Tennessee*, has an excellent chapter in volume 1 on the physiography of Tennessee.

2. Francis Asbury, *Journal and Letters*, 3 vols., ed. Elmer T. Clark et al. (London: Epworth Press, 1958), vol. 1, pp. ix, 568–570.

3. John Allison, *Dropped Stitches in Tennessee History* (1897; reprint, Johnson City, Tenn.: Overmountain Press, 1991), pp. 9–11.

4. Samuel Cole Williams, *History of the Lost State of Franklin*, rev. ed. (1933; reprint, Johnson City, Tenn.: Overmountain Press, 1993), pp. 27–44, 56–66.

5. Thomas Perkins Abernethy, *From Frontier to Plantation in Tennessee: A Study in Frontier Democracy* (Chapel Hill: University of North Carolina Press, 1932), p. 81 and passim. For commentary on Abernethy's views on land speculation, see William H. Masterson, *William Blount* (Baton Rouge: Louisiana State University Press, 1954), p. 359; Walter Faw Cannon, "Four Interpretations of the History of the State of Franklin," ETHS *Publications* 22 (1950), pp. 3–18; Stanley J. Folmsbee, *Sectionalism and Internal Improvements in Tennessee, 1796–1845*, Special Studies in Tennessee History 1 (Knoxville: East Tennessee Historical Society, 1939), p. iii.

6. John Haywood, *The Civil and Political History of the State of Tennessee from its Earliest Settlement up to the Year 1796* (Nashville: n.p., 1823), pp. 173–174.

7. Williams, *Lost State of Franklin*, p. 78.

8. Folmsbee et al., *History of Tennessee*, vol. 1, p. 164.

9. Alexander Martin to Joseph Martin, 11 February 1784, Draper Mss. 1 XX 69 (Reel 116).

10. Joseph Martin to William Russell, 1 August 1785, Draper Mss. 2 XX 5 (Reel 116).

11. Draper Mss. 3 SS 210 (Reel 105).

12. James Gettys Ramsey, *The Annals of Tennessee to the End of the Eighteenth Century* (1853; reprint, Chattanooga, Tenn.: Daughters of the American Revolution, 1926), p. 301; John P. Brown, *Old Frontiers: The Story of the Cherokee Indians from Earliest Times to the Date of Their Removal in the West 1838* (Kingsport, Tenn.: n.p., 1938), p. 240; Hubbert's name usually appears as Hubbard, but the correct spelling is used here.

13. Draper Mss. 21 S 226 (Reel 50).

14. I am indebted to Cherel Bolin Henderson for sharing with me her unpublished paper, "James Hubbert: The Tennessee Years," n.d., which is a well-researched and perceptive essay on Hubbert; I have followed it in my account of John Kirk Jr.'s revenge.

15. *Georgia Gazette,* 25 April 1789, reprinted in Williams, *Lost State of Franklin,* p. 213.

16. Henderson, "James Hubbert," p. 9.

17. Martin to Henry Knox, 21 February 1789, *ASPIA,* vol. 1, p. 48.

18. Randolph Downes, "Cherokee-American Relations in the Upper Tennessee Valley, 1776–1791," ETHS *Publications* 8 (1936), p. 49.

19. Henderson, "James Hubbert," p. 11.

20. Joseph Brown's narrative in Ramsey, *Tennessee,* pp. 508–517. Unless otherwise indicated, all quotations and paraphrasing in this section from Brown's narrative are from Ramsey on the pages cited.

21. Brown was referring to the first Christian Martyr, Stephen, who cried out as he was being stoned to death, "Lord, Jesus, receive my spirit." See Acts 6-7 (Authorized Version).

22. Draper Mss. 1 XX 48 (Reel 116).

23. *ASPIA,* vol. 1, pp. 47–49.

24. Parton, *Jackson,* vol. 1, pp. 161–162.

25. *Jackson Papers,* vol. 1, p. 12.

26. Parton, *Jackson,* vol. 1, p. 62.

27. Remini, *Jackson,* p. 39.

28. General William Lee Davidson, killed in action against Cornwallis's forces at the action at Cowan's Ford, North Carolina, 1 February 1781: see Buchanan, *Road to Guilford Courthouse,* pp. 341–348, for an account of this notable fight.

29. Parton, *Jackson,* vol. 1, p. 121.

30. Ibid., pp. 121–123; all quotations are from Parton.

31. Remini, *Jackson,* p. 40.

32. Anita Shafer Goodstein, *Nashville, 1780–1860: From Frontier to City* (Gainesville: University of Florida Press, 1989), Table 1, p. 205, for Nashville's population.

CHAPTER 4. THE CUMBERLAND SALIENT

1. The Indian is quoted in Anita Shafer Goodstein, *Nashville, 1780–1860: From Frontier to City* (Gainesville: University of Florida Press), p. 9. Goodstein's first chapter, "Leadership in a Frontier County," is a judicious and illuminating discussion of the subject and also contains a well-rounded picture of James Robertson.

2. James Leonard Highsaw, *Transcriptions from the Lyman C. Draper Manuscripts Relating to the History of Tennessee from 1769–1850* (Nashville: n.p., 1914), pp. 128–129.

3. John Woolman, *The Journal and Major Essays of John Woolman,* ed. Phillip S. Moulton (New York: Oxford University Press, 1971), p. 38.

4. Byrd to Lord Egmont, 21 July 1736, *VMHB* 36:3 (July 1928), pp. 220–221.

5. The letters are quoted in an excellent article by Gregory D. Massey, "The Limits of Antislavery Thought in the Revolutionary Lower South: John Laurens and Henry Laurens," *JSH* 63:6 (August 1997), p. 504.

6. William Cabell Bruce, *John Randolph of Roanoke, 1773–1833,* 2 vols. (1922; reprint, New York: Octagon, 1970), vol. 2, p. 203.

7. Stephen T. Rogers, "1977 Historic Site Survey" (Nashville: Tennessee Division of Archaeology, 1978), p. 38, quoting A. W. Putnam, *History of Middle Tennessee, or Life and Times of General James Robertson* (1859; reprint, Knoxville: University of Tennessee Press, n.d.), pp. 66–67.

8. Katharine R. Barnes, "James Robertson's Journey to Nashville: Tracing the Route of Fall, 1779," *Tennessee Historical Quarterly* 35:2 (Summer 1976), pp. 145–161; for the track

through the Gap, author's discussion with Jack Collier, chief ranger, Cumberland Gap National Historical Park, 4 May 1998, and National Park Service artist's rendition in the author's possession; for the weather, *Colonel William Fleming's Journal in Kentucky from Nov. 10, 1779 to May 27th 1780,* in Newton D. Mereness, ed. *Travels in the American Colonies* (New York: Macmillan, 1916), pp. 619–655, and John Carr, *Early Times in Middle Tennessee* (1857; reprint, Nashville: Parthenon Press, 1958), p. 7.

9. Harriet Simpson Arnow, *Seedtime on the Cumberland* (1960; reprint, Lexington: University of Kentucky Press, 1983), pp. 216–217, 235–240.

10. Donald Davidson, *The Tennessee,* 2 vols. (New York: Rinehart, 1946, 1948), vol. 1, pp. 152–153.

11. Unless otherwise indicated, all descriptions and quotations for the Donelson voyage are from John Donelson, *Journal of a Voyage, Intended by God's Permission, in the Good Boat Adventure, from Fort Patrick Henry on the Holston River to the French Salt Springs on Cumberland River,* in Robert T. Quarles and Robert H. White, eds., *Three Pioneer Tennessee Documents: Donelson's Journal, Cumberland Compact, Minutes of the Cumberland Court* (Nashville: Tennessee Historical Commission, 1964), pp. 1–9; for the number of boats and families on board, Carr, *Early Times,* p. 8; for the estimate of people, Arnow, *Seedtime,* p. 236.

12. Francis Baily, *Journal of a Tour in Unsettled Parts of North America in 1796 and 1797* (London: Baily Brothers, 1856), pp. 146–147, 231.

13. Ibid., p. 147; traffic on the western rivers is a fascinating subject, and two excellent books are recommended to the interested reader. The classic is Leland D. Baldwin, *The Keelboat Age on Western Waters* (Pittsburgh: University of Pittsburgh Press, 1941). The up-to-date treasure with a fine bibliographical essay is Michael Allen, *Western Rivermen, 1763–1861: Ohio and Mississippi Boatmen and the Myth of the Alligator Horse* (1990; reprint, Baton Rouge: Louisiana State University Press, 1994).

14. Carr, *Early Times,* p. 8.

15. Patrick Henry to Richard Caswell, 8 January 1779, *The State Records of North Carolina,* 26 vols., ed. William L. Saunders and Walter Clark (1907; reprint, New York: AMS Press, 1979), vol. 14, pp. 243–245; Draper Mss. 32 S 299–301.

16. Carr, *Early Times,* p. 9.

17. Folmsbee et al., *History of Tennessee,* vol. 1, p. 99.

18. Thomas Hutchins, *A Topographical Description of Virginia, Pennsylvania, Maryland, and North Carolina . . . ,* ed. Frederick Charles Hicks (1778; reprint, Cleveland: Burrows Brothers, 1904), p. 103; Davidson, *The Tennessee,* vol. 1, p. 283 (the quotation is Davidson's paraphrasing of Long).

19. These events can be followed in Buchanan, *Road to Guilford Courthouse.*

20. Carr, *Early Times,* p. 10.

21. Stanley J. Folmsbee, *Sectionalism and Internal Improvements in Tennessee, 1796–1845,* Special Studies in Tennessee History 1 (Knoxville: ETHS, 1939), p. 34.

22. James P. Pate, "The Chickamauga: A Forgotten Segment of Indian Resistance on the Southern Frontier," Ph.D. diss., Mississippi State University, 1969, pp. 80–81, 103–104.

23. Hutchins, *Topographical Description,* p. 103, describes the timber.

24. Ibid., pp. 101–102, for distance and width.

25. "Lewis Brantz's Memoranda of a Journey (1785)," in Samuel Cole Williams, ed., *Early Travels in the Tennessee Country, 1540–1800* (Johnson City, Tenn.: Watauga Press, 1928), p. 284.

26. Ibid., p. 285.

CHAPTER 5. UNDER SIEGE

1. Arnow, *Seedtime,* p. 288, citing Felix Robertson, *Nashville Journal of Medicine and Surgery,* vol. 8, pp. 452–453; Ramsey, *Tennessee,* pp. 455–456.

2. Rogers, "Survey," pp. 2–3, citing Draper Mss. 23 CC 95–97 (Reel 78). For a description of a Cumberland fortified station, see G. W. Featherstonaugh, *Excursion through the Slave States,* 2 vols. (London: John Murray, 1844), vol. 1, pp. 202–205.

3. "Articles of Agreement, or Compact of Government, entered into by Settlers on the Cumberland river, 1st May 1780," in Robert T. Quarles and Robert H. White, eds., *Three*

Pioneer Tennessee Documents: Donelson's Journal, Cumberland Compact, Minutes of the Cumberland Court (Nashville: Tennessee Historical Commission, 1964) pp. 11, 18–21; Rogers, "Survey," pp. 5, 10–12, but among the original eight Rogers omits Stone's River, which is listed in the Cumberland Compact.

4. Carr, *Early Times,* p. 12.

5. Arnow, *Seedtime,* pp. 237, 240, and n. 116, citing Draper Mss. 32 S 306 (Reel 52); Rogers, "Survey," pp. 29–30.

6. Carr, *Early Times,* p. 13.

7. Ibid.; Rogers, "Survey," p. 30.

8. James H. O'Donnell III, *Southern Indians in the American Revolution* (Knoxville: University of Tennessee Press, 1973), p. 93; Colin G. Calloway, *The American Revolution in Indian Country: Crisis and Diversity in Native American Communities* (Cambridge, U.K.: Cambridge University Press, 1995), pp. 225–226; Thomas Nairne, *Nairne's Muskhogean Journals: The 1708 Expedition to the Mississippi River,* ed. Alexander S. Moore (Jackson: University Press of Mississippi, 1988), p. 36.

9. Samuel Cole Williams, *Tennessee during the Revolutionary War* (1944; reprint, Knoxville: University of Tennessee Press, 1974), pp. 171–172; Calloway, *American Revolution in Indian Country,* p. 227.

10. Carr, *Early Times,* p. 13; Williams, *Tennessee during the Revolutionary War,* p. 172.

11. Williams, *Tennessee during the Revolutionary War,* quoting Putnam, *History of Middle Tennessee.*

12. Ibid., pp. 176–177 n. 15.

13. Ibid., pp. 173–174, and Arnow, *Seedtime,* pp. 289–292, citing various Draper Mss., tell the story of the fight at Freeland's.

14. Ibid., p. 292.

15. Draper Mss. 5 XX 14 (Reel 117), 32 S 296 (Reel 52); Putnam, *History of Middle Tennessee,* p. 66; Arnow, *Seedtime,* citing Draper Mss. 30 S 296 (Reel 51).

16. Putnam, *History of Middle Tennessee,* p. 86; Williams, *Tennessee during the Revolutionary War,* p. 177 n. 16; Rogers, "Survey," p. 25.

17. Unless otherwise indicated, my account of the Battle of the Bluffs is based primarily on accounts in the Draper Mss. 1 S 61 (Reel 47), 30 S 52 (Reel 51), 32 S 313–340 and 346 (Reel 52), 9 CC 35 (Reel 76), 6 XX 50 (Reel 117), supplemented by Carr, *Early Years,* pp. 13–15; Williams, *Tennessee during the Revolutionary War,* pp. 177–179; the number of Chickamaugas involved was estimated by Thomas Lawrence Connelly, "Indian Warfare on the Tennessee Frontier, 1776–1794: Strategy and Tactics," ETHS *Publications* 36 (1964), pp. 3–22; Arnow, *Seedtime,* p. 85, for John Buchanan Sr.'s description.

18. Connelly, "Indian Warfare on the Tennessee Frontier," pp. 13–14; James P. Pate, "The Chickamauga: A Forgotten Segment of Indian Resistance on the Southern Frontier," Ph.D. diss., Mississippi State University, 1969, p. 115.

19. Arnow, *Seedtime,* p. 296, citing Draper Mss. 6 XX (50) 17 (Reel 117).

20. Carr, *Early Times,* p. 15.

21. The quotations are from Arnow, *Seedtime,* pp. 297–298, citing Draper Mss. 6 XX (50) 17 (Reel 117), 5 S 61 (Reel 47).

22. In my chronological sequence I have closely followed Calloway, *American Revolution in Indian Country,* p. 231, citing Draper Mss. 1 XX 50 (Reel 116).

23. Quoted in ibid., p. 232.

24. For the Chickasaw peace negotiations, unless otherwise indicated, I have largely followed the account in O'Donnell, *Southern Indians in the American Revolution,* pp. 131–137; but see also Robert S. Cotterill, "The Virginia-Chickasaw Treaty of 1783," *JSH* 8 (1942), pp. 483–496.

25. Masterson, *Blount,* pp. 68–72; A. P. Whitaker, "The Muscle Shoals Speculation, 1783–1789," *MVHR* 13:3 (December 1926), pp. 365–366.

26. Quoted in Whitaker, "The Muscle Shoals Speculation," p. 365, citing Draper Mss. 4 XX 17 (Reel 116).

27. Quoted in Calloway, *American Revolution in Indian Country,* p. 233.

28. Ibid., p. 234, citing Draper Mss. 1 XX 55 and 65 (Reel 116), and pp. 213–243 for the complicated Chickasaw story, which we have only touched on.

CHAPTER 6. "I AM A NATIVE OF THIS NATION & OF RANK IN IT"

1. Caughey, *McGillivray*, pp. ix, 15, and Alexander McGillivray to Arturo O'Neill, 3 January 1784, pp. 66–67; Michael D. Green, "Alexander McGillivray," in R. David Edmunds, ed., *American Indian Leaders: Studies in Diversity* (Lincoln: University of Nebraska Press, 1980), pp. 41–42; Caleb Swann, "Position and State of Manners and Arts in the Creek, or Muscogee, Nation in 1791," in Henry Rowe Schoolcraft, ed., *Historical and Statistical Information Respecting the History, Condition, and Prospects of the Indian Tribes of the United States,* 6 vols. (Philadelphia: Lippincott, Grambo, 1851–1857), vol. 5, p. 281.

2. Caughey, *McGillivray,* pp. 9–14; Green, "Alexander McGillivray," p. 42; Louis LeClerc de Milford, *Memoir, or a Cursory Glance at My Different Travels and My Sojourn in the Creek Nation,* ed. John Francis McDermott, trans. Geraldine de Courcy (Chicago: Lakeside Press, 1956), p. 18; Edward J. Cashin, *Lachlan McGillivray, Indian Trader: The Shaping of the Southern Colonial Frontier* (Athens: University of Georgia Press, 1992), pp. 71–73, for Alexander's birthdate and his mother's parentage.

3. John Pope, *A Tour through the Southern and Western Territories of the United States of America* (1792; reprint, Gainesville: University Presses of Florida, 1979), pp. 46–49.

4. Cashin, *Lachlan McGillivray,* pp. 74–76, presents the latest research on the hazy subject of Alexander's education; Albert James Pickett, *History of Alabama, and Incidentally of Georgia and Mississippi, from the Earliest Period,* 2 vols. (Charleston, S.C.: Walker & James, 1851), vol. 2, p. 33; Caughey, *McGillivray,* pp. 13–16; Pope, *Tour,* p. 48; Johann Hinrichs, *Diary,* in Bernhard A. Uhlendorf, ed. and trans., *The Siege of Charleston . . . Diaries and Letters of Hessian Officers from the von Jungken Papers in the William L. Clements Library* (Ann Arbor: University of Michigan Press, 1938), p. 329, for description of Charleston.

5. Caughey, *McGillivray,* p. 16; Green, "McGillivray," p. 42; Cashin, *Lachlan McGillivray,* p. 298.

6. Milford, *Memoir,* pp. 94–95, and xxvii–xxx, for the editor's assessment of the work; James H. O'Donnell III, *Southern Indians in the American Revolution* (Knoxville: University of Tennessee Press, 1973), p. 81, for McGillivray's Savannah foray.

7. For the reader interested in pursuing the complex subject of the peace negotiations, three books will give a good start. Samuel Flagg Bemis, *The Diplomacy of the American Revolution* (1937; reprint, Bloomington: Indiana University Press, 1957), especially pp. 189–264; Richard B. Morris, *The Peacemakers: The Great Powers and American Independence* (New York: Harper & Row, 1965), especially the map facing p. 350; and Jonathan Dull, *A Diplomatic History of the American Revolution* (New Haven: Yale University Press, 1985), especially pp. 137–169, who charges Bemis and Morris with anti-French bias, but must also be used with care because of his pro-French bias and overheated criticism of the American commissioners. The quotations are in Morris, *Peacemakers,* p. 349, and Jonathan Dull, *The French Navy and American Independence: A Study of Arms and Diplomacy, 1774–1787* (Princeton: Princeton University Press, 1975), p. 147.

8. O'Neill to Josef de Ezpeleta, 19 October 1783, quoted in Caughey, *McGillivray,* p. 62; Pickett, *Alabama,* vol. 2, pp. 34–35, and Caughey, *McGillivray,* p. 3, for McGillivray's physical description. No image is known to exist.

9. My discussion of these subjects is based on Michael D. Green, *The Creeks: A Critical Bibliography* (Bloomington: University of Indiana Press, 1979), pp. 8–10, and Green, "McGillivray," pp. 41–63. Quotations are cited separately.

10. Green, *Critical Bibliography,* p. 8.

11. Pope, *Tour,* pp. 62, 65; Green, "McGillivray," p. 49.

12. For the economic change, see Claudio Saunt, *A New Order of Things: Property, Power, and the Transformation of the Creek Indians, 1733–1816* (Cambridge, U.K.: Cambridge University

Press, 1999), ch. 2 and passim. The reader should note, however, that the assessments in my text of McGillivray's efforts and of Hoboithle Mico and Eneah Mico are mine, not Saunt's.

13. McGillivray to Zéspedes, 15 November 1785, quoted in Caughey, *McGillivray*, p. 139.

14. McGillivray to O'Neill, 1 January 1784, and to Miró, 28 March 1784, in ibid., pp. 73–74.

15. Treaty of Pensacola, 1 July 1784, Miró to McGillivray, 7 June 1784, in ibid., pp. 75–77; William S. Coker and Thomas D. Watson, *Indian Traders of the Southeastern Spanish Borderlands: Panton, Leslie & Company and John Forbes and Company, 1783–1847* (Pensacola: University of West Florida Press, 1986), pp. 58–59.

16. The meeting is mentioned in McGillivray's letter of transmittal to the governor of Pensacola, General Arturo O'Neill, 24 July 1785, and the quotation is in "McGillivray for the Chiefs of the Creek, Chickasaw, and Cherokee Nations," 10 July 1785, from which the quotations in the following paragraph are taken, both in Caughey, *McGillivray*, pp. 90–94.

17. "McGillivray for the Chiefs of the Creek, Chickasaw, and Cherokee Nations," pp. 90–92.

18. McGillivray to O'Neill, 24 July 1785 and 1 January 1784, in Caughey, *McGillivray*, pp. 65, 93–94; Thomas Nairne, *Nairne's Muskhogeon Journals: The 1708 Expedition to the Mississippi River*, ed. Alexander S. Moore (Jackson: University Press of Mississippi, 1988), p. 75.

19. McMurphy to O'Neill, 11 July 1786, in Caughey, *McGillivray*, p. 119; Green, "McGillivray," pp. 50–51, for a clear, concise discussion; for the full story of Panton, Leslie & Co. and its relationship to McGillivray and the Creeks, see Coker and Watson, *Indian Traders of the Southeastern Borderlands*, passim.

20. Colin G. Calloway, *The American Revolution in Indian Country: Crisis and Diversity in Native American Communities* (Cambridge, U.K.: Cambridge University Press, 1995), p. 20; David J. Weber, *The Spanish Frontier in North America* (New Haven: Yale University Press, 1992), p. 272; Howard R. Lamar, ed., *The New Encyclopedia of the American West* (New Haven: Yale University Press, 1998), p. 406; McGillivray to Zéspedes, 22 May 1785, in Caughey, *McGillivray*, p. 87.

21. William Bartram, *Travels and Other Writings: Travels through North and South Carolina, Georgia, East and West Florida; Travels in Georgia and Florida, 1773–74; A Report to Dr. John Fothergill; Miscellaneous Writings*, ed. Thomas P. Slaughter (1791, 1943; reprint, New York: Library of America, 1996), pp. 357–359.

22. McGillivray to O'Neill, 5 February 1784, in Caughey, *McGillivray*, pp. 69–70.

23. McGillivray to O'Neill, 28 March 1786, in ibid., pp. 104–106.

24. McGillivray to Miró, 1 May 1786, in ibid., p. 109.

25. Miró to O'Neill, 20 June 1786, in ibid., pp. 117–118.

26. Green, "McGillivray," p. 53; McGillivray to Miró, 1 May 1786, in ibid., p. 109.

27. McGillivray to Miró, 1 May 1786; Carr, *Early Times*, pp. 21–25.

28. Walter T. Durham, *The Great Leap Westward: A History of Sumner County, Tennessee, from Its Beginnings to 1805* (Gallatin, Tenn.: Sumner County Public Library Board, 1969), pp. 89–91.

29. Ibid., p. 91; Rogers, "Survey," pp. 12, 15.

30. Durham, *Great Leap Westward*, pp. 91–93.

31. Ibid., pp. 86, 93, 95–96.

32. Pickett, *Alabama*, pp. 74–77, for the Coldwater raid; ibid., pp. 94–95.

33. William Martin to Lyman Draper, 13 May 1843, Draper Mss. 3 XX 18 (Reel 116); McGillivray to Zéspedes, 5 January 1788, in Caughey, *McGillivray*, p. 165.

34. McGillivray to O'Neill, 25 April 1788, and to John Leslie, 20 November 1788, in ibid., pp. 178–179, 207–208.

35. Ibid., pp. 34–35; Green, "McGillivray," pp. 53–54.

36. Caughey, *McGillivray*, pp. 35–36; Green, *McGillivray*, pp. 57–58; J. Leitch Wright Jr., *William Augustus Bowles: Director General of the Creek Nation* (Athens: University of Georgia Press, 1967), pp. 26–30.

37. O'Neill to Marqués de Sonoro, 20 February 1787, Miró to O'Neill, 8 July 1788, in Caughey, *McGillivray*, pp. 144, 186 n. 131, 186–187.

38. O'Neill to Miró, 22 August 1788, McGillivray to O'Neill, 19 August 1788, in ibid., pp. 197–199.

39. McGillivray to Miró, 20 September 1788, in ibid., pp. 201–202.

40. Francis Paul Prucha, *American Indian Treaties: The History of a Political Anomaly* (1994; reprint, Berkeley: University of California Press, 1997), pp. 36–40, 68–69.

41. McGillivray to John Leslie, 12 October 1789, Miró to McGillivray, 22 July 1789, McGillivray to William Panton, 8 October 1789, McGillivray to Miró, 10 December 1789, in Caughey, *McGillivray,* pp. 38, 253–255, 243, 253 n. 225; ibid., pp. 79–80.

42. McGillivray to Leslie, 12 October 1789.

43. James Lamar Appleton and Robert David Ward, "Albert James Pickett and the Case of the Secret Articles: Historians and the Treaty of New York, 1790," *Alabama Review* 51:1 (January 1998), p. 7; Hawkins to McGillivray, 6 March 1790, in Caughey, *McGillivray,* pp. 256–259.

44. McGillivray to William Panton, 8 May 1790, in Caughey, *McGillivray,* pp. 41–43, 260; Ames to Thomas Dwight, 25 July 1790, in Seth Ames, *Works of Fisher Ames,* 2 vols., ed. and enl. by W. B. Allen (1854; reprint, Indianapolis: Liberty Classics, 1983), vol. 1, p. 836; Abigail Adams to Mary Cranch, 8 August 1790, in *New Letters of Abigail Adams, 1788–1801,* ed. Stewart Mitchell (Boston: Houghton Mifflin, 1947), p. 57.

45. Prucha, *American Indian Treaties,* p. 82, for the chronology; *Pennsylvania Packet and Daily Advertiser,* 18 August 1790, in Caughey, *McGillivray,* p. 278.

46. In this paragraph I have followed the analysis of Green, "McGillivray," pp. 55–56, from which the quotations also come; cf. J. Leitch Wright Jr., "Creek-American Treaty of 1790: Alexander McGillivray and the Diplomacy of the Old Southwest," *GHQ* 51 (December 1967), pp. 379–400, by a champion of Bowles.

47. William Blount to Henry Knox, 20 March 1792, for the description of Craig, and the "Report of David Craig to William Blount," 15 March 1792, *ASPIA,* vol. 1, pp. 263–264.

48. Wright, *William Augustus Bowles,* pp. 48–54, 95–108, and passim.

49. George Hammond to Thomas Jefferson, 30 March 1792, *ASPIA,* vol. 1, p. 251.

50. Pope, *Tour,* p. 48; McGillivray to Panton, 28 October 1791, 28 November 1792, Baron de Carondelet to McGillivray, 14 December 1792, for venereal disease, McGillivray to O'Neill, 12 August 1786, in Caughey, *McGillivray,* pp. 56, 128, 300, 348, 350.

51. Panton to Carondelet, 16 February 1793, 20 February 1793, in ibid., pp. 353–354.

52. Ibid., pp. 53, 362.

CHAPTER 7. THE RISE OF ANDREW JACKSON

1. Unless otherwise indicated, my account, including quotations, of Rachel's first marriage, her meeting Jackson, and what happened thereafter follows Parton, *Jackson,* vol. 1, pp. 133, 147–154, which includes "Judge Overton's Narrative."

2. Rogers, "Survey," fig. 2 on p. 13, and p. 19 for location of Mansker's.

3. Remini, *Jackson,* p. 434 n. 8, for Stark's probable identity.

4. Ibid., pp. 60–62, 435 n. 15, for an extended discussion of this matter.

5. Ibid., pp. 44–45; Francis Baily, *Journal of a Tour in Unsettled Parts of North America in 1796 and 1797* (London: Baily Brothers, 1856), pp. 416–426.

6. Baily, *Journal of a Tour,* pp. 417–421.

7. Parton, *Jackson,* pp. 142–145, for some of the stories.

8. Ibid., p. 142.

9. Arthur Preston Whitaker, *The Spanish-American Frontier, 1783–1795: The Westward Movement and the Spanish Retreat in the Mississippi Valley* (1927; reprint, Lincoln: University of Nebraska Press, 1969), pp. 69, 90, and the map on p. 68; for the contest over Chickasaw Bluffs, see two articles by Jack D. L. Holmes in ETHS *Publications:* "Spanish-American Rivalry over Chickasaw Bluffs, 1780–1795," 34 (1962), pp. 26–57, and "The Ebb-Tide of Spanish Military Power on the Mississippi: Fort San Fernando de las Barrancas," 36 (1964), pp. 23–44.

10. For the Spanish Conspiracy a good, brief sketch is in Howard R. Lamar, ed., *The New Encyclopedia of the American West* (New Haven: Yale University Press, 1998), p. 1070; extended discussions are in Whitaker, *Spanish-American Frontier,* passim; Thomas Perkins Abernethy, *From Frontier to Plantation in Tennessee: A Study in Frontier Democracy* (Chapel Hill: University of North Carolina Press, 1932), pp. 90–102; see also Arthur Preston Whitaker, "The Muscle Shoals Speculation, 1783–1789," *MVHR* 13:3 (December 1926), pp. 365–386; an older study that

treats the conspiracy in detail is Thomas Marshall Green, *The Spanish Conspiracy: A Review of Early Spanish Movements in the Southwest* (1891; reprint, Gloucester, Mass.: Peter Smith, 1967).

11. Whitaker, *Spanish-American Frontier,* pp. 76–77; Abernethy, *From Frontier to Plantation in Tennessee,* pp. 96–97; Washington to Benjamin Harrison, 10 October 1784, in W. W. Abbot, ed., *The Papers of George Washington,* Confederation Series, 6 vols. (Charlottesville: University Press of Virginia, 1992–1997), vol. 2, p. 92.

12. Whitaker, *Spanish-American Frontier,* pp. 112–113; Remini, *Jackson,* pp. 48–50; *Jackson Papers,* vol. 1, pp. 16–17, for the letter and editorial notes on Smith and Fagot.

13. Fagot and Miró were not related: see Remini, *Jackson,* p. 50.

14. *Jackson Papers,* vol. 1, pp. 16–17 n. 2.

15. Gayoso to Valdes, 8 May 1789, in Whitaker, "The Muscle Shoals Speculation," p. 384.

16. Thomas Perkins Abernethy, *The South in the New Nation, 1789–1819* (Baton Rouge: Louisiana State University Press, 1961), pp. 53–54; Whitaker, "The Muscle Shoals Speculation," pp. 383–385; McGillivray to Vicente Folch y Juan, 22 April 1789, in Caughey, *McGillivray,* p. 227.

17. The legal documents discussed in this paragraph can be found in *Jackson Papers,* vol. 1, pp. 44, 424–428; Parton, *Jackson,* p. 152, for Overton's account, including quotations.

18. Unless otherwise indicated, my discussion follows Remini, *Jackson,* pp. 62–67, which presents the evidence and possible scenarios.

19. *Jackson Papers,* vol. 1, pp. 29–30.

20. Ibid., pp. 425–427.

21. Remini, *Jackson,* pp. 65–66.

22. Ibid., p. 63.

23. Ibid., pp. 66–67.

24. Unless otherwise indicated, this and the following paragraph on Blount's early years, including quotations, are based on Masterson, *Blount,* pp. 1–37.

25. Ibid., p. 62.

26. William Cabell Bruce, *John Randolph of Roanoke, 1773–1833,* 2 vols. (1922; reprint, New York: Octagon, 1970), vol. 2, p. 203.

27. Masterson, *Blount,* pp. 123–125, 131.

28. Ibid., 132–133; Buckner F. Melton Jr., *The First Impeachment: The Constitution's Framers and the Case of Senator William Blount* (Macon, Ga.: Mercer University Press, 1998), pp. 64–65.

29. Masterson, *Blount,* pp. 167–169.

30. Hawkins to Blount, 6 February 1790, in ibid., p. 174, 174–177; Richard Henry Lee to Patrick Henry, 10 June 1790, in James Curtis Ballagh, ed., *The Letters of Richard Henry Lee,* 2 vols. (1911, 1914; reprint, New York: Da Capo Press, 1970), vol. 2, p. 523, for hostility to Martin and the Georgia delegation.

31. Masterson, *Blount,* pp. 176–177; for the act creating the Southwest Territory, letters of support, and Blount's official appointment, see Clarence E. Carter, ed., *The Territorial Papers of the United States,* vol. 4, *The Territory South of the River Ohio, 1790–1796* (Washington, D.C.: U.S. Government Printing Office, 1936), pp. 18–20, 22–24, 33.

32. Blount to Steele, 10 July 1790, in *The Papers of John Steele,* 2 vols., ed. Henry M. Wagstaff, 2 vols. (Raleigh: Edwards & Broughton, 1924), vol. 1, pp. 67–68.

33. Jefferson to Blount, 15 June 1790, in Carter, *Territorial Papers,* vol. 4, p. 29; Masterson, *Blount,* pp. 180–181, for the preparations; George F. Bentley, "Printers and Printing in the Southwest Territory, 1790–1796," *THQ* 8 (1949), pp. 333–334.

34. Remini, *Jackson,* pp. 51–54, for a good discussion of Blount's powers.

35. Ibid., pp. 53–54; *Jackson Papers,* vol. 1, pp. 26, 37, 41.

36. Jackson to John McKee, 30 January 1793, in *Jackson Papers,* vol. 1, p. 40.

CHAPTER 8. BUCHANAN'S STATION AND NICKAJACK

1. Report of William Blount to Henry Knox, 20 March 1792, in *ASPIA,* vol. 1, p. 264; W. Stuart Harris, *Dead Towns of Alabama* (University: University of Alabama Press, 1977), p. 9.

2. William Blount to Henry Knox, 4 July 1792, in Carter, *Territorial Papers,* vol. 4, p. 159; Elijah Robertson to William Blount, 28 February 1792, in *ASPIA,* vol. 1, p. 263.

3. Knox to George Washington, 15 May 1792, in Carter, *Territorial Papers,* vol. 4, p. 150; Folmsbee et al., *History of Tennessee,* vol. 1, pp. 197–98; Francis Paul Prucha, *American Indian Treaties: The History of a Political Anomaly* (1994; reprint, Berkeley: University of California Press, 1997), pp. 86–88; Randolph C. Downes, "Cherokee-American Relations in the Upper Tennessee Valley, 1776–1791," ETHS *Publications* 8 (1936), pp. 52–53.

4. "Minutes of the Conference at Coyatee with the Chiefs and Warriors of the Cherokees, in May 1792, with the Incidental Circumstances Relative Thereto," in *ASPIA,* vol. 1, pp. 267–268.

5. Ibid.; "The Report of David Craig to William Blount," 15 March 1792, in *ASPIA,* vol. 1, pp. 263–264.

6. Knox to Washington, 28 July 1792, in Carter, *Territorial Papers,* vol. 4, pp. 159–160.

7. Blount to Knox, 16 May 1792, in ibid., p. 151.

8. Silas McBee's Account, 1 December 1843, Draper Mss. 5 XX 51; William Hall to Lyman Draper, 21 July 1845, 6 XX 8 (Reel 117); Blount to Knox, 31 August 1792, in *ASPIA,* vol. 1, pp. 275–276; Carr, *Early Times,* pp. 91–92; Arnow, *Seedtime,* p. 290 n. 31; Rogers, "Survey," p. 21.

9. Walter T. Durham, *The Great Leap Westward: A History of Sumner County, Tennessee, from Its Beginnings to 1805* (Gallatin, Tenn.: Sumner County Public Library Board, 1969), pp. 116–117, citing Draper Mss. 32 S 485 (Reel 52).

10. Blount to Knox, 31 August 1792, in *ASPIA,* vol. 1, p. 276.

11. Draper Mss. 6 XX 64 (Reel 117), for the weather.

12. Rogers, "Survey," p. 27, and James Robertson to William Blount, 3 October 1792, for location; Arnow, *Seedtime,* pp. 6, 10–12; Census Report from Governor Blount, in Carter, *Territorial Papers,* p. 81; William Martin to Lyman Draper, 13 May 1843, Draper Mss. 3 XX 18 (Reel 116), for the term *first comers;* G. W. Featherstonaugh, *Excursion through the Slave States,* 2 vols. (London: John Murray, 1844), vol. 1, pp. 205–206.

13. Rogers, "Survey," p. 39; Arnow, *Seedtime,* p. 6; Martin to Draper, 13 May 1843.

14. Martin to Draper, 13 May 1843; Arnow, *Seedtime,* p. 2.

15. Little Turkey to Blount, 2 September 1792, Sevier to Blount, 10 September 1792, Blount to Knox, 1 September 1792, in *ASPIA,* vol. 1, pp. 276–278.

16. James P. Pate, "The Chickamauga: A Forgotten Segment of Indian Resistance on the Southern Frontier," Ph.D. diss., Mississippi State University, 1969, p. 21; Bloody Fellow to Blount, 10 September 1792, Glass to Blount, 10 September 1792, in Carter, *Territorial Papers,* vol. 4, p. 184; Blount's Report, 15 November 1792, Blount to Knox, 10 October 1792, in *ASPIA,* vol. 1, pp. 294, 331.

17. Blount to Knox, 10 October 1792, in *ASPIA,* vol. 1, p. 331; Colonel Brown's Notes, 20 September 1844, Draper Mss. 5 XX 52 (Reel 117); Harriet Simpson Arnow, *Flowering of the Cumberland* (New York: Macmillan, 1963), p. 21.

18. Robertson to Blount, 3 October 1792, William Blount's Report, 5 November 1792, Blount to Knox, 10 October 1792, in *ASPIA,* vol. 1, pp. 294–295; Colonel Brown's Notes; Carr, *Early Times,* p. 95; Thomas Lawrence Connelly, "Indian Warfare on the Tennessee Frontier, 1776–1794: Strategy and Tactics," East Tennessee Historical Society *Publications* 36 (1964), p. 16; Pate, "The Chickamauga," pp. 219–221.

19. Colonel Brown's Notes; Robertson to Blount, 10 October 1792, in Arnow, *Flowering,* pp. 26–27.

20. Arthur Ferrill, *The Fall of the Roman Empire: The Military Explanation* (New York: Thames & Hudson, 1988), pp. 60–64.

21. Pate, "The Chickamauga," p. 221; Robertson to Blount, 10 October 1792, in *ASPIA,* vol. 1, p. 294.

22. Jackson to John McKee, 16 May 1794, Jackson to Monroe, 4 March 1817, in *Jackson Papers,* vol. 1, pp. 48–49; vol. 4, p. 95.

23. Deposition of Samuel Foreman, 26 January 1789, *The State Records of North Carolina,* 26 vols., ed. William L. Saunders and Walter Clark (1907; reprint, New York: AMS Press, 1979), vol. 22, p. 1007.

24. Quoted in Prucha, *American Indian Treaties,* pp. 46–47.

25. Report of Henry Knox on the northwestern Indians, 15 June 1789, in *ASPIA*, vol. 1, pp. 13–14, while referring specifically to the Wabash Indians, can be read as a statement of his overall policy. Relevant extracts can be more conveniently found in Francis Paul Prucha, ed., *Documents of United States Indian Policy*, 2nd ed., exp. (Lincoln: University of Nebraska Press, 1990), pp. 12–13.

26. Sevier to Jackson, 29 January 1797, *Jackson Papers*, vol. 1, pp. 120–121.

27. President Washington's Third Annual Message, 25 October 1791, in Prucha, *Documents of United States Indian Policy*, pp. 15–16.

28. Philander D. Chase, "A Stake in the West: George Washington as Backcountry Surveyor and Landholder," in Warren R. Hofstra, ed., *George Washington and the Virginia Backcountry* (Madison, Wisc.: Madison House, 1998), p. 181; George Washington to James Duane, 7 September 1783, in John C. Fitzpatrick, ed., *The Writings of George Washington, from the Original Manuscript Sources, 1745–1799*, 39 vols. (Washington, D.C.: U.S. Government Printing Office, 1931–1944), vol. 27, p. 133.

29. Report of Henry Knox on White Outrages, 18 July 1788, in Prucha, *Documents of United States Indian Policy*, p. 11; Knox to Call, 13 July 1791, in *ASPIA*, vol. 1, p. 125; Curtis P. Nettels, *The Emergence of a National Economy, 1775–1815* (1962; reprint, Armonk, N.Y.: M. E. Sharpe, 1989), p. 150.

30. Knox to Blount, 15 August 1792, in Carter, *Territorial Papers*, vol. 4, p. 163; Jay to Jefferson, 14 December 1786, in Julian P. Boyd, ed., *The Papers of Thomas Jefferson*, vol. 1– (Princeton: Princeton University Press, 1950–), vol. 10, pp. 598–599.

31. Quoted in Dorothy Twohig, "The Making of George Washington," and Warren R. Hofstra, " 'A Parcel of Barbarian's and an Uncooth Set of People': Settlers and Settlements of the Shenandoah Valley," in Hofstra, ed., *George Washington and the Virginia Backcountry*, pp. 15–16, 88.

32. Martin H. Quitt, "The English Cleric and the Virginia Adventurer: The Washingtons, Father and Son," *VMHB* 97 (April 1989), pp. 163–184; Douglas S. Freeman, *George Washington: A Biography*, 7 vols. (New York: Scribner's, 1948), vol. 1, pp. 15–47; Alice L. L. Ferguson, "The Susquehannock Fort on Piscataway Creek," *Maryland Historical Magazine* 36 (March 1941), pp. 1–9; Wilcomb E. Washburn, *The Governor and the Rebel: A History of Bacon's Rebellion in Virginia* (Chapel Hill: University of North Carolina Press, 1967), pp. 17–39; depositions absolving Virginia of blame are in the *William and Mary Quarterly*, 1st series, vol. 2 (1893), pp. 38–43.

33. Masterson, *Blount*, p. 267.

34. Ibid., pp. 267–268.

35. James Ore to William Blount, 24 September 1794, in *ASPIA*, vol. 1, p. 632; Sampson Williams's Account, 1 December 1843, Joseph Brown's Notes, 20 September 1844, Draper Mss. 5 XX 50, 52 (Reel 117).

36. Robertson to Watts, 20 September 1794, in *ASPIA*, vol. 1, p. 531.

CHAPTER 9.   "WHEN YOU HAVE READ THIS LETTER OVER THREE TIMES, THEN BURN IT"

1. Masterson, *Blount*, pp. 271–277; Bernard W. Sheehan, "The Indian Problem in the Northwest: From Conquest to Philanthropy," in Ronald J. Hoffman and Peter J. Albert Jr., eds., *Launching the Extended Republic: The Federalist Era* (Charlottesville: University Press of Virginia), pp. 214–222.

2. Masterson, *Blount*, pp. 274–276; Remini, *Jackson*, pp. 72–83.

3. Mitchell to Jackson, ca. 12 October 1795, in *Jackson Papers*, vol. 1, p. 75.

4. Anderson to Jackson, 3 December 1795, in ibid., p. 78.

5. Ibid., p. 83 n. 5; Remini, *Jackson*, pp. 75–79, has a good discussion of the convention and Jackson's role; Robert E. Corlew, *Tennessee: A Short History*, 2nd ed. (Knoxville: University of Tennessee Press, 1990), p. 97, for the quotation.

6. Jackson to Blount, 29 February 1796, Overton to Jackson, 10 March 1796, Election Returns for Representative to Congress, 22 October 1796, in *Jackson Papers*, pp. 82, 85, 98–99.

7. Jackson to Rachel, 9 May 1796, in ibid., pp. 91–92.

8. Jackson to Hays, 21 November 1797, and also, e.g., to Hays, 19 May and 16 December 1796, in ibid., pp. 101, 104, 152.

9. My description of Blount's financial debacle described in this and following paragraphs is based on Masterson, *Blount,* pp. 298–301; *Jackson Papers,* vol. 1, p. 58 n. 2, for David Allison; Curtis P. Nettels, *The Emergence of a National Economy, 1775–1815* (1962; reprint, Armonk, N.Y.: M. E. Sharpe, 1989), pp. 154–159.

10. Unless otherwise indicated, my description of the Blount Conspiracy is drawn from the following works: Masterson, *Blount,* pp. 301–323; Arthur P. Whitaker, *The Mississippi Question, 1795–1803: A Study in Trade, Politics, and Diplomacy* (1934; reprint, Gloucester, Mass.: Peter Smith, 1962), pp. 104–115; Buckner F. Melton, *The First Impeachment: The Constitution's Framers and the Case of Senator William Blount* (Macon, Ga.: Mercer University Pres, 1998), pp. 90–132 and passim; Andrew R. L. Clayton, " 'When Shall We Cease to Have Judases?': The Blount Conspiracy and the Limits of the Extended Republic," in Hoffman and Albert, *Launching the Extended Republic,* pp. 156–189. Chisholm's description is in Melton, *The First Impeachment,* p. 90. Only quotations are cited separately.

11. Melton, *The First Impeachment,* p. 91.

12. Masterson, *Blount,* p. 305, for the quotation.

13. Clayton, " 'When Shall We Cease to Have Judases?' " pp. 157–160, and passim, for the suggestion referred to in the text; Samuel Flagg Bemis, *Pinckney's Treaty: America's Advantage from Europe's Distress, 1783–1800,* rev. ed. (New Haven: Yale University Press, 1960), pp. 281, 294–314, and passim; Thomas Jefferson to Archibald Stuart, 25 January 1786, in Thomas Jefferson, *Writings* (New York: Library of America, 1984), p. 844. Jefferson, it should be noted, was referring to Spain's South American colonies as well as its Gulf Coast borderlands.

14. Melton, *The First Impeachment,* p. 97.

15. Ibid., pp. 99–101, prints the letter in full.

16. Ibid., p. 108.

17. Ibid., p. 126.

18. Blount to John Gray Blount, 17 November 1797, Blount to James Robertson, quoted in Remini, *Jackson,* p. 107; Certificate of Election to the United States Senate, *Jackson Papers,* vol. 1, p. 150.

19. Masterson, *Blount,* p. 346.

20. Mary McCarthy, *Venice Observed* (Paris, Lausanne: G&R Bernier, 1956), p. 84.

CHAPTER 10. MAJOR GENERAL ANDREW JACKSON

1. Jackson to Sevier, 18 May 1797, in *Jackson Papers,* vol. 1, pp. 136–137; Remini, *Jackson,* pp. 100–102, has a good discussion of the incident.

2. Jackson to Sevier, Sevier to Jackson, 8 May 1796, in *Jackson Papers,* vol. 1, p. 138.

3. Jackson to Sevier, 10 May 1797, Sevier to Jackson, 11 May 1797, in ibid., pp. 141–142.

4. Speech before the U.S. House of Representatives, 29 December 1796, in ibid., pp. 106–107.

5. Ibid., 30 December 1796, p. 108; Remini, *Jackson,* p. 97.

6. *The Revolutionary War Sketches of William R. Davie,* ed. Blackwell P. Robinson (Raleigh: North Carolina Department of Archives and History, 1976), p. 13; for other examples of militia behavior during the War of the Revolution see Buchanan, *Road to Guilford Courthouse,* pp. 181–182, 368, and passim.

7. Report of the House Select Committee on Claims, 17 January 1797, in *Jackson Papers,* vol. 1, pp. 113–148 n; Remini, *Jackson,* p. 97.

8. McNairy to Jackson, 4 May 1797, Jackson to McNairy, 12 May 1797, Jackson to McNairy, 12 May 1797, Jackson to Cocke, 9 November 1797, 24 June 1798 (2 letters), Cocke to Jackson, 25 June 1798, Jackson to Cocke, 25 June 1798, in *Jackson Papers,* vol. 1, pp. 133–135 n. 4, 138–140, 143–144, 152–153 n. 3, 199–204 n. 2.

9. Agreement with John Overton, 12 May 1794, Overton to Jackson, 8 March 1795, Agreement with Joel Rice, 5 April 1795, Agreement with David Allison, 14 May 1795, Account of Freight Expenses from Philadelphia, May–August 1795, Samuel Donelson to Jackson, 29 June 1795, Meeker, Cochrane & Company to Jackson, 11 August 1795, John B. Evans & Company to Jackson, 4 January 1796, in ibid., pp. 46–48, 54–60, 62–64, 79; Remini, *Jackson,* has a good discussion of this sorry affair.

10. *Jackson Papers,* vol. 1, p. 79 n. 1; Remini, *Jackson,* pp. 89–90.

11. Parton, *Jackson,* vol. 1, p. 219; Dumas Malone, *Jefferson and His Time,* 6 vols. (Boston: Little, Brown, 1981), vol. 6, pp. 436–437; for an interesting assessment of Webster as a source, see Arthur Schlesinger Jr., *The Age of Jackson* (Boston: Little, Brown, 1945), p. 37, esp. n. 11.

12. Jefferson to Jackson, 18 December 1823, in John Spencer Bassett, *The Life of Andrew Jackson,* 2 vols. in 1 (1931; reprint, n.p.: Archon Books, 1967), p. 329; Parton, *Jackson,* vol. 1, pp. 219–220.

13. Jackson to Robertson, 11 January 1798, in *Jackson Papers,* vol. 1, p. 165.

14. Jackson to Sevier, 18 January 1797, Sevier to Jackson 29 January 1797, in ibid., p. 117; readers interested in the naval war with France, which was in general over the rights of neutrals on the high seas, can turn to Alexander de Conde, *The Quasi-War: The Politics and Diplomacy of the Undeclared Naval War with France, 1797–1801* (New York: Scribner's, 1996).

15. Claiborne to Jackson, 20 July 1797, in *Jackson Papers,* vol. 1, p. 147.

16. Remini, *Jackson,* pp. 112–114, 441 n. 110; Sevier to Jackson, 29 January 1798, Interim Appointment as Superior Court Judge, 20 September 1798, Commission as Superior Court Judge, 22 December 1798, in *Jackson Papers,* vol. 1, pp. 209–210, 215.

17. Parton, *Jackson,* p. 227, for quotations in this paragraph, and 166–168, 228–229, for the Russell Bean story and quotations; Remini, *Jackson,* pp. 114–115.

18. Jackson Statement Regarding Land Frauds, 16 December 1797, encl. in a letter, Alexander Martin to Samuel Ashe, 7 December 1797, in *Jackson Papers,* vol. 1, pp. 157–158 n. 2. In his statement, Jackson identified his informant as John Love, but he was almost certainly mistaken: see Jackson to Samuel Ashe, 10 February 1798, and Charles Love to Jackson, 31 January 1798, in the foregoing source, pp. 179–180.

19. Jackson to John Overton, 22 January 1798, in ibid., p. 169; Remini, *Jackson,* pp. 118–119, for a discussion of Sevier's involvement.

20. David Campbell to Jackson, 25 January 1802, in *Jackson Papers,* pp. 273–274.

21. Election Returns of the Mero District for Major General of Tennessee Militia, Jackson to Sevier, 27 March 1802, Commission as Major General, 1 April 1802, *Jackson Papers,* pp. 277 n. 1, 290–292; Remini, *Jackson,* pp. 119–120.

22. Remini, *Jackson,* pp. 120–121; Parton, *Jackson,* p. 233.

23. My description of the clashes between Jackson and Sevier in this and the following paragraphs is based on Remini, *Jackson,* pp. 121–124.

24. Folmsbee et al., *History of Tennessee,* vol. 1, p. 240; Remini, ibid., pp. 123–124.

25. Ames to Christopher Gore, 16 November 1803, in Seth Ames, *Works of Fisher Ames,* 2 vols., ed. and enl. by W. B. Allen (1854; reprint, Indianapolis: Liberty Classics, 1983), vol. 2, p. 1471.

26. Leaving aside the tiresome affair of Sally Hemings, for a clear, concise, convincing defense of Jefferson, see Bernard Bailyn's review of Conor Cruise O'Brien's polemic, *The Long Affair: Thomas Jefferson and the French Revolution, 1785–1800,* in the *Times Literary Supplement,* 15 November 1996, pp. 3–4.

27. For a brief, authoritative discussion of Jefferson's Indian policy, see Reginald Horsman, *Expansion and American Indian Policy, 1783–1812* (1967; reprint, Norman: University of Oklahoma Press, 1992), ch. 7, and p. 109 for the quotation; for book-length studies see Bernard W. Sheehan, *Seeds of Extinction: Jeffersonian Philanthropy and the American Indian* (1973; reprint, New York: Norton, 1974) and Anthony F. C. Wallace, *Jefferson and the Indians: The Tragic Fate of the First Americans* (Cambridge, Mass.: Harvard University Press, 1999).

28. Jefferson to Harrison, 27 February 1803, in Thomas Jefferson, *Writings* (New York: Library of America, 1984), pp. 1118–1119.

29. Ibid., p. 1119.

30. Ibid., p. 1120.

31. Livingston to James Madison, 13 April 1803, in Henry Adams, *History of the United States of America during the Administrations of Thomas Jefferson* (1903; reprint, New York: Library of America, 1986), p. 320; Jefferson to John Colvin, 20 September 1810, in Joseph J. Ellis, *American Sphinx: The Character of Thomas Jefferson* (New York: Knopf, 1997), p. 208. For the details of the Louisiana Purchase see Adams, *History of the United States of America during the Administrations of Thomas Jefferson,* pp. 269–364, and passim, and Alexander DeConde, *This Affair of Louisiana* (New York: Scribner's, 1976); for a brief but excellent discussion of the Mississippi crisis of 1801–1803, culminating in the Purchase, see Drew R. McCoy, *The Elusive Republic: Political Economy in Jeffersonian America* (1980; reprint, New York: Norton, 1982), pp. 196–198.

32. Adams, *History of the United States of America during the Administrations of Thomas Jefferson,* p. 331.

33. Jefferson to John C. Breckenridge, 12 December 1803, in Jefferson, *Writings,* p. 1137; Turreau to Talleyrand, 27 January 1805, in Adams, *History of the United States of America during the Administrations of Thomas Jefferson,* p. 486.

34. See Bradford Perkins, *Prologue to War: England and the United States, 1805–1812* (Berkeley: University of California Press, 1968), p. 39, for the constitutional question.

35. Jackson to Jefferson, 7 August 1803, in *Jackson Papers,* vol. 1, p. 354; Remini, *Jackson,* pp. 126–127.

36. Jackson to John Coffee, 28 April 1804, in *Jackson Papers,* vol. 2, p. 19; Remini, *Jackson,* p. 128.

37. Jackson to George Washington Campbell, 28 April 1804, in *Jackson Papers,* vol. 2, pp. 18–19; Thomas Perkins Abernethy, *The South in the New Nation, 1789–1819* (Baton Rouge: Louisiana State University Press, 1961), p. 263.

38. Remini, *Jackson,* pp. 128–129.

CHAPTER 11. CONSPIRACY AND BLOOD

1. Remini, *Jackson,* pp. 129–133, and passim has clear discussions of Jackson's business interests at this and other periods of his life; Lorman A. Ratner, *Andrew Jackson and His Tennessee Lieutenants: A Study in Political Culture* (Westport: Conn.: Greenwood Press, 1997), pp. 41–42, is useful for biographical data on men close to Jackson.

2. Parton, *Jackson,* vol. 1, pp. 238–239.

3. James Parton, *The Life and Times of Aaron Burr,* 2 vols., enl. ed. (Boston: Ticknor & Fields, 1867), vol. 2, pp. 419–420; Pickett, *Alabama,* vol. 1, p. 223.

4. Parton, *Life and Times of Aaron Burr,* p. 420.

5. Hamilton to John Steele, 15 October 1792, in Harold C. Syrett, ed., *The Papers of Alexander Hamilton* (New York: Columbia University Press, 1979), vol. 12, p. 568.

6. Milton Lomask, *Aaron Burr: The Conspiracy and Years of Exile, 1805–1836* (New York: Farrar, Straus & Giroux, 1982), p. xiii.

7. Anthony Merry to Lord Harrowby, 6 August 1804, in Aaron Burr, *Political Correspondence and Public Papers of Aaron Burr,* ed. Mary-Jo Kline et al., 2 vols. (Princeton, N.J.: Princeton University Press, 1983), vol. 2, p. 883, for Burr quote, p. 891 for Merry's letter.

8. Merry to Lord Harrowby, 29 March 1805, in ibid., p. 928.

9. Jackson to William Charles Cole Claiborne, 12 November 1806, Jackson to Daniel Smith, 12 November 1806, in *Jackson Papers,* vol. 2, pp. 115–119; Burr to Harrison, 27 November 1806, in *Political Correspondence and Public Papers of Aaron Burr,* vol. 2, pp. 1005–1006; Thomas Perkins Abernethy, *The Burr Conspiracy* (New York: Oxford University Press, 1954), pp. 24, 27–28.

10. Anonymous to Jefferson, 1 December and 5 December 1805, in Abernethy, *The Burr Conspiracy,* pp. 38–39.

11. For interested readers, there are two book-length studies of the Burr Conspiracy: Thomas Perkins Abernethy's *The Burr Conspiracy* (see n. 10), and Walter Flavius McCaleb, *The Aaron Burr Conspiracy and a New Light on Aaron Burr,* rev. ed. (New York: n.p., 1966); see also Henry Adams, *History of the United States of America during the Administrations of Thomas Jefferson*

(1903; reprint, New York: Library of America, 1986), pp. 754–839, and Lomask, *Aaron Burr* (see n. 6 for full citation).

12. *Political Correspondence and Public Papers of Aaron Burr,* vol. 2, p. 936 n. 4; Parton, *Jackson,* vol. 1, p. 316.

13. Abernethy, *The Burr Conspiracy,* p. 28; Burr to Jackson, 24 March 1806, in *Jackson Papers,* pp. 92–93 n. 4.

14. *Political Correspondence and Public Papers of Aaron Burr,* vol. 2, p. 996 n. 1; Accounts with Aaron Burr, 1806, Order to Brigadier Generals of the 2nd Division, 4 October 1806, Jackson to Winchester, 4 October 1806, in *Jackson Papers,* vol. 2, pp. 110–114, 121–125.

15. Jackson to Jefferson, 5 November 1806, Jefferson to Jackson, 3 December 1806, in *Jackson Papers,* vol. 2, pp. 114–115, 121.

16. Jackson to George Washington Campbell, 15 January 1807, in ibid., pp. 148–149.

17. Jackson to Campbell, Jackson to Claiborne, 12 November 1806, in ibid., p. 116.

18. Abernethy, *The Burr Conspiracy,* pp. 221–222; *Political Correspondence and Public Papers of Aaron Burr,* vol. 2, pp. 1025–1027.

19. Jackson to William Preston Anderson, 17 June 1807, Testimony before the Grand Jury in the Case of Aaron Burr, 25 June 1807, in *Jackson Papers,* vol. 2, pp. 167–169.

20. Ibid., pp. 164–166; Parton, *Jackson,* vol. 1, pp. 333–334; Remini, *Jackson,* pp. 147–159, for an overview of Jackson's involvement.

21. Memorandum of Agreement with John Verell for the Purchase of Truxton, 11 March 1805, editorial notes, Affadavit of Joseph Erwin re Forfeit in the Truxton-Ploughboy Race, 2 January 1806, in *Jackson Papers,* vol. 2, pp. 56–57, 77–79; Parton, *Jackson,* vol. 1, pp. 267–268; Remini, *Jackson,* p. 136.

22. Editorial Notes, *Jackson Papers,* vol. 2, pp. 77–78; Parton, *Jackson,* pp. 268–269.

23. Swann Narrative, in Parton, *Jackson,* pp. 270–271; Swann to Jackson, 3 January 1806, in *Jackson Papers,* vol. 2, p. 78.

24. Jackson to Swann, 7 January 1806, in *Jackson Papers,* vol. 2, pp. 79–82; Dickinson to Jackson, 10 January 1806.

25. Swann to Jackson 12 January 1806, in ibid., pp. 82–83 n. 2; Remini, *Jackson,* pp. 137–138; Parton, *Jackson,* vol. 1, pp. 273–274, for Swann's version.

26. Parton, pp. 269–274, for Swann's statement.

27. Robertson to Jackson, 1 February 1806, in *Jackson Papers,* vol. 2, pp. 83–84.

28. Parton, *Jackson,* vol. 1, pp. 276–285.

29. Ibid., pp. 286–287.

30. Robert Purdy's account, in ibid., pp. 287–288.

31. Charles Dickinson to Thomas Eastin, 21 May 1806, Jackson to Dickinson, 23 May 1806, in *Jackson Papers.,* vol. 2, pp. 97–98; ibid., pp. 290–292.

32. Parton, *Jackson,* p. 295.

33. Arrangements of Thomas Overton and Hanson Catlett for Duel, 23 May 1806, in *Jackson Papers,* vol. 2, pp. 99–100; unless otherwise indicated, ibid., pp. 295–296, and also 297–306, for the details of the duel and all quotations in the following paragraphs to the end of the chapter.

34. For the terrible effects of this wound and others on Jackson's physical condition during the rest of his life see Robert V. Remini, *Andrew Jackson and the Course of American Freedom, 1822–1832* (New York: Harper & Row, 1981), pp. 1–3.

CHAPTER 12. OLD HICKORY

1. Isaac Brock to Lord Liverpool, 29 August 1812, in William Wood, ed., *Select British Documents of the Canadian War of 1812,* 3 vols. (Toronto: Champlain Society, 1920), vol. 1, p. 508.

2. Original sources for Tecumseh's southern trip are almost nonexistent. The best discussions are by nineteenth-century writers, especially H. S. Halbert and T. H. Ball, *The Creek War of 1813–1814,* ed. Frank L. Owsley Jr. (1895; reprint, Tuscaloosa: University of Alabama Press, 1995), pp. 40–84, which I have largely followed; see also *Woodward's Reminiscences,* passim; Pickett, *Alabama,* vol. 2, pp. 240–254; the best modern discussions are Frank L. Owsley Jr., *Struggle for the Gulf Borderlands: The Creek War and the Battle of New Orleans, 1812–1815* (Gaines-

ville: University Presses of Florida, 1981), pp. 11–17; John A. Sugden, *Tecumseh: A Life* (New York, Henry Holt, 1998), pp. 237–251; and my choice for the best book on Tecumseh, David R. Edmunds, *Tecumseh and the Quest for Indian Leadership* (Boston: Little, Brown, 1984), pp. 146–153, 219–220, whose learned "Note on Sources" guided my selection of materials. In my own discussion of the southern trip I have only cited quotations and works not listed above.

3. H&B, *Creek War,* pp. 42–43.

4. Hawkins's quotation is in Claudio Saunt, " 'Domestick . . . Quite being broke:' Gender Conflict among Creek Indians in the Eighteenth Century," in Andrew L. Clayton and Frederika J. Teute, eds., *Contact Points: American Frontiers from the Mohawk Valley to the Mississippi, 1750–1830* (Chapel Hill: University of North Carolina Press, 1998), pp. 163–164.

5. Henry DeLeon Southerland Jr. and Jerry Elijah Brown, *The Federal Road through Georgia, the Creek Nation, and Alabama, 1806–1836,* 2nd ed. (Tuscaloosa: University of Alabama Press, 1989), p. 2 and passim; Reginald Horsman, *Expansion and American Indian Policy, 1783–1812* (1967; reprint, Norman: University of Oklahoma Press, 1992), pp. 160–164; Claudio Saunt, *A New Order of Things: Property, Power, and the Transformation of the Creek Indians, 1733–1816* (Cambridge, U.K.: Cambridge University Press, 1999), pp. 216–217, 235.

6. Pickett, *Alabama,* vol. 2, pp. 242–243.

7. John Francis Hamtramck Claiborne, *Life and Times of General Sam Dale, the Mississippi Partisan* (New York: Harper & Brothers, 1860), pp. 55–61; for opposing views, see H&B, *Creek War,* pp. 69–73, and Benjamin W. Griffith Jr., *McIntosh and Weatherford, Creek Indian Leaders* (Tuscaloosa: University of Alabama Press, 1988), pp. 74–77; cf., however, Owsley, *Borderlands,* pp. 12–13.

8. For a brief discussion of the causes of the war see the excellent Donald R. Hickey, *The War of 1812: A Forgotten Conflict* (Urbana: University of Illinois Press, 1990), pp. 5–28.

9. Division Orders, 7 March 1812, in *Jackson Papers,* vol. 2, pp. 290–293.

10. Willie Blount to Jackson, 21 July 1812, William Eustis to Willie Blount, 11 July 1812, The Massacre at the Mouth of Duck River, 7 July 1812, in *Jackson Papers,* vol. 2, pp. 310–311, 315–317; Remini, *Jackson,* pp. 169–170; Owsley, *Borderlands,* p. 15.

11. Jackson to Willie Blount, 8 July 1812, Willie Blount to Jackson, 21 July 1812, Division Orders, 31 July 1812, *Jackson Papers,* vol. 2, pp. 312–313, 315–318.

12. Remini, *Jackson,* pp. 170–171; Jackson to Willie Blount, 11 November 1812, in ibid., pp. 336–338 n. 3.

13. In addition to standard biographical dictionaries for Coffee, see Gordon T. Chappell, "The Life and Activities of General John Coffee," Ph.D. diss., Vanderbilt University, 1941; for Carroll and Lewis, Lorman A. Ratner, *Andrew Jackson and His Tennessee Lieutenants: A Study in Political Culture* (Westport, Conn.: Greenwood Press, 1997), contains biographical data; R&E, *Jackson,* has biographical information on Reid.

14. Thomas Hart Benton to Jackson, 9 January 1813, Jackson to Rachel, 8 January 1813, in *Jackson Papers,* vol. 2, pp. 353–356; Jackson to William Eustis, 7 January 1813, in Parton, *Jackson,* vol. 1, p. 372.

15. Parton, *Jackson,* p. 373; Dawson A. Phelps, ed., "The Diary of a Chaplain in Andrew Jackson's Army: The Journal of the Reverend Mr. Learner Blackman—December 28, 1812—April 4, 1813," *Tennessee Historical Quarterly* 12:3 (September 1953), pp. 269 n. 14, 271–272.

16. Wilkinson to Jackson, 22 January 1813, 22 February 1813, Armstrong to Jackson, 6 February 1813, in *Jackson Papers,* vol. 2, pp. 358–359, 361, 371–372.

17. Wilkinson to Armstrong, 9 March 1813, Colonel Covington to Wilkinson, 15 March 1813, in C. Edward Skeen, *John Armstrong, Jr., 1748–1843: A Biography* (Syracuse, N.Y.: Syracuse University Press, 1981), p. 31; Parton, *Jackson,* vol. 1, p. 378; Jackson to Armstrong, 15 March 1813, in *Jackson Papers,* vol. 2, pp. 383–385 n. 3.

18. Skeen, *John Armstrong,* pp. 156–157; Parton, *Jackson,* pp. 377–380.

19. Jackson to Felix Grundy, 15 March 1813, Jackson to William Berkeley Lewis, 9 April 1813, in *Jackson Papers,* vol. 2, pp. 385–386, 401–402.

20. Jackson to Ferdinand Leigh Claiborne, 25 March 1813, for the date of departure, Jackson to Rachel, 15 March 1813, in ibid., pp. 387, 389; Parton, *Jackson,* vol. 1, pp. 381–383.

21. Parton, *Jackson,* vol. 1, pp. 381–383.

22. Ibid., p. 384.

23. Benton to Jackson, 15 June 1813, in *Jackson Papers,* vol. 2, p. 406. Benton's account of his maneuvering is in Parton, *Jackson,* pp. 384–386; Remini, *Jackson,* p. 182.

24. My discussion of this affair and what followed is based on Parton, *Jackson,* pp. 386–398; Remini, *Jackson,* pp. 180–186; Andrew Hynes to Jackson, 16 July 1813, Jackson to Thomas Hart Benton, 19 July 1813, Benton to Jackson, 25 July 1813, Jackson to Benton, 4 August 1813, Affidavit of Felix Robertson, 5 August 1813, Jackson to John M. Armstrong, 9 August 1813, Benton to the Public, 10 September 1813, James Robertson to Jackson, 16 September 1813, in *Jackson Papers,* vol. 2, pp. 411–415, 418–428. Only quotations are separately cited.

25. Jackson to John M. Armstrong, 19 August 1813, in *Jackson Papers,* vol. 2, p. 424.

26. Parton, *Jackson,* vol. 1, p. 390.

27. Ibid., p. 392.

28. Ibid., p. 393.

29. My discussion of the gunfight draws on ibid., pp. 393–394, 397–398, and Remini, *Jackson,* p. 185.

30. Parton, *Jackson,* p. 395.

CHAPTER 13. MASSACRE

1. Pickett, *Alabama,* vol. 2, p. 252; Owsley, *Borderlands,* pp. 14–15; George Stiggins, *Creek Indian History: A Historical Narrative of the Genealogy, Traditions and Downfall of the Ispocoga or Creek Indian Tribe of Indians,* ed. Virginia Pounds Brown (Birmingham, Ala.: Birmingham Public Library Press, 1989), pp. 91–93.

2. Stiggins, *Creek History,* pp. 161–162 n. 83; Deposition of Samuel S. M. Manac, 2 August 1813, in H&B, *Creek War,* p. 92.

3. Hawkins to William Eustis, 6 April 1812, 25 May 1812, in *ASPIA,* vol. 1, p. 813; Owsley, *Borderlands,* p. 15.

4. Editorial note and Thomas Johnson to Jackson, 27 May 1812, in *Jackson Papers,* vol. 2, pp. 297–299; William Henry to John J. Henry, 26 June 1812, in *ASPIA,* vol. 1, p. 814.

5. Henry to Henry, 26 June 1812.

6. Hawkins to Chiefs of the Upper Creeks, in *ASPIA,* vol. 1, p. 839.

7. Big Warrior, Alexander Cornells, and William McIntosh to Hawkins, 21 April 1813 [misdated 4/26], in ibid.

8. Nimrod Doyle to Hawkins, 13 May 1813, in ibid., p. 843.

9. Ibid.

10. Ibid., p. 844.

11. Big Warrior to Hawkins, 26 April 1813, in ibid., p. 843.

12. Hawkins to John Armstrong, 28 July 1813, in ibid., pp. 849–850.

13. Ibid., p. 850.

14. Ibid.

15. Michael D. Green, *The Politics of Indian Removal: Creek Government and Society in Crisis* (1982; reprint, Lincoln: University of Nebraska Press, 1985), pp. 41–42; *Woodward's Reminiscences,* pp. 83–84.

16. Owsley, *Borderlands,* p. 17; Stiggins, *Creek History,* pp. 88–90, 93–94.

17. Green, *Politics of Indian Removal,* pp. 39–40.

18. Hawkins to Big Warrior, 24 April 1813, in *ASPIA,* vol. 1, p. 842.

19. Big Warrior to Hawkins, 26 April 1813, in ibid., p. 843.

20. Stiggins, *Creek History,* pp. 94–95, 160 n. 78.

21. Ibid., pp. 95–96.

22. This and the preceding paragraph are based on the thorough discussion in Owsley, *Borderlands,* pp. 26–29; see also Joseph Carson to Ferdinand Leigh Claiborne, 29 July 1813, TSLA Miscellaneous Files, IV-K-I, B-1, Acc. No. 879 (typescript); Hawkins to John Armstrong, 23 August 1813, in *ASPIA,* vol. 1, p. 851, for Little Warrior's letter.

23. My discussion of the action at Burnt Corn Creek is based on Pickett, *Alabama,* vol. 2, pp. 256–260; H&B, *Creek War,* pp. 125–142 (p. 130 for Caller's description); Stiggins, *Creek History,* pp. 98–103, 161 n. 83; *Woodward's Reminiscences,* p. 85; Owsley, *Borderlands,* pp. 30–33; only quotations are cited separately.

24. Pickett, *Alabama,* vol. 2, p. 260.

25. My discussion of Fort Mims and the Red Sticks is based on ibid., pp. 264–284; Stiggins, *Creek History,* 103–114; *Woodward's Reminiscences,* pp. 80–81, 85–86; Owsley, *Borderlands,* pp. 33–41; H&B, *Creek War,* pp. 143–176; only quotations are cited separately.

26. Pickett, *Alabama,* vol. 2, p. 266, for Claiborne's orders.

27. Stiggins, *Creek History,* pp. 103–106; ibid., pp. 267–268.

28. Beasley to Claiborne, 30 August 1813, in Owsley, *Borderlands,* pp. 35–36.

29. H&B, *Creek War,* p. 152; *Woodward's Reminiscences,* p. 86.

30. Stiggins, *Creek History,* p. 110.

31. Pickett, *Alabama,* vol. 2, pp. 273–275; Report of Benjamin Hawkins, 17 September 1813, in *ASPIA,* vol. 1, p. 853.

32. Stiggins, *Creek History,* p. 113.

33. Pickett, *Alabama,* vol. 2, pp. 282–283.

CHAPTER 14. "TIME IS NOT TO BE LOST"

1. Parton, *Jackson,* vol. 1, p. 422, establishes the date, and vol. 3, pp. 610–612, prints the Parsons Ms., from which my account and the quotations are taken.

2. Robertson to Jackson, 16 September 1813, *Jackson Papers,* vol. 2, p. 427.

3. To the Tennessee Volunteers, 24 September 1813, in ibid., pp. 428–429.

4. Jackson to Leroy Pope, 31 October 1813, in ibid., p. 443.

5. The words are those of that splendid Swiss soldier Colonel Henri Bouquet, from an earlier war, in William Smith, *Historical Account of Bouquet's Expedition against the Ohio Indians in 1764,* Ohio Valley Historical Series 1 (1765; reprint, Cincinnati: Robert Clarke, 1868), p. 19.

6. Wiley Sword, *President Washington's Indian Wars: The Struggle for the Old Northwest, 1790–1795* (1985; reprint, Norman: University of Oklahoma Press, 1993), pp. 89–119, 159–195 for the Harmar and St. Clair campaigns, and pp. 183, 186 for the quotations; Richard H. Kohn, *Eagle and Sword: The Federalists and the Creation of the Military Establishment in America, 1783–1802* (New York: Free Press, 1975, pp. 115–116, and passim; Francis Paul Prucha, *The Sword of the Republic: The United States Army on the Frontier, 1783–1846* (New York: Macmillan, 1969), pp. 24–26, and passim.

7. Quimby, *The U.S. Army in the War of 1812: An Operational and Command Study,* 2 vols. (Lansing: Michigan State University Press, 1997), vol. 1, pp. 131–138, has a very clear account of Winchester's debacle; see also Harry L. Coles, *The War of 1812* (Chicago: University of Chicago Press, 1966), pp. 112–117; Statement of American Officers, 20 February 1813, in John Brannan, ed., *Official Letters of the Military and Naval Officers of the United States, during the War with Great Britain in the Years 1812, 13, 14 & 15* (n.p.: 1823), p. 135.

8. Karl von Clausewitz, *The Campaign of 1812 in Russia* (London: John Murray, 1843), p. 185, for this paragraph and the next.

9. Jackson to Coffee, 29 September 1813, in *Jackson Papers,* vol. 2, pp. 431–432.

10. Owsley, *Borderlands,* p. 62.

11. For example, Thomas D. Clark and John D. W. Guice, *The Old Southwest, 1795–1830: Frontiers in Conflict* (1989; reprint, Norman: University of Oklahoma Press, 1996), pp. 137, 139, and passim.

12. Clausewitz, *Campaign of 1812 in Russia,* pp. 252–260, with the quotations on pp. 255–256.

13. Coffee to Donelson, 22 December 1813, John Coffee Papers, MF678, Reel 2, Box 2, C-116.

14. R&E, *Jackson,* p. 77 n.

15. Jackson to Coffee, 17 October 1813, Jackson to Rachel, 11 October 1813 and 13 October 1813, in *Jackson Papers,* vol. 2, pp. 435–437.

16. Coffee to Jackson, 22 October 1813, in ibid., pp. 438–439.

17. Ibid.

18. R&E, *Jackson,* p. 39; *Jackson Papers,* p. 440 n. 5; Jackson to Chennebee, 19 October 1813, quoted in Remini, *Jackson,* p. 193.

19. R&E, *Jackson,* pp. 39–40.

20. Ibid., p. 40; *Jackson Papers,* p. 441 n. 1; Remini, *Jackson,* p. 192; Owsley, *Borderlands,* 64.

21. Coffee to Mary Coffee, 24 October 1813, Coffee Papers, MF814, Reel 5, Box 13, Folder 2; Jackson to Flournoy, 24 October 1813, in *Jackson Papers,* vol. 2, p. 441.

22. Jackson to Willie Blount, 28 October 1813, in *Jackson Papers,* vol. 2, p. 442.

23. Pathkiller to Jackson, 22 October 1813, in ibid., pp. 439–440; R&E, *Jackson,* p. 41.

24. Pathkiller to Jackson, 22 October 1813.

25. Jackson to Pathkiller, 23 October 1813, in *Jackson Papers,* vol. 2, pp. 440–441.

26. Jackson to Lewis, 24 October 1813, quoted in Remini, *Jackson,* p. 192.

27. R&E, *Jackson,* pp. 46–47, 49.

28. Ibid., pp. 49–50, for the quotations in this paragraph and the previous one.

29. David Crockett, *Life of David Crockett* (New York: n.p., 1854), p. 75.

30. Call's "Journal," quoted in Herbert J. Doherty Jr. and Richard Keith Call, *Southern Unionist* (Gainesville: University Presses of Florida, 1961), p. 6.

31. Jackson to Rachel, 4 November 1813, *Jackson Papers,* vol. 2, p. 444; Jackson to Willie Blount, 4 November 1813, quoted in Remini, *Jackson,* p. 193.

32. Alex Donelson to John Donelson, 5 November 1813, THS Miscellaneous Files, MF678, Reel 3, D-72; Jackson to Rachel, 4 November 1813, in *Jackson Papers,* vol. 2, p. 444; Owsley, *Borderlands,* p. 65; Remini, *Jackson,* pp. 193–194.

33. R&E, *Jackson,* pp. 52–53.

34. Ibid.; Pickett, *Alabama,* vol. 2, pp. 295–296; *Woodward's Reminiscences,* p. 101; Jackson to Rachel, in *Jackson Papers,* vol. 2, p. 448.

35. R&E, *Jackson,* pp. 54–55; Pickett, *Alabama,* vol. 2, p. 296; Jackson to John Lowry, 7 November 1813, Jackson to Rachel, 12 November 1813, in *Jackson Papers,* vol. 2, pp. 446, 448.

36. James White to Jackson, 7 November 1813, Jackson to Rachel, 12 November 1813, in *Jackson Papers,* vol. 2, pp. 448–449.

37. R&E, *Jackson,* p. 55; Cocke to White, 6 November 1813, quoted in Parton, *Jackson,* vol. 1, pp. 451; *Jackson Papers,* vol. 2, p. 449 n. 5.

38. Parton, ibid., pp. 448–452; Quimby, *U.S. Army,* vol. 1, pp. 408–409, 413–414.

39. R&E, *Jackson,* pp. 55–56.

40. Ibid., pp. 56–57; Jackson to Rachel, 12 November 1813, in *Jackson Papers,* vol. 2, p. 449.

41. R&E, *Jackson,* p. 57.

42. Ibid.

43. Ibid., p. 58; Jackson to Rachel, 12 November 1813, in *Jackson Papers,* vol. 2, p. 449.

44. Jackson to Rachel, 12 November 1813.

CHAPTER 15. MUTINY

1. R&E, *Jackson,* p. 60; Jackson to Rachel, 12 November 1813, in *Jackson Papers,* vol. 2, p. 448.

2. R&E, *Jackson,* pp. 60–62; Jackson to Willie Blount, 14 November 1813, in *Jackson Papers,* vol. 2, pp. 453–454.

3. R&E, *Jackson,* pp. 61, 63–66, and editor's notes, n. 49, p. xxvii; *Jackson Papers,* vol. 2, p. 453.

4. R&E, *Jackson,* p. 67.

5. Grierson to Jackson, 13–15 November 1813, in *Jackson Papers,* vol. 2, pp. 451–452.

6. Jackson to Grierson, 17 November 1813, in ibid., pp. 456–457.

7. Willie Blount to Jackson, 24 November 1813, in ibid., p. 461.

8. R&E, *Jackson,* p. 68.

9. Ibid., pp. 68–70; Parton, *Jackson,* vol. 1, p. 463.

10. R&E, *Jackson,* p. 70; Owsley, *Borderlands,* p. 69.

11. R&E, *Jackson,* pp. 70–71.

12. For this paragraph and the two following see Jackson to Cocke, 16 November 1813, 18 November 1813, Grierson to Jackson, 13–15 November 1813, Jackson to Grierson, 17

November 1813, Cocke to Jackson, 27 November 1813, and editorial comment in *Jackson Papers,* vol. 2, pp. 451–452, 454–458, 461–462; Parton, *Jackson,* vol. 1, p. 453; Quimby, *U.S. Army,* vol. 1, pp. 414–416.

13. R&E, *Jackson,* pp. 72–73.

14. Ibid., p. 73; Carroll to Jackson, 20 November 1813, in *Jackson Papers,* vol. 2, pp. 458–459.

15. Stiggins, *Creek History,* p. 115.

16. Ibid., pp. 122–124.

17. The curious name is thought to be the Creek rendition of New York, where Alexander McGillivray and other Creek leaders in 1790 signed the Treaty of New York with the United States.

18. David Adams to Peter Early, 24 December 1813, Georgia Military Affairs, vol. 3, 1801–1813 (typescript); Thomas Pinckney to Jackson, 29 November 1813, in *Jackson Papers,* vol. 2, p. 463; Owsley, *Borderlands,* pp. 51–52.

19. Floyd to Mary Floyd, 18 November 1813, John Floyd Letters; Owsley, *Borderlands,* p. 54; Stiggins, *Creek History,* p. 123; Griffith, *McIntosh and Weatherford,* p. 124; Rabbi A. J. Messing Jr., " 'Old Mordecai'—the Founder of the City of Montgomery," *Publications of the American Jewish Historical Society* 13 (1905), p. 79.

20. Floyd to Mary Floyd, 5 December 1813, John Floyd Letters; Stiggins, *Creek History,* p. 125.

21. Ibid.

22. For the battle, unless otherwise indicated, see ibid., pp. 124–127; Pickett, *Alabama,* vol. 2, pp. 300–303; Owsley, *Borderlands,* pp. 54–55; Griffith, *McIntosh and Weatherford,* pp. 125–126.

23. Peter A. Brannon, ed., "Journal of James A. Tait for the Year 1813," *Georgia Historical Quarterly* 8 (1924), pp. 234–235; Floyd to Mary Floyd, 5 December 1813, John Floyd Letters.

24. Floyd to Mary Floyd, 5 December 1813.

25. Owsley, *Borderlands,* p. 45; C. Edward Skeen, *John Armstrong, Jr., 1758–1843: A Biography* (Syracuse, N.Y.: Syracuse University Press, 1981), pp. 172–173, 175–176.

26. Pickett, *Alabama,* vol. 2, p. 314; John Francis Hamtramck Claiborne, *Life and Times of General Sam Dale, the Mississippi Partisan* (New York: Harper & Brothers, 1860), pp. 36–43.

27. Claiborne, *Life and Times of General Sam Dale,* p. 36.

28. *Woodward's Reminiscences,* p. 76.

29. Pickett, *Alabama,* vol. 2, p. 315.

30. Ibid., pp. 306–312. Unless otherwise indicated, I have followed the account in Pickett, from whom all the quotations are taken; he had it firsthand from a participant, Jeremiah Austill, and an eyewitness, Gerard W. Creagh. *Woodward's Reminiscences,* often highly critical and at times directly contradictory of Pickett's accounts, states, "The Canoe Fight was reality—I knew all the party . . ." (p. 75). Quimby, *U.S. Army,* vol. 1, pp. 400–402, has a somewhat different account that even enhances Dale's role and that I find suspect, although there are discrepancies in the various accounts that all writers must deal with. Quimby's evaluation of the Great Canoe Fight—"it proved to be the turning point in the war"—should not be taken seriously.

31. H&B, *Creek War,* pp. 201, 237, for Austill's early years and the ride.

32. Ibid., pp. 241–246.

33. Unless otherwise indicated, I have followed for these particulars and the ensuing action at the Holy Ground the following sources: Stiggins, *Creek History,* pp. 116–121; H&B, *Creek War,* pp. 264–261; Pickett, *Alabama,* vol. 2, pp. 322–325; Owsley, *Borderlands,* pp. 46–48; Griffith, *McIntosh and Weatherford,* pp. 128–132; *Woodward's Reminiscences,* pp. 87–88; for a general and sympathetic analysis of Josiah Francis and his magic see Gregory Evans Dowd, *A Spirited Resistance: The North American Indian Struggle for Unity, 1754–1815* (Baltimore: Johns Hopkins University Press, 1992), pp. 186–187.

34. The best discussion of the different versions of Weatherford's escape is in Griffith, *McIntosh and Weatherford,* pp. 129–131.

35. H&B, *Creek War,* p. 257, for the scalp pole; Owsley, *Borderlands,* p. 48, for the governor's quotation.

36. See Pickett, *Alabama,* vol. 2, pp. 325–328, for the condition of Claiborne's army, Russell's movements, and the incident of the horses; and Owsley, *Borderlands,* for an interesting discussion of Russell's march and its possibilities.

37. R&E, *Jackson,* p. 73; Jackson to Gideon Blackburn, 3 December 1813, in *Jackson Papers,* vol. 2, p. 464.

38. R&E, *Jackson,* pp. 73–74.

39. Ibid., p. 74; Jackson to Blackburn, 3 December 1813, in *Jackson Papers,* vol. 2, pp. 464–465.

40. Jackson to Cocke, 6 December 1813, in *Jackson Papers,* vol. 2, pp. 469–470, and p. 465 for James Fife being his informant.

41. Jackson to Rachel, in ibid., p. 478; R&E, *Jackson,* p. 83.

42. R&E, *Jackson,* pp. 84–85; *Jackson Papers,* vol. 2, p. 480 n. 1.

43. Jackson to Rachel, 14 December 1813, in *Jackson Papers,* vol. 2, p. 486.

44. R&E, *Jackson,* p. 85; Jackson to Rachel, 14 December 1813.

45. Jackson to Willie Blount, 15 December 1813, in *Jackson Papers,* vol. 2, p. 488.

46. Jackson to John Armstrong, 16 December 1813, in ibid., p. 493; R&E, *Jackson,* p. 90; Coffee to Jackson, 20 December 1813, quoted in Remini, *Jackson,* p. 202.

47. R&E, *Jackson,* pp. 99, 112–113; Remini, *Jackson,* pp. 202–203.

48. R&E, *Jackson,* p. 101.

49. A. L. Rowse, *Memories of Men and Women* (Lanham, Md.: University Press of America, 1980), p. 73.

50. Parton, *Jackson,* vol. 1, p. 50.

51. For the King's Mountain campaign of the American Revolution and Shelby's dominant role, see Buchanan, *Road to Guilford Courthouse,* chs. 15 and 16.

52. Jackson to Blount, 29 December 1813, in R&E, *Jackson,* pp. 102–106.

53. Jackson to Rachel, 14 December 1813, in *Jackson Papers,* vol. 2, p. 487.

CHAPTER 16. THEY "WHIPPED *CAPTAIN* JACKSON, AND RUN HIM TO THE COOSA RIVER"

1. Remini, *Jackson,* p. 207; R&E, *Jackson,* p. 120 n; Pinckney to Jackson, 24 December 1813, in *Jackson Papers,* vol. 2, pp. 502–503.

2. Jackson to Pinckney, 29 January 1814, in Parton, *Jackson,* vol. 1, pp. 486–487; R&E, *Jackson,* p. 124; Owsley, *Borderlands,* p. 75; Pickett, *Alabama,* vol. 2, p. 336.

3. R&E, *Jackson,* pp. 124–125.

4. Ibid., pp. 125–126.

5. Jackson to Pinckney, 29 January 1814, in Parton, *Jackson,* vol. 1, pp. 487–488.

6. Ibid., p. 488.

7. R&E, *Jackson,* pp. 126–127; Jackson to Rachel, 28 January 1814, in *Jackson Papers,* vol. 3, p. 18; Jackson to Pinckney, 29 January 1814, in Parton, *Jackson,* pp. 488–489; John Coffee to John Donelson, 28 January 1814, Tennessee Historical Society Miscellaneous Files, Tennessee State Library and Archives, MF678, Reel 2, Box 2, C-117.

8. R&E, *Jackson,* p. 127; Jackson to Rachel, 28 January 1814, in *Jackson Papers,* vol. 3, p. 18; Jackson to Pinckney, 29 January 1814, in Parton, *Jackson,* vol. 1, p. 489.

9. R&E, *Jackson,* pp. 127–128.

10. Jackson to Rachel, 28 January 1814, in *Jackson Papers,* vol. 3, p. 18; R&E, *Jackson,* pp. 128–129.

11. R&E, *Jackson,* pp. 129–130; Jackson to Pinckney, 29 January 1814, in Parton, *Jackson,* vol. 1, p. 490.

12. R&E, *Jackson,* p. 130 n.

13. Jackson to Rachel, 28 January 1814, in *Jackson Papers,* vol. 3, p. 19; R&E, *Jackson,* p. 130.

14. *Jackson Papers,* vol. 3, p. 21 n. 8. "Harycane" is probably the way Jackson spelled and pronounced *hurricane.* In the Adirondack Mountains of New York State a similar area is called a blowdown.

15. Jackson to Rachel, 28 January 1814, in *Jackson Papers,* vol. 3, p. 19; R&E, *Jackson,* pp. 131–132.

16. Jackson to Pinckney, 29 January 1814, in Parton, *Jackson,* vol. 1, p. 491; R&E, *Jackson,* p. 132; Jackson to Rachel, 28 January 1814, in *Jackson Papers,* vol. 3, p. 19.

17. Jackson to Rachel, 28 January 1814, in *Jackson Papers,* vol. 3, p. 19; Jackson to Pinckney, 29 January 1814, in Parton, *Jackson,* vol. 1, p. 491; R&E, *Jackson,* p. 133.

18. Jackson to Rachel, 28 January 1814, in *Jackson Papers,* vol. 3, pp. 19–20; R&E, *Jackson,* pp. 132–133; Jackson to Pinckney, 29 January 1814, in Parton, *Jackson,* vol. 1, p. 492.

19. R&E, *Jackson,* pp. 135–136; Jackson to Pinckney, 29 January 1814, in Parton, *Jackson,* vol. 1, pp. 492–493; Jackson to Rachel, 28 January 1814, in *Jackson Papers,* vol. 3, pp. 19–20.

20. Jackson to Rachel, 28 January 1814, in *Jackson Papers,* vol. 3, p. 20; R&E, *Jackson,* pp. 136–137; Jackson to Pinckney, 29 January 1814, in Parton, *Jackson,* vol. 1, pp. 493–494.

21. I must thank Lieutenant Colonel Ian McCulloch of the Canadian army, who dropped that wonderful description and its origins during a talk at the War College of the Seven Years' War, 1999, Ticonderoga, New York.

22. Pickett, *Alabama,* vol. 2, p. 335; Jackson to Pinckney, 29 January 1814, in Parton, *Jackson Papers,* vol. 1, p. 494.

23. Jackson to Rachel, 28 January 1814, in *Jackson Papers,* vol. 3, pp. 20-21 n. 13.

24. Ibid., pp. 20–21.

25. Pinckney to Armstrong, 6 February 1814, in Parton, *Jackson,* vol. 1, p. 498.

26. Unless otherwise indicated, my description of the Calabee Creek campaign follows Owsley, *Borderlands,* pp. 55–60.

27. Griffith, *McIntosh and Weatherford,* p. 133.

28. Stiggins, *Creek History,* pp. 127–128; Owsley, *Borderlands,* p. 56.

29. Griffith, *McIntosh and Weatherford,* p. 10; Pickett, *Alabama,* vol. 2, p. 336.

30. This and the following paragraphs describing the debate over Creek tactics, including all quotations, are based on Stiggins, *Creek History,* pp. 129–131, and 134 for Paddy Walsh's description. Another version of Red Eagle's plan, which states that he proposed a daytime attack while Floyd was on the march, is in *Woodward's Reminiscences,* pp. 88–89.

31. Pickett, *Alabama,* vol. 2, pp. 336–337.

32. Griffith, *McIntosh and Weatherford,* p. 135; Owsley, *Borderlands,* p. 58.

33. Stiggins, *Creek History,* p. 132; Peter A. Brannon, ed., "Journal of James A. Tait for the Year 1813," *Georgia Historical Quarterly* 8 (1924), pp. 237–238.

34. Owsley, *Borderlands,* pp. 58–59.

CHAPTER 17. HORSESHOE BEND

1. I am indebted to John Alden Reid, park ranger and interpreter, Horseshoe Bend National Military Park, for an informative letter of 18 April 1999, and for sharing with me some of his published and unpublished writings, and 39th Infantry Muster Roll; Jackson to Robert Hayes, 4 January 1814, in *Jackson Papers,* vol. 3, p. 78 n 5.

2. Parton, *Jackson,* vol. 1, p. 484.

3. Doherty to Jackson, 2 March 1814, in *Jackson Papers,* vol. 3, pp. 37–38.

4. Jackson to Pinckney, 6 March 1814, Jackson to Willie Blount, 10 March 1814, in ibid., pp. 41–42.

5. Parton, *Jackson,* vol. 1, p. 501; Quimby, *U. S. Army,* vol. 2, pp. 462–463.

6. Rachel to Jackson, 10 February 1814, in *Jackson Papers,* vol. 3, pp. 28–29; Jackson to Rachel, 21 February 1814, in *Jackson Papers,* vol. 3, p. 34.

7. Jackson to William Carroll, 17 February 1814, Samuel B. Patton, James Harris, and James H. Pickens to Jackson, 23 February 1814, and editorial note, in ibid., pp. 24–26, 31.

8. I have followed the account in Parton, *Jackson,* vol. 1, pp. 507–508.

9. Ibid., p. 509.

10. Ibid.; General Order, 14 March 1814, in *Jackson Papers,* vol. 3, pp. 48–49 n. 1.

11. R&E, *Jackson,* pp. 142–143.

12. Owsley, *Borderlands,* p. 79; R&E, ibid., pp. 139, 147; Remini, *Jackson,* p. 213; Jackson to Pinckney, 23 March 1814, in *Jackson Papers,* vol. 3, pp. 50–51 n. 4; W. Stuart Harris, *Dead Towns of Alabama* (University: University of Alabama Press, 1977), pp. 55–56; Griffith, *McIntosh and Weatherford,* p. 144.

13. Jackson to Pinckney, 23 March 1814, in *Jackson Papers,* vol. 3, p. 50.

14. My description of the Battle of Horseshoe Bend is mostly based on several eyewitness accounts, followed by my own inspection of the battlefield, some secondary works, National Park Service information available to the public, and published and unpublished papers kindly made available to me by John Alden Reid, park ranger and interpreter at Horseshoe Bend National Military Park. They are all cited in this note, below, with page numbers when relevant. The sources of the quotations are identified in the text. Jackson to Pinckney, 28 March 1814, Jackson to Rachel, 1 April 1814, Coffee to Jackson, 1 April 1814, Jackson to Tennessee Troops in the Mississippi Territory, 2 April 1814, in *Jackson Papers,* vol. 3, pp. 51–58; William Carroll, "Battle of the Horseshoe Fought 27 March 1814 as Sketched by Colo. Carroll (now Genl. Carroll) a Few Days after the Battle—to J Graham," PC 60.1, Folder 8, Joseph Graham Papers, Creek Indian War, 1814, Letterbook May 10–July 19, 1814, North Carolina Division of Archives and History; R&E, *Jackson,* pp. 148–155; Pickett, *Alabama,* vol. 2, pp. 341–346; Parton, *Jackson,* vol. 1, pp. 512–522; John Alden Reid, letter to the author, 18 April 1999, and the following unpublished papers: "The Thirty-ninth Regiment of U.S. Infantry," "Cannon at Enitachopko and Horseshoe Bend," "A Conversation with a Militiaman of the Tennessee Volunteers," "Private Dempsey Parker, Invalid Veteran of the Thirty-ninth Regiment of U.S. Infantry, Wounded at the Horseshoe," and extract from a manuscript; Thomas Kanon, "'A Slow, Laborious Slaughter': The Battle of Horseshoe Bend," *Tennessee Historical Quarterly* 58:1 (Spring 1999), pp. 3–15; Griffith, *McIntosh and Weatherford,* pp. 144–149; H&B, *Creek War,* pp. 275–278; Owsley, *Borderlands,* pp. 79–82; Remini, *Jackson,* pp. 213–217.

CHAPTER 18. "WE HAVE CONQUERED"

1. Jackson to Pinckney, 28 March 1814, Jackson to Rachel, 1 April 1814, Coffee to Jackson, 1 April 1814, in *Jackson Papers,* vol. 3, pp. 52–57; Owsley, *Borderlands,* pp. 81–82.

2. Jackson to Pinckney, 28 March 1814, Jackson to Rachel, 1 April 1814; Remini, *Jackson,* p. 216, for the story of the young warrior.

3. *Jackson Papers,* vol. 3, p. 54 n. 7; Coffee to Mary Coffee, 1 April 1814, Coffee Papers, MF814, Reel 5, Box 13, Folder 3.

4. Owsley, *Borderlands,* pp. 81–82.

5. Remini, *Jackson,* p. 216; Bradford Perkins, *The Cambridge History of American Foreign Relations,* vol. 1: *The Creation of a Republican Empire, 1776–1865* (Cambridge, U.K.: Cambridge University Press, 1995), p. 141.

6. R&E, *Jackson,* pp. 155–156; Jackson to Rachel, 1 April 1814, "To Tennessee Troops in the Mississippi Territory," 2 April 1814, Jackson to Pinckney, 1 April 1814, in *Jackson Papers,* vol. 3, pp. 54, 57–58, 62–63; Remini, *Jackson,* p. 217.

7. Jackson to Pinckney, 14 April 1814, in *Jackson Papers,* vol. 3, pp. 62–63.

8. Coffee to Mary Coffee, 18 April 1814, Coffee Papers, MF814, Reel 5, Box 13, Folder 3; Remini, *Jackson,* pp. 217–218.

9. Unless otherwise indicated, my description of Weatherford's surrender is based on R&E, *Jackson,* pp. 165–167.

10. Remini, *Jackson,* p. 219; Owsley, *Borderlands,* pp. 84–85; *Woodward's Reminiscences,* p. 89.

11. Unless otherwise indicated, my account of Pinckney's arrival and Jackson's march home is based on Parton, *Jackson,* vol. 1, pp. 539–543.

12. Armstrong to Jackson, 22 May 1814, Jackson to Armstrong, 8 June 1814, Jackson to Rachel, 10 August 1814, in *Jackson Papers,* vol. 3, pp. 76–77, 79; C. Edward Skeen, *John Armstrong, Jr., 1758–1843: A Biography* (Syracuse, N.Y.: Syracuse University Press, 1981), pp. 142–143, describes Jackson's promotions in the context of the growing tension between Armstrong and Madison; see also Remini, *Jackson,* p. 222.

13. *Woodward's Reminiscences,* p. 39.

14. Editorial note, in *Jackson Papers,* vol. 3, pp. 67–68; Owsley, *Borderlands,* pp. 86–87; Armstrong to Pinckney, 17 March 1814, 20 March 1814, in *ASPIA,* vol. 1, pp. 836–837.

15. Williams to Jackson, ca. 1 May 1814, Jackson to Williams, 18 May 1814, in *Jackson Papers,* vol. 3, pp. 68, 73–75.

16. Armstrong to Jackson, 24 May 1814, David Holmes to Jackson, 19 June 1814, in ibid., pp. 77, 82; for several reports on British activities, see William H. Robertson to Thomas Flournoy, 17 June 1814, Flournoy to Armstrong, 19 June 1814, and a series of letters from Benjamin Hawkins to Armstrong, 15 June, 21 June, 3 July, and 13 July 1814, in *ASPIA,* vol. 1, pp. 859–860.

17. Jackson to Armstrong, Jackson to Mateo González Manrique, 12 July 1814, John Gordon to Jackson, 29 July 1814, in *Jackson Papers,* vol. 3, pp. 83, 86, 98–99; R&E, *Jackson,* p. 196.

18. Jackson to Hawkins, 11 July 1814, quoted in Remini, *Jackson,* p. 224; Owsley, *Borderlands,* pp. 86–87; Jackson to the Cherokee and Creek Indians, 5 August 1814, in *Jackson Papers,* vol. 3, pp. 103–104, is a typical treaty speech, given in advance of reading the peace terms. The Cherokees were present not as signatories, but to protect their interests.

19. Armstrong to Pinckney, 17 March 1814, in *ASPIA,* vol. 1, p. 836; Owsley, *Borderlands,* pp. 86–87; Remini, *Jackson,* 226–227; Jackson to John Williams, 18 May 1814, in *Jackson Papers,* vol. 3, p. 74.

20. Jackson to Williams, 18 May 1814, in *Jackson Papers,* vol. 3, p. 75.

21. R&E, *Jackson,* pp. 188–189; Big Warrior to Hawkins, 6 August 1814, in *Jackson Papers,* vol. 3, pp. 106–109.

22. R&E, *Jackson,* pp. 189–190.

23. Ibid., p. 191; Jackson to Big Warrior, 7 August 1814, in *Jackson Papers,* vol. 3, pp. 109–111.

24. Parton, *Jackson,* vol. 1, pp. 622–623; Michael D. Green, *Politics of Indian Removal: Creek Government and Society in Crisis* (1982; reprint, Lincoln: University of Nebraska Press, 1985), p. 42; "Articles of Agreement and Capitulation," 9 August 1814, in *ASPIA,* vol. 1, pp. 826–827.

CHAPTER 19. "I ACT WITHOUT THE ORDERS OF GOVERNMENT"

1. Howell Tatum, "Major Howell Tatum's Journal while Acting Topographical Engineer (1814) to General Jackson Commanding the Seventh Military District," ed. John Spenser Bassett, *Smith College Studies in History* 8:1–3 (October 1921–April 1922), pp. 9–10; Jackson to Rachel, 5 August 1814, in *Jackson Papers,* vol. 3, p. 105.

2. Unless otherwise indicated, my description of the British plan is largely based on the excellent discussion in Owsley, *Borderlands,* pp. 92–105, but on this subject and throughout the chapter I have also drawn on the following works: Wilburt S. Brown, *The Amphibious Campaign for West Florida and Louisiana, 1814–1815: A Critical Review of Strategy and Tactics at New Orleans* (University: University of Alabama Press, 1969), pp. 21–58; Reginald Horsman, *The War of 1812* (New York: Knopf, 1969), pp. 225–236; John K. Mahon, *The War of 1812* (1972; reprint, New York: Da Capo Press, 1991), pp. 339–353; Quimby, *U.S. Army,* vol. 2, pp. 763–806.

3. Donald R. Hickey, *The War of 1812: A Forgotten Conflict* (Urbana: University of Illinois Press, 1990), pp. 197–201; George Robert Gleig, *A Subaltern in America* (London: n.p., 1833), p. 132.

4. Horsman, *The War of 1812,* pp. 138–164, has a clear account of the naval situation in 1813–1814.

5. This paragraph is based on the discussion in ibid., pp. 226–227.

6. Anonymous letter from Havana, 8 August 1814, in Arsène Lacarrière Latour, *Historical Memoir of the War in West Florida and Louisiana in 1814–1815,* expanded edition; ed. Gene A. Smith (1816; reprint, Gainesville: The Historic New Orleans Collection and University Press of Florida, 1999), pp. 184–185.

7. Ibid., p. 184; Owsley, *Borderlands,* pp. 106–107.

8. Latour, *Historical Memoir,* pp. 185–186.

9. Nicolls to Lafitte, 31 August 1814, ibid., pp. 186–187; Owsley, *Borderlands,* pp. 107–109, for an extended discussion.

10. Cochrane to Bathurst, 14 July 1814, 15 July 1814, quoted in Horsman, *The War of 1812,* p. 228.

11. "Tatum's Journal," pp. 45, 50–51; I am indebted to Michael M. Bailey, museum curator, Fort Morgan State Historic Site, for information on Fort Bowyer, Bailey to Buchanan, 15 April 1999 and encl.

12. Jackson to Rachel, 23 August 1814, Claiborne to Jackson, 12 August 1814, Jackson to Armstrong, 25 August 1814, 27 August 1814, Jackson to John Reid, 27 August 1814, in *Jackson Papers,* vol. 3, pp. 115–117, 122–125.

13. Owsley, *Borderlands,* p. 109; Latour, *Historical Memoir,* pp. 34–35; "Tatum's Journal," p. 57.

14. Owsley, *Borderlands,* pp. 109–110; William Lawrence to Jackson, 15 September 1814, in *Jackson Papers,* vol. 3, p. 137.

15. Owsley, *Borderlands,* p. 110; Latour, *Historical Memoir,* p. 37; Lawrence to Jackson, 15 September 1814, in *Jackson Papers,* vol. 3, p. 137.

16. Lawrence to Jackson, 15 September 1814, in *Jackson Papers,* vol. 3, pp. 137–139; William S. Coker, "The Last Battle of the War of 1812: New Orleans. No! Fort Bowyer," *Alabama Historical Quarterly* 43:1 (Spring 1981), pp. 52–53, for British loses; "Tatum's Journal," p. 57, for the badly burned men.

17. "Proclamation," 21 September 1814, Latour, *Historical Memoir,* p. 204; Coker, "The Last Battle," p. 53; Owsley, *Borderlands,* p. 112; Tom Kanon, "Andrew Jackson Pays the Spanish a Visit: The Capture of Pensacola, November 7, 1814," *Journal of the War of 1812 and the Era 1800 to 1840* (Spring 1999), p. 6.

18. Jackson to Leroy Pope, 31 October 1813, Jackson to Philip Pipkin, 12 September 1814, Jackson to Mateo González Manrique, 24 August 1814, in *Jackson Papers,* vol. 2, p. 443, vol. 3, pp. 120–121, 136.

19. Jackson to González Manrique, 9 September 1814, in ibid., vol. 3, p. 131.

20. Jackson to Monroe, 10 October 1814, Monroe to Jackson, 21 October 1814, in ibid., pp. 155, 170–171.

21. Jackson to Coffee, 20 October 1814, in ibid., p. 169.; "Tatum's Journal, " p. 67.

22. Jackson to Monroe, 26 October 1814, in *Jackson Papers,* vol. 3, p. 173 and p. 151 nn. 1, 2 for Cassedy.

23. "Tatum's Journal," pp. 67–68; Jackson to Monroe, 26 October 1814, Jackson to Willie Blount, 14 November 1814, in ibid., pp. 173, 185.

24. "Tatum's Journal," pp. 68–72, and 83–84 regarding Boyles; Thomas Hart Benton to Jackson, 11 September 1814 regarding Boyles; Jackson to González Manrique, 6 November 1814, González Manrique to Jackson, 6 November 1814, Jackson to Willie Blount, 14 November 1814, Jackson to Rachel, 15 November 1814, in *Jackson Papers,* vol. 3, pp. 179–181, 184–187; Owsley, *Borderlands,* pp. 112–119, covers the Pensacola operation in detail; see also two letters, each dated 15 November 1814, John Coffee to Mary Coffee, Coffee Papers, MF814, Reel 5, Box 13, Folder 3.

25. Quoted in Owsley, *Borderlands,* p. 113.

26. Jackson to Willie Blount, 14 November 1814, in *Jackson Papers,* vol. 3, p. 185.

27. Ibid; "Tatum's Journal," pp. 74–75; Latour, *Historical Memoir,* pp. 44–45.

28. Jackson to Willie Blount, 14 November 1814, Thomas Langford Butler to Henry D. Peire, 7 November 1814, in *Jackson Papers,* vol. 3, pp. 182–183, 185; "Tatum's Journal," pp. 76–85; Latour, *Historical Memoir,* pp. 45–46; Owsley, *Borderlands,* p. 118, for the casualties.

29. Cochrane's letter of 15 February 1815 to John Lambert is quoted in Owsley, *Borderlands,* p. 118. For criticism of Jackson throughout the Gulf campaign, the former secretary of war, John Armstrong, is quoted extensively in Henry Adams, *History of the United States of America during the Administrations of James Madison* (1889–1891; rev. ed. 1901, 1903, and 1904; reprint, New York: Library of America, 1986), pp. 1139, 1142, 1183. Adams himself, hardly a disinterested observer, is sharply critical of Jackson throughout ch. 12, and his line was followed by the military historian and professional soldier John R. Elting, in *Amateurs to Arms: A Military History of the War of 1812* (Chapel Hill: Algonquin Books, 1991), chs. 10 and 16. For a convenient summary of the opinions of various writers on the subject, see Quimby, *U.S. Army,* vol. 2, pp. 171–173.

30. The letter to González Manrique is quoted in Remini, *Jackson*, p. 244; "Tatum's Journal," pp. 83–86; Jackson to Monroe, 20 November 1814, in *Jackson Papers*, vol. 3, p. 193; Pickett, *Alabama*, vol. 2, p. 368.

31. "Tatum's Journal," pp. 83–86; Jackson to Monroe, 20 November 1814, in *Jackson Papers*, vol. 3, p. 193; Owsley, *Borderlands*, pp. 122–126, has an excellent discussion of Jackson's dilemma and his conduct of the campaign, and in this regard see also Horsman, *The War of 1812*, pp. 234–236.

32. Jackson to Rachel, 15 September 1814, 15 November 1814, in *Jackson Papers*, vol. 3, pp. 145, 186–188.

33. "Tatum's Journal," pp. 87–96; Jackson to Monroe, 20 November 1814, in ibid., p. 192.

34. Robin Reilly, *The British at the Gates: The New Orleans Campaign in the War of 1812* (New York: G. P. Putnam's Sons, 1974), pp. 211–212; George Robert Gleig, *Narrative of the Campaigns of the British Army at Washington and New Orleans, under Generals Ross, Pakenham, and Lambert, in the Years 1814 and 1815; with Some Account of the Countries Visited*, 2nd ed. (London: John Murray, 1826), p. 244.

35. Jackson to Monroe, 2 December 1814, in *Jackson Papers*, vol. 3, p. 199.

CHAPTER 20. "TO ARMS!"

1. Joseph G. Tregle Jr., "Early New Orleans Society: A Reappraisal," *JSH* 18:1 (February 1952), p. 29.

2. *Niles Weekly Register* vol. 29 (15 November 1812), p. 160, quoted in ibid.; on the subject of Creoles and the foreign French, in addition to Tregle's article cited above, see the essays in Arnold R. Hirsch and Joseph Logsdon, eds., *Creole New Orleans: Race and Americanization* (Baton Rouge: Louisiana State University Press, 1992), especially for our purposes the essays by Paul F. Lachance, "The Foreign French," pp. 101–130, and Joseph G. Tregle Jr., "Creoles and Americans," pp. 131–185.

3. Randolph of Roanoke quoted in Brown, *Amphibious Campaign*, p. 62; Livingston's wife described in Vincent Nolte, *The Memoirs of Vincent Nolte: Reminiscences in the Period of Anthony Adverse, or Fifty Years in Both Hemispheres* (1854; reprint, New York: G. Howard Watt, 1934), p. 89.

4. Parton, *Jackson*, vol. 2, pp. 30–31; Mrs. Livingston quoted in Owsley, *Borderlands*, p. 130.

5. British officer quoted in Donald Hickey, *The War of 1812: A Forgotten Conflict* (Urbana: University of Illinois Press, 1990), p. 154.

6. Bernard Marigny, "Reflections on New Orleans Campaign," ed. and trans. Grace King, *Louisiana Historical Quarterly* 6 (January 1923), pp. 63–64.

7. Quimby, *U.S. Army*, vol. 2, p. 822, for "least possible delay." Unless otherwise indicated, I have drawn from the following for Jackson's preparations: "Tatum's Journal," pp. 96–107; Latour, *Historical Memoir*, pp. 47–50; R&E, *Jackson*, pp. 241–284; Owsley, *Borderlands*, pp. 125–132; Brown, *Amphibious Campaign*, pp. 63–72; Quimby, *U.S. Army*, pp. 818–823; Reilly, *British at the Gates*, pp. 199–206; Remini, *Jackson*, pp. 250–254; Robert V. Remini, *The Battle of New Orleans* (New York: Viking, 1999), pp. 44–49. Quotations are cited separately.

8. Claiborne to Jackson, 12 August 1814, Jackson to Claiborne, 21 September 1814, Claiborne to Jackson, 17 October 1814, in *Jackson Papers*, vol. 3, pp. 115–116, 144–145, 164–165; Jackson's address to the free men of color, 21 September 1814, quoted in Remini, *New Orleans*, p. 18; Jackson to W. Allen, 23 December 1814, quoted in Remini, *Jackson*, p. 254.

9. "Tatum's Journal," p. 101; Latour, *Historical Memoir*, p. 48.

10. My biographical sketch of Latour is based on, and the quotations are in, the "Editor's Introduction" to Latour, *Historical Memoir*, pp. xii–xix, xxix.

11. "Tatum's Journal," pp. 98–100.

12. Jackson to Claiborne, 10 December 1814, in *Jackson Papers*, vol. 3, pp. 201–203.

13. See the Nicolls-Lafitte-Blanque-Claiborne letters and other papers in Latour, *Historical Memoir*, pp. 186–193.

14. Jackson to Claiborne, 30 September 1814, in *Jackson Papers*, vol. 3, p. 151; Nolte, *Memoirs*, p. 207.

15. There is no record of their exchange. See Latour, *Historical Memoir,* p. 58; Remini, *Jackson,* p. 253; Jane Lucas DeGrummond, *The Baratarians and the Battle of New Orleans* (Baton Rouge: Louisiana State University Press, 1961), p. 81.

16. Editorial note and Jackson to Jacques Philip Villeré, 19 December 1814, in *Jackson Papers,* vol. 3, pp. 210–211.

17. R&E, *Jackson,* p. 264.

18. "Tatum's Journal," pp. 100–101.

19. William S. Dudley, ed., *The Naval War of 1812: A Documentary History* (Washington, D.C.: Naval Historical Center, Department of the Navy, 1985), vol. 1, pp. 421–433, for samples of such letters.

20. Ibid., p. 12 n. 1.

21. Anonymous to Patterson, 5 December 1814, and Statement by Ap Catesby Jones, in Latour, *Historical Memoir,* pp. 209, 215.

22. Jones's quotation is from his report, Jones to Patterson, 12 March 1815. Unless otherwise indicated, for the ensuing action I have drawn from this letter as well as Captain Nicholas Lockyer's report, Lockyer to Admiral Cochrane, 17 December 1814, and Cochrane to John Wilson Croker, 9 March 1815, all in Latour, *Historical Memoir,* pp. 213–215, 304–307; good secondary accounts are in Owsley, *Borderlands,* pp. 138–140; Brown, *Amphibious Campaign,* pp. 77–81; Quimby, *U.S. Army,* vol. 2, pp. 823–827; Theodore Roosevelt, *The Naval War of 1812* (1882; reprint, New York: G. P. Putnam's Sons, 1902), vol. 2, pp. 72–77; and C. S. Forester, *The Age of Fighting Sail: The Story of the Naval War of 1812* (Garden City, N.Y.: Doubleday, 1956), pp. 268–270.

23. Cochrane to Croker, 9 March 1815, in Latour, *Historical Memoir,* p. 304.

24. Jones to Patterson, 12 March 1815, in ibid., p. 213.

25. Ibid., p. 214.

26. Ibid.

27. Lockyer to Cochrane, 17 December 1814, in ibid., p. 306.

28. Cochrane to Croker, 9 March 1815, in ibid., p. 305.

CHAPTER 21. "I WILL SMASH THEM, SO HELP ME GOD!"

1. Jackson to Coffee, 16 December 1814, in *Jackson Papers,* vol. 3, p. 205.

2. Coffee to Jackson, 17 December 1814, in ibid., p. 209; Coffee to Mary Coffee, 15 December 1814, Coffee Papers, MF814, Reel 5, Box 13, Folder 3.

3. Coffee to Jackson, 17 December 1814, in *Jackson Papers,* vol. 3, p. 205.

4. Coffee to Mary Coffee, 15 December 1814, Coffee Papers, MF814, Reel 5, Box 13, Folder 3.

5. Carroll to Jackson, 14 December 1814, in *Jackson Papers,* vol. 3, pp. 203–204.

6. Jackson to New Orleans Citizens and Soldiers, 15 December 1814, in ibid., pp. 204–205.

7. Parton, *Jackson,* vol. 2, pp. 58–59.

8. General Orders to New Orleans Citizens, 16 December 1814, in *Jackson Papers,* vol. 3, pp. 206–207. For a good account of the establishment of martial law and the controversy surrounding it, see Matthew Warshauer, "The Battle of New Orleans Reconsidered: Andrew Jackson and Martial Law," *Louisiana History* 39:2 (Summer 1998), pp. 261–291.

9. Gleig, *Narrative,* pp. 260–261.

10. Ibid., p. 262; John Keane to Edward Pakenham, 26 December 1814, in Latour, *Historical Memoir,* p. 308, for the dates of the transfer of troops to Isle aux Pois.

11. Gleig, *Narrative,* pp. 262–263.

12. Keane to Pakenham, 26 December 1814, in Latour, *Historical Memoir,* p. 308. Unless otherwise indicated, the ensuing actions are drawn from Keane's letter just cited, pp. 308–310; Cochrane to John Wilson Croker, 9 March 1815, also in Latour, *Historical Memoir,* pp. 304–305; Gleig, *Narrative,* pp. 272–297; Latour, *Historical Memoir,* pp. 62–83; Nolte, *Memoirs,* pp. 209–214; *Jackson Papers,* p. 217 n. 2, and editorial note, pp. 217–218; and the following secondary accounts: Parton, *Life of Jackson,* vol. 2, pp. 53–109; Brown, *Amphibious Campaign,* pp. 87–107; Quimby, *U.S. Army,* vol. 2, pp. 831–853; Reilly, *British at the Gates,* pp. 221–236; Remini, *Jack-*

son, pp. 259–265; Remini, *New Orleans,* pp. 61–84; Tim Pickles, *New Orleans, 1815* (London: Osprey, 1993); only quotations are cited separately.

13. Latour, *Historical Memoir,* pp. 62–65; John Reid to Abram Maury, 25 December 1815, John Reid Papers.

14. Latour, *Historical Memoir,* p. 66.

15. Alexander Dickson, "Journal of Operations in Louisiana, 1814–1815," ed. Carson I. A. Ritchie, *LHQ,* 44:3–4 (July–October 1961), p. 7.

16. Gleig, *Narrative,* p. 274; Latour, *Historical Memoir,* pp. 67, 308.

17. Latour, *Historical Memoir,* p. 308.

18. Quimby, *U.S. Army,* p. 838, for the "bold execution" quote; Gleig, *Narrative,* p. 242.

19. Nolte, *Memoirs,* pp. 209–210.

20. Reid to Abram Maury, 25 December 1814, John Reid Papers.

21. Jackson to James Monroe, 27 December 1814, on his fear of a "double-attack," Patterson to Monroe, 28 December 1814, Henley to Patterson, 28 December 1814, in Latour, *Historical Memoir,* pp. 227, 229, 231.

22. Coffee to Mary Coffee, 20 January 1815, MF814, Reel 5, Box 13, Folder 3; Gleig, *Narrative,* p. 283.

23. Gleig, *Narrative,* p. 284.

24. Ibid., pp. 284–285; Patterson to Monroe, 28 January 1814, Keane to Pakenham, 26 December 1814, in Latour, *Historical Memoir,* pp. 227–228, 308.

25. Gleig, *Narrative,* pp. 284–285; Jackson to Monroe, 17 December 1814, in Latour, *Historical Memoir,* p. 229.

26. Nolte, *Memoirs,* p. 210; Keane to Pakenham, 26 December 1814, in Latour, *Historical Memoir,* p. 310.

27. Gleig, *Narrative,* p. 292; Keane to Pakenham, 26 December 1814, Jackson to Monroe, 27 December 1814, in Latour, *Historical Memoir,* pp. 229–230, 309; Jackson to Robert Hays, 26 December 1814, in *Jackson Papers,* vol. 3, pp. 221–222.

28. Gleig, *Narrative,* p. 300.

29. John Reid to Abram Maury, 25 December 1814, John Reid Papers.

30. Gleig, *Narrative,* pp. 293–294.

31. Ibid., pp. 295–297.

32. Ibid., pp. 294–295.

CHAPTER 22. BEAUTY AND BOOTY

1. Remini, *New Orleans,* p. 83; Quimby, *U.S. Army,* vol. 2, p. 849.

2. E. B. O'Callaghan, ed., *Orderly Book of Lieut. Gen. John Burgoyne* (Albany: n.p., 1860), p. 3; Gleig, *Narrative,* pp. 79–80; Buchanan, *Road to Guilford Courthouse,* pp. 157–161, for a discussion of weaponry, including the bayonet, and the tactics it produced, a situation as true for the War of 1812 as for the Revolutionary War.

3. *Dictionary of National Biography.*

4. Gleig, *Narrative,* pp. 302–303, for Pakenham's reconnaissance and the physical scene; Brown, *Amphibious Campaign,* pp. 109–112, for a good discussion of Pakenham's reactions, and also Reilly, *British at the Gates,* p. 256.

5. Brown, *Amphibious Campaign,* p. 112; for hot shot, see Albert Manucy, *Artillery through the Ages: A Short Illustrated History of Cannon, Emphasizing Types Used in America* (1949; reprint, Washington, D.C.: National Park Service, 1985), pp. 69–70.

6. Henley to Daniel Patterson, 28 December 1814, in Latour, *Historical Memoir,* p. 231; "Tatum's Journal," p. 113.

7. Author's personal examination of the Chalmette battlefield and its environs. I am indebted to Wanda Lee Dickey, park ranger, Jean Lafitte National Historical Park and Preserve, for information on the landscape; "Tatum's Journal," p. 112; Latour, *Historical Memoir,* p. 87.

8. Latour, *Historical Memoir,* pp. xxiv, 86; Remini, *New Orleans,* p. 84.

9. Gleig, *Narrative,* pp. 307–309; unless otherwise indicated, my account of the action on 28 December and the quotations are drawn from Gleig, pp. 307–312; Daniel Patterson to the

Secretary of the Navy, 29 December 1814, in Latour, *Historical Memoir,* pp. 87–90, 104, 232–233; "Tatum's Journal," pp. 114–118; R&E, *Jackson,* pp. 314–318; Brown, *Amphibious Campaign,* pp. 113–117; Quimby, *U.S. Army,* pp. 867–870; Owsley, *Borderlands,* pp. 148–149; Reilly, *British at the Gates,* pp. 263–266.

10. Reilly, *British at the Gates,* p. 263, for quotation.

11. Livingston to Jackson, 25 December 1814, in *Jackson Papers,* vol. 3, pp. 220–221 n. 2.

12. Alexander Dickson, "Journal of Operations in Louisiana, 1814 and 1815," ed. Carson I. A. Ritchie, *LHQ* 44:3–4 (July–Oct. 1961), p. 38, for Rennie's description of the woods.

13. Latour, *Historical Memoir,* pp. 104–105; R&E, *Jackson,* p. 329.

14. Jackson to Monroe, 29 December 1814, in *Jackson Papers,* vol. 3, pp. 224–225.

15. Jackson to Louisiana General Assembly, 31 December 1814, in *Jackson Papers,* vol. 3, pp. 226–227.

16. Nolte, *Memoirs,* p. 214; Parton, *Jackson,* vol. 2, p. 143.

17. Patterson to the Secretary of the Navy, 2 January 1815, in Latour, *Historical Memoir,* p. 234. Good discussions of the preparations for the artillery duel, the action itself, and post-mortems are in Brown, *Amphibious Campaign,* pp. 121–128; Quimby, *U.S. Army,* pp. 870–881; Reilly, *British at the Gates,* pp. 266–273; see also Owsley, *Borderlands,* pp. 149–151.

18. Latour, *Historical Memoir,* p. 95.

19. Gleig, *Narrative,* p. 318; Reilly, *British at the Gates,* p. 274, quoting the officer; Codrington to his wife, 4 January 1815, in Quimby, *U.S. Army,* vol. 2, p. 879.

20. Jackson to Monroe, 3 January 1815, in *Jackson Papers,* vol. 3, p. 228.

21. Gleig, *Narrative,* pp. 305–307.

22. Owsley, *Borderlands,* pp. 153–156.

23. Unless otherwise indicated, for the British attack on 8 January I have drawn on the following: Jackson to Monroe, 9 January 1815, in *Jackson Papers,* vol. 3, pp. 239–240; Dispatch from General Lambert to Lord Bathurst, 10 January 1815, in Latour, *Historical Memoir,* pp. 107–121, 312–315, and return of casualties, pp. 315–317; John Coffee to Mary Coffee, 20 January 1815, Coffee Papers, MF814, Reel 5, Box 13; John Reid to Abram Maury, 9 January 1815, John Reid Papers; Gleig, *Narrative,* pp. 320–331; R&E, *Jackson,* pp. 333–350; "Tatum's Journal," pp. 125–131; "Journal of Sir John Maxwell Tylden," entries of 8 and 11 January 1815, pp. 53–55, 58–63; Brown, *Amphibious Campaign,* pp. 140–151; Owsley, *Borderlands,* pp. 156–168; Quimby, *U.S. Army,* pp. 889–906; Reilly, *British at the Gates,* pp. 282–99; Remini, *New Orleans,* pp. 130–168. Only quotations are cited.

24. Quoted in Quimby, *U.S. Army,* p. 892.

25. I have largely relied on Major Latour, supplemented by National Park Service data and the investigations of Brown and Quimby, in this paragraph and those following for the details on Jackson's line; for Dominique You and Renato Beluche see Jane Lucas DeGrummond, *The Baratarians and the Battle of New Orleans* (Baton Rouge: Louisiana State University Press, 1961), pp. 4–6.

26. The recent best judgment is Quimby's, *U.S. Army,* vol. 2, p. 891.

27. Dickson, "Journal of Operations," p. 58.

28. Reilly, *British at the Gates,* p. 285.

29. Latour, *Historical Memoir,* pp. 108–109.

30. "A Contemporary Account of the Battle of New Orleans by a Soldier in the Ranks," *LHQ* 9:1 (January 1926), pp. 11–12.

31. Latour, *Historical Memoir,* pp. 108–109.

32. Captain John Henry Cooke, *A Narrative of Events in the South of France, and of the Attack on New Orleans, in 1814 and 1815* (London: T. W. Boone, 1835), pp. 228–229.

33. "Tatum's Journal," p. 126; Latour, *Historical Memoir,* p. 110.

34. Sinclair quoted in Carson I. A. Ritchie, "The Louisiana Campaign," *LHQ* 44:1–2 (January–April 1961), p. 67.

35. Cooke, *Narrative,* p. 234.

36. Gordon quoted in Quimby, *U.S. Army,* vol. 2, pp. 903–904.

37. Latour, *Historical Memoir,* p. 109; Dickson, "Journal of Operations," p. 62.

38. Cooke, *Narrative,* pp. 235–236.

39. John Reid to Abram Maury, 9 January 1815, John Reid Papers.

40. "Contemporary Account of the Battle of New Orleans," pp. 14–15.

41. Coffee to Mary Coffee, 20 January 1815, Coffee Papers, MF814, Reel 5, Box 13; Cooke, *Narrative,* pp. 238–239.

EPILOGUE

1. Quotation in Donald Hickey, *The War of 1812: A Forgotten Conflict* (Urbana: University of Illinois Press, 1990), p. 309.

2. Remini, *Battle of New Orleans,* ch. 9, has a good discussion of what the victory meant to the nation.

3. Jackson to Jean Baptiste Plauché et al., ca. 16 March 1815, in *Jackson Papers,* vol. 3, p. 313; see also in this source Jackson's reply to the United States District Court, Louisiana, 27 March 1815, pp. 323–334; readers interested in this case should also read Remini, *Jackson,* ch. 20.

4. Jackson to Citizens and Soldiers of New Orleans, ca. 13 March 1815, in *Jackson Papers,* vol. 3, pp. 336–337.

5. Bradford Perkins, *Prologue to War: England and the United States, 1805–1812* (Berkeley: University of California Press, 1986), p. 40; John R. Elting, *Amateurs to Arms: A Military History of the War of 1812* (Chapel Hill: Algonquin Books, 1991), pp. 156–157.

6. For an excellent discussion of the establishment of Negro Fort, its destruction, and the abandonment of the Indians and blacks by the British, see Frank Owsley Jr. and Gene A. Smith, *Filibusterers and Expansionists: Jeffersonian Manifest Destiny, 1800–1821* (Tuscaloosa: University of Alabama Press, 1997), ch. 6; see also John K. Mahon, "The First Seminole War, November 21, 1817–May 24, 1818," *Florida Historical Quarterly* 57:1 (Summer 1998), pp. 62–67.

7. Calhoun to Jackson, 26 December 1817, in *Jackson Papers,* vol. 4, p. 163; Calhoun to Governor Bibb of Alabama, quoted in Remini, *Jackson,* p. 347.

8. Jackson to Monroe, 6 January 1818, in *Jackson Papers,* vol. 4, p. 167; Monroe to Jackson, quoted in Remini, *Jackson,* p. 349.

9. Jackson to Donelson, 4 February 1818, quoted in Remini, *Jackson,* p. 350; Jackson to Caso y Luengo, 4 April 1818, Caso Luengo to Jackson, 7 April 1818, *Jackson Papers,* vol. 4, pp. 186–189.

10. Jackson to Rachel, 10 April 1818, Jackson to Calhoun, 5 May 1818, in *Jackson Papers,* vol. 4, pp. 191, 199–200.

11. José Masot to Jackson, 23 May 1818, in *Jackson Papers,* vol. 4, pp. 205–206; Jackson to Calhoun, 2 June 1818, in *ASPFR,* vol. 4, pp. 602–603.

12. Quotations in Samuel Flagg Bemis, *John Quincy Adams and the Foundations of American Foreign Policy* (New York: Knopf, 1949), pp. 315–316; John Niven, *John C. Calhoun and the Price of Union: A Biography* (Baton Rouge: Louisiana State University Press, 1988), pp. 68–71.

13. Edward Gibbon, *The History of the Decline and Fall of the Roman Empire,* ed. J. B. Bury (1909; reprint, London: Methuen, 1974), vol. 1, p. 4.

14. Timothy Flint, *Recollections of the Last Ten Years Passed in Occasional Residence and Journeys in the Valley of the Mississippi* (Boston: Cummings, Hilliard, 1826), pp. 240–242. The "West in their eyes" was not Timothy Flint's phrase. It was coined by Thomas D. Clark and John D. W. Guice in their book *The Old Southwest, 1795–1830: Frontiers in Conflict* (1989; reprint, Norman: University of Oklahoma Press, 1996), to describe Flint's point of view with regard to the pioneers. I am indebted to Professor Guice for permitting me to use the phrase.

15. Gideon Lincecum, "The Autobiography of Gideon Lincecum," ed. Franklin L. Riley, *Publications of the Mississippi Historical Society,* 8 (1904), pp. 464–465.

SELECTED BIBLIOGRAPHY

MANUSCRIPTS

Georgia Department of Archives and History (selected letters)
Creek Indian Letters, Talks, and Treaties, 1705–1839, Part 3, 1813–1839
John Floyd Letters to his daughter
Georgia Military Affairs, vol. 3, 1801–1813
Governor's Letterbooks, 28 November 1809–18 May 1814.
Library of Congress (selected letters)
John Reid Papers
The New York Public Library, Manuscripts and Archives Division, Astor, Lenox
and Tilden Foundation
Tylden, Sir John Maxwell. Journal, 1814–1815
North Carolina Division of Archives and History
Joseph Graham Papers, William Carroll's report on the Battle of Horseshoe Bend
State Historical Society of Wisconsin
Draper Manuscripts
Tennessee State Library and Archives (selected letters)
John Coffee Papers (Tennessee Historical Society)
Tennessee Historical Society Miscellaneous Files
Tennessee State Library and Archives Miscellaneous Files

PRINTED SOURCES AND SECONDARY WORKS
(★ Denotes works of particular value for this book)

Aaron, Stephen. *How the West Was Lost: The Transformation of Kentucky from Daniel Boone to Henry Clay.* Baltimore: Johns Hopkins University Press, 1996.

★Abernethy, Thomas Perkins. *The Burr Conspiracy.* New York: Oxford University Press, 1954.

★———. *From Frontier to Plantation in Tennessee: A Study in Frontier Democracy.* Chapel Hill: University of North Carolina Press, 1932.

★———. *The South in the New Nation, 1789–1819.* Baton Rouge: Louisiana State University Press, 1961.

★Adair, James, *Adair's History of the American Indians.* ed. Samuel Cole Williams. 1930. Reprint, New York: Argonaut Press, 1966.

★Adams, Henry. *History of the United States of America during the Administrations of Thomas Jefferson, and History of the United States of America during the Administrations of James Madison.* 2 vols. 1889–1891; rev. ed. 1901, 1903, and 1904. Reprint, New York: Library of America, 1986.

★Alden, John. *John Stuart and the Southern Colonial Frontier: A Study of Indian Relations, War, Trade, and Land Problems in the Southern Wilderness, 1754–1775.* 1944. Reprint, New York: Gordian Press, 1966.

Allain, Mathé. *"Not Worth a Straw": French Colonial Policy and the Early Years of Louisiana.* Lafayette: Center for Louisiana Studies, University of Southwestern Louisiana, 1988.

Allison, John. *Dropped Stitches in Tennessee History.* 1897. Reprint, Johnson City, Tenn.: Overmountain Press, 1991.

★*American State Papers. Documents Legislative and Executive of the Congress of the United States . . . Commencing March 3, 1790, and Ending March 3, 1815.* Class I, Foreign Relations, 6 vols; Class II, Indian Affairs, 2 vols. Washington, D.C.: Gales & Seaton, 1832, 1834.

Appleton, James Lamar, and Robert David Ward. "Albert James Pickett and the Case of the Secret Articles: Historians and the Treaty of New York of 1790." *Alabama Review* 51:1 (January 1998), pp. 3–36.

★Arnow, Harriet Simpson. *Flowering of the Cumberland.* New York: Macmillan, 1963.

★———. *Seedtime on the Cumberland.* 1960. Reprint, Lexington: University Press of Kentucky, 1983.

★Asbury, Francis. *Journals and Letters.* 3 vols., ed. Elmer T. Clark et al. London: Epworth Press, 1958.

Axtell, James, and William C. Sturtevant. "The Unkindest Cut, or Who Invented Scalping." *William and Mary Quarterly,* 3rd ser., 37:3 (July 1980), pp. 451–472.

Badger, Reid, and Lawrence A. Clayton, eds. *Alabama and the Borderlands: From Prehistory to Statehood.* Tuscaloosa: University of Alabama Press, 1985.

★Baily, Francis. *Journal of a Tour in Unsettled Parts of North America in 1796 and 1797.* London: Baily Brothers, 1856.

Banker, Luke H. "A History of Fort Southwest Point—1792–1807." *East Tennessee Historical Society Publications* 46 (1974), pp. 19–36.

★Barnes, Katharine R. "James Robertson's Journey to Nashville: Tracing the Route of Fall, 1779." *Tennessee Historical Quarterly* 35:2 (Summer 1976), pp. 145–161.

Bartram, John. "Diary of a Journey through the Carolinas, Georgia, and Florida, from July 1, 1765, to April 10, 1766." Ed. Francis Harper. *Transactions of the American Philosophical Society,* n.s., pt. 1 (1942), pp. 1–120.

★Bartram, William. *Travels and Other Writings: Travels through North and South Carolina, Georgia, East and West Florida; Travels in Georgia and Florida, 1773–74: A Report to Dr. John Fothergill; Miscellaneous Writings.* Ed. Thomas P. Slaughter. 1791; 1943. Reprint, New York: Library of America, 1996.

Barzun, Jacques. *Clio and the Doctors: Psycho-History, Quanto-History, and History.* Chicago: n.p., 1974.

Belue, Ted Franklin. *The Long Hunt: Death of the Buffalo East of the Mississippi.* Harrisburg, Penn.: Stackpole, 1996.

★Bemis, Samuel Flagg. *The Diplomacy of the American Revolution.* 1937. Reprint, Bloomington: Indiana University Press, 1957.

★———. *John Quincy Adams and the Foundations of American Foreign Policy.* New York: Knopf, 1949.

★———. *Pinckney's Treaty: America's Advantage from Europe's Distress, 1783–1800.* Rev. ed. New Haven: Yale University Press, 1960.

Blount, William. *The Blount Journal, 1790–1796.* Nashville: Tennessee Historical Commission, 1955.

Bolton, Herbert Eugene. *The Spanish Borderlands: A Chronicle of Old Florida and the Southwest.* New Haven: Yale University Press, 1921.

★———. "Spanish Resistance to Carolina Traders in Western Georgia, 1680–1704," *Georgia Historical Quarterly* 9:2 (1925), pp. 115–130.

Bradbury, John. *Travels in the Interior of America in the Years 1809, 1810, and 1811.* 2nd ed., 1819. Reprint, Lincoln: University of Nebraska Press, 1986.

★Bradford, John. *The Voice of the Frontier: John Bradford's Notes on Kentucky.* ed. Thomas D. Clark. Lexington: University Press of Kentucky, 1993.

★Braund, Kathryn E. Holland. *Deerskins and Duffels: The Creek Indian Trade with Anglo-America, 1685–1815.* 1993. Reprint, Lincoln: University of Nebraska Press, 1996.

Brown, Roger S. *The Republic in Peril: 1812.* 1964. Reprint, New York: Norton, 1971.

★Brown, Wilburt S. *The Amphibious Campaign for West Florida and Louisiana, 1814–1815: A Critical Review of Strategy and Tactics at New Orleans.* University: University of Alabama Press, 1969.

★Burr, Aaron. *Political Correspondence and Public Papers of Aaron Burr.* 2 vols. Ed. Mary-Jo Kline et al. Princeton, N.J.: Princeton University Press, 1983.

★Calloway, Colin G. *The American Revolution in Indian Country: Crisis and Diversity in Native American Communities.* Cambridge, U.K.: Cambridge University Press, 1995.

——— . *Crown and Calumet: British-Indian Relations, 1763–1815.* Norman: University of Oklahoma Press, 1987.

★Carr, John. *Early Times in Middle Tennessee.* 1857. Reprint, Nashville: Parthenon Press, 1958.

★Carter, Clarence E., and John Porter Bloom, eds. *Territorial Papers of the United States.* 27 vols. Washington, D.C.: 1934- .

★Cashin, Edward J. *Lachlan McGillivray, Indian Trader: The Shaping of the Southern Colonial Frontier.* Athens: University of Georgia Press, 1992.

★Caughey, John Walton. *McGillivray of the Creeks.* Norman: University of Oklahoma Press, 1938.

★Claiborne, John Francis Hamtramck. *Life and Times of Gen. Sam Dale, the Mississippi Partisan.* New York: Harper & Brothers, 1860.

——— . *Mississippi as a Province, Territory, and State.* Vol. 1. Baton Rouge: Louisiana State University Press, 1964.

Clark, Jerry E. *The Shawnee.* Lexington: University Press of Kentucky, 1993.

★Clark, Thomas D., ed. *Travels in the Old South: A Bibliography, 1527–1860.* 3 vols. Norman: University of Oklahoma Press, 1956, 1959.

★Clark, Thomas D., and John D. W. Guise. *The Old Southwest, 1795–1830: Frontiers in Conflict.* 1989. Reprint, Norman: University of Oklahoma Press, 1996.

★Coker, William S., and Thomas D. Watson. *Indian Traders of the Southeastern Spanish Borderlands: Panton, Leslie and Company and John Forbes and Company, 1783–1847.* Pensacola: University of West Florida Press, 1986.

★Connelly, Thomas Lawrence. "Indian Warfare on the Tennessee Frontier, 1776–1794: Strategy and Tactics." *East Tennessee Historical Society Publications* 36 (1964), pp. 3–22.

★"A Contemporary Account of the Battle of New Orleans by a Soldier in the Ranks." *Louisiana Historical Quarterly* 9:1 (January 1926), pp. 11–15.

★Cooke, Captain John Henry. *A Narrative of Events in the South of France, and of the Attack on New Orleans, in 1814 and 1815.* London: T. W. Boone, 1835.

★Corkran, David H. *The Cherokee Frontier: Conflict and Survival, 1740–1762.* Norman: University of Oklahoma Press, 1962.

★——— . *The Creek Frontier, 1540–1783.* Norman: University of Oklahoma Press, 1967.

★Corlew, Robert E. *Tennessee: A Short History.* 2nd ed. Knoxville: University of Tennessee Press, 1990.

★Cotterill, Robert S. *The Southern Indians: The Story of the Civilized Tribes before Removal.* Norman: University of Oklahoma Press, 1954.

★——— . "The Virginia-Chickasaw Treaty of 1783." *Journal of Southern History* 8 (1942), pp. 483–496.

★Cox, Isaac Joslin. *The West Florida Controversy, 1798–1813: A Study in American Diplomacy.* Baltimore: Johns Hopkins University Press, 1918.

Crane, Verner W. "The Origin of the Name of the Creek Indians." *Journal of American History* 5 (1918), pp. 339–342.

★——— . *The Southern Frontier, 1670–1732.* 1929. Reprint, Ann Arbor: University of Michigan Press, 1956.

★——— . "The Tennessee River as the Road to Carolina: The Beginnings of Exploration and Trade." *Mississippi Valley Historical Review* 3:1 (June 1916), pp. 3–18.

Cress, Lawrence Delbert. *Citizens in Arms: The Army and Militia in American Society to the War of 1812.* Chapel Hill: University of North Carolina Press, 1982.

Dargo, George. *Jefferson's Louisiana: Politics and the Clash of Legal Traditions.* Cambridge, Mass.: Harvard University Press, 1975.

DeConde, Alexander. *This Affair of Louisiana*. New York: Scribner's, 1976.

DeGrummond, Jane Lucas. *The Baratarians and the Battle of New Orleans*. Baton Rouge: Louisiana State University Press, 1961.

★De Vorsey, Louis, Jr. "Indian Boundaries in Colonial Georgia." *Georgia Historical Quarterly* 54:1 (Spring 1970), pp. 63–78.

★——— . *The Indian Boundary in the Southern Colonies, 1763–1775*. Chapel Hill: University of North Carolina Press, 1961.

★Dickson, Alexander. "Journal of Operations in Louisiana, 1814 and 1815." Ed. Carson I. A. Ritchie. *Louisiana Historical Quarterly* 44: 3–4 (July–October 1961), pp. 1–110.

Doddridge, Joseph. *Notes on the Settlement and Indian Wars of the Western Parts of Virginia and Pennsylvania from 1763 to 1783 . . . .* 1912. Reprint, Bowie, Md.: Heritage Books, 1988.

Donelson, John. See Quarles, Robert T., and Robert H. White, eds.

★Dowd, Gregory Evans. *A Spirited Resistance: The North American Indian Struggle for Unity, 1745–1815*. Baltimore: Johns Hopkins University Press, 1992.

★Downes, Randolph C. "Cherokee-American Relations in the Upper Tennessee Valley, 1776–1791. East Tennessee Historical Society *Publications* 8 (1936), pp. 35–53.

★——— . "Creek-American Relations, 1781–1790." *Georgia Historical Quarterly* 21 (June 1937), pp. 142–184.

★——— . "Creek-American Relations, 1790–1795." *Journal of Southern History* 8:3 (August 1942), pp. 350–373.

Drake, Daniel. *Pioneer Life in Kentucky, 1785–1800*. Ed. Emmet Field Horine. New York: Henry Schuman, 1948.

Driver, Carl S. *John Sevier, Pioneer of the Old Southwest*. Chapel Hill: University of North Carolina Press, 1932.

★Dudley, William S. et al., eds. *The Naval War of 1812: A Documentary History*. Vol. 1: *1812*. Washington, D.C.: Naval Historical Center, Department of the Navy, 1985.

Dull, Jonathan. *A Diplomatic History of the American Revolution*. New Haven: Yale University Press, 1985.

★Durham, Walter T. *The Great Leap Westward: A History of Sumner County, Tennessee, from Its Beginnings to 1805*. Gallatin, Tenn.: Sumner County Public Library Board, 1969.

★Edmunds, R. David. *Tecumseh and the Quest for Indian Leadership*. Boston: Little, Brown, 1984.

★Elkins, Stanley, and Eric McKitrick. *The Age of Federalism: The Early American Republic, 1788–1800*. New York: Oxford University Press, 1993.

★Ellis, Joseph J. *American Sphinx: The Character of Thomas Jefferson*. New York: Knopf, 1997.

Filson, John. *The Discovery, Settlement and Present State of Kentucky*. 1784. Reprint, New York: Corinth Books, 1962.

★Flint, Timothy. *Recollections of the Last Ten Years, Passed in Occasional Residences and Journeyings in the Valley of the Mississippi*. Boston: Cummings, Hilliard, 1826.

Flores, Dan L., ed. *Jefferson and Southwestern Exploration: The Freeman and Custis Accounts of the Red River Expedition of 1806*. Norman: University of Oklahoma Press, 1984.

★Folmsbee, Stanley J. et al. *History of Tennessee*. 4 vols. New York: Lewis Historical Publishing, 1960.

Forrest, Charles Ramus. "Journal of the Operations Against New Orleans in 1814 and 1815." Ed. Carson I. A. Ritchie. *Louisiana Historical Quarterly* 44:3–4 (July-October 1961), pp. 111–126.

★Gibson, Arrell M. *The Chickasaws*. Norman: University of Oklahoma Press, 1971.

★Gleig, George Robert. *Narrative of the Campaigns of the British Army at Washington and New Orleans, under Generals Ross, Pakenham, and Lambert, in the Years 1814 and 1815; with Some Account of the Countries Visited*. 2nd ed. London: John Murray, 1826.

★Goodpasture, Albert V. "Indian Wars and Warriors of the Old Southwest, 1730–1807." *Tennessee Historical Quarterly* 4:1–4 (March, June, September, December 1918), pp. 3–49, 106–145, 161–210, 252–289.

★Goodstein, Anita Shafer. *Nashville, 1780–1860: From Frontier to City*. Gainesville: University of Florida Press, 1989.

★Green, Michael D. "Alexander McGillivray." In R. David Edmunds, ed., *American Indian Leaders: Studies in Diversity.* Lincoln: University of Nebraska Press, 1980.

★———. *The Creeks: A Critical Bibliography.* Bloomington: University of Indiana Press, 1979.

★———. *The Politics of Indian Removal: Creek Government and Society in Crisis.* 1982. Reprint, Lincoln: University of Nebraska Press, 1985.

Green, Thomas Marshall. *The Spanish Conspiracy: A Review of Early Spanish Movements in the Southwest.* Gloucester, Mass.: Peter Smith, 1967.

★Griffith, Benjamin W. *McIntosh and Weatherford, Creek Indian Leaders.* Tuscaloosa: University of Alabama Press, 1988.

Halbert, H. S., and T. H. Hall. *The Creek War of 1813–1814.* Ed. Frank L. Owsley Jr. 1895. Reprint, Tuscaloosa: University of Alabama Press, 1995.

Hamer, Philip M. "The British in Canada and the Southern Indians, 1790–1794." East Tennessee Historical Society *Publications* 2 (1930), pp. 107–134.

★———. "The Wataugans and the Cherokee Indians in 1776." East Tennessee Historical Society *Publications* 3 (1931), pp. 108–126.

★Hamer, Philip M., ed. "Correspondence of Henry Stuart and Alexander Cameron with the Wataugans." *Mississippi Valley Historical Review* 17 (December 1930), pp. 451–459.

Hamilton, William Baskerville. "American Beginnings in the Old Southwest: The Mississippi Phase." Ph.D. diss., Duke University, 1938.

★Harris, W. Stuart. *Dead Towns of Alabama.* University: University of Alabama Press, 1977.

Hatley, Tom. *The Dividing Paths: Cherokees and South Carolinians Through the Revolutionary Era.* New York: Oxford University Press, 1995.

Heidelberg, Nell Angela. "The Frontier in Mississippi." M.A. thesis, Louisiana State University, 1940.

Heidler, David S. and Jeanne T. *Old Hickory's War: Andrew Jackson and the Quest for Empire.* Mechanicsburg, Pa.: Stackpole, 1996.

★Henderson, Archibald. "The Treaty of the Long Island of the Holston." *North Carolina Historical Review* 8 (January 1931), pp. 55–116.

Henri, Florette. *The Southern Indians and Benjamin Hawkins, 1796–1816.* Norman: University of Oklahoma Press, 1986.

★Hickey, Donald. *The War of 1812: A Forgotten Conflict.* Urbana: University of Illinois Press, 1990.

★Hirsch, Arnold R., and Joseph Logsdon, eds. *Creole New Orleans: Race and Americanization.* Baton Rouge: Louisiana State University Press, 1992.

★Hofstra, Warren R., ed. *George Washington and the Virginia Backcountry.* Madison, Wisc.: Madison House, 1998.

★Holmes, Jack D. L. "The Ebb-Tide of Spanish Military Power on the Mississippi: Fort San Fernando de las Barrancas." East Tennessee Historical Society *Publications* 36 (1964), pp. 23–44.

★———. "Spanish-American Rivalry over Chickasaw Bluffs, 1780–1795." East Tennessee Historical Society *Publications*, 34 (1962), pp. 26–57.

★Horsman, Reginald. *Expansion and American Indian Policy, 1783–1812.* 1967. Reprint, Norman: University of Oklahoma Press, 1992.

★———. *The War of 1812.* New York: Knopf, 1969.

Hudson, Charles. *The Juan Pardo Expeditions: Explorations of the Carolinas and Tennessee, 1566–1568.* Washington, D.C.: Smithsonian Institution Press, 1990.

★———. *Knights of Spain, Warriors of the Sun: Hernando de Soto and the South's Ancient Kingdoms.* Athens: University of Georgia Press, 1997.

★———. *The Southeastern Indians.* Knoxville: University of Tennessee Press, 1976.

★Jackson, Andrew. *The Papers of Andrew Jackson.* Vol. 1. Ed. Sam B. Smith and Harriet C. Owsley. Vols. 2– . Ed. Harold D. Moser et al. Knoxville: University of Tennessee Press, 1980– .

Jacobs, James Ripley. *Tarnished Warrior: Major General James Wilkinson.* New York: Macmillan, 1938.

★Jacobs, Wilbur R. *The Appalachian Indian Frontier: The Edmund Atkin Report and Plan of 1755.* 1954. Reprint, Lincoln: University of Nebraska Press, 1967.

Jones, Dorothy V. *License for Empire: Colonialism by Treaty in Early America.* Chicago: University of Chicago Press, 1982.

★Kanon, Thomas. "Andrew Jackson Pays the Spanish a Visit: The Capture of Pensacola, November 7, 1814. *Journal of the War of 1812 and the Era 1800 to 1840* (Spring 1999), pp. 5–8.

★——— . "The Other Battle of New Orleans: Andrew Jackson and the Louisianians." Unpublished paper. 1999.

★——— . "'A Slow Laborious Slaughter': The Battle of Horseshoe Bend." *Tennessee Historical Quarterly* 58:1 (Spring 1999), pp. 2–15.

Kersey, Harry A., Jr. *The Seminole and Miccosukee Tribes: A Critical Bibliography.* Bloomington: Indiana University Press, 1987.

Latour, Arsène Lacarrière. *Historical Memoir of the War in West Florida and Louisiana in 1814–1815,* expanded edition; ed. Gene A. Smith. 1816; reprint, Gainesville: The Historic New Orleans Collection and University Press of Florida, 1999.

★Lincecum, Gideon. "The Autobiography of Gideon Lincecum." Ed. Franklin L. Riley. *Publications of the Mississippi Historical Society* 8 (1904), pp. 443–519.

★Lomask, Milton. *Aaron Burr: The Conspiracy and Years of Exile, 1805–1836.* New York: Farrar, Straus & Giroux, 1982.

Lyon, E. Wilson. *Louisiana in French Diplomacy, 1759–1804.* Norman: University of Oklahoma Press, 1934.

Mahan, A. T. *Sea Power in Its Relations to the War of 1812.* 2 vols. Boston: Little, Brown, 1905.

Mahon, John K. "The First Seminole War, November 21, 1817–May 24, 1818." *Florida Historical Quarterly* 57:1 (Summer 1998), pp. 62–67.

★——— . *The War of 1812.* 1972. Reprint, New York: Da Capo Press, 1991.

Mancall, Peter C. *Deadly Medicine: Indians and Alcohol in Early America.* Ithaca, N.Y.: Cornell University Press, 1995.

Martin, Joel W. *Sacred Revolt: The Muskogees' Struggle for a New World.* Boston: Beacon Press, 1991.

★Masterson, William H. *William Blount.* Baton Rouge: Louisiana State University Press, 1954.

Meinig, D. W. *The Shaping of America: A Geographical Perspective on 500 Years of History.* Vol. 1: *Atlantic America, 1492–1800.* Vol. 2: *Continental America, 1800–1867.* New Haven: Yale University Press, 1986, 1993.

★Melton, Buckner F., Jr. *The First Impeachment: The Constitution's Framers and the Case of Senator William Blount.* Macon, Ga.: Mercer University Press, 1998.

★Mereness, Newton D., ed. *Travels in the American Colonies.* New York: Macmillan, 1916.

★Milanich, Jerald, and Susan Milbrath, eds., *First Encounters: Spanish Explorations in the Caribbean and the United States, 1492–1570.* Gainesville: University Press of Florida, 1989.

Milford, Louis LeClerc de. *Memoir, or a Cursory Glance at My Different Travels & Sojourn in the Creek Nation.* Ed. John Francis McDermott. Trans. Geraldine de Courcy. Chicago: Lakeside Press, 1956.

★Mitchell, Robert D., ed. *Appalachian Frontiers: Settlement, Society and Development in the Preindustrial Era.* Lexington: University Press of Kentucky, 1991.

★Montgomery, James R. "The Nomenclature of the Upper Tennessee River." East Tennessee Historical Society *Publications* 51 (1979), pp. 151–162.

Montule, Edouard de. *Travels in America, 1816–1817.* Trans. Edward D. Seeber. Bloomington: Indiana University Press, 1951.

★Morris, Richard B. *The Peacemakers: The Great Powers and American Independence,* New York: Harper & Row, 1965.

★Nairne, Thomas. *Nairne's Muskhogean Journals: The 1708 Expedition to the Mississippi River.* Ed. Alexander S. Moore. Jackson: University Press of Mississippi, 1988.

Nobles, Gregory H. *American Frontiers: Cultural Encounters and Continental Conquest.* New York: Hill & Wang, 1997.

★Nolte, Vincent. *The Memoirs of Vincent Nolte: Reminiscences in the Period of Anthony Adverse, or Fifty Years in Both Hemispheres.* 1854. Reprint, New York: G. Howard Watt, 1934.

★O'Donnell, James H., III. *Southern Indians in the American Revolution.* Knoxville: University of Tennessee Press, 1973.

★Owsley, Frank L., Jr. *Struggle for the Gulf Borderlands: The Creek War and the Battle of New Orleans, 1812–1815.* Gainesville: University Presses of Florida, 1981.

★Owsley, Frank L., Jr., and Gene A. Smith. *Filibusters and Expansionists: Jefffersonian Manifest Destiny, 1800–1821.* Tuscaloosa: University of Alabama Press, 1997.

Parish, John Carl. *The Persistence of the Westward Movement and Other Essays.* Berkeley: University of California Press, 1943.

★Parton, James. *Life of Andrew Jackson.* 3 vols. New York: Mason Brothers, 1861.

Perdue, Theda, and Michael D. Green, eds. *The Cherokee Removal: A Brief History with Documents.* Boston: St. Martin's Press, 1995.

Perkins, Bradford. *The Cambridge History of American Foreign Relations.* Vol. 1: *The Creation of a Republican Empire, 1776–1865.* Cambridge, U.K.: Cambridge University Press, 1995.

———. *Prologue to War: England and the United States, 1805–1812.* Berkeley: University of California Press, 1968.

★Phelps, Dawson A. "The Chickasaws, the English and the French, 1699–1744." *Tennessee Historical Quarterly* 16:2 (1957), pp. 117–133.

———. "The Diary of a Chaplain in Andrew Jackson's Army: The Journal of the Reverend Mr. Learner Blackman—December 28, 1812–April 4, 1813." *Tennessee Historical Quarterly* 12:3 (September 1953), pp. 264–281.

Pickett, Albert James. *History of Alabama, and Incidentally of Georgia and Mississippi, from the Earliest Period.* 2 vols. Charleston, S.C.: Walker & James, 1851.

Pittman, Captain Philip. *The Present State of the European Settlements on the Mississippi.* 1770. Reprint, Gainesville: University of Florida Press, 1973.

★Pope, John. *A Tour through the Southern and Western Territories of the United States of America.* 1792. Reprint, Gainesville: University Presses of Florida, 1979.

★Prucha, Francis Paul. *American Indian Policy in the Formative Years: The Indian Trade and Intercourse Acts, 1790–1834.* Cambridge, Mass.: Harvard University Press, 1962.

★——— . *American Indian Treaties: The History of a Political Anomaly.* 1994. Reprint, Berkeley: University of California Press, 1997.

★——— . *Documents of United States Indian Policy.* 2nd ed. exp. Lincoln: University of Nebraska Press, 1990.

———. *The Sword of the Republic: The United States Army on the Frontier, 1783–1846.* New York: Macmillan, 1969.

★Quarles, Robert T., and Robert H. White, eds. *Three Pioneer Documents: Donelson's Journal, Cumberland Compact, Minutes of the Cumberland Court.* Nashville: Tennessee Historical Commission, 1964.

★Quimby, Robert S. *The U.S. Army in the War of 1812: An Operational and Command Study.* 2 vols. Lansing: Michigan State University Press, 1997.

★Ramsey, James Gettys. *The Annals of Tennessee to the End of the 18th Century.* 1853. Reprint, Chattanooga, Tenn.: Daughters of the American Revolution, 1926.

★Ranck, George Washington. *Boonesborough: Its Founding, Pioneer Struggles, Indian Experiences, Transylvania Days, and Revolutionary Annals; with Full Historical Notes and Appendix.* Filson Club Publication No. 16. Louisville, Ky.: J. P. Morton, 1901.

Ratner, Lorman A. *Andrew Jackson and His Tennessee Lieutenants: A Study in Political Culture.* Westport, Conn.: Greenwood Press, 1997.

★Read, William A. *Indian Place Names in Alabama.* Rev. ed. Tuscaloosa: University of Alabama Press, 1984.

Reeves, Carolyn Keller. *The Choctaw before Removal.* Jackson: University Press of Mississippi, 1985.

★Reid, John, and John Henry Eaton. *The Life of Andrew Jackson.* Ed. Frank L. Owsley Jr. 1817. Reprint, University: University of Alabama Press, 1974.

★Reilly, Robin. *The British at the Gates: The New Orleans Campaign in the War of 1812.* New York: G. P. Putnam's Sons, 1974.

★Remini, Robert V. *Andrew Jackson and the Course of American Empire, 1767–1821.* Vol. 1: *Andrew Jackson and the Course of American Freedom, 1822–1832.* Vol. 2: *Andrew Jackson and the Course of American Democracy, 1833–1845.* Vol. 3: New York: Harper & Row, 1977, 1981, 1984.

★——— . *The Battle of New Orleans.* New York: Viking, 1999.

★Ritchie, Carson I. A. "The Louisiana Campaign." *Louisiana Historical Quarterly* 44:1–2 (January–April 1961), pp. 13–103.

★Rogers, Stephen T. "1977 Historic Site Survey." Nashville: Tennessee Division of Archaeology, 1978.

Rogin, Michael Paul. *Fathers and Children: Andrew Jackson and the Subjugation of the American Indian.* 1975. Reprint, New Brunswick, N.J.: Transaction Publishers, 1991.

Rohrbough, Malcolm J. *The Land Office Business: The Settlement and Administration of American Public Lands, 1789–1837.* New York: Oxford University Press, 1968.

——— . *The Trans-Appalachian Frontier: People, Societies, and Institutions, 1775–1850.* New York: Oxford University Press, 1976.

Romans, Bernard. *A Concise Natural History of East and West Florida.* Ed. Kathryn E. Holland Braund. 1775. Reprint, Tuscaloosa: University of Alabama Press, 1999.

Roosevelt, Theodore. *The Winning of the West.* 4 vols. 1889–1896. Reprint, Lincoln: University of Nebraska Press, 1995.

★Rothrock, Mary U. *Carolina Traders Among the Overhill Cherokees, 1690–1760.* East Tennessee Historical Society *Publications* 51 (1929), pp. 14–29.

★Saunt, Claudio. *A New Order of Things: Property, Power, and the Transformation of the Creek Indians, 1733–1816.* Cambridge, U.K.: Cambridge University Press, 1999.

Sharp, James Roger. *American Politics in the Early Republic: The New Nation in Crisis.* New Haven: Yale University Press, 1993.

Sheehan, Bernard. *Seeds of Extinction: Jeffersonian Philanthropy and the American Indian.* 1973. Reprint, New York: Norton, 1974.

Skeen, C. Edward. *Citizen Soldiers in the War of 1812.* Lexington: University Press of Kentucky, 1999.

——— . *John Armstrong Jr., 1758–1843: A Biography.* Syracuse, N.Y.: Syracuse University Press, 1981.

★Snapp, J. Russell. *John Stuart and the Struggle for Empire on the Southern Frontier.* Baton Rouge: Louisiana State University Press, 1996.

★Sosin, Jack M. *The Revolutionary Frontier, 1763–1783.* New York: Holt, Rinehart & Winston, 1967.

——— . *Whitehall and Wilderness: The Middle West in British Colonial Policy, 1760–1775.* Lincoln: University of Nebraska Press, 1961.

★Southerland, Henry DeLeon, Jr., and Jerry Elijah Brown. *The Federal Road through Georgia, the Creek Nation, and Alabama, 1806–1836.* 2nd ed. Tuscaloosa: University of Alabama Press, 1989.

Starkey, Armstrong. *European and Native American Warfare, 1675–1815.* Norman: University of Oklahoma Press, 1998.

Starr, J. Barton. *Tories, Dons, and Rebels: The American Revolution in British West Florida.* Gainesville: University Presses of Florida, 1976.

Steele, Ian K. *Warpaths: Invasions of North America.* New York: Oxford University Press, 1994.

★Stiggins, George. *Creek Indian History: A Historical Narrative of the Genealogy, Traditions and Downfall of the Ispocoga or Creek Indian Tribe of Indians.* Ed. Virginia Pounds Brown. Birmingham, Ala.: Birmingham Public Library Press, 1989.

★Storm, Colton, ed. "Up the Tennessee in 1790: The Report of Major John Doughty to the Secretary of War." East Tennessee Historical Society *Publications* 17 (1945), pp. 119–132.

Sugden, John A. *Tecumseh: A Life.* New York: Henry Holt, 1998.

★Swann, Caleb. "Position and State of Manners and Arts in the Creek, or Muscogee, Nation in 1791." In Henry Rowe Schoolcraft, ed., *Historical and Statistical Information Respecting the History, Conditions, and Prospects of the Indian Tribes of the United States.* 6 vols. Philadelphia: Lippincott, Grambo, 1851–1857.

★Swanton, John. *Early History of the Creek Indians and Their Neighbors.* Bureau of American Ethnology Bulletin 73. Washington, D.C.: U.S. Government Printing Office, 1922.

————. *Indian Tribes of the Lower Mississippi Valley and the Adjacent Coast of the Gulf of Mexico.* Bureau of American Ethnology Bulletin 43. Washington, D.C.: U.S. Government Printing Office, 1911.

★Symonds, Craig. "The Failure of America's Indian Policy on the Southwestern Frontier, 1785–1793." *Tennessee Historical Quarterly* 35 (Spring 1976), pp. 29–45.

★Tanner, Helen Hornbeck. "Pipesmoke and Muskets: Florida Indian Intrigue of the Revolutionary Era." In Samuel Proctor, ed., *Eighteenth-Century Florida and its Borderlands.* Gainesville: University Presses of Florida, 1975.

★————. *Zéspedes in East Florida, 1784–1790.* Coral Gables, Fla.: University of Miami Press, 1963.

★Tatum, Howell. "Major Howell Tatum's Journal while Acting Topographical Engineer (1814) to General Jackson Commanding the Seventh Military District." Ed. John Spenser Bassett. *Smith College Studies in History* 8:1–3 (October 1921–April 1922), pp. 5–138.

★Thomas, Daniel H. *Fort Toulouse: The French Outpost at the Alabamas on the Coosa.* Tuscaloosa: University of Alabama Press, 1969.

Thornton, Russell. *The Cherokees: A Population History.* Lincoln: University of Nebraska Press, 1990.

★Tregle, Joseph G., Jr. "Early New Orleans Society: A Reappraisal." *Journal of Southern History* 18 (1952), pp. 20–36.

★Usner, Daniel H., Jr. *Indians, Settlers, and Slaves in a Frontier Exchange Economy: The Lower Mississippi Valley before 1783.* Chapel Hill: University of North Carolina Press, 1992.

Wallace, Anthony F. C. *Jefferson and the Indians: The Tragic Fate of the First Americans.* Cambridge, Mass.: Havard University Press, 1999.

————. *The Long, Bitter Trail: Andrew Jackson and the Indians.* New York: Hill & Wang, 1993.

Ward, John William. *Andrew Jackson: Symbol for an Age.* New York: Oxford University Press, 1962.

★Weber, David J. *The Spanish Frontier in North America.* New Haven: Yale University Press, 1992.

★Wedgewood, C. V. *Truth and Opinion: Historical Essays.* New York: Macmillan, 1960.

Wellesley, Arthur, Duke of Wellington. "Letter of the Duke of Wellington (May 22, 1815) on the Battle of New Orleans." *Louisiana Historical Quarterly* 3:1 (January 1926), pp. 5–10.

★Whitaker, Arthur Preston. "Alexander McGillivray, 1783–1789," and "Alexander McGillivray, 1789–1793." *North Carolina Historical Review* 5 (April, July 1928), pp. 181–203, 289–309.

★————. *The Mississippi Question, 1795–1803: A Study in Trade, Politics, and Diplomacy.* 1934. Reprint, Gloucester, Mass.: Peter Smith, 1962.

★————. "The Muscle Shoals Speculation, 1783–1789." *Mississippi Valley Historical Review* 13:3 (December 1926), pp. 365–386.

★————. "Spain and the Cherokee Indians, 1783–1791," *North Carolina Historical Review* 4:3 (July 1927), pp. 252–269.

★————. *The Spanish-American Frontier, 1783–1795: The Westward Movement and the Spanish Retreat in the Mississippi Valley.* 1927. Reprint, Lincoln: University of Nebraska Press, 1969.

White, Richard. *The Middle Ground: Indians, Empires, and Republics in the Great Lakes Region, 1650–1815.* Cambridge, U.K.: Cambridge University Press, 1991.

★Williams, Samuel Cole, ed. *Early Travels in the Tennessee Country, 1540–1800.* Johnson City, Tenn.: Watauga Press, 1928.

★————. *History of the Lost State of Franklin.* Rev. ed., 1933. Reprint, Johnson City, Tenn.: Overmountain Press, 1993.

————. *Tennessee during the Revolutionary War.* 1944. Reprint, Knoxville: University of Tennessee Press, 1974.

★Wilson, Samuel, Jr. *The Battle of New Orleans: Plantation Houses on the Battlefield of New Orleans.* 1965; reprint, New Orleans: Louisiana Landmarks Society, 1989.

Wokeck, Marianne S. *Trade in Strangers: The Beginnings of Mass Migration to North America.* University Park: Pennsylvania State University Press, 1999.

★Wood, Gordon S. "Launching the 'Extended Republic': The Federalist Era." In Ronald Hoffman and Peter J. Albert, *Launching the "Extended Republic": The Federalist Era.* Charlottesville: University Press of Virginia, 1996.

★———— . *The Radicalism of the American Revolution,* New York: Knopf, 1992.

★Wood, Peter H. et al., eds. *Powhatan's Mantle: Indians in the Colonial Southeast.* Lincoln: University of Nebraska Press, 1989.

★Woodward, Thomas S. *Woodward's Reminiscences of the Creek, or Muscogee Indians, Contained in Letters to Friends in Georgia and Alabama.* 1859. Reprint, Mobile, Ala.: Southern University Press, 1965.

Woolman, John. *The Journal and Major Essays of John Woolman.* Ed. Phillip S. Moulton. New York: Oxford University Press, 1971.

★Wright, J. Leitch, Jr. *Britain and the American Frontier, 1783–1815.* Athens: University of Georgia Press, 1975.

———— . "Creek-American Treaty of 1790: Alexander McGillivray and the Diplomacy of the Old Southwest." *Georgia Historical Quarterly* 51 (December 1967), pp. 379–400.

———— . *Creeks and Seminoles: The Destruction and Regeneration of the Muscogulge People.* Lincoln: University of Nebraska Press, 1986.

———— . *The Only Land They Knew: American Indians in the Old South.* 1981. Reprint, Lincoln: University of Nebraska Press, 1999.

———— . *William Augustus Bowles: Director General of the Creek Nation.* Athens: University of Georgia Press, 1967.

INDEX